W.W. Elliott and Company

History of Humboldt County, California

W.W. Elliott and Company

History of Humboldt County, California

ISBN/EAN: 9783337715250

Printed in Europe, USA, Canada, Australia, Japan

Cover: Foto ©ninafisch / pixelio.de

More available books at **www.hansebooks.com**

HISTORY OF HUMBOLDT COUNTY

CALIFORNIA,

WITH

ILLUSTRATIONS

DESCRIPTIVE OF ITS

SCENERY, FARMS, RESIDENCES, PUBLIC BUILDINGS,

Factories, Hotels, Business Houses, Schools, Churches, Etc.,

FROM ORIGINAL DRAWINGS,

INCLUDING BIOGRAPHICAL SKETCHES.

WALLACE W. ELLIOTT & CO., PUBLISHERS.

106 Leidesdorff Street, San Francisco, Cal.

1881.

A FEW WORDS OF EXPLANATION.

We have the pleasure of presenting to our patrons one of the largest and most elegant County Histories yet issued on this Coast. Not only ample in the number and beauty of its illustrations, and quality of paper and binding, but also in the extent and accuracy of its historical matter. We hope our efforts to represent the important features of this county may lead its inhabitants to understand and appreciate more fully its varied resources. We hope we have furnished information to the traveler, the tourist, or the emigrant who is seeking a location.

The book is fully illustrated, as may be seen at a glance, with views of many of the principal residences, mills and business houses of the county. Portraits of many of the pioneers appear, as well as of county officers and prominent citizens.

We are especially indebted to the following citizens for information, or for articles of value for this history which we have incorporated in the work, or given credit therefor: Hon. J. Clark, E. H. Howard, Wm. Ayers, W. F. Huestis, W. H. Wyman, J. S. Thomson, L. T. Kinsey, G. H. Shaw, J. B. Casterlin, Jackson Sawyer, Richard Johnson, W. P. Daykin, etc.

We have been in many cases unable to give proper credit for articles found floating about, or sent to us, and have therefore transferred them boldly to these columns. All history is made up from the statements and records of others. There can be no originality in the facts of history. This work contains a complete political history of the county, embraced under the following twenty general divisions, which are subdivided, as shown in the table of contents:—

1. First Discoveries by Land and Sea about Humboldt Bay.
2. Settlements made by the Gold Hunters.
3. Organization of the County Government.
4. Klamath County Formed and Disorganized.
5. Geographical Features of Country and its Soil.
6. Humboldt Bay and Harbor Described.
7. Resources and Industries of the County.
8. Redwood Forests and Lumber Business.
9. Manufacturing Interests of the County.
10. Rapid Increase in Population and Wealth.
11. Klamath, Gold Bluff and Trinity Mines.
12. Indian Difficulties, Wars, Treaties, and Reservations.
13. Descriptions of Towns and Villages.
14. Lives of Pioneer Settlers of this Region.
15. History of the Churches of the County.
16. List of Secret, Benevolent and other Organizations.
17. Sketches of Prominent Citizens of the County.
18. Public and Private Schools and their Progress.
19. The Climate and its many Advantages to Residents.
20. Botany, Zoology and Miscellaneous Matter.

The alphabetical index will be found an invaluable guide, and refers to more than 400 subdivisions of the above subjects. The first part of the work embraces a brief history of California from the discovery of the Pacific Ocean to this date.

It has been the policy of men in all ages to preserve by tradition, inscription, monument or manuscript, the memory of individuals and events associated with the settlement of a State or country. We have therefore given considerable space to the biographical department, which contains very much of interest. A few years from now it will be oftenest perused, for people delight to read of the pioneers of a country and of their trials. Each sketch contains some incidents of pioneer life, or some facts relative to the county, its soil, mode of cultivation, variety of crops, manner of harvesting, average production of different localities, and similar information not easily separated from the personal narrative, but can be found by the subheadings. Owing to the transitory state of society during the early days of California, it is impossible at this comparatively remote period, to fix the exact dates of many occurrences, or to get at the full truth of the matter. The reader will perhaps notice discrepancies in dates and incidents, and as it was impossible to adjust the differences, we have given the statements of each writer without change.

Gathering news of early events is very unsatisfactory. An "old pioneer" will enlarge by the hour upon early days, but pin him down to facts and figures, and endeavor to get a tangible historical account of any particular event of "those glorious days," and it seems to be too great an effort. Now a pioneer never would be guilty of admitting that he had forgotten anything of early times, yet get a half-dozen together to fix the date of any event, and no two of them will agree. Each will have a different date and version of the affair, and positively affirm it, as he "was there at the time." Special care has been taken, however, to avoid discrepancies, and we flatter ourselves that, in the main, the facts set forth will prove to be perfectly reliable.

We expect criticism. All that the publishers ask is that it be done in charity, after considering all the obstacles and hindrances involved in a work of this magnitude. Few persons without actual experience can comprehend the care and pains necessary to complete a book of this description.

Many old settlers, whose years of honorable toil have transformed the wild lands into harvest-laden fields, have placed us under obligations for historical and biographical incidents connected with the early history of the county.

A few years more, and all pioneers will have passed "over the river." Many now lie among the golden sands that allured them hither. Let no unmerited blot be cast upon the grand army of adventurers who covered those western shores, and brought with them the foundation of society, schools, and homes.

Our thanks are due to the citizens of the county for the cordial good feeling manifested toward our enterprise, having received from them that aid and support which can only be expected among prosperous and intelligent people.

THE PUBLISHERS.

TABLE OF CONTENTS.

LIST OF LITHOGRAPHIC ILLUSTRATIONS, MAPS, CHARTS AND DIAGRAMS.

LITHOGRAPHIC VIEWS.

Ayers William, Standard Office.... 84
Alford F. A. & W. R., Drug Store... 124
Auburnia John, Residence.......... 132
Axe Fred, Residence............... 16
Anthony A. G., Farm View......... 196
Bahnsen H. H., Farm View......... 105
Burns Hebert, Residence........... 50
Bair Thomas, Residence............ 76
Bleakinger Benjamin, Store........ 112
Benedlection L., Suburban Residence 172
Berding A., Residence............. 20
Boynton F. X., Island Home........ 32
Bullock N., Residence............. 148
Brizard A., Store et Arcata........ 80
Brown Salmon, Sheep Ranch........ 88
Boy Mill, Dolbeer & Carson........ 100
Beisner Hall...................... 32
Blocksburg Hotel.................. 56
Baron Block....................... 60
Blue Lake Hotel................... 84
Brook Farm, Mrs. G. Francis....... 105
Blocksburg Village................ 112
Churlin Clement, Blue Lake Hotel.. 84
Childs William.................... 28
Clegnane John.... Frontispiece and 180
Cuno H. A., Farm and Residence.... 116
Charles Geo. W., Residence........ 85
Carson William, Mill.............. 100
Clark Jonathan Bros., Residence... 86
Comptom William, Residence........ 216
"   Benj., Farm Residence.... 192
Cumming E. C., Store and Residence 132
Cook G. S., Home Residence........ 448
Dollison J. K., Residence......... 188
Dollaven J. J., Residence......... 124
Devlin Thomas, Residence.......... 80
Des Chua A., Farm Residence....... 132
Dent K. W., Residence............. 40
Duggan G. A., Farm................ 160
Del Norte Record.................. 180
Excelsior Mill, J. Russ & Co...... 44
Eureka Market..................... 45
Eureka Mill....................... 96
Entrance to Harbor................ 108
Enterprise Office, Ferndale....... 124
Excelsior Dairy Ranch, H. D. Smith 136
Ferndale Hotel.................... 172
Fern Cottage, Joseph Russ......... 44
Francis Mrs. G., Residence........ 105
Freese Mrs. L. A., Residence...... 148
Gilmore Alexander................. 168
Gray Geo. H., Farm and Residence.. 116
Giff A. M., Store and Warehouse... 128
Gilligan L., Star Hotel........... 80
Gold Bluff Mines....... Frontispiece
Hetherington J., City Residence... 148
Hardware Store of Robert Duras.... 60
Haynes J. P., Residence........... 56
Hicks L. S., Pleasant View........ 172
Island Mill, D. R. Jones & Co..... 68
Ivy Ranch of P. W. Robarts........ 49
Island Home of F. X. Boynton...... 32
Johnson Richard, Dairy Ranch...... 132
Jones D. R. & Co's Mill........... 68
Jones G. R., Residence............ 68
King R. F., Town Residence........ 20
Kenyon J. G., Store............... 172
Long Chas. W., Residence.......... 168
Logging Train of D. R. Jones & Co. 68
Laurel Grove Dairy Ranch.......... 152
Mad River Saw-mill of Isaac Minor. 140
Mathews James E., Residence....... 104
Monroe Mrs. A., Residence......... 104
Marsh H. W., Hotel—Arcata......... 124
Minor Isaac, Residence and Ranch.. 140
Mad River Bridge.................. 24
Norton A., Farm and Residence..... 72
Post-office at Eureka............. 16
Painter L., Biedel House.......... 64
Pierce Walter..................... 180
Putnam A., Residence.............. 132
Robinson W. S., Bridgeville Ranch. 192
Russ Joseph, Excelsior Mill....... 44
Roberts Holt. W., Home of......... 32
Roberts B. R., Ferndale Hotel..... 172
Roberts P. W., Ivy Ranch.......... 49
Roberts C. V., Home of............ 56
Rohner Henry, Residence........... 192
Robertson Mrs. H.................. 156
Southmayd J. L.................... 168
Strong Samuel, Hotel.............. 80
Sweasy Richard, Residence......... 188
Stewart Thos., Ranch Home......... 136
State Capitol..................... 217
Shaw Isabelle Mrs., Residence..... 218
Standard Office, Eureka........... 84
Sawyer Jackson, Farm Residence.... 182
Star Hotel Springville............ 52
Smith H. D., Excelsior Dairy...... 136
Ticknor H. H. Hotel............... 36
Tug-Boat Mary Ann................. 108
Tiner Office...................... 28
Trinidad Village.................. 52
Vance John, Saw-mill.............. 24
Vance Edwin P., Salmon Creek Farm. 120
Vance Hotel....................... 24
Whitmore Joel S., Ranch........... 120
Walker Jessie, Dairy Ranch........ 160
Watson John A., Residence......... 92
Winton S. F., Farm................ 180
Westbrook R., Dairy Farm.......... 207
Youmans S. T., Farm View.......... 196
Zanone Domingo Stock Ranch........ 96

PORTRAITS OF CITIZENS.

Albee Joseph P.................... 104
Brown T. M........................ 184
Bullock N......................... 176
Balme N. H........................ 164
Clark Jonathon.................... 165
Castorlin J. B.................... 184
Duff F. S......................... 165
Huestis A......................... 13
Huestis W. F...................... 13
Hansen John....................... 92
Hauna James....................... 13
Howard E. H....................... 13
Haynes J. P....................... 184
Jones D. R........................ 176
Kenyon J. G....................... 92
Kinman Seth....................... 82
Kinsey I. T....................... 184
Long Chas. W...................... 165
Monroe A.......................... 104
Minor Isaac....................... 170
Murphy Jas. E..................... 200
Mason Edgar....................... 200
Ricks C. S........................ 13
Russ Joseph....................... 44
Shaw G. M......................... 184
Smiley J. C....................... 176
Sutter J. A....................... 47
Saville William................... 200
Thomsen J. S...................... 184
Vance John........................ 24
Vrooman C......................... 165
Wyman W. H........................ 92
Woodbury W. H..................... 200
Watson John A..................... 92
Wiley Austin...................... 92

WOOD ENGRAVINGS.

Alcalde Colton and the Miner...... 87
Grist-mills of Early Settlers..... 35
Monterey in 1846.................. 33
Plow of the Native Californians... 31
San Juan Mission Buildings........ 77
Sonoma............................ 79
Spanish Ox-cart................... 33
San Joaquin River by Moonlight.... 43
Sutter, Gen. J. A. (portrait)..... 47
Sutter's Mill..................... 63
State House, San Jose, 1849....... 71
State Capitol..................... 216

MAPS, CHARTS, ETC.

Chart Showing Wind Currents....... 6
Chart Showing Size of Counties.... 76
Chart showing Coast line to Humboldt 15
Map of the State.................. 4
" Humboldt, Del Norte and Trinity 5

INDEX TO THE HISTORICAL MATTER.

Alcalde of Humboldt County........ 170
Agricultural Society.............. 212
Assessor's Report............112, 137
Arcata Village.........96, 98, 100
Alfalfa Production................ 137
Arcata Railroad................... 139
Adventure with Grizzlies—Wool..... 92
Agricultural Productions......78, 132
Attorneys of Humboldt............. 206
Altitude of Prominent Points...... 74
Anacieno Flag Raised.............. 56
Active Life of Pioneers........... 82
Alcaldes of Early Times........50, 67
Arrest of Citizens................ 40
Alcalde Colton Visits the Mines... 67
Annexation of Klamath County...... 118
Assessment Roll of 1853-54........ 142
Ayers Wm. on Lumber Business...... 142
"Arizona" Settlement.............. 196
Boundaries of Humboldt County..... 100
Bucksport Located........55, 110, 136
Big Redwood Trees................. 141
Barbecues of John Vance........... 155
Baron Block, Arcata............... 161
Bridgeville Described............. 155
Blue Lakes........................ 123
Blocksburg Village................ 150
Bear River........................ 120
Business of Crescent City......... 120
Breakwater at Harbors.........17, 19
Buckhorn Chair.................... 197
Climate of Humboldt County...164, 207
Chamber of Commerce............... 163
Crescent City and Bay........19, 120
"   " Light House........... 20
Camping in Early Days............. 84
Canoe Brig, The................... 102
County Road Contests.............. 109
Court House at Eureka............. 111
Courts in Early Times............. 112
County Expenses and Debts....113, 148
Court House at Orleans Bar........ 114
Centerville....................... 159
California Alps................... 73
Capture of Settlers............... 41
Coast Survey...................... 20
Capture of Monterey............... 68
Coal Discoveries.................. 134
Churches of the County............ 213
County Officers................... 220
Discovery of Humboldt Bay.81, 96, 122
Dairying in Humboldt County..135, 136
Democratic Standard.........217, 162
Dairying at Different Periods..32, 135
Drake's Bay....................... 14
Discovery of Cape Mendocino....... 21
Diagram of Size of Counties....... 76
Del Norte County formed......108, 119
"   "   " Progress............ 110
"   "   " Officers............ 218
"   "   " First Officers..... 119
"   "   " Resources........... 167
"   "   " Schools........121, 218
"   "   " Journalism.......... 218
"   "   " Village............. 120
Discovery of Gold at Coloma....... 63
Description of Missions........... 26
Decline of the Missions........... 25
Donner Party...................... 60
Eureka Secures County Seat........ 110
Exports for 1881.................. 137
Eureka Described.................. 101
"   Water Works................. 177
Emigrants Invited................. 127
Eureka Post-office................ 203
Eureka Guard...................... 134
Eel River...........16, 91, 97, 125, 126
Elk and Other Animals............. 87
Elk River......................... 125
Elk Horn Chair.................... 197
Emigrants Arrive.................. 33
Early Description of California... 30
Early Colonization Party.......... 30
Evacuation of Fort Ross........... 30
First White Person in Humboldt Co. 81
First Discoveries in Humboldt Co.. 65
First Discovery of Humboldt Bay... 126
First Christmas on Humboldt Bay... 90
First Party at Arcata............. 90
First Vessel Enters Trinidad Bay.. 96
First Vessel Enters Humboldt Bay.
.........................101, 175
First Election in Humboldt County. 112
First Board of Supervisors........ 113
First View of Humboldt Bay........ 176
First Lumber Mill................. 174
First Gripsstome Made............. 50
First Grist Mills................. 34
First Protestant Worship.......... 50
First Pioneer Squatter............ 34
First Ferry Boat.................. 33
First Schooner Built in California 38
First Campers on Tulare Lake...... 39
First Historian of California..... 29
First Orchard..................... 34
First Windmill.................... 35
First Tannery..................... 35
First Protestant Worship.......... 50
First American Governor........... 66
First Mission Founded............. 73
First Indian Baptism.............. 28
First Discovery of Gold........... 66
First State Constitution.......... 68
First School Teachers in State.... 77
First Officers of Del Norte County 119

TABLE OF CONTENTS OF HUMBOLDT COUNTY HISTORY.

INDEX TO THE HISTORICAL MATTER—CONTINUED.

First California Legislature	62	Herald, Rohnerville	156, 217
First Entry in Humboldt Land Office	127	Humboldt County Bank	101
First Railroads in State	139	Increase of Productions in 22 Years	147
First Child Born in Arizona	170	Indians 22, 23, 28, 45, 84, 90, 93, 182	
First Child born in Ferndale	204	Indian Reservations	158
First Sawmill on the Bay	141	" Treaties	153
First Steamer Constructed	145	" Treachery	93
First Flouring Mill	145	" Volunteers	219
First Trustees of Eureka	101	" Wars	185
First Trustees of Arcata	156	" War Claims	154
First Birth at Fort Humboldt	163	Ide Judge	57
First Schools in County	207	Independence Declared	40
First Express Lines	220	Industries of Early Times	21
First Newspapers in County	215	Immense Bands of Cattle	28
First Post Offices	208	Iron Ore Discovered	181
First Ferries Constructed	220	Jones D. R. & Co., Lumber Business	144
First Sermon Preached	213	Klamath County Organized	107, 114
First Church Erected	213	" Disorganized	100, 117
First Hotel on the Bay	178	" River	103, 122
First Alcalde of Humboldt	100	" City Located	103, 122
First school District	207	" County Bonds	117, 118
First Blacksmith of Humboldt	160	" Indian Reservation	155
First Hotel at Table Bluff	162	" County Debts Adjusted	118
Ferries of the County	220	" Indians	102
Financial Condition of Humboldt	148	List of County Officers	220
Ferndale Village	163, 217	Little River	15
Ferndale Enterprise		Light Houses	17, 21, 130
Ferndale Hotel	158	Life Stations	20, 140
Ferndale Water Works	204	Land Office of Humboldt County	126
Fort Humboldt Reminiscences	163	Largest Dairies	158
Financial Situation of Klamath	118	Lumber Business	76, 146
Fogs on the Coast	16, 28	Leather and Tanners	146
Foreigners Arrive on Coast	37	Mad River	16, 125
Gold Bluffs	19, 105, 150	Mendocino Cape	16
Great Mines	34	Mines of Trinity and Klamath	104
Golden Era	67	" of Humboldt County	141, 145, 157
Grizzly Bears of Humboldt Co	92	" of Del Norte County	119, 121
Geography of Humboldt Co	122	Mattole River	126
Gas Springs in Humboldt Co	126	Minor's Saw-Mill	127
Garberville	138	Manufacturing Business of County	143
Governors of California	72	Mining in Humboldt County	149
Grand Rush for the Gold Mines	66	Mines of T. M. Brown	149
How to Reach Humboldt County	14, 102	Miners' Laws	66
Humboldt Bay Described	53, 96, 123	Monterey Bay	25
Humboldt Harbor	17, 121	Missions Established	25
Humboldt Light House		Mining on the Beach	150
Humboldt County Organized	108, 109	Mines of John Chapman	127
Humboldt County Seat Contest	109	Marsh House, Arcata	161
Happy Camp	121	Masonic Lodges	210
Humboldt County Public Lands	127	Naming Humboldt Bay	170, 175
Humboldt Harbor Improvements	130	Newspapers of the County	215
Humboldt Port of Entry	127	Natural Wonders	79, 120
Hoopa Reservation	155	New Constitution Formed	72
Humboldt Point	162	Newspapers of Del Norte	216
Hunters and Trappers of 1832	39	
Hudson Bay Company	39	
Hydesville Village	157	
Hoosium	158	
Humboldt Times	215	

Organization of Humboldt Co.	107, 109	San Francisco and Bay	26
Orleans Bar	114, 157	Sonoma Mission	29
Oasegan Mine	151	Sale of the Missions	29
Odd Fellows' Lodges	210	San Joaquin Valley	37, 74
Organization of the State	69	Specimen Proclamation	42
Ownership of Land	78	San Joaquin Ranch	42
Overland Route to Humboldt	201	Sutter's Fort Located	40
Officers of Humboldt County	220	Strange Dream	62
Pioneers of Humboldt County	165	Sunday in San Francisco	67
Pioneer of Table Bluff	182	State House, San Jose	71
Post-office Routes	203	Secret and Benevolent Societies	210
Pioneers of California	46, 48, 49, 52, 62	Starvation Times in Mines	177
Population of the State & Co.	50, 148, 102	Shipwreck of R. H. Baine	176
Public Lands of Humboldt	127	Society, Past and Present	210
Pleasure Resorts of Humboldt	128	Snowslied	217
Productions of the County	133	Trinidad Village	101, 256
Progress of the County	137, 147	Trinidad Bay and Harbor, 18, 82, 95	
Pilot Rock	102		96, 103, 186
Petrolia	151, 163	Tides of the Coast	20
Pleasure resorts of S. Strong	187	Temperance Organizations	212
Principal Bureaus of the County	124	Trinity River	52, 96, 105, 125
Pacific Ocean First Seen	21	Trinity Bay	95
Plow of Early Settlers	31	Trinidad Mill Co	140
Pioneer Lumbermen	140	Trinity County Organized	107
Present Condition of Humboldt	148	Table Bluff	124, 129
Redwood Forests	87, 79, 140	Telegraphs, Daily and Weekly	217
Resources of Del Norte County	115	Table of California Missions	25
Redwood Creek	126	" Population of Missions	26
Rio Del Scenery	128	" Mission Indians	28
Resources of Humboldt County	132	" Missions in 1834 and 1842	30
Railroads	138, 144	" Disposition of Missions	32
Rohnerville	158	" Agricultural Products	75
" Herald	156, 217	" Altitude of Mountains	74
Rates of Taxation	147	" Barometer	206
Russians Near Fort Ross	35	" Rainfall	205
Review of the Missions	24	" County Officers	220
Roberts Hall	155	" Volunteers	219
Rainfall Tables	205	Threshing Scene of Early Times	32
Rio Del House	204	Tragic Fate of Donner Party	42
Schools of Humboldt County	207	Treaty of Peace Signed	49
Schools of Del Norte	218	Valuation from 1854 to 1882	147
Smith River	20	Vance's Railroad	138
Scenery of Humboldt County	128	Van Dusen River	102
Shipwrecks of Humboldt County	130	" Hotel	91
Sheep Ranches of Humboldt County	134	Vanle's Picnic Grounds	128
Stock-raising of Humboldt County	131	Vessels Entering Humboldt Bay	131
Saw-Mills of Humboldt County	141	View of Klamath County Jail	116
" of J. Vance	142	Villages of Humboldt	156
" of Isaac Minor	142	Votes on County Seat	110
" of J. Russ & Co	144	" Cast at Election	80
" of D. R. Jones & Co	144	" First County Election	112
" of Wm. Carson	145	Annexation of Klamath	118
Schooner Joseph Russ	145	Voyage up the Coast	13, 15
Salmon Fisheries	146	Volunteers, List of	219
Shelter Coves	150	Ward's Narrative of Discovery	81
Settlers Ordered to Leave California	40	Warrenville Started	161
Spanish Ox-Cart	33	Wool Productions	136
Strange Meeting	37	Wonders of California	79
		Wild Flowers	164

BIOGRAPHICAL NOTICES OF PROMINENT CITIZENS.

Ayers, William	217	Chapman, John	150	Jones, D. R. & Co	144	Sweasey, W. J	160
Anderson, John	102	Cass, H. S	190	Kinsey, L. T	183	Strong, Samuel	186, 187
Ave Fred	203	Carson, William	143	Kinstein, Seth	163, 197	Stewart, Thos	189
Allen J F		Culberg, Isaac		Kenyon, J. G	126, 135, 136	Shaw, Mrs. Isabella	191
Anthony, J. G	200	Devlin, Thomas	150, 146	Long, Chas. W	176	Sawyer, Jackson	194
Albert, F A		Doe, Charles A	182	Marsh, Dr. W. M	161	Shaw, G. H	47
Buhne, H. H	173	Dest, E. W	189	McCullum, W. J	188, 188	Sutter, J. A	47
Bair, Thomas	187	Duagan, G. A	179	Minor, Isaac	143, 171	Saville, Wm	200
Benedict, Geo. I.		De Haven, J. J	177	Meek, Stephen H	39, 120	Smith, H. D	202
Boynton, T. J	182	Dolliver, J. R		Marsh, Dr. John	43	Smiley, J. C	204
Bullock, N	179	Dobie, Abner	130	Murphy, Hon. J. R	198	Shaw, S. Lewis	191
Beeson John		Eccleston, Frederick A	201	Mason, Edgar	195	Simon, H. F	200
Brown, Salmon	185	Freese, Mrs L A	202	Monroe, A	205	Thomson, J. B	183
Blackburn, Wm	51	Gray, Geo. R	200	Mathews, Jas. R	201	Tickner, H. B	184, 180
Bailey, A	158, 160, 184	Gillmore, Alex		Norton, A	200	Vance, John	128, 139, 142, 145, 171
Blochberger, Benj	150, 185	Gill, A. A	158, 199	Putnam, A	184, 192	Vance, Edwin F	187
Brizard, A	161, 177	Glascock, A. A	185	Palmer, L	126, 191	Van Dyke, Walter	192
Burns, Robert	161, 196	Gibson, D. C. & Co	159	Russ, Hon. Joseph, 168, 184–3, 144–5, 168		Wyman, Hon. J. R	176
Bartschuit, Frank		Haymen, Hon. J. P	182	Robinson, W. S	170	Whitmore, Joel S	150
Brown, T. M	178, 149	Hinks, L. S	168	Roberts, Robt. W	171	Woodbury, W. H	200
Campton, Benjamin	191	Hooper Bros	157	Roberts, P. W	192	Watson, John A	162
Casterlin, J. R	183	Hacolin, A. J	107	Roberts, D. R	155, 186	Wiley, Hon. Austin	189
Cummings, E. O	207, 207	Hassin, W. F	181	Roberts, C. P	156	Whipple, S. G	206
Cook, Charles S		Hetherington	201	Holmer, Henry	186, 178	Westbrook, H	199
Clark, Jonathan	167, 183, 156	Howard, E. H	186	Robertson, Mrs. A	193	Winton, S. F	199
Coyle, C. A	158	Hanna, James	173	Ricks, Hon. C. E	172	Wargatt, C	184
Chartin, Clement	164, 185	Johnston, Richard	102	Roberts C. F		Youmans, S. T	200
				Robertson, Alexander	103	Zoanne, Domingo	165

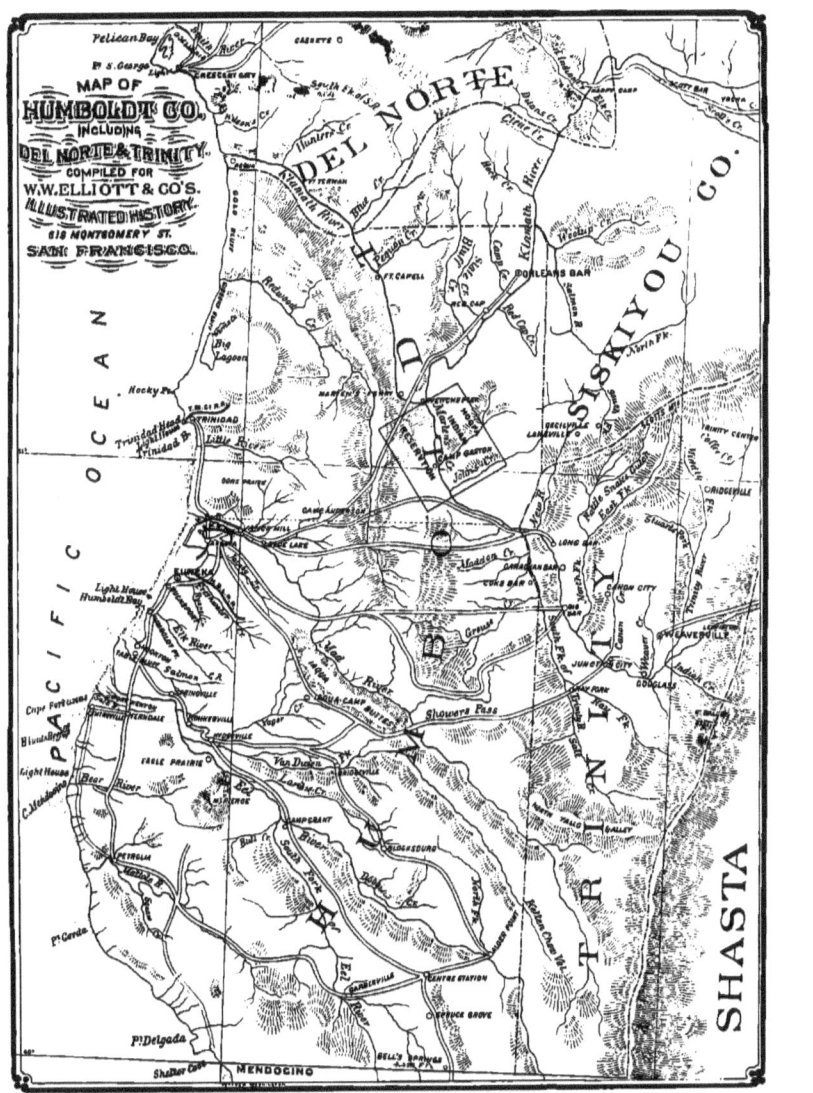

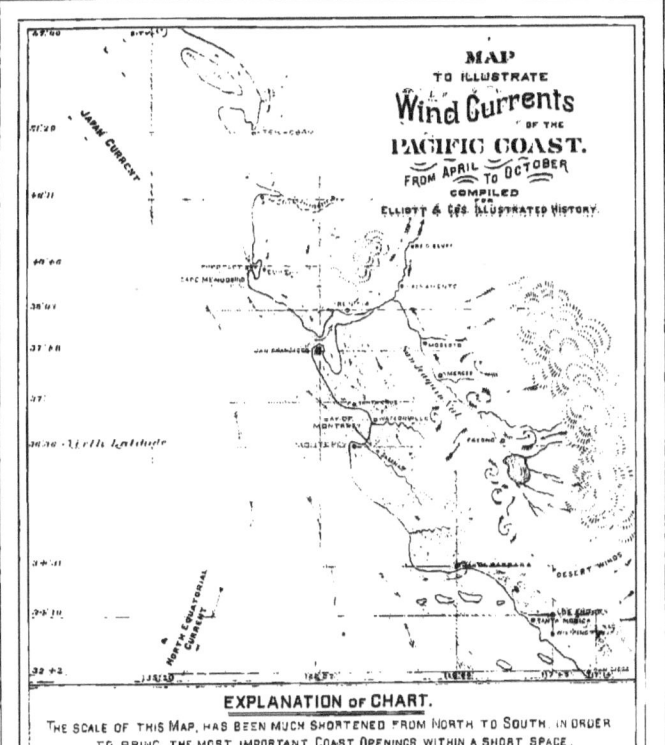

HISTORY
OF
HUMBOLDT COUNTY, CALIFORNIA,

FROM THE EARLY DAYS DOWN TO THE PRESENT TIME.

HUMBOLDT is a county of small farms and profitable homesteads, occupied by contented and prosperous owners. No soil surpasses the valley lands in productiveness. It exhibits a degree of healthful growth in the various industries and in population that will compare favorably with any rural county in the State. The climate is equable and genial. Droughts and failure of crops are unknown.

It is a county of grand scenery; of mountain and valley; hill and plain; tide marsh and sand dune; open prairie and impenetrable thicket and of giant redwoods beautiful in their native grandeur.

It is one of the best watered counties in the State. Along the whole western slope for over one hundred miles, and extending back from ten to thirty miles, lies the great redwood district of the county. This whole vast area is covered by one dense and almost impenetrable forest of giant trees from two to four hundred feet high, and from ten to sixty feet in circumference. East of this timbered section is a tract of open country of great value as a pastoral district.

At every available point for shipment stands a saw-mill turning trees into lumber, furnishing employment for labor and investment for capital.

Every little river has its fisheries and canneries, and all the valleys and bottom-lands are covered with productive farms.

The county offers peculiar inducements to tourists and pleasure seekers. This section is one of the finest hunting and fishing countries to be found. In all parts of the county, save the immediate settlements in the valleys, game of all kinds abounds.

Some of the scenery in this county is unrivaled for beauty and grandeur. Especially is this true of the coast country.

HOW TO REACH THE COUNTY.

It has no railroad facilities connecting it with the balance of the State. There are but two routes by which we can reach this important portion of our State. One is overland by stage, which in summer is a romantic and pleasant ride, but equally tedious and very uncertain in winter.

The route chiefly traveled is by ocean steamer, and is preferred on account of the quicker time made. Steamers leave San Francisco twice a week, and are possessed of good sea-going qualities and comfortable passenger accommodations. The voyage, however, on account of the liability of seasickness, is not an enjoyable one, but the steamer is a wonderful improvement on the sail vessels of a few years ago.

A very large portion of the coast carrying trade, formerly done by sailing craft, is now carried on by steamers. They carry both freight and passengers, and make frequent and regular trips. No railroads as yet interfere with the trade of that region.

A VOYAGE UP THE COAST.

Let us take a trip up the coast and in imagination see and examine all the capes, harbors and rivers that form the coast-line along this route. We shall then form some idea of the extent of the sea-coast, and of the facilities for business at the various openings along the shore. The accompanying chart of the route and of the coast-line will assist us in our observations.

The shores of the west coast, against which the waves of the great Pacific Ocean wage continual warfare, though bluff and bold and rocky for the most part, have few indentations in which the storm beset mariner may find refuge. Nature otherwise so lavish to us in its gifts in this part of the world, has denied us good harbors, and Congress, which is expected by the great American people to remedy the deficiencies of nature, has failed to provide for us artificial ones. This coast is peculiar in this respect, and there is probably no part of the world where so long a shore line presents so few available harbors.

EXPERIENCES OF THE TRIP.

The dangers to navigation are many, especially on what is usually designated the North Coast, where there is not really a single good harbor affording protection against the storm winds of the winter months until the Strait of Fuca is reached, 700 miles from San Francisco. There are a number of open roadsteads, giving partial shelter from the summer northwest winds, and several bar harbors, all of which are dangerous of access and utterly impracticable in heavy or even moderately bad weather. The outlaying dangers are all marked on the charts of the United States Coast Survey.

To the ordinary passenger, seldom on the seas, this trip is a serious undertaking and is entered upon with dread of the seasickness. To those who dwell in inland quietude, with habitations remote from the sea and out of the sound of the roar of the ocean, it may seem of slight importance; but to the sailor who must buffet about amid the angry waters, with no snug shelter into which he may guide his storm-tossed vessel; to the merchant whose effects are at the mercy of the winds and waves, a good harbor is of the utmost importance as will be seen as we proceed up the coast.

The first little place outside the Golden Gate, north of San Francisco, is Bolinas Bay, a small place very little used and that only by the small schooners.

DRAKE'S BAY.

Sir Francis Drake's Bay, behind the prominent headland of Point Reyes, affords a very fine protection from the west and northwest winds, but it is exposed to southerly storms. By anchoring in four or five fathoms, close under the north side of the point, a few small vessels lie out a winter gale, but the sea breaks a long way out at such time.

Vessels from the northward all make Point Reyes when coming here. The big bight between this point and Point Lobos, with the San Francisco bar running across it, is a difficult place for a sailing vessel to get out of in a southerly gale. When the coasters come in near enough and find the bar bad they have to claw windward to clear Point Reyes if they want sea room, and have heavy hard seas and winds to contend with. If there was a safe harbor at Drake's Bay they could always make that with ease and lie there until the weather moderated.

There is no trade from this bay, although the land in the vicinity is occupied by some of the finest dairies in the State.

TOMALES BAY AND CUFFEY'S COVE.

Tomales Bay is a bar harbor, dangerous of access, as when vessels run under the high land at the entrance, and lose the wind, they are in danger of drifting into the breakers, as has several times happened.

Cuffey's Cove, twelve miles north of Point Arena, is a good northwest harbor, has three chutes and does considerable trade. This is a great country for potatoes, large quantities being shipped from here. In the town there are a few stores, a church, hotels, bar-rooms, etc. A steam railroad brings the lumber from the saw-mills down to the landing. Great quantities of railroad ties, bark, wood, posts, etc., are shipped from this point.

MENDOCINO BAY.

Mendocino Bay is a somewhat contracted place and unpleasant from the constant heavy swell. The sea breaks in the center and southern parts of the bay, the anchorage being in the north bight close behind the point. At this place Big River enters the ocean. Some coasting schooners have been built on the river and brought over the bar at high water. Vessels load here from a chute, and sometimes in the winter from lighters. The place is only available for a few vessels at a time, and in rough weather the company do not want more than one or two there at a time. Vessels arriving are guided by signals from the shore as to the state of the harbor. If it is rough and there is room for no more vessels the flag at half mast indicates that the last comer must stay outside and wait his turn. If it is at the mast head he may come in.

The town of Mendocino City, situated at this point, is quite a good-sized village. The moorings are good and heavy. The place is owned by the Mendocino Lumber Company, and if there were any competition many vessels would go. This place has the largest lumber mill on the coast this side of Humboldt.

CASPAR CREEK.

Caspar Creek, a few miles on up the coast, has quite a little village of some three hundred inhabitants on the hill near its mouth. There is very little water in this creek at any time, but the month only closes up once in three or four years. The creek is about six miles long and empties into the ocean five miles north of Mendocino City. The first mill was erected here in 1862. The harbor is considered as good as any of its class, which is evident from the fact of their shipping lumber from there every month in the year.

This is the only place between Mendocino and Eureka where they land freight safely in winter. The moorings are examined and adjusted every fall with fresh buoys, and are very good ones. The harbor averages seven fathoms in depth, and there are no blind rocks except those which are visible at low water. The vessels generally beat out, except in calm weather; but there are three buoys to haul out by.

HUMBOLDT  **PIONEERS**

GENERAL DESCRIPTION OF THE COAST.

SHELTER COVE AND POINT DELGADA.

We now reach the first shipping places in Humboldt County. From Shelter Cove the chief exports are wool, produced in southern Humboldt and northern Mendocino.

The harbor is formed by a reef of rocks jutting out from the coast quite a distance. On the south side of this there is deep water and plenty of sea room making it a good harbor for vessels, and a place of refuge during the prevalence of northerly gales, but when southerly winds prevail it is dangerous for any craft lying at anchor.

The village of Shelter Cove is situated on a bluff overlooking the ocean and consists of only two or three houses, blacksmith, store, etc. It is thirty miles south of Cape Mendocino.

POINT GORDA AND MATTOLE RIVER.

After passing Point Gorda the mouth of Mattole River is reached. There is no harbor here. A few miles up the stream is the pretty little village of Petrolia which derived its name from the oil, or petroleum which was found in the locality. Situated within a short distance of the ocean it is fanned by its cool sea-breezes. Its situation commands some of the finest scenery on the north coast. It is in the midst of a great dairy region, to be noticed hereafter. The next point of interest on our trip is Cape Mendocino.

DENSE FOGS ON THE COAST.

The coast is often enveloped in a dense fog so that many of the points here described cannot be seen even if our vessel should keep near enough to the coast to bring them in range of our vision.

The coast fogs which prevail in summer are great drawbacks to navigation. During the height of the northwest winds the fog comes in, but the breeze by no means dispels it. This fog prevails more frequently at some points than others, but pretty much the whole coast is enveloped in it. It is more dense in summer than winter.

The fogs are low clouds whose upper surface averages 1,500 feet above the sea, and usually rising to 1,700 or 1,800 feet, with the mountains of the coast line rising like islands above the level of the fog.

It is a noticeable fact that vessels are seldom lost from gales and severe storms but mainly from running ashore in fogs. One feature, however, of winter gales is that after blowing hard from southeast it will work round to southwest with a large broken swell from the latter direction, and then finish up by heavy puffs from northwest, kicking up an ugly cross sea, very uncomfortable to small vessels and dangerous to deck-loads.

VOYAGE NOT DANGEROUS.

The voyage, however, is a safe one as the route is well known and well defined in the charts, and the only difficulty will be from fogs and at the entrance of the harbors where shifting sands form bars. Some of the coasters or small sailing craft think they know more about the coast than any book can tell them. Many of these do not even have a coast-line chart, much less detailed charts, and much of the navigation is accomplished by rule of thumb: "Stand off shore on a nor'west wind for so long, then come by the wind on the other tack and stand up the coast for so long, and strike your port." That kind of navigation is all very well sometimes, but the schooner may strike something else before the port, as it occasionally happens. A very frequent cause of wrecks in the fall of the year and winter, is the heavy sea which sometimes rolls into the smaller harbors, at a time when there is little or no wind, the result of gales off shore. At such times the schooners cannot get out and have to trust to the strength of lines and moorings. If they part the vessels pile up in the rocks. As this happens without much warning, if the moorings are not good the heavy sea coming against the vessel sometimes causes it to break loose, and a wreck is inevitable.

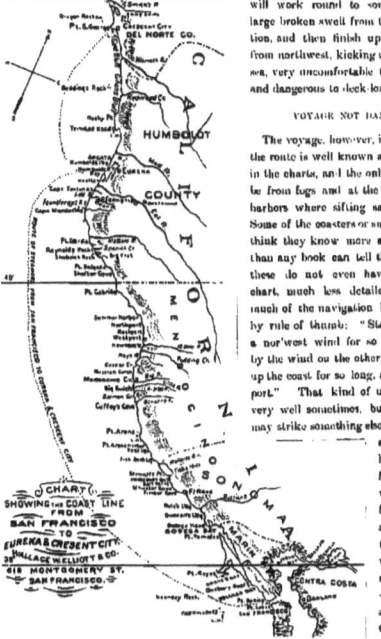

CHART SHOWING THE COAST LINE FROM SAN FRANCISCO TO EUREKA & CRESCENT CITY. WALLACE W. ELLIOTT & CO. 318 MONTGOMERY ST. SAN FRANCISCO.

CAPE MENDOCINO.

The bold mountainous headland of Cape Mendocino forms the western limit of the northwest trend of the California coast from Point Reyes, the general trend from Cape Mendocino to the Straits of Fuca being northwest. At this cape the range of coast hills from the south seems to meet a range from the east formed by ridges of 1,400 feet elevation within a mile of the sea, with peaks from 2,500 to 3,000 feet high, within two miles of the above. The whole face of the country is covered with timber.

A distinguishing feature of this cape is the large rock called the Sugar Loaf or Haystack, which is just off the point, and is about 300 feet high.

LIGHT-HOUSE OF CAPE MENDOCINO.

There is a light-house on the cape. It is flashing white of the first order, illuminating the whole horizon. The light appears for fifteen seconds and is eclipsed fifteen seconds. It is placed on a wrought iron sixteen-sided tower.

About three miles broad off this cape is Blunt's Reef, a dangerous ledge of rocks, bare at all times. In the channel between this reef and the shore are several submerged rocks, some of which show breakers at low water and some not. Although Davidson's Coast Pilot mentions this channel as a dangerous locality that should be avoided, it is pretty generally used by coasting steamers and schooners.

The old steamer *Northerner* was lost by striking one of these rocks, being beached after striking, at Cape Fortunas, where she went to pieces. In fact there are scattered sunken rocks extending nearly a mile off the coast from Shelter Cove to Cape Mendocino.

This cape is to the north coast what Point Conception is to the south, as here vessels coming to the southward meet heavier winds and rougher weather. The fact has been established by observation of the U. S. Coast Survey that in the vicinity of this cape the sea has been known to break in nine and a half fathoms of water; not snow "white water" merely, but bona fide breakers.

Five or six miles north of this is False Mendocino or Cape Fortunas, which presents the same peculiarities as Cape Mendocino, even to the rocky islets off the cape.

Bear River, one of the largest streams of this vicinity, enters the ocean near the cape. It has no harbor.

A DREADED POINT.

1543—This cape, as heretofore stated, was first discovered by Juan R. Cabrillo, February 26, 1543, and called *Cabo de Fortunas* or Cape of Perils.

This cape was formerly much dreaded by the Spanish navigators, on account of the storms usually prevailing in its vicinity; but, those fears having passed away, the cape has lost much of the respect with which it was early regarded by mariners.

CAPE VISITED BY VISCAIÑO.

1604—The *Fragata*, or small vessel belonging to Viscaiño's ship, visited this cape in 1604, under command of Aguilar. The historian says:—

"The *Fragata* parted from the *Capitana* [Viscaiño's ship,] and, supposing that she had gone onward, sailed in pursuit of her. Being in the latitude of 41°, the wind began to blow from the southwest; and the *Fraguta*, being unable to withstand the waves on her beam, ran before the wind until she found shelter under the land, and anchored near Cape Mendocino, behind a great rock, where she remained until the gale had passed over."

The historian says: "When the wind became less violent, they continued their voyage close along the shore; and on the 19th of January, the pilot Antonio Flores, found that they were in the latitude of 43°, where the land formed a cape or point, which was named *Cape Blanco*. From that point the coast begins to turn to the northwest; and near it was discovered a rapid and abundant river, with ash-trees, willows, brambles, and other trees of Castile, on its banks, which they endeavored to enter, but could not, from the force of the current." (??)

The coasts north of Mendocino, were not visited by the people of any civilized nation between the period of Cook's voyage, (1778) and 1787; and the best charts of them were those of the Spaniards, founded on the observations of Heeta and Bodega.

EEL RIVER ENTRANCE.

Eel River is the first indentation in the coast north of the cape where schooners or steamers may enter, and although a schooner went in there as early as 1850, while looking for Humboldt Bay, it is only within the past few years that much trade has developed there. The Indian name of this river was *Weeott.*

The steamer *Thomas Whitelaw* visits the river at regular intervals. There are about eleven feet of water on the bar, but the breakers are short and sharp. A vessel can go in and out here at almost any time that towage is possible on the Humboldt Bar.

The steamer *Continental* made a number of trips into this river, but was finally lost on the bar at the mouth. The *Continental* scraped on the bar a number of times on her previous passages, but the last time when she struck, her smokestack buckled forward and broke off the steam whistle pipe where it connected with the steam drum, and as the steam filled the engine room, and as pressure ran down, they lost control of the steamer, and she went ashore.

There are a number of sloughs and branches to the river, which drain a fertile section of country, mainly under cultivation. There are salmon canneries on the river. This important stream and its industries will receive more attention hereafter.

RESIDENCE OF FRED AXE, POST MASTER, EUREKA, CAL.

GENERAL DESCRIPTION OF THE COAST.

HUMBOLDT BAY.

This harbor lies about twenty-one miles above Cape Mendocino, and is an important shipping point for lumber, grain, and potatoes. Round about this bay there is considerable grazing and farming land. The products of this, and of the timber region, give the towns on the bay a large trade with San Francisco. Of the forty-nine vessels built on the coast in 1877 twelve of them were built at Humboldt, all schooners. The bay extends about nine miles north of, and four miles south of the entrance, and varies from three miles to half a mile in width. A large extent of this area, however, is mud flats, bare at low water.

The towns of Eureka, Areata and Hookton are all on the bay. Eureka is the principal port, and is about four miles from the heads. Areata is at the north end of the bay.

THE LARGEST BAY.

This is the largest bay north of San Francisco. The bar at the mouth is a very bad one, and like others undergoes irregular changes, dependent on the prevalence, direction, and strength of the wind. Vessels are often bar bound here for some time, and are generally towed out by the tugs when they go to sea, as the prevailing summer wind blows right in. The channel has shifted so often, that Davidson's Coast Pilot says: "The best advice we can offer in regard to entering the harbor, is to wait for the tug."

A SMOOTH HARBOR.

The bay affords fine shelter for vessels from all winds, when once inside, but the breakers are heavy over the shifting sands of the bar even in moderate weather, and vessels have been known to wait for a month before they could get out. No one should attempt to enter without a pilot. The shores on both sides of the entrance are low and sandy.

CONTEMPLATED IMPROVEMENTS.

The engineers, after examining this harbor, came to the conclusion that the only way to improve this entrance would be by the construction of two parallel jetties of very heavy stone, about five hundred yards apart, from the north and south spits at the entrance. If such jetties were built, the very large area of the inner bay would probably afford sufficient tidal prism to keep open a deep channel over the bar. But such construction would be attended with great difficulties and enormous expense. It was a question even with the members of the board, whether such construction would be physically possible, and one, too, on which they could not express an opinion without searching examination of all the contingencies upon which the stability or instability of such work would hinge. They did not, therefore, make any estimate of cost, as if not possible of execution. It is highly improbable that either breakwater or jetties will be attempted.

THE LIGHT-HOUSE.

The light-house at Humboldt is on the north side of the entrance, about three-quarters of a mile from the inlet, and about midway between the sea and bay shores; it is a fixed white light of the fourth order, on a conical brick tower. There is also a duplicate twelve-inch steam fog whistle here, giving alternate blasts of four and eight seconds, at intervals of twenty-eight seconds.

THE BAY UNKNOWN UNTIL 1849.

It is a little singular that so large a bay as this should have escaped the closest observations of the early explorers, and have remained unknown until a modern date, but such was the case as we shall hereafter relate.

1792—Vancouver wrote in 1792, as follows:—

"I was thoroughly convinced, as were also most persons of observation on board, that we could not possibly have passed any safe navigable opening, harbor, or place of security for shipping, on this coast, from Cape Mendocino to the promontory of Classet, [Cape Flattery, at the entrance of the Strait of Fuca.]

"So minutely has this extensive coast been inspected, that the surf has been constantly seen to break on its shores from the masthead; and it was but in a few small intervals only where our distance precluded its being visible from the deck. Whenever the weather prevented our making free with the shore, or on our hauling off for the night, the return of fine weather and of daylight uniformity brought us, if not to the identical spot we had departed from, at least within a few miles of it, and never beyond the northern limits of the coast which we had previously seen.

"An examination so directed, and circumstances happily concurring to permit its being so executed, afforded the most complete opportunity of determining its various turnings and windings, as also the position of all its conspicuous points, ascertained by meridional altitudes for the latitude, and observations for the chronometer, which we had the good fortune to make constantly once, and in general twice, every day, the preceding one only excepted. It must be considered a very singular circumstance, that, in so great an extent of sea-coast, we should not have seen the appearance of any opening in its shore which presented any certain prospect of affording a shelter, the whole coast forming one compact and nearly straight barrier against the sea."

Having performed acts of diplomacy and justice in the Sandwich Islands, Vancouver proceeded again to the American coasts; and, after examining the portion near Cape Mendocino, including the place called Port Trinidad by the Spaniards, in 1775, so as to connect his surveys north and south of that portion, he sailed to Nootka, where he arrived on the 20th of May 1793.

MAD RIVER DISCOVERED AND NAMED.

Mad River, just above Humboldt Bay, is an important stream, emptying into the ocean over the sand beach, and is fordable at the mouth. A small canal, however, has been cut from this stream to the northern part of Humboldt Bay, through which lumber is brought; and on this river are important industries, which we shall consider more fully in another place. The river was so named by a party who left the Trinity River mines and came over to the coast to discover the unknown but heard of Bay of Trinidad. This was in November, 1849.

The discovery party consisted of Dr. Josiah Gregg, L. K. Wood, D. A. Buck, —Van Duson, J. B. Truesdell, C. C. Southard. Isaac Wilson, and T. Sebring. They followed down the Bald Hills, and then crossed over to the coast, at the mouth of Mad River, which was named by them because "Gregg flew into a passion when some of the party wanted to go down the coast a few miles and examine a bay the Indians reported in that direction," which afterwards proved to be the now noted Humboldt Bay. A full account of this discovery as told by L. K. Wood will be given hereafter, as also its discovery by sea.

TRINIDAD HEAD AND HARBOR.

Trinidad Head and Bay is about seventeen miles above Humboldt, and forty miles north of Cape Mendocino. The bay, or roadstead, is somewhat contracted, but there is deep water, and the dangers are visible. It is a good summer anchorage, but dangerous in winter southeasters, a number of vessels having been lost there.

Trinidad "Head," a bold, picturesque headland, about 375 feet high, forms the western shore of the anchorland. This "head" is of metamorphic sandstone, covered about the height of eighty or ninety feet above the water with a few feet of earth, which supports a thick growth of scrub bushes. Off the western face, for nearly half a mile out, lie several high rocky islets, with one, half a mile south, (Pilot Rock,) which has nine fathoms of water close to it. In the northern part of the bay is a sand beach extending about half a mile; thence eastward the shore is rocky.

The town of Trinidad fronts on the northwest part of the roadstead, where there is a wharf. The best anchorage for a vessel, besides the permanent moorings inside of Prisoner's Rock, is on a line of that rock and the "head," in seven fathoms, muddy bottom. The harbor can be approached safely from the southeast to the southwest, taking care in coming in from the westward, when within half a mile of the head, to keep Prisoner's Rock open to the southward of it, in order to avoid the broken ground to the southward of Blank Rock, which is outside the harbor. It is customary and safe in a northwest wind to hug the land closely. This harbor is in latitude 41° .05', and about 240 nautical miles N.N.W. of San Francisco.

It is about twenty miles south of the middle point of the coast between the entrance to San Francisco Bay and the mouth of the Columbia River; it is, therefore, geographically well situated for a harbor of refuge between these two harbors.

HARBOR IMPROVEMENTS CONTEMPLATED.

The engineers say that the rock here appears to be of better quality than is generally found along the coast. The fact that it is such a bold, projecting headland, with deep water around its southern face, shows that it has been able to resist the denudation of the sea, and would seem to bear out this conclusion.

The breakwaters at this place, according to the plans submitted by the Board of Engineers, would run off from the point in a straight line in the direction of Pilot Rock for 2,000 feet, with a short piece at an angle towards the harbor 200 feet long. Between that and Pilot Rock would be an entrance to the harbor. From the other side of Pilot Rock the breakwater comes towards the shore 2,640 feet, leaving an entrance to the harbor between that end and the beach. If built as indicated this would protect an available anchorage of nearly one square mile, with good holding ground. The cost of this breakwater is estimated at $7,604,500. The rocks outside are from eighty to one hundred feet out of water, and those on the northern part of the harbor are above water also.

THE BOARD FAVORABLY IMPRESSED.

The Board of Engineers was favorably impressed with the advantages of Trinidad for a harbor of refuge, which subject is considered in a separate article.

On the head is a light of the fourth order, fixed white, varied by red flashes, at intervals of one minute. It was erected in 1871. If a harbor of refuge were built here, the light-house on Trinidad Head could be removed to Pilot Rock, and serve as a guide to enter.

TRINIDAD DISCOVERED AND NAMED.

1775.—Viceroy Bucareli ordered an expedition to examine the coasts as far as the sixty-fifth degree of latitude. The *Sentiago* was placed under the command of Captain Bruno Heceta, and a small schooner called the *Sonora*, of which Juan de Byala was in command, were fitted out. They sailed from San Blas March 15, 1775, in company with the schooner *San Carlos*, bound for Monterey.

The exploring vessels, after parting with the *San Carlos*, at Monterey, doubled Cape Mendocino, and, on the 10th of June, 1775, anchored in a small roadstead beyond that promontory, in the latitude of 41° 10'. The officers, priests, and a portion of the men, immediately landed and took possession of the country, in the name of their sovereign, with religious solemnities, bestowing upon the harbor the name Port Trinidad; and they then engaged in repairing their vessels and obtaining a supply of water, which afforded them employment for nine days.

GENERAL DESCRIPTION OF THE COAST.

LITTLE RIVER OR PIGEON RIVER.

The stream now designated as Little River on our maps is evidently the one they called Pigeon River, for during the nine days they remained in Port Trinidad the Spaniards held frequent communications with the people of the country, who dwelt principally on the banks of a small stream, named by the navigators *Rio de los Tortolos*—Pigeon River—from the multitude of these birds in its vicinity. "The Indians conducted themselves uniformly in the most peaceable manner, and appeared to be, on the whole, an inoffensive and industrious race. They were clothed, for the most part, in skins, and armed with bows and arrows, in the use of which they were very expert; their arrows were, in general, tipped with copper or iron, of which metals they had knives and other implements—whence procured the Spaniards could not learn. No signs of religious feelings, or ceremonies of any kind, could be discovered among them, unless their howling over the bodies of the dead may be considered in that light."

CROSS ERECTED AT PORT TRINIDAD.

1775. Having completed their arrangements, Hecota and Bodega sailed from Port Trinidad on the 19th of June, 1775, leaving a cross erected near the shore, with an inscription setting forth the fact of their having visited the place and taken possession of it for their sovereign. This monument the Indians promised to respect, and they kept their word, for Vancouver found it there untouched in 1793. The Spaniards considered the discovery of the place important, the harbor being, according to their journals, safe and spacious, and presenting facilities for communication between vessels and the shore; and the surrounding country fruitful and agreeable.

Vancouver, however, gives a much less favorable view of the harbor, which he pronounces to be in no respect a secure retreat for vessels, as it is entirely open to the southwest winds, which blow on that coast with the utmost violence at certain seasons of the year. The other accounts of the Spaniards, respecting the place and its inhabitants, are, in general, confirmed by those of the British navigator.

The Spaniards, after leaving Port Trinidad, were obliged to keep at a distance from the coast for three weeks, at the end of which time they again came in sight of it, in the latitude of 45° 27′, being the north part of the coast line of Washington Territory. From that parallel they examined the shore towards the south, in search of the strait said to have been discovered by Juan de Fuca in 1592, the entrance of which was placed, in Bellin's chart, between the forty-seventh and forty-eighth degrees of latitude; and, having satisfied themselves that no such opening existed there, the two vessels cast anchor near the land, though at some distance from each other, in order to obtain water and trade with the natives.

"Here a severe misfortune befell the schooner on the 14th of July. Seven of her men, who had been sent ashore in her *only boat*, though well armed, were attacked and murdered, immediately on landing, by the natives; and the schooner was herself in much danger of being taken by these savages, who surrounded her, during the whole day, in great numbers, in their canoes, and were with difficulty prevented from boarding her.

GOLD BLUFFS AND THE KLAMATH.

After leaving Trinidad we shall pass the mouth of Redwood Creek and see the noted gold bluffs, where the precious metal is washed out by the action of the waves and deposited in the sands of the sea.

The next important coast opening is a large river called the Klamath. It empties into the ocean over a beach. The stream carries a great deal of water but a sand pit runs from the south point and crowds the entrance close to the rocky bluff to the northward. The bar is extremely unreliable and although small coast vessels have entered it frequently it is generally considered dangerous and impracticable for navigation. The current at the mouth is very strong. Extensive mining operations are conducted on the Trinity River which empties into the Klamath.

CRESCENT CITY BAY.

In summer there is always some swell in this bay, and in winter it rolls fearfully and vessels have always to anchor where they can slip and run to sea. A vessel off this coast and wishing to make a harbor in a gale would never venture into Crescent City Bay, unless she knew her position accurately and was well acquainted with the coast and all its hidden dangers. The usual anchorage is on a line between the light-house and the north side of a large inlet three-quarters of a mile east of it, in three or four fathoms, hard bottom. Coast steamers run to this place, which is an important shipping point.

The Examiners for Harbor of Refuge reported unfavorably on the harbor, "first, because it is too contracted; second, on account of the many dangers sunken, and likewise both in approaching and inside; third, because of the heavy breakers in southeast and southwest weather, clear across the entrance to the harbor from Steamboat Rock to Round Rock, from Round Rock to Mussle Rock and from that to the shore." The entire harbor is feather-white with breakers in a gale of wind from the southward.

THE PROPOSED BREAKWATER.

Nevertheless, in order to have definite ideas as to the location and cost of a breakwater, the Engineers included it in the roadsteads examined with a view to improvement. They consider the best way to be to build a breakwater from the rock on which the light-house is built, off Battery Point to Steamboat Rock 1,850 feet, and from there straight out in the same line 2,640 feet, which is equivalent to extending the point artificially. The estimated cost of carrying it out is $6,022,000.

CRESENT CITY LIGHT-HOUSE.

The light here is on the seaward extremity of the inland point forming the southern and western sides of the harbor. It is a fixed white varied by white flashes, and was erected in 1856.

POINT ST. GEORGE.

The Cresent City Reefs, or Dragon Rocks, extend some six miles from Point St. George. The passage inside the reef is used by steamers. There are a few outlying rock and many sunken ones, on one of which the *Brother Jonathan* was lost, and many lives with her.

SMITH'S RIVER.

Smith's River comes into the ocean through the sand beach some fourteen miles above Cresent City. The mouth of the river shifts considerably. Inside there is a narrow channel. The river is small, but the coasting steamers have entered it lately, as have also some schooners. A salmon cannery was started here last year. It has been only of late that there has been any trade at the place, as it was supposed that the bar at the river's mouth was impracticable. There is a splendid belt of redwood in the vicinity, and the timber resources seem inexhaustible. This is the last important feature of the California Coast.

TIDES OF THE COAST.

The tides on the coast of California are of a peculiar and apparently complicated character. The Coast Survey issues annually a book of tide tables for this coast, and so also does Thomas Tennant, the chronometer maker and regulator. These coast survey tables are given for a few places, and a table of tidal contents is appended by which the stage of the tide at other locations may be computed. There are on this coast, in each twenty-four hours, or rather in each lunar day of twenty-four hours and fifty minutes, two high and two low waters, which are unequal in height, and occur at unequal intervals, differing most from each other when the moon's declination is greatest, and least when the moon is on the equator. The high and low waters generally follow each other thus:

Starting from the lowest low water the tide rises to the lower of the two high waters; then falls slightly to a low water higher than the former, and sometimes merely indicated by a long stand; then rises to the highest high water, whence it falls again to the lowest low water. The range of tide at San Francisco is about six feet. North it is greater, being about nine feet or more at spring tide at Astoria, Washington Territory.

LIFE STATIONS AND FOG SIGNALS.

The Government has established lately on this coast several life-saving stations fully equipped with life-boats and all necessary apparatus for giving assistance to shipwrecked mariners.

Those in what is known as the Twelfth District are: First—At Neeah Bay, W. T., at the entrance of the Strait of Fuca. Second—Shoalwater Bay, W. T. Third—Cape Disappointment, at the entrance of Columbia River. Fourth—Cape Arago, at the entrance of Coos Bay. Fifth—Humboldt Bay. Sixth—Bolinas Bay. Seventh—On Beach at Golden Gate Park, San Francisco. Eighth—Point Conception.

On the California Coast there are twenty-four light-houses, including those in San Francisco Bay; there are also eleven fog-whistles and three fog-bells. In the Thirteenth District, embracing Oregon and Washington Territory, there are fourteen lights, three fog-whistles and one bell. The total number of buoys on the coast and in the harbors is 109, exclusive of special buoys put down by interested parties. There are also forty-six day or unlighted beacons.

Formerly heavy guns were stationed at prominent points and could be heard a distance of some eight miles. Now the fog-horn, fog-whistle, and siren are used; the latter being most efficient. All the high light-houses like that at Cape Mendocino are useless as mere lights because situated at too great an elevation to be always seen. The light should be lower down under the fog. These light-houses and stations are indicated on our chart.

U. S. COAST SURVEY.

The Government has provided maps, charts and sailing directions for this coast, the same as it has for other parts of its territory bounding on the sea. The Coast Survey is one of the most efficient branches of the Government Departments, and its work is done thoroughly and practically whenever undertaken. On this coast it has given not only coast-line charts with location of ports, anchorages, lights, fog-bells, etc., but also finely and correctly executed detailed maps of all the principal harbors with ample sailing directions for entering them, soundings, dangers, etc., all being plainly and carefully marked.

"Davidson's Coast Pilot" is a Government publication, written by the accomplished officer who has been surveying and examining this coast for so many years. To it we are indebted for many of the items used in the preceding paragraphs.

It is a book of some 300 pages, carefully written and giving directions for entering all the principal harbors. It also gives a general description of the coast-line, and detailed descriptions of the headlands, reefs, anchorages, lights, fog signals, etc. It describes an ocean shore-line of over 3,120 miles, divided as follows: California, including the islands of the Santa Barbara Channel, 1,097 miles; Oregon, 285 miles; Washington Territory, including islands in Washington Sound, and shores of Puget Sound, 1,738 miles. The third edition of this work was published in 1869, since which time the majority of the small chute landings on the coast have been established, so it mentions few of these.

TOWN RESIDENCE OF A. BERDING, FERNDALE, HUMBOLDT COUNTY CALA.

TOWN RESIDENCE OF R. F. KING, FERNDALE, HUMBOLDT COUNTY CAL.

A GLANCE AT EARLY HISTORY.

Before entering more fully upon the history of the county it would seem appropriate to take a glance at the early history of the State, and note a little of its progress during a short decade; including the first establishment, rise and decline of the missions; the rapidity and grandeur of its wonderful rise and progress; the extent of its home and foreign commerce; the discovery and astonishing produce of gold. No county history therefore could be complete unless it included some account of the circumstances which brought each county into existence, and from whence came the men who organized and set the machinery of State and local governments in operation. It would thus be well, then, that posterity should know something of the early history of the State as well as of their own immediate neighborhood; and by placing these scenes upon record they will remain fresh in the minds of the people that otherwise, in the lapse of years, must gradually fade away.

RAPID SETTLEMENT AND PROGRESS.

One hundred years ago—almost within the memory of men now living—but very little of California's soil had been trodden by the foot of civilized man. Up to the discovery of gold in 1848, it was an afar-off land, even to those on the western border of civilization. School-boys then looked upon their maps and wondered if they might ever be permitted to traverse the "unexplored region" marked thereon. About that time, when Thomas H. Benton said the child was then born that would see a railroad connecting ocean with ocean, most people smiled and thought that the day-dream of the old man had somewhat unsettled his hitherto stalwart intellect. No dream of forty years ago, no matter how bright the colors that may have been placed before the imagination, ever pictured the California of to-day—our own, our loved California.

PACIFIC OCEAN FIRST SEEN.

1513.—The Pacific Ocean was given to the world by Vasco Nuñez de Balboa, who looked down from the heights of Panama upon its placid bosom on the 25th day of September, 1513 the same year in which Mexico was conquered by Hernando Cortes. To Balboa, therefore belongs the credit of first seeing the Pacific Ocean. He, however, supposed it to be the great Southern Ocean. In 1520, Fernando Magellan sailed through the straits that bear his name, and finding the waters so little disturbed by the storms, he was induced to give it the name of Pacific Ocean.

DISCOVERY OF CALIFORNIA.

1534.—Cortes fitted out two ships for discovery of the Pacific Coast. One was commanded by Becarra, who was murdered by his crew, led on by his own pilot Ortun, or Fortuño Zimenes.

Zimenes afterward continued the voyage of discovery, and appears to have sailed westward across the gulf, and to have touched the peninsula of California. This was in the year 1534. He therefore was the first discoverer of the country.

DISCOVERY OF CAPE MENDOCINO.

1542.—On the 27th of June, 1542, Juan Rodriguez Cabrillo, who had been one of Cortes's pilots, left Navidad, in Mexico, under instructions from Antonio de Mendoza, Viceroy of Spain, on a voyage of discovery. On the 5th of July he landed at Cape St. Lucas, in Lower California, and following the coast, he finally entered the delightful harbor of San Diego, in Upper California, on September 28th. This place he named San Miguel, which was afterwards changed by Viscaiño to that which it now bears.

1543.—He passed by the Golden Gate and reached latitude 44° on the 10th of March, 1543. The cold became so intense that he headed his ship again for Navidad. Cabrillo landed at Cape Mendocino, which he called Cabo de Fortunus (Cape of Perils), from the dangers encountered in its vicinity. This was February 26, 1543. Whatever discoveries may have been made by this navigator, were followed by no practical results.

SECOND EXPLORING EXPEDITION.

1579.—The next expedition along the coast seems to have been that of the English buccaneer, Francis Drake, afterwards knighted by Queen Elizabeth for his success in capturing and destroying the rich Spanish ships. There long existed a popular belief that Drake sailed into the harbor of San Francisco, and that the bay was named for him; but it is now well settled that the bay he entered was that of Tomales, on the coast of Marin County. This one bore the name San Francisco.

This noted English voyager, Sir Francis Drake, sailed along the coast in 1579. It is said his Spanish pilot, Morera, left him in Oregon, and thence found his way overland to Mexico, a distance of 3,500 miles. The name of New Albion was given to the country by Drake, with the evident intention of securing it for the British crown.

On the 22d of July, after repairing his ship and doubtless taking on board a goodly supply of fresh meat and water, Drake set sail for England, going by way of the Cape of Good Hope, and arriving in Plymouth November 3, 1580, having been gone about two years and ten months. He was the first Englishman who circumnavigated the globe, and was the first man who ever made the entire voyage in the same vessel. He was graciously received by Queen Elizabeth, and knighted. She also gave orders for the preservation of his ship, the *Golden Hind* that it might remain a monument to his own and his country's glory.

At the end of a century it had to be broken up, owing to decay. Of the sound timber a chair was made, which was presented by Charles II. to the Oxford University.

Sir Francis Drake died on board ship, at Nombre de Dios, in the West Indies, January 28, 1595.

DESCRIPTION OF THE ORIGINAL INHABITANTS.

1579.—The following is a highly colored description of the natives, as given by Drake: The natives bringing the Admiral (Drake) a present of feathers and cauls of net-work, he entertained them so kindly and generously that they were extremely pleased, and soon afterwards they sent him a present of feathers and bags of tobacco. A number of them coming to deliver it, gathered themselves together at the top of a small hill, from the highest point of which one of them harangued the Admiral, whose tent was placed at the bottom. When the speech was ended, they laid down their arms and came down, offering their presents, at the same time returning what the Admiral had given them. The women remaining on the hill, tearing their hair and making dreadful howlings, the Admiral supposed them engaged in making sacrifices, and thereupon ordered divine service to be performed at his tent, at which these people attended with astonishment.

The arrival of the English in California being soon known through the country, two persons in the character of ambassadors came to the Admiral and informed him, in the best manner they were able, that the King would visit him, if he might be assured of coming in safety. Being satisfied on this point, a numerous company soon appeared, in front of which was a very comely person, bearing a kind of sceptre, on which hung two crowns, and three chains of great length. The chains were of bones, and the crowns of net-work, curiously wrought with feathers of many colors.

A MAJESTIC INDIAN KING.

Next to the sceptre-bearer came the King, a handsome majestic person, surrounded by a number of tall men, dressed in skins, who were followed by the common people, who, to make the grander appearance, had painted their faces of various colors, and all of them, even the children, being loaded with presents.

The men being drawn up in line of battle, the Admiral stood ready to receive the King within the fences of his tent. The company having halted at a distance, the sceptre-bearer made a speech, half an hour long, at the end of which he began singing and dancing, in which he was followed by the King and all the people, who, continuing to sing and dance, came quite up to the tent; when sitting down, the King took off his crown of feathers, placed it on the Admiral's head, and put on him the other ensigns of royalty; and it is said that he made him a solemn tender of his whole kingdom; all of which the Admiral accepted in the name of the Queen, his sovereign, in hopes that these proceedings might, one time or other, contribute to the advantage of England.

ATTEMPT TO POSSESS THE COUNTRY.

1602.—Then there is another silence concerning this region, of twenty-four years, when Viscaíno comes, exploring more carefully, and searching for harbors.

It was not until 1602 that the Spaniards took any actual steps to possess and colonize the continent. In that year Don Sebastian Viscaíno was dispatched by the Viceroy of Mexico, acting under the instructions of his royal master, King Phillip III., on a voyage of search, in three small vessels. He visited various points on the coast, among them San Diego.

BAY OF MONTEREY FOUND AND NAMED.

1602.—It is he who finds Monterey Bay. He gets there December 16, 1602. His object was to find a port where the ships coming from the Phillipine Islands to Acapulco, a trade which had then been established some thirty years, might put in, and provide themselves with wood, water, masts, and other things of absolute necessity.

Viscaíno gave the name of Monterey to that bay. On the next day after he anchored near the site of the present town of Monterey, religious worship was held "under a large oak by the sea-side."

The description they give of the harbor says: "Near the shore is an infinite number of very large pines, straight and smooth, fit for masts, and yards, likewise oaks of a prodigious size for building ships. Here likewise are rose trees, white thorns, firs, willows and poplars; large clear lakes, and fine pastures and arable lands."

Viscaíno leaves on the 3d of January, 1603, and then follows a long silence of more than a hundred and sixty years, during which no record speaks of this region of country.

FOUNDING OF FIRST MISSION.

1763.—A great zeal for missions had sprung up, and then prevailed in Mexico for Christianizing the regions at the North. The glowing descriptions of the old navigators who touched here more than a hundred and fifty years before, were revived, and now came into existence a desire, both in Spain and Mexico, to enter into and possess the land. Two divisions of the expedition reached San Diego nearly at the same time. One by sea and the other by land, up the peninsula of Lower California.

They were at San Diego together, and founded the first of the missions of Upper California on the 16th day of July, 1769. But their zeal was too great to allow them to wait at the southernmost border of the promised land. They set their faces northward.

MONTEREY SEARCHED FOR AFTER 167 YEARS.

1769.—They had read of Viscaíno, and his glowing description of the country around the bay he named "Monterey." They proposed to set out at once to find it by land.

The expedition left San Diego July 16, 1769, and was composed of Governor Portala, Captain Revere, with twenty-seven soldiers with leathern jackets, and Lieutenant P. Fages, with seven volunteers of Catalonia, besides Engineer Constanzio, and fifteen Christian Indians, from Lower California.

Fathers Crespi and Gomez accompanied them for their spiritual consolation, and to keep a diary of their expedition. Owing to Father Crespi's diary, the principal incidents of this first journey by land up this coast are known to us. They kept near the sea-shore most of the way. They were constantly passing rancherias of Indians, whom they greeted as well as they knew how, and they were not molested by them. It was late in September when they came in sight of the Bay of Monterey, the very bay they were in search of, but they did not recognize it.

Father Crespi and the Commandant ascended a hill and looked down upon it.

MONTEREY BAY NOT RECOGNIZED.

1769.—They recognized Point Pinos, and New Year's Point as described by Cabrera, but they did not recognize the bay as Viscaino's Bay of "Monterey!" It is certainly very strange that they did not, but for some reason they did not seem to have thought of its being the very identical spot they were in search of.

The description of it by which they were guided, was of course one given by those coming into the bay by water. It may not have been detailed or definite, or suited to guide those seeking it by land.

At any rate, the soldiers explored Point Pinos on both sides, and yet never recognized the place. They searched from the 11th of November to the 9th of December.

They were all half of a mind to give up the search and go back.

But the resolution to proceed still further prevailed, and so they resumed their march. We trace them now step by step. They crossed the Salinas River. They passed several lagoons. They descended into the Pajaro Valley, and camped near the bank of the river.

DESCRIPTION OF THE NATIVES.

Moreover, in this valley they met with an encampment of Indians, numbering, as they said, five hundred.

The Indians had no notice of the arrival of strangers in their land, and were alarmed. Some took to their arms; some ran to and fro, shouting. The women fell to weeping bitterly. Sargent Ortega alighted from his horse and approached them, making signs of peace.

He picked up from the ground arrows and little flags which they had set, and they clapped their hands in signs of approbation.

They were asked for something to eat. The women hastened to their huts and began to pound seeds and make a kind of paste.

But when the fathers returned to the same spot the next day, they found only smoking remains of the Indians' camp, the Indians themselves having set fire to it and gone away.

NAMES GIVEN TO RIVERS AND TREES.

1769.—They named the river "Pajaro," because they found here an immense bird killed, stuffed with hay, measuring nine feet and three inches from tip to tip of the wings spread out. Here, too, not far from the river, they made note of finding deer.

They described the banks of the Pajaro River as they found them in the fall of 1769, thickly covered with trees. They spoke particularly of the redwood, calling it "palo colorado," on account of its color. Father Crespi says the trees are very high, and thinks they resemble the cedar of Lebanon, save that the wood has no odor. The leaves, too, he says, are different, and the wood is very brittle.

They stopped near a lake where there was a great deal of pasture, and they saw a number of cranes. They rested there three days, on account of the sick.

On the 17th of October they moved on again, walking all the time through good land, at a distance of some three miles from the sea.

At the end of that day's journey, they came to the river known as San Lorenzo. They proposed to cross it, not far from the sea. They found the banks steep. They were thickly grown with a forest of willows, cotton-wood and sycamore, so thick that they had to cut their way through.

The river was fifty-four feet wide at the point where they forded, and the water reached the belly of their horses. "It was one of the largest rivers," Father Crespi says, "that we met with on our journey."

"We camped on the north side of the river, and we had a great deal of work to cut down trees to open a little passage for our beasts. Not far from the river we saw a fertile spot, where the grass was not burnt, and it was pleasure to see the pasture, and the variety of herbs and rose bushes of Castile. We did not see near the river, nor during our journey, any Indians."

The next day about eight o'clock in the morning they moved on again.

"After proceeding about five hundred steps," Father Crespi says, "we passed a large stream of running water which had its source among high hills, and passing through a table-land, furnishes ample facility for irrigation." This creek they called "Santa Cruz." And so the little stream gave its name to the city.

Perhaps Justiniano Roxas* saw this first party of white men that ever visited this region. He must have been then about sixteen or seventeen years old.

The company remained some sixteen days near the Bay of

---

*Justiniano Roxas died at Santa Cruz, March 10, 1875, aged 123 years. His portrait and biography were inserted in Elliott's History of Santa Cruz County. From that article we learn he was for years about as destitute of flesh as a skeleton. His skin was yellow, hard and full of creases, and looked like parchment. Age had taken all expression from his countenance. His eyes were nearly closed. He walked with a staff. His last years were spent in trying to keep warm. At night he spread his blanket by the hearth, with his head toward the fire. He would not use a bed. He was cared for by the Sisters of Charity, aided by the county. He was baptised 4th of March, 1792 by the record.

Monterey. Long enough to get a very fair idea of the climate. The sky was clear and there was no fog.

They pushed on northward until they discovered San Francisco Bay and reached the Golden Gate itself.

BAY OF SAN FRANCISCO FOUND AND NAMED.

1769.—On the 1st of November, 1769, they sent a party to Point Reyes. On the 2d of November, several hunters of the expedition ascended the high mountains more towards the east; and, although we have no correct information as to the names of those hunters, it is certain that they were the first white inhabitants who saw the large arm of the sea known at present as the Bay of San Francisco.

The portion that was seen by them was that which lies between the San Bruno mountains and the estuary or creek of San Antonio (Oakland). They discovered the bay, unless the honor is accorded to the exploring party that returned on the 3d of November, who also had discovered the branch of the sea, by which they were prevented from reaching Point Reyes, and the primitive bay first called San Francisco.

On the 4th of November the whole of the expedition saw the newly discovered bay, and they tried to go around it by the south; but not being able to do so, they returned to Monterey. And so, by the merest accident, they came upon the world-renowned Bay of San Francisco.

Finding it a place answering every requirement he named it after San Francisco de Asis; and seven years later, June 27, 1776, possession was taken of the spot and a presidio established, the mission being located on the site of the present church.

MONTEREY BAY VISITED AGAIN BUT NOT RECOGNIZED.

1769.—Towards the end of November, we find them tarrying around Monterey again, not even now knowing that they were looking on the very harbor they were in search of! They even think it possible that the harbor that Viscaino found 166 years before, and described in such glowing terms, may be filled with sand, and for that reason they cannot find it. They erect a large cross near Point Pinos and place a writing at the foot of it, describing their hardships and disappointments, in case the vessel called the *San Joss* should anchor in that vicinity; and any of those on board should discover the cross and find the writing.

Finally, after many hardships, on the 24th day of January, 1770, half dead with hunger, they arrive at San Diego, after an absence of six months.

They have accomplished that long and exceedingly laborious journey; they have twice passed and looked upon the very bay they were in search of, not knowing it!

MONTEREY BAY FOUND AT LAST.

1770.—The next time Monterey Bay was searched for it was found. It was in the same year, 1770, that two new expeditions were fitted out. The two parties set out from San Diego to find it, one by land, the other by water. They find the bay this time, reaching it very nearly together.

On the 3d day of June, 1770, they take possession of the land in the name of the King of Spain.

On the same day Father Junipero begins his mission by erecting a cross, hanging bells from a tree, and saying mass under the same venerable rock where Viscaino's party celebrated it in 1602, 168 years before.

OBJECT OF THE MISSIONS.

The missions were designed by the Mexican Catholics for the civilization and conversion of the Indians. The latter were instructed in the mysteries of religion (so far as they could comprehend them) and the arts of peace. Instruction of the savages in agriculture and manufactures, as well as in prayers and elementary education, was the padre's business.

At first the Indians were exceedingly cautious about approaching or connecting themselves with this new style of civilization, but gradually their fears and superstitions were overcome, and they began to cluster about the fathers. Their old habits and manner of living were thrown off, and they contented themselves with the quiet life and somewhat laborious duties of the missions.

INDIANS NOT EASILY CIVILIZED.

The California Indian was anything but an easy subject for civilization. Knowledge he had none; his religion and morals were of the crudest form, while all in all he was the most degraded of mortals. He lived without labor, and existed for naught save his ease and pleasure. In physique he was unprepossessing; he was possessed of great endurance and strength; his features were unattractive, his hair in texture like the mane of a horse, and his complexion as dark as the Ethiop's skin.

His chief delight was the satisfying his appetite and lust, while he lacked courage enough to be war-like, and was devoid of that spirit of independence usually the principal characteristic of his race. The best portion of his life was passed in sleeping and dancing, while in the temperate California climate the fertile valleys and hill-sides grew an abundance of edible seeds and wild fruits, which were garnered, and by them held in great store.

Such means of existence being so easily obtained is, perhaps, a reason for the wonderful disinclination of Indians to perform any kind of labor. Indeed, what need was there that they should toil when nature had placed within their reach an unlimited supply of food?

MISSION RANCHOS SET APART.

Besides the missions, presidios, castillos, and pueblos, it may be remarked that there were certain public farms, called *ranchos*, set apart for the use of the soldiers. They were gen-

MAD RIVER SAW MILL, 18 MILES FROM EUREKA, HUM

BOLDT CO. CAL. JOHN VANCE, PROPRIETOR.

FOUNDING OF THE VARIOUS MISSIONS.

erally four or five leagues distant from the presidios, and were under the control of the different commandants. Little use, however, seems to have been made of these farms, and they commonly were left in a state of nature, or afforded only grazing to the few cattle and horses belonging to the presidios.

In the establishment of missions the three agencies brought to bear were the military, the civil, and the religious, being each represented by the *presidio*, or garrison; the *pueblo*, the town or civic community; and the *mission*, the church, which played the most prominent part.

TABLE OF THE UPPER CALIFORNIAN MISSIONS.

No.	Name	Date of first founding	Location
1	San Diego de Alcala	July 16, 1769	Bay of San Diego.
2	San Carlos de Monterey	June 3, 1770	Subsequently removed from Monterey to the Carmel river.
3	San Antonio de Padua	July 14, 1771	14 leagues f'm San Miguel, Monterey co.
4	San Gabriel de los Temblores	Sept. 8, 1771	9 leagues from Los Angeles, road removed to present location, also mile east of the city.
5	San Luis Obispo	Sep. 1, 1772	At present town of San Luis Obispo.
6	San Francisco (Dolores)	Oct. 9, 1776	On the Presidio ro Bay.
7	San Juan Capistrano	Nov'r 1, 1776	About midway between Los Angeles and San Diego.
8	Santa Clara	Jan'y 18, 1777	Where town of Santa Clara now stands.
9	San Buenaventura	March 31, 1782	South-east of and near Santa Barbara.
10	Santa Barbara	Dec'r 4, 1786	On the Santa Barbara channel.
11	La Purísima Concepción	Dec'r 8, 1787	On the Santa Inez river.
12	Santa Cruz	Aug't 28, 1791	Where town of Santa Cruz now stands.
13	La Soledad	Oct'r 9, 1791	In the Salinas river, Monterey county.
14	San Jose	June 11, 1797	Where the city of San Jose now is.
15	San Juan Bautista	June 24, 1797	On the San Juan river, San Benito co.
16	San Miguel	July 25, 1797	On the Salinas river, Monterey county.
17	San Fernando Rey	Sept'r 8, 1797	Twenty miles N. W. from Los Angeles.
18	San Luis Rey de Francia	June 13, 1798	Thirteen and a half leagues from San Diego.
19	Santa Inez	Sept'r 17, 1804	Twelve leagues from Santa Barbara.
20	San Rafael	Dec'r 14, 1819	North of San Francisco Bay, Marin co.
21	San Francisco de Solano	Aug't 25, 1823	Sonoma, Sonoma county.

SAN CARLOS DE MONTEREY ESTABLISHED.*

1770.—The third attempt to establish a settlement at Monterey proved successful, as heretofore noticed. The following extract from a letter of the leader of the expedition to Father Francisco Palou, gives a graphic account of the ceremonies attending the formal founding of the Mission of San Carlos de Monterey, by Padre Junipero Serra, on that memorable day, June 3, 1770.

"On the 31st of May, 1770, by favor of God, after rather a painful voyage of a month and a half, the packet San Antonio, commanded by Don Juan Perez, arrived and anchored in this beautiful port of Monterey, which is unadulterated in any degree from what it was when visited by the expedition of Don Sebastian Viscaino, in 1620. It gave me great consolation to find that the land expedition had arrived eight days before us, and that Father Crespi and all others were in good health. On the 3d of June, being the holy day of Pentecost, the whole of the officers of sea and land, and all the people, assembled on the bank at the foot of an oak, where we caused an altar to be erected, and the bells rang; we then chanted the *veni Creator*, blessed the water, erected and blessed a grand cross, hoisted the royal standard, and chanted the first mass that was ever performed in this place; we afterwards sang the *Salve* to Our Lady before an image of the illustrious Virgin, which occupied the altar; and at the same time preached a sermon, concluding the whole with a *Te Deum*. After this the officers took possession of the country in the name of the King, (Charles III.) our Lord, whom God preserve. We then all dined together in a shady place on the beach; the whole ceremony being accompanied by many volleys and salutes by the troops and vessels."

THE MISSION OF SAN ANTONIO.*

1771.—This mission was founded by Padre Junipero Serra, July 14, 1771, and is situated about twelve leagues south of Soledad, in Monterey County, on the border of an inland stream upon which it has conferred its name. The buildings were inclosed in a square, 1,200 feet on each side, and walled with adobes. Its lands were forty-eight leagues in circumference, including seven farms, with a convenient house and chapel attached to each. The stream was conducted in paved trenches twenty miles for purposes of irrigation; large crops rewarded the husbandry of the padres. In 1822 this mission owned 52,800 head of cattle, 1,800 tame horses, 3,000 mares, 500 yoke of working oxen, 600 mules, 48,000 sheep, and 1,000 swine. "The climate here is cold in winter and intensely hot in summer. This mission on its secularization fell into the hands of an administrator who neglected its farms, drove off its cattle, and left its poor Indians to starve."—*Walter Colton's Three Years in California.*

The mission grapes were very sweet; wine and aguardiente were made from them in early days, and the grapes were brought to Monterey for sale. The vineyard and garden walls are now gone, and the cattle have destroyed the vines; many of the buildings are down, and the tiles have been removed to roof houses on some of the adjoining ranches. The church is still in good repair. There was formerly a good grist-mill at the mission, but that also, like the mission, is a thing of the past.

THE MISSION OF SOLEDAD.

1791.—Mission Soledad was founded October 9, 1791, and is situated fifteen leagues southwest of Monterey on the left bank of the Salinas River, in a fertile plain known by the name of the "Llano del Rey." The priest was an indefatigable agriculturist. To obviate the summer drought, he constructed, through the labor of his Indians, an aqueduct extending fifteen miles, by which he could water 20,000 acres.

IMMENSE BANDS OF CATTLE.

In 1826 the mission owned about 36,000 head of cattle, and a greater number of horses and mares than any other mission in the country.

So great was the reproduction of these animals that they were not only given away, but also driven in bands into the Bay of Monterey, in order to preserve the pasturage for the cattle. It had about 70,000 sheep and 300 yoke of tame oxen.

---
*An extended history of these missions will be found in the "History of Monterey County," by Elliott & Co.

In 1819 the major-domo of this mission gathered 3,400 bushels of wheat from thirty-eight bushels sown. Its secularization has been followed by decay and ruin.—*Walter Colton.*

The mission possessed a fine orchard of 1,000 trees, but very few were left in 1849. There was also a vineyard about six miles from the mission in a gorge of the mountains.

MISSION SAN JUAN BAUTISTA.*

1794.—This mission looms over a rich valley ten leagues from Monterey—founded 1794. Its lands swept the broad interval and adjacent hills. In 1820 it owned 43,870 head of cattle, 1,360 tame horses, 4,870 mares, colts and fillies. It had seven sheep farms, containing 69,530 sheep; while the Indians attached to the mission drove 321 yoke of working oxen. Its store-house contained $75,000 in goods and $20,000 in specie.

REIGN OF DESOLATION AT SAN JUAN.

This mission was secularized in 1834; its cattle slaughtered for the hides and tallow, its sheep left to the wolves, its horses taken by the dandies, its Indians left to hunt acorns, while the wind sighs over the grave of its last padre.—*Walter Colton.*

This melancholy picture is not too highly colored. Doubtless the secularization laws were intended to benefit the Indians of the mission, nor does it seem that they were conceived in a spirit of unfriendliness to the padres.

HOW THE BUILDING MATERIAL WAS PREPARED.

None of this building stone was found in the vicinity of San Juan Bautista, so that its church is built entirely of *adobe* (sun-dried brick) and *ladrillo*, a species of brick that was baked in a subterranean kiln. The adobe was made out of a species of soil, common to most parts of California. The material was mixed with straw, thoroughly kneaded by hand and foot, moulded into the desired dimensions and afterwards spread upon the earth to dry in the sun, being turned twice in the process of drying, to prevent cracking. The regulation adobe was about thirty inches long by sixteen wide and four thick, and weighed fifty pounds. The bricks were made of clay, mixed and kneaded like the adobe, and baked in subterranean kilns, with a slow fire. These brick were twelve inches long by eight wide and two thick, and are wonderfully durable, as may be seen in the mission church and corridor; the floors of which (being laid with this brick) are hardly abraded by the wear and tear of three-quarters of a century.

DESCRIPTION OF MISSIONS.

The missions were usually quadrilateral buildings, two stories high, including a court-yard ornamented with fountains and trees. The whole consisting of the church, father's apartments, store-houses, barracks, etc. The quadrilateral sides were each about 600 feet in length, one of which was partly occupied by the church.

*An extended history of these missions will be found in the "History of San Benito County," by Elliott & Co.

And so they began their work, surrounded by beautiful scenery, but in seclusion and loneliness. They lived under the shadow of the hills. The sun rose bright and the air was mild, as now, and the music of the surf, and the roar of the ocean in times of storm—these things must have been as familiar to them as they are now to us.

But there must have been something of sublimity about them when all around was in a condition of nature, that we miss in our more artificial life.

They go about their work. They get together the Indians as soon as possible, to communicate with them. They teach them some rude approach to the arts of civilized life. They teach the men to use tools, and the women to weave.

TABLE SHOWING POPULATION OF THE MISSIONS IN YEAR 1802. MOSTLY CHRISTIANIZED INDIANS.

DATE OF FOUNDING	NAME OF MISSION.	MALES.	FEMALES.	TOTAL.
1769	San Diego	737	822	1559
1798	San Luis Rey de Francia	256	276	532
1776	San Juan Capistrano	502	511	1013
1771	San Gabriel	532	515	1047
1797	San Fernando	317	297	614
1782	San Buenaventura	436	502	938
1786	Santa Barbara	521	572	1093
1787	La Purissima Conception	457	571	1028
1772	San Luis Obispo	374	325	699
1797	San Miguel	309	305	614
1791	Soledad	296	267	563
1771	San Antonio de Padua	568	484	1052
1770	San Carlos de Monterey	376	312	688
1797	San Juan Bautista	530	428	958
1794	Santa Cruz	238	199	437
1777	Santa Clara	736	555	1291
1797	San Jose	327	295	622
1776	San Francisco	433	381	814
1804	Santa Inez	...	...	...
1817	San Rafael Archangel	...	...	...
1823	San Francisco de Solano	...	...	...
	Totals	7945	7617	15562

BUILDING MISSION CHURCHES.

Time passes away and we find them with a great work on their hands. It is nothing less than the building of a church. We think that to be no small undertaking even now, with all our facilities. But it is not easy for us to imagine what it was to them, with nothing but hand labor; and that of a very rude sort.

Fifteen years seems a long time to devote to the erection of a church, even when we consider the character of the laborers and the rude tools and appliances used in its construction.

But they set about it. They make adobes. They cut down the trees. They hew out the timber. By some means they get it up to the spot. No small undertaking that as we can see now by examining those very beams, in what remains of those old churches.

Nor did the hewing lack in skill and accuracy, as you can

DESCRIPTION OF THE MISSION CHURCHES.

also see, and the solid adobe walls, you can measure them, and you will find them to be five feet thick. It took often several years to build a church. And so life at the mission began in earnest. Other buildings were erected as they came to be needed.

MISSION DAILY LIFE.

The daily routine at all the missions was very much alike and was about as follows:—

They rose at sunrise and proceeded to the church, to attend morning prayers. Breakfast followed. Then the day's work. Towards noon they returned to the mission and passed the time till two o'clock in the afternoon, between dinner and repose.

After that hour they resumed work and continued it till about sunset. Then all betook themselves to the church for evening devotions, and then to supper.

After supper came amusements till the hour for retiring.

Their diet consisted of beef and mutton, with vegetables in the season. Wheaten cakes and puddings or porridge, called atole and pinole, formed a portion of the repast.

Government Order No. 6, issued from Monterey July 20, 1798, is "to cause the arrest of Jose Arriola, and send him, under guard, so that he be at this place during the coming Sunday, from there to go to Santa Barbara, there to comply with his promise he made a young woman of that place to marry her."

The records do not inform us whether Jose fulfilled his agreement with the young lady or not!

Extract from a letter dated Monterey, June 3, 1799:—

* * * "I send you by the wife of the pensioner, Josef Brabo, one piece of cotton goods and one ounce of sewing

VIEW OF MISSION BUILDINGS AT SAN JUAN.

The dress was, for the males, linen shirt, trousers, and a blanket. The women had each two undergarments a year, a gown and a blanket.

What a dreamy secluded life it must have been, with communication with the outer world only at intervals.

LAWS FOR THE COLONISTS.

We make the following extracts from laws sent the colonists and bearing date Monterey, March 23, 1816:—

"All persons must attend mass, and respond in a loud voice, and if any person should fail to do so, without good cause, they will be put in the stocks for three hours."

"Living in adultery, gaming and drunkenness will not be allowed, and he who commits such vices shall be punished."

Another order required every colonist to possess "two yoke of oxen, two plows, two points or plowshares (see engraving of plow), two hoes for tilling the ground, and they must provide themselves with six hens and one cock."

silk. There are no combs, and I have no hope of receiving any for three years.   HERMENEGILDO SAL,
"Military Governor."

Just think of the colonists being without combs for three years!

DESCRIPTION OF MISSION CONVERTS.

Captain Beechey, in 1826, visited the missions, and says:—

"If any of the captured Indians show a repugnance to conversion, it is the practice to imprison them for a few days, and then allow them to breathe a little fresh air in a walk around the missions, to observe the happy mode of life of their converted countrymen; after which they are again shut up, and thus continue incarcerated until they declare their readiness to renounce the religion of their fathers."

"In the aisles and passages of the church, zealous beadles of the converted race are stationed, armed with sundry weapons of potent influence in effecting silence and attention, and which are not sparingly used on the refractory. These consist of sticks and whips, long goads, etc., and they are not idle in the hands of the officials."

"Sometimes they break their bonds and escape into their original haunts. When brought back to the mission he is always flogged and then has an iron clog attached to one of his legs, which has the effect of preventing his running away and marking him out *in terrorem* to others." Notwithstanding this dark picture, it must not be imagined that life was one of much hardship, or that they even thought so.

THE FIRST INDIAN BAPTISM.

1770.—Of those who came oftenest among them at San Diego, was an Indian about fifteen years of age, who was at last induced to eat whatever was given him without fear. Father Junipero had a desire to teach him, and after understanding a little of the language he desired him to try and bring some little one for baptism. He was told to tell the parents that by allowing a little water to be put on the head the child would become a son of God, be clothed and become equal to the Spaniards. He returned with several Indians, one of whom brought the child for baptism. Full of joy the child was clothed, and the venerable priest ordered the soldiers to attend this first baptism. The ceremony proceeded, and as the water was about to be poured the Indians suddenly snatched away the child and made off in great haste, leaving the father in amazement, with the water in his hands unused.

It was not, however, until the 26th of December, 1770, that the first baptism of the Indians was celebrated at Monterey, which turned out better than the first attempt at San Diego. But at the end of three years only 175 were baptized, showing that the Indians received civilization slowly.

MISSION OF SAN FRANCISCO.

1776.—On September 17, 1776, the presidio and mission of San Francisco were founded, on what was then the extreme boundary of California, the former in a manner being a frontier command, having a jurisdiction which extended to the farthest limits of Spanish discovery.

In its early day the whole military force in Upper California did not number more than from two to three hundred men, divided between the four presidios of San Diego, Santa Barbara, Monterey, and San Francisco, while there were but two towns or pueblos, Los Angeles and San Jose.

When Junipero Serra and his band of missionaries entered Upper California from the lower territory, they brought with them a number of horses, mules, and cattle, wherewith to stock the proposed missions. These were duly distributed, and in time asses, sheep, goats, and swine were added.

RICH MEN OF 1793.

1793.—An inventory of the rich men of the presidio of San Francisco, bearing date 1793, was discovered some years since,
showing that the entire number of stock owned by fourteen wealthy Spaniards, was 115 cattle, 298 sheep and 17 mares.

These are the men who laid the foundation of those immense hordes of cattle which were wont to roam about the entire State, and who were the fathers of those whom we now term native Californians.

As year succeeded year so did their stock increase. They recieved tracts of land "almost for the asking."

Vast bands of cattle roamed about at will over the plains and among the mountains. Once a year these had to be driven in and *rodeod*, i. e., branded, a work of considerable danger, and one requiring much nerve. The occasion of *rodeoing*, however, was the signal for a feast; a large beeve would be slaughtered, and all would make merry until it was consumed. The rule or law concerning branded cattle in those early days was very strict.

If any one was known to have branded his neighbor's cattle with his own mark, common usage called upon him to return in kind fourfold.

Not only did this apply to cattle alone, but to all other kinds of live-stock.

TABLE SHOWING NUMBER OF MISSION INDIANS BETWEEN 1802 AND 1822.

NAME OF MISSION.	BAPTIZED.	MARRIED.	DIED.	EXISTING.
San Diego	5,452	1,460	3,186	1,096
San Luis Rey	4,024	922	1,507	2,063
San Juan Capistrano	3,879	1,026	2,531	1,052
Santa Catarina	6,006	1,638	4,635	1,593
San Fernando	2,519	709	1,503	1,001
San Gabriel	3,608	973	2,606	973
Santa Barbara	4,917	1,298	3,224	1,010
San Buenaventura	1,195	330	896	582
Purisima Conception	3,100	919	2,173	704
San Luis Obispo	2,562	715	1,954	467
San Miguel	2,205	632	1,336	926
San Antonio de Padua	4,119	1,037	317	834
Our Lady of Soledad	1,932	584	1,333	532
San Carlos	3,267	912	2,432	341
San Juan Bautista	3,270	823	1,853	1,222
Santa Cruz	2,136	718	1,541	499
Santa Clara	7,324	2,056	6,565	1,394
San Jose	4,573	1,376	2,933	1,620
San Francisco	6,804	2,050	5,202	958
San Rafael	829	244	183	830
Totals	74,621	20,412	47,925	20,958

DECLINE OF THE MISSIONS.

1803.—In this year one of the missions had become the scene of a revolt; and earlier still, as we learn from an unpublished correspondence of the fathers, it was not unusual for some of the converted Indians to abandon the missions and return to their former wandering life. It was customary on these occasions to pursue the deserters, and compel them to return.

1813.—The extinction of the missions was decreed by act of the Spanish Cortes in 1813, and again in 1828; also, by the

VIEW OF THE VILLAGE OF TRINIDAD, HUMBOLDT CO. CAL.

OFFICE OF THE DAILY HUMBOLDT TIMES, W. H. WYMAN, PROPRIETOR.

SECULARIZATION OF THE MISSIONS.

Mexican Congress in 1833. Year after year they were despoiled of their property, until their final overthrow in 1845.

Each successive revolution in Mexico had recourse to the rich California missions for plunder.

In 1813, when the contest for national independence was being waged on Mexican territory, Spain resolved upon dispensing with the services of the fathers, by placing the missions in the hands of the secular clergy. The professed object of this secularization scheme was, indeed, the welfare of the Indians and colonists; but how little this accorded with the real intentions of the Government, is seen from the seventh section of the decree passed by the cortes, wherein it is stated that one-half of the land was to be hypothecated for the payment of the national debt. This decree of the Government was not carried out at the time, yet it had its effect on the state and well-being of the missions in general.

REIGN OF DISORDER BEGINS.

1826.—In 1826 instructions were forwarded by the Federal Government to the authorities of California for the liberation of the Indians. This was followed a few years later by another Act of the Legislature, ordering the whole of the missions to be secularized and the religious to withdraw. The ostensible object assigned by the authors of this measure, was the execution of the original plan formed by the Government. The missions, it was alleged, were never intended to be permanent establishments.

Meantime, the internal state of the missions was becoming more and more complex and disordered. The desertions were more frequent and numerous, the hostilities of the unconverted more daring, and the general disposition of the people inclined to revolt. American traders and freebooters had entered the country, spread themselves all over the province, and sowed the seeds of discord and revolt among the inhabitants. Many of the more reckless and evil-minded readily listened to their suggestions, adopted their counsels, and broke out into open hostilities.

In 1802, when Humboldt visited California, he estimated the whole population of the upper country as follows: Converted Indians, 15,562; whites and mulattoes, 1,300; total, 66,802. Wild Indians, or beetios (beasts), as they were called, were quite numerous, but being unbaptized were considered beneath the notice of reasonable beings.

ATTACKS ON SEVERAL MISSIONS.

Their hostile attack was first directed against the mission of Santa Cruz, which was captured and plundered, when they directed their course to Monterey, and, in common with their American friends, attacked and plundered that place. From these and other like occurrences, it was clear that the condition of the missions was one of the greatest peril. The spirit of discord had spread among the people, hostility to the authority of the fathers had become common, while desertion from the villages was of frequent and almost constant occurrence.

SECULARIZATION OF THE MISSIONS.

1833.—The Mexican Congress passed a bill to secularize the missions in Upper and Lower California, August 17, 1833.

MISSION CHURCH AND BUILDINGS AT SONOMA.

This took away from the friars the control of the mission property, placing it in charge of administrators; it gave the civil officers predominance over the priestly class. The President of the Republic issued his instructions to Governor Figueroa, of California, who in turn, August 9, 1834, issued a decree that in August, 1835, ten of the missions would be converted into pueblos or towns. A portion of the mission property was then divided among the resident Indians, and the decree issued for the liberation of all the Indians was immediately put in force. The dispersion and demoralization of the people were the immediate results. Released from all restraint, the Indians proved idle, shiftless, and dissipated, wholly incapable of self-control, and a nuisance both to themselves and to every one with whom they came in contact. Within eight years after the execution of the decree, the number of Christians diminished from 30,650 to 4,450!

A REVIEW OF THE MISSIONS.

At the end of sixty-five years, Hon. John W. Dwinelle tells us, in Centennial Memoirs, page 89, that the missionaries of Upper California found themselves in possession of twenty-one prosperous missions, planted upon a line of about 700 miles, running from San Diego north to the latitude of Sonoma. More than 30,000 Indian converts were lodged in the mission buildings, receiving religious culture, assisting at divine worship, and cheerfully performing their easy tasks. Over 700,000 cattle of various species, pastured upon the plains as well as 60,000 horses. One hundred and twenty thousand bushels of wheat were raised annually, which, with maize, beans, peas, and the like, made up an annual crop of 180,000 bushels; while, according to the climate, the different missions rivaled each other in the production of wine, brandy, soap, leather, hides, wool, oil, cotton, hemp, linen, tobacco, salt and soda.

Of 200,000 horned cattle annually slaughtered, the missions furnished about one-half, whose hides, hoofs, horns and tallow were sold at a net result of $10 each, making $1,000,000 dollars from that source alone; while the other articles of which no definite statistics can be obtained, doubtless reached an equal value, making a total production by the missions themselves of $2,000,000.

RAPID DECLINE OF CONVERTS.

It will thus be observed that out of the 74,621 converts received into the missions, the large number of 47,925 had succumbed to disease. What the nature of this plague was it is hard to establish; the missionaries themselves could assign no cause. It was, in all probability, caused by a sudden change in their lives from a free, wandering existence, to a state of settled quietude.

EARLY COLONIZATION PARTY.

1834.—During the year 1834, one Jose Maria Hijar was dispatched from Mexico with a colonization party, bound for Upper California. The ship touched at San Diego, and here a portion of the party disembarked. The remainder proceeded to Monterey, and, a storm arising, their ship was wrecked upon the beach. Hijar now presented his credentials, and was astonished to find that a messenger overland from Mexico had already arrived bringing news of Santa Ana's revolution, together with dispatches from the new president revoking his (Hijar's) appointment; and continuing to keep Figueroa in office.

In the bitter discussion that followed, it came out that Hijar had been authorized to pay for his ship, the *Natalia*,* in mission *tallow*; that the colonists were organized into a company, duly authorized to take charge of the missions, squeeze out of them the requisite capital, and control the business of the territory. The plan had miscarried by a chance, but it showed the missionaries what they had to expect.

With the energy born of despair, eager at any cost to outwit those who sought to profit by their ruin, the mission fathers hastened to destroy that, which through more than half a century, thousands of human beings had spent their lives to accumulate.

---

*The identical vessel in which Napoleon escaped from the Isle of Elba—1815.

TABLE EXPLAINING THE CONTRAST BETWEEN THE ADMINISTRATION OF THE MISSIONS BY THE FATHERS IN 1834 AND THAT OF THE CIVIL AUTHORITIES IN 1842.

NAMES OF THE MISSIONS	NUMBER OF INDIANS		NUMBER OF HORNED CATTLE		NUMBER OF HORSES		NO. OF SHEEP, GOATS AND SWINE		BUSHELS OF GRAIN
	1831	1842	1834	1842	1834	1842	1834	1842	1834
San Diego	2,500	500	12,000	20	1,800	100	17,000	200	18,000
San Luis Rey	3,500	400	80,000	2,500	10,000	400	100,000	4,000	14,000
San Juan Capistrano	1,700	100	70,000	500	1,900	150	10,000	200	10,000
San Gabriel	2,740	500	105,000	700	20,000	300	40,000	2,500	20,000
San Fernando	1,500	400	14,000	1,500	5,000	400	7,000	2,000	7,000
San Buenaventura	1,100	300	4,000	200	1,000	40	6,000	400	7,000
Santa Barbara	1,200	400	5,200	1,800	1,200	160	2,000	400	7,000
Santa Ines	1,370	750	14,000	10,000	1,500	500	12,000	4,000	3,500
La Purisima Concepcion	900	90	15,000	300	2,000	100	14,000	3,500	6,000
San Luis Obispo	1,250	80	9,000	300	4,000	200	7,000	500	4,000
San Miguel	1,300	80	4,000	40	2,500	50	10,000	400	5,500
San Antonio	1,400	150	12,000	50	2,500	100	14,000	1,000	5,000
Nostra Senora de la Soledad	700	20	6,000	...	1,300	...	7,000	...	2,500
Mission del Carmel	500	40	3,000	...	700	...	7,000	...	2,400
San Juan Bautista	1,410	80	9,000	...	1,200	...	9,000	...	3,500
Santa Cruz	500	30	8,000	...	700	...	10,000	...	5,500
Santa Clara	1,800	300	13,000	1,500	1,300	250	15,000	3,000	6,000
San Jose	2,400	400	14,000	8,000	1,100	200	19,000	7,000	10,000
Dolores de San Francisco	500	20	5,000	6	1,000	...	4,000	500	2,000
San Rafael	1,250	20	3,000	...	400	...	4,400	...	1,000
San Francisco Solano	1,300	70	3,000	...	700	...	5,000	...	5,000
Totals	31,812	4,450	390,400	20,820	72,800	3,520	321,500	31,000	122,500

GREAT SLAUGHTER OF CATTLE.

Hitherto, cattle had been killed only as their meat was needed for use; or, at long intervals perhaps, for the hides and tallow alone, when an overplus of stock rendered such action necessary. Now they were slaughtered in herds. There was no market for the meat, and this was considered worthless. The creature was lassoed, thrown, its throat cut; and while yet writhing in the death agony its hide was stripped and pegged upon the ground to dry. There were no vessels to contain the tallow, and this was run into great pits dug for that purpose, to be spaded out anon, and shipped with the hides to market.

Whites and natives alike revelled in gore, and vied with each other in destruction. So many cattle were there to kill, it seemed as though this profitable and pleasant work must last forever. The white settlers were especially pleased with the turn affairs had taken, and many of them did not scruple unceremoniously to appropriate large herds of young cattle wherewith to stock their ranches. Such were the scenes being enacted on the plains.

MISSION BUILDINGS DESTROYED.

At all the missions a similar work was going on. The outer buildings were unroofed, and the timber converted into firewood. Olive groves and orchards were cut down; shrubberies and vineyards torn up. Where the axe and vandal hands failed, fire was applied to complete the work of destruction. Then the solitary bell left hanging on each solitary and dismantled church, called their assistants to a last session of praise and prayer, and the worthy padres rested from their labors.

When the government administrators came, there was but little left; and when they went away, there was *nothing*.

MISSIONS ORDERED ABANDONED.

1845.—A proclamation of Governor Pico, June 5, 1845, provides:—

FINAL DISPOSITION OF THE MISSIONS.

1. That the governor should call together the neophytes of the following-named missions: San Rafael, Dolores, Soledad, San Miguel and La Purisima; and in case those missions were abandoned by their neophytes, that he should give them one month's notice, by proclamation, to return and cultivate said missions, which if they did not do, the missions should be declared abandoned, and the Assembly and governor dispose of them for the good of the Department.

2. That the missions of Carmel, San Juan Bautista, San Juan Capistrano and San Francisco Solano, should be considered as *pueblos*, or villages, which was their present condition; and that the property which remained to them, the governor, after separating sufficient for the curate's house, for churches and their pertinents, and for a municipal house, should sell at public auction, the product to be applied, first to paying the debts of the establishments, and the remainder, if any, to the benefit of divine worship.

3. That the remainder of the missions to San Diego, inclusive, should be rented at the discretion of the governor.

SALE OF THE MISSIONS.

1845.—On the 28th of October of this year, Governor Pico gave public notice for the sale to the highest bidder of five missions, viz: San Rafael, Dolores, Soledad, San Miguel and La Purisima; likewise for the sale of the remaining buildings in the pueblos (formerly missions) of San Luis Obispo, Carmel, San Juan Bautista, and San Juan Capistrano, after separating the churches and their appurtenances, and a curate's, municipal and school house. The auctions were appointed to take place, those of San Luis Obispo, Purisima and San Juan Capistrano, the first four days of December following (1845); those of San Rafael, Dolores, San Juan Bautista, Carmel, Soledad and San Miguel, the 23d and 24th of January, 1846; meanwhile, the Government would receive and take into consideration proposals in relation to said missions.

The final disposition of the missions at the date of 1846 will be seen in the following:—

TABLE SHOWING THE FINAL DISPOSITION OF MISSIONS.

No.	Name of Mission.	How Disposed of at the Government.
1	San Diego	Sold to Santiago Arguello, June 8, 1846.
2	San Luis Rey	Sold to Antonio Cot and Andres Pico, May 18, 1846.
3	San Juan Capistrano	Purchased and rented as a sale to John Forster and James McKinley, December 6, 1845.
4	San Gabriel	Sold to Julian Workman and Hugo Reid, June 16, 1846.
5	San Fernando	Rented to Andres Pico, for nine years from December, 1845, and sold to Juan Celis, June, 1846.
6	San Buenaventura	Sold to Joseph Arnaz.
7	Santa Barbara	Rented for nine years, from June 5, 1846, to Nich's Den.
8	Santa Ynez	Rented to Joaquin Carrillo.
9	La Purisima	Sold to John Temple, December 6, 1845.
10	San Luis Obispo	Pueblo.
11	San Miguel	Unavailable.
12	San Antonio	Vacant.
13	Soledad	House and garden sold to Sobranes, January 4, 1846.
14	Carmel de Monterey	Pueblo.
15	San Juan Bautista	Pueblo.
16	Santa Cruz	Vacant.
17	Santa Clara	In charge of priest.
18	San Jose	In charge of priest.
19	Dolores, (San Francisco)	Pueblo.
20	San Rafael	Mission in charge of priest.
21	San Francisco Solano	Mission in charge of priest.

Industries of Early Times.

FARMING in California was in a very primitive state up to its occupation by the Americans. What farming the Californians did was of a very rude description; their plow was a primitive contrivance, their vehicles unwieldy. Such articles of husbandry as reapers, mowers and headers had not entered their dreams, and they were perfectly independent of their advantages.

Grain was cut with a short, stumpy, smooth-edged sickle; it was threshed by the tramping of horses. One of their few evils was the depredations of the wild Indians, who would sometimes steal their horses, and then the cattle would have to perform the work of separation. The cleaning of grain was performed by throwing it in the air with wooden shovels, and allowing the wind to carry off the chaff.

In a work published in London in 1839, by Alexander Forbes, are some interesting descriptions of the country about the Bay of Monterey, and the condition of farming as witnessed by him in 1835.

PLOW USED BY CALIFORNIANS.

The plow used at that time must have been of great antiquity. It was composed of two principal pieces; one, called the main piece, was formed out of a crooked branch of timber, cut from a tree of such a natural shape. This plow had only one handle, and no mould-board or other contrivance for turning over the furrow, and was, therefore, only capable of making a simple cut, equal on both sides.

PLOW USED BY NATIVE CALIFORNIANS.

The only iron about the plow was a small piece fitted to the point of the stile, and of the shape seen in the detached part of the engraving. The beam was of great length, so as to reach the yoke of the oxen. This beam was also composed of a natural piece of wood, cut from a tree of proper dimensions, and had no dressing, except taking off the bark. This beam was inserted into the upper part of the main piece, and connected with it by a small upright piece of wood, on which it slides, and is fixed by two wedges; by withdrawing these wedges the beam was elevated or lowered, and depth of furrow regulated.

The long beam passes between the two oxen, like the pole of a carriage, and no chain is used. A pin is put through the point of the beam, and the yoke is tied to that by thongs of rawhide. The plow-man goes at one side, holding the handle with his right hand, and managing the goad and cattle with his left. The manner of yoking the oxen was by putting the yoke (a straight stick of wood) on the top of the head, close behind the horns, and tied firmly to their roots and to the forehead by thongs, so that, instead of drawing by the shoulders, as with us now, they drew by the roots of the horns and forehead. They had no freedom to move their heads, and went with the nose turned up, and seemed to be in pain.

With this plow only a sort of a rut could be made, and the soil was broken by successive crossing and recrossing many times. Plowing could only be done after the rains came, and an immense number of plows had to be employed.

MODERN FARMING TOOLS UNKNOWN.

The harrow was totally unknown, and a bush was drawn over the field to cover in the seed; but in some places a long, heavy log of wood was drawn over the field, something of the plan of a roller, but dragging without turning round, so as to carry a portion of the soil over the seed.

INDUSTRIES OF NATIVE CALIFORNIANS.

The Californians were not without their native manufactures, and they did not, as is generally supposed, rely altogether upon the slaughter of cattle and the sale of hides and tallow. The missionaries had taught them the cultivation of the grape and manufacture of wine. Hemp, flax, cotton and tobacco were grown in small quantities. Soap, leather, oil, brandy, wool, salt, soda, harness, saddles, wagons, blankets, etc., were manufactured.

Of California it may be truly said, that before the admission of foreign settlers, neither the potato nor green vegetables were cultivated as articles of food.

DAIRYING IN EARLY TIMES.

The management of the dairy was totally unknown. There was hardly any such thing in use as butter and cheese. The butter was an execrable compound of sour milk and cream mixed together; the butter being made of the cream on top of the milk, and a large portion of the sour, heat up together by hand, and without a churn. It was of a dirty gray color, and very disagreeable flavor, and always rancid.

They had an awkward way of milking, as they thought it absolutely necessary to use the calf to induce the cow to give milk; so they let the calf suck for some time alone, and then lay hold of the teats as they could, while the calf was still sucking, and by a kind of stealth procured a portion of the milk.

The supercargo of a British ship from India, bound to the coast of Mexico, informed Alexander Forbes* in 1832, that on making the coast of California, they touched at the Russian settlement, called La Bodega (Sonoma County), and which borders on the Spanish territory—or rather of right belongs to it, and although the part which the Russians possess is sterile in comparison to the fine plains occupied by the Spaniards, yet they found immediately on their arrival a present sent on board by the Russian Governor, of most excellent butter, fat mutton, and

* Now a resident of Oakland. See Biography, page 31.

good vegetables, all things most desirable to people arriving from a long voyage. They soon proceeded to Monterey, the capital of Spanish California, where they could find nothing but hull beef; neither bread, butter, cheese, or vegetables could be procured. As late as 1834 Monterey was supplied with butter and cheese from the Russian settlement at Bodega.

PRIMITIVE THRESHING SCENE.

When the crops were ripe, they were cut with a sickle, or any other convenient weapon, and then it became necessary to thresh them. Now for the *modus operandi*. The floor of the corral into which it was customary to drive the horses and cattle in order to lasso them, from constant use had become hardened. Into this inclosure the grain would be piled, and upon it the *manatha*, or hand of mares, would be turned loose to tramp out the grain. The wildest horses would be turned adrift upon the pile of straw, when would ensue a scene of the wildest confusion; the excited animals being driven, amidst the yelling of the *vaqueros* and the cracking of whips, here, there, and everywhere, around, across, and lengthwise, until the whole was trampled, leaving naught but the grain and chaff.

The most difficult part of the operation, however, was the separating of the grain from the chaff. Owing to the length of the dry season, there was no urgent haste to effect this; therefore when the wind was high enough, the Indians, who soon fell into the ways of the white pioneers, more especially where they were paid in kind and kindness, would toss the trampled mass into the air with large wooden forks, cut from the adjacent oaks, and the wind carried away the lighter chaff, leaving the heavier grain. With a favorable wind, several bushels of wheat could thus be winnowed in the course of one day.

How insignificant this scene appears when contrasted with a San Joaquin farmer's outfit of a 24-horse reaper and thresher combined, which is fully described further on in this work, and represented in several engravings.

GOLDEN AGE OF NATIVE CALIFORNIANS.

Mr. William Halley says: From 1833 to 1850 may be set down as the golden age of the native Californians. Not till then did the settlement of the rancheros become general. The missions were breaking up, the presidios deserted, the population dispersed, and land could be had almost for the asking. Never before, and never since, did a people settle down under the blessings of more diverse advantages.

The country was lovely, the climate delightful; the valleys were filled with horses and cattle; wants were few, and no one dreaded dearth. There was meat for the pot and wine for the cup, and wild game in abundance. No one was in a hurry. "Bills payable" or the state of the stocks troubled no one, and Arcadia seems to have temporarily made this her seat. The people did not, necessarily, even have to stir the soil for a livelihood, because the abundance of their stock furnished them

"BELMORE HALL", HOME OF ROBERT W. ROBARTS, FERNDALE, HUMBOLDT CO. CAL.

ISLAND HOME OF F. Z. BOYNTON 4 MILES FROM FERNDALE, HUMBOLDT CO. CAL.

with food and enough hides and tallow to procure money for every purpose. They had also the advantage of cheap and docile labor in the Indians, already trained to work at the missions. And had they looked in the earth for gold, they could have found it in abundance.

They were exceedingly hospitable and sociable. Every guest was welcomed. The sparsity of the population made them rely on each other, and they had many occasions to bring them together.

SCENES OF FESTIVITY AND GAYETY.

Church days, bull-fights, rodeos, were all occasions of festivity. Horsemanship was practiced as it was never before out of Arabia; dancing found a ball-room in every house, and music was not unknown. For a *caballero* to pick up a silver coin from the ground at full gallop, was not considered a feat; and any native youth could perform the mustang riding which was lately accomplished with such credit by young Peralta, in New York. To fasten down a mad bull with a *lariat*, or even subdue him single-handed in a *corral*, were every-day performances. The branding and selecting of cattle in *rodeos* was a gala occasion.

While the young men found means to gratify their tastes for highly-wrought saddles and elegant bridles, the women had their fill of finery, furnished by the Yankee vessels that visited them regularly for trade every year. Few schools were established, but the rudiments of education were given at home. The law was administered by Alcaldes, Prefects, and Governor. Murder was very rare, suicide unknown, and San Francisco was without a jail.

FAVORITE NATIVE LIQUOR.

Wine was plentiful, and so was brandy. There was a native liquor in use, that was very intoxicating. It was a sort of cognac, which was very agreeable and very volatile, and went like a flash to the brain. It was expensive, and those selling it made a large profit. This liquor was known as *aguadiente*, and was the favorite tipple until supplanted by the whisky of the Americanos. It was mostly made in Los Angeles, where the larger part of the grapes raised were used for it.

THE ADOBE RESIDENCES.

The walls were fashioned of large sun-dried bricks, made of that black loam known to settlers in the Golden State as adobe soil, mixed with straw, with no particularity as to species, measuring about eighteen inches square and three in thickness; these were cemented with mud, plastered within with the same substance, and whitewashed when finished. The rafters and joists were of rough timber, with the bark simply peeled off and placed in the requisite position; while the residences of the wealthier classes were roofed with tiles of a convex shape, placed so that the one should overlap the other, and thus make a water-shed; or, later, with shingles, the poor contenting themselves with a thatch of *tule*, fastened down with thongs of bullock's hide. The former modes of covering were expensive, and none but the opulent could afford the luxury of tiles. When completed, however, these mud dwellings will stand the brunt and wear and tear of many decades, as can be evidenced by the number which are still occupied.

There were occasional political troubles, but these did not much interfere with the profound quiet into which the people had settled. The change from a monarchy into a republic scarcely produced a ripple. The invasions of the Americans did not stir them very profoundly. But they have received such a shock in their slumbers that they, too, like their predecessors, the Indians, are rapidly passing away.

SPANISH OX-CART.

The form of the ox-cart was as rude as that of the plow. The pole was of very heavy dimensions, and fastened to the yoke and oxen the same as the plow. The animals had to bear the weight of the load on their heads. This added greatly to the distress of the poor animals, as they felt every jerk and twist of the cart in the most sensitive manner; and as the roads were full of ruts and stones, it is a wonder that the animals' heads were not twisted off.

OLD FASHIONED SPANISH OX-CART.

The wheels of this cart were of the most singular construction. They had no spokes and were made of three pieces of timber. The middle piece was hewn out of a large tree, of size to form the nave and middle of the wheel, all in one. The other two pieces were made of timber bent and joined by keys of wood. There does not enter into the construction of this cart a particle of iron, not even a nail, for the axle is of wood and the lynch-pin of the same material.

Walter Colton says: "The ox-cart of the Californian is quite unique and primitive. The wheels are cut transversely from the butt end of a tree, and have holes through the center for a huge wood axle, as seen in our engraving. The oxen draw by the head and horns instead of the chest; and they draw enormous loads.

"On gala days it was swept out and covered with mats: a deep body put on, which is arched with hoop-poles, and over these a pair of sheets are extended for a covering. Into this the ladies are tumbled with the children, and they start ahead."

An old settler writes to us that "Many of our people will

recollect the carts used in early days by the Californians. They usually traveled from place to place on horseback; but when the family desired to visit a neighbor or go to town, the family coach was called into use. The vehicle consisted of two immense wooden wheels, cut or sawed off a log, with holes as near the center as convenient for the axle-tree, with a tongue lashed to the axle with rawhide thongs. Upon this a frame, as wide as the wheels would permit, and from seven to twelve feet in length, was placed, upon which was securely fastened one or two rawhides with the flesh side down, and a rude frame over the top, upon which to stretch an awning, with rawhide thongs woven around the sides to keep the children from tumbling out.

"The female portion of the family, with the small children, would seat themselves in the cart, to which was attached a pair of the best traveling oxen on the ranch. An Indian would drive, or rather lead the oxen (for he usually walked ahead of them). In this simple, rude contrivance the family would travel twenty or thirty miles in a day with as much comfort, apparently, as people now take in riding in our modern vehicles. Sometimes several families would ride in a single cart, and visit their friends, go to town for the purpose of shopping, or to attend church, etc."

SPANISH GRIST-MILL.

Wheat and corn were generally ground or pounded in the common hand stone mortar; but in larger settlements horse-power was used in turning or rolling one large stone upon another, as shown in the engraving on page 35.

Water-power mills for grinding flour in Upper California were but few, and of the most primitive description; but none better are to be found in the other parts of Spanish America not even in Chili where wheat abounds. These mills consist of an upright axle, to the lower end of which is fixed a horizontal water-wheel placed under the building, and to the upper end of the mill-stone; and as there is no intermediate machinery to increase the velocity, it is evident that the mill-stone can make only the same number of revolutions as the water-wheel. This makes it necessary that the wheel should be of very small diameter, otherwise no power of water thrown upon it could make it go at a rate sufficient to give the mill-stone the requisite velocity. It is therefore made of very small dimensions, and is constructed in the following manner; A set of what is called *cucharas* (spoons) is stuck in the periphery of the wheel which serve in place of float-boards; they are made of pieces of timber in something of the shape of spoons, the handles being inserted in mortises on the edge of the wheel, and the bowls of the spoons made to receive the water, which spouts on them laterally and forces the small wheel around with nearly the whole velocity of the water which impinges upon it. Of this style of mill even there were not more than three in all California as late as 1835.

Russian Settlements in Sonoma.

1811.—In January, 1811, Alexander Koskoff, took possession of the country about Bodega, Sonoma County, on the fragile pleas that he had been refused a supply of water at Yerba Buena, and that he had obtained, by right of purchase from the Indians, all the land lying between Point Reyes and Point Arena, and for a distance of three leagues inland. Here he remained for a while, and to Bodega gave the name of Romanzoff, calling the stream now known as Russian River, Slavianka.

Although repeatedly ordered to depart by the King of Spain, who claimed all the territory north of Fuca Straits, they continued to remain for a lengthened period, possessors of the land.

FIRST PIONEER SQUATTERS.

And as General Vallejo remarks: "As the new-comers came without permission from the Spanish Government, they may be termed the pioneer 'squatters' of California." So far indeed was it from the intention of the unwelcome Muscovite to move, that we find them extending their trapping expeditions along the coast, to the north and south, and for a considerable distance inland.

At Fort Ross, in Sonoma County, they constructed a quadrilateral stockade, which was deemed strong enough to resist the possible attacks of Spaniards or Indians. It had within its walls quarters for the commandant, officers, and men, an arsenal, store-houses, a Greek church, surmounted with a cross and provided with a chime of bells.

ONE OF THE FIRST ORCHARDS.

About a mile distant from the fort there was an inclosure containing about five acres, which was inclosed by a fence about eight feet high, made of redwood slabs about two inches in thickness, these being driven into the ground, while the tops were nailed firmly to girders extending from post to post, set about ten feet apart. Within the inclosure there was an orchard, consisting of apple, prune, and cherry trees. Of these, fifty of the first and nine of the last-named, moss-grown and gray with age, still remain, while it is said that all the old stock of German prunes in California came from seed produced there.

FIRST INDUSTRY NORTH OF SAN FRANCISCO.

We may safely assert, that to these Russians belongs the honor of erecting the first church in California, north of the Bay of San Francisco; but this is not all; to them belongs the credit of first planting fruit, raising grain, and working in leather, wood and iron, within the limits of the same territory. With these industries in hand, there is not the remotest doubt that the Russians looked to a future permanent possession of northern California. At this time, too, they made considerable annual shipments of grain to Sitka from Fort Ross and Bodega.

INDUSTRY AND THRIFT OF THE RUSSIANS.

RUSSIANS LOCATE AND FORTIFY.

The location once chosen they set to work to prepare their new homes. A site was chosen for the stockade near the shore of the ocean, and in such a position as to protect all their ships lying in the little cove, and prevent any vessel inimical to them from landing. The plat of ground inclosed in this stockade was a parallelogram, 280 feet wide and 312 feet long, and containing about two acres. Its angles were placed very nearly upon the cardinal points of the compass. At the north and south angle there was constructed an octagonal bastion, two stories high, and furnished with six pieces of artillery. These bastions were built exactly alike, and were about twenty-four feet in diameter.

The walls were formed of hewed logs, mortised together at the corners, and were about eight inches in thickness. The roof was conical shaped, having a small flag-staff at the apex. The stockade approached these towers in such a way that one-half of them was within the inclosure and the other half on the outside, the entrance to them being through small doors on the inside, while there were embrasures both on the inside and outside. They were thus arranged so as to protect those within from an outside enemy. All around the stockade there were embrasures suitable for the use of muskets or carronades, of which latter it is said, several were in the fortress.

RUSSIAN CHAPEL AT FORT ROSS.

On the northern side of the eastern angle there was erected a chapel which it is said was used by the officers of the garrison alone. It was 25x31 feet in dimensions, and strongly built, the outer wall forming part of the stockade, and the round port-holes for the use of carronades, are peculiar looking openings in a house of worship. The entrance was on the inside of the fort, and consisted of a rude, heavy wooden door, held upon wooden hinges. There was a vestibule about 10x25 feet in size, thus leaving the auditorium 21x25 feet. From the vestibule a narrow stair-way led to a low loft, while the building was surmounted with two domes, one of which was round and the other pentagonal in shape, in which it is said the Muscovites had hung a chime of bells. The roof was made of long planks, either sawed or rove from redwood, likewise the side of the chapel in the fort.

The frame-work of all the buildings was made of very large, heavy timbers, many of them being twelve inches square. The rafters were all great, ponderous, round pine logs, a considerable number of them being six inches in diameter.

FIRST WINDMILL FOR GRINDING WHEAT.

To the northward of, and near the village, situated on an eminence, was a windmill, which was the motor for driving a single run of buhrs, and also for a stamping machine used for grinding tan-bark. The windmill produced all the flour used in that and the Bodega settlements, and probably a considerable amount was also sent with the annual shipment to Sitka.

FIRST TANNERY ERECTED.

To the south of the stockade, and in a deep gulch at the *debouchure* of a small stream into the ocean, there stood a very large building, probably 80x100 feet in size, the rear half of which was used for the purpose of tanning leather. There were six vats in all, constructed of heavy, rough redwood slabs, and each with a capacity of fifty barrels; there was also the usual appliances necessary to conduct a tannery, but these implements were large and rough in their make; still with these they were able to manufacture a good quality of leather in large quantities.

The front half of the building, or that fronting on the ocean, was used as a work-shop for the construction of ships. Ways were constructed on a sand beach at this point leading into deep water, and upon them were built a number of staunch vessels, and from here was launched the very first sea-going craft built in California. Still further to the south, and near the ocean shore, stood a building 80x100, which bore all

GRIST-MILL OF EARLY SETTLERS.

the marks of having been used as a store-house; it was, however, unfortunately blown down by a storm on July 16, 1878, and before many years there will be nothing left to mark its former site.

THE RUSSIAN FARMERS.

The Russians had farmed very extensively at this place, having at least 2,000 acres under fence, besides a great deal that was not fenced. These fences were chiefly of that kind known as rail and post.

Their agricultural processes were as crude as any of their other work. Their plow was very similar to the old Spanish implement, described on page 31, so common in this country at that time, and still extant in Mexico, with the exception that the Muscovite instrument possessed a mold-board. They employed oxen and cows as draft animals, using the old Spanish yoke adjusted to their horns, instead of to their necks. We have no account of any attempt at constructing either cart or wagon by them, but it is probable that they had vehicles the same as those described heretofore, as being in use among the Californians at that time.

THRESHING AS DONE BY RUSSIANS.

Threshing was done on a floor composed of heavy puncheons, circular in shape, and elevated somewhat above the ground. Between the puncheons were interstices through which the grain fell under the floor as it was released from the head. The threshing was done in this wise: A layer of grain, in the straw, of a foot or two in thickness, was placed upon the floor. Oxen were then driven over it, hitched to a log with rows of wooden pegs inserted into it. As the log revolved, these pegs acted well the part of a flail, and the straw was expeditiously relieved of its burden of grain. It was, doubtless, no hard job to winnow the grain after it was threshed, as the wind blows a stiff breeze at that point during all the summer months.

The Russians constructed a wharf at the northern side of the little cove, and graded a road down the steep ocean shore to it. Its line is still to be seen, as it passed much of the way through solid rock. This wharf was made fast to the rock on which it was constructed with long iron bolts, of which only a few that were driven into the hard surface now remain; the wharf itself is gone, hence we are unable to give its dimensions, or further details concerning it.

FIRST LUMBER MADE NORTH OF SAN FRANCISCO.

1812.—These old Muscovites, doubtless, produced the first lumber with a saw ever made north of San Francisco Bay, for they had both a pit and a whip-saw, the former of which can be seen to this day. Judging from the number of stumps still standing, and the extent of territory over which they extended their logging operations, they evidently consumed large quantities of lumber. The timber was only about one mile distant from the ship-yard and landing, while the stumps of trees cut by them are still standing, and beside them from one to six shoots have sprung up, many of which have now reached a size sufficient for lumber purposes. This growth has been remarkable, and goes to show that if proper care were taken, each half century would see a new crop of redwoods, sufficiently large for all practical purposes, while ten decades would see gigantic trees.

For more than a quarter of a century they continued to hold undisturbed possession of the disputed territory, and prosecuted their farming, stock-raising, hunting, trapping and ship-building enterprises, and whatever may have been the causes which led to it, there finally came a time when the Russian authorities had decided to withdraw the California colony.

RUSSIANS SELL OUT TO GENERAL SUTTER.

The proposition was made first by them to the government authorities at Monterey, to dispose of their interests at Bodega and Fort Ross, including their title to the land; but, as the authorities had never recognized their right or title, and did not wish to do so at that late date, they refused to purchase. Application was next made to General M. J. Vallejo, but on the same grounds he refused to purchase.

They then applied to Captain John A. Sutter, a gentleman at that time residing near where Sacramento City now stands, and who had made a journey from Sitka, some years before, in one of their vessels. They persuaded Sutter into the belief that their title was good, and could be maintained; so, after making out a full invoice of the articles they had for disposal, including all the land lying between Point Reyes and Point Mendocino, and one league inland, as well as cattle, farming and mechanical implements, also, a schooner of 180 tons burthen, some arms, a four-pound brass field-piece, etc., a price was decided upon, the sum being $30,000, which, however, was not paid at one time, but in cash installments of a few thousand dollars, the last payment being made through Governor Burnett, in 1849.

All the stipulations of the sale having been arranged satisfactorily to both parties, the transfer was duly made, and Sutter became, as he thought, the greatest landholder in California. In 1859, Sutter disposed of his Russian claim which was a six-eighths interest in the lands mentioned above, to William Muldrew, George R. Moore and Daniel W. Welty; but they only succeeded in getting $6,000 out of one settler, and the remainder refusing to pay, the claim was dropped.

EVACUATION OF FORT ROSS.

Orders were sent to the settlers at Fort Ross to repair at once to San Francisco Bay, and ships were dispatched to bring them there, where whaling vessels, which were bound for the northwest whaling grounds, had been chartered to convey them to Sitka. The vessels arrived at an early hour in the day, and the orders shown to the commander, Rotscheff, who immediately caused the bells in the chapel tower to be rung, and the cannon to be discharged, this being the usual method of convocating the people at an unusual hour, or for some special purpose, so everything was suspended just there—the husbandman left his plow standing in the half-turned furrow, and unloosed his oxen, never again to yoke them, leaving them to wander at will over the fields; the mechanic dropped his planes and saws on the bench, leaving the half-smoothed board still in the vise; the tanner left his tools where he was using them, and doffed his apron to don it no more in the State of California.

As soon as the population had assembled, Rotscheff arose and read the orders. Very sad and unwelcome, indeed, was this intelligence; but the edict had emanated from a source which could not be gainsaid, and the only alternative was a speedy and complete compliance, however reluctant it might be—and thus 400 people were made homeless by the fiat of a single word. Time was only given to gather up a few household effects.

BLOCKSBURG HOTEL, CAP. H.H.TICKNOR, PROPRIETOR. BLOCKSBURG, HUMBOLDT CO. CAL.

SALMON BROWN'S SHEEP RANCH, TWO MILES FROM BRIDGEVILLE, HUMBOLDT CO. CAL.

Foreigners Begin to Come.

The early success of the missions advertised the attractiveness of California to the world. It became known not only in Mexico, but through the early adventurers and traders, in the United States. They not only traded in hides and tallow, but told the story of the mission wealth—the herds and flocks and fruits, and they told of the furs to be procured.

The valleys of California were, during the early part of this century, occupied and traversed by bands of trappers in the employ of the American and foreign fur companies. The stories of their wanderings and experiences are mostly related in the form of sensational novels, whose authenticity and accuracy must be taken with a great degree of allowance.

Few records concerning these fur hunters remain which are within the reach of the historian, and the information given has been gleaned, in part, from personal interviews with those whose knowledge of the subject was gained by actual experience or by a personal acquaintance with those who belonged to the parties. In many cases their stories differ widely in regard to facts and names.

We here give the date of arrival of some of the most important of the pioneers, and incidents connected with their movements.

1814.—John Gilroy arrived at Monterey on the 8th of February, 1814. His baptismal name was John Cameron; but he assumed the name of John Gilroy in consequence of certain circumstances connected with his birth.

He spent most of his life around Monterey, and resided at what is called "Old Gilroy," a short distance from Gilroy, in Santa Clara County, which places are named from him.

UPPER SAN JOAQUIN VALLEY EXPLORED.

1820.—As early as this date, Tulare, San Joaquin and Sacramento Valleys were occupied by trappers, who had wandered there while searching for the Columbia River. Captain Sutter, in 1834, while in New Mexico, heard from these California trappers, of the Sacramento Valley, which afterwards became so reputed as his home. The disputes arising in regard to the occupation of the northern part of the Pacific Coast trapping region in Oregon, led the American hunters to occupy the territory in and about the Rocky Mountains.

A TOUCHING LITTLE EPISODE.

1822.—About the year 1822, an Englishman landed at Santa Cruz, known by the name of William Thompson. He is employed in the hide business. There is a touching little story connected with him. His native place was London. His father was a sail-maker. And there lived the family—mother, brothers, sisters and all. William went to sea. They parted with him with regret and sorrow, and after a time they ceased to hear from him. Years went by and they could get no tidings of him. The family grieved; and the mother pined for her son. But time went on, and no tidings came. By and by his brother Samuel proposed to go in search of him. Though he did not know where on the globe he might be, if still alive, yet he thought he could go to sea, and make voyages to different parts, and somewhere fall in with him, or hear of him. His plan was agreed to, and he started. Just how long he sailed, and where he went, is unknown; but after a while he was on a ship that came into the port of Santa Cruz. Here was anchored, at that time, another ship, taking on board a cargo of hides.

Samuel then came ashore and inquired for the captain of that ship. When he found him, he asked him if among his crew there was one William Thompson. The captain said he didn't know certainly whether he had a man by that name "but there the men are," said he, pointing to them at work on the beach, carrying hides, "you can go and see." Samuel went, and the very first man he met was William! We can imagine Samuel's joy at the meeting, after so long a search; and the joy, also, that the account of it caused in that home in London, when it reached there. But it appears, instead of Samuel getting William to go home, that they both remained on this coast. They shipped together and went down to South America, and then returned to Santa Cruz.

STRANGE MEETING ON THE MERCED.

1823.—The Ashley expedition was fitted out in 1823, at St. Louis, for the fur trade. This party entered the San Joaquin Valley, and hunted and trapped along the Merced, Stanislaus and Tuolumne Rivers.

Belonging to this company was Joshua Griffith and William Hawkins, who met first at St. Louis, and afterwards hunted in the San Joaquin Valley.

Years rolled on and they were widely separated, and after many vicissitudes, of wild adventure, through scenes of peril, among hostile Indians and various hair-breadth escapes—strange to say, we find them after years had passed away, in 1874, settled down to quiet life, each with a family, on the Merced River, which locality seems to have impressed them as the choicest of the State. They were living there as late as 1878.

Captain Juan B. R. Cooper came to Monterey in 1823, and obtained a license to hunt otters, as also did some others.

1824.—Santiago McKinly, a native of Scotland, arrived in Los Angeles during the year 1824. He was at that time twenty-one years of age. He became a merchant, and his name appears on a list of foreigners resident in Los Angeles in 1836, now on file in the city archives. He afterwards went to Monterey, and was reported dead some years ago.

From Scotland came David Spence, in 1824, with the view of establishing a packing house in Monterey for a Lima firm.

SAN JOAQUIN VALLEY.

1825.—In the spring of this year, Jedediah Smith, with a party of forty trappers and Indians, started from the headquarters on Green River, traveling westward, crossed the Sierra Nevada Mountains, and in July entered the Upper San Joaquin Valley. The country from the Tulare to the American Fork of the Sacramento River was traversed in trapping for Beaver. They found at the fork another party of American trappers encamped, and located their own rendezvous near the present town of Folsom. In October, Smith, leaving the remainder of the party at the camp, returned to the company's headquarters on Green River.

1826.—In May, 1826, Smith again set out for the new trapping region taking a route further south than on the first trip, but when in the Mohave settlement on the Colorado, all the party, except Smith, Galbraith, and Turner, were killed by Indians. These three escaped to San Gabriel Mission, and December 26, 1826, were arrested as spies or filibusters. They were taken to the presidio at San Diego, where they were detained until the following certificate from Americans then in San Francisco was presented:—

"We, the undersigned, having been requested by Captain Jedediah S. Smith to state our opinion regarding his entering the Province of California, do not hesitate to say that we have no doubt but that he was compelled to, for want of provisions and water, having entered so far into the barren country that lies between the latitudes of forty-two and forty-three west that he found it impossible to return by the route he came, as his horses had most of them perished for want of food and water; he was therefore under the necessity of pushing forward to California—it being the nearest place where he could procure supplies to enable him to return.

"In testimony whereof we have hereunto set our hand and seal, this 20th day of December, 1826.

WILLIAM G. DANA, Captain of schooner *Waverly*.
WILLIAM H. CUNNINGHAM, Captain of ship *Courier*.
WILLIAM HENDERSON, Captain of brig *Olive Branch*.
JAMES SCOTT.
THOMAS M. ROBINS, Mate of schooner *Waverly*.
THOMAS SHAW, Supercargo of ship *Courier*."

Smith was liberated, and during the summer of 1827 with his party left the San Joaquin Valley, journeying toward the Columbia River.

John J. Read, when but a mere lad, was taken by his uncle, who was a sailor, on a voyage to Mexico, from thence to California, sailing from Acapulco, arriving in the State in the year 1826, just after attaining his twenty-first year, and, after staying a short time in Los Angeles, proceeded northward until he reached Saucelito, and there took up his residence. He next, in 1827, removed to Sonoma County, and tilled a portion of the Cotate Rancho, at the same time making application for the grant; but he was not permitted to remain, for the Indians drove him off, destroyed his crop, and buried his implements.

FIRST FERRY-BOAT ON THE BAY.

Mr. Read came to Saucelito to reside in 1832, erecting, for his accommodation, near the *old town* a wooden shanty, from whence he plied a small boat regularly to the opposite shore of Yerba Buena, and established the first ferry on the Bay of San Francisco. Mr. Read married, October 13, 1836, at the Church of the Mission Dolores, the Señorita Hilarita, the youngest daughter of Don Jose Antonio Sanchez, Commander of the Presidio at San Francisco.

PIONEER MERCHANT AT LOS ANGELES.

1827.—John Temple, who may justly rank as the pioneer merchant of Los Angeles, was a native of Reading, Mass., and for several years prior to his advent on this coast, resided at the Sandwich Islands. He came to Los Angeles about the year 1827, formed a partnership with George Rice, and opened the first store of general merchandise ever established in the pueblo.

ANOTHER PIONEER.

1828.—Abel Stearns, a native of Salem, Mass., spent considerable time in Mexico, and settled in Los Angeles as a merchant in the year 1828. He married Doña Arcadia, daughter of Don Juan Bandini. He obtained large grants of land throughout the territory, and accumulated much wealth. He was a member of the Constitutional Convention, 1849, and of the State Legislature, 1851; also 1861. He died at San Francisco, August 23, 1871. His widow subsequently married Col. R. S. Baker—residence, Los Angeles.

SAN JOAQUIN VALLEY VISITED.

1830.—Ewing Young, who had trapped with parties on the upper part of the Del Norte, the eastern part of the Grand and the Colorado Rivers, pursuing the route formerly traversed by Smith, in the winter of 1829–30, entered the San Joaquin Valley and hunted on the Tulare Lake, and the adjacent streams.

1832.—During the last part of 1832, or early in 1833, Young, having again entered the San Joaquin Valley and trapped on the streams, finally arrived at the Sacramento River, about ten miles below the mouth of the American. He followed up the Sacramento to the Feather River, and from there crossed over to the coast. The coast-line was traveled till they reached the mouth of the Umpqua, where they crossed the mountains to the inland. Entering the upper portion of the Sacramento Valley, they proceeded southerly till they reached the American River. Then they followed up through the San Joaquin Valley, and passed out through the Tejon Pass in the winter of 1833–34.

Besides these parties and leaders mentioned, during this period there were several trappers, or "lone traders," who explored and hunted through the valleys.

FIRST SCHOONER BUILT.

1831.—William Wolfskill was born March 20, 1798, near Richmond, Kentucky. Until the year 1831 he roamed through the great West as a hunter and trapper. In February of that year he reached Los Angeles with a number of others, and here the party broke up. Aided by Friar Sanchez, then in charge of San Gabriel Mission, he, in company with Nathaniel Pryor, Richard Laughlin, Samuel Prentiss, and George Young, late of Napa County, (all Americans) built a schooner at San Pedro for the purpose of hunting sea-otter.

FIRST BILLIARD TABLES MADE.

1832.—Joseph Pawhling was a native of Maryland, and entered California from New Mexico in the winter of 1832-33, by way of the Gila River. He afterwards traveled a good deal in both countries. He was a carpenter by trade, and made the first two billiard tables ever made in California; the first for George Rice, and the second for John Rhea. He died at Los Angeles, June 2, 1860.

HUNTERS AND TRAPPERS OF 1832.

About the middle of 1832 another band of trappers, under Michael Laframboise, came into San Joaquin Valley from the north, and until the next spring spent the time in trapping on the streams flowing through the great valley. The Hudson Bay Company continued sending out its employés into this region until about the year 1845. Their trappers in California belonged to the "Southern Trapping Party of the Hudson Bay Company," and were divided into smaller parties composed of Canadians and Indians with their wives. The trapping was carried on during the winter in order to secure a good class of furs.

The free trappers were paid ten shillings sterling for a prime beaver skin, while the Indians received a moderate compensation for their services.

The outfits and portions of their food were purchased from the company.

HUDSON BAY COMPANY.

The Hudson Bay Company employed about ninety or one hundred men in this State. The greater part of the Indians were fugitives from the missions, and were honest and peaceably inclined, from the fact that it was mainly to their interest to be so.

From 1832 the chief rendezvous was at French Camp, about five miles south of Stockton. About 1841, the company bought of Jacob P. Leese, the building he had erected for a store in San Francisco, and made that their business center for this territory.

The agents were Alexander Forbes and William G. Ray. The latter committed suicide in 1845. His death, and the scarcity of beaver and otter, caused the company to wind up their agency and business in the territory.

FIRST ENGLISH HISTORIAN OF CALIFORNIA.

Alexander Forbes was for a long series of years the British Consul at San Francisco, and by his genial manners, superior culture, and finished education, made a record which places him among the noted men of the State. This gentleman resided in Oakland; and, although seventy-five years of age, his faculties were as strong as ever. His memory was wonderful, and the power of retention, with the vast fund of knowledge possessed, has been of great service to the historian. He had the honor of being the first English historian of California, his "California," published in London in 1839, being written in Mexico four years previous to the date of its publication. He died in 1879.

In 1832 came Thomas O. Larkin from Boston, intending to manufacture flour. Mr. Larkin's home was in Monterey, and he probably did far more to bring California under the United States flag than any other man.

1833.—James Peace, a Scotchman, came into the country in 1833, having left a ship of the Hudson Bay Company. He was of a somewhat roving disposition, and became acquainted with all the earlier pioneers from Monterey to the Sonoma District. Was with his countryman, John Gilroy, in Santa Clara County; was with Robert Livermore, an English seaman, who settled and gave the name to the Livermore Valley in Alameda County, and was at New Helvetia, the establishment of General Sutter.

FIRST CAMPERS ON TULARE LAKE.

Stephen Hall Meek, the famous hunter and trapper, who now resides on Scott Creek in Siskiyou County, spent the winter of 1833 on the shores of Tulare Lake. He is the only one of the large trapping party now living who wintered there.

There is probably not now living a mountain man who has had so varied an experience and so many wild adventures, hairbreadth escapes and battles with savage animals and no less savage men, as the veteran trapper, Stephen H. Meek. He was born in Washington County, Virginia, on the Fourth of July, 1807, and is a relative of President Polk. He attended the common schools of the day when young. When scarcely twenty years of age he became imbued with that restless spirit of adventure that has since been a marked characteristic of his life, and left his home for the then comparatively unknown West.

We have not space to relate his travels all over California and Oregon. In the spring of 1831 the party went up a tributary of the Yellowstone; then to Green River, and finally wintered on Snake River, where Fort Hall was afterwards built. In the spring he trapped Salmon, Snake and Poin Neuf, and then went to Green River rendezvous. There he hired to Capt. B. L. E. Bouneville to accompany an expedition of thirty-four men under Joseph Walker to explore the Great Salt Lake. They got too far west and finally started down the Mary's or Humboldt River for California, over a country entirely unknown to the trappers. They discovered Truckee, Carson and Walker Rivers, Donner Lake and Walker's Pass, through which they went and pitched their camp for the winter on the shore of Tulare Lake, in December, 1833.

FIRST AMERICAN RESIDENTS IN SAN FRANCISCO.

1835.—William A. Richardson moved from Saucelito to Yerba Buena (San Francisco), opened a store, and began trading in hides and tallow in the summer of 1835.

1836.—Jacob P. Leese, for a number of years a resident of Los Angeles, in July, 1836, built a store in Yerba Buena. He had previously met many obstacles in obtaining a grant of land upon which to locate the building, but by the authority of Governor Chico, this was finally effected.

Previous to the location of Richardson and Leese, the only inhabitants of the pueblo and mission at Yerba Buena were Spaniards, Mexicans and Indians.

EARLY IMMIGRATION SOCIETIES.

1837.—As early as 1837 several societies were organized in the American States to promote immigration to the Pacific Coast. During that and ensuing years, thousands of emigrants journeyed across the rocky and snowy mountains, enduring toils and hardships indescribable, to settle in California and Oregon. Others came by the way of Mexico or Cape Horn, and soon the valleys of the northern rivers were peopled by American agriculturists; and the southern and coast towns by American traders, who speedily monopolized the whole business of the country, and even in some communities formed the numerical strength of the white population.

The Mexican Congress, feeling that California was about to slip from their country as Texas had done before, passed laws against the intrusion of foreigners; but there was no power in the State competent to put these edicts into execution.

We have mentioned a few of the early pioneers so as to give an idea of the extent and kind of settlers up to about 1840, at which time numerous companies of settlers arrived, and we shall now only mention those of the most importance, and who took an active part in political affairs.

FIRST SAW-MILL ERECTED.

1833.—Isaac Graham came from Hardin County, Kentucky, to California in 1833. He settled near Monterey, and his name is intimately associated with Santa Cruz and vicinity.

It is said that he erected on the San Lorenzo, somewhere in the neighborhood of where the powder works now are, the first saw-mill in California.

Early in life he went to New Mexico, and Benjamin D. Wilson met him at Taos. Mr. Wilson has described him as being at that time a very disreputable character. He also says that Graham left a family in Tennessee, being obliged to flee that State to escape the consequences of some offense he had committed.

He reached Los Angeles in company with Henry Naile about 1835, and remained there until the following year, when he removed to "Natividad," Monterey County, and (according to Mr. Wilson) "established a small distillery in a *tule* hut which soon became a nuisance owing to the disreputable character of those who frequented it."

Graham was a brave and adventurous man, a thorough frontiersman, at home with his rifle in his hand, and this had become known to the native officials in Monterey.

When, in 1836, Juan B. Alvarado, a subordinate customs officer, was plotting revolution and contemplated the expulsion of Governor Guiterrez, he came to Graham and sought his assistance, and that of the foreigners who acted with him in the matter.

INDEPENDENCE OF MEXICO CONTEMPLATED.

On condition that all connection with Mexico should be severed, and that California should become independent, the assistance of Graham and others was promised, and in due time it was rendered. And by means of it Guiterrez was sent away, and Alvarado and his party soon became masters of the situation. Now was the time for the fulfillment of the promise of independence of Mexico, but Mexico, instead of punishing Alvarado, proposes to confirm him in his usurped authority. Alvarado, pleased and flattered by this, quickly breaks his promise to Graham, but in so doing, he feels a wholesome fear of those rifles, by the assistance of which he had himself gained his promotion.

His first care seems to have been to disable that little force of foreigners, and to put it out of their power to punish his breach of faith.

GENERAL ARREST OF FOREIGNERS.

1840.—Orders are sent out secretly to all the Alcaldes in this part of the country simultaneously, on a certain night to arrest foreigners and bring them to Monterey. Jose Castro himself heads the party for the arrest of Graham.

It was on the morning of the 7th of April, 1840, before light, that the party reached Graham's dwelling. They broke in the doors and shattered the windows, firing at the inmates as they saw them rising from their beds. One of the assailants thinking to make sure of Graham himself, discharged a pair of pistols aimed at his heart, the muzzles touching his cloak, which he had hastily thrown over his shoulders.

This assassin was amazingly surprised afterwards on seeing Graham alive, and he could not account for it till he examined his holsters, then he found the reason. There, sure enough, were the balls in the holsters! The pistols had been badly loaded, and that it was that saved Isaac Graham from instant death.

MOUNTAIN VIEW, RES. OF EDWIN W. DENT, 2 MILES WEST OF FERNDALE, HUMBOLDT CO. CAL.

P. W. ROBARTS, "IVY RANCH," 1 MILE WEST OF FERNDALE, HUMBOLDT CO. CAL.
BREEDER OF SPANISH MERINO SHEEP.

He was however hurried to Monterey and placed in confinement, as also were other foreigners, arrested on that same night.

What followed is best told in a memorial which these same prisoners afterwards addressed to the Government of the United States, asking that Mexico be required to restore their property, and compensate them for their injuries and lost time.

We quote from an unpublished manuscript, which Rev. S. H. Willey obtained in Monterey in 1849, and furnished for publication in Elliott's History of Monterey.

APPEAL TO THE UNITED STATES GOVERNMENT.

MONTEREY, November, 1842.

To his Excellency, John Tyler, President of the United States:

"On the morning of the seventh of April, one thousand eight hundred and forty, we, your petitioners, citizens of the United States of North America, and many more of our countrymen, together with several of H. B. M. subjects, engaged in business in Monterey and its vicinity, were, without any just cause or provocation, most illegally seized and taken from our lawful occupation, (many being married to natives of the country,) and incarcerated in a loathsome prison in Monterey. The number was subsequently increased by the arrival of others for the space of some ten or twelve days. No warrant or civil process was either read or shown to them (at the time of their seizure) nor has the Government of California concealed to this present day in any official manner, why or wherefore that our persons were thus seized, our property taken from us, what crime we had committed, and why transported like so many criminals to a province in Mexico.

"The perpetrators of this most outrageous action against the rights and privileges allowed to American citizens (according to treaty) were principally officers and soldiers appertaining to this Government and acting by authority and command (as the undersigns have heard and firmly believe), of his Excellency, Don Juan Bautista Alvarado, Governor of the two Californias.

"Some of us were marched on foot to prison, some forced to go on their own animals, and, on their arrival at the prison door, said animals and equipments taken from them, including what was found in their pockets, and with menacing, thrust into prison. The room in which we were confined, being about twenty feet square, without being floored, became very damp and offensive, thereby endangering our health, at times. One had to stand while another slept, and during the first three days not a mouthful of food found or offered us by our oppressors, but living on the charity of them that pitied us.

"To our countryman, Mr. Thomas O. Larkin, we are bound in conscience to acknowledge that he assisted us not only in food, but in what other necessaries we at the time stood in need of and what was allowed to be introduced; some of us were taken out of prison from time to time and released by the intercession of friends or through sickness.

PRISONERS EXAMINED BY THE AUTHORITIES

"Eight of the prisoners were separately called upon and examined by the authorities of Monterey, having as interpreter, a native of the country (who himself frequently needs in his occupation one to interpret for him), there being at the same time, men far more equivalent for the purpose than he was, but they were not permitted; the above-mentioned eight were, after examination, taken to another apartment and there manacled to an iron bar during their imprisonment in this port. After fifteen days' confinement, we were sent on board of a vessel bearing the Mexican flag, every six men being shackled to an iron bar, and in that condition put into the hold of said vessel and taken to Santa Barbara, a sea-port of this province, and there again imprisoned in company with the mate of an American vessel, recently arrived from Boston, in the United States, (and part of the crew) said vessel being sold to a Mexican, resident in this territory, without, as before mentioned, any just or legal cause being assigned, why or wherefore.

"On arriving at Santa Barbara, we were landed and taken some distance; three of us in irons were put into an ox-cart, the remainder on foot; among the latter some were chained in pairs, in consequence reached the prison with much difficulty. Here we were put into a room without light or means of air entering only through a small hole in the roof. For the first twenty-four hours we were not allowed food or water, although we had been some time walking in a warm sun. One of the prisoners became so completely prostrated, that for some time he could not speak, nor swallow when water was brought to him, and would have expired but for the exertions of a Doctor Den, an Irish gentleman living in the town who, with much difficulty, obtained admittance to the sufferer. By his influence and some Americans in the place, food and water were at last sent us.

"In Santa Barbara our number was increased by the addition of more of our countrymen; some of those brought from Monterey were discharged and received passports to return; the remainder were marched to the beach, again put in the hold of a vessel (in irons), and in this manner taken to the port of San Blas, landed, and from thence, in the midsummer of a tropical climate, marched on foot sixty miles to the city of Tepic, and there imprisoned. Some time after our arrival we were discharged by the Mexican Governor, and in the space of four hundred and fifty-five days from the commencement of our imprisonment, we again returned to Monterey. From the day we were taken up until our return we had no opportunity to take care of our property; we were not even allowed, when ordered on board in Monterey, to send for a single garment of clothing, nor permitted to carry any into the prison, but such as we had on; and not once during our said imprisonment in Monterey, although in a filthy and emaciated condition, permitted to shave or wash ourselves.

"When in prison, in the hold of the vessel, and on our march, we were frequently threatened, pricked and struck with swords by the subaltern officers of the Mexican Government.

SUFFERINGS OF THE PRISONERS.

"Our sufferings in prison, on board ship, and when drove on foot in a warm sun, then ordered to sleep out at night in the dew, after being exhausted by the heat and dust, surpass our power of description, and none but those who were with us can realize or form a just conception of our distressed situation.

"For many weeks we were fed in a manner different from the common mode, kept in a filthy and disgusting condition, which, combined with the unhealthy state of the country where we were taken to, has caused death to some, and rendered unhealthy for life, others of our companions. * * * *

"Since our return to California from our confinement in Mexico, Captains Forest and Aulick have visited this port at different periods, in command of United States vessels. Each of those gentlemen took up the subject of our claims and ill-treatment, and, as we believe, received fair promise from the Governor of the province; but the stay of those officers at Monterey having been limited to a few days only, was entirely too short to effect any good. The Governor's promise, orally, made by a deputy to Captain Aulick, on the eve of his departure, so far from being complied with or adhered to, was, as we have reason to believe, abrogated by his orders to Alcaldes, not to listen to the complaints of Americans, i. e., citizens of the United States. * * * * * * *

"We, the undersigned, citizens of the United States, aforesaid, were among the prisoners, some of us to the last day, and have never given provocation to the Mexican Government for such cruel treatment, nor do we know of any given by our companions, and respectfully submit to your notice, the foregoing statement of facts, in hopes that through your means, this affair will be fully represented, so that the Government of the United States will take prompt measures to secure to us indemnity for the past, and security for the future, according to the rights and privileges guaranteed to us by treaty, existing between our Government and Mexico.

"ISAAC GRAHAM,   WILLIAM BARTON,
"WILLIAM CHARD,   ALVIN WILSON,
"JOSEPH L. MAJORS, CHARLES H. COUPER,
"CHARLES BROWN,   AMBROSE Z. TOMILSON,
"WILLIAM HANCE,   HENRY NAILE.

"Monterey, Upper California, the 9th of November, 1842."

Two years later these persons were returned to California, the charges not having been proven; and Mexico was obliged to pay them a heavy indemnity to avoid serious complication with the American Government. All these died several years ago.

It appears that after Alvarado, Castro and company, had got their dreaded company of foreigners in confinement on board a vessel ready to sail to Mexico, seven citizens of note, of California, signed and issued the following proclamation, which is a curiosity in itself and illustrative of the men and the times:—

A SPECIMEN PROCLAMATION.

"PROCLAMATION MADE BY THE UNDERSIGNED. Eternal Glory to the Illustrious Champion and Liberator of the Department of Alta California, Don Jose Castro, the Guardian of Order, and the Supporter of our Superior Government.

"*Fellow-Citizens and Friends*: To-day, the eighth of May, of the present year of 1840, has been and will be eternally glorious to all the inhabitants of this soil, in contemplating the glorious expedition of our fellow-countryman, Don Jose Castro, who goes to present himself before the Superior Government of the Mexican nation, carrying with him a number of suspicious Americans, who under the mask of deceit, and filled with ambition, were warping us in a web of misfortune; plunging us into the greatest confusion and danger; desiring to terminate the life of our Governor and all his subalterns; and, finally, to drive us from our asylums; from our country; from our pleasures, and from our hearths.

"The bark which carries this valorous hero on his grand commission goes filled with laurels and crowned with triumphs, ploughing the waves and publishing in distinct voices to the passing billows the loud *vivas* and rejoicings which will resound to the remotest bounds of the universe. Yes, fellow-citizens and friends, again we say, that this glorious Chief should have a place in the innermost recesses of our hearts, and in the name of all the inhabitants, make known the great rejoicings with which we are filled, giving, at the same time, to our Superior Government the present proclamation, which we make for said worthy Chief; and that our Governor may remain satisfied, that if he (Castro) has embarked for the interior of the Republic, there still remain under his (the Governor's) orders all his fellow-countrymen, companions in arms, etc., etc."

DISAPPOINTMENT AND HUMILIATION.

But a great disappointment awaited this heralded hero on his arrival in Mexico. We find the description of it in another manuscript, as follows:—

"Commandant Castro and his three or four official friends rode into Tepic in triumph, as they thought, and inquired for the house of the Governor. On their arrival at his Excellency's they were refused admittance and ordered to go to prison, which one of them said could not be compared in comfort to the meanest jail or hole in all California. Here they had time to reflect on their scandalous conduct to so many human beings. Castro was then ordered to the City of Mexico and tried for his life, Mr. Packenham, the English Minister, having every hope of his being sent a prisoner for life to the prison of San Juan de Ulca in Vera Cruz. The culprit himself afterwards confessed that such would have been his fate had Mr. Ellis, the American Minister, exerted himself equally with Packenham.

"After an absence of two years and expending eight or ten thousand dollars, he returned to California a wiser and better man than when he left it, and never was afterwards known to raise a hand or voice against a foreigner. His officers and soldiers returned to California in the best manner they could, leaving their country as jailers and returning prisoners."

FIRST SETTLERS IN SAN JOAQUIN VALLEY.

1835.—Dr. John Marsh arrived at the foot of Mount Diablo and purchased the "Rancho los Meganos" in 1837, of three square leagues of land, and settled upon it in the same year, and occupied it afterwards until his death, which occurred in 1856. The doctor lived in a small adobe house near where he afterwards constructed what is known as the "Marsh Stone Home." So that the doctor was the first born native American citizen who ever resided permanently in that section. It would be difficult now to conceive of a more lonely and inhospitable place to live.

Until about 1847, Dr. Marsh had no American neighbors nearer than within about forty miles, and dwellings on adjoining Spanish ranches were from twelve to fifteen miles distant.

All early emigrant parties made Dr. Marsh's ranch an objective point, as it was so easily sighted, being at the foot of Mount Diablo. All parties met with a cordial reception.

Sutter's Fort and Marsh's Ranch were the two prominent settlements in northern California at that date. Dr. Marsh was an educated man and an able writer, as will be seen from the following letter.

DR. JOHN MARSH TO HON. LEWIS CASS.*

FARM OF PULPUNES, NEAR ST. FRANCISCO,
UPPER CALIFORNIA, 1844.

"HON. LEWIS CASS—*Dear Sir*: You will probably be somewhat surprised to receive a letter from an individual from whom you have not heard, or even thought of, for nearly twenty years; yet although the lapse of time has wrought many changes, both in men and things, the personal identity of us both has probably been left. You will, I think, remember a youth whom you met at Green Bay in 1825, who, having left his Alma Mater, had spent a year or two in the "far, far, West," and was then returning to his New England home, and whom you induced to turn his face again toward the setting sun; that youth, who, but for your influence, would probably now have been administering pills in some quiet Yankee village, is now a gray-haired man, breeding cattle and cultivating grape-vines on the shores of the Pacific. Your benevolence prompted you to take an interest in the fortunes of that youth, and it is therefore presumed you may not be unwilling to hear from him again.

*This interesting letter descriptive of California did much to call public attention to this then unknown region. The letter was written from the Marsh Grant, at the foot of Mount Diablo, in Contra Costa County, and published in Elliott's History of Contra Costa County.

"I left the United States in 1835, and came to New Mexico, and thence traversing the States of Chihuahua and Sonora crossed the Rio Colorado at its junction with the Gila, near the tide-water of Gulph, and entered this territory at its southern part. Any more direct route was at that time unknown and considered impracticable.

FIRST SAN JOAQUIN RANCH.

"I have now been more than ten years in this country, and have travelled over all the inhabited and most of the uninhabited parts of it. I have resided eight years where I now live, near the Bay of San Francisco, and at the point where the rivers Sacramento and San Joaquin unite together to meet the tide-water of the bay, about forty miles from the ocean. I possess at this place a farm about ten miles by twelve in extent one side of which borders on the river, which is navigable to this point for sea-going vessels. I have at last found the far West, and intend to end my ramblings here. * * *

VIEW OF SAN JOAQUIN RIVER BY MOONLIGHT.

"The Government of the United States, in encouraging and facilitating immigration to Oregon is, in fact, helping to people California. It is like the British Government sending settlers to Canada. The emigrants are well aware of the vast superiority of California, both in soil and climate, and I may add, facility of access. Every year shorter and better routes are being discovered, and this year the great desideratum of a good and practical road for wheel carriages has been found. Fifty-three wagons, with that number of families, have arrived safely, and more than a month earlier than any previous company. The American Government encourages immigration to Oregon by giving gratuitously some five or six hundred acres of land to each family of actual settlers. California, too, gives lands, not by acres, but by leagues, and has some thousands of leagues more to give to anybody who will occupy them. Never in any instance has less than one league been given to any individual and the wide world from which to select from all the unoccupied lands in the territory. While Colonel Almonte, the Mexican Minister to Washington, is publishing his proclamations in the American newspapers forbidding people to immigrate to California, and telling them that no lands will be given them, the actual Government here is doing just the contrary. In fact they care about as much for the Government of Mexico as for that of Japan. * * * * * * *

EARLY IMPRESSIONS OF CLIMATE.

"The climate of California is remarkably different from that of the United States. The great distinguishing difference is its regularity and uniformity. From May to October the wind is invariably from the northwest, and during this time it never rains, and the sky is brilliantly clear and serene. The weather during this time is temperate, and rarely oppressively warm. The nights are always agreeably cool, and many of the inhabitants sleep in the open air the whole year round. From October to May the southeast wind frequently blows, and is always accompanied by rain. Snow never falls excepting in the mountains. Frost is rare except in December or January. A proof of the mildness of the winter this moment presents itself in the shape of a humming-bird, which I just saw from the open window, and this is in latitude 38° on the first day of February. Wheat is sown from October until March, and maize from March until July. As respects human health and comfort, the climate is incomparably better than that of any part of the United States. It is much the most healthy country I have ever seen or have any knowledge of. There is no disease whatever that can be attributed to the influence of the climate.

"The face of the country differs as much from the United States as the climate. The whole territory is traversed by ranges of mountains, which run parallel to each other and to the coast. The highest points may be about 6,000 feet above the sea, in most places much lower, and in many parts they dwindle to low hills. They are everywhere covered with grass and vegetation, and many of the valleys and northern declivities abound with the finest timber trees. Between these ranges of mountains are level valleys, or rather plains of every width, from five miles to fifty. The magnificent valley through which flows the rivers San Joaquin and Sacramento is 500 miles long, with an average of width of forty or fifty. It is intersected laterally by many smaller rivers, abounding with salmon.

The only inhabitants of this valley, which is capable of supporting a nation, are about 150 Americans and a few Indians. No published maps that I have seen give any correct idea of the country, excepting the outline of the coast.

SAN FRANCISCO BAY DESCRIBED.

"The Bay of San Francisco is considered by nautical men as one of the finest harbors in the world. It consists of two principal arms, diverging from the entrance in nearly opposite directions, and each about fifty miles long, with an average width of eight or ten. It is perfectly sheltered from every wind, has great depth of water, is easily accessible at all times, and space enough for half the ships in the world. The entrance is less than a mile wide, and could be easily fortified so as to make it entirely impregnable. The vicinity abounds in the finest timber for ship-building, and in fact everything necessary to make it a great naval and commercial depot. If it were in the hands of a nation who knew how to make use of it, its influence would soon be felt on all the western coast of America, and probably through the whole Pacific. * * *

"The agricultural capabilities of California are but very imperfectly developed. The whole of it is remarkably adapted to the culture of the vine. Wine and brandy of excellent quality are made in considerable quantities. Olives, figs and almonds grow well. Apples, pears and peaches are abundant, and in the southern part, oranges. Cotton is beginning to be cultivated, and succeeds well. It is the finest country for wheat I have ever seen. Fifty for one is an average crop, with very imperfect cultivation. One hundred fold is not uncommon, and even 150 has been produced. Maize produces tolerably well but not equal to some parts of the United States. Hemp, flax and tobacco have been cultivated on a small scale, and succeed well. The raising of cattle is the principal pursuit of the inhabitants, and the most profitable.

PIONEERS ESTIMATE ON CALIFORNIA.

The foreign commerce of Upper California employs from ten to fifteen sail of vessels, mostly large ships. Some what more than half of these are American, and belong exclusively to the port of Boston. The others are English, French, Russian, Mexican, Peruvian and Hawaiian. The French from their islands in the Pacific and the Russians from Kamtschatka, and their establishments on the northwest coast, resort here for provisions and live-stock. The exports consist of hides and tallow, cows, lard, wheat, soap, timber and furs. There are slaughtered annually about 100,000 head of cattle, worth $800,000. The whole value of the exports annually amounts to about $1,000,000. The largest item of imports is American cotton goods. The duties on imports are enormously high, amounting on the most important articles to 150 per cent. on the original cost, and in many instances to 400 or 500. Thus, as in most Spanish countries, a high bounty is paid to encourage smuggling. Whale ships visit St. Francisco annually in considerable numbers for refreshments, and fail to profit by the facilities for illicit commerce.

CALIFORNIA WILL BE A STATE.

"California, although nominally belonging to Mexico, 1844, is about as independent of it as Texas, and must erelong share the same fate. Since my residence here, no less than four Mexican Governors have been driven from the country by force of

THE EXCELSIOR MILL ON GUNTER'S ISLAND, HUMBOLDT BAY, OPPOSITE

"FERN COTTAGE" RES OF JOSEPH RUSS, OCEAN AVENUE 24 MILES WEST OF FERNDALE, HUMBOLDT CO. CAL. 1882.

A, HUMBOLDT CO. CAL. JOSEPH RUSS & CO. PROPRIETORS, 1882.

arms. The last of these, Micheltorena, with about 400 of his soldiers and 100 employés, were driven away about a year ago. This occurred at the time that the rest of the nation was expelling his master, Santa Ana, although nothing of this was known here at the time. The new administration, therefore, with a good grace, highly approved of our conduct. In fact, the successive administrations in Mexico have already shown a disposition to sanction and approve of whatever we may do here, from a conscious inability to retain even a nominal dominion over the country by any other means. Upper California has been governed for the last year entirely by its own citizens. Lower California is in general an uninhabited and uninhabitable desert. The scanty population it contains lives near the extremity of the Cape, and has no connection and little intercourse with this part of the country. * * * *

INDIANS IN CALIFORNIA.

"I know not, since you have been so long engaged in more weighty concerns, if you take the same interest as formerly in Indian affairs, but since I have supposed your personal identity to remain, I shall venture a few remarks on the Aborigines of California. In stature the California Indian rather exceeds the average of the tribes east of the mountains. He is heavier limbed and stouter built. They are a hairy race, and some of them have beards that would do honor to a Turk. The color similar to that of the Algonquin race, or perhaps rather lighter. The visage, short and broad, with wide mouth, thick lips, short, broad nose, and extremely low forehead. In some individuals the hair grows quite down to the eyebrows, and they may be said to have no forehead at all. Some few have that peculiar conformation of the eye so remarkable in the Chinese and Tartar races, and entirely different from the common American Indian or the Polynesian; and with this unpromising set of features, some have an animated and agreeable expression of countenance. The general expression of the wild Indian has nothing of the proud and lofty bearing, or the haughtiness and ferocity so often seen east of the mountains. It is more commonly indicative of timidity and stupidity.

"The men and children are absolutely and entirely naked, and the dress of the women is the least possible or conceivable remove from nudity. Their food varies with the season. In February and March they live on grass and herbage; clover and wild pea-vine are among the best kinds of their pasturage. I have often seen hundreds of them grazing together in a meadow, like so many cattle. [Descendants of Nebuchadnezzar.—ED.]

"They are very poor hunters of the larger animals, but very skillful in making and managing nets for fish and food. They also collect in their season great quantities of the seeds of various grasses, which are particularly abundant. Acorns are another principal article of food, which are larger, more abundant, and of better quality than I have seen elsewhere. The Californian is not more different from the tribes east of the mountains in his physical than in his moral and intellectual qualities. They are easily domesticated, not averse to labor, have a natural aptitude to learn mechanical trades, and, I believe, universally a fondness for music, and a facility in acquiring it.

INDIANS OF THE MISSIONS AT LABOR.

"The Mission of St. Joseph, when in its prosperity, had 100 plough-men, and I have seen them all at work in one field each with his plough. It had also fifty weavers, twenty tanners, thirty shoe-makers, forty masons, twenty carpenters, ten blacksmiths, and various other mechanics. They are not nearly so much addicted to intoxication as is common to other Indians. I was for some years of the opinion that they were of an entirely different race from those east of the mountains, and they certainly have but little similarity. The only thing that caused me to think differently is that they have the same Moccasin game that is so common on the Mississippi, and what is more remarkable, they accompany it by singing precisely the same tune! The diversity of language among them is very great. It is seldom an Indian can understand another who lives fifty miles distant; within the limits of California are at least 100 dialects, apparently entirely dissimilar. Few or no white persons have taken any pains to learn them, as there are individuals in all the tribes which have communication with the settlements who speak Spanish.

INDIANS EASILY DOMESTICATED.

"The children, when caught young, are most easily domesticated and manifest a great aptitude to learn whatever is taught them; when taken into Spanish families, and treated with kindness, in a few months they learn the language and habits of their masters. When they come to maturity they show no disposition to return to the savage state. The mind of the wild Indian of whatever age, appears to be a *tabula rasa*, on which no impressions, except those of mere animal nature, have been made, and ready to receive any impress whatever. I remember a remark of yours some years ago, that "Indians were only grown-up children." Here we have a real race of infants. In many recent instances when a family of white people have taken a farm in the vicinity of an Indian village, in a short time they would have the whole tribe for willing serfs. They submit to flagellation with more humility than the negroes. Nothing more is necessary for their complete subjugation but kindness in the beginning, and a little well-timed severity when manifestly deserved. It is common for the white man to ask the Indian, when the latter has committed any fault, how many lashes he thinks he deserves.

INDIAN SIMPLICITY.

"The Indian, with a simplicity and humility almost inconceivable, replies ten or twenty, according to his opinion of the magnitude of the offense. The white man then orders another

Indian to inflict the punishment, which is received without the least sign of resentment or discontent. This I have myself witnessed or I could hardly have believed it. Throughout all California the Indians are the principal laborers; without them the business of the country could hardly be carried on.

"I fear the unexpected length of this desultory epistle will be tedious to you, but I hope it will serve at least to diversify your correspondence. If I can afford you any information, or be serviceable to you in any way, I beg you to command me. Any communication to me can be sent through the American Minister at Mexico, or the Commanding Officer of the Squadron in the Pacific, directed to the care of T. O. Larkin, Esq., American Consul in Monterey. I am, sir, very respectfully,

"Your obedient servant,

"HON. LEWIS CASS.   JOHN MARSH."

[Dr. Marsh was murdered on the 24th of September, 1856. It occasioned much excitement at the time, as the Doctor was one of the oldest residents of the State. The murderers were Mexicans, who followed him as he was on the road towards home from Pacheco. The discovery of the horse and buggy in Martinez at early daylight, was the first knowledge of the affair. One of the murderers was arrested the next day. He was tried, but escaped from jail and eluded pursuit for ten years. He was again arrested, with his accomplice, P. Moreno, who was sentenced to State Prison for life, while the first was discharged. —EDITOR.]

INCREASED IMMIGRATION.

1840.—In the first five years of the decade commencing with 1840, there began to settle in the vast Californian valleys that intrepid band of pioneers, who, having scaled the Sierra Nevada with their wagons, trains, and cattle, began the civilizing influences of progress on the Pacific Coast. Many of them had left their homes in the Atlantic and Southern States, with the avowed intention of proceeding direct to Oregon. On arrival at Fort Hall, however, they heard glowing accounts of the salubrity of the Californian climate and the fertility of its soil; they therefore turned their heads southward, and steered for the wished-for haven. At length, after weary days of toil and anxiety, fatigued and foot-sore, the promised land was gained. And what was it like?

CALIFORNIA IN A STATE OF NATURE.

The valleys were an interminable grain field; mile upon mile, and acre after acre, wild oats grew in marvelous profusion, in many places to a prodigious height—one glorious green of wild waving corn—high overhead of the wayfarer on foot, and shoulder-high with the equestrian; wild flowers of every prismatic shade charmed the eye, while they vied with each other in the gorgeousness of their colors, and blended into dazzling splendor.

One breath of wind and the wild emerald expanse rippled itself into space, while with the heavier breeze came a swell whose rolling waves beat against the mountain sides, and, being hurled back, were lost in the far-away horizon; shadow pursued shadow in a long, merry chase.

The air was filled with the hum of bees, the chirrup of birds and an overpowering fragrance from various plants. The hillsides, overrun as they were with a dense mass of tangled jungle, were hard to penetrate, while in some portions the deep dark gloom of the forest trees lent relief to the eye. The almost boundless range was intersected throughout with divergent trails, whereby the traveler moved from point to point, progress being, as it were, in darkness on account of the height of the oats on either side, and rendered dangerous in the valleys by the bands of untamed cattle, sprung from the stock introduced by the missions and early Spanish settlers. These found food and shelter on the plains during the night; at dawn they repaired to the higher grounds to chew the cud and bask in the sunshine.

THE HARDY PIONEERS.

What a life was that of the early pioneer, and how much of life was often crowded into a year, or, sometimes, even into a day of their existence! Now, that the roads are all made, and the dim trail has been supplanted by well-beaten and much-traveled highways, how complacently we talk and write and read of their deeds and exploits.

It has been theirs to subdue the wilderness, and change it into smiling fields of bright growing grain. Toil and privations, such as we can little appreciate now, was their lot for years. Poor houses, and even no houses at all, but a simple tent, or even an Indian wickiup, sheltered them from the rigors of the storm and the inclemancy of the weather. The wild beasts of the woods were their night visitors, prowling about and making night hideous with their unearthly noises, and working the nerves of women, and often, perhaps of men, up to a tension that precluded the possibility of sleep and rest. Neighbors lived many miles away, and visits were rare and highly appreciated.

LAW AND ORDER PREVAILED.

Law and order prevailed almost exclusively, and locks and bars to doors were then unknown, and the only thing to fear in human shape were the petty depredations by Indians. For food they had the fruit of the chase, which afforded them ample meat, but bread was sometimes a rarity, and appreciated when had as only those things are which tend most to our comfort, and which we are able to enjoy the least amount of. But they were happy in that life of freedom from the environments of society and social usage. They breathed the pure, fresh air, untainted by any odor of civilization; they ate the first fruits of the virgin soil, and grew strong and free on its strength and freedom.

ARRIVAL OF CAPTAIN SUTTER.

The southern portion of California was essentially Spanish and Mexican in its population, while the northern part was left to the occupation of foreigners. The Sacramento Valley was

ARRIVAL OF PIONEER PARTIES.

comparatively unnoticed until after the settlement of Captain John A. Sutter at New Helvetia, but following that event, it became the theater for grand operations and achievements. Sutter's Fort was the nucleus about which congregated nearly all of the early emigrants, and the annexation of California is largely due to the influence of that gentleman and those associated with him. Ever hospitable and generous, he was a friend to whom the early settlers and explorers repaired for advice and sustenance.

1839.—Captain John Augustus Sutter was born in Baden Germany, at midnight, February 28, 1803, of Swiss parents. After the completion of his education he became a Captain in the French army, but becoming tired of the superficial nature of French society and customs, he set out for America, to find some secluded spot where he might surround himself with a home and associations more in consonance with his ideas and tastes. New York was reached in July, 1834, and from there, after a sojourn of only one month, the Captain went to the far-famed "West." From here he journeyed to New Mexico and having heard of the marvelous beauty and fertility of California, he joined a party of trappers, expecting soon to reach his destination. But the journey ended at Fort Vancouver, and Captain Sutter's only way to reach California was to go to the Sandwich Islands and from there to take a sailing ship to Monterey. After waiting a long time in Honolulu he took passage in a ship bound for Sitka. By singular good luck the vessel was driven into San Francisco Bay, July 2, 1839.

Captain Sutter, having reached the goal of his ambition, received permission from the Mexican authorities to select a place for settlement in the Sacramento Valley. After much difficulty he finally succeeded in reaching the junction of the Sacramento and American Rivers.

SUTTER'S FORT LOCATED

1840.—A location was made, and Captain Sutter commenced the construction of a house. The spot was named "New Helvetia," in honor of his mother country. On account of the strength, armament and formidable appearance of the buildings, the place was called by all the early settlers, "Sutter's Fort," which name is even now the most general one. This fort was commenced in 1842 and finished in 1844. In 1841, when his grant of land was to be made, it became necessary to have a map of the tract, and he employed for that purpose Captain Jean Vioget, a seaman and Swiss by birth. The survey was made by lines of latitude and longitude. Sutter made his application under this survey of 1841, the same year the map was completed. The Mexican laws allowed only eleven leagues to be granted to any one person, but Sutter's map contained fifty leagues or more. Nevertheless he got the idea that he could hold it, and with this came the idea that he could sell it. The original claim embraced a considerable portion of Sacramento and Placer Counties, all of Sutter, the valley portion of Yuba, and a little point of Colusa.

PIONEER PARTY OF 1839.

1839—In the early part of 1839 a company was made up in St. Louis, Missouri, to cross the plains to California, consisting of D. G. Johnson, Charles Klein, David D. Dutton, mentioned earlier as having come to the country with Captain Smith and William Wiggins. Fearing the treachery of the Indians this little band determined to await the departure of a party of traders in the employ of the American Fur Company, on their annual tour to the Rocky Mountains. At Westport they were joined by Messrs. Wright, Gegger, a Doctor Wiselzenius and his German companion, and Peter Lassen, also two missionaries with their wives and hired man, en route for Oregon, as well as a lot of what were termed fur trappers, bound for the mountains, the entire company consisting of twenty-seven men and two women. At Fort Hall, Klein and Wiselzenius returned, thus reducing the number to twenty-five.

GEN. JOHN A. SUTTER.

In September, the company reached Oregon, and sojourned there during the winter of that year; but in May, 1840, a vessel arrived with missionaries from England, designing to touch at California on her return. Mr. William Wiggins, now of Monterey, the narrator of this expedition, and his three companions from Missouri, among whom was David D. Dutton, at present a resident of Vacaville, Solano County, got on board.

The vessel put in at Bodega, where the Russians were. The Mexican Commandant sent a party of soldiers to prevent them from landing. At this crisis, the Russian Governor ordered the Mexican soldiers to leave or be shot down. They then retired.

Here our travelers were at a stand-still, with no means of proceeding on their journey, or of finding their way out of the inhospitable country; they therefore penned the following communication to the American Consul, then at Monterey:—

PORT BODEGA, July 25, 1840.

"*To the American Consul of California*—

"DEAR SIR: We, the undersigned citizens of the United States, being desirous to land in the country, and having been refused a passport, and been opposed by the Government, we write to you, sir, for advice, and claim your protection. Being short of funds, we are not able to proceed further on the ship. We have concluded to land under the protection of the Russians; we will remain there fifteen days, or until we receive an answer from you, which we hope will be as soon as the circumstances of the case will permit. We have been refused a passport from General Vallejo. Our object is to get to the settlements, or to obtain a pass to return to our own country. Should we receive no relief, we will take up our arms and travel, consider ourselves in an enemy's country, and defend ourselves with our guns.

"We subscribe ourselves,
"Most respectfully,
"DAVID DUTTON, WM. WIGGINS,
"JOHN STEVENS, J. WRIGHT."
"PETER LASSEN.

PIONEER PARTY OF 1841.

1841.—May 8, a party of thirty-six persons left Independence Missouri, bound for California. They passed near Salt Lake to Carson River, and then to the main channel of Walker's River. Near its source they crossed the Sierras, and descended into the San Joaquin Valley. They crossed the San Joaquin River at the site of the present railroad bridge; and, reaching the ranch of Dr. Marsh, at the base of Mount Diablo, the eyes of the party were refreshed with the first signs of civilization which had greeted them from the time of leaving Fort Laramie.

Of this adventurous little band who braved the hardships and dangers of a journey, then occupying months, which can now be compassed within a week, a number are still living in California, among whom may be mentioned General John Bidwell of Chico—of which he is the honored founder—having filled high public stations which mark the esteem and confidence reposed in him by his fellow-citizens, not only of his own immediate home, but of the entire State; Captain Charles M. Weber, one of the most prominent of the pioneer citizens of Stockton, who died in 1880; Josiah Belden, one of the oldest residents of San Jose.

This party disbanded at Dr. Marsh's, and became scattered throughout the State. Many of these emigrants have played such important parts in the early history of California that a few of the principal names are appended:—

COL. J. B. BARTLESON,	Captain of the party. Returned to Missouri. Is now dead.
GEN. JOHN BIDWELL,	Resides in Chico, Butte County.
COL. JOSEPH B. CHILDS,	Resides in St. Helena, Napa County.
JOSIAH BELDEN,	Resides at San José and S. F.
CHARLES M. WEBER,	Resided in Stockton. Died in 1880.
CHARLES HOPPER,	Resides in Yountville, Napa County.
HENRY HUBER,	Resides in San Francisco.
MICHAEL C. NYE,	Resides in Oregon.
GREEN MCMAHON,	Resides in Vacaville, Solano County.
BENJ. KELSEY and wife,	Reside in Santa Barbara County.
ANDREW KELSEY,	Killed by the Indians at Clear Lake.
ROBERT H. THOMES,	Died March 26, 1878, at Tehama.
ELIAS BARNETT,	Lives in Yountville, Napa County.
J. P. SPRINGER,	Died at or near Santa Cruz.

FIRST SETTLEMENTS IN THE VALLEY.

1841.—It is a fact that there was not a house in the Sacramento or San Joaquin Valleys in 1841, except those of Sutter and Dr. Marsh. Sutter had one adobe house and a few huts, but his fort was not completed until sometime afterwards.

After the settlement of New Helvetia, the next point where a dwelling was located was about two miles northeast of the fort on the American River, in 1841. This was settled by John Sinclair for Captain Elias Grimes and Hiram Grimes, to whom Sutter afterwards sold it. It made a fine ranch and farm, and was extensively stocked.

1842.—Nicolaus Allgeier, in 1842, was placed on what is known as the town of Nicolaus, on the east bank of Feather River. The next two places of Gordon and Baca were settled in the fall of this year. Hock Farm, which subsequently became the home of Captain Sutter, was established and made his principal stock-farm, the animals ranging over that part of Sutter County lying west of Feather River, and south of the Butte Mountains.

The land in the vicinity of Marysville was leased to Theodore Cordua. Cordua made a stock-farm of it to a limited extent. Marysville is located where he erected, at what is now the foot of D Street, an adobe dwelling-house, a store-house or trading room, culinary department and out-houses. The walls of the dwelling were thick, and well constructed for withstanding a siege. The spot was named "New Mecklenburg" by Captain Sutter, in honor of the place of nativity of Cordua. It soon became known, however, as Cordua's Ranch.

William Gordon settled on his ranch on Cache Creek, in Yolo County, in the fall of 1842. The place now known as Vacaville was settled about the same time by Manual Baca, from New Mexico.

PIONEER PARTY OF 1843.

1843.—In the fall of this year, a party arrived across the plains via Fort Boise and Pit River. They came down the west bank of the Sacramento River into what is now Colusa County, crossed the river below the mouth of Stony Creek.

Major P. B. Redding, who was with this party, sketched the land about the mouth of Stony Creek, and not being entitled to receive a grant himself, gave the map to the wife of Dr. Stokes, of Monterey, who was a Mexican woman, and she obtained a grant, giving Redding two leagues, or perhaps half the grant, for his locations. This was the first grant made within the limits of Colusa County, and the first settler on the grant was a man by the name of Bryant, who built a house and raised some corn in 1846.

"FERNDALE" RESIDENCE OF MRS. ISABELLA SHAW, FERNDALE, HUMBOLDT CO. CAL.

PIONEERS SETTLE IN ALL PARTS OF THE STATE.

Wolfskill settled on his grant on Putah Creek, south of Cache Creek, and south of Gordon's grant, in 1843.

General John Bidwell says: "In my trip up the valley, in 1843, I went as far as the present town of Red Bluff I was in pursuit of some stolen animals, and was in haste to overtake a party going to Oregon, which I did, and recovered the animals. My party consisted of Peter Lassen, James Bruham, and an Indian.

"In the summer of 1843, a company arrived from 'the States' via Oregon, where they had wintered. This party was under the lead of L. W. Hastings, and N. Coombs, of Napa, was one of the party. Hastings was so well pleased with the land lying on the west bank of the Sacramento River just below the present town of Colusa, that he got me to make a map of it, intending to apply for a grant. He did not succeed, however. Some two or three of Hastings' party—their names I do not now recall—were in the habit of shooting at Indians, and had killed two or three before reaching the Colusa village, which was the only known point within about forty miles above, and thirty miles below, where horses could be watered from the river. At last the Indians became alarmed, and the tribe ahead had notice of the coming of the Oregon party. On attempting to approach the river at Colusa the Indians attacked them. For this they were reported hostile, and Sutter went with about forty men—mostly Indians whom he had taught the use of fire-arms and whom he employed as hunters and trappers—and punished them severely. Many Indians were killed—mostly of the Willy tribe. Sutter's forces crossed the river six or seven miles above Colusa on a bridge built by the Indians—the Doc-Docs, I believe—for fishing purposes. This bridge was about sixty feet wide and very long, for the river was wide but not deep.

"On my return from Red Bluff in March, 1843, I made a map of this Upper Sacramento Valley, on which most of the streams were laid down, and they have since borne the names then given them.

FIRST SETTLEMENT NORTH OF SUTTER'S FORT.

"Peter Lassen then selected what afterward became his grant on Deer Creek (now in Tehama County), and it was the first place selected and settled north of Sutter's grant. He started there in December, 1843, but camped at Sutter's Buttes (now called Marysville Buttes or Butte Mountains) till January or February, 1844, before proceeding to his destination. Several other places were examined and mapped in 1843, but little was done in this line till 1844, because those who wanted the land had not been here long enough to become citizens and be entitled to receive a grant."

Knight's grant, on the Sacramento River, was settled by himself, in 1844. The settlement by Samuel Neal and David Dutton on Butte Creek, about seven miles south of Chico, was made in 1844. About the same time Edward A. Farwell, with Thomas Fallon, settled on his grant on Chico Creek, about a mile below the present town site of Chico. The same year, but a little later, a settlement was made on the present property of General John Bidwell, by William Dickey, who obtained the grant.

PIONEER PARTY OF 1844.

1844.—This party consisted of eleven wagons, twenty-six men, eight women and about a dozen children. Let us give the names: Dr. John Townsend and wife; Martin Murphy, Sr.; Martin Murphy, wife and four sons—James, Martin S., Patrick W., Bernard D.; James Murphy, wife and one child—Mary F.; Bernard Murphy (unfortunately killed on board the *Jenny Lind* in 1853); Miss Ellen Murphy (the present Mrs. Weber, of Stockton); John M. Murphy, Daniel Murphy, Jas. Miller, wife and four children; Allen Montgomery and wife, Captain Stevens, Mr. Hitchcock, Mrs. Peterson and family, Mat Harbin, Moses Schallenberger, John Sullivan, his sister and two brothers, Robert and Mike; John Flomboy, Joseph Foster, Oliver and Francis Marguet, Mr. Mastin, Sr., Dennis Mastin, Pat Mastin, John and Brittain Greenwood, and old Mr. Greenwood. About May 1, 1843, these intrepid pioneers started from Council Bluffs to undertake the untried journey which lay before them, little thinking of its thousand dangers and vicissitudes, hardships enough to deter the bravest.

From December until March, 1844, the party encamped near Donner Lake, and while at this place the first child of white parents born in California saw the light. This was a daughter to Mr. and Mrs. Martin Murphy, a young lady who received the name of Elizabeth, and afterwards became Mrs. William P. Taffe.

Martin Murphy purchased a property on the American Fork, from a man named Rufus, comprising two leagues, and there dwelt until 1850, when he disposed of it and removed to Santa Clara Valley, where he purchased the homestead on which he now resides.

The golden anniversary of their wedding was celebrated on the 18th of July, 1881, with all the *éclat* that wealth could throw around it, and the thousands of friends who paid their respects on that day loudly demonstrated the high estimation in which Martin Murphy and his family are held by the people of California, who look upon him who first broke a wagon trail across the Sierras as the *avant courier* of a higher civilization.

TRUCKEE, THE INDIAN GUIDE.

The dangers of the plains and mountains were passed, and the party reached the Humboldt River, when an Indian named Truckee presented himself and offered to guide them to California. After questioning him closely, they employed him as their guide, and as they progressed found that the statements he had made about the route were fully verified. He soon became a great favorite among them, and when they reached the lower crossing of the Truckee River, now Wadsworth, they gave his name to the beautiful stream, so pleased were they by the pure water and abundance of fish to which he had directed them. The stream will ever live, in history, as the Truckee River.

CONSTRUCTION OF VESSELS.

1845.—William Hardy came ashore from a whale-ship in the latter part of the year 1845. He first went to work as a carpenter for Thomas O. Larkin, in Monterey. He had not been employed in this way long before Roselean and Sansevain sent over to Monterey for carpenters to come to Santa Cruz and build a schooner. Mr. Hardy came, among others, and they went to work on the vessel. The vessel was completed in 1846, and was called the *Santa Cruz*, and sailed to the Sandwich Islands to be coppered. She returned, and was lost at sea.

THE FIRST GRINDSTONES.

Mr. W. C. Moon settled at "Moon's Ranch," in Tehama County, in 1845, and with him a noted hunter and Indian fighter by the name of Merritt. They, with Peter Lassen, made a large canoe-load of grindstones, on Stony Creek, in Colusa County, in 1845, and packed them on mules over twenty miles to the river. They sold a few at Sutter's Fort, and peddled the rest out all round the Bay of San Francisco. When the canoe left Sacramento it was laden to within six inches of the top. As they proceeded from point to point the canoe became lighter, of course; but, at first, it seemed anything but safe, even for inland navigation.

THE CELEBRATED ALCALDE.

In the year 1845 Mr. William Blackburn came to Santa Cruz. He came over the plains from Independence, Missouri, and arrived here in October. He was a native of Virginia, born in 1814. He came over the country in company with Jacob R. Snyder, George McDougal and Harvey Speel.

They stopped together on the Zyante and went to making shingles. William Blackburn was a cabinet-maker by trade, and in the year 1844 worked at that business in New Orleans. But men arriving in California, of course, took hold of any business that would pay. So these men seem to have been still engaged in lumbering and shingle-making when the Bear flag went up in Sonoma.

When the Bear Flag Battalion came marching down towards Monterey, early in July, 1846, William Blackburn and his associates joined it. Just now, too, the United States flag went up in Monterey, and the battalion went south to see that its authority was acknowledged. In due time Blackburn returned to Santa Cruz and went into the merchandizing business, establishing himself in the old adobe building fronting on the upper plaza.

In the year 1847 he was appointed alcalde by Governor Mason, and for a year or two dispensed justice in a way peculiarly his own, as some of the old records of his court will show.

BLACKBURN AS ALCALDE.

Many curious illustrations of it could be given, but we will instance one or two. Many enlarged stories have been told of Judge Blackburn, but those here mentioned are taken from the records, or from living witnesses' statements.

The alcalde records in the County Clerk's office of Santa Cruz of date of August 14, 1847, show that on that day a jury tried Pedro Gomez for the murder of his wife, Barbara Gomez, and found him guilty.

Sentence of the Court: "That the prisoner be conducted back to prison, there to remain until Monday, the 16th of August (two days only), and then be taken out and shot."

"August 17. Sentence carried into effect on the 16th accordingly. W. BLACKBURN, Alcalde."

Pretty summary justice that! It should, perhaps, be stated that, according to law, Judge Blackburn ought to have reported the trial of this criminal to the higher Court in Monterey, and have had the action of his Court sanctioned, before the execution. For some reason he did not do this, but had the criminal shot, and then reported both the trial and execution to headquarters!

This did not quite suit Governor Mason's ideas of propriety, even in that lawless time, and some pretty sharp correspondence followed between the Governor and Judge Blackburn. This exact course of procedure does not seem to have been repeated!

A TOUCHING SCENE.

But there was a sequence, on the 21st of August, before the Court, that is touching, indeed. Josepha Gomez and Balinda Gomez, orphan children of a murdered father and murdered mother, were brought into Court—two little girls—to be disposed of by the Court.

The Court gave Balinda, eleven years old, to Jacinto Castro "to raise" until she was twenty-one years of age, unless she was sooner married; the said Jacinto Castro obligating himself to give her a good education, and three cows and calves at her marriage, or when she arrives of age.

The Court gave Josepha, nine years old, to Alexander Rodriguez, with some similar provision for her education and care. But it is a sorry feeling that comes over us as we seem to see these poor little orphan girls parted there to go among strangers. It is hoped their lives have been less a grief than their childhood.

SERVED HIM RIGHT.

But in Court, still further, November 27, 1847, the case of A. Rodriguez vs. one C———; plaintiff sued defendant, a boy, for shearing his horse's mane and tail off. It was proved that the defendant did the shearing.

An eye-witness of the trial says that when it came to the matter of the sentence, Judge Blackburn looked very grave, and his eyes twinkled a good deal, and he turned to his law book, and examined it here and there, as if looking up authorities touching a very important and perplexing case. All at once he shut up his book, sat back in his chair, and, speaking with a solemn tone, said:

"I find no law in any of the statutes applicable to this case, except in the laws of Moses—'An eye for an eye and a tooth for a tooth.' Let the prisoner be taken out in front of this office and there be sheared close."

The sentence was literally carried into effect, to the great satisfaction and amusement of the native inhabitants, who expressed their approval by saying, "It served him right."

BLACKBURN'S CAREER.

In the year 1845 he crossed the plains from Independence, Missouri, to California, in the company of Jacob R. Snyder, George Williams, George McDougal and Henry Speel, all being leading men in the company. They arrived in this county in October of that year, and settled on the Zyante, where Blackburn, Snyder and McDougal engaged in the shingle business. Speel left the party at Fort Hall for Oregon, but arrived in California in 1846.

Blackburn, with all of these fellow-travelers, was in Fremont's battalion, under the Bear flag, Blackburn being First Lieutenant of Artillery, Company F—Captain McLane. At the battle of Buenaventura, Lieutenant Blackburn fired the first gun, loading and handling it. During that campaign Snyder was the Quartermaster. They continued in the service till the treaty of Couenga, when they returned to Santa Cruz as their home, Blackburn opening a store on the old plaza, which was also an open hotel, for no white man was ever asked pay for supper or lodging; but anything there was in the house was at the service of the guest; open-handed hospitality being the character of host and people in those primitive times, here as elsewhere, throughout California. McDougal settled in Gilroy.

BLACKBURN AS JUDGE.

During those stormy periods of anarchy and lawlessness he performed the duties of the office to the entire satisfaction of all; and although his decisions cover points of all the varied questions of jurisprudence, we believe none have ever yet been reversed by any higher Court. His pretensions were not based on Coke or Littleton, but on common sense and justice. The records of his Court are as amusing as the jokes of "Punch."

Blackburn, as a Judge, was always anxious that the law and justice should be fully and quickly vindicated, and, after passing sentence, would give no delay to its execution; for, although it was the rule for his decisions to be sent to the Governor for approval, they were generally sent after the execution, so that there should be no chance for a delay of justice. Although that might seem to be summary proceeding, yet it met the approval of the people over whom he governed, but at times was the cause of some sharp and terse correspondence between himself and his superiors.

In 1848 he resigned his office to go to the gold region. He returned to Santa Cruz in 1849, and was appointed a Justice of the Peace under the Territorial Government.

BLACKBURN'S FARMING PROFITABLE.

In 1851 he settled on his homestead in Santa Cruz, and commenced farming in company with his brother, Daniel Blackburn, and they planted the bottom with potatoes, and such was the enormous yield of the whole bottom that at thirteen cents per pound, the then price of potatoes, the yield was nearly $100,000; and for several years the profits of potato raising were enormous. Where the house now stands four acres yielded $1,200 worth of potatoes to the acre; they were early, and brought 12½ cents per pound. Next year thirteen acres were rented to Thomas Weeks at $100 per acre, full payment in advance.

BLACKBURN'S PREMIUM POTATOES.

From this place the Judge sent samples of potatoes of four pounds weight (which was a general average), to the Crystal Palace Fair at New York, and received a premium for the finest potatoes ever known. From here also was derived the fame which Santa Cruz now holds of producing fine potatoes.

In 1848 Judge Blackburn built a vessel, a schooner of about fifty tons burden, called the *Zach Taylor*, and Captain Vincent commanded it. When Monterey ceased to be the headquarters of the Pacific, the vessel was run on the Sacramento River. He was also concerned in building the first saw-mill up the Blackburn Gulch.

He was considered a man of enterprise and improvement, and we find him from his start towards the Pacific to have been a man of note, first as one of the leaders in the train with which he journeyed; again a commander and soldier in the first war towards the generation of a Pacific Government; then, as a jurist, his history is recorded in the archives of the country; finally as an agriculturist, his mark was made and is on record in the proceedings of the Crystal Palace World's Fair, New York, which was also probably the first visible knowledge demonstrating to the East the capabilities of California to raise her own food.

FIRST PROTESTANT WORSHIP.

1846.—Mr. A. A. Hecox appears to have commenced the first Protestant public worship in California. He was an authorized Christian minister in the Methodist Episcopal Church. Worship was first held at the house of John D. Green, in August, 1847, and after that in the house of J. C. T. Dunleavy.

Mr. Hecox thinks he preached the first Protestant sermon in California at the funeral of a Miss Hitchcock, who died at San Jose, about December, 1846.* Feeble in body and leaning upon a staff he made his way to the house of mourning, where he found a few of the relatives of the deceased, who had assembled to bid farewell to their departed sister, who had fallen far,

*See Elliott's History of Santa Cruz County.

far from home. His remarks were based upon the following words: "Remember how short my time is."

The first Methodist class was formed in the latter part of February, 1848, and the Rev. E. Anthony elected preacher, and Mr. Hecox appointed in charge of the work in San Jose.

The gold discovery, however, drew off the people very suddenly in the latter part of the year, and public worship was practically suspended for the time.

Alfred Baldwin came in 1846. When a boy, living in Delaware County, New York, he got very much interested in this Pacific region through reading Lewis and Clark's journal.

The desire to see this country that was said to have no cold winters, grew upon him. Being in St. Louis in 1845, when a party was starting overland to Oregon, he embraced the opportunity and joined it.

They reached their destination in the fall of 1845. Mr. Baldwin came to San Francisco early in 1846. He very soon enlisted under Purser James H. Watmough, purser of the sloop of war *Portsmouth*, with others, to see that there was no resistance to the flag of the United States, which had then just been raised. They were stationed at San Jose.

THE SAN JOAQUIN.

While they were there news came down from the Mission San Jose, that Indians from the San Joaquin neighborhood were making their usual raids and stealing all the horses they could lay hands on.

This was an old habit of the Indians, and frontier ranches, like Marsh's or Livermore's, could not keep horses.

The spirit of the new flag did not propose to submit to these depredations. So, very promptly, Captain Watmough organized a party to go and look after these matters. It consisted of some twenty-five or thirty men.

They went to the Indians' lurking place on the Stanislaus River, and there camped for the night. By and by, in the darkness, a band of horses came rushing on them.

The Indians had stolen them from around the mission, as before remarked, and now as they thought they were driving them into their own secure retreat, they were driving them into the hands of our encamped force. The horses were secured and brought back, but the Indians themselves succeeded in getting away into the willows and thickets.

Returning to San Jose, the party was ordered at once to go south in a vessel named *Sterling* to help take care of things there. Getting a little below Monterey, they met the *Vandalia* coming up with orders that they should return to Monterey, and there fit out an expedition and proceed, in force, down the coast by land. Back to Monterey they came. Men were sent to the Sacramento Valley to get horses to mount the expedition. Mr. Baldwin, meanwhile, worked at his trade in Monterey, getting the harnesses ready for the hauling of the cannon.

STRUGGLE FOR AMERICAN RULE.

In the month of November, 1846, the requisite number of horses having been obtained, they were about to be driven across the Salinas plain toward Monterey.

But just here, Pio Pico, who had heard of this coming band of horses, confronts them with a force of Californians.

Before he gets the horses, however, the men in charge of them turn them aside to a rancho in the hills, and on the next day go out to disperse the opposing California forces.

The battle of the Salinas resulted, and it went very hard with our few men. It is said to have been the only battle during the struggle for American rule in California that did go hard with our forces. The record is that Captain Foster, the officer in command, was killed, and eleven of his men. But the horses were not captured. That night their faithful Indian guide, "Tom," broke through and carried the news to Monterey. The entire force there marched immediately over to the Salinas, but no enemy was any longer to be found. The horses were obtained, the expedition was gotten ready, and moved down the country. Of course in December and onward they encountered the rainy season, and the storms in the St. Ines Mountains were terrible; but they got through at last, and accomplished the object of their equipment.

WORDS OF A PIONEER.

Hon. Elam Brown, who resides at Lafayette, Contra Costa County, was prominent and active in aiding to establish the rule of the Americans. He was a member of the convention that formed the Constitution at Monterey.

Mr. Brown participated in the first two sessions of the Legislature. What he lacked in ability and knowledge, he in a great measure made up in industry and economy.

Mr Brown tells us: "I was eighty-three years old the 10th day of last June. I labor under the same embarrassment that the hunter did who could not shoot a duck; for when he took aim at one, another would put its head in the way. I find much less difficulty in collecting than in selecting incidents. My own and Mr Nathaniel Jones' families were the first Americans that settled within the present bounds of this, Contra Costa, County. There were no white families nearer than San José Mission. I settled on my present farm in 1848, and I expect to remain on it the balance of my time on earth." *

Mr. Brown disclaims any praise over the tens of thousands of others who have equally participated and aided in the great work of reclaiming the vast waste of wilderness, that seventy-six years ago was almost entirely occupied by the native Indians and wild beasts, but now covered over with organized States, counties, cities, towns and farms, with all the comforts and conveniences of art and science that civilization confers. Being an eye-witness in the front line of a long march, the picture is plain. The work is large to those who have not seen

---
*Elliott's History of Contra Costa County.

HUNTER AND TRAPER OF HUMBOLDT CO CAL

the beginning and end of the whole extraordinary advance of settlement and civilization in America from the year 1804 to 1880.

FIRST CAST PLOW.

1846—Elihu Anthony came to California in 1846, from Indiana. He stopped first in San Jose, but moved with his family to Santa Cruz in January, 1848.

Mr. Anthony's foundry made the first cast-iron plows ever constructed in California. Patterns were obtained from the East in 1848, and the castings made and attached to the proper wood-work. Previous to this they had been imported and sold at high figures. The modern plow was at this time supplanting the old Mexican affair, illustrated and described elsewhere.

FIRST MINING PICK.

At this same foundry were made, in the spring of 1848, the first picks for mining purposes. As soon as the report of gold discovery was known in Santa Cruz, Anthony went to manufacturing picks for miners' use. He made seven and a half dozen. They were light and weighed only about three pounds each.

Thomas Fallon, now of San Jose, took them with his family in an ox-team across the mountains to the Sutter mines, or mill, to dispose of them. He sold nearly all of them at three ounces of gold each; but the last of the lot brought only two ounces each, as by this time other parties had packed in a lot from Oregon.

These were some of the men who were at the head of affairs here in that stirring transition period between the two flags, the Mexican and that of the United States, and the introduction of California as a State of the American Union. This brings us to what is known as the Bear Flag War.

FIRST WHITE WOMAN ARRIVED.

Mrs. Mary A. Kelsey crossed the plains at the age of eighteen years. She left Jasper County, Missouri, with her husband, Benjamin Kelsey, in the spring of 1841. She was the only woman in that party, which consisted of thirty-three persons, of which General Bidwell and others were members, as mentioned on page 48. She and her husband remained at Sutter's Fort until 1843. They then went to Oregon and resided in Willamette Valley until 1844. Getting dissatisfied with that locality they moved to Napa, and Kelsey was present at the capture of Sonora in 1846. In 1851 they again went to Oregon and remained until 1855, and then again returned to California. In 1856 they pulled out for Texas, which State they reached in 1858, and remained there several years. Finally they decided that no place was like California, and returned and located near Stockton.

We have now given the names of some of the leading arrivals previous to the discovery of gold, and leading incidents in their native lives.

Bear Flag War.

DURING the year 1846, the American settlers, many of whom had married Spanish ladies, learned that it was the intention of General Castro, then Governor of California, to take measures for the expulsion of the foreign element, and more especially of the Americans. Lieut. John C. Fremont of the United States Topographical engineers, was then camped at the north end of the Buttes, being on his way to Oregon. The settlers sent a deputation to him, asking him to remain and give them the protection of his presence. He was afraid of a court-martial; but they argued with him that if he would take back to Washington his broken Lieutenant's commission in one hand and California in the other, he would be the greatest man in the nation. The bait was a tempting one. Fremont hesitated; but they kept alluring him nearer to the scene of action. On the 9th of June, 1846, there were some thirteen settlers in his camp at the mouth of the Feather River, when William Knight, who had arrived in the country from Missouri in 1841, and had married a Spanish lady, came and informed them that Lieutenant Arci had passed his place—now Knight's Landing—that morning, going south, with a band of horses, to be used against the Americans in California.

THE SETTLERS ORGANIZE.

The settlers organized a company with Ezekiel Merritt, the oldest man among them, as captain, and gave chase to Arci. They overtook him on the Cosumne River, and captured him and his horses. The Rubicon was now passed, and there was nothing to do but to go ahead. When they got back to Fremont's camp they found other settlers there, and on consultation it was determined to capture Sonoma, the headquarters of General M. G Vallejo, the military commander of Northern California. They gathered strength as they marched along, and when they got to John Grigsby's place in Napa Valley, they numbered thirty-three men. Here the company was reorganized and addressed by Dr. Robert Semple, afterwards President of the Constitutional Convention. We give the account of the capture in General Vallejo's own words, at the Centennial exercises held at Santa Rosa, July 4. 1876.

"I have now to say something of the epoch which inaugurated a new era for this country. A little before dawn on June 14, 1846, a party of hunters and trappers, with some foreign settlers, under command of Captain Merritt, Doctor Semple, and William B. Ide, surrounded my residence at Sonoma, and without firing a shot, made prisoners of myself, then commander of the northern frontier, of Lieutenant-Colonel Victor Prudon, Captain Salvador Vallejo, and Jacob P. Leese. I should here state that down to October, 1843, I had maintained at my own expense a respectable garrison at Sonoma, which often, in union with the settlers, did good service in campaigns against the Indians: but at last, tired of spending money which the

Mexican Government never refunded, I disbanded the force, and most of the soldiers who had constituted it left Sonoma. Thus in June, 1846, the plaza was entirely unprotected, although there were ten pieces of artillery, with other arms and munitions of war. The parties who unfurled the Bear Flag were well aware that Sonoma was without defense, and lost no time in taking advantage of this fact, and carrying out their plans.

"Years before, I had urgently represented to the Government of Mexico the necessity of stationing a sufficient force on the frontier, else Sonoma would be lost, which would be equivalent to leaving the rest of the country an easy prey to the invader. What think you, my friends, were the instructions sent me in reply to my repeated demands for means to fortify the country? These instructions were that I should at once force the emigrants to recross the Sierra Nevada, and depart from the territory of the Republic. To say nothing of the inhumanity of these orders, their execution was physically impossible—first, because the immigrants came in autumn, when snow covered the Sierras so quickly as to make a return impracticable.

"Under the circumstances, not only I, but Commandante General Castro, resolved to provide the immigrants with letters of security, that they might remain temporarily in the country. We always made a show of authority, but well convinced all the time that we had no power to resist the invasion which was coming upon us. With the frankness of a soldier I can assure you that the American immigrants never had cause to complain of the treatment they received at the hands of either authorities or citizens. They carried us as prisoners to Sacramento, and kept us in a calaboose for sixty days or more, until the authority of the United States made itself respected, and the honorable and humane Commodore Stockton returned us to our hearths."

FIRST MOVEMENT FOR INDEPENDENCE.

On the seizure of their prisoners the revolutionists at once took steps to appoint a Captain, who was found in the person of John Grigsby, for Ezekiel Merritt wished not to retain the permanent command. A meeting was then called at the barracks, situated at the northeast corner of the plaza, under the presidency of William B. Ide, Dr. Robert Semple being Secretary.

At this conference Semple urged the independence of the country, stating that having once commenced they must proceed, for to turn back was certain death. Before the dissolution of the convention, however, rumors were rife that secret emissaries were being dispatched to the Mexican rancheros, to inform them of the recent occurrences, therefore to prevent any attempt at a rescue, it was deemed best to transfer their prisoners to Sutter's Fort, where the danger of such would be less.

RESOLVED TO ESTABLISH A GOVERNMENT.

Before transferring their prisoners, however, a treaty, or agreement was entered into between the captives and captors, which will appear in the annexed document kindly furnished to us by General Vallejo, and which have never before been given to the public.

"We, the undersigned, having resolved to establish a government upon Republican principles in connection with others of our fellow-citizens, and having taken up arms to support it, we have taken three Mexican officers as prisoners: Gen. M. G. Vallejo, Lieut. Col. Victor Prudon, and Capt. D. Salvador Vallejo; having formed and published to the world no regular plan of government, we feel it our duty to say that it is not our intention to take or injure any person who is not found in opposition to the cause, nor will we take or destroy the property of private individuals further than is necessary for our immediate support.

"EZEKIEL MERRITT,   WILLIAM FALLON,
"R. SEMPLE,   SAMUEL KELSEY."

GEN. VALLEJO A PRISONER IN SUTTER'S FORT.

But to proceed with our narrative of the removal of the General, his brother and Prudon to Sutter's Fort. A guard consisting of William B. Ide, as Captain, Captain Grigsby, Captain Merritt, Kit Carson, William Hargrave, and five others left Sonoma for Sutter's Fort, with their prisoners upon horses actually supplied by General Vallejo himself. We are told that on the first night after leaving Sonoma with their prisoners, the revolutionists, with singular inconsistency, encamped and went to sleep without setting sentinel or guard; that during the night they were surrounded by a party under the command of Juan de Padilla, who crept up stealthily and awoke one of the prisoners, telling him that there was with him close at hand a strong and well-armed force of rancheros, who, if need be, could surprise and slay the Americans before there was time for them to fly to arms, but that he, Padilla, before giving such instructions waited the orders of General Vallejo, whose rank entitled him to the command of any such demonstration.

The General was cautiously aroused and the scheme divulged to him, but with a self-sacrifice which cannot be too highly commended, answered that he should go voluntarily with his guards, that he anticipated a speedy and satisfactory settlement of the whole matter, advised Padilla to return to his rancho and disperse his band, and positively refused to permit any violence to the guard, as he was convinced that such would lead to disastrous consequences, and probably involve the rancheros and their families in ruin, without accomplishing any good result.

Having traveled about two-thirds of the way from Sutter's Fort, Captain Merritt and Kit Carson rode on ahead with the news of the capture of Sonoma, desiring that arrangements be made for the reception of the prisoners. They entered the fort early in the morning of June 16th.

MAKING OF THE BEAR FLAG.

On the seizure of the citadel of Sonoma, the Independents found floating from the flag-staff-head the flag of Mexico, a fact which had escaped notice during the hustle of the morning. It was at once lowered, and they set to work to devise a banner which they should claim as their own. They were as one on the subject of there being a star on the groundwork, but they taxed their ingenuity to have some other device, for the "lone star" had already been appropriated by Texas.

So many accounts of the manufacture of this insignia have been published that we give the reader those quoted by the writer in *The Pioneer*:—

"A piece of cotton cloth," says Mr. Lancy, "was obtained, and a man by the name of Todd proceeded to paint from a pot of red paint a star in the corner. Before it was finished, Henry L. Ford, one of the party, proposed to paint on the center, facing the star, a grizzly bear. This was unanimously agreed to, and the grizzly bear was painted accordingly. When it was done the flag was taken to the flag-staff, and hoisted amid the hurrahs of the little party, who swore to defend it with their lives."

Of this matter Lieutenant Revere says: "A flag was also hoisted bearing a grizzly bear rampant, with one stripe below, and the words, 'Republic of California,' above the bear, and a single star in the union." This is the evidence of the officer who hauled down the Bear flag and replaced it with the Stars and Stripes on July 9, 1846.

The *Western Shore Gazetteer* has the following version: "On the 14th of June, 1846, this little handful of men proclaimed California a free and independent Republic, and on that day hoisted their flag, known as the 'Bear flag;' this consisted of a strip of worn-out cotton domestic, furnished by Mrs. Kelley, bordered with red flannel, furnished by Mrs. John Sears, who had fled from some distant part to Sonoma for safety upon hearing that war had been thus commenced. In the center of the flag was a representation of a bear, *en passant*, painted with Venetian red, and in one corner was painted a star of the same color. Under the bear were inscribed the words, 'Republic of California,' put on with common writing ink. This flag is preserved by the California Pioneer Association, and may be seen at their rooms in San Francisco. It was designed and executed by W. L. Todd."

The *Sonoma Democrat* under the caption, "A True History of the Bear Flag," tells its story: "The rest of the revolutionary party remained in possession of the town. Among them were three young men,—Todd, Benjamin Duell, and Thomas Cowie. A few days after the capture, in a casual conversation between these young men, the matter of a flag came up. They had no authority to raise the American flag, and they determined to make one. Their general idea was to imitate, without following too closely their national ensign. Mrs. W. B. Elliott had been brought to the town of Sonoma by her husband from his ranch on Mark West Creek for safety. The old Elliott cabin may be seen to this day on Mark West Creek, about a mile above the Springs. From Mrs. Elliott, Benjamin Duell got a piece of new red flannel, some white domestic, needles, and thread. A piece of blue drilling was also obtained.

So from this material, without consultation with any one else, these three young men made the Bear flag. Cowie had been a saddler. Duell had also served a short time at the same trade. To form the flag, Duell and Cowie sewed together alternate strips of red, white and blue. Todd drew in the upper corner a star, and painted on the lower a rude picture of a grizzly bear, which was not standing as has been sometimes represented, but was drawn with head down. The bear was afterwards adopted as the design of the great seal of the State of California. On the original flag it was so rudely executed that two of those who saw it raised have told us that it looked more like a hog than a bear. Be that as it may, its meaning was plain—that the revolutionary party would, if necessary, fight their way through at all hazards. In the language of our informant, it meant that there was no back-out; they intended to fight it out. There were no halyards on the flag-staff, which stood in front of the barracks. It was again reared, and the flag, which was soon to be replaced by that of the Republic, for the first time floated on the breeze."

William Winter, Secretary of the Association of Territorial Pioneers of California, and Mr. Lancey, questioned the correctness of these dates, and entered into correspondence with all the men known to be alive, who were of that party, and others who were likely to throw any light on the subject. Among many answers received, we quote the following portion of a letter from James O. Bleak:—

"St. George, Utah, 16th of April, 1878.

"*To William Winter, Esq., Secretary of Association 'Territorial Pioneers of California'*—

"Dear Sir: Your communication of the 3d instant is placed in my hands by the widow of a departed friend—James M. Ide, son of William B.—as I have at present in my charge some of his papers. In reply to your question asking for 'the correct date' of raising the 'Bear flag' at Sonoma, in 1846 I will quote from the writing of William B. Ide, deceased:—

"'The said Bear flag (was) made of plane (plain) cotton cloth, and ornamented with the red flannel of a shirt from the back of one of the men, and christened by the "California Republic," in red paint letters on both sides; (it) was raised upon the standard where had floated on the breeze the Mexican flag aforetime; it was the 14th of June, '46. Our whole number was twenty-four, all told. The mechanism of the flag was performed by William L. Todd of Illinois. The grizzly bear was chosen as an emblem of strength and unyielding resistance.'

"James G. Bleak."

W. B. IDE'S REMARKABLE SPEECH.

The garrison being now in possession, it was necessary to elect officers; therefore, Henry L. Ford was elected First Lieutenant; Granville P. Swift, First Sergeant; and Samuel Gibson, Second Sergeant. Sentries were posted and a system of military routine inaugurated. In the forenoon, while on parade, Lieutenant Ford addressed the company in these words:—

"My countrymen! We have taken upon ourselves a very responsible duty. We have entered into a war with the Mexican nation. We are bound to defend each other or be shot! There's no half-way place about it. Each of you has had a voice in choosing your officers. Now they are chosen they must be obeyed!"

To which the entire band responded that the authority of the officers should be supported. For point and brevity this is almost equal to the speech put in the mouths of some of his military heroes by Tacitus, the great Roman historian.

CAPTAIN IDE ORGANIZES THE FORCES.

The works of William B. Ide throw further light upon the machinery of the civil-military force: "The men were divided into two companies of ten men each. The First Artillery were busily engaged in putting the cannons in order, which were doubly charged with grape and canister. The First Rifle Company were busied in cleaning, repairing and loading the small arms. The commander, after setting a guard and posting a sentinel on one of the highest buildings to watch the approach of any persons who might feel a curiosity to inspect our operations, directed his leisure to the establishment of some system of finance, whereby all the defenders' families might be brought within the lines of our garrison and supported. Ten thousand pounds of flour were purchased on the credit of the Government, and deposited with the garrison. And an account was opened, on terms agreed upon, for a supply of beef and a few barrels of salt which constituted our main supplies. Whisky was contrabanded altogether. After the first round of duties was performed, as many as could be spared off guard, were called together and our situation fully explained to the men by the commanders of the garrison.

Will S. Green says: "We have seen it stated by some writers, that Capt. John Grigsby was chosen to the command after the capture of Sonoma, and also that Ide was so chosen but both of them went with the prisoners to Sutter's Fort. We have talked with both Ide and Semple about the Bear Flag War, and we are certain that Ide was not the military commander, but that it was in a civil capacity that he issued the proclamation above given. Ford, although nominally a Lieutenant, was the real military leader of the Bear Flag Party. He had served four years as Sergeant in the U. S. Dragoons, and understood the drill and discipline better than those more able to direct the policy to be pursued. Ide and Semple were the leaders in that."

A messenger was dispatched to San Francisco to inform Captain Montgomery, of the United States ship *Portsmouth*, of the action taken by them, he further stating that it was the intention of the insurgents never to lay down their arms until the independence of their adopted country had been established.

A TRAGIC AND FEARFUL DEATH.

Lieutenant Ford finding that the magazine was short of powder, sent two men, named Cowie and Fowler, to the Sotoyome Rancho, at Healdsburg, owned by H. D. Fitch, for a bag of rifle powder. Two miles from Santa Rosa, they were attacked and slaughtered by a party of Californians. Two others were dispatched on special duty; they, too, were captured, but were treated better. Receiving no intelligence from either of the parties, foul play was suspected; therefore on the morning of the 20th of June, Sergeant Gibson was ordered, with four men, to proceed to the Sotoyome Rancho, learn if possible, the whereabouts of the missing men, and procure the powder. They went as directed, secured the ammunition, but got no news of the missing men. As they were passing Santa Rosa, on their return, they were attacked at daylight by a few Californians, and turning upon their assailants, captured two of them, Blas Angelina and Barnadino Garcia, *alias* Three-fingered Jack, and took them to Sonoma. They told of the taking and slaying of Cowie and Fowler.

The story of their death is a sad one. After Cowie and Fowler had been seized by the Californians, they encamped for the night, and the following morning determined in council what should be the fate of their captives. A swarthy New Mexican named Mesa Juan Pedilla, and Three-fingered Jack, the Californians, were loudest in their denunciation of the prisoners as deserving of death; and, unhappily, their counsels prevailed. The unfortunate young men were then led out, stripped naked, bound to a tree with a lariat, while for a time, the inhuman monsters practiced knife-throwing at their naked bodies, the victims, the while, praying to be shot. They then commenced throwing stones at them, one of which broke the jaw of Fowler. The fiend, Three-fingered Jack, then advancing, thrust the end of his riata (a rawhide rope) through the mouth, cut an incision in the throat, and then made a tie, by which the jaw was dragged out. They next proceeded to kill them slowly with their knives. Cowie, who had fainted, had the flesh stripped from his arms and shoulders, and pieces of flesh were cut from their bodies and crammed into their mouths, they finally being disemboweled. Their mutilated remains were afterwards found and buried where they fell, upon the farm now owned by George Moore, two miles north of Santa Rosa.

No stone marks the grave of these pioneers, one of whom took so conspicuous a part in the event which gave to the Union the great State of California.

Three-fingered Jack was killed by Captain Harry Love's Rangers, July 27, 1853, at Pinola Pass, near the Merced River,

PROCLAMATION FOR REPUBLICAN GOVERNMENT.

with the bandit Joaquin Murietta; while Ramon Carrillo met his death at the hands of the Vigilantes, between Los Angeles and San Diego, May 21, 1864.

W. B. IDE'S PROCLAMATION.

At Sonoma Capt. William B. Ide, with the consent of the garrison, issued the following:—

"*A Proclamation to all persons and citizens of the District of Sonoma, requesting them to remain at peace, and follow their rightful occupations without fear of molestation.*

"The commander-in-chief of the troops assembled at the fortress of Sonoma, gives his inviolable pledge to all persons in California, not found under arms, that they shall not be disturbed in their persons, their property, or social relations, one with another, by men under his command.

"He also solemnly declares his object to be: first, to defend himself and companions in arms, who were invited to this country by a promise of lands on which to settle themselves and families; who were also promised a republican government; when, having arrived in California, they were denied the privilege of buying or renting lands of their friends; who instead of being allowed to participate in, or being protected by a republican government, were oppressed by a military despotism; who were even threatened by proclamation, by the chief officers of the aforesaid despotism, with extermination, if they should not depart out of the country, leaving all their property, arms, and beasts of burden; and thus deprived of their means of flight or defense, were to be driven through deserts inhabited by hostile Indians, to certain destruction.

"To overthrow a government which has seized upon the property of the missions for its individual aggrandizement; which has ruined and shamefully oppressed the laboring people of California, by enormous exactions on goods imported into the country, is the determined purpose of the brave men who are associated under my command.

"I also solemnly declare my object, in the second place, to be to invite all peaceable and good citizens of California, who are friendly to the maintenance of good order and equal rights, and I do hereby invite them to repair to my camp at Sonoma, without delay, to assist us in establishing and perpetuating a republican government, which shall secure to all civil and religious liberty; which shall encourage virtue and literature; which shall leave unshackled by fetters agriculture, commerce, and manufactures.

"I further declare that I rely upon the rectitude of our intentions, the favor of heaven, and the bravery of those who are bound and associated with me by the principles of self-preservation, by the love of truth and the hatred of tyranny, for my hopes of success.

"I furthermore declare that I believe that a government to be prosperous and happy must originate with the people who are friendly to its existence; that the citizens are its guardians, the officers its servants, its glory its reward.

"WILLIAM B. IDE.

"Headquarters, Sonoma, June 18, 1846."

JUDGE W. B. IDE'S HISTORY.

Capt. William B. Ide was born in Ohio; came overland, reaching Sutter's Fort in October, 1845. June 7, 1847, Governor Mason appointed him land surveyor for the northern district of California, and the same month he was appointed Justice of the Peace at Cache Creek. At an early day he got a grant of land which was called the Rancho Barranca Colorado, just below Red Creek, in Colusa County, as it was then organized. In 1851 he was elected County Treasurer, with an assessment roll of $373,206. Moved with the county seat to Monroeville, at the mouth of Stony Creek, September 3, 1851; was elected County Judge of Colusa County, and practiced law, having a license. Judge Ide died of small-pox at Monroeville, Colusa County, on Saturday, December 18, 1852, aged fifty years.

ANECDOTE OF JUDGE IDE.[*]

Ide was the presiding Judge and Deputy Clerk, and Huls was Associate Justice and Deputy Sheriff. The prisoner was brought into court by Huls, and the indictment read to him by Ide as Clerk. He was on trial for horse-stealing; the penalty at that time was death. The Judge mounted the bench and informed the prisoner of his rights, including that of having counsel assigned him for his defense. This the prisoner asked. Here was a dilemma. There was no licensed attorney, nearer than Butte County, to be had. The Court (Ide and two Associate Judges) held a consultation on the situation. Ide, however, was always equal to any emergency, and he suggested that he himself had been over at Hamilton a few days before attending Judge Sherwood's Court, and had been admitted as a practicing attorney, and he did not see why he should not defend the prisoner.

This was suggested to the defendant at the bar, who was delighted with the arrangement of being defended by the presiding Judge. There being no District Attorney present, it was expected that the presiding Judge would also look out for the interests of the people. With the Court thus organized, the trial began. Ide would question the witnesses, raise his points of law on either side, and then get on the bench to help decide them, take exceptions to his own ruling, and then as Clerk make the entries.

When the testimony was all in Ide addressed the jury, presenting first the side of the prosecution, and then of the defense, winding up with a plea for mercy. Then he got on the bench again, and instructed the jury calmly and impartially as to the law in the case. The jury retired, and in a few moments brought in a verdict of "guilty."

[*] Written by Will S. Green, of the *Colusa Sun*, for Elliott's History of Colusa County.

When the time for sentence came, the Judge ordered the prisoner to stand up, and he addressed him in substance as follows: "You have had a fair and impartial trial by a jury of your peers. You have been ably defended by counsel appointed by this Court. The jury have found you guilty of grand larceny, the penalty of which, under the benign laws of this State, is death. It is, therefore, the judgment of this Court that you be taken by the Sheriff to some convenient place, on the — day of ——, and then and there hanged by the neck, until you are dead, dead, dead, and may the Lord have mercy on your soul."

Turning to Associate Huls, he ordered the Sheriff to take charge of the prisoner. A day or so before that set for the execution Huls went over after his prisoner, but found that he had been pardoned out by the Governor, without the officers of Colusa County knowing anything about it.

ONLY FIGHT UNDER THE BEAR FLAG.

1846.—The only real fight of the war occurred on the twenty-fifth of June, between a body of about eighty Californians and some twenty men under command of Lieutenant Ford. These few men were put to flight, and continued their march across the bay. Fremont arrived at Sonoma two days after the fight, still hesitating. He wanted, so we are told by Semple and Ide, (who informed Will S. Green, of Colusa,) to occupy a position where he might reap the benefit of a victory and not suffer from defeat.

After the return of the Californians across the bay, the Bear Flag Party urged Fremont to capture the ship *Moscow*, then lying at Saucelito, cross the bay, capture Castro, and by one bold stroke end the war. Captain Phelp, of the *Moscow*, was in full sympathy with the movement, and even went so far as to put a lot of provisions on a launch near enough to them to be captured by the party of revolutionists.

Com. John D. Sloat took possession of Monterey, and three days afterwards the Bear Flag Party heard of it, and the Stars and Stripes took the place of the Bear at Sonoma.

AMERICAN FLAG RAISED IN MONTEREY.

On Saturday, July 11, 1846, came the astounding news from Monterey that Commodore Sloat had arrived there in the United States frigate *Savannah*, and had raised the United States flag, and had taken possession of the country in consequence of war, which had broken out between the United States and Mexico. It was understood that Commodore Sloat requested Captain Fremont to go with all possible dispatch to Monterey.

The United States flag was raised in Monterey on July 7th. If the messenger started immediately, he was four days on his way to Fremont's camp. But Fremont appears to have been nine days on the way to Monterey, reaching there on Sunday, July 19th. If the question is asked, why this slowness, when speed would be so certainly looked for, the reply must be that no answer is apparent.

CAPTURE OF MONTEREY.*

"Concerning the capture of Monterey," says Will S. Green, "we were fortunate enough to hear the recital by Commodore Sloat himself. War was anticipated between the United States and Mexico long before it occurred, and Commodore Jones, then in command on this coast, was instructed to take Monterey, the capital of California, as soon as he heard hostilities had commenced. As we have seen, he acted too hurriedly, and, on the instance of the American Minister, he was removed. Sloat, who succeeded, had the same instructions, and was lying at Mazatlan with a frigate and sloop-of-war anxiously watching the signs of the times. It was known that there was an arrangement with England to take possession of California, and hold it for Mexico in case of war. Admiral Seymour, of the British navy, with the line-o'-battle ship *Collingwood*, was also at Mazatlan waiting orders. One day Seymour got dispatches, and Sloat got none. Sloat set a watch on the Admiral's movements, and found him in close consultation with the leading Mexicans, who avoided the American commander. He guessed that hostility had commenced, and when Seymour went on board his vessel and began to make ready for departure, he felt certain of the fact; and the white sails of the *Collingwood* had not disappeared in the distance before the two small American vessels were under way for Monterey. Every possible inch of canvas was spread and a quick voyage was made. On arriving at Monterey a demand was made for the surrender of the place, which was complied with without the firing of a gun. In a day or so the lookout announced the approach of the *Collingwood*. Not knowing how the Admiral would interpret his order to take possession of Monterey, the Commodore had his two small vessels got in readiness for action. The huge Englishman sailed up between the two American vessels and dropped anchor. Sloat sent an officer on board with his compliments to the Admiral, and the latter came in person to see the Commodore. He told Sloat that he knew that he had received no official information of the existence of war, and added that no officer in the British navy would have taken the responsibility he had done. He then asked Sloat, in a sort of bantering way, what he would have done if he had come into port and found the British flag flying. "I would have had you sink these two little ships for me," was the Commodore's reply. It was thus owing to the prompt action and courage of Commodore Sloat that we became possessed of California.

WHERE FIRST AMERICAN FLAG WAS RAISED.

"The soil of San Benito County claims the honor of having sustained the first American flag of conquest ever unfurled to a California 'breeze.' General Fremont having

---

* More fully given in the local "History of Colusa County," by Elliott & Co.

floated the United States flag on the Gabilan Peak in March, 1846."

Judge James F. Breen, one of the survivors of the Donner party, in preparing a history for us of San Benito County, says: "This statement has been often challenged as not being a historical fact. But I believe a careful examination of the facts connected with the conquest and possession of California by the United States will justify the above assertion."

General Fremont had been ordered out of the country by General Castro. Matters began to look serious, and Captain Fremont concluded to retire, at his leisure, however, but to leave nothing undone to make an available defense if attacked. He accordingly abandoned the Mission of San Juan, and led his company, with their horses, provisions, and such munitions of war as he had, up the steep acclivities leading to the Gabilan, or Fremont's Peak, as it is often and more appropriately called, which overlooks the towns of Hollister and San Juan. He there camped, erected a flag-staff and unfurled the Stars and Stripes, and calmly awaited the attack. But the attack was not delivered.

The spot where Captain Fremont halted his company, and raised the flag, is on the San Benito side of the division line between Monterey and San Benito Counties; and the prominent peak which rises just above the spot is to-day better known as Fremont's Peak than as the Gabilan Peak, as it was called by the Californians. And so it is that San Benito County claims, with justice, that her soil supported the first American flag of conquest that was ever unfurled to a California breeze. It is to be borne in mind that Commodore Sloat did not raise the American flag over Monterey until July 10, 1846; and that the famous "Bear Flag," which was American in sentiment if not in design, was not raised by Ide at Sonoma until June of the same year.

WAR DECLARED AGAINST MEXICO.

In the meantime Congress had (unknown to these parties) declared war against Mexico, and an expedition 1,600 strong, under Gen. Stephen W. Kearney, was traversing the continent in the direction of the Pacific. Simultaneously with Fremont's action in the north, Commodore Sloat seized upon Monterey; and his successor—Commodore Stockton—prepared at once for the reduction of the then principal city of Los Angeles.

CAPTURE OF LOS ANGELES.

With this end in view he organized a battalion of mounted riflemen, of which Fremont was appointed Major, and Gillespie Captain. This force was embarked on the sloop-of-war *Cyane*, and dispatched to San Diego with orders to co-operate with the Commodore in his proposed movement on the *Ciudad de Los Angeles*. On August 1st Stockton sailed in the *Congress*, and on the sixth arrived at San Pedro, having taken possession of Santa Barbara on his way. He now learned that the enemy under Generals Castro and Andres Pico were strongly posted near Los Angeles with a force estimated at 1,500 men. He learned further that Major Fremont had landed at San Diego, but was unable to procure horses, and therefore could not join him. In the absence of Fremont's battalion, Stockton was wholly destitute of cavalry; yet, impressed with the importance of celerity of movement, he disembarked his men. The force consisted only of from 300 to 400 marines, wholly ignorant of military drill; and their only artillery—six small guns, rudely mounted and dragged by hand.

A few days after landing, a flag of truce approached over the hills, borne by commissioners from Castro. Desiring to impress these with an exaggerated idea of the strength of his force, Stockton directed his little army to march at intervals of twenty or thirty paces apart, to a position where they would be sheltered from observation. In this manner the commissioners were completely deceived, and when on their arrival they were marched up to the mouth of an immense mortar, shrouded in skins save its huge aperture, their terror and discomfiture were plainly discernible.

Stockton received them with a stern and forbidding countenance, harshly demanding their mission, which they disclosed in great confusion. They bore a letter from Castro proposing a truce; each party to hold its own possessions until a general pacification should be had. This proposal Stockton rejected with contempt, and dismissed the commissioners with the assurance that only an immediate disbandment of his forces and an unconditional surrender, would shield Castro.

CALIFORNIA DECLARED A U. S. TERRITORY.

After some skirmishing of the two forces Castro surrendered, and the soldiers were permitted to go at large on their parole of honor—not again to bear arms against the United States. Commodore Stockton now issued a proclamation declaring California a territory of the United States; and, as all resistance had ceased, proceeded to organize a civil and military government, himself retaining the position of Commander-in-chief and Governor.

About this time Stockton first learned that war had been declared between the United States and Mexico; and leaving fifty men under command of Lieut. A. H. Gillespie to garrison Los Angeles, he proceeded north, to look after affairs in that quarter. Thus the whole great territory of Upper California had been subjected to American rule without bloodshed *or even the firing of a gun.*

TREATY OF PEACE SIGNED.

The treaty of peace between the United States and Mexico was signed at Guadalupe Hidalgo, February 2, 1848; ratifications were exchanged at Queretaro, May 30th, following. Under this treaty the United States assumed the Mexican debt to American subjects, and paid into the Mexican Treasury

$15,000,000 in money receiving in exchange Texas, New Mexico, and Upper California, and the right of free navigation on the Colorado River and the Gulf of California.

FIRST AMERICAN GOVERNOR.

1846.—Sloat proclaimed himself Governor of California, and acted as such until the 17th of August, 1846, when he was superseded by Com. R. F. Stockton, who commenced at once a vigorous campaign against the Mexicans under Flores, whom he defeated January 8 and 9, 1847. In January, 1847, Stockton appointed Fremont Governor, but this of right belonged to Gen. S. W. Kearney, who, on March 1st, assumed that office. He was succeeded by Colonel Mason in May, and on the 15th of April, 1849, Gen. Bennett Riley was appointed Governor, and continued in office until he was succeeded by Peter H. Burnett, under the State Constitution.

CALIFORNIA IN TRANSITION.

The year 1846 was the crisis-year in the destiny of California. In looking back on the events of that year, touching this country, from this distance of time, their main purpose stands out clearly revealed, as it did not when those events were transpiring. It is plain enough now, that they were inspired from Washington.

The Government of the United States had kept a careful watch of what was going on on this coast for many years. Ever after the famous explorations of Lewis and Clarke, who were sent out by President Jefferson, in 1804, our Government had kept itself thoroughly informed of everything that concerned California.

The hopes of England to acquire California were also well known, and all her movements having that end in view, were carefully observed.

Meanwhile the Government at Washington continued to seek all possible information concerning this country, then so remote and unexplored. Thomas O. Larkin, who came here from Massachusetts in 1832, seems to have had a fancy and a tact for gathering up facts and statistics. These he freely communicated to the Government.

By this means, as well as in other ways, they were made acquainted, not only with the geography and natural resources of the country, but with its inhabitants, both the native born and the foreign.

THE DONNER PARTY.

The following incidents were furnished us by Superior Judge Breen, of Hollister, one of the survivors of the party:—

There are many stories of human trial and suffering whose deep interest no amount of repetition can render stale, and such a story is the record of the ill-fated party of immigrants which furnished the actors in the terrible tragedy of Donner Lake. Portions of the tale have been written by many hands. They have differed widely, and many have been plainly colored for effect.

The story of the Donner party, in its general features, is too well known on this coast to need repetition. Too many suffered the hardships of crossing the plains to allow the recollections of those days to die out. For years after the great rush of immigration in '49 no story was told more frequently or was listened to with more eager interest than the misfortunes of that party.

The Donner party proper was formed in Sangamon County, Illinois, and was composed of ninety persons. Numerous additions were made to the train on its way, and when it left Independence, Missouri, it numbered between 200 and 300 wagons, and was over two miles in length. The journey to Salt Lake was made without any noticeable incidents, save the extreme slowness of the march. At Fort Bridger the woes of the Donner party began. Eighty-seven persons—the survivors of the original ninety—determined to go by way of the Hastings Cut-off, instead of following the old trail. The remainder of the train clung to the old route, and reached California in safety. The cut-off was by way of Weber Cañon and was said to rejoin the old emigrant road on the Humboldt, making a saving of 300 miles. It proved to be in a wretched condition, and the record of the party from this time was one long series of disasters. Their oxen became exhausted—they were forced to make frequent halts; the stock of provisions ran low. Finally, in the Salt Lake Desert, the emigrants saw plainly that they would never reach the Pacific Coast without assistance. Two of their number were despatched with letters to Captain Sutter imploring aid.

THE FATAL REST.

At the present site of Reno, the party concluded to rest. Three or four days' time was lost. This was the fatal act. The storm-clouds were already brewing upon the mountains, only a few miles distant. The ascent was ominous. Thick and thicker grew the clouds, outstripping in threatening battalions the now eager feet of the alarmed emigrants, until at Prosser Creek, three miles below Truckee, October 28, 1846, a month earlier than usual, the storm set in, and they found themselves in six inches of newly-fallen snow. On the summit it was already from two to five feet deep.

The party, in much confusion, finally reached Donner Lake in disordered fragments. Frequent and desperate attempts were made to cross the mountain tops, but at last, baffled and despairing, they returned to camp at the lake. The storm now descended in all its pitiless fury upon the ill-fated immigrants. Its dreadful import was well understood, as laden with omens of suffering and death. With slight interruptions, the storm continued for several days. The animals were literally buried alive and frozen in the drifts. Meat was hastily prepared from their carcasses, and cabins rudely built. One cabin (Moses Schallenberger's, now a resident of San Jose), erected November, 1844, was already standing about a quarter of a mile below the lake. This the Breen family appropriated. Judge Breen, now of San Juan, gives his reminiscences of the

RESIDENCE OF ROBERT BURNS, ARCATA, HUMBOLDT CO. CAL.

Donner party in our history of San Benito County. The Murphys erected one 300 yards from the lake, marked by a large stone twelve feet high. The Graves family built theirs near Donner Creek, farther down the stream, the three forming the apexes of a triangle, and distant 150 yards or more.

The Donner Brothers, with their families, hastily constructed a brush shed in Alder Creek Valley, six or seven miles from the lake.

The Mr. Donner who had charge of one company, was an Illinoisan, sixty years of age, a man of high respectability and abundant means. His wife was a woman of education and refinement, and much younger than he.

Of course these were soon utterly destitute of food, for they could not tell where the cattle were buried, and there was no hope of game on a desert so piled with snow that nothing without wings could move. The number of those who were thus storm-stayed, at the very threshold of the land whose winters are one long spring, was eighty, of whom thirty were females, and several, children. Much of the time the tops of the cabins were below the snow level.

FORLORN HOPE RESCUE PARTY.

It was six weeks after the halt was made that a party of fifteen, including five women and two Indians, who acted as guides, set out on snow-shoes to cross the mountains, and give notice to the people of the California settlements of the condition of their friends. At first the snow was so light and feathery that even in snow-shoes they sank nearly a foot at every step. On the second day they crossed the "divide," finding the snow at the summit twelve feet deep. Pushing forward with the courage of despair, they made from four to eight miles a day.

Within a week they got entirely out of provisions; and three of them, succumbing to cold, weariness, and starvation, had died. Then a heavy snow-storm came on, which compelled them to lie still, buried between their blankets under the snow, for thirty-six hours. By the evening of the tenth day three more had died, and the living had been four days without food. The horrid alternative was accepted—they took the flesh from the bones of their dead, remained in camp two days to dry it, and then pushed on.

On New Year's, the sixteenth day since leaving Truckee Lake, they were toiling up a steep mountain. Their feet were frozen. Every step was marked with blood. On the second of January, their food again gave out. On the 3d, they had nothing to eat but the strings of their snow-shoes. On the 4th, the Indians eloped, justly suspicious that they might be sacrificed for food. On the 5th, they shot a deer, and that day one of their number died. Soon after three others died, and every death now eked out the existence of the survivors. On the 17th, all gave out, and concluded their wanderings useless, except one. He, guided by two friendly Indians, dragged himself on till he reached Johnson's Ranch on Bear River, the first settlement on the western slope of the Sierras, when relief was sent back as soon as possible, and the remaining six survivors were brought in next day. It had been thirty-two days since they left Donner Lake. No tongue can tell, no pen portray, the awful suffering, the terrible and appalling straits, as well as the noble deeds of heroism that characterized this march of death. The eternal mountains, whose granite faces bore witness to their sufferings, are fit monuments to mark the last resting-place of this heroic party.

SEVERAL RELIEF PARTIES FITTED OUT.

The story that there were immigrants perishing on the other side of the snowy barrier, ran swiftly down the Sacramento Valley to New Helvetia, and Captain Sutter, at his own expense, fitted out an expedition of men and of mules ladened with provisions, to cross the mountains and relieve them. It ran on to San Francisco, and the people rallying in public meeting, raised $1,500, and with it fitted out another expedition. The naval commandant of the port fitted out still others.

First of the relief parties, under Capt. J. P. Tucker, reached Truckee Lake on the 19th of February. Ten of the people in the nearest camp were dead. For four weeks those who were still alive had fed only on bullocks' hides. At Donner's camp they had but one hide remaining. The visitors left a small supply of provisions with the twenty-nine whom they could not take with them and started back with the remainder. Four of the children they carried on their backs.

Second of the relief parties, under J. F. Reed, reached Truckee Lake on the 1st of March. They immediately started back with seventeen of the sufferers; but, a heavy snow-storm overtaking them, they left all, except three of the children, on the road.

The third party, under John Stark, went after those who were left on the way; found three of them dead, and the rest sustaining life by feeding on the flesh of the dead.

THE LAST SURVIVOR.

Last relief party reached Donner's camp late in April, when the snows had melted so that the earth appeared in spots. The main cabin was empty, but some miles distant they found the last survivor of all lying on the cabin floor smoking his pipe. "He was ferocious in aspect, savage and repulsive in manner. His camp-kettle was over the fire and in it his meal of human flesh preparing. The stripped bones of his fellow-sufferers lay around him. He refused to return with the party, and only consented when he saw there was no escape."

This person was Louis Keseberg, who has been execrated as a cannibal, and whose motive in remaining behind has been ascribed to plunder. Never until now has he made any attempt to refute these stories. He says:—

"For nearly two months I was alone in that dismal cabin.

"* * * Five of my companions had died in my cabin, and their stark and ghastly bodies lay there day and night, seemingly gazing at me with their glazed and staring eyes. I was too weak to move them had I tried. I endured a thousand deaths. To have one's suffering prolonged inch by inch; to be deserted, forsaken, hopeless; to see that loathsome food ever before my eyes was almost too much for human endurance."

For two months he lived there entirely alone, boiling the flesh of his dead companions. When the last relief party came they found him the sole survivor.

If he were guilty of the crimes charged to him he has certainly paid the penalty. To use his own words: " Wherever I have gone people have cried,' Stone him! stone him!' Even little children in the streets have mocked me and thrown stones at me as I passed. Only a man conscious of his own innocence would not have succumbed to the terrible things which have been said of me—would not have committed suicide. Mortification, disgrace, disaster, and unheard-of misfortune have followed and overwhelmed me."

Keseberg has lost several fortunes, and is now living in poverty at Brighton, Sacramento County, with two idiotic children.

FATE OF DONNER AND WIFE.

When the third relief party arrived at Donner Lake, the sole survivors at Alder Creek were George Donner, the Captain of the company, and his heroic wife, whose devotion to her dying husband caused her own death during the last and fearful days of waiting for the fourth relief. George Donner knew that he was dying, and urged his wife to save her life and go with her little ones with the third relief, but she refused. Nothing was more heart-rending than her sad parting with her beloved little ones, who wound their childish arms lovingly around her neck, and besought her with mingled tears and kisses to join them. But duty prevailed over affection, and she retraced the weary distance to die with him whom she had promised to love and honor to the end.

Mrs. Donner was the last to die. Her husband's body, carefully laid out and wrapped in a sheet, was found in his tent. Circumstances led to the suspicion that the survivor (Keseberg) had killed Mrs. Donner for her flesh and her money; and when "he was threatened with hanging, and the rope tightened around his neck, he produced over five hundred dollars in gold, which probably he had appropriated from her store."

STRANGE AND EVENTFUL DREAM.

George Yount was the pioneer settler of Napa County. He, in the winter of 1846, dreamed that a party of immigrants were snow-bound in the Sierra Nevadas, high up in the mountains, where they were suffering the most distressing privations from cold and want of food. The locality where his dream had placed these unhappy mortals, he had never visited, yet so clear was his vision that he described the sheet of water surrounded by lofty peaks, deep-covered with snow, while on every hand towering pine trees reared their heads far above the limitless waste. In his sleep he saw the hungry human beings ravenously tear the flesh from the bones of their fellow-creatures, slain to satisfy their craving appetites, in the midst of a gloomy desolation. He dreamed his dream on three successive nights, after which he related it to others, among whom were a few who had been on hunting expeditions to the Sierras. These wished for a precise description of the scene foreshadowed to him. They recognized the Truckee, now the Donner Lake. On the strength of this recognition, Mr. Yount fitted out a search expedition, and with these men as guides, went to the place indicated; and prodigious to relate, was one of the successful relieving parties to reach the ill-fated Donner Party.

Of the eighty-seven persons who reached Donner Lake, only forty-eight escaped. Of these twenty-six are known to be living in this State and in Oregon.

SCENE OF THE DISASTER.

The best description of the scene of the disaster was given by Edwin Bryant, who accompanied General Kearney's expedition in 1847 to bury the remains. He says: " Near the principal cabins, I saw two bodies entire, with the exception that the abdomens had been cut open and the entrails extracted. The flesh had been either wasted by famine or evaporated by exposure to the dry atmosphere, and they presented the appearance of mummies. Strewn around the cabins were dislocated and broken skulls (in some instances sawed asunder with care for the purpose of extracting the brains), human skeletons, in short, in every variety of mutilation. A more revolting and appalling spectacle I never witnessed. The cabins were burned, the bodies buried, and now there is nothing to mark the place save the tall stumps, from ten to twenty feet in height, which surround some of the rocks on the lake's shore."

TRIALS OF THE PIONEERS.

It was in the few years prior to the discovery of gold that the genuine pioneers of California braved the unknown dangers of the plains and mountains, with the intention of settling in the fair valley, of which so much was said and so little known, and building a home for themselves and their children. Many of these immigrants crossed the mountains by nearly the same route pursued by the Central Pacific Railroad, except that they followed down Bear River to the plains.

The first settlement reached by them was that of Theodore Sicard, at Johnson's Crossing, on the Placer County side, and a few miles below Camp Far West. This settlement was made in 1844, and was the first point reached by the members of the ill-starred Donner Party in 1847. Opposite Sicard's settlement was Johnson's ranch, owned by William Johnson and Sebastian Kyser, who settled there in 1845. Johnson's Crossing was for years a favorite landmark and rallying point.

The Discovery of Gold.

No HISTORY of the State, or of a county in California would be complete without a record of the rush to this coast at the time of what is so aptly termed the "gold fever."

The finding of gold at Coloma by Marshall was not the real discovery of the precious metal in the territory. But the time and circumstances connected with it, together with the existing state of affairs, caused the rapid dissemination of the news. People were ready and eager for some new excitement, and this proved to be the means of satisfying the desire. From all parts of California, the coast of the United States, and in fact thence to the Butte Mountains up the Sacramento Valley, as far as the location of Chico.

While passing over the black adobe land lying between the Butte Mountains and Butte Creek, which resembled the gold wash in Brazil, Dr. Sandels remarked: "Judging from the Butte Mountains, I believe that there is gold in this country, but I do not think there will ever be enough to pay for the working." Dr. Sandels was hurried, as the vessel upon which he was to take passage was soon to sail, and he could not spare the time to pursue his search to any more definite end.

GEN. BIDWELL KNEW OF GOLD.

1844.—When General Bidwell was in charge of Hock Farm, in the month of March or April, 1844, a Mexican by the name

SUTTER'S MILL, WHERE GOLD WAS DISCOVERED.

the world, poured in vast hordes of gold-seekers. The precious metal had been found in many places.

DR. SANDELS' SEARCH FOR GOLD.

1843.—In the summer of 1843, there came to this coast from England, a very learned gentleman named Dr. Sandels. He was a Swede by birth. Soon after his arrival on this coast, the Doctor visited Captain Sutter. The Captain always thought there must be mineral in the country, and requested Dr. Sandels to go out into the mountains and find him a gold mine; the Doctor discouraged him by relating his experience in Mexico, and the uncertainty of mining operations, as far as his knowledge extended, in Mexico, Brazil, and other parts of South America. He advised Sutter never to think of having anything to do with the mines; that the best mine was the soil, which was inexhaustible. However, at Sutter's solicitation, Dr. Sandels went up through his grant to Hock Farm, and

of Pablo Gutierrez was with him, having immediate supervision of the Indian vaqueros, taking care of the stock on the plains, "breaking" wild horses, and performing other duties common to a California rancho. This Mexican had some knowledge of gold mining in Mexico, where he had lived, and after returning from the mountains on Bear River at the time mentioned, he informed General Bidwell that there was gold up there.

As heretofore mentioned, Dr. Marsh describes gold and silver mines as early as 1842.

SUTTER'S SAW-MILL CONSTRUCTED.

1847.—Captain Sutter always had an unconquerable desire for the possession of a saw-mill, by which he could himself furnish the necessary material for the construction of more improved buildings than the facilities of the country could at that time afford. Around his fort in 1847, was a person named James W.

Marshall, who had a natural taste for mechanical contrivances, and was able to construct, with the few crude tools and appliances at hand, almost any kind of a machine ordinarily desired. It was to this man that Sutter intrusted the erection of the long-contemplated and much needed saw-mill. The contract was written by Mr. John Bidwell, then Captain Sutter's Secretary, and signed by the parties. Marshall started out in November, 1847, equipped with tools and provisions for his men. He reported the distance of the selected site to be thirty miles, but he occupied two weeks in reaching his destination in Coloma. In the course of the winter a dam and race were made, but when the water was let on, the tail-race was too narrow. To widen and deepen it, Marshall let in a strong current of water directly to the race, which bore a large body of mud and gravel to the foot.

MARSHALL'S DISCOVERY OF GOLD.

1848.—On the 19th of January, 1848, Marshall observed some glittering particles in the race, which he was curious enough to examine. He called five carpenters on the mill to see them; but though they talked over the possibility of its being gold, the vision did not inflame them.

One lump weighed about seventeen grains. It was malleable, heavier than silver, and in all respects resembled gold. About 4 o'clock in the evening Marshall exhibited his find to the circle composing the mill company laborers. Their names were James W. Marshall, P. L. Wimmer, Mrs. A. Wimmer, J. Barger, Ira Willis, Sydney Willis, A. Stephens, James Brown, Ezekiah F. Persons, H. Bigler, Israel Smith, William Johnson, George Evans, C. Bennett, and William Scott. The conference resulted in a rejection of the idea that it was gold. Mrs. Wimmer tested it by boiling it in strong lye. Marshall afterwards tested it with nitric acid. It was gold, sure enough, and the discoverer found its like in all the surrounding gulches wherever he dug for it. The secret could not be kept long. It was known at Yerba Buena three months after the discovery.

TWO IMPORTANT EVENTS.

1848.—The treaty of Guadalupe Hidalgo, by which California was ceded to the United States, was concluded in Mexico, on February 2, 1848. It proves to have been on that very day, the 2d of February, 1848, that here in California, Marshall rides in from Sutter's Mill, situated at what is now Coloma, forty miles to Sutter's Fort, his horse in a foam and himself all bespattered with mud; and finding Captain Sutter alone, takes from his pocket a pouch, from which he pours upon the table about an ounce of yellow grains of metal, which he thought would prove to be gold. It did prove to be gold, and there was a great deal more where that came from. General Bidwell writes: "I myself first took the news to San Francisco. I went by way of Sonoma. I told General Vallejo. He told me to say to Sutter 'that he hoped the gold would flow into his purse as the water through his mill-race.'"

WHAT MIGHT HAVE BEEN.

We cannot observe the coincidence of the date of this great discovery, with that of the negotiation of the treaty of peace with Mexico, by which California was acquired by the United States, without thinking. What if the gold discovery had come first? What if the events of the war had postponed the conclusion of peace for a few months? What if Mexico had heard the news before agreeing upon terms? What if Mexico's large creditor, England, had also learned that there was abundance of gold here in California? Who can tell, when in that case, there would have been peace, and upon what terms, and with what disposition of territory.

THE DISCOVERY OF GOLD DOUBTED.

In the bar room at Weber's Hotel in San Jose, one day in February, 1848, a man came in, and to pay for something he had purchased, offered some gold-dust, saying that gold had been discovered at Sutter's Mill on American River, and all were going to work. The people were very incredulous and would not believe the story. An old Georgia miner said that what the man had was really gold, and requested him to investigate the matter. When he arrived at Sutter's Mill, he asked Sutter regarding it, and the Captain assured him that it was a certainty, and that a man could make five dollars a day. He carried the news to San Jose and the place was almost deserted, every one hastening to the mines.

The people were suspicious regarding the quality and amount of the gold. As the weeks passed, confidence was gained and the belief that there might possibly be precious minerals in other localities was strengthened.

Prospectors gradually pushed out beyond the narrow limits of the first mining district, and thus commenced the opening up of the vast mining fields of California and the Pacific Coast.

SPECIMEN PIECES OF GOLD.

A Frenchman fishing in a prospect hole for frogs for his breakfast, at Mokelumne Hill, in November, 1848, discovered a speck of gold on the side of the excavation, which he dug out with his pocket-knife and sold for $2,150.

Three sailors who had deserted took out $10,000 in five days on Weber Creek. Such strokes of good fortune turned all classes into miners, including the lawyers, doctors and preachers.

The exports of gold-dust in exchange for produce and merchandise amounted to $500,000 by the 25th of September. The ruling price of gold-dust was $15 per ounce, though its intrinsic value was from $19 to $20.

The first piece of gold found in California weighed 50 cents, and the second $5. Since that time one nugget worth $43,000, two $21,000, one $10,000, two $8,000, one $6,500, four $5,000, twelve worth from $2,000 to $4,000, and eighteen from $1,000 to $2,000 have been found and recorded in the History of the

State. In addition to the above, numberless nuggets worth from $100 to $500 are mentioned in the annals of California gold mining during the last thirty years. The first two referred to were exchanged for bread, and all trace of them was lost. The finder of one of the $8,000 pieces became insane the following day, and was confined in the hospital at Stockton.

MERCHANTS REFUSE GOLD-DUST.

A meeting of citizens in San Francisco, presided over by T. M. Leavenworth and addressed by Samuel Brannan, passed resolutions in September, 1848, not to patronize merchants who refused to take gold-dust at $16 per ounce. A memorial was also sent from San Francisco to Congress in that month for a branch mint here. It stated, among other things, the opinion that by July 1, 1849, $5,000,000 worth of dust at $16 per ounce would be taken out of the mines. The figures were millions too low.

ADVANCE IN REAL ESTATE.

Real estate in San Francisco took a sudden rise. A lot on Montgomery Street near Washington, sold in July for $10,000, and was resold in November with a shanty on it for $27,000. Lots in Sacramento, or New Helvetia, also came up to fabulous prices that winter. By the month of October the rush from Oregon caused the Oregon City papers to stop publication. In December, the Kanakas and Sonorians came in swarms. A Honolulu letter, November 11th, said:—

"Such another excitement as the news from California created here the world never saw. I think not less than 500 persons will leave before January 1st, and if the news continues good, the whole foreign population except missionaries will go."

The news did continue good, and they came, some missionaries included. Soon there came up from the mines complaint of outrage and lawlessness, mostly against Kanakas and other foreigners. How well they were founded, to what they led, and how they were suddenly and summarily silenced, is a story that covers a very interesting part of the history of California and the progress of civilization in America.

On the 29th of May, the *Californian* issued a slip stating that its further publication, for the present, would cease, because nearly all its patrons had gone to the mines.

SAN FRANCISCO DESERTED.

A month later there were but five persons—women and children—left in Yerba Buena. The first rush was for Sutter's Mill, since christened Coloma, or Culluma, after a tribe of Indians who lived in that region. From there they scattered in all directions. A large stream of them went over to Weber Creek, that empties into the American some ten or twelve miles below Coloma. Others went up or down the river. Some, more adventurous, crossed the ridge over to the north and middle forks of the American.

By the close of June the discoveries had extended to all the forks of the American, Weber Creek, Hangtown Creek, the Cosumnes (known then as the Makosumé), the Mokelumne, Tnolumne, the Yuba from *uvas*, or *yuvas*—grape), called in 1848 the "Yuba," or "Ajuba," and Feather River.

On July 15th, the editor of the *Californian* returned and issued the first number of his paper after its suspension. It contained a description of the mines from personal observation. He said:—

"The country from the Ajuba Yuba to the San Joaquin, a distance of about 120 miles, and from the base toward the summit of the mountains, as far as Snow Hill [meaning Nevada], about seventy miles, has been explored and gold found on every part. There are now probably 3,000 people, including Indians, engaged in collecting gold. The amount collected by each man ranges from $10 to $350 per day. The publisher of this paper collected, with the aid of a shovel, pick, and a tin pan, from $44 to $128 per day—averaging $100. The gross amount collected may exceed $600,000; of which amount our merchants have received about $250,000, all for goods, and in eight weeks. The largest piece known to be found weighs eight pounds.

NUMBER OF MINERS AND THEIR SUCCESS.

1848.—On the 14th of August, the number of white miners was estimated at 4,000. Many of them were of Stevenson's Regiment and the disbanded Mormon Battalion. The *Californian* remarked on that day that "when a man with his pan or basket does not average $30 to $40 a day, he moves to another place.

Four thousand ounces a day was the estimated production of the mines five months after the secret leaked out. In April the price of flour here was $4 per hundred. In August it had risen to $16. All other subsistence supplies rose in the same proportion. Here is a part of a letter from Sonoma, to the *Californian*, August 14th:—

"I have heard from one of our citizens who has been at the placers only a few weeks, and collected $1,500, still averaging $100 a day. Another, who shut up his hotel here some five or six weeks since, has returned with $2,200, collected with a spade, pick, and Indian basket. A man and his wife and boy collected $500 in one day."

Sam Brannan laid exclusive claim to Mormon Island, in the American, about twenty-eight miles above its mouth, and levied a royalty of thirty per cent. on all the gold taken there by the Mormons, who paid it for awhile, but refused after they came to a better understanding of the rules of the mines. By September the news had spread to Oregon and the southern coast and on the 2d of that month the *Californian* notes that 125 persons had arrived in town "by ship" since August, 26th. In the "Dry Diggings" near Auburn, during the month of August, one man got $16,000 out of five cart-loads of dirt in the same diggings a good many were collecting from $800 to $1,500 a day.

In the fall of 1848, John Murphy, now of San Jose, discovered Murphy's Camp Diggings in Calaveras, and some soldiers of Stevenson's Regiment discovered Rich Gulch at Mokelumne Hill. That winter one miner at Murphy's realized $80,000. It was common report that John Murphy, who mined a number of Indians on wages, had collected over $1,500,000 in gold-dust before the close of the wet season of 1848.

The following notice of the discovery is from the *Californian*, of San Francisco, on the 19th of April, 1848:—

NEW GOLD MINE.—It is stated that a new gold mine has been discovered on the American Fork of the Sacramento, supposed to be [it was not] on the land of William A. Leidesdorff, Esq., of this place. A specimen of the gold has been exhibited and is represented to be very pure.

May opened with accounts of new discoveries. The *Californian* of May 3d said: "Seven men, with picks and spades, gathered $1,600 worth in fifteen days." That was a little more than $15 per man per day. On the 17th of May the same paper said:—

"Many persons have already left the coast for the diggings. Considerable excitement exists here. Merchants and mechanics are closing doors. Lawyers and alcaldes are leaving their desks, farmers are neglecting their crops, and whole families are forsaking their homes, for the diggings."

By May 24th gold-dust had become an article of merchandise, the price being from $14 to $16 per ounce. The *Californian* of that date had these advertisements:—

GOLD! GOLD!! GOLD!!!—Cash will be paid for California gold by H. R. BUCKALEW, Watchmaker and Jeweler, San Francisco.

GOLD! GOLD!! GOLD!!!—Messrs. DICKSON & HAY are purchasers of Sacramento gold. A liberal price given. BEE HIVE.

THE SECRET WOULD NOT KEEP.

Before Sutter had quite satisfied himself that the metal found was gold, he went up to the mill, and, with Marshall, made a treaty with the Indians, buying of them their titles to the region round about for a certain amount of goods. There was an effort made to keep the secret inside the little circle that knew it, but it soon leaked out. They had many misgivings and much discussion whether they were not making themselves ridiculous; yet by common consent all began to hunt, though with no great spirit, for the "yellow stuff" that might prove such a prize.

Slowly and surely, however, did these discoveries creep into the minds of those at home and abroad; the whole civilized world was set agog with the startling news from the shores of the Pacific. Young and old were seized with the California fever; high and low, rich and poor, were infected by it; the prospect was altogether too gorgeous to contemplate. Why, they could actually pick up a fortune for the seeking!

GRAND RUSH FOR THE GOLD

While the real argonauts of 1848 were wandering around among the hills and gulches that flank the western slope of the Sierra Nevada, armed with pan, spoon, and butcher-knife, testing the scope and capabilities of the gold mines, the news of discovery was speeding on its way to the Eastern States, by two routes simultaneously.

It reached the frontier of Missouri and Iowa by the Mormon scouts and moving trappers about the same time that vessels sailing round Cape Horn took it to New York and Boston, which was in the late autumn of 1848. The first reports repeatedly confirmed and enlarged upon, threw the whole country into the wildest excitement. In the city of New York and the extreme Western States the fever was hottest.

EMIGRANT COMPANIES FORMED.

1849.—The adventurers generally formed companies, expecting to go overland or by sea to the mines, and to dissolve partnership only after a first trial of luck together in the "diggings." In the Eastern and Middle States they would often buy up an old whaling ship, just ready to be condemned to the wreckers, put in a cargo of such stuff as they must need themselves, and provisions, tools, or goods, that must be sure to bring returns enough to make the venture profitable. Of course, the whole fleet rushing together through the Golden Gate, made most of these ventures profitless, even when the guess was happy as to the kind of supplies needed by the Californians. It can hardly be believed what sieves of ships started, and how many of them actually made the voyage.

Hundreds of farms were mortgaged to buy tickets for the land of gold. Some insured their lives and pledged their policies for an outfit. The wild boy was packed off hopefully. The black sheep of the flock was dismissed with a blessing, and the forlorn hope that, with a change of skies, there might be a change of manners. The stay of the happy household said "Good-bye, but only for a year or two," to his charge. Unhappy husbands availed themselves cheerfully of this cheap and reputable method of divorce, trusting time to mend matters in their absence. Here was a chance to begin life anew.

THE MINERS' LAWS.

The miners found no governmental machinery competent to protect their lives or their property, and hence each mining camp made a law unto itself. The punishment, of course, was sure and swift, and, as a consequence, there was but little of it. Gold was left in deep cañons with no one to watch it, and every opportunity was afforded for theft; but if there were any disposed to take what did not belong to them, the knowledge that their lives would pay the forfeit if detected, deterred them from it. The excitement of the times led to gambling. It seemed that almost everybody, even those who had been leading church members at the East, were seized with the mania for gambling. Tables for this purpose were set out in every hotel, and one corner of many of the stores, both in mines and cities, were set apart for the monte table.

SAN FRANCISCO ON SUNDAY.

Sunday in the time of the mining excitement differed little from other days. Banks were open; expresses were running; stores were open for the most part; auctioneers were crying their wares, and the town was full of business and noise. Gambling saloons were thronged day and night. The plaza was surrounded with them on two sides, and partly on a third. Music of every sort was heard from them, sometimes of the finest kind, and now and then the noise of violence and the sound of pistol shots. The whole city was a strange and almost bewildering scene to a stranger.

THE GOLDEN ERA OF 1849.

"The 'fall of '49 and the spring of '50' is the era of California history, which the pioneer always speaks of with warmth. It was the free-and-easy age when everybody was flush, and fortune, if not in the palm, was only just beyond the grasp of all. Men lived chiefly in tents, or in cabins scarcely more durable, and behaved themselves like a generation of bachelors. The family was beyond the mountains; the restraints of society had not yet arrived. Men threw off the masks they had lived behind and appeared out in their true character. A few did not discharge the consciences and convictions they brought with them. More rollicked in a perfect freedom from those bonds which good men cheerfully assume in settled society for the good of the greater number. Some afterwards resumed their temperate, steady habits, but hosts were wrecked before the period of their license expired.

"Very rarely did men on their arrival in the country, begin to work at their old trade or profession. To the mines first. If fortune favored, they soon quit for more congenial employment. If she frowned, they might depart disgusted, if they were able; but oftener, from sheer inability to leave the business, they kept on, drifting from bar to bar, living fast, reckless, improvident, half-civilized lives; comparatively rich to-day, poor to-morrow; tormented with rheumatisms and agues, remembering dimly the joys of the old homestead; nearly weaned from the friends at home, who, because they were never heard from, soon became like dead men in their memory; seeing little of women and nothing of churches; self-reliant, yet satisfied that there was nowhere any 'show' for them; full of enterprise in the direct line of their business, and utterly lost in the threshold of any other; genial companions, morbidly craving after newspapers; good fellows, but short-lived."

A REVIEW OF EVENTS.

At this day it seems strange that the news of this great discovery did not fly abroad more swiftly than it did. It would not seem so very strange, however, if it could be remembered how very improbable the truth of the gold stories then were.

And it appeared to be most improbable, that if gold was really found, it would be in quantities sufficient to pay for going after it. People were a little slow to commit themselves, at first, respecting it. Even as late as May 24, 1848, a correspondent writing in the *Californian*, a paper then published in San Francisco, expressed the opinion of some people thus:—

"What evil effects may not result from this mania, and the consequent abandonment of all useful pursuits, in a wild-goose chase after gold!"

A good many people, far and near, looked upon the matter in this light for some time. The slowness with which the news traveled in the beginning, is seen in this:—

Monterey, then the seat of government, is not more than four or five days' travel from the place where gold was first discovered. The discovery took place not later than the 1st of February, 1848. And yet Alcalde Walter Colton says, in his journal under date, May 29th, "Our town was startled out

ALCALDE COLTON MEETS THE MINER. (See next page.)

of its quiet dreams to-day by the announcement that gold had been discovered on the American Fork."

If it took four months for the news of the discovery of gold to travel as far as Monterey, the capital town of the country, it is not surprising that it hardly got over to the Atlantic States within the year 1848. There was then an express that advertised to take letters through to Independence, Missouri, in sixty days, at fifty cents apiece.

If the gold news had been thoroughly credited here, it might have been published all through the East by the first of May; but it was not. In the early fall of 1848, however, the rumor began to get abroad there, through private sources. At first it was laughed at, and those who credited it at all had no idea that gold existed here in sufficient quantities to be worth digging.

ALCALDE COLTON'S VISIT TO THE MINES.

Walter Colton, the alcalde of Monterey, and writer of "Three Years in California," hearing of the discovery of gold, visited the mines. From his descriptions we gain an insight into those days. We copy his journal for a few days:—

"1848 October 12.—We are camped in the center of the gold mines, in the heart of the richest deposits, where many hundreds are at work. All the gold-diggers were excited by the report that a solid pocket of gold had been found on the Stanislaus. In half an hour a motley crowd, with crow-bars, pick-axes, spades, and wash-bowls went over the hills in the direction of the new deposit. I remained and picked out from a small crevice of slate rock, a piece weighing a half-ounce.

"October 13. I started for the Stanislaus diggings. It was an uproarious life; the monte-table, with its piles of gold, glimmering in the shade. The keeper of the bank was a woman. The bank consisted of a pile of gold, weighing, perhaps, a hundred pounds. They seemed to play for the excitement, caring little whether they won or lost.

"It was in this ravine that, a few weeks since, the largest lump of gold found in California was discovered. Its weight was twenty-three (23) pounds, and in nearly a pure state. Its discovery shook the whole mines. (Query—Does any one know the name of the finder?)

"October 14.—A new deposit was discovered this morning near the falls of the Stanislaus. An Irishman had gone there to bathe, and in throwing off his clothes, had dropped his knife, which slipped into a crevice, and in getting it, picked up gold-dust. He was soon tracked out, and a storm of picks were splitting the rocks.

PRICES OF PROVISIONS.

"October 15.—Quite a sensation was produced by the arrival from Stockton of a load of provisions and whisky. The price of the former was: flour, $2 per pound; sugar and coffee, $4. The whisky was $20 per quart. Coffee-pots and sauce-pans were in demand, while one fellow offered $10 to let him suck with a straw from the bung. All were soon in every variety of inebriety.

"October 16.—I encountered to-day, in a ravine some three miles distant, among the gold washers, a woman from San Jose. She was at work with a large wooden bowl, by the side of a stream. I asked her how long she had been there, and how much gold she averaged per day. She replied: "Three weeks, and an ounce."

"October 18.—A German, this morning, picking a hole in the ground near our camping tree, struck a piece of gold weighing about three ounces. As soon as it was known, some forty picks were flying into the earth, but not another piece was found. In a ravine, a little girl this morning picked up what she thought a curious stone, and brought it to her mother, who found it a lump of gold, weighing six or seven pounds.

"October 20.—I encountered this morning, in the person of a Welshman, a marked specimen of the gold-digger. He stood some six feet eight in his shoes, with giant limbs and frame. A slender strap fastened his coarse trowsers above his hips, and confined the flowing bunt of his flannel shirt. A broad-rimmed hat sheltered his browny features, while his unshorn beard and hair flowed in tangled confusion to his waist. To his back was lashed a blanket and bag of provisions; on one shoulder rested a huge crow-bar, to which was hung a gold washer and skillet; on the other rested a rifle, a spade, and a pick, from which dangled a cup and a pair of heavy shoes. He recognized me as the magistrate who had once arrested him for breach of the peace. "Well, Alcalde," said he, "I am glad to see you in these diggings. I was on a buster; you did your duty, and I respect you for it; and now let me settle the difference between us with a bit of gold; it shall be the first I strike under this log." Before I could reply, his traps were on the ground, and his pick was tearing up bog after bog. These removed, he struck a layer of clay. "Here she comes," he ejaculated, and turned out a piece of gold that would weigh an ounce or more. "There Alcalde, accept that, and when you reach home have a bracelet made for your good lady." He continued digging around the same place for the hour I remained, but never found another piece—not a particle. No uncommon thing to find only one piece, and never another near it."

THE DESERTED CLAIMS.

Scattered all up and down through the mining districts of California are hundreds of such spots as that represented by Colton. Time was when the same place was full of life and activity; when the flume ran; when the cabins were tenanted; when the loud voices of men rose, and the sounds of labor kept the birds away that now fly so fearlessly around the tumbling ruins. But the claim gave out, and the miners, gathering their tools together, vamosed for some other spot, and desolation set in. The unused flume dropped to pieces, ownerless huts became forlorn, and the *debris* only added to the dismalness of the place. Or who knows, some dark deed may have led to the abandonment of the claim, for surely the spot looks uncanny and gloomy enough for twenty murders.

FIRST DISCOVERIES OF GOLD.

The first actually known of the metals was the reported discovery, as early as 1802, of silver at Alizal, in Monterey County. In 1825, Jedediah S. Smith, at the head of a party of American trappers, while crossing the Sierra Nevada in the vicinity of Mono Lake, "found placer gold in quantities and brought much of it with him to the encampment on Green River."

This is the first known discovery of gold in California, and much of the honor that is showered upon James W. Marshal, should properly fall upon this intrepid and enterprising pioneer trapper, Jedediah S. Smith.

In 1828, at San Isador, in San Diego County, and in 1833, in the western limits of Santa Clara County, gold was also found.

Gold placers were discovered in 1841, by a Canadian, near the Mission of San Fernando, forty-five miles northeast of Los Angeles, and were worked until 1848, in a small way, yielding some $6,000 annually.

CO. EUREKA, HUMBOLDT CO. CAL.

Organization of the Government.

1846.—Thomas O. Larkin, the American Consul at Monterey, who under instructions had gained a great amount of influence among the leading native Californians, suggested and caused the issuance of a circular by Governor Pico, in May, 1846, calling a convention of thirty of the more prominent men in the country. This assemblage was to discuss the condition of affairs and to petition the Mexican authorities for an improved government; if the request met with a refusal, the territory was to be sold to some other power. The tendency of this discussion would be towards the transfer of the territory to the United States. The convention did not meet, however, as events transpired which precluded the possibility of a peaceful transfer. Lieut. John C. Fremont arrived in that year, and soon became embroiled in a wordy conflict with the authorities, and he and his party declared a revolution at Sonoma as heretofore mentioned.

The more intelligent settlers of California saw at an early day the urgent necessity of a regular constitution and laws. The provisional government existing since the conquest of 1847 was but a temporary affair and by no means able to satisfy the wants of a great, growing, and dangerous population which had now so strangely and suddenly gathered together. The inhabitants could not wait the slow movements of Congress. Attempts were made by the citizens of San Francisco, Sonoma, and San Jose to form legislatures for themselves, which they invested with supreme authority. It was quickly found that these independent legislative bodies came into collision with each other, and nothing less than a general constitution would be satisfactory to the people.

Great meetings for these purposes were held at San Jose, San Francisco, Monterey, Sonoma, and other places, in the months of December and January, 1848-49. It was resolved that delegates be chosen by popular election from all parts of the State to meet at San Jose. These delegates were to form a Constitution. These movements were general on the part of all citizens, and no partizan feeling was shown in the matter.

CONVENTION CALLED AT MONTEREY.

1849.—While the people were thus working out for themselves this great problem, the then great Military Governor, General Riley, saw fit to issue on the 3d of June, 1849, a proclamation calling a Convention to meet at Monterey on the 1st of September, to frame a Constitution.

These delegates were forty-eight in number, and while they represented all parts of the State, they were also representatives of every State in the Union. They were men not much used to those deliberations expected of such a body, but they determined to do their duty in the best possible manner.

The delegates, at their first regular meeting on the 4th of September, chose, by a large majority of votes, Dr. Robert Semple as President of the Convention; Capt. William G. Marcy was then appointed Secretary, and the other necessary offices were properly filled up. After rather more than a month's constant labor and discussion, the existing Constitution of California was drafted, and finally adopted by the Convention.

THE FIRST STATE CONSTITUTION.

This document was formed after the model of the most approved State Constitutions of the Union, and was framed in strict accordance with the most liberal and independent opinions of the age.

On the 13th of October, 1849, the delegates signed the instrument, and a salute of *thirty-one* guns was fired.

The house in which the delegates met was a large, handsome two-story stone erection, called "Colton Hall," and was, perhaps, the best fitted for their purposes of any building in the country. It was erected by Walter Colton, who was the Alcalde of Monterey, having been appointed by Commodore Stockton July 28, 1846. The building is still standing in a good state of preservation.

The Constitution was submitted to the people and was adopted on the 13th of November, a Governor being elected at the same time:—

For the Constitution	12,064
Against the Constitution	811
For Governor, Peter H. Burnett	6,716
" W. Scott Sherwood	3,188
" J. W. Geary	1,475
" John A. Sutter	2,201
" William M. Stewart	719
Total vote on Constitution	12,875
Total vote for Governor	14,290

This vote was light, and was chiefly cast at San Francisco, Los Angeles, San Diego, Santa Barbara, San Jose, Stockton, Sacramento, and the mines most convenient to the latter places. The miners were moving about from place to place, were scattered along the rivers and in the mountains, and on account of the limited facilities for communication and the short time between the adjournment of the Convention and the day of the election, there was no opportunity offered to thousands to exercise the right of franchise on this occasion, but they gladly acquiesced in the decision of their countrymen.

FIRST CALIFORNIA LEGISLATURE.

On Saturday, the 15th of December, 1849, the first Legislature of the State of California met at San Jose. The Assembly occupied the second story of the State House, but the lower portion, which was designed for the Senate Chamber, not being ready, the latter body held their sittings, for a short period, in the house of Isaac Branham, on the southwest corner of Market Plaza. The State House proper was a building

MEETING OF THE FIRST LEGISLATURE.

sixty-five feet long, forty feet wide, two stories high and adorned with a piazza in front. The upper story was simply a large room with a stairway leading thereto. This was the Assembly Chamber. The lower story was divided into four rooms; the largest, 20x40 feet, was designed for the Senate Chamber, and the others were used by the Secretary of State and the various committees. The building was destroyed by fire on the 29th of April, 1853, at four o'clock in the morning.

SOLONS DISSATISFIED WITH SAN JOSE.

On the first day of the first legislative session only six Senators were present, and perhaps twice as many Assemblymen. On Sunday, Governor Riley and Secretary Hallock arrived, and by Monday nearly all the members were present. Number of members: Senate, 16; Assembly, 36. Total, 52. No sooner was the Legislature fairly organized than the members began to growl about their accommodations. They didn't like the legislative building, and swore terribly, between drinks, at the accommodations of the town generally. Many of the solons expressed a desire to move the Capitol from San Jose immediately. On the 19th instant George B. Tingley, a member of the House from Sacramento, offered a bill to the effect that the Legislature remove the Capitol at once to Monterey. The bill passed its first reading and was laid over for further action.

FIRST STATE SENATORS ELECTED.

On the 20th Governor Riley resigned his gubernatorial office, and by his order, dated Headquarters Tenth Military Department, San Jose, California, December 20, 1849, (Order No. 41), Capt. H. W. Hallock, afterwards a General in the war of the Rebellion, was relieved as Secretary of State. On the same day Gov. Peter Burnett was sworn by K. H. Dimick, Judge of the Court of First Instance.

The same day, also, Col. J. C. Fremont received a majority of six votes, and Dr. M. Gwin a majority of two for Senators of the United States. The respective candidates for the United States Senate kept *ranches*, as they were termed; that is, they kept open house. All who entered drank free and freely. Under the circumstances they could afford to. Every man who drank of course wished that the owner of the establishment might be the successful candidate for the Senate. That wish would be expressed half a dozen times a day in as many different houses. A great deal of solicitude would be indicated just about the time for drinks.

FIRST INAUGURAL BALL.

On the evening of the 27th the citizens of San Jose, having become somewhat alarmed at the continued grumbling of the strangers within their gates, determined that it was necessary to do something to content the assembled wisdom of the State, and accordingly arranged for a grand ball, which was given in the Assembly Chamber. As ladies were very scarce, the country about was literally ' raked," to use the expression of the historian of that period, "for señoritas," and their red and yellow flannel petticoats so variegated the whirl of the dance that the American-dressed ladies, and in fact the solons themselves, were actually bewildered, and finally captivated, for, as the record further states, " now and then was given a sly wink of the eye between some American ladies, and between them and a friend of the other sex, as the señoritas, bewitching and graceful in motion, glided by with a captured member." But, notwithstanding this rivalry, the first California inaugural ball was a success. " The dance went on as merry as a marriage bell. All were in high glee. Spirits were plenty. Some hovered where you saw them not, but the sound thereof was not lost."

THE NOTED LEGISLATURE.

Speaking of the appellation applied to the first body of California law-makers, *i.e.*, " The Legislature of a Thousand Drinks," the same quaint writer says, "with no disrespect for the members of that body, I never heard one of them deny that the baptismal name was improperly bestowed upon them. They were good drinkers—they drank like men. If they could not stand the ceremony on any particular occasion they would lie down to it with becoming grace. I knew one to be laid out with a white sheet spread over him, and six lighted candles around him. He appeared to be in the spirit land. He was really *on* land with the spirits in him—too full for utterance. But to do justice to this body of men, there were but a very few among them who were given to drinking habitually, and as for official labor, they performed probably more than any subsequent legislative body of the State in the same given time.

In the State House there was many a trick played, many a joke passed, the recollection of which produces a smile upon the faces of those who witnessed them. It was not infrequently that as a person was walking up stairs with a lighted candle, a shot from a revolver would extinguish it. Then what shouts of laughter rang through the building at the scared individual. Those who fired were marksmen; their aim was true and they knew it."

THE FANDANGO PATRONIZED.

Speaking of the way in which these gay and festive legislators passed their evenings, a writer says: "The almost nightly amusement was the fandango. There were some respectable ones, and some which at this day would not be called respectable. The term might be considered relative in its signification. It depended a good deal on the spirit of the times and the notion of the attendant of such places. Those fandangos, where the members kept their hats on and treated their partners after each dance, were not considered of a high-toned character (modern members will please bear this in mind).

There were frequent parties where a little more gentility was exhibited. In truth, considering the times and the coun-

ACTS AND AMUSEMENTS OF EARLY LEGISLATORS.

try, they were very agreeable. The difference in language, in some degree prohibited a free exchange of ideas between the two sexes when the Americans were in excess. But then, what one could not say in so many words he imagined, guessed, or made signs, and, on the whole, the parties were novel and interesting.

AMUSEMENTS FOR THE MEMBERS.

The grand out-door amusements were the bull and bear fights. They took place sometimes on St. James, and sometimes on Market Square. Sunday was the usual day for bull-fights.

On the 3d day of February the legislators were entertained by a great exhibition of a fellow-man putting himself on a level with a beast. In the month of March there was a good deal of amusement, mixed with a considerable amount of excitement.

It was reported all over the Capital that gold had been discovered in the bed of Coyote Creek. There was a general rush. Picks, shovels, crow-bars and pans had a large sale. Members of the Legislature, officials, clerks, and lobbyists concluded suddenly to change their vocation. Even the sixteen dollars per day which they had voted themselves was no inducement to keep them away from Coyote Creek. But they soon came back again, and half of those who went away would never own it after the excitement was over. Beyond the above interesting and presumably prominent facts history gives us very little concerning the meeting of our first Legislature except that the session lasted 129 days, an adjournment having been effected on the 22d of April, 1850.

SECOND SESSION OF LEGISLATURE.

1851.—The Second Legislature assembled on the 6th of January, 1851. On the 8th the Governor tendered his resignation to the Legislature, and John McDougal was sworn in as his successor. The question of the removal of the capital from San Jose was one of the important ones of the session, so much so that the citizens of San Jose were remarkably active in catering to the wishes of the members of the legislative body. They offered extravagant bids of land for the capital grounds, promised all manner of buildings and accommodations, and even took the State scrip in payment for Legislators' board. But it was of no use.

Vallejo was determined to have the capital, and began bribing members right and left with all the city lots they wanted. The act of removal was passed February 14th, and after that date the Legislators had to suffer. The people refused to take State scrip for San Jose board, charged double prices for everything; and when, on the 16th of May, the Solons finally pulled up stakes and left, there was not thrown after them the traditional old shoe, but an assorted lot of mongrel oaths and Mexican maledictions greeted them on their long-wished-for departure.

REMOVALS OF THE CAPITAL.

Third Session—Convened at Vallejo, the new Capital, January 5, 1852. Number of members: Senate, 27; Assembly, 62 Total, 89.

Fourth Session—Convened at Vallejo, January 2, 1853 removed to Benicia, February 4, 1853.

Fifth Session—Convened at Benicia, January 2, 1854, removed to Sacramento, February 25, 1854, where it has since remained.

PRESENT CAPITOL BUILDING.

In the beginning of 1860, the citizens of Sacramento deeded to the State, lots of land in the city on which a new State Capitol could be built. Work commenced the 15th day of May, 1861, and the corner-stone was laid with Masonic ceremonies, conducted by N. Green Curtis, then Grand Master of the Order. In a few years other blocks were added, so that now the grounds extend from Tenth to Fifteenth and from L to N Streets. For

STATE HOUSE AT SAN JOSE, 1849.

this addition the citizens subscribed $30,000, the State appropriation not being sufficient to fully pay for the land. The original architect was Reuben Clark, to whom the greatest meed of praise should be given for the beautiful building that now adorns the city and is an honor to the State. After the dedication ceremonies, work was discontinued on it for some time, and it was not until 1865, that labor was recommenced in earnest. Up to November 1, 1873, the cost, added to the usual items for repairs and improvements, amounted to $2,449,-428.31. The building is 240 feet in height, the height of the main building being 94 feet. Its depth is 149 feet and its length 282. The Assembly Chamber is 75 by 75, with a height of 48 feet, the Senate 75 by 56, with the same height. The first or ground story of the building, is 16 feet above level of the surrounding streets.

The State Capitol, one of the prettiest in America, stands in a park of eight blocks, terraced and ornamented with walks, drives, trees, shrubs, and plants, forming one of the prettiest spots in the country. This fine structure cost about $2,500,000, and its towering dome, surmounted by the Temple and Goddess

A NEW CONSTITUTION ADOPTED.

of Liberty, rises 240 feet, and is the first object presented to view in the distance from whatever direction the traveler approaches the city. A fine engraving of this building will be found as a frontispiece.

The State Capitol Park, in which are located the Capitol building, the State Armory, and the State Printing Office, embraces ten full blocks of land, and the breadth of four streets, running north and south. Recent improvements lay out the grounds in a graceful landscape style, of extensive lawn and clumps of trees, and arranges them more especially as a drive. The main drive is in the form of an ellipse, the roadway being forty feet in width, and estimated to be about two-thirds of a mile in length. It is bordered by a double row of trees, and the grounds intervening between the roadway and the fences are being tastefully laid out in the best style of landscape gardening.

FORMING OF A NEW CONSTITUTION.

The Constitution which was framed at Monterey, when the State was yet in its swaddling clothes, answered every purpose for a number of years, but the entire body politic had changed, and the popular voice became clamorous for a change in the organic law of the State. The question had often been before mooted, and votes taken upon calling a convention for the purpose of framing a new Constitution, but public sentiment did not reach the requisite condition until the general election of 1877, at which time "Constitutional Convention, Yes," carried with an overwhelming majority. During the session of the Legislature, which followed this election, a bill was framed and passed, which provided for the election of delegates to the convention, and which was approved March 30, 1878. Thirty-two of the delegates were to be elected from the State at large, not more than eight of whom should reside in any one Congressional district. In accordance with a proclamation issued by the Governor, an election for the purpose of choosing delegates to the convention was held June 19, 1878. The body comprising the Constitutional Convention, met at Sacramento City, September 28th of that year, and continued in session 175 days. The day set for the people of the State to adopt or reject the result of the labors of the Convention was May 7, 1879, and there was a very strong, and in some instances, a bitter fight made over it; those opposing it, citing wherein the old Constitution had proved satisfactory, and wherein the new organic law would prove disastrous; while those who desired its adoption were as ready to show up the weak points of the old, and its inadequacy to the demands of the present advanced state of affairs, and wherein a new would almost prove a panacea for all our ills, both social, moral, and political. Thus the matter continued to be agitated until the day had come on which the die should be cast, and greatly to the surprise of everybody, the decision of the people of the State was in favor of the new law.

LIST OF CALIFORNIA GOVERNORS.

The Governors of California since its settlement to the present time were as follows:—

SPANISH RULE.

Gaspar de Portala	1767–1771
Felipe de Barri	1771–1774
Felipe de Neve	1774–1782
Pedro Fajes	1782–1790
Jose Antonio Romeu	1790–1792
*Jose J. de Arrillaga	1792–1794
Diego de Borica	1794–1800
Jose J. de Arrillaga	1800–1814
*Jose Arguello	1814–1815
Pablo Vincente de Sola	1815–1822

MEXICAN RULE.

Pablo Vincente de Sola	1822–1823
Luis Arguello	1823–1825
Jose Maria de Echeandia	June, 1825–Jan., 1831
Manuel Victoria	Jan., 1831–Jan., 1832
*Pio Pico	Jan., 1832–Jan., 1833
Jose Figueroa	Jan., 1833–Aug., 1835
*Jose Castro	Aug., 1835–Jan., 1836
Nicolas Gutierrez	Jan., 1836–Apr., 1836
Mariano Chico	Apr., 1836–Aug., 1836
Nicolas Gutierrez	Aug., 1836–Nov., 1836
Juan B. Alvarado	Nov., 1836–Dec., 1842
Manuel Michelterena	Dec., 1842–Feb., 1845
Pio Pico	Feb., 1845–July 1846

AMERICAN RULE—TERRITORIAL.

Com. John D. Sloat	July 7, 1846–Aug. 17, 1846
Com. R. F. Stockton	Aug. 17, 1846–Jan. —, 1847
Col. John C. Fremont	Jan. —, 1847–Mar. 1, 1847
Gen. S. W. Kearny	Mar. 1, 1847–May 31, 1847
Col. Richard B. Mason	May 31, 1847–Apr. 13, 1849
Gen. Bennet Riley	Apr. 13, 1849–Dec. 20, 1849

STATE—GOVERNORS.

NAME	INAUGURATED
†Peter H. Burnett	Dec. 20, 1849
John McDougal	Jan. 9, 1851
John Bigler	Jan. 8, 1852
John Bigler	Jan. 8, 1854
J. Neely Johnson	Jan. 8, 1856
John B. Weller	Jan. 8, 1858
†Milton S. Latham	Jan. 8, 1860
John G. Downey	Jan. 14, 1860
Leland Stanford	Jan. 8, 1862
‡Frederick F. Low	Dec. 2, 1863
Henry H. Haight	Dec. 5, 1867
†Newton Booth	Dec. 8, 1871
Romualdo Pacheco	Feb. 27, 1875
William Irwin	Dec. 9, 1875
George C. Perkins	Jan. 5, 1880

* Ad interim.   † Resigned.   ‡ Term increased from two to four years.

FARM OF A. NORTON, ON MAD RIVER, NEAR BLUE LAKE, HUMBOLDT CO. CAL.
RESIDENCE OF A. NORTON, BLUE LAKE.

Geographical Features.

The Coast Range of mountains runs parallel to the ocean, and has an altitude of from 2,000 to 4,000 feet above the sea, and an average width of twenty to forty miles.

On the general eastern boundary of California, and running nearly its entire length, lies the Sierra Nevada (snowy range), its summit being generally above the region of perpetual snow. In this State it is about 450 miles long and 80 miles wide, with an altitude varying from 5,000 to 15,000 feet above the level of the sea. Nearly its whole width is occupied with its western slope, descending to a level of 500 feet above the sea; its eastern slope, five or six miles wide, terminating abruptly in the great interior basin, which is 5,000 feet above the sea level. The sides of the Sierra Nevada, to the height of about 8,000 feet, are covered with dense forests of valuable timber, which is unexceeded by rugged granite and perpetual snow.

THE CALIFORNIA ALPS.

John Muir says of the region about the head-waters of King's River:—

"Few portions of the California Alps are, strictly speaking picturesque. The whole massive uplift of the range, 450 miles long by about seventy miles wide, is one grand picture, not clearly divisible into smaller ones; in this respect it differs greatly from the older and riper mountains of the Coast Range. All the landscapes of the Sierra were remodeled deep down to the roots of their granite foundations by the developing icefloods of the last geological winter.

"On the head-waters of the King's River is a group of wild Alps on which the geologist may say the sun has but just begun to shine, yet in a high degree picturesque, and in all its main features so regular and evenly balanced as almost to appear conventional—one somber cluster of snow-laden peaks with gray pine-fringed granite bosses braided around its base, the whole surging free into the sky from the head of a magnificent valley, whose lofty walls are beveled away on both sides so as to embrace it all without admitting anything not strictly belonging to it. The foreground was now all aflame with autumn colors, brown and purple and gold, ripe with the mellow sunshine; contrasting brightly with the deep, cobalt blue of the sky, and the black and gray and pure, spiritual white of the rocks and glaciers. Down through the midst the young river was seen pouring from its crystal fountains, now resting in glassy pools as if changing back again into ice; now leaping in white cascades as if turning to snow; gliding right and left between the granite bosses, then sweeping on through the smooth meadowy levels of the valley, swaying pensively from side to side with calm, stately gestures, past dipping willows and sedges, and around groves of arrowy pine; and throughout its whole eventful course, flowing fast or slow, singing loud or low, ever filling the landscape with spiritual animation, and manifesting the grandeur of its sources in every movement and tone."

MOUNT DIABLO.

The most familiar peak in the State is, however, Mount Diablo, being very near its geographical center, and towering above all other peaks—prominent from its inaccessibility and magnificent panoramic sweep from its top—prominent from its selection by the Government as the initial point of base and meridian lines in the land survey, it being the reference point in about two-thirds of the State.

It stands out boldly 3,856 feet high, overlooking the tranquil ocean, thirty miles due east from the Golden Gate, serving as a beacon to the weary, sea-tossed mariner, far out on the blue, briny billows, pointing him to a haven of security in the great harbor through the Golden Gate itself; and even on through bay and strait to anchorages safe and deep, up to where the foot-stones of the great pile meet and kiss the brackish waters. Grand old mountain, majestic, silent, yet a trumpet-tongued preacher! Who is there of the prosperous dwellers upon its slopes, or near its grateful shadows, that, going or coming by land or sea, does not look upon that blue receding or advancing pile with a full heart?

It is believed there are few points on the earth's surface from which so extensive an area can be seen as from this mountain. The writer has from its summit, counted thirty-five cities and villages, where reside two-thirds of the inhabitants of the State.

The two great mountain ranges unite at the northern and southern part of the State, each connecting range having a lofty peak.

MOUNT SHASTA.

In the northern connecting link is Mount Shasta, 14,442 feet high. It rears its great craggy snow-covered summit high in the air, and is often seen at a distance of 200 miles at the southwest. It takes about three days to reach its summit and return. You can ride to the snow line the first day, ascend to the top the following morning, descend to your camp in the afternoon, and return to the valley on the third day. Mount Shasta has a glacier, almost, if not quite, the only one within the limits of the United States. The mountain is an extinct volcano. Its summit is composed of lava, and the eye can easily trace the now broken lines of this old crater when viewed from the north. Mount Shasta is clothed with snow for a virtual mile down from its summit during most of the year.

MOUNTS WHITNEY AND SAN BERNARDINO.

Mount Whitney is the highest point in the United States (14,000 feet); but Mount Shasta (14,442 feet) makes a more imposing appearance because it rises in solitary grandeur 7,000 feet above any mountains near it. A signal station has lately been established on Mount Whitney. In the Sierra Nevada Range are more than 100 peaks over 10,000 feet high, according to the

State Geographical Survey. In the southern connecting link is snow-capped Mount San Bernardino 11,600 feet above the sea level.

GREAT SAN JOAQUIN VALLEY.

Between these two great mountain ranges, lies the great interior basin of the State, comprising the Sacramento and San Joaquin Valleys, really but one geographical formation, drained by the two great rivers bearing their respective names, and their tributaries; an uninterrupted level country of exceeding fertility, and the great future wheat growing section of the State. This basin extends north and south about 400 miles, with an average breadth of from fifty to sixty miles, rising into undulating slopes and low hills as the mountains are approached on either side. It is covered with a diluvium from 400 to 1,500 feet deep, and presents evidences of having once been the bed of a vast lake.

Innumerable valleys are formed by spurs shooting off from the western slope of the Sierra Nevada Range, and from the Coast Range on either side, extending the entire length of the State; well watered by springs and living streams, possessing a good soil and climate, and every way adapted to profitable mixed husbandry.

This great valley is drained from the north by the Sacramento River, and from the south by the San Joaquin, which, after meeting and uniting in the center of the basin, break through the Coast Range to the Pacific. At the southern extremity are the Tulare Lakes and marshes which, in the wet season, cover a large extent of surface. Along the great rivers the valleys are generally low and level, and extremely fertile rising into undulating slopes and low hills as the mountains are approached on either side, and broken on the east by numerous spurs from the Sierras. The following table gives the most noted elevations in the State and their distance from San Francisco.

ALTITUDE OF PROMINENT POINTS IN THE STATE

NAMES OF PLACES. (SIERRA NEVADA RANGE.)	Distance fr'm S. F.	Altitude ab've sea	NAMES OF PLACES. (COAST RANGE.)	Distance fr'm S. F.	Altitude ab've sea
Mount Whitney	173	14,900	Snow Mountain	114	7,560
Mount Shasta	244	14,442	Mount St. John	96	4,500
Mount Tyndall	160	14,386	Mount Hamilton	52	4,400
Mount Dana	148	13,227	Mount St. Helena	70	4,343
Mount Lyell	144	13,217	Mount Diablo	32	3,856
Mount Brewer	162	13,886	Mount Loma Prieta	54	4,040
Mount Silliman	130	11,623	Mount Bailey	260	6,375
Lassen Butte	183	10,577	Mount Tamalpais	15	2,604
Stanislaus Peak	125	11,500	Marysville Butte	92	2,030
Round Top	120	10,050	Farallone Islands	34	200
Downieville Butte	157	9,720	Clay Street Hill		357
Colfax Village	144	2,431	Red Bluff	225	307
Sacramento	90	30	Redding	260	558

THE STAPLE PRODUCTIONS.

Prior to 1864, no very marked results were reached in farming in California, the export of agricultural products, with the exception of wool, not having been such as to attract attention abroad. And owing to the drought that prevailed in 1863 and 1864, California had but little grain or other farm produce to spare, flour having been to some extent imported. The large extent, undoubted fertility, and known capabilities of the lands of the San Joaquin, Sacramento and Salinas Valleys give assurance that agriculture will become the predominant interest of its people.

The principal staples which the soil and climate of these valleys favor are the cereal grains. Wild oats are indigenous to the country, and on lands allowed to run wild, will run out other small grains, but are cultivated only as a forage plant which, cut while green, makes an excellent hay. Barley also thrives well, and, in a green state, is often cut for hay. But the great staple, from being "the staff of life," and the ease of cultivation over other products in this climate, is wheat. In a moderately rainy season it is capable of perfecting its growth before the heats of summer have evaporated the moisture from the roots, and a crop is nearly sure of being made. No disease. rust, or insect harms the grain, although smut was in early days very prevalent, but, by proper treatment has nearly disappeared. There has always been a good demand for the surplus crop of this cereal, in the mines and for export, and its cultivation has been profitable.

Cotton cultivation has been experimented upon in Fresno County, and in the Tulare Basin, where the yield has averaged 500 pounds to the acre of a fine textile fibre.

Next to the cultivation of cereals, the vine engrosses the minds of California agriculturists more than any other production, the product of her vineyards finding favor in all parts of the world.

Nearly a thousand vessels enter the port of San Francisco in a year, and a large number of these are required to carry the wheat to Europe. Some $15,000,000 is annually received for wheat alone, and it is shipped to the following countries, arranged in order according to the amount which was sent them: Great Britain, Belgium, France, Australia, Spain, South America, New Zealand, China, Germany, Hawaiian Islands, British Columbia, Tahiti, and Mexico. By this list it is seen that we contribute breadstuffs to nearly every country of the globe.

CALIFORNIA'S VARIED INDUSTRIES.

California has now a total area of 7,000,000 acres inclosed, 4,000,000 cultivated—nine-tenths of the cultivated land being in cereals, and 90,000 in grape-vines. She has 2,500,000 bearing trees of temperate fruits—apple, pear, peach, plum, prune, apricot, nectarine, and cherry—300,000 bearing trees of semi-tropical fruits—orange, lemon, lime, fig, and olive—400,000 almond and English walnut trees, 4,400 miles of mining ditchs, 260 gold quartz-mills, 300 saw-mills and 140 grist-mills. Among her annual products are 12,000 tons of wool, 5,000 of butter, 1,500 of cheese and 500 of honey, 6,000,000 gallons of wine and 14,000,000 of beer, and 500,000,000 feet of sawn lumber. The assessed value of her property is $578,000,000, of which half is in San Francisco and its suburbs.

AGRICULTURAL STATISTICS OF THE STATE.

AGRICULTURAL PRODUCTIONS.

It is as an agricultural State now, however, that California is attracting attention, and to show what we are doing in that line we append a table of receipts and exports from San Francisco of wheat, flour, barley, oats, beans and potatoes since 1856.

Each year terminates with June 30th:—

WHEAT AND FLOUR.

Date.	RECEIPTS. Equal to bbls. Flour.	Date.	EXPORTS. Equal to bbls. Flour.
1857	151,470	1857	43,960
1858	116,474	1858	6,654
1859	212,888	1859	20,018
1860	419,740	1860	186,182
1861	834,020	1861	707,156
1862	500,304	1862	385,600
1863	781,138	1863	402,724
1864	715,075	1864	509,723
1865	310,691	1865	99,032
1866	917,217	1866	626,060
1867	1,967,197	1867	1,697,402
1868	1,878,508	1868	1,694,115
1869	2,238,800	1869	1,912,093
1870	2,244,061	1870	1,974,280
1871	1,597,756	1871	1,386,831
1872	937,203	1872	758,200
1873	3,815,911	1873	3,537,874
1874	3,079,473	1874	3,069,123
1875	3,731,104	1875	3,413,669
1876	2,852,461	1876	2,430,033
1877	4,115,554	1877	4,029,253
1878	1,864,644	1878	1,765,304
1879	3,839,180	1879	3,867,955
1880	2,891,660	1880	2,591,543

BARLEY AND OATS.

	BARLEY.			OATS.	
	Receipts, in centals.	Exports, in centals.		Receipts, in centals.	Exports, in centals.
1857	453,823	66,768	1857	187,344	8,370
1858	637,568	142,612	1858	186,039	107,650
1859	779,870	295,836	1859	320,248	218,647
1860	540,293	69,246	1860	216,808	90,682
1861	677,455	339,530	1861	315,078	116,467
1862	611,227	188,617	1862	351,635	154,885
1863	492,293	49,809	1863	177,105	39,986
1864	611,143	40,329	1864	304,044	91,186
1865	498,432	13,920	1865	273,979	3,366
1866	1,037,209	340,900	1866	349,042	113,966
1867	730,112	142,154	1867	328,478	80,331
1868	638,920	31,342	1868	221,811	5,685
1869	608,088	91,202	1869	234,498	21,934
1870	752,418	300,598	1870	290,143	13,937
1871	701,639	138,008	1871	304,155	13,227
1872	792,198	16,707	1872	358,531	11,707
1873	981,028	226,928	1873	200,345	5,437
1874	1,127,390	243,752	1874	243,400	27,640
1875	1,249,657	182,146	1875	305,844	56,929
1876	1,142,154	204,131	1876	293,960	3,101
1877	1,352,765	282,875	1877	210,257	4,470
1878	858,867	88,887	1878	145,413	10,756
1879	1,732,712	468,835	1879	253,892	20,253
1880	1,191,481	411,145	1880	143,396	5,372

BEANS AND POTATOES

	BEANS.			POTATOES.	
	Receipts, in sacks.	Exports, in sacks.		Receipts, in sacks.	Exports, in sacks.
1857	55,265	438	1857	343,681	
1858	65,076	6,721	1858	330,307	
1859	69,682	22,933	1859	292,458	
1860	38,714	8,300	1860	326,073	11,055
1861	34,188	4,675	1861	317,419	4,397
1862	58,294	11,789	1862	293,074	5,815
1863	59,620	2,863	1863	364,423	14,952
1864	82,568	21,619	1864	376,046	22,161
1865	47,822	4,244	1865	346,854	5,976
1866	43,717	6,062	1866	315,807	16,984
1867	50,678	2,921	1867	549,193	7,278
1868	50,698	12,917	1868	692,986	19,133
1869	53,711	1,899	1869	604,302	24,360
1870	99,585	7,890	1870	701,960	24,710
1871	85,618	21,800	1871	790,122	18,880
1872	56,390	7,479	1872	729,077	36,378
1873	70,048	5,997	1873	779,379	27,986
1874	80,091	5,739	1874	781,049	33,772
1875	113,577	8,156	1875	752,436	29,444
1876	115,128	17,296	1876	731,207	25,684
1877	117,860	10,512	1877	810,576	30,818
1878	80,116	12,705	1878	624,353	18,840
1879	207,103	17,871	1879	750,211	23,440
1880	108,249	28,740	1880	590,611	36,290

STATE LANDS AND HOW DIVIDED.

State Surveyor-General, William Minis, places the area of the State at 100,500,000 acres, divided as follows:—

Agricultural and mineral lands surveyed to June 30, 1879	40,054,114
Agricultural and mineral lands unsurveyed	39,065,754
Private grants surveyed to June 30, 1879	8,459,694
Mission Church property	40,767
Pueblo Lands	188,049
Private grants unsurveyed	15,000
Indian and military reservations	318,631
Lakes, islands, bays and navigable rivers	1,561,700
Swamp and overflowed lands unsurveyed	110,714
Salt marsh and tide lands around San Francisco bay	100,000
Salt marsh and tide lands around Humboldt bay	5,000
Aggregate	100,500,000

OWNERSHIP AND CULTIVATION OF LAND.

From various official sources we have compiled the subjoined table, showing the total area, the area sold by the Government (that is, held by private ownership), the area enclosed, and the area cultivated, in every county of the State—all in square miles. The figures are not exact, nor is it possible to make them so from any official records now in existence. The area "sold" is that treated as subject to taxation in the several counties, and the areas enclosed and cultivated are reported annually in the Assessor's reports.

In some cases, considerable quantities of land have been disposed of by the Federal Government, but in such a manner that they are not subject to taxation. Thus, the Southern Pacific Railroad Company has built 150 miles of its road in San Diego county, and is entitled to twenty square miles of land as subsidy for each mile of the road, making a total of 3,000 square miles; but this land has not yet been conveyed by patent, and nobody is authorized to say precisely which section will pass under the grant. The total areas as given in the following table, are taken from calculations made by J. H. Wible, E. q.

SIZE AND WEALTH OF EACH OF THE COUNTIES.

DIAGRAM SHOWING COMPARATIVE SIZE OF COUNTIES.
Prepared for Elliott & Moore's County History.

Arranged in square miles, each square represents 50 square miles land.

Each black ■ square represents 50 square miles cultivated, fractions omitted.

Each dotted ▣ square represents 50 square miles sold but not cultivated.

Each open □ square represents 50 square miles unsold land, not assessed.

The areas in the table are not exact. The cultivated and assessed land and valuations are from Assessor's reports. About one twenty-fourth of the State is cultivated, and about one-fourth belongs to individuals.

NAME.	AREA.	CULTIVATED.	SOLD.	VALUATION. Real and Personal.
Santa Cruz.	432	35	380	$ 5,010,553
San Mateo.	450	90	450	6,107,210
Marin.	575	25	490	7,868,917
Sutter.	570	325	575	3,906,293
Yuba.	600	90	300	4,258,250
Amador.	700	45	290	2,794,449
Contra Costa.	739	180	700	7,720,292
Alameda.	800	105	650	37,459,230
Solano.	800	190	790	8,071,022
Napa.	820	40	350	7,873,926
Merced.	830	4	140	751,205
Calaveras.	850	35	820	1,820,865
Lake.	875	30	230	1,213,084
San Benito.	1,000	55	480	2,771,603
Sacramento.	1,020	170	980	18,578,385
Nevada.	1,050	50	800	6,921,300
Yolo.	1,150	215	850	9,010,507
Santa Clara.	1,300	350	850	23,028,345
San Joaquin.	1,350	470	1,350	16,675,504
Stanislaus.	1,350	690	1,320	6,031,988
Ventura.	1,380	75	700	2,857,383
Placer.	1,380	150	600	5,832,925
Sonoma.	1,400	310	1,200	15,178,121
Mariposa.	1,410	9	350	1,290,950
Del Norte.	1,440	2	80	695,850
Butte.	1,453	370	750	10,685,007
Trinity.	1,600	12	100	598,510
El Dorado.	1,872	20	330	2,341,460
Tuolumne.	1,950	50	290	1,640,071
Merced.	1,975	480	1,500	5,712,651
Humboldt.	2,800	45	1,100	3,355,028
Colusa.	2,870	425	1,500	10,516,712
Plumas.	2,736	10	200	1,926,154
Tehama.	2,800	300	750	4,192,348
Siskiyou.	3,040	48	300	2,651,367

NAME.	AREA.	CULTIVATED.	SOLD.	VALUATION.
San Luis Obispo.	3,160	90	1,800	$1,137,570
Monterey.	3,300	300	1,100	7,183,185
Santa Barbara.	3,510	90	1,800	4,479,820
Mendocino.	3,810	95	1,100	5,508,080
Mono.	4,185	10	80	1,021,770
Shasta.	4,500	55	1,800	1,963,320
Lassen.	4,942	40	320	1,213,184
Tulare.	5,500	130	1,900	4,054,250
Inyo.	5,832	10	110	972,401
Los Angeles.	6,000	170	2,200	16,100,988
Modoc.	7,360	40	230	1,239,132
Kern.	8,000	40	2,000	4,485,007
Fresno.	8,730	110	2,600	6,055,062
San Diego.	15,100	28	600	3,181,177
San Bernardino.	22,472	85	700	2,601,321
Total.	164,031	6,911	41,550	$376,630,214

By way of comparison, on same scale, to show the vast size of California, we represent the State of Rhode Island, 1,306 square miles.

SCHOOLS AND EDUCATIONAL ADVANTAGES. 77

EDUCATIONAL ADVANTAGES.

California has 2,749 public schools, with an attendance of 144,805, and 210,464 children on the census roll. In the year 1878-79 there was $2,285,732.38 paid to teachers as salaries. Since the organization of California as a State, she has paid for the support of schools $38,500,000—not a bad showing.

The educational system of the State has received much attention and care from those in authority. Our public schools and higher institutions of learning are liberally endowed, and generally efficient. The profession of teaching is held in high repute, and teachers command good salaries. We are justified, we think, in saying that the system of public schools established by the laws of California is in no respect inferior to the best in any other State in the Union.

FIRST YANKEE SCHOOL-MASTER.

In April, 1847, the first English school was opened in a small shanty on the block bounded by Dupont, Broadway, Pacific and Stockton Streets. Here were collected from twenty to thirty pupils, who then comprised nearly all the children of the city. It was a private institution and was supported by tuition fees from the pupils, and by the contributions of the citizens. It was taught by Mr. Marsden, who is entitled to the honor of being the first Yankee school-master upon the Pacific Coast. Although he continued his school but a few months, he performed an important part as a pioneer in establishing our schools, which should cause his name to be held in grateful remembrance by every friend of education.

THE PIONEER LADY TEACHER.

In January, 1848, Mrs. Mary A. Case located in Santa Cruz and opened a school in her own house, and taught two terms, when the discovery of gold broke up her school by the removal of families. Mrs. Case was, in 1879, still living in Santa Cruz. She was a native of Connecticut, and came to California in 1847. Her husband, B. A. Case, died at Long Valley, California, in 1871.

FIRST PUBLIC SCHOOL.

Late in the fall of 1847, active measures were first taken by the citizens of San Francisco to organize a public school, which resulted in erecting a humble one-story school-house on the south-west part of Portsmouth Square, fronting on Clay Street, near where it joins Brenham Place. An engraving of this first public school-house in San Francisco has been preserved in the "Annals of San Francisco." The history of this old building is cherished by the early pioneers with many pleasing associations. Here germinated every new enterprise; here the town meetings and political conventions were held; here the churches first held their gatherings, and the first public amusements were given. After the discovery of gold it was deserted for school purposes, and was used as a Court House under Judge Almond. It was afterwards degraded into a public office and used as a station-house. It was demolished by the city in 1850.

On the 3d of April, 1848, the school was opened in the building described, under the instruction of Mr. Thomas Douglass, now residing in San Jose, an able and zealous pioneer in the cause of education. He was appointed teacher by the Board of School Trustees, at a salary of $1,000 per month. The population at this time was 812, of whom sixty were children of a suitable age for attending school. Although it was a public school under the control of regularly elected officers, it was mainly supported by tuition from the pupils. The success and usefulness of this school were soon paralyzed by the great discovery of gold, which for a time depopulated the town, leaving the teacher minus pupils, trustees and salary. He therefore closed his school and joined in the general exodus for the mines, the new El Dorado of untold wealth.

In the general excitement and confusion which followed the first rush for the "diggings," the school enterprise was for a time abandoned. The education of the children, who were rapidly increasing from the flood of emigration pouring into San Francisco from every part of the world, was entirely neglected until the 23d of April, 1849, when the Rev. Albert Williams opened a school in his church.

In October, 1849, Mr. J. C. Pelton and wife opened a school in the basement of the Baptist Church, on Washington, near Stockton Street, and in July, 1850, the "Happy Valley School" was opened in a little dilapidated building, in what was then called "Happy Valley."

THE STATE UNIVERSITY.

This important institution is situated at Berkeley, Alameda County, and is endowed by the various gifts of Congress with Seminary, Building and Agricultural College lands; also with a State endowment from the sale of tide lands, which yields an annual income of $52,000. Its production fund is larger than that of the University of Michigan. It has an able corps of Professors and instructors, some of whom have a national reputation. The names of 336 students are upon its catalogue, distributed in the various departments of science and art. Its buildings and grounds are extensive, and for beauty of situation, or the thoroughness of its instruction in literature and science, it cannot be excelled. Its Medical Department is in the city of San Francisco. The University is free to both sexes.

The Normal School, at San Jose, is one of the most admirably managed of our State Institutions. It has an excellent faculty and over 400 students. An additional Normal School is about to be erected at Los Angeles.

California has, besides these State Institutions, fifteen colleges endowed or maintained by the different religious denominations.

DIMENSIONS OF CALIFORNIA.

Width on the north end, 216 miles; extreme extension from west to east, 352 miles; average width, about 235 miles; extension from north to south, 655 miles. A direct line from the northwest corner of the State to Fort Yuma, being the longest line in the State, is 830 miles; a direct line from San Francisco to Los Angeles, 342 miles; a direct line from San Francisco to San Diego, 451 miles. San Diego lies 350 miles south, and 285 miles east of San Francisco. Los Angeles lies 258 miles south, and 223 miles east of San Francisco. Cape Mendocino, the most westerly point in the State, is 96 miles west of San Francisco and 185 miles north.

California has an area of 164,981 square miles, or 100,947,840 acres, of which 80,000,000 acres are suited to some kind of profitable husbandry. It is four times greater in area than Cuba. It will make four States as large as New York, which has a population of nearly 5,000,000. It will make five States the size of Kentucky, which has a population of 1,321,000. It will make 24 States the size of Massachusetts, having a population of 1,500,000. It has an area of 144 times as great as Rhode Island. It is four-fifths the size of Austria, and nearly as large as France, each having a population of 36,000,000. It is nearly twice the size of Italy, with 27,000,000 inhabitants, and is one and one-half times greater than Great Britain and Ireland, having a population of 32,000,000. Its comparative size is best shown by the diagram on page 76.

California needs population—she is susceptible of sustaining millions where she now has thousands.

With industry, economy, sobriety, and honesty of purpose, no man in this State, with rare exceptions, will fail of success in the ordinary pursuits of life.

BAYS, HARBORS, ISLANDS, AND LAKES.

California has a sea-coast extending the whole length of the State, amounting, following the indentations, to somewhat over 700 miles. The principal bays and harbors, beginning on the south, are San Diego, Santa Barbara, San Luis Obispo, Monterey, San Francisco, Tomales, Bodega, Humboldt, Trinidad and Crescent City Bay.

San Francisco Bay, the most capacious and best protected harbor on the western coast of North America, is nearly fifty miles long (including its extension, San Pablo Bay,) and about nine miles wide. The entrance to the bay is through a strait about five miles long and a mile wide, and is named Chrysopyire, or Golden Gate.

There are few lakes worthy of mention in California. The largest is Tulare, in the southern part of the State, which is very shoal. It is about thirty-three miles long by twenty-two wide, though in the wet season it covers a much larger area. Owens, Kern, and Buena Vista are much smaller lakes, in the same vicinity.

Lake Tahoe, in Placer County, thirteen hours from Sacramento by rail, is visited by the tourist, attracted by the wonders of the scenery, oftener than the invalid; has a pure mountain air, with a most charming summer climate, there being no excessive heat, and only an occasional and enjoyable thunder-storm. Here, besides the lake and the streams, are the waters of mountain springs and hot and cold mineral springs. There is trout fishing in the streams as well as in the lake, where a number of fish are taken—trout of several kinds, from a quarter of a pound to five pounds in weight, minnows, white fish, and several other sorts. Several of the beaches or bays of the lake are of interest, as Emerald and Carnelian Bays, carnelian stones being picked up that are very pretty. The lake is more than 6,000 feet above the level of the sea, and it twenty-two by twelve miles in size. Its greatest measured depth is something over 1,500 feet, and this great depth makes the principal wonder of the lake. The water is fresh, varying from thirty-nine to sixty degrees in temperature, and the extreme cold of the depth, which prevents drowned bodies from decomposing and rising to the surface, has given rise to the erroneous belief that the water is not buoyant, and will not float any object.

Donner Lake, near the scene of the Donner tragedy, is a small body of water much visited by tourists, situated near the eastern border of the State.

Lake Mono, fourteen miles long from east to west and nine miles wide, lies in Mono County, east of the Sierra Nevada. The water, being saturated with various mineral substances, the chief of which are salt, lime, borax, and carbonate of soda, is intensely bitter and saline, and of such high specific gravity that the human body floats in it very lightly. No living thing except the larvæ of a small fly and a small crustacean, inhabits this lake, which is sometimes called the Dead Sea of California.

The other lakes are: Clear, in Lake County, in the western part of the State, about ten miles long; and Klamath and Goose Lakes, lying partly in Oregon.

CHIEF NAVIGABLE STREAMS.

The Sacramento is about 370 miles long, and is navigable for large steamboats at all seasons to Sacramento, ninety miles from its mouth, or 120 miles from San Francisco, and for smaller craft to Red Bluff, 150 or 200 miles above Sacramento.

The San Joaquin, about 350 miles long, is navigable for ordinary steamers to Stockton, and for small craft during the rainy season to the mouth of the Tulare Slough, about 150 miles. The Calaveras, Stanislaus, Tuolumne, and Merced empty into the San Joaquin. Tule and swamp lands line the banks of the river. The soil is rich and needs only to be protected against high waters, to equal any in the State for production. The tules are a sort of tall rush, and in early times, fires swept over them as on a prairie. The effect is faintly indicated in our engraving on page 43.

THE NATURAL WONDERS.

Among the many remarkable natural curiosities of California is the valley of the Yo Semite.

This far-famed valley is 140 miles east of San Francisco, and is a cañon a mile wide and eight miles long. The bottom of the valley is more than 4,000 feet above sea level, and the walls rise as high as 4,000 feet. Its principal water fall (though not the only one, nor the most beautiful), has 2,000 feet to fall. Great cliffs, rising 6,000 feet high, and gigantic dome-shaped mountains, are gathered in this narrow valley, which are supposed to have been formed suddenly one day by a fissure, or crack, in the solid mountain chain. The valley scenery is of great beauty, and the summer climate is cool, with snow in winter. People camping in tents have an inclosure in Yo Semite set apart for them, and may also locate themselves in other parts of the valley, always under the stated regulations, which provide that fire-wood may be picked up, but never cut down; that fires must not be left burning; that fish may be taken with hook and line only, and that birds must not be killed. In the valley are three hotels, three stores, four livery stables, a blacksmith, a cabinetmaker, four photographers, a saloon, a bathing house, three carpenters and four laundries.

The Big Trees of Mariposa, only one of several interesting groups in the State, are sixteen miles from Yo Semite. The tallest tree in this grove is 325 feet high, and the thickest is twenty-seven feet through. The age of the oldest one, which has been counted by rings, is 1,300 years old, its seed having taken root in this California valley, in the sixth century after Christ, when the world's history (so called) was confined to that narrow strip of land along the Mediterranean Sea, with the barbarous nations on its borders. These trees are of the *Sequoia Gigantea*, and only the *Eucalyptus Amygdalena* of Australia ever grows so large.

The Geysers are also remarkable natural phenomena. There is a collection of hot sulphur springs, more than 300 in number, covering about 200 acres, in a deep gorge, in the northeast part of Sonoma County. They are about 1,700 feet above the sea, and are surrounded by mountains from 3,000 to 4,000 feet high. Hot and cold, quiet and boiling springs are found within a few feet of each other.

There are five natural bridges in California. The largest is on a small creek emptying into the Hay Fork of Trinity River. It is eighty feet long, with its top 170 feet above the water. In Siskiyou County there are two, about thirty feet apart, ninety feet long; and there are two more on Coyote Creek, in Tuolumne County, the larger 285 feet long.

The most noted caves are the Alabaster Cave in Placer County, containing two chambers, the larger 200 feet long by 100 feet wide; the Bower Cave in Mariposa County, having a chamber about 100 feet square, reached by an entrance seventy feet long.

The most recently discovered of the great natural wonders of the State is the petrified forest, about seventy-five miles north of San Francisco, the existence of which was first made public in 1870.

TIMBER FORESTS.

California is noted for its large forests of excellent timber, and for trees of mammoth size. The sides of the Sierra Nevada, to the height of 2,500 feet, are covered with oaks, manzanita and nut pine and above this, to a height of 8,000 feet, with dense forests of pine, fir, cypress, hemlock, and other coniferous trees.

Dense forests of redwood exist on the coast north of latitude thirty-seven degrees, chiefly in Humboldt County. This timber is used for fence posts, railroad ties, and furnishes lumber for all building purposes. It answers the same for house material in California as Wisconsin and Michigan pine does in the Mississippi Valley. There is a large amount of timber of the various species named in the mountains and valleys in the northern part of the State, from the Sierra Nevada Range to the ocean.

The redwood, bearing a strong resemblance to the mammoth, frequently grows to a height of 300 feet, and a diameter of fifteen feet. These forests are fully described in the local history of the County.

White and live oak abound in large quantities on the west slope of the Coast Range, and in the intervening valleys south of latitude 37°, in the counties of Monterey, San Luis Obispo, and Santa Barbara. This wood is chiefly used for fuel and is of little value for building or fencing purposes.

A great part of the Sacramento and San Joaquin Valleys, the Colorado Basin, the east slope of the Coast Mountains, and the Coast Range south of Point Conception, are treeless.

The sugar pine is a large tree, and one of the most graceful of evergreens. It grows about 200 feet high and twelve feet in diameter. This wood grows in the Sierra Nevada, is free-splitting and valuable for timber. The yellow pine and white cedar are all large trees, growing more than 200 feet high and six or eight feet in diameter.

The story is told of two men who were engaged in the cutting of one of these immense trees into logs, with a cross-cut saw. After they had sawed themselves out of sight of each other, one of them became impressed with the belief that the saw was not running as easily as it ought, when he crawled on top of the tree to remonstrate with his partner, whom he discovered to be fast asleep.

The visitor to California has not seen it all until he has spent a week in the deep recesses of a redwood forest. It is then, standing beside the towering monarch of the forest, that a man will realize his utter insignificance, and how inestimably ephemeral he is compared with many other of God's handiwork. He looks upon a tree that stood when Christ was yet in his youth, the circles of whose growth but mark the cycles of time almost since the first man was, and on whose tablets might have been written the records of the mighty men of old.

POPULATION AND ITS INCREASE.

In 1831, the entire population of the State was estimated at 23,025, of whom 18,683 were Indian converts. During the years 1843, '44, '45 and '46 a great many emigrants from the United States settled in California. In January, 1847, the white population was estimated at from 12,000 to 15,000. Its population in 1850 was probably 150,000. The population of the State in 1880 was 858,864. There are, on the average, six inhabitants to the square mile, but the distribution of the settlement over the State is unequal. Thus, San Francisco has about 8,000 people to the square mile, while those portions of San Diego and San Bernardino Counties in the Colorado Desert and inclosed basin, with an area of 14,000 square miles, have at least seven square miles to each white inhabitant. The counties of San Francisco, San Mateo, Santa Clara, Contra Costa, San Joaquin, Sacramento, Yolo, Solano, Napa, Sonoma, and Marin, fronting on San Francisco, San Pablo, and Suisun Bays, and the deltas of the Sacramento and San Joaquin Rivers, all within thirty miles of Mount Diablo, and distinctly visible from its summit, have 580,800 inhabitants, or about fifty-eight to the mile, leaving a little more than two to the square mile for the remainder of the State.

TABLE OF VOTES CAST BY CALIFORNIA AT ALL THE PRESIDENTIAL ELECTIONS.

DATE.	NAME OF CANDIDATES.	No. OF VOTES.	MAJORITY.
1852	Scott and Graham	35,407	
"	Pierce and King	40,026	5,219
"	Hale and Julian	100	
	Total	76,133	
1856	Fremont and Dayton	20,691	
"	Buchanan and Breckinridge	53,365	17,200
"	Fillmore and Donelson	36,165	
	Total	110,921	
1860	Lincoln and Hamlin	38,734	
"	Breckinridge and Lane	38,023	711
"	Douglas and Johnson	33,975	
"	Bell and Everett	9,136	
	Total	119,868	
1864	Lincoln and Johnson	62,134	13,273
"	McClellan and Pendleton	48,841	
	Total	110,875	
1868	Grant and Colfax	54,583	506
"	Seymour and Blair	54,077	
	Total	108,660	
1872	Grant and Wilson	54,020	3,302
"	Greeley and Brown	40,718	
	Total	94,738	
1876	Hayes and Wheeler	79,306	2,842
"	Tilden and Hendricks	76,460	
"	Cooper	47	
	Total	155,821	
1880	Garfield and Arthur	80,207	
"	Hancock and English	80,332	65
"	Weaver	3,381	
	Total	163,980	

For 1880, it is the average vote on elections. One Republican elector was elected and five of the Democratic election, and the vote was cast accordingly.

CENSUS OF THE STATE BY COUNTIES
SINCE ITS ORGANIZATION.

	COUNTIES	1850.	1860.	1870.	1880.	Increase in Last 10 years.
1	Alameda		8,927	24,237	62,636	39,402
2	Alpine (a)			685	539	dec 146
3	Amador		10,930	9,582	11,386	1,804
4	Butte	3,574	12,106	11,403	18,721	7,308
5	Calaveras	16,884	16,299	8,895	8,980	85
6	Colusa	115	2,274	6,165	13,118	6,953
7	Contra Costa		5,328	8,461	12,525	4,044
8	Del Norte		1,003	2,022	2,499	628
9	El Dorado	20,057	20,562	10,309	10,047	338
10	Fresno		4,605	6,336	9,478	3,142
11	Humboldt		2,694	6,140	15,515	9,375
12	Inyo (c)			1,956	2,928	477
13	Kern (b)			2,925	5,600	2,675
14	Klamath (i)		1,803	1,686		
15	Lake (c)			2,969	6,643	3,674
16	Lassen (d)			1,327	3,341	2,014
17	Los Angeles	3,530	11,333	15,309	33,392	18,083
18	Marin	323	3,334	6,903	11,326	4,423
19	Mariposa	4,379	6,243	4,572	4,399	dec 173
20	Mendocino (e)	55	3,067	7,545	11,000	3,455
21	Merced		1,141	2,807	5,657	2,850
22	Mono (f)			430	5,416	5,013
23	Monterey	1,872	4,739	9,876	11,309	1,433
24	Modoc (j)				4,700	4,700
25	Napa (c)	405	5,521	7,163	12,894	5,713
26	Nevada		16,446	19,134	20,534	1,400
27	Placer		13,270	11,357	14,278	2,921
28	Plumas (d)		4,363	4,489	6,881	2,392
29	Sacramento	9,087	24,142	26,830	36,200	9,370
30	San Benito (k)				5,584	5,584
31	San Bernardino		5,551	3,988	7,800	3,812
32	San Diego		4,324	4,951	8,620	3,669
33	San Francisco (g)		56,802	149,473	233,956	84,483
34	San Joaquin (h)	3,647	9,435	21,050	24,323	3,273
35	San Luis Obispo	336	1,782	4,772	8,142	3,370
36	San Mateo (g)		3,214	6,635	8,717	2,082
37	Santa Barbara	1,185	3,543	7,784	9,478	1,694
38	Santa Clara		11,912	20,246	35,113	6,864
39	Santa Cruz	643	4,944	8,743	12,808	4,605
40	Shasta (d)	378	4,360	4,173	9,700	5,527
41	Sierra		11,387	5,619	6,617	998
42	Siskiyou		7,629	6,648	8,401	1,553
43	Solano	580	7,169	16,871	18,475	1,604
44	Sonoma	560	11,867	19,819	25,925	6,106
45	Stanislaus (h)		2,245	6,499	8,951	2,452
46	Sutter	3,444	3,390	5,030	5,212	182
47	Tehama		4,044	3,587	9,414	5,827
48	Trinity	1,635	5,125	3,213	4,982	1,769
49	Tulare		4,638	4,533	11,281	6,748
50	Tuolumne (h)	8,351	16,229	8,150	7,843	dec 307
51	Ventura (j)				5,088	5,088
52	Yolo	1,086	4,716	9,899	11,580	1,981
53	Yuba	9,073	13,668	10,851	11,540	689
	The State	92,597	379,994	560,247	864,686	304,439
	White	91,635	323,177	499,424	767,266	267,842
	Colored	962	4,086	4,272	6,265	1,993
	Chinese		34,933	49,310	75,025	25,715
	Indians		17,908	7,241	16,130	8,889

The returns of 1850 for Contra Costa and Santa Clara were lost on the way to the Census Office, and those for San Francisco were destroyed by fire. The corrected State census of 1852 gives the population of these three counties as follows: Contra Costa, 2,740; San Francisco, 36,154; and Santa Clara, 6,764; and gives the total population of the State (save 33 D mds), not returned) 255,122. El Dorado was estimated at 40,000, which would make the total population at that date 255,122. [Vide Doc. No. 14, Appendix to Senate Journal, 4th session Legislature.]
(a) In 1862 Alpine from Amador, Calaveras, El Dorado, and Mono.
(b) In 1866 organized.
(c) In 1861 Lake from Napa.
(d) In 1863 Lassen from Plumas and Shasta.
(e) In 1860 organized.
(f) In 1848 organized.
(g) In 1857 San Mateo from San Francisco.
(h) In 1854 Stanislaus from San Joaquin and Tuolumne.
(i) Divided and attached to other counties.
(j) Organized 1873.
(k) Organized in 1874 from Monterey.

The census of 1880 gives Indians, 816,971; females, 348,415; natives, 575,000; foreigners, 291,840.

Discoveries and Settlements.

First Exploring Parties; Rush for Trinity Mines by Sea and Land; Rapid Increase in Population; Discovery and Naming of Bays and Rivers; Narratives of L. K. Wood, Lieut. Ottinger, E. H. Howard, and Other Explorers; Gold Bluff Excitement, Etc., Etc.

It is but little more than thirty years since the first white foot pressed the soil about Humboldt Bay, and left any definite record of its visit. Whether at any time before the visit of the discovery party of L. K. Wood, whose narrative we shall give in full, Humboldt Bay was ever visited by white people, is not definitely known. But, from our investigations, there seems no doubt but what the shores of the bay were trod by the trappers and hunters of early days. This region was then in a state of nature, abounding with deer, antelope, elk, and bear. The streams were alive with beaver, and other fur-bearing animals.

FIRST WHITE PERSONS IN HUMBOLDT COUNTY.

1827.—Doubtless the Jedediah S. Smith party were the first Americans who ever entered the present limits of Humboldt County. He was the first white man to lead a party overland to California. In the spring of 1825, he led a company of forty men into the Sacramento Valley. He collected a large quantity of furs, and established his headquarters on the American River, near Folsom. In 1826, he trapped in the San Joaquin.

In 1827, he started with the company for the Columbia River. He passed through what is now Yolo County, "up the Cache Creek, and reached the ocean near the mouth of Russian River, and followed the coast line as far as Umpqua River," near Cape Arago, when all (forty) but himself, Daniel Prior, and Richard Laughlin, were treacherously murdered by the Indians, and all their traps and furs were lost.

These men escaped to Fort Vancouver and related their misadventure to Dr. McLaughlin, the agent of the Hudson Bay Company. Smith proposed to the agent that if he would send a party to punish the Indians and recover his property, he would conduct them to the rich trapping grounds he had just left; and for this reason as well as because it was the policy of that corporation never to let an outrage go unpunished, an expedition was sent out, which chastised the savages and recovered most of the stolen property.

OTHER PARTIES VISIT HUMBOLDT.

Smith and a portion of this company returned to Vancouver, while the Indians, led by Alexander Roderick McLeod, entered California "that fall by the route Smith had come, and trapped on the streams."

After Smith took his leave on Lewis River in 1828, Ogden's party continued southwest through Utah and Nevada, and entered the San Joaquin Valley through Walker's Pass. "They trapped up the valley and then passed over to the coast and up to Vancouver, by the route Smith had formerly traveled."

In the spring of 1832, Michael Laframbois entered the Sacramento Valley at the head of a party of Hudson Bay Company's trappers, "visiting the streams as far south as Tulare Lake, and returned over the usual route along the coast to Fort Vancouver the following spring."

There can be no other conclusion than this, that the Smith party must have visited Humboldt Bay. They could not have well avoided it. No historian ever accompanied these parties, and their reports were only given at headquarters in a general sort of a way, and so no definite account is given us of the exact route traveled. But after reaching the mouth of Russian River, it is hardly probable they followed the coast or attempted to do so. Their business would have led them to some stream bearing north; so we will suppose they reached the head-waters of Eel River, and thus followed down that stream to the ocean, and thence to Humboldt Bay. These several parties mentioned doubtless trapped the Eel, Trinity, and Klamath Rivers. The Russians were at Ft. Ross thirty years, and it is probable that they visited Humboldt Bay, but this is only a supposition.

LAST RESTING-PLACE OF THE PIONEER.

Captain Smith sold his interest in the Rocky Mountain Company in 1830, and, in 1831, was treacherously killed by Indians while digging for water in the dry bed of the Cimeron River, near Taos, New Mexico, and was buried there by his companions. This is the last resting-place of the pioneer overland traveler to the beautiful valley of California, and of the first American who ever gazed upon the grand forests of Humboldt, or trod its grass-carpeted valleys. But whether these parties actually visited Humboldt Bay is not positively known; and we must give credit to the discovery party of 1849, whose very interesting adventures and discoveries are so graphically described by L. K. Wood.

SETTLEMENT BY GOLD SEEKERS.

To what is generally known as the Trinity excitement, we must look for the opening up and settlement of this region. The Trinity mines and the anxiety to get to them, led to many expeditions along the coast, the discovery of Trinidad and Humboldt Bays, the mouth of the Klamath, and Salmon and Scott Rivers, bringing thousands into this region, and transforming it in one year from a beautiful wilderness to the home of civilization, and making its hills resound to the unaccustomed sound of the axe, the rattle of the rocker, the shout of the packer, and the merry laugh of the miner.

In 1858, Maj. Pearson B. Reading, the old trapper and pioneer Californian, who settled upon his ranch in Cottonwood Creek, Shasta County, in 1847, gave the following account of the first mining in northern California. At the time he named it, Trinity River was not an unknown stream to the trappers of the Hudson Bay Company, who were familiar with every stream of consequence in this portion of the State; that they had ever given it a name, however, is uncertain; if so, it is unknown to history:—

DISCOVERY OF TRINITY RIVER.

"In the spring of 1845, I left Sutter's Fort for the purpose of trapping the waters of Upper California and Oregon. My party consisted of thirty men, with 100 head of horses.

"In the month of May, I crossed the mountains from the Sacramento River, near a point now called the Backbone; in about twenty miles' travel reached the banks of a large stream, which I called the Trinity, supposing it led into Trinidad Bay, as marked on the old Spanish charts. I remained on the river about three weeks, engaged in trapping beaver and otter; found the Indians very numerous, but friendly disposed. On leaving the Trinity I crossed the mountains at a point which led me to the Sacramento River, about ten miles below the Soda Springs. I then passed into the Shasta and Klamath settlements, prosecuting my hunt. Having been successful, returned in the fall to Sutter's Fort.

"In the month of July, 1848, I crossed the mountains of the Coast Range, at the head of middle Cottonwood Creek; struck the Trinity at what is now called Reading's Bar; prospected for two days, and found the bars rich in gold; returned to my house on Cottonwood, and in ten days fitted out an expedition for mining purposes; crossed the mountains where the trail passed from Shasta to Weaver.

"My party consisted of three white men, one Delaware, one Walla Walla, one Chinook, and about sixty Indians from the Sacramento Valley. With this force I worked the bar bearing my name. I had with me 120 head of cattle, with an abundant supply of other provisions. After about six weeks' work, parties came in from Oregon, who at once protested against my Indian labor. I then left the stream and returned to my home, where I have since remained, in the enjoyment of the tranquil life of a farmer."

Mr. Reading has, no doubt, placed his mining expedition one year too early, and should have said in 1849, or else he went back again the next year, something that his language implies, though it does not positively state he did not do. Oregonians could not have disturbed him in 1848, as news of the gold discovery did not reach Oregon until September of that year.

At all events he did go to Trinity River in the summer of 1849, for a report of his trip was given by the *Placer Times* of Sacramento in August of that year.

EXPLORATION OF TRINITY RIVER.

In June 1849, Major Reading started from his ranch with a small party for the purpose of exploring this stream. They went up Clear Creek and then crossed the mountains to the river, going up the stream some distance and finding gold in abundance. About the first of August they returned to the Sacramento Valley, and reported that they had made forty dollars per day to the man, for the few days they had worked. They also laid considerable stress on the fact that in crossing the summit they had camped one night above the snow line.

TRINITY MINES WORKED IN 1849.

The effect of such a statement as this can well be imagined. Emigrants were then coming down from Oregon, or entering the upper end of the Sacramento Valley by the Lassen route from across the plains, and while most of these preferred to go on to the well-known mines farther south, a few were venturesome enough to cross the high mountain to Trinity River. In this way quite a number of miners gathered and worked on the banks of the Trinity in the fall of 1849. The report sent out and brought out by these men created quite a fever of excitement, but the fear of the rigors of winter were so great that few dared to go into the mountains until spring, and the majority of those who were on the river in the fall went back to the valley for the same reason.

MINERS ATTEMPT TO FIND TRINIDAD.

The error made by Major Reading in supposing that the river he had named Trinity flowed into the old Trinidad Bay of the Spanish explorers was communicated to others and became the general opinion. It was then conceived that the best route to the mines must be to go to Trinidad Bay in a vessel and thence up the river to the mines. All that was known of the bay was the record of the explorers and the indication of such a place at an indefinite point on the northern coast. To find Trinidad Bay, then, became the next and the all-absorbing question. It had been discovered by an exploring expedition, consisting of a frigate commanded by Bruno Ezorta and a sloop under Juan de la Quadra Y. Bodega, on the eleventh of June, 1775. This was the Sunday of the Holy Trinity, and the bay was named Trinidad in consequence, and was fully mentioned on page eighteen.

As early as March, 1848, a call was made in San Francisco for a public meeting to take steps to re-discover and explore Trinidad Bay, to see what kind of a harbor it presented and what was the character of the country tributary to it. The announcement of the gold discovery at Sutter's Mill, however, put an end to all such designs, and the matter lay in abeyance until the reports from the Trinity Mines revived it.

DISCOVERY OF HUMBOLDT BAY.

In the month of November, 1849, two parties left the Trinity Mines to discover the desired harbor.

One of these went over to the Sacramento Valley, and down to San Francisco, where they commenced fitting out a sea expedition. The other party followed down the Trinity to the Bald Hills, and then crossed over to the coast, thus failing to discover the fact that the Trinity did not empty into the ocean direct.

The following very interesting narrative of this expedition was prepared by L. K. Wood for the *Humboldt Times*, and was first printed in 1856. It was afterward revised and printed in the *West Coast Signal*, copies of which were furnished us by Jonathan Clark, Esq.:—

"The month of October, 1849, found me on Trinity River, at a point now called 'Rich Bar,' without provisions, poorly clad, and worse than all in this condition at the commencement of a California winter. The company at this place numbered some forty persons, the most of whom were in much the same situation and condition as myself. Near this bar was an Indian ranch, from which, during the prevalence of the rain that was now pouring down as if in contemplation of a second flood, we received frequent visits. From them we learned that the ocean was distant from this place not more than eight days' travel, and that there was a large and beautiful bay, surrounded by fine and extensive prairie lands.

The rainy season, having now set in all appearances, a scanty supply of provisions for the number of persons now here, and scarcely a probability of the stock being replenished before the rains should cease, the idea was conceived of undertaking an expedition, with the view to ascertain whether the bay, of which the Indians had given a description, in reality existed.

JOSIAH GREGG CHOSEN LEADER.

Among the first and most active in getting up and organizing the expedition, was a gentleman by the name of Josiah Gregg, a physician by profession, formerly of Missouri. He had with him all the implements necessary to guide us through the uninhabited, trackless region of country that lay between us and the point to be sought. No one seemed better qualified to guide and direct an expedition of this kind than he. Upon him, therefore, the choice fell to take command. The number of persons that had expressed a desire to join the company up to this time, were twenty-four.

The day fixed upon by the Captain for setting out was the 5th day of November. In the meantime whatever preparations were necessary, and in our power, were made. The Captain had negotiated with the chief of the rancheria for two of his men to act as guides. Nothing more remained to be done —all were anxiously awaiting the arrival of the day fixed upon, and a cessation of the rain, which was still falling in torrents.

The day of departure arrived, but with it came no change in the weather, save an occasional change from rain to snow. Many of the party now began to exhibit marked symptoms of a desire to withdraw and abandon the expedition.

The two Indian guides refused to go, assigning as a reason, that the great storm we had experienced on the river, had been a continuous snow-storm in the mountains, and that the depth of the snow would present an insuperable barrier to our progress, and endanger the safety of the whole party to attempt the passage. This was sufficient for those who had manifested a desire to withdraw; and the number of the company was speedily reduced to eight men, including the Captain whose determination was only the more firmly fixed, because so large a number had abandoned the expedition.

NAMES OF THE EXPLORERS.

The company now consisted of the following persons: Dr. Josiah Gregg, Captain; Thomas Sebring, of Ottawa, Illinois; David A. Buck, of New York; J. B. Truesdell, of Oregon; — Van Duzen; Charles C. Southard, of Boston; Isaac Wilson, of Missouri, and L. K. Wood, of Mason County, Kentucky.

Owing to this great diminution in the number of the party, it became necessary before setting out to examine the condition of our commissary department, from which it was ascertained that the stock of provisions had suffered even greater diminution than had the company in point of numbers. The articles found were flour, pork, and beans, and of these scarcely sufficient for ten days' rations. Notwithstanding this, an advance was determined upon, and, accordingly, we broke up camp.

Here commenced an expedition, the marked and prominent features of which were constant and unmitigated toil, hardship, privation and suffering. Before us, stretching as far as the eye could reach, lay mountains, high and rugged, deep valleys and difficult cañons, now filled with water by the recent, heavy rains. After leaving Trinity River we struck up the mountain, in the direction indicated by the Indians that were to have been our guides. The ascent, at any time tedious, was now particularly difficult.

Without any other trail or pathway than an occasional elk or Indian trail through the dense stunted undergrowth, the ground for a long distance up the mountain completely saturated with water from the great quantity of rain that had fallen, our ascent, as might be expected, was not only tedious and difficult, but extremely fatiguing. Before reaching the summit, however, the character of the ascent was materially changed. Snow had taken the place of slippery mud, which had completely obliterated all there was of a trail, its depth increasing in preparation to the altitude gained. We now had to grope our way as best we might; slowly and silently we continued to ascend the steepest part of the mountain in order to shorten the distance.

At length we reached the summit. Our first glances were cast in the direction indicated to us as our course. As I gazed upon the wild and rugged country spread out before us, and that all these snow-crested mountains lay between us and the place of our destination, a feeling of dread came over me. I could hardly refrain from giving expression to the feelings of doubt with which I was impressed, as to the result of the expedition we had undertaken, but the time for reconsideration had passed.

CAMPING IN EARLY DAYS.

As it was about sunset when the summit was gained, preparations were made for going into camp. Now, "camping" in California is not precisely the same thing implied by that term in other countries. It consists of nothing more than taking your saddle and blankets from the animal and depositing them on the first convenient spot of Mother Earth, or, as applied to us this night, on snow. To have a choice in ground on which to camp would be deemed fastidious, and to form a hut from bushes a foolish expenditure of time and labor. Unpacking animals and getting supper were the things first to be attended to; this being done, our blankets were spread, and in them we passed the first night of our expedition.

At an early hour in the morning, having breakfasted and packed our animals, we resumed our journey, descending the mountain, keeping as near our course as the nature of the country would permit. It would have been to us a source of some encouragement, if when we had attained the summit of a mountain, or mountain ridge, our course would have permitted us to continue on such ridge—but the case was otherwise. The ridges or mountains that constitute and are denominated the Coast Range, are nearly parallel with the coast; therefore, as the general direction of the coast is nearly north and south, and the mountain ridges the same, and our course nearly west, we were compelled to pass over a constant succession of mountains, now over the top of one, then through the deep valley beneath, and again climbing the steep side of another.

Nothing beyond the ordinary routine of constant traveling by day, and stretching our wearied limbs upon the snow or cold wet ground by night, occurred during the succeeding four days worthy of notice.

Towards the evening of the fifth day, while passing over a sterile, rugged, rocky country, we heard what appeared to be the rolling and breaking of the surf upon the distant sea shore, or the roaring of some water-fall. A halt was therefore determined upon, and we resolved to ascertain the cause of this before proceeding further, and here pitched our camp.

Early next morning Mr. Buck left camp alone, for the purpose above expressed, and before night returned, bringing with him a quantity of sand, which from its appearance, as well as that of the place where it was gathered, he thought indicated the presence of gold; but not being on a gold hunting expedition, we thought it the better discretion to use all possible dispatch in reaching the coast. The result of his search was that he found a stream at the foot of a rugged descent, whose now swollen waters rushed with terrific speed and violence. This, then, was what we heard. The gleam of hope that for the moment animated us was soon dispelled. This stream is the South Fork of Trinity.

Having ascertained that it was impossible to effect a crossing at or near this place, we continued on down, keeping as near as it was possible, until we came to its junction with the Trinity River. Here we succeeded in crossing.

Upon gaining the opposite shore, we had a steep bank to ascend. As we reached the top of this bank, we came suddenly upon an Indian rancheria. To us this was entirely unexpected, and undoubtedly not less so to them. Had it not been for the strange, I might say ludicrous, scene that followed immediately upon their discovering us, I would not vouch but that some if not most of the company, would have betrayed signs of timidity, if not actual fear, for our fire-arms had been rendered completely unfit for use, from constant exposure to the rain, which continued through the whole of this day. Knowing this we were fully conscious that should they meditate any harm towards us, we could make but a sorry show at a defense. A moment's consideration, however, taught us that it was not necessary, nor was it likely, that these savages should know our precise situation, and that it was our policy to give them to understand we were in no fear of them.

INDIANS' FIRST VIEW OF WHITE MEN.

But the scene that followed for the moment wholly divested our minds of all apprehension of danger, for as soon as they saw us, men, women and children, fled in the wildest confusion, and in every direction; some plunging headlong into the river, not venturing to look behind them until they had reached a considerable elevation upon the mountain on the opposite side of the river, while others sought refuge in the thickets and among the rocks, leaving everything behind them. So soon as they had stopped in their flight, those who were yet in view we endeavored by signs to induce to return, giving them to understand as best we could, that we intended them no harm; but for the present it was all to no purpose.

They had never before seen a white man, nor had they received any intelligence of our coming; and to their being thus suddenly brought in contact with a race of beings so totally different in color, dress, and appearance, from any they had ever seen or heard of, is attributable the overwhelming fear they betrayed.

Our stock of provisions was now nearly or quite exhausted, and what portion of our journey had been accomplished we

were of course entirely ignorant; one thing, however, was apparent, that from this forward, upon Providence and our good rifles our dependence for food must rest. Having failed to induce the Indians to return to their rancheria, and observing that they had considerable quantities of salmon in their huts, which they had obtained and cured for their subsistence during the winter, we helped ourselves to as much as was wanted, leaving in its place a quantity of venison that had been killed by some of our party a short time previous, invoking as a justification for so doing the old adage, "a fair exchange is no robbery," and pressed forward on our journey with all diligence.

We had hoped that the Indians would not care to become better acquainted with us, and would allow us to pass on unmolested. Imagine our surprise, then, when as we were about camping for the night, there came marching towards us some seventy-five or eighty warriors, their faces and bodies painted, looking like so many demons, and armed and prepared for battle. There needed no calling a counsel of war on our part to arrange plans to determine the course to pursue in the emergency that now presented itself to us. Our guns were available at this moment for no other purpose than to use as clubs, for the reasons before stated.

The only alternative, therefore, left to us, was to assume an air of perfect indifference at their approach. This we did, but when they had advanced to within one hundred yards of us, we by signs forbid their coming nearer, and in obedience to our command they halted. Two of our company now advanced towards them, holding up to their view, beads and other fancy articles which we fortunately had in our possession. With these they appeared highly pleased, and were persuaded that it was neither our desire or intention to disturb or injure them, and soon became quiet and apparently friendly.

INDIANS' FIRST KNOWLEDGE OF FIRE-ARMS.

They represented to us that their people were very numerous, and seemed desirous of impressing upon our minds that we were in their power and at their mercy, and in order to make this more evident they assured us that at any moment they wished they could kill the whole company. I need scarce tell you that we lost little time in disabusing their minds on this subject.

It was a matter not only of surprise but evident curiosity with them, to know how so small a number of men could successfully resist a force so vastly superior. The secret was in our weapons. The use of these, however, they could not understand. In order to accomplish our object, we gave them to understand that one of our guns would kill as many of them at a single shot, as could stand one behind the other. This however, did not seem to satisfy them—they seemed disposed to doubt the correctness of our representations. As an evidence of this, they insisted upon our giving them an opportunity of witnessing the effects produced by shooting at a mark. This we declined to do, not desiring to attempt a display of our skill with guns that perhaps would require fifteen minutes to discharge, but promised to gratify them the next morning.

Prudence and a reasonable regard for our safety, compelled us to keep a careful watch during the night; notwithstanding this, and the fact that some of the company felt little inclined to sleep, one of these expert thieves, aided by the pitchy darkness of the night, crept stealthily to the spot where we were encamped, and took from beneath the blankets a Colt's revolver, without detection—to the surprise of all and particularly the loser, who, by the way, was one of those who were so little disposed to sleep.

At the first glimpse of dawn we were prepared for the start, but not, however, in time to avoid our engagement made the evening before; for, as if anticipating our intention, they, together with a host of their women and children, as early made their appearance.

We proceeded without delay to satisfy their curiosity and fulfill our promise. Handing a piece of paper, about two and a half inches in diameter, to one of the Indians, directing him to place the same upon a tree about sixty paces distant, they in the meantime having arranged themselves on either side the shot was made. Not expecting any report, they were completely terror-stricken, particularly the women and children, who set up a terrible yelling, at the same time scattering in every direction. After looking about them and discovering that none of their number had been injured, they at length returned, and being curious to see what effect the gun produced, approached the tree and examined the paper, which the ball had perforated, and the tree where the same had entered and disappeared. They now seemed disposed to treat us with greater respect than they had done.

Taking advantage of the impression created upon their minds by what they had just witnessed, we endeavored to fasten upon them the conviction that our small company were able to cope with all they could bring against us, and told them that the force of a ball thrown from one of our guns, and the amount of execution it would do, was as much greater, in proportion, than that of an arrow shot from one of their bows, as the report of one was louder than the other.

THE JOURNEY RESUMED.

It had been our intention to follow the river down, although its course being from this point northwest, was not in the direction we desired to take. Against this, however, the Indians cautioned us, asserting that there were numerous tribes scattered along the river to its mouth, who would certainly oppose our passing through their country, besides on being made to understand the object we had in view, they informed us that our best route, both in point of distance and on account of the Indians, was to leave the river and strike westward.

This advice, we, upon the whole, thought the most prudent to follow, and accordingly commenced the ascent of the mountain that now lay in our path.

The night of the second day after leaving the river, having pitched our camp, we set about preparing a supper. I would not consume the time in detailing so minutely these unimportant items, but a portion of the material of that night's meal, although a morsel delicate and palatable in comparison with some of which we partook later in our journey, and it being the first time within my experience where necessity had reduced me to a like extremity, it made an impression upon my mind which to-day is as fresh as if it occurred but yesterday. Our stock of flour was exhausted; the almost continual rain, however, had so saturated our entire camp equipage—the flour among the rest—and there had formed on the inner surface of the sacks in which it had been carried, a kind of paste which the dampness had soured and moulded.

This paste was carefully *peeled off*, softened with water, and equally divided among the party—when each one, after the same had been submitted to a process of hardening before the fire, devoured his portion with an avidity that would have astonished and shocked mortals with appetites more delicate than ours. Nothing now remained of the stock of provisions that constituted our outfit—flour, pork, beans—all were gone. The night of the 13th of November, the eighth day, we were compelled to retire to our blankets supperless.

Our animals, however, had been without feed for the previous two days, but were now luxuriating in fine grass, which fact tended to render our situation the more supportable, for preservation of our animals, next to food for ourselves, was of the highest importance, because upon them we depended for the packing of our blankets and provisions, when fortunate enough to find any of the latter.

PROPOSITION TO RETURN OVERRULED.

During the succeeding day, a halt was several times called to consider the proposition submitted by some to return; but as often as it was made it was overruled, upon the belief that the coast could certainly be reached in much less time than it would require to return to the river. After picking our way the whole of this day through an almost impenetrable forest, we came to a small prairie. This we reached about sunset, worn down with fatigue, and feeling but too acutely the painful sensations occasioned by a long abstinence from food. Here we determined to remain awhile, to hunt for something upon which to subsist.

On leaving the South Fork of the Trinity, we had hoped by this time to have gained the sea-shore, but in this expectation we were doomed to disappointment. The dim outline of the distant mountains still marked the horizon, the same as when our first glance was cast in the direction of our route, upon reaching the summit of the first mountain.

In the morning all the party, save a guard for the camp, started out in search of food, and after a short hunt succeeded in killing several deer. A quantity of venison steak broiled or cooked in the ashes, soon appeased the extreme hunger from which we were suffering.

Here we remained several days for the purpose of recovering our nearly exhausted strength. During our stay at this place, we cured a quantity of venison with which, upon resuming our journey, we packed the animals, and proceeded on foot ourselves, thinking that by so doing we could certainly take sufficient to last, if not until we should get through, at least until more could be obtained. But no; on we toiled, faithfully and constantly, until the last of the venison was consumed, and the first, and second, and third day of fasting came and passed.

SUFFERING FOR WANT OF FOOD.

During all this time our animals suffered intensely from want of food. The only kind that could be obtained for them was leaves, and in places even these could not be procured only by cutting down trees. Two of them, however, were too far reduced to go further, and we were compelled to leave them behind.

Again we had the good fortune to reach a piece of mountain prairie where we found an abundance of game for ourselves, and plenty of grass for the animals. At this place we remained three days, collecting and preparing meat for use while traveling. We had now two animals less in number, and consequently were obliged to increase the loads of those remaining in order to pack sufficient to keep soul and body together for a reasonable length of time, for as when we left one camping place, when or where another would be found was of course uncertain, and to pack our provisions ourselves was a thing out of the question, in our present condition.

Having prepared as large a quantity of meat as our animals could carry, on we went. Disappointment seemed to be our constant companion. Without following us day after day in our zigzag course, and detailing the occurrences that transpired, suffice it to say ten days passed away without being favored with the sight of any living thing that could be made available or useful for food.

Again was our stock of provisions exhausted. For several days we subsisted upon a species of nut resembling the acorn, but far more bitter and unpalatable. The only way that they could be used was by roasting them in the fire until crisp and dry. A dose of these was found to be from six to ten, and to be taken about every fifteen minutes—a larger dose or oftener was sure to operate as an emetic.

Our drink was for a greater part of the time, a tea made of *yerba buena*—an herb that resembles mint. It seemed that each scene of toil and suffering which we had been compelled to undergo after leaving these recruiting places—that were to us like oases to the traveler crossing the sandy desert—was but the prelude to another of a worse and more trying character. Not one was without its quota of hardship, privation, and almost starvation.

ELK, DEER, AND GRIZZLIES.

At length we reached another opening in this world-wide forest, and without first selecting a camping place, as was usual with us, we hastened to search for food. We ascended a rocky eminence that overlooked the country for a considerable distance around. Upon gaining the summit one of the most attractive and inviting scenes opened to our view. On one side were feeding little knots of deer, on another and nearer to us were a large herd of elk, and still in another direction both were to be seen. After a few moments' consultation, we determined to attack the elk, and accordingly separated in order to approach them from opposite directions.

Scarcely a half hour had elapsed, before I heard the report of a rifle, and two more in quick succession. From the direction I supposed it to be Van Duzen, and from the rapid succession in which the shots were fired, I was fearful that some danger had befallen him, and immediately hastened to his assistance. I shall not soon forget the scene that was here presented to me.

There stood Van Duzen reloading his rifle; near by lay three grizzly bears, two dead and the third with his back broken. Two others stood near by, grinning and snarling in a most unamiable manner, looking first upon their fallen companions and then upon us. As this was my first introduction to Bruin, and the meeting being so sudden and unexpected, I hesitated a moment whether to approach and become better acquainted, or remain a spectator. There was a certain something in their appearance that involuntarily brought to mind the many tales I had heard related of their ferocity, when disturbed, and particularly when wounded. I, however, concluded to venture a shot at one of them, and with that intention advanced towards them.

Van Duzen perceiving this, called on me to stop, fearing that we might get into trouble. Heedless of his caution, I approached slowly, intently watching their movements, until within fifteen steps of one of them when I stopped and fired. The shot was a fatal one, the shaggy monster fell, with a howl, dead upon the ground. At the same moment Wilson, whom the frequent firing had likewise attracted to the spot, sent a ball through the heart of the remaining bear with a similar result. This you will say was pretty good shooting, to kill five grizzly bears with as many shots out of one band. But it is nevertheless true. As for myself I can say without boasting—although it was my first experience in hunting this kind of game, and although I was conscious of the fact, that should my shot fail to be a fatal one, the bear would in all probability be upon me before I could get ten steps from the place where I stood—that I felt indifferent to danger. Our situation had become so desperate, and the conviction fast settling upon our minds that each day passed in the mountains lessened the probability of reaching any settlement in safety, that recklessness and indifference had become a second nature to me.

Our attention had been so completely engrossed in the encounter with the grizzlies, that the band of elk were forgotten, and we lost the opportunity of getting any of them. However, before night we succeeded in bringing several deer into camp. At this place we remained five days, feasting and fattening on bear meat, and preparing venison for future use.

Our progress up to this time had been very slow. The distance travelled per day did not exceed an average of seven miles. The appearance of the country now seemed to change, the mountain ridges were less high and abrupt than those over which we had passed, but much more densely covered with timber. Our belief now was that twelve miles further travel would bring us, if not to the coast, at least to a more level country, when our advance would be more rapid and attended with less difficulty and suffering. We therefore resumed our journey with lighter hearts and more buoyant hopes. Our calculation of the distance to the coast or valley, subsequently proved to be not far from correct.

DENSE REDWOOD FOREST ENTERED.

The redwood forests, however, through which we had to pass, were more dense and difficult to penetrate than any before, consequently our progress was in proportion retarded. Dr. Gregg frequently expressed a desire to measure the circumference of some of these giants of the forest, and occasionally called upon some one of us to assist him. Not being in the most amiable state of mind and feeling at this time, and having neither ambition to gratify nor desire to enlighten the curious world, we not unfrequently answered his calls with shameful abuse. His obstinate perseverance, however, in one or two instances, resulted in success. One redwood tree was measured whose diameter was found to be twenty-two feet, and it was no unusual thing to find these trees reaching the enormous height of 300 feet. This may excite incredulity abroad, but trees have since been found in this redwood forest, of much greater dimensions.

Through this forest we could not travel to exceed two miles a day. The reason of this was the immense quantity of fallen timber that lay upon the ground in every conceivable shape and direction, and in very many instances one piled upon another so that the only alternative left us was literally to cut our way through. To go around them was often as impossible as to go over them. We were obliged, therefore, constantly to keep two men ahead with axes, who, as occasion required, would chop into and slab off sufficient to construct a sort of platform by means of which the animals were driven upon the log and forced to jump off on the opposite side. There was not the least sign indicative of the presence of any of the animal creation; indeed it was almost as impenetrable for them as for us, and doubtless was never resorted to save for purposes of shelter.

WELCOME ROAR OF THE OCEAN.

On the evening of the third day from our bear camp, as we called it, our ears were greeted with the welcome sound of the surf rolling and beating upon the sea-shore. There was no doubt or mistake about it this time. The lofty tree tops caught the sound, which the deep stillness of a night in the forest rendered the more plainly audible, and echoed it back to our attentive ears.

The following morning, Messrs. Wilson and Van Duzen proposed to go to the coast in advance of the company, and at the same time to mark out the best route for the animals; to which proposition all agreed, and accordingly they left camp. In the evening of the same day they returned, bringing the glad tidings that they had reached the sea-shore, and that it was not more than six miles distant.

At an early hour in the morning we resumed our journey with renewed spirits and courage. For three long, weary days did we toil in these redwoods. Exhaustion and almost starvation, had reduced the animals to the last extremity. Three had just died, and the remainder were so much weakened and reduced, that it constituted no small part of our labor and annoyance in assisting them to get up when they had fallen, which happened every time they were unfortunate enough to stumble against the smallest obstacle that lay in their path, and not one single effort would they make to recover their feet, until that assistance came. At length we issued from this dismal forest prison, in which we had so long been shut up, into the open country, and at the same instant in full view of that vast world of water—*the Pacific Ocean.*

PACIFIC OCEAN REACHED AT LAST.

Never shall I forget the thrill of joy and delight that animated me as I stood upon the sandy barrier that bounds and restrains those mighty waters.

It seemed like meeting some dear old friend, whose memory, with joy, I had treasured during long years of separation, and as the well-spent surf glided upon the beach, bathing my very feet, a thousand recollections, like magic, flooded my mind. I felt as though there was yet some hope of deliverance from these sufferings.

Our appetites, having again been sharpened by more than two days' fasting, soon awakened us from our pleasing reveries, and reminded us of the necessity of immediately going in search for food.

Not long after we had separated for that purpose, Van Duzen shot a bald eagle, and Southard a raven, which was devouring a dead fish thrown upon the beach by the surf. These they brought into camp, and all, eagle, raven, and half-devoured fish, were stewed together for our supper, after partaking of which we retired to our blankets and enjoyed a good night's rest.

Our prospects for a meal the next day were anything but flattering. Dr. Gregg therefore requested me to return to my mule which had fallen down the day before and been left to die, and take out his heart and liver and bring them to camp. I accordingly went, but judge of my surprise, when approaching the spot where I had left him, to find him quietly feeding. I determined for once not to obey my orders, and instead thereof, drove him into camp.

LITTLE RIVER DISCOVERED.

The point at which we struck the coast was at the mouth of a small stream now known by the name of Little River. From this point we pushed on northward, following the coast about eleven miles, when a small lake (Big Lagoon) arrested our progress. Finding it impossible to proceed further without again encountering the redwood forest, which we were not in the least inclined to do, it was determined that we should retrace our steps and proceed south, following the coast, to San Francisco, if such a course were possible. Traveling south about eight miles, we made a halt at a point or headland, which we had passed on our way up from where we first struck the coast. This we called "Gregg's Point," and is now known as Trinidad Head.

During our journey over the mountains, the old Doctor took several observations in order to prevent, as much as possible, a departure from the general course given us by the Indians. As we advanced, and our toil and sufferings accumulated, we gradually cultivated a distaste for such matters, and at an early day regarded his scientific experiments with indifference, while later in our journey they were looked upon with contempt. It was not unusual, therefore, for us to condemn him in most measured terms, for wasting his time and energies about that which would neither benefit him nor us in the least, or be of any service to others.

From an observation taken on the plateau, where the town of Trinidad is now situated, this point was found to be in latitude 40° 6' north. This the old gentleman took the trouble to engrave upon the trunk of a tree standing near by, for the benefit, as he said, of those who might hereafter visit the spot, if perchance such an occurrence should ever happen.* Here we remained two days, living on mussels and dried salmon, which we obtained from the Indians, of whom we found many.

EVERY MAN FOR HIMSELF.

Again we resumed our journey. In crossing a deep gulch, a short distance from the Point, the Doctor had the misfortune to have two of his animals mire down. He called lustily for assistance, but no one of the company would aid him to rescue them. We had been annoyed so much, and detained so long, in lifting fallen mules—some remembered the treatment they received when in a similar predicament—that one and all declared they would no longer lend assistance to man or beast,

---

* Discovered by the crew of the *Cameo*, and mentioned in that narrative.

RESIDENCE OF GEORGE W. CHARLES, HUMBOLDT CO. CAL.

and that from this forward each would constitute a company by himself, under obligations to no one, and free to act as best suited his notions.

In obedience to this resolve, I immediately set about making arrangements in regard to myself.

Having for some time noticed the rapid strides the company were making towards disruption, and anticipating a result similar to that which had just transpired, I visited the chief of a tribe of Indians who lived close at hand, and explained to him, as best I could, what I wanted and intended to do, provided we could agree. I gave him to understand that I desired to remain with him awhile, and that if he would protect me and take care of my mule, and give me a place in his wigwam, I would furnish him with all the elk meat he wanted. To this he readily acquiesced, and in addition returned many assurances that nothing should harm either me or mine.

When the company were again about starting—for they all seemed bound in the same direction, whether in conformity to an agreed plan, or involuntarily, I did not know—they discovered that I was not prepared to accompany them, and demanded to know the reason why I did not get ready. I then informed them of my determination, and the agreement I had made with the Indian chief. All were violently opposed to the arrangement, and urged as a reason why I should not persist in such a determination, that when altogether we were not sufficiently strong to pass through the Indian country in safety, should they see fit to oppose us, and that to remain with them would be to abandon myself to certain destruction, while at the same time it would lessen the probability of any of them reaching the settlements in safety. I told them I had no horse that could travel, I was not able to walk, and that I would as soon be killed by Indians as again to incur the risk of starvation, or, perhaps, that which was worse, fall a victim to cannibalism.

Truesdell, who had two animals left, offered to sell me one of them for one hundred dollars, if I would continue with them. I finally accepted the offer and proceeded with them.

MAD RIVER DISCOVERED AND NAMED.

Little River was soon recrossed, after which nothing occurred to interrupt our progress until we reached another stream, which was then a large river, being swollen by the heavy rains. Its banks ran full, and its waters, near the mouth, appeared deep, and moved so slowly and gently that we concluded it must be a navigable stream. Our next difficulty was to cross this river. Here the harmony that had existed for so short a time was again disturbed.

The Doctor wished to ascertain the latitude of the mouth of the river, in order hereafter to know where it was. This was of course opposed by the rest of the company. Regardless of this opposition, he proceeded to take his observation. We were, however equally obstinate in adhering to the determination of proceeding without delay. Thus decided, our animals were speedily crossed over, and our blankets and ourselves placed in canoes—which we had procured from the Indians for this purpose—ready to cross. As the canoes were about pushing off, the Doctor, as if convinced that we would carry our determination into effect, and he be left behind, hastily caught up his instruments and ran for the canoe, to reach which, however, he was compelled to wade several steps in the water. His cup of wrath was now filled to the brim; but he remained silent until the opposite shore was gained, when he opened upon us a perfect battery of the most withering and violent abuse. Several times during the ebullition of the old man's passion, he indulged in such insulting language and comparisons, that some of the party, at best not any too amiable in their disposition, came very near inflicting upon him summary punishment by consigning him, instruments and all, to his beautiful river. Fortunately for the old gentleman, pacific counsels prevailed, and we were soon ready and off again. This stream, in commemoration of the difficulty I have just related, we called Mad River.

OBJECT OF THE EXPEDITION FORGOTTEN.

We continued on down the beach a short time, when night overtaking us, we camped. So long a time had elapsed since our departure from the Trinity River, and the constant suffering, toil and danger to which we had been exposed, that the main object of the expedition had been quite forgotten; and our only thought and sole aim seemed to be, how we should extricate ourselves from the situation we were in, and when we might exchange it for one of more comfort and less exposure and danger.

Immediately after halting, Buck and myself went in search of water. It had been our custom, wherever night happened to overtake us, there to camp—the almost ceaseless falling of the rain affording us a continual supply of water. This night, however, we camped in some sand hills, about a mile back from the beach, without giving a thought how we should get water. A short distance from the camp we separated, Buck going in one direction and I in another. I soon found slough water, which although not agreeable and pleasant to the taste, I concluded would answer our purpose, and returned with some of it to camp. Not long after Buck came in and placed his kettle before us without anything being said. The Doctor not relishing the water I had brought, and being somewhat thirsty, was the first to taste the other. The suddenness with which the water was spit out after it had passed his lips, was a sufficient warning to the rest of us.

FIRST DISCOVERY OF HUMBOLDT BAY.

The Doctor asked Mr. B. where he had got that water, Buck replied, "about half a mile from here." The Doctor remarked: "You certainly did not get it out of the ocean, and we would like to know where you did get it." Buck answered:

"I dipped it out of a bay of smooth water." This excited our curiosity, and Buck seemed, at the time, to be rather dogged, and not much disposed to gratify us by explanations. It was dusk, and he could not tell the extent of the bay. This was the night of the 20th of December, 1849, and was undoubtedly the first discovery of the bay by Americans, notwithstanding Capt. Douglass Ottinger claims to have first discovered it. We gave it the name of "Trinity Bay," but before we could return (the next year), Captain Ottinger, with a party by water, discovered it and gave it the name of "Humboldt Bay," the name which it still retains.

The next morning, by daylight, we were up and moved our camp over to the bay, and stopped there during the day. This was opposite the point where Bucksport now stands. (On the strip of sand west of the bay.) We encamped the night previous under a group of small trees in the sand-hills lying between the bay and the ocean, on the strip of land now known as the "Peninsula," or "North Beach." The reason we had not discovered the bay the day previous, in traveling down from the mouth of Mad River, was because we followed the beach—it being hard sand and easy traveling—and the low hills and timber on the strip of land, lying between the ocean and the bay, shut out the latter entirely from our view.

During the day we remained here, the Indians came to our camp, and we learned from them that we could not follow down the beach on account of the entrance to the bay, which was just below us. Mr. Buck, however, to satisfy ourselves, took an Indian with him and started down to the entrance. When he returned, he reported quite a large and apparently deep stream connecting the bay with the ocean, and considerable swell setting in, which he thought would make it dangerous to attempt to cross. The Indians also represented that it was deeper than the trees growing on the Peninsula were tall; so we abandoned the idea of attempting to cross it.

Where we were camped was the narrowest part of the bay, being the channel abreast of Bucksport, and the Indians assured us that we could swim our animals across there, and offered to take us across in their canoes. Most of the party, including Dr. Gregg, were of the same opinion; but some of the company opposing the project, we packed up next morning and started northward, keeping as near the bay as the small sloughs would permit, for the purpose of heading it.

FIRST PARTY EVER AT ARCATA.

After making our way through brush and swamp, swimming sloughs and nearly drowning ourselves and animals, we arrived towards night of the second day, after leaving our camp opposite Bucksport, on a beautiful plateau near the highland and redwoods, at the northeast end of the bay. At this point which commands a fine view of the bay, stretching out to the southwest, we made a halt, and it being nearly night, pitched our camp. This plateau is the present site of the town of Union (now Arcata).

Our camp was near the little spring, about two hundred yards from the east side of the Plaza, towards the woods. I have seen some of the old tent pins, still remaining there, within the last year (1856).

As soon as we had unpacked, some of the party started in search of game, and soon came across a fine band of elk, a little north of our camp, about where the cemetery now is, and fired several shots, wounding two or three, but they succeeded in reaching the thicket in the edge of the redwoods, and dark setting in, they could not be found. We therefore did not get any supper that night. The next morning, early, some went in search of the elk and found one of them in the brush dead, and brought it to camp.

FIRST CHRISTMAS ON HUMBOLDT BAY.

Next morning, 25th of December, 1849, we roasted the elk's head in the ashes, and this constituted our Christmas feast. This was my first Christmas in California, and having been reduced so often to the point of starvation, we enjoyed this simple fare, yet you may rest assured, it was not that "Merry Christmas" I had been accustomed to in Kentucky with the "old folks at home." This day we moved down to the point of high prairie, near the mouth of Freshwater Slough at the east side of the bay, and there camped.

The next day we made our way through the woods, following an indistinct Indian trail, back of where the town of Eureka is now situated, and came out at the open space in the rear of where Bucksport now stands, which place derives its name from one of our party, David A. Buck. We pitched our camp near the bluff, on the top of which is at present Fort Humboldt.

The next day we followed down the bay, crossing Elk River, to Humboldt Point.

THE INDIANS FRIENDLY.

Here we were visited by the Chief of the tribe of Indians in the vicinity of the bay, who was an elderly and very dignified and intelligent Indian. He appeared very friendly and seemed disposed to afford us every means of comfort in his power. He supplied us with a quantity of clams, upon which we feasted sumptuously. The evening we arrived here, some of the party went out on the slope of prairie, to the east of our camp, and killed an elk, and while there taking care of it, we sent a note over to them, and received one in return, by this Chief, who would not allow any other Indian to carry them, but insisted upon being the bearer himself. He seemed anxious to arrive at the secret of this means of communication, and would watch to see what effect the piece of written paper would have on the one to whom he delivered it. This old man's name we learn was Ki-we-lat-tah. He is still living on the bay (1856), and has always been known as a quiet and friendly Indian.

It had been our intention at the outset, if we succeeded in

discovering the bay, and provided the surrounding country was adapted to agricultural purposes, and was sufficiently extensive, to locate claims for ourselves, and lay out a town; but the deplorable condition in which we now found ourselves, reduced in strength, health impaired, our ammunition nearly exhausted—upon which we were entirely dependent, as well for the little food we could obtain, as for our defense and protection—and destitute of either farming or mechanical implements, induced us to abandon such intention, at least for the present, and use all possible dispatch in making our way to the settlements.

Accordingly, having remained at this camping place one day, we turned our faces toward the South. Our progress was extremely slow, as the rain was falling almost incessantly, rendering traveling difficult and fatiguing.

EEL AND VAN DUZEN RIVERS DISCOVERED AND NAMED.

The third day after leaving the bay we reached another river, which arrested our advance in that direction.

Upon approaching this river, we came suddenly upon two very old Indians, who, at seeing us fell to the ground as if they had been shot. We dismounted and made them get up, giving them to understand that we were their friends; but it was with much difficulty that we succeeded in quieting their fears. They were loaded with eels, which they informed us they obtained from this river. Our appetites being in just such a condition, that anything not absolutely poisonous, upon which a meal could be made, was palatable, without asking many questions, we helped ourselves to nearly the whole of their load.

In exchange for these we gave them a few beads and some small pieces of iron. They seemed to value these pieces of iron more highly than anything else we had to dispose of. I took an old frying-pan that had been rendered comparatively useless, having lost its handle and being otherwise considerably damaged, and broke into small strips. With these I kept the company supplied with eels during our stay, often obtaining as many as three dozen for one piece. We gave to this stream the name of Eel River.

Near the place where we met these Indians, we got them with their canoes, to set us across the river, which was at this time a large stream, the water being high. We swam our animals as usual.

The point where we crossed was just below the junction of Van Duzen's Fork, which latter stream takes its name from one of our party. Here we remained two days, during which time we lived upon eels obtained from the Indians.

DISAGREEMENT AND SEPARATION.

At this camp a controversy arose among us in relation to the course now to be pursued. Some contended that we should follow the coast down to San Francisco. Others again urged, as the shortest and most advantageous route, to proceed up this river as far as its course seemed to suit, and then leave it and strike southerly for the nearest settlement. Neither party seemed inclined to yield to the other. Not all the arguments that the more peaceably disposed members of the company could adduce, could quell the storm that was gathering. Harsh words passed and threats were interchanged. As all prospects of a reconciliation had been abandoned, Seabring, Buck, Wilson and myself resolved to continue on our journey together, over the route we had advocated. Accordingly we separated, and although the rain was falling in torrents, we left the camp.

As before stated, our intention was to continue along the river, believing that by so doing our progress would be more rapid, and that the chances for obtaining food would be better. In this, however, we were sadly disappointed, for, as we advanced, the country became more and more uneven, and at last mountainous. The spurs from the mountains extending down to the river's edge, became so abrupt, and the ravines between so deep, as to render it extremely difficult to get our animals over them. We toiled along, however, until the third day, when we determined to leave the river. Our hope was to find some mountain ridge leading in a southeasterly direction—that being about the course we desired to take—and with this view we ascended the mountain.

PROGRESS OF THE "WOOD" PARTY.

The day after we left the river it commenced snowing, which, in a short time, so completely obliterated all there was of a trail, and shut from our view every landmark that could guide us in our course, that we were compelled to camp. Our situation now was indeed deplorable. At no time before had we been so completely destitute, and never had our prospects been so gloomy and disheartening. Fast being hemmed in with snow, without food either for ourselves or our animals, it seemed to us inevitable that our only alternative was to apply to that resource which we had with so much trouble and care preserved and kept with us—namely, our mules. We had for some time past thought that a misfortune like that which now seemed imminent, might overtake us, and therefore looked upon them as serving us in the additional capacity of food, when necessity might compel us to resort to them.

While the snow was yet not too deep, the animals with their feet pawed the grass bare, and thus obtained all there was to eat. We, too, were fortunate enough to kill a small deer. Five days elapsed before we were able to move from this camping place, and then not in the direction we desired, for the great quantity of snow that had fallen presented an impassable barrier to our progress, consequently we were compelled to return to the river.

The small supply which the deer afforded us was no more than sufficient to sooth the hunger pains with which we had, with little interruption, been suffering; and by the time we had extricated ourselves from our unfortunate situation in the snow, nothing remained of the deer but the skin.

We continued our course up the river, as best we could, sometimes aided by an Indian or elk trail, at others literally cutting our way along. For several days all that we had or could obtain to subsist upon, was the deer-skin which we had saved, and a few buckeyes. The former we cut up and boiled in water, and afterwards drank the water in which it had been boiled, and chewed the hide.

DISASTROUS ADVENTURE WITH GRIZZLIES.

Upon passing from the forest into a small opening, we came suddenly upon five grizzly bears. Wilson and myself immediately went in pursuit of them, but unfortunately met with no further success than to wound one of them severely. The day following this, while traveling over a piece of mountain prairie, and passing a small ravine or gulch, we espied a group of no less than eight more of these animals. Although exhausted from fatigue, and so reduced in strength that we were scarcely able to drag ourselves along, yet we determined to attack these grim customers.

Wilson, Seabring, and myself prepared for the conflict, which it was altogether probable we should have, before the matter was ended, and advanced towards them. While yet a long distance from them, Seabring sought shelter for himself by climbing a tree, not wishing to hazard the chances of a hand to hand contest with bruin. Wilson and myself advanced until within about one hundred yards of the nearest of them, when a consultation was again held in relation to the mode of making the attack.

THEIR MODE OF ATTACKING BEARS.

It was arranged that I should approach as near as possible, and fire; then make the best of my way to some tree for safety. The latter part of the arrangement I did not assent to, for one very good reason—I was so completely prostrated from exposure and starvation, that had I the will to run, my limbs would scarcely have been able to execute their functions. We continued to approach our antagonists until within about fifty paces, when I leveled my rifle at the one nearest me, and after a careful aim, fired. The shot was to all appearances, a fatal one, for the huge monster fell, biting and tearing the earth with all the fury of one struggling in death. So soon as I had fired, Wilson said to me, in a low tone of voice—"run! run!" Instead however of yielding to his advice, I immediately commenced reloading my rifle. Wilson now discharged his gun at another with equal success.

When I fired, five of the bears started up the mountain. Two now lay upon the ground before us, and a third yet remained, deliberately sitting back upon her haunches, and evidently determined not to yield the ground without a contest, looking first upon her fallen companions and then upon us.

USELESS ATTEMPTS TO ESCAPE.

Wilson now thought it was time to retreat, and accordingly made the best of his way to a tree. Unfortunately for me, I could not get the ball down upon the powder, and in this predicament, so soon as Wilson started to run, the bear came dashing at me with fury. I succeeded however in getting beyond her reach in a small buckeye tree. I now made another effort to force the ball down my rifle, but with no better success than at first, and was therefore compelled to use it to beat the bear off as she attacked the tree, for the purpose of breaking it down or shaking me out of it. She kept me busy at this for two or three minutes, when to my astonishment, the bear I had shot down, having recovered sufficiently from the effects of the wound, came bounding towards me with all the violence and ferocity that agony and revenge could engender. No blow that I could inflict upon the head of the maddened monster with my gun could resist or even check her. The first spring she made upon the tree broke it down. I had the good fortune to gain my feet before they could get hold of me, and ran down the mountain in the direction of a small tree, standing about thirty yards distant. Every jump I made I thought must be my last, as I could distinctly feel the breath of the wounded bear as she grabbed at my heels. I kept clear of her while running, but the race was a short one. On reaching the tree, or rather bush, I seized hold of the trunk of it and swung my body around so as to afford the bear room to pass me, which she did, and went headlong down the hill some twenty paces before she could turn back. I exerted all my energies to climb this tree, but before I could get six feet from the ground, the hindermost bear caught me by the right ankle and dragged me down again. By this time the wounded bear had returned, and, as I fell, grabbed at my face. I however dodged, and she caught me by the left shoulder. The moments that followed were the most critical and perilous of my life. Here, then, thought I, was the end of all things to me! That I must perish—be mangled and torn in pieces—seemed inevitable. During all the time I was thus situated, my presence of mind did not forsake me.

TERRIFIC ENCOUNTER WITH GRIZZLIES.

Immediately after the second bear had caught me by the shoulder, the other still having hold of my ankle, the two pulled against each other as if to draw me in pieces; but my clothes and their grip giving way, occasionally saved me. In this way they continued until they had stripped me of my clothes, except a part of my coat and shirt, dislocated my hip, and inflicted many flesh wounds—none of the latter, however, being very serious. They seemed unwilling to take hold of my flesh, for, after they had divested me of my clothes, they both left me—one going away entirely, and the other (the wounded bear) walking slowly up the hill, about one hundred yards from

me, and then, deliberately seated herself, and fastened her gaze upon me, as I lay upon the ground perfectly still.

THE BEAR RESUMES THE ATTACK.

After remaining thus several minutes, I ventured to move, which, I suppose, she must have seen, for the first motion brought her pell-mell upon me again, tearing every jump as loud as she could roar. At this moment, I must confess, my presence of mind nearly forsook me. I knew that if she again attacked or took hold of me, it must be upon my naked flesh. The moment left me was one of fearful suspense. No sooner had she reached me than she placed her nose violently against my side, and then raised her head and gave vent to two of the most frightful, hideous, and unearthly yells that were ever heard by mortal man. I remained perfectly quiet, hoping that by so doing she would leave me, and in this hope I was not disappointed, for after standing over me a short time, she again walked away. I now thought she had left for good, and determined to place myself, if possible, beyond her reach, should she, however, make up her mind to again return and continue the attack.

Up to this time I was unconscious of the extent of the injury I had received; that an accident had befallen my leg I was well aware, but not until I attempted to get up was my true situation manifest to me. I then found that I could not use my right leg, and supposed it was broken.

Turning to look about me, to assure myself that my enemy had retired, imagine my surprise at seeing her again not more than 100 yards distant, sitting back upon her haunches and her eyes glaring full at me. With my leg in the condition I have related, I dragged myself to the buckeye bush, from which I had been pulled down by the bear, and after much difficulty succeeded in climbing up about eight feet. So soon as Wilson had discovered me up the tree, he left his tree and came to me. The bear seeing him came bounding towards us with the greatest ferocity. Wilson remarked, "What in the name of God shall I do?" I replied that he could come up the limb of the adjoining tree, and he was barely enabled to get beyond reach, before she arrived. She deliberately seated herself immediately beneath us, and kept her eyes steadily upon us, and as either one or the other of us happened to move, she would utter an angry growl. I observed Wilson present his rifle at her, and not shooting immediately, I remarked: "Shoot her—for God's sake, shoot her—for she is the beast that did me all the injury I have received!" He watched her eyes closely for a moment, with his aim still fixed upon her, and when I again repeated my request for him to shoot, he replied —"No sir; let her go—let her go, if she will."

After having detained us in this situation for a few minutes, she went away, and disappeared altogether, much to our joy and relief—thereby giving me an opportunity to get down from the tree.

A DISTRESSING SITUATION.

Now that all the fear of further interruption from our late visitor was past, I began fully to realize my true condition. The wounds I had received became momentarily more painful. So soon as the remainder of the party came up, I was carried some distance down the mountain, to a place suitable for camping. Here we remained twelve days, subsisting entirely upon the meat afforded by the bear Wilson shot in the late encounter.

It now became a source of much anxiety, to know when and how we should leave this place, or what disposition they would make of me, as I seemed to grow worse, instead of better. It was thought that by remaining in camp ten or twelve days, my wounds would have so far healed as to enable us to resume our journey; but no one, not even myself, supposed that the injuries I had received were of so serious a character as they now proved to be. Finding, however, at the expiration of that time, that my condition had in nowise improved, they consulted me in relation to the course that should be adopted. That it was necessary, absolutely so, that no more time should be lost, all insisted, as we were almost entirely stripped of clothing and without shoes to protect our feet from the thorns and briars that were ever in our path. All were becoming aware of the fact that their strength and health were fast failing, and although we had, from the outset, been gradually trained to bear cold, hunger and pain, yet it was too evident that our powers of endurance were seriously impaired. They urged, as a further reason, that our ammunition was nearly or quite exhausted, upon which our sole dependence rested for the scanty supply of food that we could obtain.

The meaning of this was obvious to me, and in reply I said to them, that they had remained with me as long as I could expect or ask; that they were bound to save themselves if they could, and that they ought not to allow me to be in their way; but as they had seen proper to speak of the matter, I would ask of them one other favor.

INDIAN TREACHERY.

I suggested two ways in which they could dispose of me, either of which I would prefer to being abandoned to my fate in the condition and place in which I now was. The first, was to induce the Indians, who had visited us during our stay here, to take care of me until they could go to a settlement and return; and a second was to put an end to my sufferings.

They cheerfully sought the chief of these Indians, and explained to him what they desired to do, and in turn what they required of him, to all of which he apparently readily assented, and promised faithfully to attend to me and supply me with food until they could return. He agreed to come the next morning and convey me to his ranch, which was about three miles distant, and situated upon the river.

At the appointed time the old chief presented himself,

together with three of his men, and expressed his readiness to fulfill his agreement. One of them gave me several varieties of herbs, which I accepted and ate, and gave him to understand that they were very good. Before taking me, however, they demanded some presents as a compensation for the services they were about to render. All the beads and trinkets in our possession were gathered together and given to them. These, however, were not sufficient, and more were required. Their demand for more was repeated, and compliance on our part yielded, until everything we had, save such things as necessity absolutely required us to retain—even blankets that had been allotted to me—were given up to them, in order, if possible, to avoid offending them. At length they seemed satisfied that they had gotten all they could, when the chief very coolly turned to his men and bade them return to their home, he following after them, leaving us to regret the folly and indiscretion committed, in reposing too much confidence in a race of beings, known by all experience to be totally unworthy of it.

While these preliminaries were being arranged, I was busied in dragging myself upon a litter that had been prepared for me. This was a difficult task. I could not endure assistance my leg was so much swollen and inflamed, and so exceedingly sensitive in getting upon it. I however finally succeeded, and had prepared myself to bid farewell, most likely forever, to my companions who had so patiently submitted to the great delay to which they had been subjected, through the misfortune that had overtaken me, and who had so calmly and quietly—without a single murmur—endured intense sufferings. When, however, I saw these treacherous villains leave us with their ill-gotten booty, my heart for a moment ceased to beat. The first thought that possessed my brain, was that my fate was sealed—that death awaited me. Either I should be abandoned in these desolate solitudes, to endure the gnawing pangs of hunger, and at last to perish alone, a victim of starvation, or they would release me from these accumulated tortures by shooting me; for in this light I viewed it, and therefore preferred the latter alternative.

A BRAVE AND NOBLE COMPANION.

A solemn and profound silence now prevailed with all—a silence which no one seemed disposed to interrupt. I turned my face from my companions, that they might not be embarrassed in their consultation, or in carrying into execution any determination they might arrive at, particularly if it should be to relieve me of my sufferings by shooting me.

Their conversation was carried on in a low, indistinct tone of voice, for some time. Occasionly detached portions of sentences would reach my ears, enough, however, to satisfy my mind that there was a difference of opinion in relation to the course they should now adopt.

At length Wilson's voice rose above the rest, saying, "No!—I will not leave him!—I'll remain with him, if it is alone, or I will pack him if he is able and willing to bear the pain!" This terminated the conversation, and in a few moments after Seabring came to me and inquired what should now be done. I told him they might pack me to the river, where they had hacked out a canoe for the purpose of crossing, and I would then tell them whether I could continue with them, and in the event of my being unable to endure being packed further, all I had to ask of them was to leave me in the canoe to drift whither fate might direct.

He said, "we cannot pack you, for you have never allowed us to touch you, even; how then can you bear to be placed upon a horse and packed?"

"You are not to consult my wishes in the matter," I replied. "If you have decided not to abandon me, you must do with me as you will. Much longer delay in this place and at this season of the year, may prove fatal to all; self-preservation, therefore, must demand an immediate resumption of our journey, if it be at the risk, and even expense, of the life of one."

PAINFUL JOURNEY COMMENCED.

Wilson then requested me to select whichever animal I preferred; I however chose my own. They now lifted me into the saddle, and spent much time in placing me in a position that would give me the least pain. None, however, seemed to suit, and I asked Seabring, as a particular favor, to exchange saddles, for I thought his would make me more comfortable, and was certain it could not be worse than mine. They laid me upon the ground, changed the saddles, and again placed me upon my horse. I said nothing, but the agony I suffered no language can describe. The exchange of saddles aggravated my misery, but I had determined to be satisfied with this, let it be as it would. Seabring led my horse down the mountain, and after a long and tedious march, we reached the river. Here we camped.

When the bear that Wilson had killed in the late encounter, had been cut up and brought into camp, the entrails were likewise brought in, carefully cleaned and preserved; the blubber or fat was boiled out and put up in these skins and laid aside. On resuming our journey these were taken along, and this we were compelled to drink, as a substitute for other food, before we reached the settlements.

The next morning I was again consulted, and asked if I was able to continue on with them. I replied that as long as I lived, if it so pleased them, I desired to have them pack me, and should I die, that they should cut the cords that bound me to my horse and pass on. I could not ask or expect them to bury me, for there were no tools among the company with which to dig a grave.

Again was I bound upon my horse and packed until another camp was reached, enjoying only an occasional respite, to allow my benumbed limbs, to recover from the effects produced by being confined in one position for so long a time.

In this manner we continued on, with little or no change in the occurrences that happened, for the period of ten days, following down the Russian River a long distance, and then striking across towards Sonoma. At the expiration of this time, we arrived at the ranch of Mrs. Mark West, about thirty miles from the town of Sonoma, on the 17th day of February 1850. Here I remained six weeks, until sufficiently recovered to proceed to San Francisco, and was treated with the greatest kindness by every member of the family.

PROGRESS OF THE "OREGON" PARTY.

I must now tell you something of the other four, Messrs. Gregg, Van Duzen, Southard and Truesdell, whom we left on Eel River, and within twenty miles of the bay or coast.

They attempted to follow along the mountains near the coast, but were very slow in their progress on account of the snow on the high ridges. Finding the country very much broken along the coast, making it continually necessary to cross abrupt, rocky points, and deep gulches and cañons, after struggling along for several days, they concluded to abandon that route and strike easterly, towards the Sacramento Valley.

Having very little ammunition, they all came nigh perishing from starvation, and—as Mr. Southard related to me—Dr. Gregg continued to grow weaker, from the time of our separation, until, one day, he fell from his horse, and died in a few hours without speaking—died from starvation—had had no ment for several days—had been living entirely upon acorns and herbs. They dug a hole with sticks and put him under ground, then carried rock and piled upon his grave to keep animals from digging him up. They got through to the Sacramento Valley a few days later than we reached Sonoma Valley. Thus ended our expedition.

THE BAY WAS NAMED TRINITY.

When our party first discovered this bay, Dr. Gregg called it Trinity Bay, because, as he said, he believed it was the same bay which he had seen laid down upon the old Spanish charts under that name. This was on the 20th day of December, 1849, and on the 21st we made our camp close to the bay, and opposite the present town of Bucksport. We had been in camp but a short time when the chief Ki-we-lat-tah, alias "Ohl Coonskin," his two wives, and his brother Shuscpee, came in a canoe from the headland known as Humboldt Point, to see us, and from them we learned that no white persons had ever been on the shores of the bay before, but that a long time ago, when they were children, a sail vessel had entered, remained a short time, went to sea and never returned. During our whole stay here of about ten days, the chief and his party remained with us night and day, except the two days we were camped at the head of the bay where Arcata now stands.

We left the bay on our way south on the 1st day of January, 1850, and arrived at Sonoma on the 17th day of February, from whence two of our party went to San Francisco.

SECOND EXPLORING PARTY.

The others immediately set about recruiting a company to return, and soon succeeded in making the party about thirty strong, and in the early part of March, 1850, when about to start, four of the recruits were arrested for murder (Indian killing), which delayed us. "Six should have been arrested, and five of the six hanged, as they never quit Indian killing, but kept it up after reaching here, which was the first cause of our Indian troubles.) These worthies were taken to Benicia and confined on board a man-of-war, but by some means were released and soon returned to us, and we made our start the latter part of March, reaching the bay about the 19th day of April, 1850.

FIRST SETTLERS OF BUCKSPORT AND ARCATA.

We saw that the schooner *Laura Virginia* was inside, and that Humboldt Point was occupied by her party. They did not see us, and that they should not, we shifted our course more to the north, coming upon the shore of the bay where Bucksport now stands. Here we left four of our number to occupy and make improvements upon the land, the rest proceeding as fast as possible across the bay at this point, by the help of the Indians, and made our way on foot to the head of the bay where Arcata now stands, and which we considered the only place for a town. We arrived here on the 21st of April, and stayed about three days, laying foundations for houses, posting notices with names, dates, etc., in order to show that the land was claimed and occupied, then all hands returned by the east side of the bay to where we had left the four, and on our way we came upon a small company of the *Laura Virginia* party encamped upon that piece of prairie on the point of land north of Ryan's Slough." So ends Wood's narrative.

SEARCH BY SEA FOR TRINIDAD.

Meanwhile, the other party that had come down to San Francisco in November had chartered the brig *Cameo*, and sailed on the ninth of December. They utterly failed to find any such bay, and returned with the report that Trinidad was a myth, only to be greeted by the appearance of the land party and the assurance that it certainly did exist. Away sailed the *Cameo* again, followed by the others as rapidly as they could be gotten ready.

Up and down the coast they sailed, meeting with numerous adventures and mishaps, but failing utterly to find any bay. Some of them returned with reports of their ill success, claiming the bay to be a myth, while others still maintained the search. The return of the unsuccessful searchers did not restrain others from attempting the voyage. Ships sailed loaded with adventurers, some of them being on the coöperative plan, while others charged from fifty to one hundred dollars for passengers. In this way the *Cameo*, *Sierra Nevada*, *James R. Whiting*, *Isabel*, *Arabian*, *General Morgan*, *Hector*, *California*, *Parugon*, *Laura Virginia*, *Jacob M. Ryerson*, *Mulleroy*,

Galinda, and Patapsco, had all gone in search of the mysterious bay.

FIRST VESSEL ENTERS TRINIDAD BAY.

By the first of April, 1850, the news of the discovery of Trinidad Bay reached San Francisco from passengers of the Cameo, which was the first to sail and the first to discover, though not till three months afterwards, the long-sought harbor. On the sixteenth of March, 1850, the Cameo rounded to off Trinidad heads and sent a boat's crew to examine a point that made out into the sea. This crew, among whom was W. G. R. Smith, rounded the point and found the entrance to a harbor which they believed to be the long-sought Trinidad. The Cameo was compelled to sail on account of the stormy weather thus deserting the small boat and crew and proceeded to Point St. George where she landed her passengers, unaware that the men in the boat had discovered the bay. The men who were deserted explored the bay, near the head of which they found a tree with the following inscription:—

Lat. 41° 3' 32"
Barometer 29° 86'
Ther. Feb. 48° at 12 M.
Dec. 7, 1849.   J. Gregg.

This was the record by the party as mentioned in Wood's narrative and proved the truth of their story about having seen the bay.

SUPPOSED DISCOVERY OF TRINITY RIVER.

Some twenty miles north of the bay they discovered a river entering the ocean, which they supposed to be the Trinity. They were on shore eight days and were nearly starved, when the Laura Virginia arrived in the offing and was piloted in by the hungry explorers, being the first vessel to enter the harbor. She was soon followed by the James R. Whiting and California. The California sailed for San Francisco on March 28th, with news that the bay had been found and the Cameo supposed to be lost.

GREAT EXCITEMENT FOLLOWS THE DISCOVERY.

The reception of this news created great excitement, and a large number of vessels were at once advertised to sail for Trinidad with freight and passengers. The excitement caused by the return of the Gregg party was by no means confined to San Francisco, nor to expeditions by sea. A party left Napa Valley for Trinidad overland, early in April, followed soon by another. The following communication appeared in the Alta, April 10:—

"HO ! FOR TRINITY !

"MESSRS. EDITORS:—From the reports of persons who lately came into Napa and Sonoma Valleys from an exploration of the country around the Trinity, there remains no doubt of the great richness of the mines in that region. Already large bodies of practical and experienced miners are on the move in that direction. The mines are reached by an easy route, only 150 miles distant from the head of Napa Valley, in an almost northerly course, passing on the westerly side of Clear Lake, some five or six miles above the head of the lake, through a prairie gap to the head-waters of the Russian River, and thence by a good trail to a branch of the Trinity, where rich deposits of gold are found. By this route a large party, headed by Charles Hopper, left Napa Valley at the close of last month. Another party will leave Napa on the eleventh of the month by the Clear Lake road, among whom are John Walker and that old mountaineer, Aaron Adams.   Yours, etc.,   J. W. B."

DISCOVERY OF HUMBOLDT BAY BY SEA.

On the twenty-ninth of March, 1850 the day after the California sailed from Trinidad with the news of its discovery, Capt. Douglass Ottinger, of the Laura Virginia, also weighed anchor and sailed from the harbor to see what else he could find. A few days later he discovered and entered a fine bay a few miles to the south which he named Humboldt, after the renowned traveler, and located the town of Humboldt.

We are indebted to Dr. Jonathan Clark for the following interesting scrap of Humboldt history, which he furnished for publication in 1870, in the Northern Independent:—

"SAN FRANCISCO, Cal., April 25, 1850.
"To the Hon. Wm. M. Meredith, Secretary of the Treasury—

"SIR: Although on furlough, yet I feel that when I can give what I believe to be useful information to the Department, it is my duty to do so, and therefore take the liberty of sending you a brief report of my late voyage for the purpose of exploring the coast of California from Bodega Bay to the anchorage at Cape St. George.

"I sailed from this port in command of the schooner Laura Virginia, with a party of gentlemen, for Trinity Bay, and also to make examinations for the mouth of Trinity River. The schooner under my command being well adapted for coasting, gave me considerable advantage over the numerous vessels that had preceded me, and no doubt contributed much to my ultimate success.

"During the first two days of my voyage, the weather was thick, and our progress slow; but from Pinnacle Rock, in latitude 39° 07', I had an opportunity of seeing most of the shore. The timber begins to show itself some distance to the south of Pinnacle Rock, and as we proceeded north, became more dense, and the trees nearer to the ocean. The coast, generally, is rocky, but safe for the purposes of navigation, as all danger seemed to show itself. The sea-breeze blows from the northwest, but not regular, and comes in generally about 11 A. M., and ceases at 5 P. M., which renders the coast particularly well suited for steam navigation, as it is almost calm, within four miles of the land, eighteen hours in the day; and the further we went north, the less regular we found the northwest trade

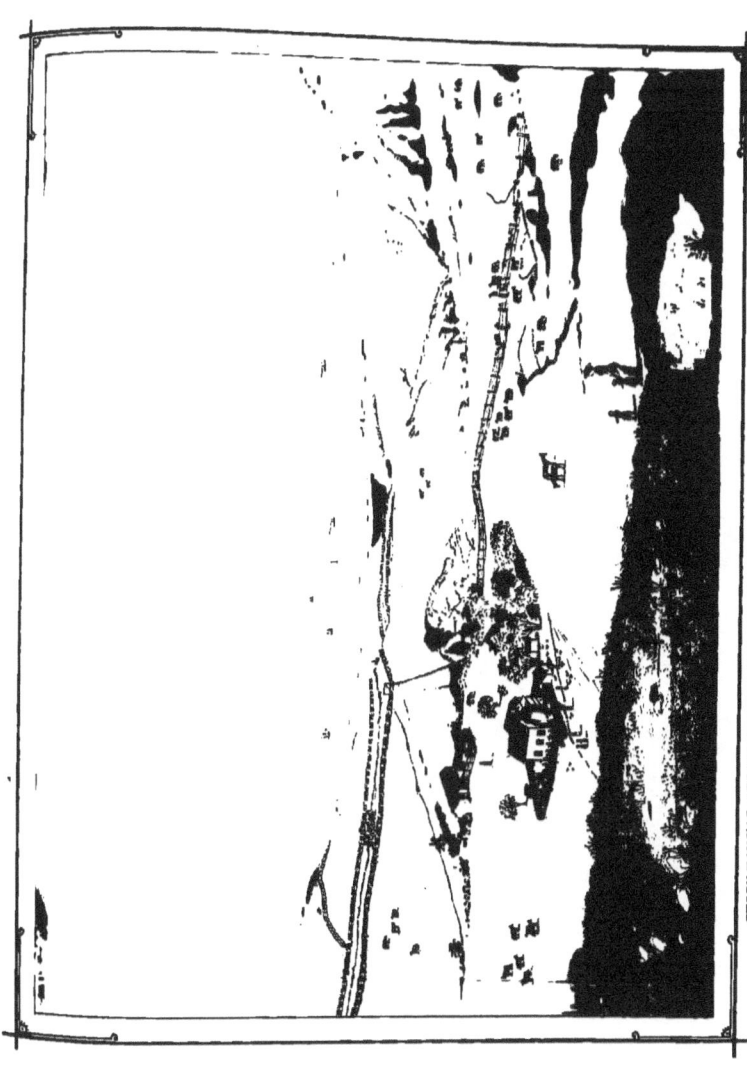

STOCK RANCH & RES. OF DOMINGO ZANONE, 5 MILES FROM PETROLIA & CAPE MENDOCINO LIGHT HOUSE, HUMBOLDT CO. CAL.

winds. After passing Cape Mendocino about six miles, which is in latitude 40° 20', the land trends to the eastward, and forms a considerable indentation or bay with a valley of some ten or fifteen miles in width, and running back as far as the eye could reach.

DISCOVERY OF EEL RIVER.

"We now ran along within half a mile of a low sand beach, upon which the sea was breaking heavily, expecting to find a river of considerable magnitude from such topography, and soon had the satisfaction of seeing a large stream winding its way among the woodlands.

"I spent two days in sounding and waiting for a smooth sea to get over the bar, latitude 40° 41', and finally attempted it, but had the misfortune to upset one of our boats, by which accident a valuable life was lost. I was in the other boat, and succeeded in saving the remaining gentlemen composing the crew. I was satisfied, however, that my vessel could enter with safety, but the great difficulty which presented itself was to get her out, for there seemed a heavy and constant run of breakers at its mouth, sufficient to render a sail craft unmanageable. I have since been informed by persons competent to judge, that this river is navigable for forty or fifty miles, and that it passes through a section of country diversified with hill and valley, woodland and prairie, with a soil so rich and deep that ages of culture will not exhaust it.

FIRST VIEW OF THE BAY.

"We again stood to the northward, and after passing a headland, which I have named Ridge Point, I noticed that the country continued open near the ocean, and from the masthead discovered inside of a sand bank a large bay but no clear entrance showed itself. I was, however, of the opinion that so large a sheet of water must have an outlet of considerable depth; and from the anchorage at Trinity Bay, latitude 41° 03' 55", a party was dispatched overland on the 4th of April to examine the topography on the shores of the bay, and to gain some knowledge of the channel." The adventures of this party were written for our history by one of the company.

FIRST VESSEL ENTERS THE BAY.

"On April 8th they returned to Trinidad Bay, and I again proceeded to the entrance of the large bay, latitude 40° 48', and after sounding the bar and channel, sent in my boats and landed a party—did not find less than four fathoms of water on the bar, which, after crossing, deepened to ten fathoms. I spent two days in sounding the depth of the water, and examining the capacity of this beautiful bay, which is about sixteen miles in length, and from one to five in breadth, with safe anchorage for two or three hundred sail of ships. Latitude of the point where our first tent was pitched, 40° 42' 30".

"In both the northern and southern parts of the bay there are extensive flats, dry at low water, but the country surrounding its shores has been pronounced by persons competent to judge as possessing in the highest degree all that is requisite for a flourishing agricultural district, as well as to furnish timber for all the cities in California. And so far as appearance goes it is one of the most beautiful sections of country that I have ever looked upon, being well watered and possessing as much prairie as would probably be needed for culture for some years.

"The woods abound with elk, deer, and small game, and the water with shell and other fish. In addition to the advantages above mentioned, its proximity to the rich gold mines on the Trinity River will doubtless give it some immediate commercial importance; and, under this belief, I have taken the liberty of making this report to the head of the Department to which I am attached.

"I would further state that, so far as I have examined the line of country bordering on the sea-coast, it appears to be well adapted to agricultural purposes. The timber is of the most abundant and stupendous growth, and streams of sufficient power and fall to drive large gangs of saws, emptying into the ocean within every three or four miles.

HARBOR OF CRESCENT CITY.

"I have examined with great care, the coast from Cape Mendocino to Cape St. George, at which last-named point I found a brig at anchor and a schooner ashore, having parted her cables in a gale. From persons on board these vessels, I first learned of the death of Lieut. R. Bache, and Lieut. R. Browning, U. S. Navy, and three other persons who were drowned by the upsetting of a boat whilst attempting to land through the surf. The body of Lieutenant Bache had been recovered and buried on the sand beach, but was removed from thence and reinterred on the high land by our party, the particulars of which I have written to his brother, A. D, Bache, Esq., Superintendent of U. S. Coast Survey. The land, timber, and streams at this point are nearly the same as those already described; but the anchorage is not good, as the bottom of the bay appears to be composed of quicksand. Latitude of same 41° 42' 23".

KLAMATH RIVER DISCOVERED.

"I would also mention a river of considerable magnitude in latitude 41° 33', with but little breakers on its bar, and not less than three fathoms, so far as I had an opportunity of sounding. This stream, I have no doubt, can be safely entered by vessels of fifty or one hundred tons, and rafts of timber floated to ships, outside where the anchorage is good, and the current strong from the river at three-quarters of a mile from the beach. In about latitude 41° 19' there is also a considerable stream, but not of sufficient magnitude for commercial purposes, further than rafting down timber. The lands in the neighborhood of all these rivers appear to be of the highest character for agriculture, and the coast by no means dangerous to navigate.

"The Indians, though numerous, appear to be harmless, except their propensity to pilfer, and they received us kindly at every point we visited. The climate so far as I could judge, is quite temperate even in winter, although the second range of mountains, which are in some places within twenty miles of the coast, were covered with snow on the 20th instant. One circumstance which influences me in coming to the conclusion that the temperature is very low on this part of the coast, is, that the Indians are almost without clothing of any kind to protect them from the inclemency of the weather.

"I have the honor to inclose herewith a sketch of the bay and her harbor, which we have named, "Humboldt."

"I am, very respectfully, sir, your obedient servant,

"DOUGLASS OTTINGER,
"Captain U. S. R. Marine."

The following detailed account of the movements and discoveries of the party sent out by Lieutenant Ottinger, has been prepared for our history by E. H. Howard Esq., Commander of the party.

THE CRUISE OF THE "LAURA."

The Laura Virginia Association was one of the first organized for the exploration by water and settlement of the coast north of the Golden Gate. Its members were mostly citizens of San Francisco, who projected the enterprise with a view of obtaining a more thorough knowledge of that portion of the coast belonging to our newly acquired territory on the Pacific, but having special reference to the selection, if possible, of some point with harbor advantages as a depot for the distribution of merchandise for the mining districts of northern California—a largely productive mining field already occupied, and being developed with a promise of permanent returns, to a population still more numerous, for many generations to come.

WEAVERVILLE THE MINING CENTER.

At this time, Weaverville was a young but flourishing mining camp, with a population, approximately stated, of 4,000, and situated in a basin on the Trinity River, about ninety miles from the coast. Its subsequent history entitled it to rank as one of the most productive "gold centers" in the State. Lying farther north were other regions of mineral wealth, on Salmon and Klamath Rivers, making an aggregate population in the northern part of the State, of 15,000. To these distant localities the transportation of supplies was chiefly carried on by the way of Red Bluff, at the head of Sacramento Valley, and thence by pack-mules over a succession of different mountains, and swarming with hostiles.

To divert the present large and prospective trade of this part of the State into a more economical and expeditious channel by the coast, as well as to open an easier route to travel for any who, for settlement or adventure, might seek this ultimate frontier of civilization, seemed to the Company a sufficient warrant for the undertaking, especially when supplemented by the possible dividends that might drop into the purse of individual members. Private enterprise, purely in the interest of geographical discovery, or any scientific research, was not on the business programme of those days—certainly not on the "Laura's."

TITLE AND OBJECTS OF THE ASSOCIATION.

The Association adopted the prefix of "Laura Virginia," the name of a staunch Baltimore-built, rakish-looking craft, of 120 tons, which was chartered for the cruise, with Lieut. Douglass Ottinger (of U. S. Revenue Cutter *Frolic*) as Commander. Having a miscellaneous cargo of lumber and general merchandise, and provisioned for a two months' voyage, for about fifty passengers, the jaunty vessel, on the 10th of March, 1850, left the foot of Long Wharf for the " Heads," which were speedily passed, and soon only to be dimly outlined in the distance. The *Laura* was a splendid sailor, without a rival on the coast for speed; and her Captain, drilled to the thorough seamanship of the Revenue Marine, delighted in a charge that so admirably answered to his skill. When beyond Fort Ross his course was governed much by the appearance of the shore, not omitting, however, to lay close to such places as invited nearer inspection, or offered an approach either for landing or shelter. The dense fogs, lying low under the prominent coast ridges, effectually cut off from view their terminal shore-line, and proved an aggravating damper to observation. But now the skies became bright again, and the distant land looked happy. From below the higher mountain tops, the rounded hills threw out their shoulders to the sensuous sun-beams, stretching in graceful declivities to the shore.

Their sloping sides of verdure, in many places, were literally covered with deer and elk, which were easily seen without a glass, roaming or resting in the freedom of their native pastures.

CHARACTER OF THE COAST.

Point Gordon is now passed—next the scene is shifted—and, suddenly thrust out on the theatrical stage of waters, Mendocino stands before you, the boldest sentinel of the coast, to challenge the formality of a distant salute. So far as seen from the ship, the coast up to this latitude had shown neither break nor depression that indicated any considerable valley or affluent to the sea. But here the uniformity ended. Clearly profiled against the eastern sky, and retreating far to the interior, the mountains sweep grandly round to the north, forming an amphitheater of varied beauty of landscape in the foreground, and advancing to the coast again some forty miles to the north, terminate at Trinity Heads. Truly the hosts of Israel were not more impatient under the guidance of their grand old pioneer of Hebrew civilization, to the new fields of promise, than were the "Laura" party to reach what might prove to be their promised land. The time, however, was not yet. Breakers and rocks, sheeted with billows of foam, told plainly enough, "Keep off." At the same time, the fog came sweeping down the coast, and soon the Captain was standing out to sea, and the passengers, one by one, subsided to their close-packed quarters, in surly resignation or disgust.

For several weary days every prospect was shut out, and there was enforced imprisonment on the drizzled deck, or the dungeon-like dive below. To most of the passengers this was strongly suggestive of the horrors of the slave ship, in which piratical character the *Laura* was sailing, when, with all her ghastly cargo, she was captured by one of our cruisers off the African Coast, some years before, a fact that had but lately come to their knowledge. The blank sea was still more dismal as the spectacle of some formless, giant redwood, looming up in the mist, from whose broken, stubbed branches the scared sea-fowl would dart down with a shriek, and be seen no more, might readily be transformed, by fancy, into some storm-shattered hulk from whose skeleton spars the despairing crew leaped down to a watery grave. But dyspeptic dreams and bad weather at last came to an end.

The view was again unclouded. The ocean on every side was strewn with the fragmentary drift and grass of fresh-water affluents, whose turbid torrents were mixed with the sea to a distance of several leagues. These were the first unmistakable signs of any considerable stream whose entrance was near at hand, that the party had discovered. A field of tumbling, tumultuous breakers stretched far out from the shore, and seemed to forbid approach near enough to distinguish its low, uncertain outlines; and it was, on consultation, determined to extend the voyage further up the coast, and, returning, dispatch a party of explorers from Trinidad by land.

THE "LAURA" GOES UP THE COAST.

The *Laura* accordingly proceeded north to the bay, or roadstead, on which Crescent City is now situated, where, with a fearful ground-swell running, she swung to her straining cable for the first time since leaving San Francisco. Here it was learned from the Indians that a "big canoe" had, a few days before, visited the place, and, in trying to make a landing, several persons were lost.

A stroll to the south along the beach resulted in finding the body of one of the unfortunate party, which proved to be that of Lieut. R. Bache, of the U. S. Coast Survey, then lately assigned to duty on the Pacific. A plain coffin was prepared, and the remains were interred after the ritual service of the Protestant Episcopal Church, Captain Ottinger officiating.

The *Laura* now weighed anchor and stood for Trinidad, where, in a few hours, she was quietly lying in the roadstead. Among the volunteers for prospecting the coast from this point, as before agreed upon, E. H. Howard, who had the charge of this expedition, selected the following-named gentlemen, to wit: H. W. Havens, Samuel B. Tucker, H. Lamott, S. W. Shaw (artist), and Mr. Peeldes. Duly provided for the defensive against the assaults of either savages or hunger, the party took their march southerly along the beach, while the schooner was to keep in readiness near the shore until the tenth day therefrom, when, unless signaled before, she was to return, and take the detachment on board.

GREAT NUMBERS OF INDIANS.

Three or four hours' travel brought them to a muddy, angry stream, 150 yards in width, whose southern bank was lined with canoes, drawn up on the land, and numerous Indian rancherias. In a moment the approaching party were discovered, and yell answering yell rang out from the dark forest, bringing down, as if by magic, groups of its excited dusky denizens. Squaws, with their papooses, were seen scampering from their wigwams to the rear, while the bucks, panoplied with bows and well-filled quivers, with frantic gesticulations gathered on the bank in hasty pow-wow, as if debating whether the "wougas" strange apparition boded to them "intents wicked or charitable." In a figurative fashion the olive branch was held out to them across the dividing torrent, and tardily tokens of peace responded from the other shore, from which several canoes now struck out, dancing and whirling in the perfidious eddies, and each manned by two stalwart fellows, whose guttural explosives of "ugh!" "ugh!" kept time with the labored stroke of their paddles. After an exchange of quite a miscellaneous, if not intelligible stock of pantomime between the parties, the schedule price of ferriage was fixed, and the service duly performed "on time," though not without an attempt by the canoe party to divide their passengers, and take them across one at a time. To this arrangement the latter, for obvious reasons, made vigorous protest on the spot, and the diggers, with seeming reluctance, carried them as directed. Being now safely over, and in the midst of throngs of natives, curiously, if not treacherously bent, the little band applied themselves to the solution of the problem of making one-half dozen equal a dozen dozen. Their arithmetic proved equal to the emergency. It was soon figured out to their satisfaction that six white men, with each a rifle and revolver, with an unlimited supply of ammunition and brains, could face a thousand Indians. Yet they would have felt a little more confidence in their conclusion if they were once sure that the poor devils believed it also. Thanks to the superiority of race, the promises of the white man's logic at least might be taught on the object lesson theory.

Besides the fire-arms, as just intimated, we also carried a surveyor's compass. These must do duty for the occasion. The superstition of the red man, known always to be intense, must be reached through his senses by some striking device.

that, to their intellects, would seem a proof of gifts supernatural. The lesson is begun. The compass is opened in presence of an eager circle of bucks. They watch the needle trembling on its pivot and then settling to a perfect rest.

THE AWE-STRUCK SAVAGES.

The time had now come to carry out the role of "medicine man" (as we shall call our manipulator), and one of the party comes forward and begins his part, by moving the point of a knife blade around the disk of the instrument. The natives watch the needle's point follow with obedient impulse. The knife is withdrawn, and they see the needle flutter back to rest as before. Then our medicine man consults his compass, as if to learn what message it may tell him of all their thoughts, their secret plans and feelings toward their new visitors. Such, at least, he would have them understand had been whispered to him by the Wonder Spirit of the *Wuugo*, through the little glancing arrow that had turned round and round toward every part of the crowd, and taken account of its numbers and what it was intent on doing. Their curiosity has grown by this time into something akin to awe. The firearms, having been exposed to wet, needed fresh loading. Another trial might now be made upon their emotional natures.

Awe must be intensified into fear. A man's figure is drawn upon a huge redwood puncheon, and the next object lesson is begun. Bullet after bullet at sixty yards, crashed through the effigy tearing it off in splinters, and along the ground beyond.

Another shot at a passing flock of geese and a fluttering "honker," dropped with a thud upon the ground within a few feet of where they stand. To the mystery of knowledge has been added the mystery of power. For the present, intelligence has imposed on the credulity of superstition, and comes off master.

THEY DISCOVER HUMBOLDT BAY.

Leaving a few presents among what appeared to be the "big Injuns," the company proceeded on their way, keeping to the beach which was smooth and comparatively free from any chance surprise which the sand-hills on the east might afford the natives. Some of the latter followed for several miles, stealing from hillock to hillock on a parallel tract and now and then one could be seen with his head just raised above some distant drift of sand watching every movement of the party. Late in the afternoon might have been seen a veritable stampede, not from an enemy, nor of an enemy. Two who happened to be detached from the party and were some 200 yards in the lead, with a whoop that would have done credit to a Comanche, sprung to a brisk trot and then to a downright run, to the wonder of their companions in the rear. *They had caught sight of the entrance to Humboldt Bay*, as since called. Upon reaching it they threw themselves not on their knees, as some great discoverers have devoutly done, but flat on their stomachs beside the noble stream that was set out by a broad, smooth, clearly defined channel to the open sea.

After a moment's breathing, the first impulse was to sample its quality. It was somewhat turbid it is true, but was it fresh or salt? They thought it too much of the latter for drinking, and yet was fresh enough for the mouth of a river emptying into the sea, and a river they believed it to be.

Following the shore line inland this impression was strengthened by the general appearance of the opposite shore and seeming uniformity of width of the channel which stretched away to the northward. It then for the first time occurred to them that they had been for the last hour traveling unconsciously within a fourth of a mile from the stream ignorant of its existence and only separated from it by narrow patches of timber and low sand-hills. The upper and eastern bank was not visible on account of a heavy fog and to the south of the entrance for the same reason a few hundred yards limited the prospect in that direction. The party had now reached the ultimate point of their excursion and felt satisfied so far with its result. Camping over night near by where the present light-house stands and the site of an abandoned rancheria, on the morning of the next day, as little of the opposite land could be seen on account of the prevailing fog they took at once to the ocean beach and the same day arrived at Trinidad.

Fortunately on the next day the *Laura* was sighted close in, coming up the coast, and in a few hours their signal was answered, and the ship's boat was dispatched to take the party on board. The report of the expedition was hailed with every demonstration of joy and Captain Ottinger, without delay, put directly for the "entrance" of which such a favorable account had been given.

FIRST VESSEL TO ENTER EEL RIVER.

In the meantime another vessel, the *J. M. Ryerson* had followed the *Laura Virginia* from San Francisco and for a couple of days past had been in her company at this place. It was ascertained that her aim was to make a port at the mouth of what is now know as Eel River, five miles to the south of the *Laura's* objective point.

Captain Ottinger seemed to favor the impression of the *Ryerson* that he also was seeking the same entrance. Unfortunately, in carrying out this strategy, a boat manned by a volunteer crew from the passengers was swamped in the surf in attempting to go over the bar at the mouth of the river, and one of them was lost. N. P. Dupern, Esq., a gentleman since well known at the French Consulate in San Francisco, and in the business community of that city, was one of those rescued, having clung to the boat's bottom, with others, till another boat was sent to their relief. After a little game of fast and loose between the vessels near shore, the *Laura* playing the "make believe," but the *Ryerson* in dead

"BROOK FARM" OF MRS. G. FRANCIS, FERNDALE, HUMBOLDT CO. CAL. 1882.

"BAY MILL" & RESIDENCE OF DOLBEER & CARSON, EUREKA, CAL. CONSTRUCTED, 1878.
CUTTING CAPACITY, PER DAY 60,000.
" " YEAR 8,580,000.
" SHINGLE " 2,800,000.

earnest, to get into the river first the latter saw her opportunity, put her bows straight for the bar, which, after some fifty floundering in the breakers, she safely passed, and was soon seen at anchor in smooth water.

FIRST VESSEL ENTERS HUMBOLDT BAY.

Having got rid of his competitor, Captain Ottinger now lays directly for the channel on the north, and wind and tide being favorable, crosses the bar, which was smooth with three and one-half fathoms of water, and, without scarcely a variation of course, passes in between two low headlands, and, keeping to the south, anchors within cable length of what is now called Humboldt Point, April 9, 1850."

Many other parties visited this region at that time, and made numerous explorations and discoveries; among the most important were the following vessels and parties.

EXPLORATION OF EEL RIVER.

Late in March, 1850, Selim Franklin, C. E. Gordon, Captain McDonald and G. Chandler, with two sailors, left San Francisco in a whale boat in search of Trinidad. Early in April they came to the mouth of Eel River, which they supposed to be the Trinity. The schooner *Jacob M. Ryerson* appeared a few hours later, and the two companies united in exploring the stream a distance of forty miles, finding deep water. A town was laid out, and some of the men went overland to Trinidad to get goods that had been shipped to that point. Franklin returned from there to San Francisco to procure supplies and to advertise the new town, which he did by assuring every one that the river led direct to the mines, though he had no evidence of the fact beyond his hope that it was true.

SECOND DISCOVERY OF EEL RIVER.

A few days prior to this, however, Eel River had again been discovered and named. Samuel Brannan had fitted out the schooner *General Morgan*, commanded by his brother John, and on the 5th of April, 1850, anchored off the mouth of Eel River, the *Laura Virginia* also coming to anchor there. Two boats, each commanded by a Brannan, entered the river which they named Brannan River, followed by a boat from Ottinger's vessel, which was swamped in the surf and Julius S. Rowen drowned. The *Laura Virginia* then sailed north and found and entered Humboldt Bay, as before mentioned.

The Brannans explored the river some distance, and the next day crossed a neck of land at the foot of a high bluff, which they named Brannan Bluff (Table Bluff), dragging their boat after them, and entered Humboldt Bay. To this they gave the name of Mendocino Bay, after the cape not far distant, apparently forgetting to apply the name Brannan to it also. They rowed to the head of the bay and then walked along the coast to Trinidad, where R. A. Parker and his company received them hospitably.

ATTEMPT TO START A CITY

Parker had entered Trinidad with the schooner *James R. Whiting*, accompanied by Charles C. Southard, of the Gregg party, J. C. Campbell, living at Etna, Frank Lemmon, Thomas J. Roach, Robert Atherton, Myers, a surveyor, and William Hawks. This party had commenced to lay out a city, and invited Brannan's company to unite with them. This was done; and all was harmonious until the question of a division of lots was raised, and then there was trouble. Parker's party was much smaller than the other, and wanted half the lots, while Brannan insisted they should be divided in proportion to the number of men. The controversy ended in Brannan getting very angry, swearing considerably, and he was an artistic swearer, and taking his departure with his whole company, and thus the only capitalist in both parties was driven away. He went to Point St. George and then to San Francisco in disgust. Members of his company decided to start a town on Mendocino (Humboldt) Bay and cut a canal through to Brannan (Eel) River, which was to be their highway to the mines.

THE CITY OF WARNERSVILLE.

The following letter from Captain Warner, taken from the *Alta* dated at Trinidad Bay, April 10, 1850, gives an idea of the situation of the new town on Trinidad Bay.

"I arrived here to-day in the brig *Isabel*; immediately went on shore and laid out part of a town. I surveyed about ten fifty-vara lots, taking R. A. Parker's south base line for my north line and his west lines for my west lines, bordering on the Indian village to the east, and running down to the water. I immediately built a house, and erected the American flag some sixty or seventy feet above the hill. This hill or knoll I intended for an observatory.

"We have called our location Warnersville. Below we have a fine valley, dotted with many fine trees and a fine soil. Already we have made many improvements, put up several houses and made a road to the hill. This place we call Isabel Valley, at which we have left some men to improve in our absence. Trinidad possesses a fine climate and soil adapted to cultivation. As yet we have not learned the correct distance to the mines, but believe it to be about forty miles.

HOUSES ERECTED AND OFFICERS ELECTED.

"Improvements are progressing with the utmost rapidity. Mr. R. A. Parker put up the first house, Mr. Van Wyck the second, and myself the third. We had an election on the 13th, and chose an Alcalde, Second Alcalde, and Sheriff. We polled 140 votes. What do you think of that for a town three days old? This place has fine streams of good fresh water.

"A party of Canadians have just arrived, consisting of fourteen men and two females, with sixteen fine pack horses. They bring flattering news from Trinity River. This place abounds with all kinds of game and fine woodlands. The bay is a good harbor with all winds except south and south-west; those blow directly into the harbor. The correct latitude of the bay is 41° 5′ 56″.

"We found a number of Indians but they are inclined to be peaceable. Bark *Galinda* lost three passengers, brig *Arabian* five, and schooner *General Morgan* one. These men were lost in landing in the breakers below the port.

"Yours, CAPTAIN R. V. WARNER.
"Of brig *Isabel.*"

Captain Warner was mistaken about the men lost, for it was the *Laura Virginia* and not the *General Morgan* that lost a man off the mouth of Eel River. The five men lost by the *Arabian* were Lieutenant Bache, United States Navy, Lieutenant Browning, United States Navy, John H. Peoples, W. W. Cheshire, and John Purdy, their boat being capsized in the surf, four miles below Point St George. Besides these disasters the *Paragon, Eclipse* and several other vessels ran aground on the bar at the entrance of Humboldt Bay, or else were stranded in the surf off Trinidad. This, with the supposed loss of the *Cameo*, made quite a string of disasters, and gave rise to the following briny yarn, whose author is unknown, the *Alta* publishing it June 14, 1850. The *Cameo* did not meet the watery grave it was supposed to be resting in at the date the "machine" ground out the following doggerel.

THE LEGEND OF THE CAMEO;
—OR—
THE PHANTOM BRIG.

RESPECTFULLY DEDICATED TO SIR ROBERT RIDLEY.

'Twas many years ago,
  In San Francisco Bay,
A vessel called the *Cameo*
  With many others lay;
For stories of our golden sands
  Had spread throughout the world,
And vessels there from every land,
  Lay with their sails unfurled.

Full many a mountain steep was scaled,
  And many a rock was cleft;
Some few found gold, but many failed,
  And were of life bereft;
But death and danger still were spurned,
  The tide still onward rolled,
And all creation was upturned,
  In that mad search for gold.

Ere long the country was o'errun,
  And gold could not be had,
And many people then began
  To talk of 'Trinidad';
And some affirmed that they had seen
  A man, who heard one say
He knew a person who had been
  In sight of that same bay,
And that some forty miles from there,
  He dug ten thousand pounds
Of gold, and any one might share
  Who'd go and ship it round.

The story spread, like any lie,
  A party sailed in haste,
But soon returned—the reason why,
  They could not find the place.
Sir Robert Ridley then did swear

That he was bound to go,
  And he would carry people there
In the old *Cameo.*

The victims rushed their fare to pay,
  For Robert did them tell,
That he would surely "find the bay,
  Or run the brig to h—l";
And which of these two things he did
  Will soon appear before ye,
If ye will but take pains to read
  The rest of this true story.

The day of sailing came at last,
  And all were there on board;
The sails were set and soon they passed
  The outmost point of land.
The grog was good, they all felt gay,
  And all things promised well;
Says Bob, "We'll either find the bay,
  Or run the brig to h—l."

One day they came in sight of land;
  A party went on shore;
But none of all that lucky band
  E'er saw the *Cameo* more;
But many a sailor tells a tale
  Of the old *Cameo's* host,
Doomed to the end of time to sail
  Along the northwest coast.

Long days, and weeks, and months passed on
  The *Cameo* ne'er came back;
A schooner, called the *Paragon,*
  Was started on her track;
For still the golden fever raged,
  And people were so mad
As ships and pilots to engage.
  To go to Trinidad;
And all along that rocky shore,
  Where'er a boat could land,
Some one would start a canvas store,
  And a large city plan.

The *Paragon* had sailed some time,
  When one morn, just at light,
The wind being fair, the weather fine,
  A vessel hove in sight;
And with a glass they did discern,
  What much they wished to know,
Her name, for upon her stern
  It was, the *Cameo.*

The men on board the *Paragon*
  Gazed on the brig with fear,
And as they slowly moved along,
  Each moment drawing near,
And saw the strange, unearthly look
  Of vessel and of crew,
Their limbs as with an ague shook,
  And pale their faces grew;
For in those forms that looked so wan,
  These pale and death-like faces,
They recognized full many a man
  They'd seen in other places.

Sir Robert soon the schooner hailed,
  And wished to know her name,
Where she was bound and when she sailed,
  And from what port she came;
And when the answers all were given,
  He cried in accents sad,
"There is no harbor under heaven
  Called 'Bay of Trinidad.'"

And sighs, and groans and shrieks were heard,
  As down from mortal view,
Beneath the wave they disappeared,
  That phantom brig and crew;
And while they gazed in sore dismay,
  There rose a sulph'rous smell,
And loud was heard "We'll find the bay,
  Or run the brig to h—l."

That night the schooner anchored near,
  And there arose a gale,
Which gave the crew new cause of fear,
  And made stout hearts to quail;
For ragged rocks were all around,
  'Gainst which the waters roared,
Which certainly was not a sound,

> To comfort those on board;
> And all prepared to meet their fate,
> And thought that hope was vain,
> And thronged upon the deck to wait
> The parting of the chain.
>
> The schooner trembled like a reed,
> Then with an awful shock,
> The chain gave way, and on with speed
> She hastened towards the rock.
> But cool and calm, devoid of fear,
> Did her bold captain stand,
> And clear of rock her course did steer
> Direct upon the sand.
> The crew were saved, but there she lays,
> Dismantled and forlorn,
> The prettiest schooner of these days,
> The famous *Paragon*.
>
> The brig *Arabian* next did meet
> The *Cameo* on the wave,
> And of her crew, ere sun had set,
> Five found a watery grave;
> For when the phantom brig appears,
> Most dire is the effect;
> The sight of her has been for years
> Forerunner of a wreck.
>
> But onward she is doomed to sail,
> Along the rock-bound coast,
> And when most loudly roars the gale,
> Is seen the *Cameo's* ghost;
> And then a voice is heard to say,
> With loud, unearthly yell,
> "By G—d, we'll either find the bay,
> Or run the brig to h—l."
>
> *May 1, 1850.*

The news that Trinidad Bay had been discovered spread like wild-fire, and a dozen expeditions began to fit out, a few by land but most of them by sea, some of them having members of the late exploring party connected with them, and some "going it blind" on general principles.

Besides the town of Humboldt, two others were laid out on Humboldt Bay in April, 1850, Eureka and Union, that became its rivals as well as Trinidad. During the same month the town of Reading was laid out on the Sacramento River by Major P. B. Reading, as a supply point for the Trinity Mines. During all this time the Trinity Mines were fast filling up by men from the Sacramento Valley. A number had wintered there, and as early as February they began to pour in across Trinity Mountain, settling generally on the North Fork. Many were induced not only to embark in the sea expeditions, but to hasten overland to the new mines, by such letters as the following in the Sacramento and San Francisco papers:—

"SACRAMENTO CITY, March 9, 1850.

"The latest news from Trinity is that seven men and two boys have just arrived in this city from there with $150,000. Mr. J. D. Baker, formerly proprietor of the Brannan House, is now in my office and tells me that he has seen the gold, which is in some forty large-sized bags. Mr. Moran, one of the party, has deposited his portion at Mr. Lee's store (formerly Priest, Lee & Co.), of this city. The party left here in the latter part of December, 1849. Two of the men are from New York, two from New Jersey, and the others from Oregon. Beat this from the southern mines if you can.

"When communication was opened between the new towns on the coast and the mines, which was not effected until May, there were about 2,000 miners on the river.'"

MIXED TOPOGRAPHY STRAIGHTENED

It did not take long then to get the topography of the country straightened out. It was found that Eel River was by no means a highway to the mines, and that both Trinidad and Humboldt Bays were of little use to the miners on Trinity River, who could communicate more easily and cheaply with the Sacramento Valley than with the sea. It was also found that the Trinity River, whose eccentric course had so deceived the early prospectors, did not enter the ocean at all, but was simply a tributary of the Klamath. To see how this became known we must go back a little.

Among those who wintered on the Trinity were Robert O. Shaw, James Chick, Samuel Jackson and Julius Holtzwart. These men started down the river on the 1st of March, 1850, intending to go to its mouth in a canoe. They had progressed some thirty miles, when the canoe overturned, and all but Shaw were drowned. Thus was the knowledge of the location of Trinity and Klamath Rivers delayed till they were entered from the sea in April. On the 3d of April Captain Ottinger of the *Laura Virginia* had discovered the mouth of the Klamath, but could not enter it. He located it in 41° 33' and supposed it to be the Rogue River, as he considered it too far north for the Trinity. Fremont had given the latitude of the Klamath at its source as 42° 27', and for this reason it was supposed to lie much farther to the north, in Oregon.

DISCOVERIES MADE BY THE CAMEO.

When the *Cameo* was driven from off Trinidad in March and supposed to be lost, she proceeded to Point St. George, near Crescent City and landed a part of the passengers consisting of B. W. Bullett, Herman Ehrenberg, J. T. Tyson, A. Heepe and Mr. Gunns, explored the coast to the south on foot, and on the 10th of April reached the Klamath, which they supposed at first to be the Trinity. They explored the river up beyond the mouth of the Trinity, and parties coming down that stream soon settled the identity of both rivers. A few miles above the mouth of the Klamath they took up 160 acres of land each, on the south bank, and then started down the coast for Trinidad. They reached that place on the 13th and told of the discovery of the river.

KLAMATH CITY LAID OUT.

A number of others of the *Cameo* returned with them to lay out the new town, which they called Klamath City. Here they learned the fate of five others of the *Cameo* party who had followed them down from Point St. George in a boat. They had been upset in the surf and four of them drowned, Eugene Du Bertrand alone being rescued by an Indian.

This river was variously called Rogue, Chester, Trinity and

Klamath, the latter name being found the correct one. A party explored it for a long distance in May, passing the mouth of of the Trinity, and returning the same month, have been driven out by hostile Indians. Miners on Upper Trinity River, with their usual restlessness, pushed down that stream, and thus settled the much-mooted point of where the mouth of the river was. Prospecting parties up the Klamath and others down the Trinity soon set at rest all doubt as to the location and names of the two streams.

Klamath City had but a brief and inglorious career. It was soon discovered that the shifting sands at the mouth kept so incessantly altering and obstructing the channel, that it was a matter of considerable uncertainty when a vessel could enter, and when once inside it was just as uncertain when it could get out again. No sooner was this fact realized than the people, to use an expressive phrase, "slid out," and the beautiful metropolis, with its projected parks, boulevards and institutions of learning became again a mountain wild, and so remains at the present time.

RIVAL TOWNS ON BOTH BAYS.

The towns of Trinidad and Humboldt Bays vied with each other in their endeavors to secure trade and travel. Every issue of the San Francisco *Alta* contained letters from both, lauding their advantages to the skies and decrying the rivals. The Humboldt people said that Trinidad Bay was not a safe harbor, in fact, no harbor at all, while the Trinidad proprietors asserted that a vessel could pass neither in nor out of Humboldt Bay in safety, because of the bar at the entrance. Both claimed to be nearest to the mines and to have the best road to them, and they also both claimed to be doing all the business that was done.

The fact was that neither of them was in a situation favorable to do much business with the mines on Trinity River, but the discovery of gold on the Klamath, Salmon, and Scott Rivers during the spring and summer, to which region they were the most accessible points, saved them from wasting away like a plucked rose.

RICH DIGGINGS ARE FOUND.

Early in June a number of men crossed the ridge from the north fork of the Trinity and came upon the south fork of the Salmon River, which they followed down to the forks and there struck rich diggings. Several hundred men collected there and spread up the north fork, working at various points along the stream. During the same month a party consisting of Rufus Johnson, James Duffy, —— Van Duzen, —— Dollarhide and a number of others, went on an exploring expedition up the Klamath from its mouth. They proceeded about as far as Happy Camp, when the Indians became so hostile they had to turn back. Leaving the river they struck across the mountains and reached the forks of Salmon River.

PROSPECTING UP THE KLAMATH.

They related wonderful stories of the richness of the bars on the Klamath River, asserting that a man could make two ounces a day. This was enough. A company of some forty men was formed to go on a prospecting tour on the Klamath, in search of two-ounce diggings.

The party left the forks of the Salmon in July, and struck across the country in a northwesterly direction, reaching the Klamath, which there runs nearly south, a distance above the mouth of Salmon River. Their first move was to cross the stream to the west side, which they did by making a raft of two logs, secured by a lariat, upon which their effects were placed, and which they pushed across the stream, the men and stock swimming. This method of transportation was used in all their frequent crossings of the river. They had secured a Klamath Indian or two for guides, being able to maintain an aggravating and uncertain conversation with them by means of the Chinook jargon, with which they were all slightly familiar. They then started up the stream, following an Indian trail, knowing that the best routes would there be found, sometimes going directly away from the river, across a spur of mountains, but always getting back to it again. Their Indian guides would go with them as far as the limits of the range of their tribe or band and then stop, but others soon appeared in camp.

Major Cook, probably to be provided for any emergency, was driving along a good fat steer, but one day it commenced rolling down a steep declivity, and when it reached the bottom it was quickly resolved from steer into minced beef, being left for the Indians to regale themselves upon, if they chanced to find it. In this way they passed up the stream, prospecting in a superficial and unsatisfactory way all the bars and streams they passed, frequently crossing the river for that purpose, and always getting "color," but never finding any two-ounce diggings. One noon they camped a little more than half a mile below Scott River, and a few of them swam over to Hamburg Bar, where were congregated a large number of Shasta Indians, with whom they talked and visited. After prospecting a little on the bar, they returned to camp, and the company resumed its journey. All are familiar with the bend in the river where Scott River empties into it, and it will be readily understood how, in following the trail over the spur of the mountain, around which the river makes a broad sweep, they missed seeing Scott River, although passing within half a mile of its mouth.

The next day near Oak Bar, where they also prospected, they lost a man by means of the Indians, and after that had considerable difficulty with them, the details of which will be given in another place. The highest point reached was a mile above the mouth of the Shasta River. Here they were overtaken and joined by the party of Rufus Johnson, which had been

RESIDENCE OF MRS. A. MONROE, COR OF E AND 9TH STS. EUREKA, CAL.

reorganized, the united company being above sixty strong. They then crossed to the south side, and started for Shasta Valley, a glimpse of which they had obtained from the opposite hills. As the beautiful valley with its wealth of tall, waving grass and its snow-crowned king, grand old Shasta, opened before their vision, it seemed like a veritable Garden of Eden, so different was it from the rugged and precipitous mountains through which they had been passing. After considerable prospecting they finally settled down for the winter at Middletown, where were also quartered hundreds of others, who penetrated this region the next spring.

EXPLORATIONS OF KLAMATH AND TRINITY.

Rufus Johnson went down the Klamath and reorganized his party, and again started up the stream. At the mouth of the Trinity he fell in with Charles McDermit, Abisha Swain, John W. Burke, Stevens, Charles D. Moore, and Buck, who went with him as far as the mouth of the Salmon, where they stopped to mine, while the Johnson party continued up the Klamath. They prospected in a number of places, and finally came to Scott River and did a little work there. In this party of some forty men there were Rufus Johnson, Dollarhide, Duffy, Snyder, and Van Duzen. They left Scott River and continued up the Klamath, overtaking and joining the Jones and Bean party near the mouth of Shasta River.

But a few days after the departure of Johnson's party from Scott River, a small company of men from the forks of Salmon, led by John Scott, arrived there and went to work, the place being named by them Scott Bar. They had, however, worked here but a short time when the Indians made such hostile demonstrations as to induce them, being few in number, to abandon the river.

They went up the stream to the valley, and then over the divide to the north fork of Salmon, and thence over to Trinity where the news of their discovery soon spread and several parties were organized to find the river, some of them led by members of the Scott party. Some of this company went to Trinidad and others to Reading's Springs, and in this way the fame of Scott Bar was rapidly spread abroad, and as it was considered dangerous to winter in the mountains many made a silent resolve to go to Scott Bar early in the spring as was safe.

A few days after Scott's party was chased off the river Jesse J. Pool was working on the north fork of Salmon River, when an Indian, arrayed simply in a breech-clout, appeared before him and opened a conversation in Chinook, which Pool could not understand. "Close tum tum," said he, smiting himself on the breast and smiling in a winning way, "Boston man, Hi you, Shasta," pointing over the mountains to the northeast. Seeing that he was not fully understood, he took Pool's pan, put in some small stones and began shaking the implement as if washing dirt, all the time laughing and saying, "Hi you Boston man. Hi you, Hi you, Shasta." Pool decided that he was trying to tell him there was a party of white men mining on Shasta River, and that they were finding coarse lumps of gold. That there was such a river as Shasta, all the miners knew, and they expected to find it to the east, in fact when Salmon River was first found it was supposed to be the Shasta. He is satisfied that the Indian referred to Scott's party on Scott Bar, and by "Shasta" meant over towards Mount Shasta. He told his partner, Moses Dusenberry, what he thought, and they went up the stream a short distance and got eleven more to join them in a trip over the mountains. A careful search revealed a fresh trail. This they followed into Scott Valley, where they were delayed three days by reason of Indians stealing some of their stock, and then continued on till they reached Scott Bar, where they found a party of about fifty men had arrived but the day before.

At the head of this company was Doctor Goodwin, and they had come direct from Trinity River, where they had been informed of the discovery here by some members of Scott's party. It was probably due to their coming over the trail that made the confusion of tracks. Doctor Goodwin, Pool, Dusenberry and ten others formed a company and put in a wing dam. This was just below the bridge on the opposite side from the present town of Scott Bar. They made hand-barrows of beef hides. From that time till the present day mining has been carried on unremittingly along Scott River.

THE GOLD BLUFF EXCITEMENT.

There is one other element that entered into the development of this region that must not be overlooked, and that is the Gold Bluff excitement. In the month of May, 1850, B. Nonlheimer, J. H. Stinchfield, Charles D. Moore, and a number of others, were going up the sea-shore from Trinidad to the new town of Klamath City, when they observed gold in the sand on the ocean beach. They took some of this, but it was so mixed with fine gray and black sand that they could do nothing with it. They passed on, and no attempt was made to work the sea-shore deposit. In the fall, J. M. Maxwell and —— Richardson went to the bluff and began operations. They soon found that it was but occasionally that the gold was visible. The bluff is several miles long and 400 feet high, with but few feet between it and the sea. In times of storm at high tide the surf beats against the bluff and washes down the quartz that partially composes it. The fine grains of gold that thus become mixed with the sand are sometimes brought to the surface by the action of the water, and sometimes buried out of sight. Maxwell and Richardson watched their opportunity, and when the glistening particles appeared on top of the sand, they filled buckskins bags with the mixture of sand and gold, and carried it back on the bluff to be worked over at their leisure. The gold was so fine and the sand so heavy that they only saved a small per cent of what the mixture contained.

MOST WONDERFUL GOLD STORIES.

News of the wonderful beach of gold went to San Francisco, and a company was organized, that chartered the steamer *Chesapeake*, to explore the place. She arrived off Gold Bluff on the 23d of December, 1850, and the next morning sent a boat ashore. This was broken up in the surf, but the occupants succeeded in reaching the beach in safety. The others, not wishing to land in such a damp and dangerous manner, sailed for the mouth of the Klamath, but could not cross the bar. They then returned to Trinidad and went up the coast on foot with pack-mules owned by J. C. Campbell. The *Chesapeake* then returned to San Francisco to report the success of the expedition. The *Alta California* contained the following, January 9, 1851:—

"A NEW EL DORADO.—We have been all along prepared to hear marvelous accounts of discoveries of gold; that it would be as abundant as lead seemed not altogether improbable; and we have looked forward to a time when a man would have to give a cart-load of the precious metal in exchange for a barrel of wheat. But there is nothing left for credulity now. The world has never heard of such wealth as lies on the shores of the Pacific.

"It is well known that the steamer *Chesapeake*, with about thirty adventurers, left this port on the 21st ultimo, for the Klamath, and in yesterday's paper we gave some account of her progress. Scarcely was our paper issued when the *Chesapeake* came into port, bringing back five or six of the 'prospectors,' Gen. John Wilson and John C. Collins, Esq., among the number. A meeting of the stockholders was called, to hear the result of the expedition, which meeting we attended, and if we can bring our ideas down to anything like reason after hearing the wonderful details, we will let the public into the secret.

GOLD BLUFF MINES.

"Twenty-seven miles beyond the Trinity, there is a beach several miles in extent and bounded by a high bluff. The sands of this beach are mixed with gold, to an extent almost beyond belief. The sands are of two kinds, a fine black sand and a gray sand. The gray sand can be separated very easily from the black sand, and this seems to be a desirable object. The gold is mixed with the black sand in proportions from ten cents to ten dollars to the pound. At times when the surf is high, the gold is not easily discovered, but in the spring of the year, after a succession of calms, the entire beach is covered with a bright and yellow gold. Mr. Collins, the Secretary of the Pacific Mining Company, measured a patch of gold and sand, and estimates it will give to each member of the company the snug little sum of $43,000,000, and this estimate is formed upon a calculation that the sand holds out to be one-tenth as rich as observation warrants them in supposing.

"The Pacific Mining Company (the adventurers of the Chesapeake have banded themselves together under this title) found some nineteen men at these diggings. The men had no disposition to dig, for the gold was all ready for them whenever they felt disposed to take it. Besides, such is the character of the roads, that they cannot take away more than seventy-five to 100 pounds apiece—an amount too trifling for their consideration. They had erected a comfortable log cabin, and designed watching this claim till spring, and then take a ship-load of the gold and travel to some country where the metal was not so abundant. Mr. Collins saw a man who had accumulated 50,000 pounds, or 50,000 tons—he did not recollect which—of the richest kind of black sand.

"General Wilson says that thousands of men cannot exhaust this gold in thousands of years, and he gives all who doubt his statements the liberty of going and ascertaining these facts.

"The company will send up 100 additional laborers as speedily as they can be embarked. They also design purchasing a steamer and running her up to the "Gold Bluffs." Sixty men are now at the scene of operations. We await with anxiety further reports. Numerous specimens of the sand and gold were exhibited to stockholders at the meeting last evening."

In addition to the long article in the *Alta*, Mr. Collins published two affidavits he had secured while at the wonderful beach. One was signed by M. C. Thompson and C. W. Kinsey, and the other by Edwin A. Rowe, both attested by L. B. Gilkey, Justice of the Peace of Trinity County. They spoke of the nature and richness of the beach, and Rowe's contained the following passage: "I am now, however, confident that with the proper arrangements for amalgamating the gold, on a scale as extensive as your company is capable of doing, millions upon millions of dollars can be easily obtained every year for more than a century to come."

A RUSH FOR THE GOLD BLUFFS.

The next day shares demanded a premium. On the 18th, the steamers *Chesapeake* and *General Warren* sailed for Gold Bluff, and a few days later the bark *Chester*. A great many companies were formed and vessels chartered to take them to the auriferous beach. Hundreds reached Trinidad *en route* to the bluff, but were met with the news that the gold could not be separated from the black sand, and that it was a waste of time and money to attempt it. Still many went to be convinced by experience, and when so convinced pushed on up the Klamath to the Salmon Mines. It was principally these adventurers, unprovided with supplies, who crowded into the Salmon country and produced the starvation times there. All efforts to work the beach on an extensive scale failed and were abandoned. Every year, however, a few men have worked there at a favorable season and made good wages, and they are doing the same at the present time; but how the "millions upon millions" have dwindled. The Gold Bluff Mines of later times will be more fully mentioned hereafter.

ORGANIZATION OF THE COUNTY.

The First Counties Organized; Rapid Increase of Population; Constant Change of Boundaries; Humboldt Organized; First County Seat Contest; First Courts, Officers, etc., etc.

The first election held in the State, in 1849, was not participated in by residents of this region, if any there were. At that time the State was not organized, and election precincts were established only in those interior towns and mining camps that had sprung into recognized prominence during the few short months that had elapsed since had begun that tumultuous rush for the gold-fields of California. As yet the venturesome foot of the prospector had not pressed the grassy carpet of these northern altitudes. Of those who were to become the founders of the county, some were in the early southern mines, some were toiling wearily westward, or tossing upon the heaving bosom of the ocean, eager to reach the land of gold and sunshine, while others were still in their eastern homes, with scarce a thought of that far-off land so soon to beckon them away.

Let no unmerited blot be cast upon the grand army of adventurers who reached these western shores and brought with them the foundations of our society, schools, churches, and homes, and here established a great State.

NORTHERN CALIFORNIA.

Upon the subdivision of the State into counties in 1850, Mr. Wathall, member of Assembly of the delegation from the Sacramento District, which included the Sacramento Valley to the Oregon line, proposed the names of Shasta and Trinity for the northern part of the State, which at that time included what is now Del Norte, Humboldt, Trinity, Siskiyou, Modoc, Lassen, Shasta, and a part of Butte County.

Our history must of necessity include the territory which was at one time Trinity, Klamath, and Del Norte.

For the purpose of explaining the changes which have taken place in the two northern counties of the State since its first organization, we present a series of diagrams. They will help to show the geographical changes which have taken place at different dates.

When the State was divided into counties by the Act of February 18, 1850, this region was a *terra incognita* to the legislators. The Trinity excitement was then at its height, but still little was known of that region, the population having progressed but little beyond the diggings on the Sacramento River and Clear Creek, and about Shasta, all the northeastern part of this territory was erected into one county called Shasta, with the county seat at Reading's Ranch. The northwestern part was called Trinity County, with the county seat at Trinidad, and the territory was divided as in the following diagram:—

NORTHERN CALIFORNIA IN 1850.

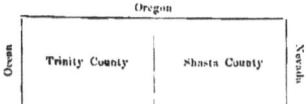

All that portion of the State lying west of Shasta County, and embracing what afterwards formed Trinity, Humboldt, Klamath and Del Norte Counties, was created Trinity County, but as it was yet a comparatively unknown region, it was attached to Shasta for judicial purposes. This action was taken because it was expected that a large population would soon be found on Trinity River and about the Bay of Trinidad.

KLAMATH COUNTY ORGANIZED.

Trinity County was divided in 1852. All south of a line due east from the mouth of Mad River being Trinity, and all north of that line Klamath County.

The California Legislature of 1850–51 provided for the organization of Klamath County, and ordered an election to be held on the second Monday in June, 1851. The act was approved on May 28, 1851, and R. A. Parker, W. W. Hawks, Edward Fletcher, Smith Clark and B. W. Dullitt, of said county, were appointed and constituted a Board of Commissioners to designate the election precincts for such election. The officers were duly elected and the county government took effect immediately after.

This act also reorganized Trinity County, and the territory assumed the following shape:—

NORTHERN CALIFORNIA IN 1851.

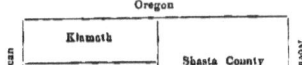

The Legislature appointed commissioners to designate election precincts and superintend the election. Five commissioners were appointed, none of whom were from what is now Trinity County; two were from Humboldt City, two from Eureka and one from Union (Arcata).

The following were the first officers elected for Klamath: County Judge, Dr. Johnson Price; District Attorney, William Cunningham; County Clerk, John C. Burch; Sheriff, Wm. H Dixon; Assessor, J. W. McGee; Treasurer, Thos. L. Bell.

A contest immediately arose as to the location of the county seat. By a famous poll book from a precinct called Simpson's Hole, which polled seventy-five votes for Eureka, it received a majority of the votes. But the Judge ordered a new election, and Weaverville became the victor. Some irregularity occurred at this election and another vote was had in the fall of 1852, but Weaverville was finally crowned the victor.

SISKIYOU COUNTY ORGANIZED.

When the Legislature met in 1852, it created several new counties in the State, and among others Siskiyou. So rapidly did the population increase in 1851, that it became absolutely necessary to form a new county. The county seat of Shasta was too far away, and the inconvenience of doing official business there was so great that the need of a new county was imperative. By Act of March 22, 1852, the County of Siskiyou was created and an election called for May 3, 1852, to select the first officers. Wilson T. Smith, H. G. Ferris, D. H. Lowry, Charles M. Tutt and Theodore F. Rowe were appointed commissioners under the act, to supervise the election and organize the county.

The commissioners held their meetings and canvassed the votes in the Verandah, the most popular saloon in Yreka, and seemed to give as much satisfaction as in the most elaborate temple of justice ever erected. The Act of Organization also provided for the assumption by Siskiyou County of its just proportion of the debt of Shasta County, contracted while it was a portion of that body. The territory now formed four counties as per diagram:—

NORTHERN CALIFORNIA IN 1852.

Oregon

| | Klamath | Siskiyou | |
|Ocean| Trinity | Shasta |Nevada|

The exact location of the boundary line between California and Oregon was not definitely determined upon until the fall of 1868, when the line was run by the surveyors of the United States Government. In a number of localities bordering upon the line, the collection of taxes had been for some time a matter of difficulty. The establishment of the line by the Government settled the point beyond all controversy, and monuments now mark the spots where the line crosses the traveled highways and other points of importance.

HUMBOLDT COUNTY FORMED.

By act of the Legislature, approved May 12, 1853, Trinity County was divided into two parts. The western portion was organized into Humboldt County, and the eastern part retained the name of Trinity. The Clerk of Trinity was required to restore to the Clerk of Humboldt County the books, records, maps and papers held by Trinity County, and the same became part of the records of Humboldt, including maps of the towns of Union (Arcata), Eureka and Bucksport. This change in boundaries made the territory into five counties as follows:—

NORTHERN CALIFORNIA IN 1853.

Oregon

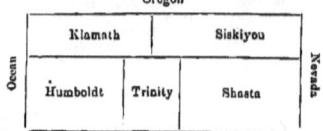

The act provided its boundaries shall commence at a point in the ocean three miles due west of Mad River, thence due east from the point of beginning to the Trinity River (this old line is shown on our county map) thence up the Trinity River to the mouth of Grouse Creek; thence south to the north line of Mendocino County, and thence to the ocean. This boundary was rather indefinite and caused considerable trouble as we shall see hereafter.

The territory cut off comprised all that part of Trinity County that lay between the south fork of the Trinity River and the coast, being "a strip some fifty or sixty miles along the coast of rough wooded country," as described at that time. The organization of Humboldt will be fully described in another place.

DEL NORTE COUNTY FORMED.

In 1857 the Legislature decided that there should be a new county formed with the county seat at Crescent City. Now begins the disintegration of Klamath which finally disappears from the map. Del Norte was formed from the northern portion of Klamath County, as per diagram:—

NORTHERN CALIFORNIA IN 1857.

Oregon.

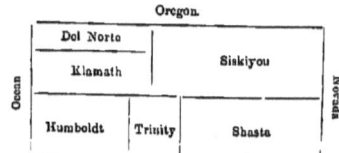

Officers of Del Norte were elected in May, 1857. The county was divided into three Supervisor Districts. The County Judge was to receive $1,000 per annum. The county was attached to Klamath for representative purposes, and to the 12th Senatorial District, and to the 8th Judicial District. It was first named "Buchanan," but the Committee on Counties and County Boundaries, to whom was referred a bill to establish the new county and define its boundaries, reported it back with the amendment, the name of the county, "Buchanan," be struck out and that "Del Norte" be inserted in its stead. Other names had been suggested. One was "Alta."

RES. OF CAP. H. H. BUHNE, EUREKA.

"MARY ANN BUHNE" EUREKA, CAL.

NE, HUMBOLDT CO. CAL.

ORGANIZATION OF HUMBOLDT COUNTY.

Another, "Altissima," as it was the farthest county north. Among others was the name "Rincon," and "Del Merritt." The boundaries embraced all the country on both sides of the Klamath River as high as a point five miles above the mouth of Indian Creek, and as far down that river as a point half-way between Clear Creek and Dillon's Creek, taking in Elk Creek and the mining country thereabouts; in fact including the points of Happy Camp, Elk Creek, Wingate's Bar, Spanish Bar, Clear Creek, Indian Creek, Forks of Smith's River, and Crescent City and the adjoining country.

U. B. Fremmer, J. T. Hayes, Peter Darby, H. B. Morford and P. H. Puveler were appointed a Board of Commissioners to divide the county into three Supervisor Districts.

KLAMATH BLOTTED OUT.

In 1874 Humboldt and Siskiyou Counties acquired the territory of "Old Klamath," and it no longer appears on our maps. In 1874 it was disorganized, divided, and attached to Siskiyou and Humboldt. Much the larger part was attached to the latter county, and at this date the territory of the original two counties has become seven counties, and one has disappeared.

NORTHERN CALIFORNIA IN 1874 AND 1882.

	Oregon			
Del Norte	Siskiyou		Modoc	
Humboldt	Trinity	Shasta	Lassen	Nevada

Ocean

In 1863 Lassen County was formed with Susanville as the county seat. Assemblyman Cressler introduced a bill in 1874, to create the new County of Canby, out of the east end of Siskiyou and the north end of Lassen.

The bill was defeated in consideration of the inability of Lassen County to spare any of its territory, and another bill to meet the requirements of the situation was immediately framed. This provided for the formation of the County of Summit out of the eastern portion of Siskiyou. In this shape the bill passed the Assembly and went to the Senate, where it was amended by changing the name to Modoc County, and then passed. February 17, 1874, it received the signature of the Governor and became a law.

ORGANIZATION OF HUMBOLDT COUNTY.

Until the exploring party of 1849, whose history has just been given as written by Wood, Humboldt County was unknown to the civilized race. The Indian roamed over its wilds, hunting, fishing and fighting as occasion required, fearless of anything save the grizzlies or a rival tribe.

Instead of following the usual laws of settlements of a new State, commencing at the frontier and pushing back regularly, the emigrants to this State scattered here and there—to the extremes as well as the center—in their wild pursuit after the rich treasures of the earth. There were no mountains too high and rugged, and no cañons too deep to interrupt their progress. Towns and settlements sprang up as by magic, and political organizations were soon demanded for proper government of the rapidly increasing population.

As has been already noticed, the search for the mines was the magnet which drew hither the bands of explorers who discovered and located the various points on the bay. The first trade was done wholly upon the Lower Trinity. Soon other places began to attract the floating population of miners. Settlements began to extend lower down the Trinity River and on to New River. The Klamath opened a new field for trade and enterprise, and its tributary, the Salmon, came next. On all these rivers the miners made from one to six ounces per day. The western portion of Trinity along the bay so increased in population that a new county was a matter of necessity and Trinity was made into two counties.

BOUNDARIES OF THE COUNTY.

The Act of May 12, 1853, organizing Humboldt County, provided that the line is "to commence at a point in the ocean, three miles due west of the mouth of Mad River; thence due east from the point of beginning to the Trinity River; thence up the Trinity River to the mouth of the north fork of said Trinity River, running along the eastern side of said north fork 100 feet above high water mark to the mouth of Grouse Creek, and thence in a due south direction to the fortieth degree of north latitude and thence west to the ocean, etc." These lines were somewhat indefinite and for a while considerable conflict of authority and double taxation occurred along the Trinity River and on the northern boundaries. But they were finally amicably settled by the lines being more definitely determined.

COUNTY SEAT CONTEST.

Very naturally there arose a great contest over the location of the county seat of the new county. Rival towns along the bay exerted themselves to the utmost to secure the coveted prize, and great bitterness of feeling was engendered as the contest deepened.

Union, as it was then called, was designated as the seat of justice. Bucksport and Eureka were not pleased, and became jealous rivals. At the first contest for location of county seat, the people of Eel River in conjunction with all the rural districts of that part of the county joined with Bucksport and supported that place for the location, but Union (Arcata) bore off the prize. The air was filled with charges of fraud and dishonest voting.

A petition containing over one-third of the voters of the county was readily obtained and application made for another contest, which was entered into with great zeal on both sides. An election to settle the matter by popular vote was called.

COUNTY JUDGE CALLS ELECTION.

Whereas a petition, signed by qualified electors of the County of Humboldt, equal to at least one-third of all the votes in the county at the last general election, has been duly presented to the undersigned County Judge of said county, praying for the removal of the seat of justice from the place where it is now fixed, and that an election be held to determine to what place such removal shall be made. Therefore, in pursuance of an act entitled "An Act to provide for the permanent location of Seats of Justice of the several counties," passed April 11, 1850, and of an act amendatory thereof, passed May 13, 1854, I do hereby give notice to the electors of Humboldt County, that an election will be holden on the 25th day of October, 1854, for the purpose of determining whether, and to what place the removal of the seat of justice of Humboldt County shall be made.

J. E. WYMAN,
County Judge, Humboldt County.
Dated September 14, 1854.

EUREKA CLAIMS COUNTY SEAT.

A meeting of the citizens of Eel River was held at the house of A. B. Liles on the 19th of September, 1854, with B. T. Jamison Chairman, and E. L. Dorris Secretary. It was resolved that the south end of the county was materially injured by the selection of Union Town, and "we the citizens of Eel River take this method of expressing our preference for Eureka." The following committee were appointed to issue an address: Messrs. L. W. Fish, E. L. Davis, J. N. Borden, B. J. Jamison and J. Burrell. In their address they say: "We believe Eureka will poll a greater number of votes for herself than Bucksport can possibly do for herself, and that Union Town will poll a greater number of votes in favor of that *delectable* village than at the last election. And now we ask you to consider whether you ought or not to join us in support of Eureka, and thus try once more to overbalance, by honest votes, the frauds which will—to judge by the past—inevitably be practiced in Union."

The citizens of Bucksport and vicinity pledged themselves that in case Eureka received at the first election a larger number of votes than Bucksport, that at the second election they would vote for Eureka, and *vice versa*, but the arrangement does not seem to have been carried out.

BUCKSPORT CLAIMS COUNTY SEAT.

A committee of citizens interested in giving the county seat to Bucksport, issued an address, in which they say:—

"That Bucksport is the most appropriate place for county seat in Humboldt County. It has the best town site, the best natural advantages for a commercial city, and by far the best water on the bay for shipping purposes. That it is the nearest central of any of the places proposed, and most accessible; that it will accommodate the citizens generally better than any other place, produce more general quiet, and that, when once established, will be far more likely to remain permanent than any other place on the bay; are facts of so general notoriety and so well established in the minds of most unbiased persons, that arguments to substantiate them are unnecessary."

In the *Humboldt Times* of October 14, 1854, is published a conveyance from Wm. Roberts to the committee for the purpose of laying such honorable motives before the public as shall secure the election of Bucksport for county seat.

Wm. Roberts agreed to convey by deed to the trustees named below, a large portion of his quarter section of land at Bucksport, on which is situated that most beautiful plateau overlooking the bay and ocean. The deed provided for surveying into lots fifty by one hundred feet, and that every citizen of the county outside of Bucksport precinct, *shall be entitled to a lot of that size for the nominal price of one dollar, if he support Bucksport for county seat,* and it he elected as such.

It provided also that the county be entitled to a choice block of land anywhere on his premises for county buildings, to be selected by the County Judge, or such commissioners as may be duly appointed. Signed by following committee:—

S. B. KNOX,   A. CALDWELL,
J. C. MARTIN, C. A. PINE,
A. J. HUESTIS, J. CLARKE,
WM. EDGAR.

October 21, 1854.

RESULT OF THE VOTE.

The result of the matter was that neither place received a majority of all the votes cast, as will be seen by the following table:—

	For Union.	For Bucksport.	For Eureka.
Union	205	16	
Eureka	3	13	389
Bucksport	14	221	1
Eel River	2	12	45
Table Bluff	1	12	26
Pacific	—	12	7
Angel's Ranch	25		
South Fork	60	1	1
Total	310	288	469

ANOTHER ELECTION ORDERED.

It became the duty of the County Judge under the law, to select the two towns obtaining the highest vote, and to order another election. Union and Eureka therefore became the contestants, and the following notice of a new election was given:—

"It appearing to me, from the certificate of Lewis K. Wood, County Clerk of Humboldt County, that no particular place received a majority of all the votes cast at the election held on the 25th ult. for the purpose of determining whether and to what place the county seat shall be removed, and that the towns of Eureka and Union received the greatest number of votes at said election, I do hereby order that a new election be held on the 20th of November, 1854, to determine which of said places, Eureka or Union, shall be the county seat."

J. E. WYMAN, *County Judge.*

Dated November 4, 1854.

Each of the rival candidates went actively at work for a final contest. It was charged by people of Union that every precinct except theirs, cast illegal votes. That soldiers voted at Bucksport; sailors at Eureka; Klamath County miners at South Fork, and foreigners at Angel's Ranch.

In the meantime, as will be seen by the number of votes cast, that the population of the county had rapidly increased since the last vote was taken.

RESULT OF THE SECOND VOTE.

	For Union.	For Eureka.
Union	429	5
Eureka	6	1,713
South Fork	207	2
Angel's Ranch	2,136	—
Bucksport	319	9
Eel River	1	31
Table Bluff	9	24
Total	3,107	1,804

It was evident that wholesale frauds had been committed at this election. Four thousand eight hundred and twenty-eight votes cast in five precincts, where there could not, at most, have been over 800 legal voters, and yet reputable citizens certified to these votes as being cast.

The County Judge gave notice that "it appearing by the certificate of the County Clerk, to me issued and directed, that at the election held November 20, 1854, to determine which of the two places received the greatest number of votes cast for county seat, a majority of all the votes were given in favor of Union, and I do hereby declare the town of Union to be the county seat from and after this date."

The County rented rooms and were paying as follows:—

For Court Room per annum	$500.00
Clerk's Office	" 180.00
Treasurer's	" 120.00
Sheriff's	" 120.00
	$920.00

The people of Union were anxious for the erection of a Court House but the Supervisors declined to take any action. The result was that the contest was continued, and at one time it was proposed to divide the county so that each place could have a county seat. The proposed division " to commence at the center of the channel at the entrance and run up to the north end of Indian Island and across to the mouth of Big Slough and up to its head, and thence across to a point on the south fork of the Trinity and down that stream to the Trinity, down the Trinity to the Klamath thence to the ocean and along the coast to the place of beginning." But this plan did not work and the matter was finally settled by the Legislature.

EUREKA GAINS THE COUNTY SEAT.

Union retained the location until the Act of the Legislature of 1856, removing it from that place to Eureka, which act took effect on May 1, 1856.

The Board of Supervisors at special meeting, April 12, 1856, accepted the proposal of R. W. Brett, to furnish the county with a court room, two jury rooms, Clerk's, Treasurer's and Sheriff's offices at Eureka for one year from the first day of May, 1856. Mr. Brett reserved to himself the use of the court room and with this reservation furnished the rooms mentioned for $200 per annum.

On Thursday the first day of May, L. K. Wood, County Clerk and *ex officio* Recorder, removed the records, books, files, safes, etc. belonging to those two offices to Eureka in accordance with the Act declaring Eureka the county seat of Humboldt County from and after that day.

R. W. Brett who owned the buildings at Eureka occupied by the county for court room and offices, had them improved in January, 1857, by having the court room extended through to the front of the building, the same height and width, making a very spacious room, some seventy-five by twenty-five feet and sixteen feet high. These rooms were used until the Court House was built.

PRESENT COURT HOUSE.

The county in 1860, purchased the block of ground lying between Second Street and the bay—being above the termination of First Street—and between I Street on the west and K on the east, with a large frame building thereon, built by Hinkle & Co.

A contract was then entered into for placing this building suitably on the block, adding wings thereto and finishing the whole for court room and all the county offices according to plans and specifications. The contractor performed the job faithfully and to the entire satisfaction of the Board of Supervisors.

The main building is eighty feet in length parallel with Second Street, by twenty-four deep. In the center there is a front projection, for entry-way, etc., extending towards Second Street twelve feet by twenty-six feet in width. On the opposite or bay side, there is a wing of the same width (twenty-six feet) by thirty in length, giving the building the shape of a cross. It is three stories high and finished throughout.

The court room is 46x25 feet in the clear. The jail is over the jailer's department, consisting of one large room and three cells very substantially arranged. The grand jury room occupies the third floor in the eastern end of the main building.

On the front projection are large, gothic windows. The court room is lighted by six large, plain windows, three sash each, hung on pulleys.

The building is surmounted with a belfry rising from the

intersection of the roofs. It is a good frame structure and rests upon a solid and extremely well-built stone foundation.

The entire cost of the ground and building together was $5,507.00.

It must, however, be admitted that the building is hardly up to the times or creditable to a wealthy and prosperous county.

COURT OF SESSIONS.

The affairs of the county were managed by the Court of Sessions from the organization in 1853, until 1855, when they passed into the hands of the Board of Supervisors.

The County Judge as Chief Justice, and two Justices of the Peace, as Associate Justices, composed the Court of Sessions. Annually the County Judge convened the Justices of the Peace of the county, who selected from their own number, two who should act as Associate Justices of the Court of Sessions for the ensuing year. In case of a vacancy or a failure to attend, the County Judge appointed another Justice, and as this frequently occurred, some years half a dozen gentlemen occupied the position.

DUTIES OF THE COURT OF SESSIONS.

The duties of this Court of Sessions at first were chiefly to administer the affairs of the county, a function now discharged by a Board of Supervisors. In 1851 a radical change was made in the powers of this court by conferring upon it the criminal jurisdiction previously exercised by the District Court. It had the power to inquire into all criminal offenses by means of a Grand Jury, and to try all indictments found by that body, save those for murder, manslaughter, and arson, which were certified to the District Court. In 1855 the Legislature created Boards of Supervisors in the various counties, leaving to the Court of Sessions only its criminal jurisdiction. In 1863 the Court was abolished and its powers were conferred upon the County Court.

DISTRICT COURT.

This was the highest local tribunal of original jurisdiction, embracing chancery, civil and criminal causes. As at first created it had original cognizance of all cases in equity, and its civil jurisdiction embraced all causes where the amount in question exceeded $200, causes involving the title to real property or the validity of any tax, and issues of fact joined in the Probate Court. It had power to inquire into criminal offenses by means of a grand jury, and to try indictments, found by that body. In 1851, the Legislature took from this Court its criminal jurisdiction and conferred it upon the Court of Sessions, leaving it the power of hearing appeals from that Court on criminal matters, and the power to try all indictments for murder, manslaughter, arson, and any cases in which the members of the Court of Sessions were personally interested.

ADJUSTMENT OF THE DEBT OF TRINITY.

By the Act of 1853 for the division of Trinity County and the organization of Humboldt out of the western portion thereof, one-half of the debt of the old county was apportioned to the new.

The whole amount of the debt was ascertained by the officers to be between $12,000 and $13,000; that chargeable to Humboldt County being therefore something over $6,000. This last amount was funded, under an act passed subsequently, and bonds were issued for the same, bearing interest at the rate of ten per cent. per annum. A special tax was also provided to pay the interest and ultimately redeem the bonds.

FIRST COUNTY ELECTION.

We here give the vote in full of the first election after the organization of the county, as it shows very nearly the total voters of the county at that time and the different precincts. Election September, 1854.

TABLE OF VOTES CAST AT FIRST COUNTY ELECTION.

PRECINCTS.		Union	Eureka	Bucksport	Table Bluff	Eel River	Pacific	South Fork	Total	Majority
For Clerk of Supreme Court	Z. R. Beard, Whig	98	68	53	12	23	5	16	274	
	Chas. A. Leake, Dem.	69	110	71	12	28	11	4	304	31
For the Assembly	A. H. Murdock, Whig	157	61	59	0	13	1	15	303	33
	A. Flanders, Dem.	15	114	72	17	36	12	4	270	
For Dist. Attorney	Walter Van Dyke, Whig	88	107	54	11	21	3	15	298	43
	E. H. Howard, Dem.	79	59	64	11	26	12	3	256	
For Treasurer	John Vance, Whig	42	106	37	13	17	5	14	234	
	M. Spencer, Dem.	127	62	80	11	30	11	5	326	92
For Coroner	H. D. P. Allen, Whig	87	56	53	—	23	5	15	239	
	J. Johnson, Dem.	70	57	70	23	28	11	4	263	24

JUSTICES OF THE PEACE.

Union, J. H. Cowan, Dem., J. A. Whaley, Dem.; Eureka, D. F. Gilbert, Whig, Thos. Dean, Whig; Bucksport, A. Caldwell, Dem., J. C. Murdock, Whig; Table Bluff, Wm. Espie, Whig, J. Jones, Whig; Eel River, A. D. Sevier, Whig, L. W. Fish, Whig; Pacific, Cutler Hatch, Whig, N. Patrick, Whig; South Fork, J. A. Drake, Whig, N. B. Hill, Whig.

REPORT OF ASSESSOR FOR 1854.

The following report of the Assessor will give a very good idea of the condition of the county at that date.

The quantity of land under cultivation in this county is probably about 2,500 acres; this is chiefly situated in the valley of Eel River and Mad River bordering on the bay. The area of land adapted to grazing is very extensive; I can give no information as to the quantity.

Bordering on the bay and coast the country is principally covered with timber and of excellent quality, consisting chiefly of redwood, pine and spruce.

This is probably the best as well as the most extensive lumbering district in the State. The soil is of excellent quality,

ORGANIZATION OF HUMBOLDT COUNTY.

producing grains and esculents in great abundance and variety. The exact limits and boundaries of this county are not defined in consequence of no survey being completed. Owing to this fact there are continual disputes as to the whereabouts of the boundaries between this and Klamath. As yet but little fruit has been raised, but another year or two will add greatly to this branch of agriculture. There is a large number of fruit trees of every variety adapted to the climate in fine growth, and some have already borne fruit.

The quantity of mineral lands known in this county is small. The number of horses, cattle, etc., of the county, as stated below, is as correct as possible, although many immigrants have located in the county since these were enumerated, and have added to the number somewhat.

FIRST BOARD OF SUPERVISORS.

Under the law of 1855, organizing Boards of Supervisors, the County Judge, J. E. Wyman, gave notice that the county was divided into three districts, corresponding with the number of Supervisors to be elected, which were as follows, to wit: Eel River, Pacific and Table Bluff Townships constituting the first; Bucksport and Eureka Townships constituting the second; and Union and South Fork Townships constituting the third district. The election was called to be held on the second Monday of April, 1855, and the places of holding the polls, and the Inspectors and Judges of election, were as follows:

FIRST DISTRICT—*Eel River*.—Polls at R. R. Roberts' house.—Inspector, H. F. Jamison; Judges, L. W. Fish and T. D. Felt.

Pacific.—Polls at the house of S. L. Shaw.—Inspector, S. L. Shaw; Judges, Uri Williams and N. Patrick.

Table Bluff.—Polls at Table Bluff House.—Inspector, J. Van Avenain; Judges, J. D. Myers and John Jones.

SECOND DISTRICT—*Bucksport.*—Polls at school house.—Inspector, Dr. J. Clark; Judges, J. C. Murdock and A. Cadwell.

Eureka.—Polls at Brett's Hotel.—Inspector J. M. Eddy; Judges, John Chamberlin and G. H. Knight.

THIRD DISTRICT—*Union.*—Polls at A. Packsher & Co.'s Hotel.—Inspector, H. S. Daniels; Judges, J. H. Cowan, and H. W. McNay.

South Fork.—Polls at Drake & Baggott's Ferry House.—Inspector, N. Hill; Judges, J. A. Drake and —— McCann.

FIRST MEETING OF SUPERVISORS.

At this election the following persons were chosen: First District, John Quick; Second District, Jonathan Clark; Third District, J. S. Bowles.

The Board met May 6, 1855, and elected John Quick, Chairman.

They continued in session seven hours each day, and disposed of a large amount of business.

They commenced the examination of all the affairs of the county since its organization. They passed an order requiring some of the county officers to give additional bonds. In some cases the securities were dead, had left the county, or were men of straw, from whom not a dollar could be collected by compulsion. They carefully examined the books, accounts, and vouchers of the county officers from the organization of the county, and found them correct. Every cent received and disbursed by them was accounted for.

At this first meeting they abolished the election precincts at Angel's Ranch and South Fork on account of the frauds committed at those places at last county seat election.

The County Assessor was allowed ten dollars per day for assessing; the Clerk of the Board $200 per year; the District Attorney, $750 per year. Byron Deming was appointed Coroner, and Benj. F. Myran Public Administrator.

They divided the county into six townships, named as follows: Pacific, Table Bluff, Eel River, Bucksport, Eureka, and Union. And organized six Road Districts bounded same as the Townships.

The Clerk of the county reported the indebtedness of the county, May 1, 1855, as follows:—

Warrants outstanding	$4,532.05
Bonds not redeemed	5,150.00
Balance of money due estate	591.00
Total debt	$10,273.05

COUNTY EXPENSES UP TO 1855.

The following statement was furnished to the Board by Hon. J. E Wyman, County Judge, of the liabilities of the county, from its organization July 1, 1853, to the 1st of May, 1855, twenty-two months, and for what such liabilities were incurred:

Salary of County Judge	$3,300.00
Rent of court room, offices, etc.	859.50
Furniture and stationery for court room	48.88
Expenses of elections	612.50
Per diem fees of Associate Justice	776.00
Grand and trial jurors' fees	845.00
Salary of District Attorney	1,081.66
Proportion of Trinity County debt apportioned to Humboldt County	6,150.01
Expenses of commission to ascertain Trinity County debt	492.65
County Clerk, Auditor and Recorder's fees	1,520.80
Books, safe, furniture, etc, for Clerk's office	781.65
Sheriff's fees	849.50
To Sheriff expenses of guarding and supporting prisoners	1,204.00
Books, furniture for Treasurer's office	65.20
Expense of carrying lunatic to State Insane Asylum	280.00
Compensation to School Marshal	52.00
Expenses of inquest upon the body of Blaisdell	82.50
Advertising and printing bonds	45.00
	$22,329.00

It will be seen that the annual expenses of the County Government in a county numbering less than 1,000 men, women and children, amounted to $9,682.80.

KLAMATH FORMED AND DISORGANIZED.

Formation of Klamath County; County Seat Contests; Hopelessly in Debt; Conduct of Officers; Final Disorganization and Disappearance, etc.

KLAMATH FROM ORGANIZATION TO DISINTEGRATION.

As heretofore shown in the diagram on page 107, Klamath County was taken from north half of Trinity in 1852, the year previous to the organization of Humboldt. This county seemed to have an unfortunate career, and after losing the northern part of its territory in 1857, it was finally blotted out in 1874.

The first county seat was established at Trinidad, but in 1854, the Legislature declared Crescent City the county seat, and legalized the acts of the County Judge in changing the seat of justice from Trinidad to Crescent City.

Notwithstanding Crescent City had the honor of being the county seat, it was six days' hard travel to reach a distant portion of the county like the tributaries of the Salmon River, and so much dissatisfaction existed that by order of the County Judge an election was held September 5, 1855, for choosing a county seat.

The people living on the Klamath River were also much dissatisfied, and urged that the county seat be removed to Orleans Bar.

At this election a large majority of the voters of Klamath County declared themselves in favor of removing the county seat of said county from Crescent City to Orleans Bar. It was therefore enacted, "That from and after the passage hereof, Orleans Bar shall be, and is hereby declared to be the county seat of Klamath County. That the order of the County Judge, removing the county seat on the 4th day of December, 1855, is hereby ratified and approved.

COUNTY BUILDINGS AT ORLEANS BAR.

County buildings were constructed at Orleans Bar in 1856, which were "considered an ornament to the county seat." Considerable taste was manifested in the selection of ground for the county buildings, being a square in the rear of the main street, and at an elevation of some twenty feet above the flat on which the town was built, affording a fine view of the place and surrounding country.

This place is about 150 miles from Crescent City, the former county seat, and is situated in the midst of a mining district on the Klamath River.

Orleans Bar, the new county seat, became the scene of unusual activity. Hundreds of pack mules passed through the place, destined for the upper Klamath and Salmon. Traders were driving a brisk business, miners were doing well, several new buildings were in the process of construction, and competition among the business men ran very high. Goods were plenty and cheap, and good living could be had at a lower rate than at any other place on the coast.

The population of the county at this time, 1856, was estimated as follows: Happy Camp, mining population, 100; Indian Creek, 450; other localities down to the mouth of Salmon River, 250; Salmon River, 1,200; Smith's River Valley and Redwood Diggings, mining and farming population, 200; Crescent City, 800; total, 11,700.

BOUNDARIES AND CONDITION.

The Legislature in 1855 amended the act forming the County of Klamath so as to have it "begin at a point in the ocean, three miles due west of Mad River, and running thence due east along the northern boundary of Humboldt to Trinity County, thence due north to the northwestern corner of Trinity, thence easterly along said county to Siskiyou, thence northerly to the parallel of 42° (State line) and thence west to the ocean."

Klamath County was as badly governed as any county in in the State. Many and loud were the complaints in regard to the financial condition of the county, and much attention was called to the fact that Klamath County, although not quite four years old, was badly in debt, without roads, without county buildings, even without a proper safe for her records.

The Court of Sessions of Klamath County had, so far as the administration and general supervision of county affairs was concerned, made a complete failure in that particular line of business, and involved the county in debt at a time when it should have had a balance standing in its favor.

It is no wonder, then, that a change in the county government was hailed with satisfaction by the tax-payers of the county. The change consisted in an act by the Legislature, transferring the management of county affairs to a Board of Supervisors.

FINANCIAL SITUATION.

The Board of Supervisors in August, 1855, reported the county $25,000 in debt. They ratified and confirmed all the acts and proceedings of the Court of Sessions except the proceedings of the term of Court held at Trinidad long after the county seat had been removed to Crescent City. It was at this term of said Court that the $4,000 was allowed to the County Judge for six months' salary. Upon this the famous scrip was issued that afterwards became so celebrated in the San Francisco stock market.

The Treasurer's books had not been properly made up, and according to the books of the Auditor, a large amount of money had been unaccounted for by the Sheriff. In view of these facts, the Board refused to levy any county tax for that year. The Sheriff had already reported that no property taxes had been collected for the past year.

All this may have been very pleasing to the tax payers, but it was certainly the means of involving the county in a maze of financial difficulties, which it required years to set right.

One of the members of the Board assigned as a reason for this step that "the county would be just as well off without our citizens throwing away their money for taxes, for what had been collected heretofore had never done any good as they could get no correct account of it."

THE TREASURER'S STATEMENT.

The County Treasurer, W. T. Wood, published the following card:—

"I was elected to the office of County Treasurer in 1852, with the general ticket of that year. All the moneys that have ever been paid me I safely deposited with the State Treasurer, where it belonged, and in return had his receipt given. It matters not how much I paid in, be the same more or less, it was all I had paid me.

"I even went to the great expense and trouble to travel to Sacramento City in 1854, to make such settlement. There was then a small balance due the State from the County. All the past years the county has had no charges against her, that is, from '53. All the funds of this State for 1854 were paid over to J. P. Haynes, District Attorney, except a small balance yet due from that year, which has not been paid me. For the year 1855, no settlement was ever had with the Controller of the State, which was from the fact that no money was ever in my hands belonging from the county to the State chargeable to me on the State's account."

BAD STATE OF AFFAIRS.

The tax payers having lost all confidence in the officers intrusted with the collection of revenue, refused generally to to pay their taxes. They said they paid their taxes year after year without benefiting the county or her creditors a farthing, and until a new order of things is established, they would not pay. There was such a strong sentiment in the county, in support of this refusal to pay that it was impossible for the officers to enforce the collection under the law, and they collected only from such as would pay voluntarily.

The people of Klamath County had been outraged beyond measure by some of her officers.

In 1857, the Supervisors of Klamath County were authorized to issue bonds of not less than fifty dollars nor more than $500, to the amount of the then county indebtedness, with rate of interest at ten per cent. per annum.

JUDGE FLETCHER'S REMARKABLE CHARGE TO JURY.

The Court of Sessions, consisting of Judge Fletcher and Associate Justices Darling and Mathews, met April 14, 1857, at which time a Grand Jury was impanelled. Judge Fletcher delivered an extempore charge, which, though brief, was most decidedly emphatic and to the point. He said Klamath County had become a by-word and a reproach among all decent men on account of the corruption and rascality that had been practiced, and said it was time to put a stop to it and charged them to inquire strictly into the conduct of the county officers, and to be influenced neither by fear, favor, or affection, or by the wealth or social position of any person.

He also recommended to their special attention those persons who have been in the habit of maltreating Indians and the vagabonds who travel up and down the river without any business or means of support except gambling.

He stated that within the last three years, sixteen murders had been committed without the least notice having been taken of any of them, and he thought it high time that such a state of affairs should be brought to an end.

REPORT OF THE GRAND JURY.

The Grand Jury say that they find the financial condition of the county much embarrassed.

The Sheriff absent from the county and delinquent in the sum of $32,461.27.

The Treasurer's books in such a confused state that they are unable to make anything out of them, and the Assessor is delinquent in the sum of $39.

Speaking of county officers they say: "In the examination of the official acts of the officer and the clearness and accuracy of his accounts, we find the County Clerk deserving our highest approval; and in giving us the information we have required of him in our investigations of the accounts in his office, he has displayed a commendable frankness and courtesy.

DISORGANIZATION THE REMEDY.

The above statements will give some idea of the situation the county had gradually approached, and it is no wonder the question of disorganization was considered by some the only available remedy. Many attempts were made to adjust matters and get the county in a flourishing condition, but without permanent success.

As early as 1871, the question of the disorganization of Klamath County was widely discussed by the newspapers of the northern portion of the State. The majority of the people of that county were in favor of the action. The population had become so reduced, and the assessment valuation was so low, that it was a great burden upon the people to maintain a county government, and an impossibility to pay the debt, that already amounted to over $20,000, and was annually increasing. Under these circumstances it was deemed best to disorganize the county and to annex the territory to the surrounding counties as would be the most convenient and for the best interest of the citizens. A bill to submit the question of disorganization to a popular vote of Klamath County was introduced into the Legislature of 1872, but failed to pass.

KLAMATH FORMED AND DISORGANIZED

So expensive was everything used in the early days, and so great were the fees allowed for official services, that not only the State but every county, also, run badly into debt during the first few years of its existence. The amount of tangible taxable property was small, and the rate of tax at first imposed entirely inadequate to raise a sum sufficient to meet the current expenses of the county government. The population was of an active and energetic character, whose chief capital was enterprise and hope, and whose property consisted mainly of mining claims.

The county had not been long enough settled to admit of the creation of valuable property to serve as a financial basis for a government. Services were performed and materials furnished at a high price, but there was not money enough in the treasury to meet a tithe of the warrants issued therefor.

PLANS FOR DISORGANIZING.

The matter remained in abeyance, although being more or less discussed, until the Legislature again met in 1874.

A petition of the citizens of Klamath County was then presented, praying that the county be disorganized and annexed to Siskiyou, Trinity, Humboldt and Del Norte Counties. After considerable discussion, this resulted in the introduction of a bill by Assemblyman Tulley, for annexation to the Counties of Siskiyou and Humboldt.

A remonstrance was presented by some of the citizens of Klamath County, who preferred to be united to Trinity or Del Norte, the county seats of the others being almost inaccessible to their locality in winter. The bill was referred to the Klamath delegation.

SISKIYOU OPPOSES THE ANNEXATION.

Humboldt County seemed to look with favor upon the scheme, while in Siskiyou there was a great diversity of opinion. Political feeling entered into the matter as well as local interests.

It was claimed by the Republicans that it was a Democratic scheme to retain control of the county, as the section proposed to be added to Siskiyou had a large Democratic majority, which would atone to that party for the votes lost by the segregation of Modoc. Again the scheme was bitterly opposed in Yreka for local reasons. It was feared that the annexation of this section would make the western end of Siskiyou so strong, that the next move would be to take the county seat away from Yreka and locate it in Scott Valley. Although any intention of this kind was disclaimed by the people of that valley, still they were arrayed on one side of the question, and the people of Yreka and Shasta Valley on the other.

Petitions for and against the proposed action were sent by both factions to the Legislature, and the discussion was warmly maintained, both in the newspapers and on the street.

It was argued with a great deal of force by the opponents of the measure, that the proposed territory was separated from the county by the Salmon Mountains, to cross which, in winter, was almost, and sometimes entirely, impossible, save upon snowshoes, thus leaving it and its inhabitants completely isolated from the main part of the county a portion of the year; that the collection of taxes, the administration of county affairs and the conduct of legal business of that section, would be difficult, expensive and annoying; and, finally, that the county would have to assume a debt of $10,000 or $12,000 which the value of the acquired assessable property was not sufficient to justify.

DISINTEGRATION DECIDED BY SISKIYOU.

However well founded these objections seemed to be, they did not prevent the passage of the bill, although it was so amended as to have it take effect only upon a favorable vote of the people of Siskiyou County.

The Act of March 28, 1874, provided for an election to be held in Siskiyou County upon the question of receiving a portion of the territory of Klamath, and if the result was favorable to the measure, the act was to take effect, and not otherwise. The division was as follows:—

Commencing at the point where the present boundary of Klamath and Del Norte crosses the Klamath River; thence running easterly in a direct line to where the Salmon River enters the Klamath River; thence in a southerly direction, following the ridge of the mountain that divides the waters of the Salmon and its tributaries from the waters of the Klamath and Trinity Rivers and their tributaries, to the northern boundary line of Trinity County.

All the Klamath County north and east of this line was to become a portion of Siskiyou County, and all south and west a portion of Humboldt.

Causes in the courts were to be transferred to the proper tribunals in the two counties, and two commissioners each were to be appointed by Humboldt and Siskiyou, to apportion the debt and cash on hand in proportion to the valuation of property in each section. County property was to be sold.

As the day set for the election approached the discussion grew warmer, the question narrowed down to a trial of strength between the eastern and western portions of Siskiyou County. The vote was taken May 30, 1874.

VOTE ON THE QUESTION OF ANNEXATION.

	FOR	AGAINST
Fort Jones	104	10
Oro Fino	63	1
Rough and Ready (Etna)	120	0
Callahan's	50	3
McAdam's Creek	28	2
Buckeye Bar	32	16
Scott River	36	34
Cottonwood	16	13
Humbug	13	15
Butteville	3	62
Table Rock	10	39
Bogus	1	8
Willow Creek	2	11
Yreka	52	278
Total	529	491
Majority	37	

FARM & RESIDENCE OF G. H. GRAY, ADJOINING HYDESVILLE, HUMBOLDT CO. CAL.

FARM & RESIDENCE OF H. S. CASE, 1½ MILES FROM HYDESVILLE, HUMBOLDT CO. CAL.

Dissatisfied citizens of Klamath County took legal steps to contest the act. An injunction was issued by the County Judge, J. T. Cary, in June, restraining the Boards of Supervisors of the three interested counties from taking any action in the matter until the constitutionality of the act could be tested in the Supreme Court.

This did not prevent the appointment of the Commissioners and on the 24th of August, Hon E. Steele and A. Swain, on the part of Siskiyou County, met John A. Watson and John Keleher, Commissioners of Humboldt County, at Orleans Bar, to carry out the provisions of the act.

They found that in obedience to the injunction the Supervisors and officers of Klamath County had taken no steps towards settling the affairs of the county. They were refused access to the books by P. W. Wasmuth, the Treasurer, and were unable to accomplish the task that had been assigned them. Under these circumstances they adjourned and reported the situation to their respective boards. Nothing further was done until the decision of the Supreme Court was rendered.

The ground upon which the law was contested was, that it was a delegation of legislative power to the people, as it made the disorganization of Klamath County, and the taking effect of the law, dependent upon a vote of the people of Siskiyou. In March, 1875, a decision was rendered, fully sustaining the legality of the act, deciding that it was not a delegation of authority, but the making of the act to take effect upon the happening of a contingent event, namely, the affirmative vote of Siskiyou County to receive a portion of the territory and assume a portion of the debt.

THE DIFFICULTIES FINALLY SETTLED.

It now remained to carry the law into effect. After considerable correspondence and a failure to meet, Commissioners Steele and Swain resigned, and H. B. Warren and W. T. Laird were appointed.

A meeting was arranged for October, but the Siskiyou Commissioners failed to be present, and the matter still remained unsettled. The next winter a bill was introduced into the Legislature by Assemblyman J. Clark, of Humboldt.

It authorized the Humboldt County Supervisors to settle the affairs of Klamath County, and apportion the debt; made it obligatory upon Siskiyou to assume the portion thus assigned to it; provided for a tax in both counties to pay the Klamath County bonds; provided for the transfer of causes in the courts to the courts of Humboldt County; and donated the county real estate to the Orleans Bar School District.

Assemblyman Harris, of Siskiyou, submitted a substitute, which differed from the original bill by placing the settlement and apportionment in the hands of four Commissioners, two from each county, and providing for the sale of the county real estate at auction. The act was passed as thus amended.

The Supervisors of Siskiyou appointed John Dagget and John V Brown May 22, 1876, to serve as Commissioners under the act, which called for a meeting June 5th, at Orleans Bar.

The Commissioners of Humboldt County, W. J. McNamara and W. P. Hanna, were there at the appointed time, but Daggett and Brown failed to appear, the expenses of the meeting, according to a provision in the law, falling upon Siskiyou County, through whose laches it had been rendered futile.

After this failure, new Commissioners were appointed by both counties, James Beith, Jr., and Hudson B. Gillis on the part of Siskiyou, and Thomas Cutler and William P. Hanna for Humboldt. They met in Orleans Bar, August 14, 1876, examined the books, settled up the county affairs, and made the following apportionment:—

VALUATION—Portion in Siskiyou...........$428,018
     "   "   Humboldt   273,511
                                           $601,529
OUTSTANDING DEBT—To Siskiyou.........$13,063.27
     "   "   Humboldt 10,892.59
                                           $23,955.86
CASH ON HAND—Apportioned to Siskiyou...$2,414.81
     "   "   "   Humboldt.. 2,013.54
                                           $4,428.33

The report of the Commissioners was accepted by both counties, and Klamath County became a thing of the past.

KLAMATH COUNTY BONDS.

From a late number of the *Times*, we take the following article about the Klamath County bonds of 1857.

When Klamath County was wiped from its existence on the map and its territory divided between Siskiyou and Humboldt Counties, the debt had to be assumed by the counties in which it was included. The portion due by Humboldt County when Mr. Stateler's warrant shall have been paid, will all be paid, with the exception of about $1,200.

The bonds which were held by Mr. Stateler, have something of a history. The owner of them lived many years ago in Del Norte County and had warrants to the amount of $825.90 against the County of Klamath. The indebtedness of the county was bonded and bonds given him for the amount of the warrants. He subsequently moved to Virginia City, and was there in business as a banker. Like most men who have had dealings with mining stocks, he led a chequered life. More than once he was very wealthy and then lost all his money by unfortunate speculation or bad loans. The little bonds against the County of Klamath were laid away and forgotten.

It is supposed that they were burned in 1865, when Mr. Stateler's place of business was destroyed. Some of our county officers were talking over the bonds which had never been payed and Mr. Stateler's name was mentioned as the owner of three. One of the gentlemen present had known him in years gone by, and wrote to him about the bonds. Mr. Stateler put the matter into the hands of Mr. DeHaven and has secured a warrant for $2,640, the yearly interest since 1857 at 10 per cent. being more than double the principal.

DEL NORTE COUNTY ORGANIZED.

First Officers; Courts; Its Prosperity and Progress; Its Resources; Present Condition; Future Prospects, etc.

ORGANIZATION OF DEL NORTE.

The Crescent City *Herald* of the 23d of February, 1856, advocated a division of Klamath County and the formation of a new county out of the northwestern part to be called Requa, including in the new county that portion lying north and west of a line drawn from Spanish Bar, on the Upper Klamath, to the mouth of Blue Creek, on the lower, thence to the ocean, including the Indian reservation.

The paper alluded to attributes the great financial embarrassment of that county to the peculiar topographical nature of the same; certainly it was a heavy load of sin to impose upon the mountains, cañons and ravines of Klamath.

The Legislature of 1857 passed the Act organizing Del Norte County, and this bill located the seat of justice at Crescent City, and ordered an election held in May, 1857, for the election of county officers. The bill also provided that Del Norte pay one-third of the indebtedness of Klamath County, and that it was to issue bonds therefor, bearing ten per cent. per annum interest to Klamath County. Twenty per cent. of the taxes and other moneys received by the Treasurer of Del Norte was ordered to be set aside as a sinking fund for the redemption of the bonds; and the sum arising from this twenty per cent. was to be appropriated annually to their redemption. The Board of Supervisors of Del Norte County was authorized to levy a special tax, not to exceed twenty-five cents on each one hundred dollars of valuation of taxable property in the county; the fund arising from the special tax to be applied in liquidation of the debt of Klamath.

KLAMATH COUNTY DEBTS ADJUSTED.

The Board of Examiners appointed under the provisions of the Act of the Legislature of 1856-57 dividing Klamath County and creating the new county of Del Norte, consisted of Messrs. Lewis, Peveler, McDonald and Buel. They met at Orleans Bar on the third Monday in September, and proceeded to the discharge of their duties. They first went to work to ascertain the indebtedness of Klamath County prior to the 4th day of May, 1857. This they found to be $5,534.93. But the more the Board investigated the further they were from agreeing upon any basis of settlement.

The Board then endeavored to agree upon a fifth man to decide the point, but there they failed again, and adjourned without accomplishing anything more than the ascertaining the amount of debt to be divided.

The whole debt outstanding of Klamath County on the 4th day of May, 1857, of which Del Norte had to pay its portion, was $26,843.54. The Board having failed to divide this, the only thing now to be done under the provisions of the Division Act, was for the County Auditor of Del Norte to draw his warrant on the Treasurer of his county for one-third of this amount, being $8,948.

The Legislature of 1858-59 appointed Commissioners to apportion the Funded Debt of Klamath County, and the interest thereon, between the counties of Klamath and Del Norte. This question had long been a bone of contention between the two counties, and several attempts to settle the matter had been made without success.

The Commissioners, W. M. Buel, on the part of Klamath County, and Ben F. Dorris, on the part of Del Norte County, declined to act in the premises, alleging as a reason, that, in their opinion, a just and equitable settlement could not be made on the basis of the revenue of seven months of each county. In their report to the Board of Supervisors of Del Norte County, they stated, that upon an examination of the statements furnished them by the Auditors of the two counties showing the net revenues of both, they found that seven months taken as a basis would work greatly to the prejudice of Klamath County. They therefore proposed, after a due consideration of all the circumstances attending the embarrassed condition of affairs, to take the revenue of the first year, namely, from May 4, 1857, to May 4, 1858, as the basis of settlement. The apportionment on this proposition was as follows: Joint debt of Klamath and Del Norte Counties, as ascertained from the books of Funding Commission, $31,986.54; amount of revenue collected in both counties from May 4, 1857, to May 4, 1858, $14,067.00; apportionment of the debt according to the above basis — Klamath County $20,307.00; Del Norte County, $11,679.54; interest to be calculated to the 11th of June, 1859.

Finally in 1859, the Legislature passed an act amending the boundary between Klamath and Del Norte, and providing for the payment of the debt existing at the time of the organization of Del Norte.

PROGRESS OF THE COUNTY.

The people had much to congratulate themselves upon, and had good reason to expect a great increase in population, business, and wealth during the years to come. The division of Klamath County had been accomplished and the new county of Del Norte created; and above all, the determination shown by the judicial officers of the new county to punish and thereby prevent crime, augured a new era in the administration of county affairs, and an improvement in the moral tone of the community.

The month of April, 1857, brought the heaviest immigration

to Del Norte that had ever been known during the same length of time. Over 450 passengers were landed at the port of Crescent City within three days.

During the months of March, April and May, the first business months of the year, there were landed at Crescent City 1,278 tons of freight and 1,717 passengers. And the above may be taken as a fair criterion of the average business of the town in 1857.

FIRST COUNTY OFFICERS.

On Monday, May 4, 1857, the election for the first county officers for the new county of Del Norte took place, and the persons elected were: County Judge, F. E. Weston; County Clerk, Ben Reynolds; Sheriff, N. Tack; District Attorney, John P. Haynes; Treasurer, E. Y. Naylor; Assessor, Solon Hall; Coroner, Jasper Houck; Surveyor, D. C. Lewis; Public Administrator, John T. Hayes. The Supervisors elected were: First district, Wm. Saville; Second, Ward Bradford; Third, P. H. Pveeler.

Under their administration, the new county was reasonably prosperous, and has so continued under succeeding administrations. The present (1882) officers are James Murphy, Superior Judge; W. H. Mason, Assemblyman; Treasurer, William Saville; Sheriff, Chas. E. Hughes; Assessor, W. H. Woolbury; County Clerk, P. H. Poveler; District Attorney, E. Mason; Superintendent of Schools, John Miller.

RESOURCES OF DEL NORTE.

The county is exceedingly well timbered with redwood, spruce, hemlock, cedar and pine. In the eastern part of the county the surface is much more broken and mountainous, with less timber. The Siskiyou Mountains, in the eastern and central portion of the county, attain an altitude of 6,000 feet, many peaks reaching from 4,000 to 5,000 feet; along the coast the mountains seldom reaching more than from 700 to 1,000 feet; the latter are covered with very heavy redwood and spruce timber.

A comparatively small amount of land is cultivated, dairying being the great industry which requires nearly all the land for grazing purposes.

Views and descriptions of the principal dairies of Smith River are given in this work.

Owing to dairying the amount of grain raised in the county is very small. Potatoes could be raised in great quantities, new land yielding from eight to ten tons to the acre, but the home market at present does not warrant the farmer to plant very many.

There is small amount of arable land in the eastern portion of the county in the vicinity of Happy Camp and Indian Creek, and is mostly farmed to vegetables, which find ready sale among the mines in the vicinity.

The extent of farming land in the county now surveyed will amount to about 15,000 acres; this, taking all the surveyed land in the county, would only make about 100,838 acres. A great portion of the unsurveyed lands are excellent timber.

Toward the mouth of Smith River, is the Occidental and Oriental Fish Packing Company, largely engaged in canning salmon fish, which are caught, canned, and shipped to all parts of the world. The company employ from sixty to seventy-five hands, and caught and canned last year 158,750 cans, or 7,000 cases, valued at $43,500.

There are several saw-mills in the county. Two of the largest near Crescent City. The Elk River Mill, owned by Hobbs, Wall & Co., is the largest, being a two-story steam mill, the upper story being occupied by the saw-mill, the lower story by the most extensive box factory on the coast. The mill has a capacity of 30,000 feet of lumber, per day. It has an iron track railroad one mile long from the mill to the end of the wharf.

J. Wenger & Co.'s mill is located at the lower end of Lake Earl. The logs are rafted down on the lake to the mill; on arriving they are hauled up by steam, converted into lumber, and thence, by tramway, to the wharf, and from there to vessels. This mill has a capacity of 32,000 feet per day.

There are miles and miles of redwood forests in the county, so thickly wooded that one can scarcely see a dozen yards, that the lumberman has never entered, "and" says the *Record*, "we are inclined to believe that this generation will have passed away long before there will be a scarcity of this timber. Although the saw-mills in this county have been running many years and have cut a vast amount of this species of lumber, still all of their lumbering has been done on the low lands within two or three miles of the ocean, never having gone back to the hills, where the finest growth of timber can be found.

MINES AND MINING IN DEL NORTE.

The production of gold for the county annually is about $230,000 from placer mines in all parts of the county.

Copper mines are also valuable. One owned by M. F. Jewett of San Francisco is considered a very rich mine; extensive developments are now being made. Copper ore was first discovered in 1860, in the northwestern part of the county.

Hon. James E. Murphy has a number of miners employed in developing his copper mine, which is now, beyond doubt, one of the finest mining properties on the coast, the ore yielding from thirty to forty per cent. pure copper. The ore is easily smelted in a blacksmith's forge, and requires nothing at all for fluxing. There are croppings of copper ore all over Mineral Point which are easily traced for over a mile in length. If a more easy and accessible way were opened, there might be from 10,000 to 15,000 tons of copper ore exported annually from these mines.

The chrome mines of Del Norte County are situated in the vicinity of the copper mines. The first shipment being made by the Tyson Smelting Company, of Baltimore, Md., in 1869, which has control of the chrome business in the United States. There are extensive deposits of chrome in this county.

Deposits of iron ore, of various grades and classes, are found in different parts of the county, the bulk of which is in the vicinity of the copper and chrome mines. These iron ores have been tested by scientific men, who pronounce them of a very high grade.

Coal was discovered several years ago, a few miles north from Crescent City.

GREATEST NEED OF DEL NORTE.

What Del Norte County most needs is harbor improvements at Crescent City. That will bring in people with capital who will improve her many water powers, saw up her immense forests of redwood into lumber, and unlock the great vaults in which her vast minerals are now sleeping. The now sparsely-settled country will then teem with many industries which, at present, are scarcely thought of; then her gold, iron, chrome, fish, lumber and butter will be sent by her own ships to all parts of the world.

The harbor is at Crescent City, which is located on a small bay in latitude 41° 44', longitude 120° 10', which is 280 miles north of San Francisco by water.

The harbor is an open roadstead, with no bar to cross, and affords tolerable good shelter for vessels during the summer months, when the wind generally blows from the northwest, but is open and unprotected against the southerly gales which prevail during the winter months on this coast, and, at times cause a heavy sea to set in from the southwest, dangerous to vessels in the harbor. There is considerable of a bay here, with several large rocks, which are from one-fourth to one-half mile from the shore.

Crescent City Described.

When the town was located it was named Crescent City, because the bay on which it is situated is a semicircle.

In February, 1853, the land was surveyed by T. P. Robinson and divided up into town lots.

M. Rosborough purchased a land warrant in J. F. Wendell's name, for the 320 acres of land on which Crescent City now stands.

The grant which Wendell had purchased from the State was, however, afterwards declared to be void, the United States Government claimed the right to the land, and those who had invested in town lots were in danger of losing both their lots and money. An arrangement was finally effected by which the Common Council of Crescent City purchased the land from the United States, at $2.50 per acre. The Council then issued certificates of title to all those who had bought town lots from Wendell, and to those who were originally interested in the location of the town.

FIRST BUSINESS IN CRESCENT CITY.

The first mercantile firms who opened business at Crescent City were S. H. Gruhler, Gilbert & Farrington, Hamilton City & Co., and a short time afterward Gilkey & Co. R. F. Knox & Co., of San Francisco, sent F. E. Weston to represent and take charge of their interests. They bought and shipped in his charge on the *Pomona*, a small saw-mill, which he immediately erected near what is now the corner of C and Third Streets. That mill made the lumber of which the first houses in Crescent City were constructed. A year or two later they built a larger saw-mill near the corner of G and Seventh Streets, and in 1856, they added a grist-mill.

The first sack of flour ever ground in this county, was turned out of the Crescent City Mills in October, 1856. In 1857, Mr. Weston left and S. G. Kingsland took his place in charge of the property and business. In 1860, these mills were burned down, with all the surrounding improvements with the exception of the house now occupied by Judge Hamilton, and a large amount of lumber and grain was consumed at the same time.

The first vessel built at Crescent City was, in 1854, the *Rosalie*, commanded by E. A. Babcock. She was built of spruce and hemlock.

From March 16, to October 22, 1854, the number of arrivals, according to the Custom House reports, were, steamers, 39; sailing vessels, 9; total, 48. Amount of freight carried by steamers, 3,385 tons; by sailing vessels, 540; total, 3,925; or, in round numbers, 4,000 tons of merchandise.

During the same period the number of passengers carried from San Francisco to Crescent City, according to the Purser's reports, was 2,286.

Thus it will be seen that the travel to this part of the State was large, and that its many natural advantages were at that time receiving considerable attention, and the place for a few years had a rapid growth.

The city has two churches, Methodist and Catholic, where the usual services are conducted.

Crescent City Lodge, No. 398, I. O. G. T., meets every Saturday evening.

Del Norte Lodge, No. 183, A. O. U. W., meets every Tuesday evening.

Klamath Lodge, No. 41, I. O. O. F., meets every Thursday evening.

Crescent Lodge, No. 45, F. and A. M., meets on the Monday evening of, or next preceding the full of the moon. The Masons have a fine hall, the largest building in town, and the Order is in a prosperous condition.

The schools of Crescent City are among the best in the State, and at the Centennial Exhibition in 1876, Crescent City received credit for the best exhibit of work done in the schools of California. From the report of the public schools of Crescent City for the month ending December 22, 1880, by H. H.

SALMON CREEK FARM, PROPERTY OF E. P. VANCE, 1 MILE FROM TABLE BLUFF, HUMBOLDT CO. CAL.

RANCH OF JOEL S. WHITMORE, 16 MILES FROM HYDESVILLE, HUMBOLDT CO. CAL.

Heath, Principal, it appears that the whole number of children enrolled in the school is 120; three teachers are employed. The number of children in the county in 1880 was 477; the amount of money appropriated by the State was $629.64

On the 10th of June, 1854, that necessity of all civilized communities, a local newspaper, was established, with Messrs B. F. Fechtig and W. B. Freaner as publishers. It was called the Crescent City *Herald*, was a five-column paper, published all at home, and ably edited.

The Valedictory of the Crescent City *Courier*, which had been purchased by Mason & Tack from Walter H. Thorpe, and published by them for a period of one year, appeared in the issue of March 13, 1875. The publishers had probably found it up-hill work publishing a country newspaper, and had thought it the better part of valor to retire from the lists. The *Courier* was resurrected in November, 1878, by Silas White, as publisher and proprietor, who discontinued it in the fall of 1881. The *Del Norte Herald* is the only paper now published in the county. It is ably managed by J. E. Eldridge as editor and proprietor, who gleans all the local news worthy of record. It is in its 4th year of publication.

Crescent City contains a population of about 1,000, and the district polls a vote of 305. It is well laid out and compactly built. The buildings are nearly all of wood, superior lumber being manufactured here for building purposes. Spruce and fir are mostly used, redwood not being suitable for that purpose. There are twelve brick buildings and one stone warehouse.

HAPPY CAMP.

The noted Happy Camp was the first settlement made within the present limits of Del Norte. In the spring of 1851, a party consisting of Captain Gwin, R. Tomkins, Robert L. Williams, Capt. Chas. McDermott, Charles D. Moore, Thos. J. Roach, Charles Wilson, Charles Southard, W. Taggart, George Wood, W. T. Stevens, William Rumley, W. A. J. Moore, Jerry Lane, John Cox, S. S. Whipple, J. W. Burke, James Buck, Abisha Swain, L. H. March, J. H. Stimbfield, Jeremiah Martin, William Bagley, Daniel McDougall, Jack McDougall, William McMahone, and several others, started from Trinidad, worked their way up the Klamath River, camping on every bar which showed the color of the gold they were seeking, and continually compelled to keep guard against the prowling and treacherous Indians. Notwithstanding all the precautions taken by the company, three young men of the party were killed by the Indians. In return an attack was made on an Indian village, and it was believed all were murdered. The company then passed on up and located Happy Camp. They built a cabin which they used as a storehouse, and Cochrane remained there to look after the property and mules while the others scattered along the river mining. Soon the original party was increased by large additions. The name of this place was said to arise from the miners having a "good time" one evening at a gathering in the cabin. Some one proposed the place have a name, and another suggested it be called "Happy Camp." This was received with cheers and the "drinks" were had over the christening.

RECOLLECTIONS OF HAPPY CAMP.

A late number of the Crescent City *Record* gives some reminiscences of life there in 1852, by an "old inhabitant," and we here make some extracts, as it shows the general character of those early miners' camps.

"During the first four months of the year, 1852, we had one express, and one only, with newspapers and letters from home. This was in the early part of April. Frank Rogers, of Cram, Rogers & Co.'s Express, came up the river from Trinidad, bound with the express for Yreka. The weather had been checkered the numerous streams to be crossed more or less swollen, and the facilities for crossing being poor, rendered his progress slow and tedious. How long he had been on the road I do not know, nor does it matter. He put up at the 'Pelican House,' and it soon spread to every nook and corner of the camp that the long-looked-for express had arrived. We had not seen a newspaper since the previous November, in Yreka, and of course we were all anxious to hear from the 'States.' We made a general grand rush for the express office, the 'Pelican House,' and procured some of the latest dates. One would buy the St. Louis *Republican*, another the New York *Herald*, third man the *Tribune*, and still another the New Orleans *Delta*, etc. We would read one through and then exchange with our neighbors. Those who happened to be so fortunate, received letters from anxious parents, brothers and sisters in the far distant East. These letters and papers cost us $2.50 each; but notwithstanding the high prices, papers were eagerly sought for and their contents devoured with the avidity of a hungry wolf after a sheep's carcass.

EARLY MINING.

"Winter passed, and spring opened fine and pleasant. The most of us went to work in the cañon, some five miles below, leaving Happy Camp nearly deserted. Each mess or company of two to four partners had a tent, with frying-pan, camp kettle, tin cup, etc., picks, shovels, pans, and rocker. We strung along the river, up and down the cañon, on both sides of the stream, at no great distance from each other—perhaps half a mile between the most distant camps. There was a canoe—a kind of dugout—at the upper end of the cañon for the accommodation of those who worked on the left bank of the river. The water was high in the river, caused by the melting of the snow in the mountains, running with a strong and rapid current, with many sucks, eddies, and whirlpools on either side, rendering the crossing with a canoe, especially with inexperienced and green hands, extremely difficult—in fact, dangerous. But that insatiable appetite for gold, sordid gold, causes mankind to lose sight of danger, however palpable the same may be.

"Notwithstanding the high stage of the water in the river, we did well. Two men with one rocker made on an average about half an ounce ($8) a day each, and not work very hard at that. But those good old days are passed and gone, never more to return. Happy Camp was our base of supplies. We had cabins there, with some blankets and cooking utensils, for be it known that we did not move all our plunder to our temporary camp in the cañon. We, at least some of us, generally went to Happy Camp on Saturday evening, and the following Sunday returned with sufficient supplies to do us through the week.

"There were at Happy Camp about half a dozen fixtures who remained there all the while. Madam Cochrane (known to the old Crescentonians) and her man were running the 'Pelican House.' She kept some 'chain lightning' (known on Front Street as 'benzine'). The 'Pelican House' was situated immediately on the bank of Indian Creek.

"Then there was Maltese Green, with a shirt-tail load of goods and a keg of 'knock-'em-stiff'—perhaps of his own manufacture. He was also familiar with the route to Indian Creek's waters' edge. During Sunday the boys amused themselves in various ways, such as shooting at a target, a social game of euchre, and sometimes a scrub horse race. I never in all my life knew a happier and more contented people. Everything was merriment and fun, and such a thing as a row was totally unknown amongst them."

The town is built on both sides of Indian Creek, near its junction with the Klamath River, and surrounded by mountains, the only means of reaching the place being by mountain trails. The country around it is rich in gold; mining being its support. It has quite a thriving trade, there being four stores, three kept by white men and one by Chinese. It is ninety miles west of Crescent City.

KLAMATH CITY.

A short time after the settlement of Happy Camp, a settlement was made at the mouth of the Klamath River, a stream emptying into the ocean some twenty miles south of Crescent City. The Klamath was visited, in 1850, by a schooner on a voyage of exploration, which anchored off the mouth of the river and sent a small boat with a crew of fifteen or twenty to make an attempt to cross the bar. The bar being rough at the time, the boat was swamped, and all the crew were drowned with the exception of one man, who was rescued by the Indians. Afterwards, in the year 1851, another schooner arrived and a settlement was formed.

It was named Klamath City, and it had a rapid growth.

It was supposed that Klamath River was rich in gold, and the new town soon became the headquarters of explorers, prospectors and others.

The frames of houses, ready to be put together on arrival, were shipped by sail vessels from San Francisco, and it is said that one iron house was imported and erected in the town. For what purpose it was intended or used is not known. As the Indians were living there in great numbers, it is supposed that the owner intended to guard against their attacks by erecting a castle which would be proof against shot and fire.

Klamath City had a rapid growth, and soon became a place of considerable importance. But its growth was not more rapid than its decline, and it had but a brief existence. Prospectors at the mouth of the river did not meet with the success they had anticipated, and they soon began to seek other mining localities. In 1852, the iron house was re-shipped to San Francisco, and a short time afterwards, Klamath City belonged to the list of deserted mining towns.

DEL NORTE VILLAGE.

Del Norte, sometimes called "Smith River Corners," is located sixteen miles northeast of Crescent City. It contains about 200 inhabitants. This place is right in the midst of the dairy country, and is more fully described elsewhere.

CONDITION OF THE COUNTY.

The present condition of Del Norte may be partially gathered from the Assessment Roll for 1880.

Value of land, $285,667; number of acres, 61,139; value of improvements on land, $13,512; town lots and blocks $30,010; improvements on lots and blocks, $99,875; deduction on mortgages, $55,807; value of personal property, $308,240; money, $22,048; improvements on all property assessed to other than the owner of the land, $1,745; amount of deductions, $27,152; total value of all property, $899,738; value after all deductions, $804,144.

Value of script, $6,893; money, $27,373; fourteen bee-hives, $39; 1,070 gallons liquor, $3,326; 525 gallons, $2,737; beef cattle, 975; 770 stock cattle, $7,961; colts, $2,040; 2,311 cows $44,646; 126 utensils, $1,147; 137 goats, $402; 912 hogs, $2,258; 475 horses, $21,788; 135 mules, $4,875; 77 oxen, $2,570; 334 poultry, $808; 1,404 sheep, $2,675; total value $126,827.

The levy of taxes for State purposes for the year 1880, was sixty-four cents on each and every $100 of taxable property. Add to the State tax a levy for county purposes of $1.86, and we have a total taxation of $2.50 on each and every $100 of taxable property.

The principal exports are butter and lumber, of which 10,000,000 feet of lumber was shipped to San Francisco in 1880, and 322,000 pounds of butter. About $200,000 in gold-dust is also exported annually from the mines in the county. The imports are small, probably 3,000 tons of general merchandise per year.

The population of Del Norte in 1860, was 1,993; in 1870, 2,022; in 1880, 2,499, showing an increase in ten years of 628. The voting population is about 700.

Geographical Features of Humboldt.

Its Mountains, Valleys, Rivers, Bays, Capes, Public Lands, Scenery, Harbor Improvements, Etc.

HUMBOLDT COUNTY contains 3,500 square miles, or 2,297,600 acres of land. Its length from north to south is 108 miles, and its greatest breadth is forty-seven miles. It has more than 175 miles of meander coast line. It is three times as large as the State of Rhode Island, and more than one-half as large as Massachusetts. The farming land with few exceptions, lies along the rivers, formed by sedimentary deposits, owing to the constant shifting of the water channel.

For general small farming, dairying, stock-raising and lumbering, it is not excelled by any county in the State. Perhaps one-tenth of the area might be called waste land, and is the rocky cliffs along the sea-shore, and some of the tallest mountains in the eastern part of the county. The balance of the unsurveyed lands are what might be called grazing lands, the most of it being covered with an inferior growth of stunted timber, while some of it may come under the head of mineral lands, which are located in the north end of the county, and consisting of gold, silver and quartz lodges. There are no large valleys. The whole consists of rounded ridges, with their prairies on top, and wooded sides and small valleys between.

The largest area of level land is in the vicinity of Humboldt Bay, which is on the coast about midway between the north and south lines of the county. Between Eureka and Arcata, there are thousands of acres of swamp and overflowed lands. From Eureka, south, are what is known as the Hookton Flats. There is another large tract of land, from the island to Mad River and the marsh south of Eureka to Humboldt Point, and still further south to the mouth of Eel River, all of which would be easy to reclaim, but is yet in a state of nature.

MOUNTAINS AND HILLS.

Twenty miles below Petrolia, on the coast, arises a high mountain known as King's Peak, lying parallel with the beach. Immediately inland, and running six or seven miles in the same direction, is a twin brother, Wilder Ridge.

Below Eel River, down the coast, there are no long streams, and consequently no long ridges till you arrive at Bear River Ridge, a distance of ten or twelve miles. The river and ridge lie at right angles with the coast, consequently their course is east and west, the ridge being on the north side of the river. This ridge preserves a distinct demarkation for twenty-five miles and terminates at its juncture with the dividing ridge of the South Fork, which point is familiarly known as the Monument.

On the south side of Bear River and parallel with that stream, are Southmayd and then Rainbow Ridge, being really the same ridge, which extends eastward till it joins the South Fork divide, at the head of Bull Creek, south of the Monument, and here it also connects, at right angles, with that great grazing region known as Elk Ridge. It runs northerly and southerly, twelve to fifteen miles from the coast, and is the main dividing ridge between the South Fork and Mattole River.

There seems to be a break in the great redwood belt. The country is in conformation, like the rest of the county, hilly, with rounded ridges and sloping ravines. It is covered by straggling oaks, ash and spruce. The land is not rocky, but a soil extends over the whole. This supports a nutritious grass, known as mesquite. Being in the fog belt, the growth of herbage is immense, and the country is occupied by dairy farms, producing large quantities of butter, shipped from Humboldt Bay or Shelter Cove.

The Coast Range commences at the ocean, and falls back from the coast, increasing gradually in height, until it reaches an elevation of some 1,440 feet, known as the Bald Hills. They retreat slightly from the ocean around Humboldt Bay.

For a long distance from north to south, through the county are the Bald Hills. Seen from the summit of the first range of hills to the east, or from the valleys at points whence they are visible, the Bald Hills present anything but an inviting appearance. They look bare and withered and comfortless for they lose their verdure far earlier than the regions nearer the sea. Nevertheless they constitute one of the great reserves of wealth with which this county is so bountifully endowed They are now for the most part devoted to the grazing of flocks and herds.

On the south line of the county is Bell Spring Mountain, on the Overland Road, 4,400 feet elevation, from which a very extended view is obtained of the ocean and a large extent of country This mountain has here and there peaks formed out of smooth round pebbles and bowlders that were once a river bed, and which have been thrown up by volcanic action, and solidified, but are now loosening from each other. As they fall away they pile around the base of the peak in a loose, shifting heap.

Quartz is seen protruding from the surface and suggests that gold may yet be found in paying quantities in the Coast Range. The stone that marks the line dividing Humboldt from Mendocino, is planted on this mountain.

The mountains extend near to the coast in the lower part of the county, below Mattole River, and are some 3,000 feet high, and generally covered with chaparral. There are very many peaks scattered about the country of various heights.

TABLE BLUFF.

The following description was furnished us by Jackson Sawyer, Esq.:—

The Table Bluff, as its name would indicate, is an elevated portion of land some one and a half miles wide and seven in length. It rises in quite a steep bluff from the ocean beach, and with varied elevations and depressions, extending in a southeasterly direction, reaches the redwoods, where it terminates at an elevation of 500 or 600 feet. The surface of Table Bluff, is very much broken by gulches running in various directions, containing an abundance of the best of water and groves of alder trees, with some spruce and fir. The surface of the land as first seen by white men, was covered in some places with grass and hazel brush, but mostly with a dense growth of fern and myrtle brush. The soil is black and of a light loamy nature, and on the level from two to three feet deep.

LAKES AND LAGOONS.

About nine miles above the town of Trinidad are several lakes—three in number—which are deep, have well defined shores, are not intruded upon by marshes, abound with all the fish native to this section, and would afford magnificent and safe yachting. The largest of these, known as Big Lagoon, is six miles long and four miles wide, is completely inclosed from the ocean, and is fed by Maple Creek. On the south side it is bounded by rolling hills, and on the north by a very high hill, commanding a full, grand ocean prospect from north to south The lake is three-cornered, narrowing to a point where the creek discharges. Warren Creek empties into this lagoon.

Blue Lake is another of the most beautiful sheets of water in the county. It is on the east side of Mad River. A hotel is here kept as a pleasure resort by Clement Chartin. It has a charming situation upon the banks of the beautiful lake from which it takes its name. It is the most enchanting rural resort in Humboldt County.

THE RIVER SYSTEM.

The river system of the county consists of a system of parallel streams running northwest through the county into the Pacific. Going up these rivers, they pass transversely through the redwoods towards the southeast. The river channels run through cañons in places so narrow as to afford only passage way for the winter floods, but widen at intervals, leaving strips of bottom-land from one-quarter of a mile to a mile in width between the edge of the channels and the mountains. In some places the gorges of the streams are absolutely frightful to contemplate.

The large streams have a general course towards the northwest. The Klamath, Mad, Mattole and Eel Rivers have their head-waters outside of the county lines.

None of these rivers will ever be of much service for navigation, for the reason they all have a steep grade; their cañons are free from rocks, and the channels nearly, in every instance, pass over strips of sand, and are hedged in by walls of redwood timber. The current, during the season of floods, is terrific. The cañons are then but conduits for a seething flood, bearing on its surface the debris of the forest's huge redwood trees, undermined along the banks and swept along by the flood; old logs, dislodged from the drifts, where they had lain for years, are carried out into the ocean. These rivers rise very suddenly with the heavy rains in winter.

We will give brief descriptions of these rivers, beginning at the north end of the county.

THE GREAT KLAMATH RIVER.

The great Klamath River rises in the lake of the same name, and in its windings through the mountains takes a general westerly course until it pours into the ocean near Crescent City the combined waters of the Klamath, Shasta, Scott, Salmon, and Trinity Rivers, with their hundreds of tributaries. The volume of water that goes surging through its rocky gorges and precipitous cañons in the winter season is tremendous, and the slowly melting snows on the mountain peaks keep the stream a rushing torrent till late in the summer.

The name "Klamath" is of Indian origin, and was first applied to the stream near its source by the early trappers, who asked the natives there what they called the stream, and were answered "Klamat," or "Tlamat." It is spelled by Fremont "Tlamath." The tribes that lived along the stream each had its name for the great river, but the name adopted by the whites soon became known from the mouth to the source, and was also applied to the lakes from which it springs, though for these the Klamath tribe that inhabited their borders had different and distinct appellations. This stream, as well as its first important tributary, the Shasta, was known to the trappers.

The Klamath drains a large extent of territory, and carries a volume of water truly wonderful. Between its precipitous banks the waters, augmented by the winter's storms, rush and tumble and foam to the sea, falling ten feet to the mile, and furnishing water-power enough to turn every factory wheel in the world. Through this narrow outlet flows all the water that falls in Upper California, enough, could it be pent up, to make a lake of vast volume and extent. When a heavy rain continues for several days without abating, the streams are unable to carry the water that runs so rapidly down the mountains into the valleys and cañons. The creeks and rivers overflow their banks, and mountain torrents rush through gulch and cañon to collect and form a lake in every valley towards which they run. The same is true when a warm rain brings down the melted snow from the mountains faster than the river can carry it away. These floods now do considerable damage to the crops and farms in the valleys and to the mining claims along the river.

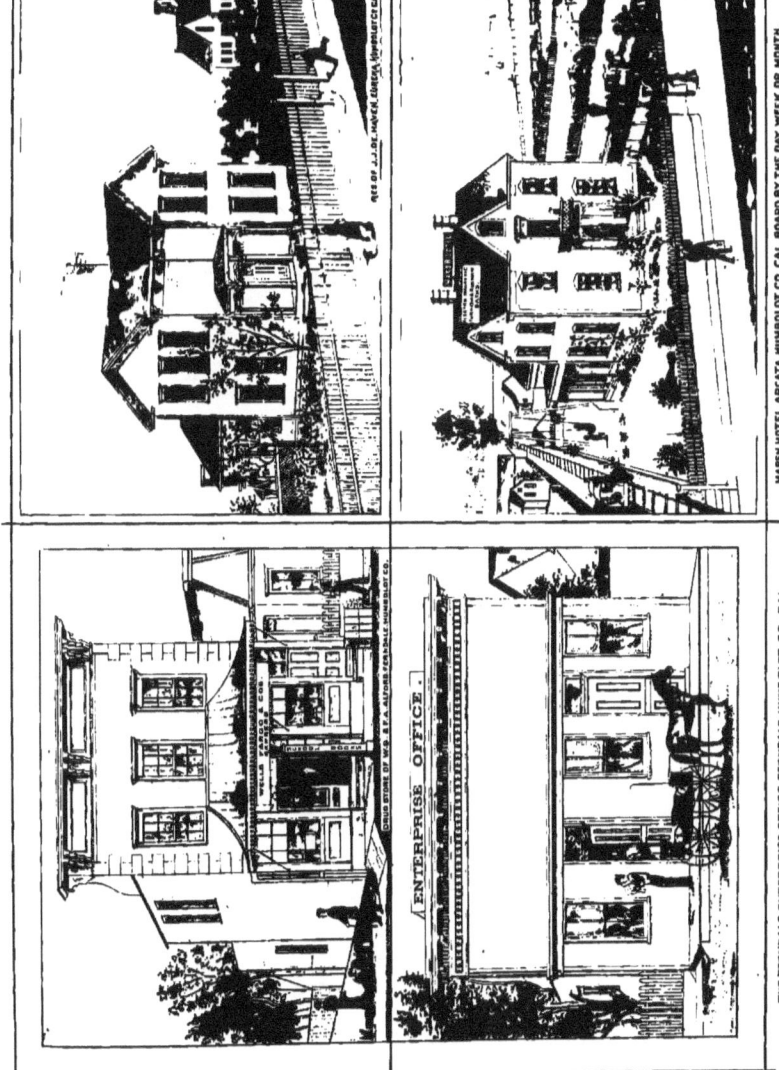

FIRST TRIP DOWN THE KLAMATH.

Two parties who had been living at Scott's Bar, on the Klamath, intending to visit the Fraser River mines, concluded to attempt what had never before been done—the descent of the Klamath River. They accordingly built a boat at Scott's Bar, embarked with their traps and made entire voyage down the Klamath to its mouth. The distance is about 175 miles. They had to make two portages, and should have made another, but, attempting to come over the rapids, they capsized, and all their plunder was lost, though they sustained no personal injury.

The Klamath enters at the northeastern corner of the county and takes a southwestern course into Humboldt County, for a distance of about forty miles, where the Trinity and several other streams flow into it; thence taking a northwestern course for a distance of forty-five miles. The latter twenty-five miles are within the boundaries of Del Norte County. The Klamath River, near to the mouth, is the second largest river in the State. It was declared navigable by the State Legislature for a distance of sixty miles, to Orleans Bar. It has a course of some eighty or ninety miles in all in Humboldt County. The Klamath is now navigable thirty five miles from the entrance, and flows water enough for navigation at all seasons of the year, and, with some obstructions removed from the bed of the stream, would be navigable for sixty or eighty miles.

TRINITY RIVER.

The principal tributary of the Klamath is the Trinity, which flows more than fifty miles in the county, and joins the Klamath near the middle of the northern boundary of Hoopa Reservation. It received its name from Major P. B. Reading who trapped on its head-waters in 1845, and named it Trinity because he supposed it to empty into Trinidad Bay, discovered by the early Spanish explorers, an error which misled thousands of gold seekers in 1849 and 1850, who sought to reach its famous mines by entering the bay in vessels and passing up the stream from its mouth, as related in preceding chapter.

Grouse Creek is one of the chief branches of the Trinity in this county, being some thirty miles long and running about due east. Another branch a little further north is Madden Creek. In this section are placer mines along the Trinity and branches.

REDWOOD CREEK.

The stream called Redwood Creek, which from its length could well be styled a river, has a course of more than 100 miles in the county, and empties into the ocean twenty-five miles south of the mouth of the Klamath.

On Redwood Creek there are from 3,000 to 5,000 acres of bottom-land good as any in the country. It was in early times covered with a dense growth of cottonwood, alder and salmon brush, and some spruce. There has been much headway made in clearing up the dense jungles which cover the ground, which give promise of developing into valuable ranches. Prairie Creek is the main large north branch of the Redwood.

Little River empties into the ocean four miles north of Trinidad. The course is almost due west and it has a length of forty miles or more, with numerous small branches.

MAD RIVER.

Mad River has a course of over 100 miles in the county. It rises in Trinity County. Its general course is northwest. All its tributaries flow in from the north side, as it flows on the south close to a sharp range of hills called, for part of the way, "Iaqua Bluffs." It empties into the ocean just above Humboldt Bay. It is one of the most important streams in the county. Its discovery and naming has already been related.

The next stream in order going south is Jacoby Creek, and so named from a pioneer settler, who located on its banks.

Freshwater Creek enters the bay near Eureka. Both these streams are twelve or fifteen miles in length.

ELK RIVER.

Elk River has its origin in the mountains from numerous springs, forming two distinct streams at its source, divided by a mountain ridge, and forming a junction about four miles from its mouth. These tributaries are commonly known as the North and South Fork of Elk River. The difference in the volume of water flowing in these feeders is hardly distinguishable; the North Fork, however, is several miles the longest.

In winter, when the rains swell this stream into a deep, swift body of water, it serves as a medium for conveying the logs from this section to the mills on the bay. But in summer the stream becomes shrunken to a mere brook, with its crystal waters rippling over gravelly beds from one pool to another. Its cool, clear waters are the home of the speckled and mountain trout, and of the ocean salmon and other fish in winter and spring.

Salmon Creek is of about the same characteristics as Elk River. It is about midway between Elk River and Eel River.

EEL RIVER.

Eel River has its source in the center of Mendocino County, and along the line of Lake, Colusa and Tehama Counties, which bound Mendocino on the east. This grand, wild and ever-flowing stream waters but little arable or bottom-land in that county in proportion to the immense area it drains. Hundreds of miles of its tributaries flow through rocky gorges or leave the base of steep, open hill-sides of rich grazing-land, with miles upon miles of their length without enough valley for the foundation of a cartway. Having its source in the summit of the Coast Range, with the snows of Sanhedrim, Mount Hood, Hull Mountain, Yola Bola, and the Trinity range to feed it, its waters are cold, clear and rapid, flowing freely all summer.

It has a course of more than 125 miles in the county, and, with its tributaries, Van Dusen, Larabee, South Fork and

Yager, each about 100 miles in length, constitute an important physical feature of the county.

Eel is an exceedingly crooked river, but its general course is northward, bearing somewhat to the west, and emptying into the Pacific a few miles south of Humboldt Bay. It is most prolific in crooks and rapids. The bed of the river is obstructed by rocks, often of the most massive kind, so that it cannot be followed down by animals, and only forded at rare intervals. Eel River has been known to rise in its banks from twenty to thirty feet within a few hours. The Indian name of the river was "Wee-ot-lolla" (many eels). A town was laid out hy Sam Brannan, in 1850, on this river and named Trinity City.

EEL RIVER ENTRANCE.

The shipping point is on Salt River, which empties into Eel about one mile from its mouth. It would be impossible to exaggerate or overestimate the beauty, fertility and importance of the region round about Eel River.

J. G. Kenyon, the original owner of the land upon which the shipping point known as Port Kenyon is situated, struggled long and bravely to establish the fact of the navigability of the bar. He finally enlisted T. P. H. Whitelaw of San Francisco in the matter, and the result was a staunch and well-constructed steamer of excellent sea-going qualities, the *Thos. A. Whitelaw*, which for a time made regular trips.

The citizens of Ferndale and vicinity lately took active steps toward having the entrance of Eel River improved, in order to render the same navigable for steamers at all times. At their late meeting a committee was appointed to collect statistics and information, which report we clip from the *Enterprise*:—

To the Honorable, the Senate and House of Representatives in Congress assembled—

WE, the undersigned, and residents of Eel River Valley, County of Humboldt, State of California, would most respectfully represent,

That, Eel River and its tributaries drain a large section of country, rich in natural resources, consisting of the finest agricultural, grazing and timber lands;

That, the country has been thickly settled by a hard-working class of people who are using their best endeavors to develop these resources;

That, for years vessels have entered Eel River Harbor, and at times steamers have run between said river and San Francisco regularly;

That, at the present time a steamer, built by the people and costing $60,000, is plying between said ports;

That, at this time the entrance to our harbor is dangerous and unsafe, causing an interruption of communication with San Francisco.

We would, therefore, most respectfully ask that the sum of $100,000 be appropriated for the purpose of making our harbor permanently safe for vessels to enter at all times.

BEAR RIVER.

This river rises at the foot of Mount Pierce and has a due west course emptying into the ocean near Cape Mendocino. There is not much bottom-land on this river. It lays in patches of from five to twenty acres, and at some places the bills push down to the river's edge. There are about a dozen ranches located on the river in a distance of about six miles. The hill-sides, as usual on the north side of the river, presenting a south face to the sun, are open and covered with grass; on the south side of the river, presenting a north face, covered with timber. Pepperwood, maple and spruce are scattered along the river.

WONDERFUL GAS SPRING.

At a point on the ridge about six miles up from the county road, a trail makes down one of the side ridges towards Bear River. About half way down this ridge, turning sharp to the left and descending to the gulch below, a distance of half a mile, is one of the wonders of California. It is the gas spring, jet or whatever you may call it, of Bear River. There are several, but this is the principal one. It is one mass of blue flame, covering over ten feet square of ground. It is a strange sight to see the blue flame thus burning in so large a body, upon the bare ground, particularly when we consider the fact that it had burned continuously some six or seven years. The spectator cannot help gazing and wondering, and speculating in his mind as to the source of this fiery fount. The fact remains, however, that a large amount of coal oil gas escapes from these gulches, and there are abundant evidences of the presence of coal oil, which must have been expressed from some vast bed of coal lying back near the South Fork.

MATTOLE RIVER.

In 1854, John Hill, in a trip to the south part of the county, found a river that had been heretofore unknown. It was called by the Indians "Mattole," which signifies clear water. The Indians had apparently never seen a white man at that time. He reported the valley of the river in glowing terms, as having open prairie ready for settlers, the table-land easy to clear.

Near the river cottonwood was the principal growth, but as you recede spruce, pine and redwood predominate. The prairie patches were then covered with the finest specimens of clover which grew to an almost unheard of height. The timbered lands were covered with wild oats and several varieties of grass. The Mattole rises in Mendocino and seventy-five miles of its one hundred lies in this county.

LAND-OFFICE AND PUBLIC LANDS.

As early as 1850 the Legislature passed a resolution to establish an additional land district in the northern part of the State, and that a land-office be established in Humboldt County.

PUBLIC LANDS OF HUMBOLDT COUNTY.

By Act of Congress a land-office was opened in 1858, and Wm. McDaniels and Major Hook were Register and Receiver. The officers thought it their duty under their instructions to open the office at "Humboldt Point," until they should receive orders from the department at Washington to remove it to Eureka, in accordance with a petition previously forwarded. No authority having arrived for such removal, and the winter season approaching, the officers found it necessary to find new quarters. At Humboldt Point they had no other conveniences, either for themselves or persons wishing to do business before them, than found in any ordinary private family. They selected Bucksport, and moved there October, 1858, as the nearest point to the imaginary town of "Humboldt Point," at which place they were instructed to open the office. Humboldt City failed away, like many another western city, and the office found its way to Eureka, though we believe no official transfer was ever made.

Since the office has been established here there have been seven Registers and three Receivers, the present incumbent, Mr. Cooper, having been in the office for fourteen years, and C. P. Roberts, the Register, for ten years. A new building, constructed at the northeast corner of Fourth and F Streets, will be used as the United States Land Office. The lot is owned by Solomon Cooper, Receiver of the Land Office.

FIRST ENTRY IN LAND OFFICE.

The first entry in the Land Office was as follows: "No. 1, October 14, Seth Kinsman of Humboldt County, the south half of the NW. quarter, of Section 36, Township No. 4 N., of Range No. 2 W., 80 acres."

During the twenty-four years of its existence there have been 6,562 entries made in Humboldt Land Office, as follows:—

Homestead Applications.............................. 1,838
Pre-emption Declaratory Statements filed............. 4,653
Mining Applications................................. 71

Total entries........................... 6,562

For the same time 4,578 cash entries—that is, final proofs—have been made, 521 being homesteads, the balance, pre-emptions and mining claims. Allowing 160 acres to each claim, the total entries for the twenty-four years would amount to 749,920 acres for the district. At the average price of $1.25 per acre this would give the sum of $935,400. But the value is probably much more than this, because a portion of the land described is held at $2.50 per acre. The business of the office for the year ending December 31st, has been as follows:—

	Acres
246 Pre-emption Declaratory Statements	39,680
102 Homestead Entries	15,686
9 Mining Applications	917
99 Final Homestead Certificates Issued	15,423

The number of acres disposed of was 28,844, for which the Government received $30,164.30.

HUMBOLDT DISTRICT.

This district includes Humboldt and Del Norte Counties, and those portions of Trinity and Siskiyou that lie west of range 10 west, Mount Diablo Meridian. Register C. P. Roberts approximates the unsold Government land in his district in the following proportions:—

Humboldt County (acres)	1,250,000
Del Norte	1,250,000
Trinity	1,750,000
Siskiyou	750,000
Total (acres)	5,000,000

In regard to the peculiarities of the land, it contains mineral of untold wealth, while there is no limit to the timber area, the only difficulty being inability to get it to market. The mountain grazing country is claimed to be too cold to winter stock without preparing food for winter use. There is very little valley land susceptible of cultivation that is not taken up.

A FIELD FOR EMIGRATION.

As a field for emigration Mr. Roberts does not give a very glowing account as reported in the San Francisco papers. He says: " We have little to offer as an inducement for emigration in the way of Government lands, for many reasons. First, the cost of getting here by steamer is ten dollars; second, the lack of roads to enable a person to get around over the country. If the land were surveyed and we had a railroad, there is room for thousands of families who could make a good living. As it is, many who went into the hills years ago with the intention of making themselves homes, found upon trial that they were not living in the proper sense. They were only staying away from churches, schools and society, all of which privileges and advantages they could have, and yet make a good living, by coming nearer the towns and settlements. As a natural consequence they have mostly sold out to some stock-raiser and left the hills. There is not one family in the hills now where ten could be found eight or ten years ago. Business of all kinds has been good for the past year—work for all, and every one well paid. The three leading industries of the country, lumber, wool and dairying, are in a flourishing condition; never better. The farmers who depend upon the raising of grain and potatoes have not done so well, owing to short crops caused by blight, as well as too heavy freight charges. Taken as a whole, our county is in a prosperous condition, and will compare favorably with any in the State, all things considered."

The *Times* remarks on the above as follows: "The timber land is of little value for farming, for the reason that the stumps and roots never decay and cannot be removed. There is a good deal of land now used for cattle and sheep ranges that would make good agricultural land, but the owners do not care to dispose of these ranges. There are small patches here and there where fine farms can be made at reasonable expense. It is safe to say that the resources of the county are almost

THE SCENERY, AND PLEASURE RESORTS.

wholly undeveloped. They consist chiefly in forest, mining, agricultural and grazing lands, any one of which is sufficient in point of value and extent to insure a prosperous growth.

SCENERY AND RESORTS.

In speaking of the natural endowments of the county, the Humboldt *Standard* says:—

Yo Semite and other mountain gorges having surpassing romantic attractions, have become public resorts; some of our lakes in the interior of the State have also become the rendezvous for the summer tourists. Others have been beautified and retained as private homes or country residences. Thus far the seeming isolation of Humboldt County has prevented the improvement of any of her natural beauties. And yet we have them, rare gems of romantic grandeur, claiming both mountain hill and glen, river, lake and ocean, beach and bluff. The almost certainty of the advent of the railroad through our county in the near future, brings these points of attraction more forcibly to mind, for we have some unsurpassed locations, particularly on the coast north of Trinidad. About nine miles above the town named are several lakes—three in number—which are deep, have well-defined shores, are not intruded upon by marshes, abound with all the fish native to that section, and would afford magnificent and safe yachting.

THE BLUE LAKES.

Blue Lake, near Arcata, is one of the most important resorts in the county. A hotel is kept here by Clement Chartin. The house is roomy and cheerful, and has been built with an especial regard to the comfort of pleasure seekers. The neighborhood is one of the most romantic and inviting spots on the North Pacific Coast. Parties and families desiring to spend a short time in the country will find a well-provided table, with every comfort and convenience desired and every attention shown. Complete accommodations for wayfarers and travelers. The Blue Lake Hotel is situated on the north side of Mad River, on the Mad River road, about eight miles from Arcata. Stage connects with the Arcata boat daily, Sundays excepted. This is the only direct route to Green Point, Willow Creek, Hoopa Valley, New River, Orleans Bar, Sawyer's Bar, Weaverville and the lumbering part of Mad River, and a trip out to Blue Lake will afford a fine view of the redwoods and other scenery. Our artist has given a sketch of this beautiful and romantic resort.

RIO DELL SCENERY.

For another view of the country we recommend a ride to Rio Dell, a charming country retreat, situated on Eel River, which offers unsurpassed attractions to the tourist and pleasure seeker.

Here he will find a comfortably furnished and well-kept inn, where he can loll in the sunshine, eat fruit to his heart's content and the satisfaction of his inner man.

If he wants a boat ride he can take one on the limpid waters of Eel River, which, for the space of a mile or more, seems to have given up its idea of wandering over the whole adjacent country. It forms a summer lake and makes a beautiful sheet of water. The hotel is kept by L. Painter, and is illustrated and fully described elsewhere. The visitor will enjoy himself and live on an abundance of fresh fruit, milk, and butter from the home, garden, and dairy. Stage runs regularly from Ferndale and Eureka during the summer season.

VANCE'S PICNIC GROUNDS.

An annual picnic, engineered and managed by John Vance, Esq., has been held for several years. This trips affords a delightful view of the redwood forests and other scenery. It is thus mentioned by a correspondent: "The company started from the city wharf on three barges, drawn by steamers *Ada* and *Little Jones*, having on board about 1,000 persons, and at the landing took the cars on Vance's railroad. During the run of about six miles many changes of climate and scenery were apparent. The beautiful little engine, a perfect model of the larger ones used on ordinary railroads, carried us along at times with a high rate of speed. Rushing suddenly from the level prairie shores of the bay, which are swept by northern winds, we plunge into a jungle of almost tropical richness, through which a road is cut, barely wide enough for the track, on either side of which is seen a dense growth of vegetation, interspersed with giant trees towering above the mass of verdure, silent monitors, who have come down to us perhaps from the antediluvian.

Soon we enter upon a curving line of trestle-work and cross the rapid stream of Mad River on a covered bridge, then winding up the north bank of this wild and romantic river, through deep cuts and narrow vales, where cosy farm-houses loom out from sheltered nooks and warm valleys, clothed with yellow harvests, gardens and orchards, where the coast winds never penetrate.

The picnic grounds are well arranged, and located just below the busy mill and village. Within the inclosure are abundant facilities for rest and comfort in the way of seats and tables, sunshine and shade, with an extensive view down into the river and up the mountain sides, also a commodious platform for dancing and promenading. The Eureka band and Kauson's orchestra accompanied the picnicers, and played during the trip to and fro, and also at the grounds.

DESCRIPTION OF HUMBOLDT BAY.

The Bureau of the United States Coast Survey, A. D. Bache Superintendent, published the following: "Sailing directions—this harbor may be easily recognized by a remarkable red bluff* facing the entrance, with a perpendicular front to the

---

* The Red Bluff mentioned is generally called "Howard's Bluff," from the fact that it was embraced in the premises of Maj. E. H. Howard.

STORE AND WAREHOUSE OF A. M. GILL, ROHNERVILLE, HUMBOLDT CO. CAL.

FARM & RESIDENCE OF WILLIAM CAMPTON, RHONERVILLE, HUMBOLDT CO. CAL.

sea of ninety-six feet, and by the head-land, known as Table Bluff, five miles to the southward. To enter the harbor, bring Howard's house (Maj. E. H. Howard, still a resident of Eureka , a large white four-story house, to bear by compass, SE., and well on with a point of trees on the highlands, two miles back. Run it on this range until across the bar, when the breakers on either side of the channel will be a sufficient guide to the anchorage."

Latitude of Humboldt entrance 40° 46′ 05″. Longitude West from Greenwich, 124° 12′ 21″. Variations of the Magnetic Needle, 17° 04″ East. Captain Ottinger, of the U. S Revenue Marine, reported (1850) eighteen feet at low water on the bar.

Humboldt Bay divides, one portion running northeast from Humboldt Point about twenty miles, from one to eight miles wide, dotted over with beautiful islands. The bay is the shape of a pear with the stem towards the sea, with a depth of water sufficient for vessels to lay anywhere close up to the bluff shores safe from any and all gales that may blow. The anchorage grounds are equal to any port in the world. Ships are not compelled to discharge freight at the "ship's tackles," one or two miles from land, but come directly to the wharves.

The other portion of the bay runs from Humboldt Point southeast, with two channels. This bay is comparatively long and narrow. Its length is something over twenty miles, with a width ranging from less than a mile to eight miles. The area of the bay is from thirty-six to forty square miles, a portion of which is very shallow tide water. The exit to the sea is at the south end. The sand ridge between the bay and the ocean is covered with a stunted growth of trees, which breaks the force of the storm coming over the ocean. The depth of the bay about Eureka ranges from ten to thirty feet of water, but much of this bay is extremely shallow. However, in the vicinity of Eureka, the largest sea-going vessels will easily float when once in the bay.

WHO FIRST DISCOVERED HUMBOLDT BAY.

In preparing the early history of Humboldt Bay, we corresponded with Stephen H. Meek, the veteran trapper and hunter. He came on a trapping expedition to California in 1832. He wintered on Tulare Lake in 1833. He followed trapping all over California. In 1835 he trapped for the Hudson Bay Fur Company on Rogue River, Trinity, Scott, Pit, Yuba, Feather, American and other streams. In 1842 he wintered in Oregon. In 1845 he conducted the first large train of 480 wagons to Oregon. It is very evident that he knew if there were any trappers about Humboldt Bay at that time. He is still hunting and trapping the streams of Northern California, and we inquired of him if he knew anything about Humboldt Bay at that date, and received the following reply:—

"ETNA, Siskiyou Co., Cal., January 4, 1882.

"PUBLISHER OF COUNTY HISTORY—*Dear Sir:* As regards the early history of Humboldt Bay, it is very clear that the first explorations along that coast, and within the bay itself, was made by Mr. William G. Ray, a factor of the Hudson Bay Company, who was sent down the coast from Vancouver to attempt the establishment of one or more stations on the coast, about the year 1830 or 1831. He entered this bay ,being under the impression that it was Drake's Bay), passing close under the bluff called Table Bluff, and discovered what he named Clearwater Bay, on account of the purity of its waters. On landing he found the Indians so hostile that no permanent station was established at that time, whereupon he sailed farther south and established a post at Drake's Bay, which is there yet, I believe. This same Mr. Ray, as good a man as ever lived, at the beginning of the Mexican war, being still an employé of the Hudson Bay Company, took sides with the Americans in the contest, contrary to the wishes of his employers, for which action he was cashiered. This disgrace preyed upon his mind to such an extent that he committed suicide in his own house in San Francisco, and was buried in the garden of the old establishment, from whence his remains have been removed to a cemetery.

"Yours truly, STEPHEN H. MEEK."

DANGEROUS ENTRANCE TO BAY.

The danger at Humboldt Bay is at the entrance. It cannot be denied that the condition of the bar and entrance present a very serious question to the shippers and to every resident of Eureka, and of the whole county.

The North and South Sprits are, for a mile on each side of the entrance, subject to occasional irruptions by the ocean, which materially widen the space and cause shoal water. The channel, after crossing the bar, is but one-fourth of a mile in width for some distance. While the North and South Sprits remain in their present condition three tidal currents, one from the bay proper (north), one from Elk River (east), and the other from the south bay, meet at the entrance.

Capt. H. H. Buhne, whose experience as a pilot in this harbor dates back to its earliest discovery, and who was the first to sound the entrance and enter the bay in a whale boat from the sea, does not speak very encouragingly of the possibility of building a breakwater.

On the 18th of November, 1881, sixteen sailing vessels were lying laden with lumber waiting for an opportunity to cross the bar. The ocean breaks upon this bar, and it is often very difficult to get over, and always very rough. The depth upon the bar varies from ten to sixteen feet. In seasons of heavy storms the ocean waves gain the ascendancy, and the minimum depth prevails.

Hon. J. T. Ryan's *Mary Ann* was the first tug which towed vessels in and out in 1852.

NUMBER OF SHIPWRECKS.

The following record of the number of shipwrecks on or near Humboldt Bar was prepared for us by W. P. Daykin:—

1850—*Eclipse*, brig *San Jacinto*, schooner *Sarah Wardwell*.
1851—Bark *Jane*, steamer *Commodore Preble*.
1852—Steamer *Sea Gull*, bark *Home*, bark *Cornwallis*, brig *John Clifford*.
1853—Schooner *Mexican*.
1855—Schooner *Piedmont*, schooner *Sierra Nevada*.
1858—Schooner *Toronto*.
1859—Schooner *J. W. Ryerson*.
1860—Bark *Success*, steamer *Northerner*, thirty lives lost, near Centreville.
1862—Schooner *T. H. Allen*, one life lost; brig *Eolus*.
1863—Steam tug *Merrimac*, thirteen lives lost; schooner *Dashaway*, fourteen lives lost at sea.
1864—Bark *Hartford*.
1876—Schooner *Albert & Edward*, five lives lost, one saved.
1877—Schooner *Marrietta*, all saved.
1878—Schooner *Laura Pike*, seven lives lost.
1879—Scow *Sura*, lost at sea off Crescent City.
1880—Schooner *Edward Parker*, two lives lost, four saved.

HUMBOLDT BAY LIGHTHOUSE.

The light was exhibited for the first time on the night of the 20th of December, 1856, and was thus described:—

At the entrance of Humboldt Bay is a fixed, white light, fourth order of fresnel, illuminating the entire horizon. The house is situated on the north sands, three-fourths of a mile from the inlet, and about midway between the bay and sea-shores. It consists of a keeper's dwelling of one story and a half, with a tower rising twenty-one feet above the roof from the center, both plastered and white-washed and surmounted by an iron lantern painted red.

The light is fifty-three feet above high water of spring tides, and should be seen in clear weather from the deck of a sea-going vessel twelve nautical or fourteen statue miles.

The present keeper of the lighthouse, is Capt. W. P. Daykin. He keeps a record of the weather and of the number of vessels entering and departing, and much other useful information which he has furnished for our history.

LIFE-SAVING STATION.

At the entrance to the bay at the lighthouse is a life-saving station. The apparatus is thus described;—

There is a brass mortar, by which a strong cord can be immediately attached to an ingeniously contrived projectile and thrown 700 feet from the shore or life-boat. The mortar, only weighing 100 pounds, can be carried quickly to almost any point on the Peninsula, quickly arranged and the cord sent to its destination in one second from the time when fired. By means of this cord attached to a larger one, and this to a still larger one, and so on, persons upon a wrecked vessel could soon have a powerful cable connecting the wreck with the shore. The life-car is attached to this heavy cable by means of the cable passing through two iron rings, one at each end and top part of the boat, or car, by which means and the use of a cord attached to the car, and connecting with the shore and wreck, a rapid and safe transit can be kept up, and precious lives saved that otherwise would be destroyed. In this iron car can be placed several persons, and so securely locked up that the car in its transit may tumble, roll, and remained submerged, and its occupants are safe.

This department is rendered largely ineffective for the want of a rail track from the boat-house to low tide water, that the boat may be got to sea when necessary. When the *Edward Parks* was wrecked, the life-boat got stuck between the boat-house and the water, and had to be abandoned, and a lighter boat, one that could be handled, taken in its place.

HARBOR IMPROVEMENTS.

The *Standard* says:—

"The march of improvement which has carried other sections of our country onward and upward with such rapid strides and which left Humboldt out in the cold for so many years, now seems to have been permanently turned toward our county.

"In the fall of 1877, we commenced the agitation of the subject of harbor improvement, and for the purpose of showing the importance of the improvement published a series of articles extending over two months, describing our coast line, territory, navigable rivers, ports, shipping points, area, productions, exports, resources, distances, capacity for the maintenance of population and increase of productions, and the effect that improved avenues of commerce and trade would have upon all these.

"In the winter of 1878–79, we entered into correspondence with Capt. James B. Eads, relative to a survey and study of our bar as a preliminary and foundation to the securing of a Government appropriation for its improvement. Mr. Eads made a favorable reply, but through the apathy of some of our leading men his services were not obtained. The movement, however, had the effect of bringing our harbor into prominent notice.

"The Government is at work on the bay, the growing commerce at last having attracted attention. In carrying out the orders of the Department for the survey, Colonel Mendall, of the corps of U. S. Engineers, made an inspection of the bay in person. Although the advantages and capacity of the harbor, the volume of commerce and crying necessity for Government aid, had been sounded in every possible key, yet that gentleman was much surprised at what he found here, the importance of the position, resources and commerce. Appreciating the requirements, he directed the work of the survey of the harbor with a view to greatly extending improvements.

"The sum of $40,000 was appropriated by the Government for dredging. The present contract requires the bay in front of the wharves to be dredged so that the water will be of a uniform depth of ten feet at low tide. A second appropriation has been recommended by the United States Engineers for the Pacific Coast, the amount to be $50,000. It is expected that this will also be expended in needed improvements.

The commerce of the bay during the entire year keeps a fleet of sailing vessels plying to San Francisco and also to foreign ports in the Pacific. During a portion of the year two steamers are constantly running between Eureka and San Francisco, and one steamer is kept busy during the remainder of the year. The most noticeable feature in the carrying trade from this place at the present time is the extensive business with foreign ports. The field for export from this place seems to have been gradually enlarging. Demand has sprung up in new places for lumber, to be supplied from this county and shipped from Eureka. The principal foreign trade has been for years with the Hawaiian Islands and Mexico.

NUMBER OF VESSELS ENTERING THE BAY.

During the year terminating on the 30th of June, 1854, there were 183 arrivals of vessels in Humboldt Bay. For the next twenty years we could obtain no definite information.

The following record of the number of vessels that have crossed Humboldt Bar was furnished us by W. P. Daykin. It covers a space of eight years, and gives some idea of the amount of business transacted:—

1874, May to December		514
1875, January to December		781
1876, " " "		1,196
1877, " " "		832
1878, " " "		762
1879, " " "		737
1880, " " "		766
1881, " " " 31		746
		6,264

LIVELY BUSINESS ON THE BAY.

The following items, taken from the *Times* in regard to the shipping business of Humboldt Bay, show the amount of business there transacted, and speaks more emphatically than anything we can say with reference to the importance of this port and its growing business.

"October 26, 1881, there were twenty-five vessels in port. The schooners *Ida McKay*, *Lottie Carson*, *W. H. Stevens*, and *Fairy Queen* were loaded and ready for sea. The schooner *Jennie Thelin* was discharging ballast at Bairal's Wharf, and the *Western Home* and *Ivanhoe* were loading at the Occidental Mill. The schooners *Emma* and *Louisa* are loading at Hookton, and the schooners *James Townsend* and *Bonanza* at the Arcata Wharf. At Carson's Mill, the schooners *Sparkling Sea*, *John Hancock*, *A. P. Jordan*, and *Halcyon* (new) were taking cargo. The *Mary Buhne* was discharging coal at Buhne's Wharf. The brig *Josephine* and schooners *Sparrow* and *Mary Swan* were loading at Vance's Mill; the schooners *Mary E. Russ* and *Serena Thayer* at Russ & Co's Mill, and the schooners *Jessie Nickerson*, *Eva*, and *Isabel*, and brig *Hesperian*, at Jones & Co's Mill on the Island. The barkentine *C. L. Taylor* and the schooners *Laura Pike*, *Vanderbilt*, and *N. L. Drew* were outside yesterday, but the rough condition of the bar prevented bringing them into port.

"The first iron sailing vessel that ever entered Humboldt Bay, arrived November 19, 1881. The *Ferrea*, Capt. Schutt, came directly from Victoria, British Columbia, whither she had gone from China with a cargo of merchandise. The capacity of the vessel is 400,000 feet of lumber in the hold. This amount of lumber will be purchased by Captain Schutt and taken to Melbourne. The ballast consisted of gravel, and was used on the streets of the city.

"The British bark *Woodville* and British brig *Restless* arrived in the bay. Both vessels will carry lumber to Sydney. The *Woodville* has an order for 210,000 feet, and will carry enough more to make a full cargo. The *Restless* will take a cargo of 260,000 feet or thereabouts."

E. H. Howard's valuable statistics show the arrival, for 1881, of twenty-two vessels from foreign ports, and thirty cleared for foreign ports. The foreign ports cleared for were as follows: Honolulu, Mexico, Central America, Fiji Islands, Victoria, Tahiti, Sidney, Valparaiso, Panama, and Australia.

PORT OF ENTRY.

As long ago as 1854, a joint resolution of our Legislature declared that

WHEREAS, The manufacturing and commercial interests of Humboldt Bay are rapidly growing in importance, showing from official statistics as large an exportation of lumber as from any point on the coast; and *whereas*, the agricultural, mineral, and lumbering districts depending upon this port for their supplies, are being developed by a large and increasing population, who will require increase of importations of merchandise; and *whereas*, to secure the benefits arising from improved facilities for manufacturing, other than domestic markets must be sought, in which to dispose of the proceeds of the one and supply the demand of the other; therefore,

Resolved, that Congress be urged to create a new Collection District, with its port of entry at Humboldt Bay.

The above has been true for many years, and still the people are getting up petitions calling for a port of entry which shall comprise all the waters and shores of the State of California north of the south boundary line of Humboldt County, for the reason that many vessels are built and owned at Humboldt Bay, and ought to be registered there. The nearest port of entry is at San Francisco, a distance of over two hundred miles. The new law proposed provides that the Fourth District shall be the District of Humboldt; to comprise all the waters and shores of the counties of Humboldt and Del Norte, in which Eureka, on the Bay of Humboldt, shall be the sole port of entry, and Crescent City a port of delivery. In the District of Humboldt there shall be a Collector, who shall reside at Eureka, and one Inspector, to be appointed by the Collector, with the approval of the Secretary of the Treasury, for the port of Crescent City.

RESOURCES AND INDUSTRIES.

Character of Soil—Chief Productions—Stock-Raising, General Farming, Dairying—Progress of Twenty Years—Exports, Etc.

The resources and industries of Humboldt are of great variety. The four principal ones being agriculture, stock-raising, mining and manufacturing. These to a great extent support each other, and were it not for the home markets created by the mines and mills, agriculture would not have been so far developed as it is to-day. Without a railroad, the farmers of this county are thrown chiefly upon the home demand to furnish a market for a large share of their produce, as lumbering and mining creates a demand for what the farmer raises.

THREE DIVISIONS OF SOIL.

The land is naturally divided into three parts. The first division includes the lowlands near the coast, the alluvial lands on the rivers, and the sloping lands near the coast, which in some places form a connecting link between the lowlands and the high timbered ridges.

This division contains some of the richest soil in the world. It is nearly all agricultural land.

Professor Hilgard, who analyzed the soil of the Eel River bottom, said:—

"There is very little difference between the soil and subsoil down to thirty inches depth. I am inclined to think that the soil and subsoil have been exchanged, for the differences between them, according to the usual state of things, appear to be the wrong way, the surface soil being somewhat more clayey than the subsoil.

"The soil and subsoil are very rich in potash, and contain a respectable amount of phosphates. A somewhat extraordinary amount of magnesia, and of sulphuric acid, giving rise to the suspicion that in low spots there will be sometimes an "alkali," consisting largely of Epsom salt coming to the surface.

The soil is remarkably poor in lime for one of its character; so much so that I would recommend the application of lime as one of its foremost needs, both as respects tillage and the making up of the other deficiency, viz., vegetable matter or humus. The latter, after liming, can be introduced by green manuring—plowing in of green crops. With the aid of these, your soil ought to hold out for a long time."

SECOND DIVISION OF LAND.

The second division includes the belt of timbered lands, which skirt the coast, at a greater or less distance from it. It approaches quite near to the coast in some places, and in others it recedes several miles from it; it varies in width from eight to fifteen miles, and rising, as it does, one ridge above another, and being densely timbered with evergreen trees, it gives the country, when viewed from the ocean, that dark sombre appearance for which it is so remarkable, and almost entirely hides from view, the still higher mountains in the interior, known as the Bald Mountains.

This country is very uneven, being cut at short intervals by the numerous streams coming down from the interior to the coast with sharp ridges between them; the earth is of a clayey character generally, but volcanic rocks make their appearance on the tops of some of the highest ridges; the hills and ridges are invariably steep, but seldom or never precipitous; it contains scarcely any agricultural land, a few small open spots on the different streams being all that can be found worthy of cultivation.

THIRD DIVISION OF THE LANDS.

The third division embraces the open mountain country, farther in the interior. This division is much the largest of the three. Though it is termed the Bald Mountain country, in contradistinction to the densely timbered lands between it and the coast, it is by no means destitute of timber, scrub oaks being scattered all over the ridges; groves of spruce and firs are found on the cool, shady sides of the ridges, generally in the moist places and near the springs in the gorges. At a greater elevation, near the sources of the streams, the long-leafed pine makes its appearance.

The soil has generally a burnt red appearance, showing unmistakable evidence of having undergone the action of fire, and in some places masses of volcanic rocks protrude from the tops of the ridges. This country is chiefly for practical purposes, being covered in all places with grass of an excellent quality; near the tops of the poorest ridges, before it was used so much for stock range, grows a grass that bears a seed nearly as large as oats. The lower moist spots, and particularly the alluvial spots near the streams, grow grass and clover of indescribable exhuberance, not surpassed by any cultivated meadow in the Atlantic States.

This region is exceedingly well watered; besides the streams already mentioned, and their numerous tributaries, running in all directions, springs are numerous, even near the tops of the high ridges.

PLENTY OF WATER.

One of the features of Humboldt County is its wealth in pure water. One finds it everywhere—pure and cold as the fountains of the upper Sierra. An old resident says there is not, he thinks, 160 acres in the county without a permanent spring of fine water. The springs of pure, cold water about this county are a marvel, and it is impossible to fully describe their beauty and usefulness. There are thousands and thousands. Every hill and mountain side teems with them, and

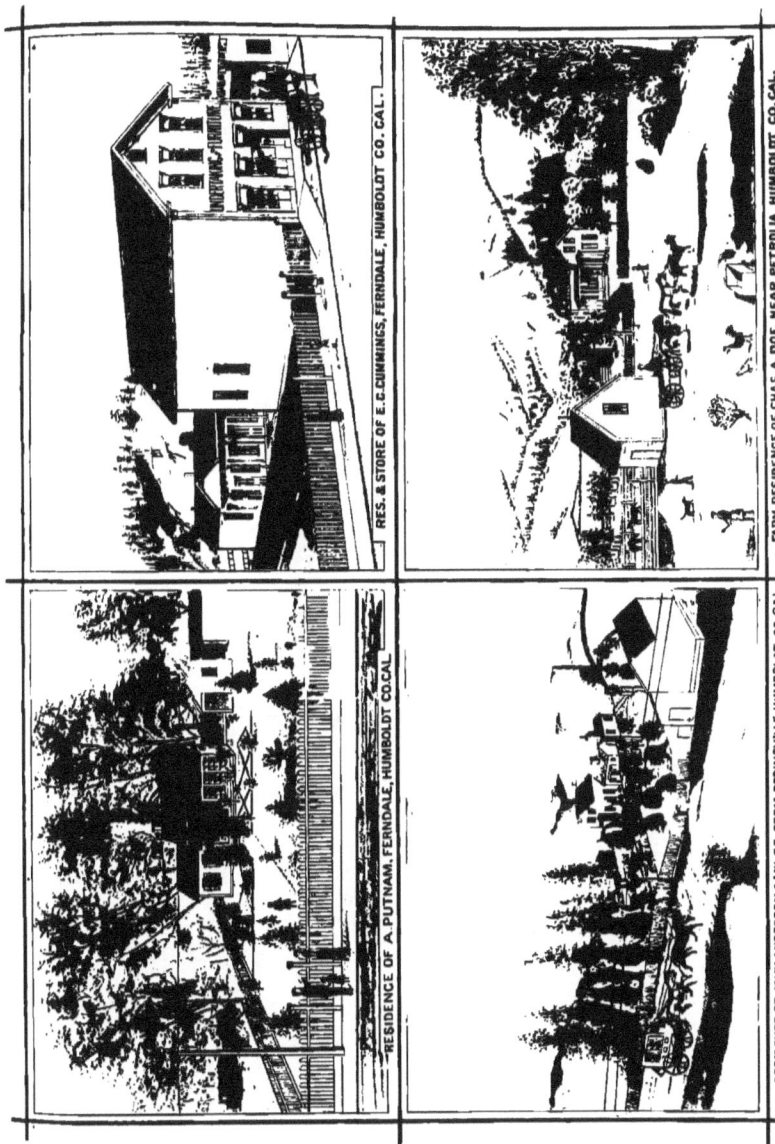

the weary traveler and his thirsty beast find streams of pure water, cool and fresh, gushing from the wayside banks, and gathered into troughs for his convenience. The flow of these springs vary from a few gallons a day to barrels per minute.

Whence comes all this grand body of pure water which is hourly poured from the mountain sides of Humboldt and adjoining counties? It is evident that the fountain head is far away from the outlet, and far above it also. The snow melting on the far away Sierras, must be the grand center of supply, and when we come to contemplate what a wonderful system of channels and veins there are in the surface of the earth, and how perfectly they all work, it is a fit subject for reverential meditation. How it gushes from the rock in its pure and crystalline beauty, glittering and glistening in the sunshine as it dances down the hill-side, refreshing and cheering the the thirsty world, making the flowers to spring up in their glorious grandeur, making the grass to put forth its greenest shoots the whole year through. What a glorious mission on earth has this spring of water! To man, and beast, and bird, and tree, and shrub, and grass, and flower, and fruit—to all that exists on the face of the earth, it proves a grand, glorious, inestimable boon.

THE PRINCIPAL VALLEYS.

There are hundreds of small valleys and productive prairies in all parts of the county, but the principal ones are those of Eel, Mad, Elk, Mattole, and Lower Trinity Rivers.

Elk River Valley, on the main stream, is about a mile wide and ranging from a few rods to a quarter of a mile on its forks.

The soil is of a clayey loam, heavily supplied with alluvial deposits, possessing extraordinary durability and fertility, yet that portion of this rich and lovely valley occupied by the husbandman hardly extends upward to the forks of the stream, the balance of the valleys and adjacent hills for several miles further up having been logged and burned over, and its space, occupied by an extraordinary supply of black, thimble, salmon, sallal, and other berry fruits, besides furnishing an excellent range of pasturage for immense bands of wild and domestic cattle.

Eel River Valley is the most noted and productive in the the county. In the entire valley are nearly 140 square miles, most of which are tillable and in a few years will be brought under cultivation. The soil is inexhaustable alluvial loam and there is no end to its productions. The Upper Eel River is a narrow, wild stream, without any valley land except in very small patches.

Mattole Valley is about wide enough for a good-sized farm where the river runs close to the mountain. Its fertility is equal to any in the county and produces abundant crops, principally wheat and oats. The valley is inclosed by lofty hills. The principal industries are farming and dairying, and some sheep-raising. The products of the dairies in the Mattole rank among the first in the county.

Hoopa Valley was formerly called Eden Valley or the Garden of Eden. It lies a little north of the parallel of 41° north latitude, and on Trinity River some eight miles above its junction with the Klamath. The distance to the ocean by the way of the river is about sixty miles. The Indians navigate the river with their canoes, some of which will carry two tons of freight, from the coast to some thirty miles above Hoopa Valley.

There are few falls or rapids, however, at which they have to make portages. The distance from the valley to Humboldt Bay is about forty miles. The valley is small, embracing only about six square miles of level land, which is mostly rich prairie, with some groves of white and evergreen oaks, some cottonwood, elder, maple, ash and willow.

The mountains rise gradually on all sides to a considerable height, and are mostly covered with pine and oak and an undergrowth of hazel, manzanita, oak and other brush, with openings of prairie which produce an abundance of excellent grass. There are a number of beautiful streams of the purest water flowing from the mountains across the valley. The climate of the valley is very mild. Snow seldom falls in the valley, and when it does, it lays but a short time. In summer it is dry and warm and not subject to fogs which prevail along the coast.

AGRICULTURAL PRODUCTIONS OF THE COUNTY.

We now mention the most prominent productions of these valleys and fertile prairies.

WHEAT—There is considerable wheat being grown throughout every agricultural portion of the county. But it is not the chief crop, as in most other counties of the State. All the county susceptible of cultivation will produce wheat. The bottom land near the bay will grow larger crops of wheat, even ninety to 100 bushels to the acre, but on account of the fogs the yield of flour is small, and that of bran, large. It does not present that hard, flinty appearance, such as gives character and notoriety to California wheat.

As a wheat-growing section this county is a decided success, but it has never been cultivated up to its capacity, and perhaps never will be. The yield per acre is greater than in any other portion of the State. More attention is given to this crop every year.

PEAS—There is probably no country in the world where the climate is so exactly suited to the culture of peas as Humboldt County. The yield is greater, the kernel is more fully developed, and is a surer crop than in any other country we know of in the world. The demand for split peas and the adulteration of coffee is from 3,000 to 3,500 sacks per year. The yield is enormous. Heretofore this county has supplied San Francisco market almost entirely alone. When they ripen, many farmers, instead of harvesting them, turn hogs on them, and an increased weight of an excellent quality of pork is the result.

BARLEY—Nearly all the land in Humboldt County not covered by redwood is well adapted to the raising of barley. As the lands are very prolific its cultivation has generally proved a good investment. The larger part sold is used at home by the mill men, this is generally ground before feeding.

MESQUIT SEED—The immense success of this article as a pasture grass is beyond parallel. No grass ever sown in the county has equaled it. It has been introduced as a pasture grass generally throughout the county. It flourishes on hill land or on bottoms. It will grow in any nook or corner which is worthless, except as a pasture. It will support more stock to the acre of pasturage than any grass grown in the county. Steep hillsides which cannot be cultivated, if burned over and sown with this seed, are made as valuable as any of the other lands. Any place that it has been sown in this county, the crop improves with age. It is equal to bunch grass for sweetness and palatability for stock.

POTATOES—Humboldt County is perhaps, the best potato-growing county in the State. Three hundred and twenty-four sacks per acre have been grown, in weight twenty-one and a half tons to an acre. In the times when potatoes succeeded the best in this county, an average crop on bottom land was eight to ten tons per acre. It was discovered at an early day that this was a great country for potatoes. In 1857, Wm. Chapman raised from a patch of less than an acre, 30,000 pounds—fifteen tons. On the Bates Ranch 19,000 pounds was raised on three-fourths of an acre.

Along the coast are alluvial benches varying from half a mile to three miles in width, which are exceedingly fertile from the washing of the ridges, the soil being of a black, rich vegetable mold, light and friable, and in places twenty feet deep. On this ground are raised the fine potatoes which market under the name of "Humboldt Spuds."

In earlier times Humboldt, in the potato market, was king. Everybody could own a piece of land if he wished, and might reckon on his $300 or $400 for every acre cultivated. Good land for this crop and eligibly situated became enormously high in price. Fortunes were made in the business and all diversified forms of farming were dropped and disappeared in this. The end, of course, soon came; some retired in time, others with less prudence ventured on.

Potatoes are no longer the leading article of farm export. Wool, oats and butter have all outstripped potatoes in commercial importance.

OATS—All the bottom lands in Humboldt County will produce 100 bushels per acre of this grain. The many new mills and other enterprises which have been added to the industries of the county during the past years, have created a home market for oats, so as to cut off exports considerably. The climate appears peculiarly adapted to the production of oats. The heavy fogs near the coast which have deleterious influence on wheat for flour-making purposes, appear to be just what is needed to make a good crop of oats. Oats will do well on any of the land, but the hill land will not produce as well as the bottom lands, but they will produce more than any of the States east of the Rocky Mountains. They are a good paying crop in this county.

PRINCIPAL FRUITS RAISED.

No particular attention has been given to raising of fruit for a foreign market. Most kinds of fruit do well, and almost every farmer has more or less orchard and garden. The principal apple-producing portion of the county is Eel River Valley, where the trees are somewhat sheltered from the ocean breeze. There is also considerable cider made, but none to ship. The capabilities of the county in the way of producing this fruit are enormous. Anywhere in the county, apples, pears, and plums luxuriate, except when exposed to the direct blasts of the northwest trade-winds on the ocean tank. In the interior all other fruits do well, save apricots, which are often caught by late spring frosts. Heavy fogs mark the coast during the summer months, and heavy rains may be looked for from October to May.

The above are the principal productions of the county. A full list is given in the statistical list of productions.

For several years past agriculture has shown the largest export footing, leading the lumber trade by a few hundred thousand, but with the present boom in lumber on the one hand, and the ceasing of the potato crop and shipment on the other, lumber is likely to take the lead for the next two or three years.

SHEEP AND WOOL.

The wool production has increased in a wonderful manner during the past ten years. The total product of the county in 1870 was 51,867 pounds, while the export in 1880 from Eureka alone reached the aggregate of 900,000 pounds, while the bulk from the southern portion of the county went out by the way of Shelter Cove; and no statistics are attainable. Much attention is being paid to the grading of flocks, many very fine bucks having been brought into the county during past seasons.

Humboldt wool commands the highest market prices, ranging from four to seventeen cents higher than any other section of the Pacific Coast except Sonoma and Mendocino Counties. The wool is free from dirt, burrs and other deleterious substances.

THE LARGEST SHEEP RANCH.

The Fort Baker sheep ranch, owned by Russ, Porter & Hanson, is considered the largest in the county. When shearing time comes it is said that Fort Baker is as lively as a village. In 1881, shearing commenced the 6th and ended the 17th of June. Among the number of men on the ranch, thirty-eight were shearers, one doctor to doctor sheep, three men to drive the sheep into the pens, two men to gather them up on the range, one man to hand horses for the shearers, making a total of over fifty men. They sheared 14,000 sheep; the biggest day's work was 3,090 head; the two men that baled wool put up sixty-two bales of wool that day, which is considered the biggest day's work ever done on any ranch in the county. The largest tally for any one man was 120 sheep in one day's shearing. Russ, Hanson & Porter had a good crop of wool, which was hard to beat for cleanliness and length of staple.

Like all other sheep-owners in the mountains, they keep a large number of dogs for the protection of the stock. A well-trained hound that will lead the pack is worth $150. He must not only be trained to follow a bear or coyote persistently, but be taught to pay no heed to either sheep or deer. He is to wage war against destructive "varments" alone. These dogs are fed on cold mush, without cream and sugar, with only an occasional feast of meat.

Other large sheep-raisers are mentioned elsewhere.

PRICES OF WOOL.

The lowest average price of wool for eleven years past was in 1870, when it was quoted at fourteen cents. The two highest years were 1871 and 1872, when the average price of California wool went up to twenty-six and one-half and twenty-nine cents. Wool brought a higher price in 1872 than it did during 1880. The largest wool clip ever known in California was in 1876, when it amounted to a total of 56,550,970 pounds, and although the clip was much larger that year than in 1880 when it amounted to 46,074,154 pounds, or more than 10,000,000 pounds difference, yet the money value of the crop of 1880 exceeded the total value of that of 1876 by nearly $2,000,000. The average price of wool during 1880 was twenty-two cents, and the total production of the State for the past eleven years amounted to 423,701,905 pounds, which produced in cash $78,632,830. The average price of California wool has been steadily increasing.

The wool-growing interest in the county is comparatively of modern growth. Until within the last fifteen years it has assumed no proportions worthy of note.

STOCK-RAISING.

In earlier years grazing was a favorite business, and the rich pasture ranges in the eastern part of the county and an unequalled climate invited large herds of cattle from the central and southern parts of the State; but the great losses sustained from Indian depredations in the first years of its settlement came to be a certain and serious factor in the calculation of profits. With the disappearance of the Indians came a revival of stock-raising—with its usual adjunct, dairying, both of which, under the improved conditions of management of late years, have become sure and steady sources of profit to owners.

A great deal of pasture land is used as ranges for stock cattle that will eventually be used for dairying purposes as the business expands. From these hills are annually gathered large bands of cattle, which are driven south to San Francisco and other markets.

THE DAIRYING BUSINESS.

Butter-making is fast becoming a leading enterprise in the county. The grasses are especially adapted for dairying, and grazing for cattle or sheep. The territory is large, the grazing crop never fails, the climate is not severe on cattle, cows yield milk copiously, and we know of no more promising or inviting place for the intelligent dairyman to operate in than in this county.

Humboldt butter commands the highest rates, a large section of the country near Ferndale being devoted to that industry entirely. The country is hilly, but not particularly rough. Stock feeds on its highest hills almost the year round. Dairy products have reached a high figure at times, while the average prices have afforded a good return for the labor, time and capital involved. Dairying in Humboldt County, says the *Times*, has become one of our leading industries, employing, as it does, a large amount of capital and labor, and its chief product—butter—has established for itself a reputation second to none in the State. The climate of Humboldt is peculiarly adapted to dairying, especially along the coast belt—a strip say fifteen miles wide, and extending from Mendocino on the south to Del Norte on the north, a distance of one hundred miles. There are no extremes of heat or cold to which interior sections are subject, while the ranges are covered with nutritious grasses—native clover and filaree, which are kept green and thrifty by the fogs and moist sea air well into the fall, admitting of longer dairy seasons than would otherwise be possible.

There are still considerable tracts of good dairy land in Bear River and Mattole sections—at least what will make good dairy land when cleared up and seeded with red clover, or English white clover mixed with timothy or cheat grass. Some of this land lies in the hills bordering the Eel River Valley, southeast of Bear River.

THE LARGEST DAIRIES.

Hon. Joseph Russ owns thousands of acres which he has divided into suitable ranges, and he is still laying out new farms on Cape and Bear River ridges, where the largest dairies are situated.

Mr. Russ is fitting up a dairy in the heart of the Bear River country, which will be one of the largest in the county. All this country is well supplied with spring water for stock and dairy use.

Of the eighty-one dairies in the Bear River country, Mr. Russ owns twenty, nineteen of which are leased. On these eighty-one dairies, 4,580 cows are milked, being an average of a trifle over fifty-six cows to the dairy. These 4,580 cows

IMPORTANCE OF THE DAIRYING INTEREST.

yielded 732,800 pounds of butter for the season of 1881, being an average of 100 pounds to the cow. The average price for which this butter was sold was twenty-eight cents per pound. This makes the product of each cow $44.80 for the season, which is a very fair return, considering that the cow would not cost more than one-half or two-thirds of that amount. The total sales of butter from this district for the past season amounted to $205,184. The great bulk of this butter is shipped to Eureka and San Francisco markets.

Capt. H. H. Buhne, at his ranch seven miles from this city, also has fine large buildings, and will be able, with the improvements now making, to tie up nearly one hundred head of stock. He is breeding Jerseys and Short Horns, with which he has been quite successful.

We make the following extracts from an article furnished us on the subject of butter-making by Richard Johnson of Capetown, one of the oldest dairymen of that section:—

"It is found out by experienced dairymen that the best butter is made from milk skimmed at the right time, which varies from thirty-six to forty-eight hours, entirely depending on the temperature at which the milk is kept, which ought to be from 60° to 70° Fahrenheit. There is a great deal said in books about dairying, or rather the theory of dairying, which is not worth the paper it is written upon to the practical man. Some of these book-writers say that it is essentially necessary to wash the cow's udder before milking, etc., in the winter time. It may be so occasionally, but not always; and then again 'that the milker ought to have his hands and face washed, hair combed and have a white apron on while he milks.' So far as his hands are concerned it is all well enough, but the other appendages are, to say the least, superfluous and impracticable, and if there was no other reason, the proprietor could not afford to pay thirty or forty dollars a month to keep his hired help in the shape of milkers dressed and cleaned with white aprons. It is right and proper to have everything around the dairy house clean and sweet as circumstances will permit, so as to be able to send a No. 1 article of butter to the market.

"My method of dairying is to have the cows milked clean in as short a time as possible. A good milker will milk twenty cows in two hours and a half, or three hours at the farthest. I have the milk strained into a hundred or more gallon vat which stands in the dairy house, or on the porch of the dairy house, and have it strained by one man all the time, and into pans that will hold six or seven quarts, set on revolving racks. The milk stands from thirty-six to sixty hours, depending on the temperature. We churn every day by horse power, wash the butter thoroughly with water in the churn. We do not let the butter gather in a lump in the churn until it is washed. It is churned until it gets in little round lumps about the size of a pea, then draw off the buttermilk, put in plenty of water to keep it in that state until the buttermilk is all washed out of it, then turn the churn round half a dozen or more times, which will gather it up in a lump fit to be taken out on to the butter table to be worked and salted, which ought to be done as quickly as possible, only just working it enough to mix the salt well through it, so that there will be no white streaks in it. It is either moulded into what is called two pound rolls, or put down solid. If put into rolls, there is about six pounds of salt put to the hundred pounds of butter. If put down solid, eight pounds of salt put to the one hundred pounds of butter."

DEFICIENCY IN WEIGHT OF BUTTER.

"I do earnestly hope that the time is not far distant when there will be a law passed that will make the two-pound roll of butter weigh two pounds. As it is now, the box of fifty rolls of butter which ought to weigh 100 pounds, ranges from ninety-three to ninety-seven pounds, which is all in favor of the retail dealer, at least so says the commission man.

"A dairy of 100 cows requires the labor of five men for about five months, and four men for another month, and three men until the cows are dried up, except when they feed. The milking season lasts in Humboldt County on Bear River, seven months. On the Mattole from five to six months. On the farming land in the valleys, longer.

"On Bear River, Mattole, and in some other places, we dairy altogether on the natural grasses, which are found to be very nutritious.

"Our present dairy region is not very extensive, but from all the information I can obtain from other places, we can keep more stock to the acre than any other county in the State. We milk now, in this county, about 5,000 cows, and on the increase every year, and in ten years from now I have no doubt there will be 10,000 dairy cows in the county. There is quite a difference now and when I came to the county in 1856. I do not think there were 200 cows, all told, dairied in the county then, and butter was made in a way that would not bring the highest market price. Then it was thought that if the buyers objected to a few hairs or a few specks of dirt, that they were getting too particular. One man, an acquaintance of mine, gave up the business on that account.

"There is one fact that every dairyman knows, that the longer we remain in the business the more proficient we become. I have dairied for nearly a quarter of a century, and I am still learning every year something more about it. As yet we have not the experience in feeding that they have in other places. We depend upon the natural grass, which will keep a cow in good condition the year round to every four acres. In some places it will require more, but on most of the dairy ranches on Bear River, a cow can be kept on every four acres. The valley or farm land, which is a rich, alluvial deposit—when properly subdued, cultivated, and put down in timothy grass, clover, alfalfa or lucern, can be made to keep a cow to the acre.

RANCH HOME OF THOMAS STEWART, ON BEAR RIVER, 15 MILES FROM FERNDALE, HUMBOLDT CO. CAL.

EXCELSIOR DAIRY RANCH, OF H. D. SMITH, BEAR RIVER, HUMBOLDT CO. CAL.

PROGRESS OF THE LEADING INDUSTRIES.

ALFALFA FOR COWS.

"It is being found out that the valley land will produce alfalfa. I visited a farmer the other day that had about an acre, and he told me that he had cut it three times, a couple of tons each time, and, although our climate is moist, he told me that the yield would be more if irrigated. If alfalfa can be successfully raised, our county is only in its infancy. Every year farmers become more convinced of the profits of dairy husbandry.

"The climate, soil, and surroundings are better adapted to this branch of farming than any other, as the facility for getting bulky produce to market is very expensive, taking into consideration the expense of getting it to a shipping port and thence to San Francisco.

"By putting the products of the farm into butter and pork, for they both go together, his freight to and from a shipping point, is nothing in comparison to that of grain and potatoes. This is well known to every intelligent farmer in the county, and I have not a doubt in my mind, but in the not distant future dairying will be one of our principal industries. There is a great need of a creamery and cheese factory, one or more in the Kel River Valley, which to my mind, for the small dairy farmer, would be a much cheaper way to convert their cream into butter, than by doing so at home.

"It takes a long time to get most of our farmers out of the old rut or way of getting along. The milk and beef qualities of our stock perhaps, are equal to any other dairy stock of a common quality, and, perhaps, it is not saying too much that they are equal to fancy stock in milk and butter qualifications. In a portion of the dairy season we can make from one and one-quarter to one and one-half pounds to the cow. To sum it all up, we can make as many pounds of butter to the cow, and of as good a quality as is made in any other part of the State or the United States."

PROGRESS FOR TWENTY YEARS.

The following statistics of the leading industries will show how the county has progressed in twenty years. It is not claimed these figures are entirely correct; but are as near as could be obtained at the time by the Assessors. The statistics of 1860 were reported by J. J. DeHaven, Assessor, and those of 1880 were furnished us by Geo. H. Shaw, Esq., present County Assessor:—

	1860	1880
Land enclosed	10,975	105,347
Land cultivated	3,547	27,897
Wheat in acres	1,564	3,705
Wheat in bushels	40,564	86,600
Barley in acres	58	3,289
Barley in bushels	1,991	54,418
Oats in acres	542	7,193
Oats in bushels	15,723	260,774
Corn in acres	63	364
Corn in bushels	1,990	10,223
Peas in acres	883	656
Peas in bushels	31,584	17,321
Potatoes in acres	208	1,706
Potatoes in bushels	56,692	*4,714
Hay in acres	744	3,890
Hay in tons	1,233	7,724
Butter in pounds	34,400	96,750
Cheese in pounds	6,800	1,400
Apple trees	15,888	10,457
Peach trees	2,370	2,550
Pear trees	367	927
Plum trees	568	1,223

LIVE STOCK.

	1860	1880
Number of horses	1,658	4,914
Number of mules	328	1,003
Number of horned cattle	19,205	26,623
Number of sheep	523	170,829
Number of goats	18	372
Number of hogs	8,194	7,267

IMPROVEMENTS.

	1860	1880
Grist-mills, steam	2	2
Grist-mills, water power	2	2
Grist-mills, run of stone	4	4
Grain ground in bushels	16,500-bbls. flr.	3,000
Saw-mills, steam power	7	18
Saw-mills, water power	2	3
Lumber sawed, feet	9,575,000	32,349,000
Shingles made		25,110,500
Total assessed valuation	$1,309,801	86,239,452

PRODUCTIONS AND EXPORTS.

It has been the custom of the *Times* for several years past to furnish its readers with a statement of the productions and exports of the county, and from the valuable tables thus gathered we take the summary for the year. Humboldt has three recognized ports, namely, Trinidad, Humboldt Bay, and Eel River. Her shipping points that are directly available to deep water communication are Klamath River, Trinidad, which can accommodate the largest craft of the merchant marine, Arcata, Eureka, Fairhaven, Hookton, Southport, Port Kenyon and Shelter Cove.

EXPORTS FOR THE YEAR 1881.

Articles	Weight in Pounds.
Potatoes	9,030,700
Oats	7,735,650
Wheat	1,386,280
Peas	560,840
Wool	869,550
Barley	7,560
Apples	24,300
Hides, dry	5,830
Hides, salt	85,100
Deer skins	12,395
Bacon	90,000
Pork	36,100

*Tons.

Lard	15,500
Tallow	24,400
Butter	468,440
Leather	23,600
Beef	103,460
Fish	85,200
Salmon, ½ bbls	191,800
Salmon, cases	277,900
Tan Bark	33,600
Charcoal	25,000
Flax Seed	6,710
Total lbs	21,110,915

Articles.	Quantity.
Poultry, 97 coops, av 3 doz	291
Eggs, 1,301 boxes, av 30 doz	39,030
Mouldings, bdls	3,558
Redwood doors	4,061
Shakes	3,114,000
Shingles	9,410,000
Box material, bdls	230
Starch, boxes	204
Horses	54
Calves	373
Sheep	87
Hogs	153
Pelts, bdls	25
Skins and furs, bdls	91
Lumber, in feet	48,630,121

The export from the mills of the Trinidad Mill Co., Falk, Chandler & Co., and the Milford Lumber Co., are not included in the report of the lumber shipments.

To show the increase of business in Humboldt County for the last five years we give from the *Times* a comparative table showing the shipments of 1877 and 1881.

Articles.	1877.	1881.
Potatoes	3,189,690	9,039,700
Oats	4,232,185	7,735,650
Wheat	85,500	1,386,280
Peas	413,412	500,840
Wool	1,551,880	869,550
Butter	135,015	468,440
Fish	140,600	85,200
Hides, dry	21,990	5,830
Hides, salt	97,300	85,100
Salmon, ½ bbls	276,300	191,800
Eggs, doz	1,650	39,030

In the past year the county has made a good showing, take it all in all, and the present outlook for 1882 is most encouraging. Attention is being paid to every industry, and everything looks bright and prosperous.

The *Standard* gives the summary of exports for the entire county for 1881 as follows:—

In conclusion we have, of the items specified, the summary of exports for the county to be:—

Lumber, feet	146,000,000
Shingles	13,648,000
Shakes	5,044,000
Posts	238,000
Wool, pounds	1,015,000
Butter, pounds	570,000

The arrivals in port, 322, exclusive of steamers. The total tonnage, 92,450 tons.

Railroads of Humboldt.

WHAT Humboldt County needs is railroad communication with the rest of the world. But this is a question of time only. The large and increasing business will soon demand some step towards its construction.

FIRST RAILROADS IN THE STATE.

But it must not be supposed by the outside world that Humboldt has no railroads. The fact is the first railroads in this State were constructed here in 1854. At that date there were upwards of twenty miles of good, graded, substantial roads built by loggers, and used to convey logs to the waters' edge. Since that date iron rails have been laid and locomotives used on most of them.

THE VANCE RAILROAD.

John Vance, one of the active and most enterprising citizens of the county, many years ago, asked the public for the right of way and a small subsidy, as a guarantee, and in return would construct and equip a road from Eureka up Eel River Valley. The offer was not accepted, many being diametrically opposed to granting subsidies, while others owning land along the route demanded nearly as much damages for the narrow strip of land necessary, as their whole property was worth. Of course, the project was abandoned.

He did not, however, abandon the idea of a railroad, but constructed one as a private enterprise. It extends from tidewater to his mills on Mad River. This road was commenced in 1874. Besides opening up a large section of fine farming land it has made the fortunate proprietor altogether independent of other sources of supply of logs for his mills, of which he has two. The road is five miles long and cost the proprietor $15,000 per mile. Mr. Vance has a Baldwin locomotive and about thirty truck cars, upon which are transported the immense redwood logs and large quantities of lumber. At the tide-water terminus of this road lighters receive the lumber and are floated with the outgoing tide to a point eight miles above Eureka, where vessels of a capacity of 300,000 feet receive their loads, and are towed to the city wharves by Mr. Vance's steamer.

He recently made the road a public one and built a warehouse for the reception of freight. He will doubtless extend the road into the dense redwoods of Mad River and also northwestwardly to the valuable timber of Little River. This road crosses Mad River on a Howe Truss Bridge heretofore mentioned and illustrated.

H. B. AND L. RAILROAD.

In 1875, the South Bay Railroad Company had a track laid from the marsh on South Bay, up Salmon Creek a distance of five miles. The road was built for logging purposes. The road was standard gauge, built of forty-pound T iron and cost,

THE RAILROADS OF HUMBOLDT COUNTY.

equipped, $15,000 per mile. It was operated by a tank engine, weighing eighteen tons, built at the Baldwin Works, Philadelphia. Eighteen truck cars of massive build were used in working this road. A log thirty-six feet long and twelve feet in diameter, weighing twenty-five tons, was transported on two of the trucks. The grade of the road was very steep, sometimes being as much as 200 feet to the mile. The officers of the company were President, Calvin Page, of San Francisco; Secretary, Charles Nelson; Treasurer, John Kentfield; Superintendent, J. W. Henderson; Directors, C. Page, J. Page, Jno. Kentfield, Chas. Nelson, H. H. Buhne and J. W. Henderson.

The body of timber up Salmon Creek was not so extensive as was supposed, and in the short time of three years the supply for railroad purposes was practically exhausted. The Directors proposed extending the road up the Eel River Valley. From many they received encouragement; but others held their land at a valuation far exceeding its real worth. Some were found who said that they had taken up their land in early days, fought Indians and high water, and now, just as they were getting fixed comfortably, and wanted to live in peace and quiet, a railroad was talked of, and they were asked to give or sell a right of way. They were opposed to a railroad, and would not do anything. Meeting with such a reception, the company gave up the idea of the Eel River Road, took up their track, moved all the appurtenances, and invested their capital in the H. B. and L. Railroad.

This road has recently been built on Freshwater Creek, and reaches from tide-water on Humboldt Bay a distance of some four miles. The company own a Baldwin locomotive and a number of trucks.

ARCATA AND MAD RIVER RAILROAD.

Articles of incorporation were filed July 22, 1881, of the Arcata and Mad River Railroad Company. The purposes of the corporation are set forth to be the construction of a single track narrow-gauge railroad to be operated by steam and horse power, the same to be constructed from the main ship channel at the northerly end of Humboldt Bay, to the north fork of Mad River, passing through the town of Arcata for the transportation of freight and passengers. The Directors for the first year were G. W. B. Yocom, R. M. Fernald, B. Deming, Austin Wiley and E. A. Deming. The capital stock is $60,000.

This road is an extension of the Arcata Transportation Company's road, the initial point being Isaac Miner's Mill, on Mad River, three and one-half miles beyond the Dolly Varden Mill. The company have extended this road a distance of fifteen miles up Mad River, where the new mill is built, right in the redwood timber country.

Their wharf is said to be the longest in the United States. The company's steamer makes connection from Arcata to Eureka, a distance of five miles. This road was to be completed, the full length, by the first of March, 1882, for passengers, freight, lumber, etc., Yocum & Fernald, proprietors.

JACOBY CREEK RAILROAD.

This road is about two miles in length, on Jacoby Creek, and will be extended as the timber is cut. The line of the railroad crosses the Arcata Road. This railroad is to be extended from tide-water up into the dense forests that cover the slopes and fringe the hill-tops. The logs brought down by the railroad will be rafted to mill.

Dolbeer & Carson are constructing this road. It is built of standard gauge of T iron, with a grade which allows the loaded cars to reach tide-water by their own momentum; horses are then used to return the cars to the upper end of the road. This constitutes the railroads in the vicinity of Humboldt Bay.

A large area of fine redwood and spruce lumber is tributary to this road which will be extended as occasion requires. About 2,000,000 feet of logs have been transported over the road this year. It has ample facilities for transporting six times the amount mentioned.

TRINIDAD MILL COMPANY RAILROAD.

The Trinidad Mill Company is composed of Messrs. F. T. Hooper, J. A. Hooper and J. C. Smith of San Francisco, and Josiah Bell of Trinidad, the latter being the Superintendent. They have extended their railroad into the redwoods at a cost of $15,000 a mile, including rolling stock, and will insure a supply of lumber to the mills for twenty years. The company own and control about 10,000 acres of first-class redwood land. It is claimed that there is a belt of redwood, spruce and pine forty miles in length, extending from Little River north to a considerable distance above Trinidad, which must necessarily find an outlet at Trinidad.

The tramway from the mill to the wharf is half a mile long, a considerable portion of it running over trestle work sixty feet high. They use twenty-four trucks of massive build in transporting lumber from the mill to the wharf, and eight still heavier trucks for logging purposes. This is shown in our view of the village of Trinidad.

The mill company own two mills of the respective capacity of thirty-five thousand and thirty thousand per day. Also a shingle mill, capacity, thirty thousand per day. They also manufacture shakes, fence-posts, pickets, etc. They employ on an average 200 men in the woods and mills. Their pay roll averages $8,000 per month for ten months of the year. They use thirty yoke of oxen and thirty-five mules in the iroperations. They use twenty-four trucks of massive build in transporting lumber from the mill to the wharf, and eight still heavier trucks for logging purposes.

The roads above mentioned, exclusive of a number of tramways, constitute the railroad system of Humboldt County, and its needs and possibilities in this direction.

THE LUMBER BUSINESS.

Redwood Forests—Large Logs and Trees—
First Saw-Mill—Business of 1881—
Future Supply of Redwood—
Description of Mills—Exports of Lumber, Etc.

THESE old Muscovites, who settled at Bodega Bay, in 1812, produced the first lumber with a saw ever made north of San Francisco Bay, for they had both a pit and whip-saw, the former of which can be seen to this day. Judging from the number of stumps still standing, and the extent of territory over which they extended their logging operations, they evidently consumed large quantities of lumber. The timber was only about one mile distant from the ship-yard and landing, while the stumps of trees cut by them are still standing, and beside them from one to six shoots have sprung up, many of which have now reached a size sufficient for lumber purposes. This growth has been remarkable, and goes to show that if proper care were taken, each half century would see a new crop of redwoods, sufficiently large for all practical purposes, while ten decades would see gigantic trees.

HUMBOLDT REDWOODS.

Humboldt is the home of the redwood. It grows in dense forests. Where there is timber it is all timber, consisting of immense trees, running from 200 to 400 feet high, and varying in circumference from thirty to seventy feet. Near the coast it consists of spruce, fir, Oregon pine, hemlock, and a species of cedar; as the land becomes elevated, redwood takes the place of the other varieties, and as the elevation becomes still greater, a species of the live-oak is found mingled with it. At a still greater elevation, and near the termination of this belt of timber, it almost entirely displaces the redwood; a dense undergrowth covers it at all places. Surely Humboldt has something of which she may justly be proud, and from which she is and will continue to receive an ever-increasing revenue until the last is fallen. But they, like the elk they have sheltered, and the poor Indian whose wigwam they have built, are doomed to fall before the advance of civilization.

VISIT TO A REDWOOD FOREST.

A visitor to one of these forests says: No one can contemplate the wholesale destruction of these glorious forests without the saddest feelings. Nothing can be more majestic and impressive than the land clothed with them, nor more naked, desolate, ragged and uncouth than the land after it is stripped of them. It is in the one case peace, beauty, plenty, virginity and bounty; in the other rags, fire, destruction, rapine, ghastliness and most unsightly death. There are not, I think, more impressive forests in the world. The land is actually darkened with them. You walk in some of them on a bright, sunshiny day as you might in the gloom and darkness of Alaskan forests.

The impression that the atmosphere above is draped in fog, or is overspread with the cloud darkness preceding rain, is constant, except where an occasional opening allows the sun to break through. Nowhere in our forests is sunshine more acceptable or beautiful. It comes in long, yellow splinters, or open, clear bars, lighting up the dead-gray bark of the redwoods, the luminated cork-like bark of the pines, and showering ineffable beauty on the clear, green undergrowth, particularly on the fleur-de-lis-shaped circles of immense ferns which everywhere in the shade cover the ground. The effect of this coming out into a break of sunshine from the gloom of the forests, is very peculiar. It seems out of place in its suddenness—as if one were instantaneously to emerge from the darkness and gloom of rain into clear sunshine.

SILENT AND GRAND.

Not a sound of bird, beast or wind disturbs the silence, and even the most of the streams steal quietly seaward. It is a place where silence itself might feel the need of going on tiptoe. Fancy going mile after mile through trees 150 to 300 feet high packed as closely, one sometimes thinks, as trees can conveniently stand, and *breathe*—where deep shade prevails, and where no noise, not even a leafy rustle or tree-shaken whisper is heard—and it can be imagined how different the feeling is than when in open ground and in full sunshine. After walking for half an hour thus, to have a break of sunshine slant in with its yellow light and color illumination, the invariable feeling is that the sun is bending to send in a salutation of light peace and glory.

VENERABLE GIANTS.

But the size of these redwood trees, their number, their grandeur, their immovably-rooted bases, their beauty, their litheness, their remarkable straightness—none nor all of these are anything like so impressive as their age. They are 900 to 1,500 years old. Here are trees standing, not in ruins, nor even in the senility, loss of strength and color of age, but with intense exhibition of almost immortal strength, spanning and bridging past centuries. Holy men of old walked, it is said, with God; these trees have stood with and worshipped before him, while almost countless generations have come, gone and passed away. Age and strength, age and beauty, age and straightness, age and flexibility, here stand hand in hand, harmonizing the apparently irreconcilable, making apparent impossibilities possible and natural.

Think of single trees yielding 50,000 feet of redwood, and single acres of land yielding 1,000,000 feet of lumber. Indeed, in a radius of 150 feet, we in one place counted sixty trees, some

RESIDENCE AND RANCH OF ISAAC MINOR, ONE

SAW MILL ON MAD RIVER.

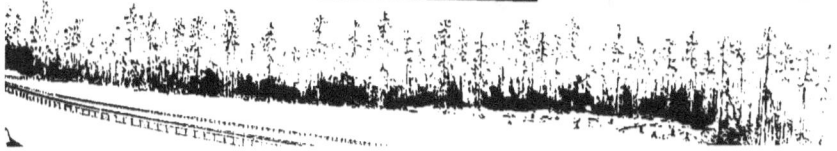

of them 300 feet high, and with a circumference of sixty feet two or three feet from the ground. All of the trees there are large. The acre of land on which those trees stood would yield much more than 1,000,000 feet of lumber, or say enough to load four of the largest three-masted schooners. The size quality and grandeur of the redwood trees of California, and the extent of the redwood forests, have been the theme of many writers and the admiration and wonder of the lovers of nature, until their fame is world-wide.

But a slight conception can be had of their size and height until they are seen. All accounts seem fabulous until one stands amidst a forest of these monsters; stands at the base of a tree sixteen feet in diameter and four hundred feet in height, straight as an arrow, covered with massive layers of bark twelve to twenty inches thick.

WILL THE SUPPLY FAIL?

The calamity which will befall the people of Humboldt County by the exhaustion of the forests of redwoods could be in a great measure averted, if the growth of the young redwoods were fostered.

But no care is taken; and, in fact, it seems that an effort is made to thoroughly eradicate all traces of the forests. The stumps are fired just to see them burn, and fire runs over the land every fall, which serves to completely destroy the young shoots. The protection of our forests should be a charge of our Legislature; for, while the men of to-day may not remain to suffer for the want of these forest trees, the commonwealth of the State will remain, and its future weal should be cared for by the present generation.

LARGE LOGS AND TREES.

Messrs. W. H. Stayneast & Co., of Humboldt Bay, sawed in 1854, a "spruce-pine log," twenty-six feet long, which turned 4,000 feet clear stuff, without knot or wind-shakes. The tree turned out 13,000 feet clear lumber. There are trees of other woods much larger—for instance the redwood—that are estimated will turn out upwards of 100,000 feet. That one tree will build two houses, each two stories high and fifty feet square, furnishing all the square timber, planks, shingles, &c., would not be credited in the Atlantic States.

Four redwood logs, containing by actual measurement 26,902 feet of lumber, were hauled by a ten-ox team on a logging claim, a distance of three-quarters of a mile. It is claimed that this is the largest load ever hauled in the county by ten oxen.

To give an idea of the size of the trees we give an account of a tree cut down by a citizen of Arcata in 1855, which stood within two hundred yards of the *Times* newspaper office. From it a man built a house 24x30 feet, two stories high. The frame, siding, floors, doors, windows and roof were made from lumber split from one tree. Also lumber to build garden fence and out-house. He sold lumber enough to build his brother-in-law a one-story house. He only used sixty feet of the body of the redwood. The editor adds: The house is now (1855) occupied by Mr. Stokes. The tree was small, and Mr. Underwood, who cut it down, was troubled to find a smaller one.

THE BIG TREE.

Hutching's Magazine in 1856 says: On the trail from Trinidad to Salmon River there is a hollow tree measuring thirty-three feet in diameter. The tree is situated between Trinidad and Elk Camp, near Redwood Creek, and about midway in one of the densest forests probably on the continent, and it is unnecessary to say that it would be a very choice range for hungry animals. Men have frequently camped in that tree, not from choice, however, but because they were caught by night, whose dark mantle falls upon the wayfarer in those sombre old woods much sooner than in the open country, or perhaps a sudden rise in Redwood Creek during a portion of the year would carry away the bridge, consisting of a fallen tree across the stream, with the rough bark on the upper side hewn off.

The old tree would afford a very good shelter to those bound down from the mines until a crossing could be effected. We could quote stories from reliable gentlemen in the county that we scarcely believe ourselves, in reference to the size of trees.

FIRST SAW-MILL AND LOG.

The first mill on Humboldt Bay was the "Tauppoos," which after a two years' trial, was abandoned. The Ryan, Duff & Co.'s mill was made from the old steamer *Santa Clara*, and was the first successful mill on Humboldt Bay. It had four gangs of saws, one circular, one edger, one cross-cut saw, two double lath machines, one shingle machine, one planing machine, turning lathes, etc. Its daily capacity with double gangs of men was an average of 60,000 feet of lumber, board measure, and 40,000 laths. The capital invested was $100,000, and the number of men employed in the mill was from thirty-five to forty. Since then improvements have continued until perfection has been nearly attained in modern mills.

The first saw-log cut on Humboldt Bay was felled in November, 1850, by George Carson and Alexander Gilmore. It was a spruce, and measured 140 feet to the first limb.

The amount of lumber exported for year ending June 30, 1854 was 20,567,000 feet. This was at the end of only two years' development.

MILLS AND BUSINESS FOR 1881.

Within the boundaries of Humboldt County there are twenty-two saw-mills. The motive power in seventeen of these is steam and in remaining five, water. The official returns show that during 1880 the lumber sawed was 41,969,766 feet, and the number of shingles made was 19,018,000.

For 1881 the lumber exported from the county amounted

to the following, according to E. H. Howard, who carefully collected statistics:—

Lumber in feet	141,000,000
Shingles	13,648,000
Shakes	5,644,000
Posts	268,000

THE LUMBER BUSINESS.

The following facts from the *Democratic Standard* of May 7, 1881, relative to the lumber business, were prepared by William Ayers, the Editor, especially for our History.

"Seven or eight months ago the *Standard* published several articles setting forth the extent and productiveness of the territory that was being laid with railroads along the Southern Pacific; the number of railroad connections with Pacific deepwater ports; the marvelous development of latent wealth, and the consequent activity which must by force of circumstances, be created along the redwood belt of California, and particularly around its most eligible shipping points. While some thought our predictions "rose colored" and high flown, yet, they were founded upon careful calculation, and at this early day they have not only proven to be correct, but we did not tell half the story. Mill men with whom we have conversed within the last two weeks have told us: "Why, we cannot supply the demand! If it keeps on this way we cannot fill half the orders!" There is no mystery about the condition of things, for it is the result of conjunction of events and conditions which have conspired to bring about the fact in a very natural way. Let any one who is interested in the advancement of Northern California in general, and the redwood lumber interests in particular, consider what has been in the past, and is developing, and will be in the next few years, the market for our redwood lumber. California has been the main consumer, with occasional cargoes to South America and the Islands. Glance over the map of the United States and Mexico and make a comparison of the territory that has required our lumber heretofore, with what is now coming rapidly in reach by water and rail. The problem is too plain to require any argument that the demand for lumber of all kinds for the six to ten will be four to six times greater yearly than at any previous time. Arizona, New Mexico and Colorado alone, more than treble the field, and when there is added to this the whole of Mexico and Central America, which are now throbbing with the march of improvement, and all of which are devoid of everything that can take the place of redwood as a finishing material, the market that is opening to our doors is at once apparent. And yet even this is not all.

FUTURE TIMBER SUPPLY.

"Let us look for a moment at the sources of supply for finishing lumber. We know that the coast redwood belt reaching from Del Norte to Sonoma, is the only body of this timber available to commerce. East of the Rocky Mountains—Maine, Michigan, Minnesota and Wisconsin—are the only States that have a supply of lumber sufficient for export beyond their own borders.

"All the rest are either devoid of lumber or consume all they are able to produce. Michigan, Minnesota and Wisconsin, by the best calculations, are estimated to have 13,000,000,000 of lumber, all told, and of this amount the combination which controls the lumber business in these States cut, last year, 1,564,000,000 feet. At this rate it is very certain that the sources of supply to satisfy the demand of the entire Atlantic seaboard and interior States cannot long hold out, and the price has already reached a figure which permits the shipment of redwood lumber and shingles across the continent by rail, and though not generally known, a few manufacturers and dealers are already driving a profitable trade in this direction. All these facts are conspiring to make a wonderful activity in the redwood lumber manufacturing business, and that activity, as a matter of course, will be greatest when the lumber is most available.

"Humboldt Bay is the best shipping point along the entire belt. It is true that the Oregon lumber will enter the same market, but nothing can take the place of redwood as a finishing material, except cedar, and the supply of that timber is too limited to affect the case. At one glance there, it will be readily seen that our opportunities are greater than ever before, and that Humboldt Bay and County stand at the head as a supply depot and shipping point. This revival will stimulate other branches of industry, and we hope, encourage the investment of a great amount of manufacturing capital.

AVAILABLE HUMBOLDT REDWOOD.

"The timber lands of Humboldt are of themselves a mine of incalculable wealth to their owners. Let us for a moment make a calculation of the available redwood lands of Humboldt County, which will be as follows:

Number of acres on Humboldt Bay	125,000
" " " Eel River	100,000
" " " Van Duzen & Yager	75,000
" " " Redwood Creek	100,000
" " " Little River	40,000
" " " Mad River	30,000
" " " Around Trinidad	40,000
Total	510,000

"There are what may be termed the available redwood lands of Humboldt County. There are some outside bodies of timber, perhaps 100,000 acres in all, not including the above enumeration, which will not be reached for many years. That which can be easily reached is ample to supply all possible demand for a long time to come, but the cutting capacity of our mills is not equal to the demands."   W. A.

JOHN VANCE'S MILL.

John Vance's mill, on Mad River, constructed in 1875, is one of the most important mills of Humboldt, with a cutting capacity of 40,000 feet per day. There is also an extensive shingle mill in operation. The mill is situated at the end of Vance's railroad. A feature of this road which our artist has sketched and which forms a beautiful scene in one of our views, is the Howe Truss Bridge, over Mad River, two spans of 120 feet each, built by the Pacific Bridge Company, at a cost of about $10,000. He has so planned his mill as to obtain the advantages of a logging pond of large extent, which holds in reserve a large stock of logs. On Mad River he has a large timber tract of 3,000 acres.

Mr. Vance has another large mill in Eureka which cuts large amounts of lumber. It would at first thought appear that the supply for these mills would soon be exhausted. Mr. Vance employs a large force of men, sometimes as many as 150, in his extensive operations. The total amount of lumber cut in 1881 was 11,143,389 feet; total number of shakes, 508,925, and of shingles, 7,550,250.

For nearly three decades men have been plunging into the depths of these grand old redwood forests, and utilizing these stately trees. Steadily with the growth of California this interest has increased until it stands to-day a marvel on the commercial catalogue of the State. Millions of feet are cut yearly, and yet the source seems practically inexhaustible. All along the streams putting back from the coast of the old Pacific this industry teems, and many mills have been built, and thousands of men find daily employment, and millions of dollars are thus yearly earned and distributed among the laboring classes. To the city market it rolls in one unceasing tide, thence it is distributed to all parts of the State. Day and night the hum of this industry is heard in every mountain glen, and continues in one grand unceasing round, and the sharp ring of the glistening steel as it cleaves the mighty bolt makes mellow music to him whose home is in the redwood forests.

REDWOOD LUMBER FOR DOORS.

John Vance informs us that he is shipping redwood lumber to San Francisco, to be used in the manufacture of doors. This is a new departure. Doors are usually made from pine, and the custom has been so general and so long in vogue that it seemed like heresy to suggest that redwood be substituted. The principal argument used against redwood in door-making is that it is too soft to hold screws for the hinges. This may be the beginning of a large demand for redwood to be used in the manufacture of doors.

The price of all grades of lumber has advanced at intervals throughout the year, until now it is from two to three dollars higher per thousand feet than it was at the close of 1880.

When the lumbering business was new here, the cheapest and easiest means of transporting logs was by water. As a consequence, all the timber skirting the streams was cut off. Then railroads had to be constructed for hauling logs. These are fully described under the head of railroads. They demonstrated the practicability of transporting logs to tide water at such cost as renders their manufacture into lumber, at living rates, possible.

LOGGING BY STEAM.

Messrs. Dolbeer & Carson have lately employed a logging machine of their own invention or conception which has already more than realized their greatest expectations. It is at work in the woods at Salmon Creek, where it can be seen by any one who is anxious enough to visit the camp. It bids fair to change very considerably the system of logging. The idea of such a "contrivance" was laughed at by practical men, and when the machine was set down among the "crew" at Salmon Creek it was pronounced utterly impracticable. But the inventors had faith in the new machine, and put it in motion. It has performed its work to perfection from the first, and is now a "regular hand" in the Salmon Creek woods.

The machine is designed to be used in blocking out roads, hauling out of the way all waste material and hauling logs into the roads and coupling them together ready for the ox team to take away. It consists of an upright boiler and engine.

To those who are familiar with the logging woods, or who have been accustomed all their lives to see the unwieldy ox-team tugging at the great logs it must seem a great innovation. The Millford Mill, at Salmon Creek, manufactured for 1881—

Lumber, ft.	3,207,459
Shingles	2,391,230
Shakes	496,000
Posts	5,746

The other mill of Dolbeer & Carson is of the largest capacity of any on the Bay.

ISAAC MINOR & CO'S. MILL.

A new mill has been erected by this firm on Mad River, a view of which is given on another page. The mill building proper, is 130x135 feet with the necessary sheds and outbuildings added. All the modern improvements are placed in the mill, and is considered one of the most compact, complete and easiest working mills on the bay. Besides the mill there are other improvements on an extensive scale. A massive dam has been built across the creek, thus forming a pond or receptacle for logs, and it is built in such a substantial manner that no doubts are entertained but what it will stand the highest water or greatest freshets. The capacity of the pond will be from ten to fifteen million feet of logs. The outlook for the company owning this property is very flattering, as they have almost every advantage known in logging and milling in this county.

The mill is located right in the midst of the timber; the logs for the first year or two can be felled into the pond at a very small expense, thus enabling the company to manufacture lumber at a cost of several dollars less on a thousand feet than other manufactories. The machinery works very satisfactorily. It is claimed that 50,000 feet can be sawed per day and the capacity of the mill was intended to be only 30,000 feet per day. A steam donkey engine is used on the side hills to move the logs.

THE LUMBER INDUSTRIES OF HUMBOLDT.

J. RUSS & CO'S. MILL.

This energetic firm have on the "Island" one of the most perfectly constructed mills on the Pacific Coast, called the Excelsior Mill. The old rigs for sawing lumber have had to give place to the most improved devices that could be found in this country. The logs are hauled into the mill on an improved car track and rig. They are then placed on the most perfect double circular saw to be found in any mill on the coast. Here is where the first "Prescott Direct Steam Feed" was used this side of the Rocky Mountains, a perfect machine for shoving the carriage both ways. This machine has many other minor improvements not to be found in other mills, such as saw relief, carriage, trucks, track, guides, etc. From these saws all lumber six inches thick and less passes through an improved edger, thus ripping and edging it to the proper width in passing it once through the machine, after which the edgings are separated from the good, the waste passing to one side are placed in an elevator, which takes them to the fire outside; the lumber going to the other side, passes over or through an ingenious gang trimmer, cutting both ends of it at once, making each length exact and alike.

There are two engines, one, eighteen inches bore, by twenty inches stroke, running 160 revolutions a minute; the other, fourteen inches bore by thirty inches stroke, making 110 revolutions. This last one is considered much too small for the work and is soon to be replaced by another considerable larger, of twenty-inch bore and same stroke, thus making the power complete. The steam is generated by six flue boilers, forty-two inches diameter and twenty-four feet long, set in two nests' thus making it essential to have two smoke-stacks. The fires burn the wet redwood sawdust placed on the fire by an ingenious method. Thus it can be seen the fires are kept burning by machinery—none of the laborious shoveling to be seen in this mill. Steam is easily kept up at the desirable figure, about eighty pounds. In connection with the boiler there is an improved heater, it also being the first in use on this bay. This is peculiar insomuch that it condenses nearly all the steam coming from the engines and other machines, to be re-used, and at the same time filters all the new or fresh water wanted to keep the supply good from all wastage. The class of mechanics and workmen engaged in this mill are fully up to the standard of the improved machinery. All intelligent men, understanding their positions and qualified to fill them.

Our space will not permit an extended description of this mill and its improved machinery, and we close with the following remarks made by Hon. J. Russ at the dinner on "Opening Day," which shows the honesty of the man and his positive sympathy with all working men, and especially those in his employ. He lays out a well-considered system for both the employer and employes to follow.

"After having made a careful examination of the old mill, I concluded that she was behind the times and too slow for the age. Therefore I obtained Mr. Evans to remodel, rebuild, and reconstruct the mill and everything in connection with it. I am well pleased with his work, and we seem to have a model mill in every sense of the word.

"While Mr. Evans was remodeling the mill, I saw that there were many other things of great importance that needed remodeling. I saw that there was no proper place provided for the men to sleep, and that wrong I determined to right. I try always to measure such things as I would have them measured out to me. After working hard all day I want a good room and a good bed to sleep in, and I want every man that works for me to have just as good a room and just as good a bed to sleep in as I have myself. This feeling has prompted me to have a house erected containing forty bedrooms, furnished with good spring beds, bedding and other furniture necessary to make it comfortable and pleasant. Also a reading room and all the other comforts possible to provide under the circumstances.

"I also observed in connection with the boarding-house that the time allowed for meals was much too limited for comfort or health. Therefore I have arranged for the men to have as much time to eat their meals as I have to eat mine. Your physical and your mental powers are your capital, and I have endeavored by these changes to so protect that capital that you will realize the greatest results possible from investments.

"I have long been of the opinion that the relation between employer and employe should be readjusted in many respects. At present it seems to be the sole aim of employers to obtain the greatest amount of work at the least possible cost, while those employed too often take no further interest in their work than to put in his allotted hours, with that characteristic slowness of those whose sole interest is his hire. I am convinced that labor adjusted on this basis has a constant and almost inevitable tendency to engender and precipitate the strikes and other harsh and desperate remedies for supposed and actual grievances. The remedy for this is a community of interest between employer and employe. I do not mean by this co-operation as used in its popular sense. I regard that as impracticable, unless in exceptional lines of industry, but I mean such a common interest as will make those in prosperity a common benefit. There must be capital and there must be labor. Without capital, labor is useless, and without labor the greatest capitalist is but a helpless man at most. So capital should cherish labor because it is its hands and feet, its eyes and ears, and the strong arm of labor should always be ready to defend capital, for without it labor is but a body without breath in its lungs or blood in its veins.

"And in conclusion may I not express the hope that this step in the right direction may be followed up until it is the rule and not the exception, and until the path here marked out becomes a broad highway along which capital and labor, hand in hand, shall move around in peace and prosperity."

The Lumber Business of D. R. Jones & Co.

In Eureka, in 1860, David R. Jones, in company with Mr. John Kentfield, of San Francisco, under the firm name of D. R. Jones & Co., purchased a small saw-mill in Eureka from Mr. S. L. Mastick, known in those days as the "Bailey" mill. It was what is called a "sash" mill, having a sash saw as the principal saw, and by which the logs were sawed into boards and then placed on a small edger to be edged and ripped into boards of the required dimensions. The cutting capacity of this mill was then about 3,000 feet per day of twelve hours, cutting only spruce and pine lumber. Shortly after they improved the mill, putting in the first circular saw on the bay for sawing cants; also a Hawkins' patent log carriage. These improvements increased the cutting capacity to about 25,000 feet per day.

HUMBOLDT REDWOOD INTRODUCED.

In 1861 they sawed and shipped on the schooner *Dashaway* the first full cargo of redwood lumber that had been shipped from Humboldt Bay. Previous to this, the redwood in Humboldt County was considered to be of no value, and unfit for any purpose, but now is considered the best on the coast.

The demand for it is increasing steadily every year. During the last few years there has been from 40,000,000 to 60,000,000 feet shipped from the bay annually. A great deal of it is now being shipped to such ports as foreign as Mexico, South America, Sandwich Islands, Australia and other places, the demand increasing steadily as the people learn the many advantages of the redwood. New York and other eastern cities are also beginning to use redwood lumber and redwood shingles.

MILL ON INDIAN ISLAND.

In 1866, Mr. Jones and Mr. Kentfield took Captain H. H Buhne as a third partner, the firm name remaining the same, and built the large double mill on Indian Island, about a half mile from Eureka, the cutting capacity of which is about 90,000 feet per day. The supply of logs for the mills was then obtained from the forests along the edges of the bay and the small streams emptying into it. But after several years the timber along the edges of the bay and the small streams becoming exhausted, they found it would become necessary to go further back for their supply of logs, and to provide some means of transporting them to the bay.

SOUTH BAY R. R. AND LAND CO.

In 1875 they, in company with two other gentlemen incorporated the South Bay Railroad and Land Company, and built the South Bay Railroad from the bay up Salmon Creek, D. R. Jones & Co. holding half the stock. This was the first steam railroad introduced in the county. The rolling stock consisted of one large Baldwin locomotive and several cars. In 1878, the old sash mill being pretty well worn out, it was found necessary either to make very extensive repairs on it or build a new mill. They finally decided to build a new mill, so the old one was torn down and a fine new one was built on the same site, having all the latest improvements and saw-mill machinery, and a cutting capacity of 50,000 feet of lumber per day.

HUMBOLDT LOGGING RAILWAY CO.

In 1880, all their timber on Salmon Creek became exhausted, and they moved the South Bay Railroad to Fresh Water Creek changing the name also to the Humboldt Logging Railway Company, but the stockholders remained the same. In the early part of this spring (1882), D. R. Jones & Co. bought the entire stock of the company, making them the sole owners of the road, and they immediately set to work to extend the road and increase the capacity. The road is now about seven miles long, and the rolling stock consists of two large locomotives and twenty-eight cars.

IMMENSE LUMBER OPERATIONS.

They expect to haul this year (1882), about 20,000,000 to 25,000,000 feet of logs.

In one year D. R. Jones & Co. sawed and shipped to San Francisco and various foreign markets 20,000,000 feet of redwood lumber and shingles, valued at over a quarter of a million dollars. During the year they will employ about 250 men in the various branches of their business. Besides the two large saw-mills and the railroad they own about 11,000 acres of timber land, the tug-boat *Lillie Jones*, employed in towing rafts, vessels, etc., on the bay, and the controlling interests in several fine sailing vessels, employed principally in the coasting trade. Among the several vessels which they have built and own is the barkentine *Eureka*, one of the finest vessels on the coast; she is now in the trade between San Francisco and Honolulu. At present they are building a fine, large three masted schooner at their mill on Indian Island.

BIOGRAPHY OF DAVID R. JONES.

DAVID R. JONES.

David R. Jones was born May 31, 1820, in Montgomeryshire, North Wales. He was one of five children, two girls and three boys. His younger brother died when about ten years old, and soon after his mother also died. The family circle being broken, home was no more "what it used to be." Some time after his mother's death his father married his second wife. At the age of nineteen Mr. Jones started for America, on the bark *Caledonian*, arriving in New York, where he met his eldest sister, who had arrived there some time before. Here he engaged with a Mr. McCormick, to learn the carpenter trade, and for whom he worked about seven years.

In 1847 he started from New York for New Orleans, going through Albany, Utica, Buffalo, Pittsburg, Cincinnati and several other principal cities, at some of which he remained a short time, but finally arrived at New Orleans, where, during the great cholera plague, he also contracted the disease, and for some time his life was despaired of, but after a while he began to recover and was advised to take a sea trip to repair his broken health. In the hope of fully regaining his health, he embarked on a sailing vessel for New York, where his sister was living, besides a great many friends.

During the voyage they encountered a succession of heavy storms, and when the vessel was about a month overdue and not appearing, she was given up for lost with all on board, and Mr. Jones' funeral sermon was preached in New York, in the church of which he was a regular attendant during his residence there. After being out forty-eight days on the passage, the vessel, with all on board, arrived in New York on a Sunday, and Mr. Jones surprised his sister and friends by walking into church just as the services begun, where his funeral sermon had been preached the week previous.

Remaining in New York a short while, and having fully recovered his health, he again went to New Orleans, where he remained until the winter of 1849.

D. R. JONES ARRIVES IN SAN FRANCISCO.

He, like many others, hearing of the gold excitement in California, determined to seek his fortune there also. He took passage at New Orleans on the steamer *Ohio* for Chagres, and there went by boat some distance up the Chagres River, and then on foot traveled the balance of the way across the isthmus to Panama, where he expected to take the steamer which was about to sail for San Francisco. But the steamer having all the passengers she could carry, he had to wait in Panama about three weeks, when a small brig was chartered to take a large number of passengers that were waiting for an opportunity to get to California. Taking passage on the little brig, he arrived in March, 1850, in San Francisco, after a pleasant voyage of about forty-five days. When he arrived there he engaged as a carpenter, at $16.00 per day, to help build a steamer that was to run between San Francisco and Sacramento.

VISIT TO THE KLAMATH MINES.

After working a while at his trade, he, like many others, got the gold fever; and a few days after the great fire in San Francisco, of May, 1850, by which nearly the whole city was destroyed, he started on the schooner *Laura Virginia* for Humboldt Bay, which had just been discovered, bound for the Klamath mines; but when a few miles outside of the Golden Gate, and during the night, the vessel struck on Duxberry Reef, where she laid hard and fast on the rocks until the next morning, floating off at high tide. Leaking very badly, the Captain decided to return to San Francisco for repairs. After some hard work at the pumps to keep the vessel free, they succeeded in getting back to San Francisco.

He started again for Humboldt Bay on the brig *Reindeer* Captain Batchelder; and after a very rough trip they arrived about the first of June, 1850, in the bay, and landed at what was then known as Humboldt City, situated at the Humboldt Point, opposite the entrance to the bay. This city is now almost entirely destroyed, only one house remaining, which is still owned by Capt. H. H. Buhne, the discoverer of Humboldt Bay. At this time there were no houses where Eureka now stands. Mr. Jones celebrated the Fourth of July, 1850 on the spot where the city of Eureka now stands.

Shortly after he started for the Klamath mines, where he remained only a few months, as the Indians were very troublesome. Having several fights with the Indians, he became disgusted, and with his little bag of gold, which he dug while there, returned by way of Humboldt Bay to San Francisco, arriving there in the fall of the same year.

CHURCHES OF SAN FRANCISCO IN 1851.

He again resumed his trade—house-building and contracting. Early in the year 1851, he built himself a small residence in the city, which was destroyed by the great fire of May 4, 1851. During the same year, among other buildings, he built the First Presbyterian Church, on Stockton Street, between Jackson and Pacific, and the Welsh Presbyterian Church on Vallejo Street, between Kearny and Dupont.

In 1852 he married Miss Ann Williams, who afterwards died in Eureka, in 1875, and by whom he had five children three girls and two boys, all of whom are still living. In 1881 the eldest daughter, May Jane, married Mr. Z. U. Dodge, of San Francisco.

Mr. Jones continued to work at his trade until 1853, when he, in company with others, purchased a small saw-mill for $30,000, in San Mateo County, which they run until 1858, when the mill was totally destroyed by fire; but notwithstanding the misfortune, they immediately rebuilt the mill and continued to run it until 1860, when Mr. Jones sold out and returned to Eureka, Humboldt Bay, where he still lives, and is identified with most of the principal enterprises of the city.

He is one of the founders of the Humboldt County Bank, and for several years has been one of its Directors.

Manufacturing Business of the County.

HUMBOLDT is quite a manufacturing community. Besides the manufacture of lumber there are several other industries. The *Standard* says: "Ship-building is becoming one of the important industries. During the year one steamer and several schooners have been launched from the ways into the waters of the harbors, and several others are now on the stocks in process of construction, while others are contemplated."

There are five ship-yards in the vicinity of Eureka. Oregon pine, as it is called, is very valuable for ship-building, preferred indeed, to the article found in higher latitudes. The material is here in abundance, such as long timber, saw-mills, lumber etc., for conducting this business extensively.

H. D. Bendixon, whose yard is near the Government lighthouse, has built more vessels than any man in the county.

FIRST STEAMER CONSTRUCTED.

The first steamer ever built on Humboldt Bay was by Messrs. Allen & Co., in 1854, and named the *Glide*, and was built for the Eureka and Arcata trade. "Fare, one dollar each way until July 7th, when it will be two dollars."

Including vessels nearly completed there have been constructed in Humboldt Bay seventy-nine vessels, as follows: sixty-three schooners, three stern-wheel steamers, two propellers, three barkentines, two brigs, one scow and one tug.

THE SCHOONER JOSEPH RUSS.

The schooner *Joseph Russ* was launched from Cousin's ship-yard in July, 1881. The craft is a three-master, with a capacity of carrying 375,000 feet of lumber. The dimensions are 122 feet keel, ten feet depth of hold and 31 feet beam. The cost of construction was $22,000. She was loaded with some 376,000 feet of redwood lumber and sailed for San Diego. This is one of the largest sized vessels going out of the harbor of Humboldt Bay, and is the pride of her builders and owner. The *Enterprise*, who witnessed the launching says:—

"We noticed the pleasant countenance of Hon. Joseph Russ, after whom the vessel was named, standing upon the forecastle deck looking as calm and composed as a sea-faring man of sixty. During this time the workmen were busily engaged in knocking the wedges from under her, when suddenly and without a moment's warning the vessel gave a slight shock, then began to move slowly and beautifully down into the water amid the cheers of the admiring crowd. As she made her first movement, Mr. Russ stepped to the bow and performed the usual ceremony of 'breaking the bottle.'

"The *Joseph Russ* has been about six months in the course of construction and continually under the supervision of Mr. Cousins the well-known ship builder. The *Joseph Russ* is certainly a model of beauty in the ship-building line, having all the features that could be combined to form beauty and durability."

JOHN VANCE'S BARKENTINE.

Charles Murry launched the largest vessel of the kind ever built in California. She was built for John Vance Esq., and was launched in December, 1881. The *Times* thus describes the vessel and its launching.

"As the time for high tide approached, the vessel was wedged up and finally the last block was knocked from under, and the barkentine slowly started for the water. With every instant the speed accelerated and she dipped into the water with a splash and then floated out into the bay. The voices of the people on shore and on board joined in an uproarious cheer to the successful launch.

"Miss Maggie Graham dashed a bottle of champagne over the bows and christened her *Uncle John*.

"The vessel is owned by Mr. John Vance and the name given her is a sobriquet by which Mr. Vance is known among his many employes and others, as well. The *Uncle John* was built by Mr. Murry, a veteran ship-builder. Captain Manson will be the commander. The dimensions are: Length, over all, 150 feet; breadth of beam, thirty-four feet and depth of hold ten and a half feet. The registered tonnage is 334 tons and the capacity 430,000 feet of lumber. She is a beautiful craft, the prettiest ever launched in Humboldt waters. She is a staunch vessel, and will be a serviceable ship, being constructed of timber from Mr. Vance's own land, and selected by him and mostly sawed at his mills.

FLOURING MILLS.

The first flouring mill was erected in September 1854, on a tributary of the Van Dusen fork, by Messrs. Corwine, Burlow and Price. The mill was swept away by high water in September 1856.

The Humboldt Flouring Mill, owned by William R. Duff, was completed in September 1854, at Eureka, and began turning out fifty barrels of flour per day.

J. A. Kleiser established a flouring mill in Hoopa Valley in 1855.

There are four flouring mills in the county, each with only two run of stone. They do a good deal of custom work, and in 1880 turned out about 3,000 barrels of flour.

WILLOW-WARE FACTORY.

There exists a thrifty and rapidly-expanding business of willow-ware manufacture by the Genn-Irot Brothers. No better article than they make in this department of skilled labor can be found in the State, and its ready sale in local and San Francisco markets is only limited by their ability to supply them. Their wares are made from a variety of willow imported expressly for their special use, of which they have many acres in cultivation, and of as perfect growth of twig as can be found in any of the fine nurseries of the southern portion of Europe.

THE VARIOUS MANUFACTURING INTERESTS.

LEATHER AND TANNERIES.

Mr. Thomas Devlin has a tannery at Arcata where a good article of leather is manufactured, but on a small scale, and one totally incommensurate with the facilities at hand. He uses about 100 tons of bark a year. He supplies the local dealers with a considerable portion of their stock. Mr. Devlin deserves great credit for his energy and enterprise in starting and developing this business, thus demonstrating that it can he successfully carried on and become a large business. There is no earthly reason why one of the largest and most successful tanneries in the country should not be in operation at Arcata and other points, unless the timidity of capital and the failure of its possessors to appreciate great advantages may be assigned for reasons. There are only two tanneries in operation in the county. The one at Eureka uses about twenty tons of bark per year.

CANNING OF SALMON.

There are four canneries on Eel River, where are annually put up large quantities of salmon in cans. Cutting & Co. have the largest establishment with a capacity of 200 cases per day. In 1880 the number of cases put up amounted to 3,000. They employ sixty hands, mostly Chinamen.

Messrs. Swett & Adams do quite an extensive business in salting and smoking salmon. Their cooper-shops and salting and smoking building is 100x30 feet with a warehouse attached 60x30. They make their own barrels, employing during the season from twelve to eighteen men—white labor exclusively—paying their hands from thirty to thirty-five dollars per month. They have thirty-three large tanks with a capacity of salting 700 barrels.

As soon as the "run of fish" commences the news travels round, and in a day or two the non-quiet river banks are lined with men and dotted with tents and brush and clapboard shanties. Two or three hundred men find employment during the season.

SEAL AND SHARK FISHERIES.

In 1878 Captain Stephen Smith carried on the business of seal fishing near Cape Mendocino, quite extensively. The taking of these animals is confined to the shelves and benches on the seaward side of Cape Rock. The benches fall in succession to the water, on which is the grand parade ground of the sea-lions. The oil averages to the producer about fifty cents to the gallon. From ten to thirty gallons are obtained from a single fish. The bulls weigh from 1,000 to 3,000 pounds. The cows from 500 to 1,000 pounds. The rocks upon which the seals display themselves are covered with hair from their shedding coats. The operation of taking sea-lions and rendering the oil is not only laborious but is attended with much exposure and danger.

The fisheries of Humboldt County are assuming greater proportions each year. Salmon swarm in all our streams with the first winter rains. Large amounts of salmon are shipped fresh to San Francisco, as well as halibut and flounders.

VARIOUS MANUFACTORIES.

The Lincoln Mills were lately established. Mouldings and doors are made at the mill and shipped to Australia, via steamer to San Francisco and sailing vessels across the ocean. On every trip the steamer *Humboldt* carries away large quantities of the manufactures from this mill. The moulding is made from refuse lumber, obtained with little expense from the lumher mills in the county. The Lincoln mill shipped, in 1881, to Australia, via San Francisco, 1,035,417 feet of mouldings and 4,029 doors, manufactured from redwood lumber. About 200,000 feet of moulding and a large number of doors made hy this mill have been used in this county.

The manufacture of furniture has grown to be quite an important industry. This company had to build furniture warerooms, dry-house, steam chest, buy necessary wood for manufacture, and work the same up into furniture, and yet with four hands at work the firm has made cash sales, during the six months mentioned, to the sum of nearly $5,000, besides have several thousand dollars' worth of goods on hand.

The moulding business and ornamental house finish enter as large items in their trade.

Mr. J. P. McKenna, the Manager and Superintendent of the Humboldt Pork Packing Company, furnishes the following statement of the business done at that company's works from January 1, 1880 to January 1, 1881. Number of hogs killed, 2,416. They shipped the following: 138 barrels lard, 143 kegs pigs feet, 26 kegs pigs tongue, 296 barrels pickled pork, 227 cases bacon, 62 cases hams, 5 cases shoulders; amounting to 225,175 pounds. The above is intended to show the amount shipped from the county. It is safe to say that this institution has handled and sold over 400,000 pounds of pork.

The manufacture of tan-bark is likely to prove a large business. About five years ago some attention began to be given to this business. John M. Sass built a bark mill on his place, on Kneeland Prairie, and engaged in the business of cutting, grinding and shipping. The chestnut oak is considered the best for tan-bark. It grows in quite large forests in this county. It is estimated that there are from fifteen to twenty thousand acres and the localities in the neighborhood of Trinidad and Upper Eel River, the Mattole region and Kneeland Prairie. The tan-bark made on the Pacific Coast is considered the best in the United States, as a better quality of leather can be made from it. There are about 28,000 cords of tan-bark used in California each year, of which amount San Francisco requires 16,000 cords.

There are several breweries which manufactured some 25,000 gallons of beer in 1880, and the usual number of small manufacturers, of which we have no reports.

RAPID INCREASE IN PROSPERITY.

Real and Personal Property, Rates of Taxation, Progress of the County, Increase in Population, Etc.

YEAR by year the Assessor's reports show a marked increase in the assessed valuation of all property. Nor is this to be wondered at, when we mark the strides made by mechanical invention in perfecting the tools with which the farmer works. But thirty years have elapsed since the Mexican fastened the crooked branch of a tree to the horns of his ox by thongs, and therewith lightly scratched the bosom of Mother Earth; then laboriously dropped the seed, one by one, in the tiny furrows he had made. See illustrations of these tools on page 31.

Now, behold the mighty gang-plows, yoked to a score of snorting steeds, cutting a broad swath of brown mold across the green prairie, from horizon to horizon. Next the automatic seeder scatters the germs by millions; and where once was seen but the Mexican's tiny acre of scanty stalks, now waves a billowy ocean of yellow grain, far as the eye can reach. Not the slow sickle, or puny scythe must reap this harvest. The swift headers come, with waving wings and rattling blades rejecting the treasured straw of the Eastern farmer, and daintily choosing only the golden heads. And last—no wooden flail with feeble beat, nor old-time fanning-mill, but the mighty steam separator, devouring heads by millions, and making immediate return in hundreds of tons of clean, bright grain.

Note also the wonderful increase of schools, churches and all those institutions calculated to elevate and benefit mankind.

The same relative increase in all productions is shown by export returns, and the largely increased amount of taxable property within the county limits, and there can be little doubt that the next decade will double the population, if not treble it. Its population is as good as any State in the Union can produce. Humboldt is the place of the poor and the rich. It invites honest, industrious and intelligent citizens from other States to come and make homes within its limits.

TOTAL VALUATION FROM 1854 TO 1882.

No one thing will more clearly show the rapid and substantial progress of Humboldt County from its organization to the present time than the increase in total valuation of property The following statement, prepared for this history by County Assessor, Geo. H. Shaw, shows the value and increase of real estate and personal property in the county from its organization down to the present date, as also the rate of taxation. A large amount of land is unoccupied or untaxed, as may be seen in the table of "Comparative Sizes of Counties," on page 76:

INCREASE OF TWENTY YEARS.

Date.	Kind of Property.		Total Valuat'n	Tax Rate
1853-54	Real Estate and Improvements Personal Property	$199,785 382,775	$582,560	$1.10
1854-55			632,831	1.50
1855-57			467,161	1.80
1856-57			618,335	
1857-58			823,000	1.70
1859-60			1,068,905	1.10
1860-61	Real Estate Improvements Personal Property	293,973 297,618 717,910	1,308,501	1.37
1862-63	Real Estate Improvements Personal Property	251,846 236,674 781,741	1,346,361	.95
1863-64	Real Estate Improvements Personal Property	285,295 265,290 578,680	1,129,265	2.37
1864-65	Real Estate Improvements Personal	277,975 566,920 258,270	1,102,965	2.20
1865-66	Real Estate Improvements Personal	372,364 279,106 730,123	1,383,594	2.10
1866-67	Real Estate Improvements Personal	419,130 332,270 953,658	1,705,058	2.40
1867-68	Real Estate Improvements Personal	407,965 354,260 899,315	1,661,540	2.46
1868-69	Real Estate Improvements Personal	450,950 568,340 572,427	1,691,787	2.33
1869-70	Real Estate Improvements Personal	680,050 425,545 1,066,005	2,071,600	2.33
1870-71	Real Estate Improvements Personal	643,250 456,170 1,163,120	2,281,540	2.50
1871-72	Real Estate Improvements Personal	786,975 499,450 1,246,486	2,532,911	2.48
1872-73	Real Estate Improvements Personal	1,602,671 782,260 2,218,876	4,603,707	1.97
1873-74	Real Estate Improvements Personal	1,741,802 756,231 1,346,067	3,844,100	1.90
1874-75	Real Estate Improvements Personal	1,707,004 758,475 1,950,718	4,416,197	2.17
1875-76	Real Estate Improvements Personal	1,885,858 859,770 2,149,482	4,894,310	2.20
1876-77	Real Estate Improvements Personal	2,247,739 1,017,915 1,695,583	4,961,687	2.30
1877-78	Real Estate Improvements Personal	2,379,908 1,144,609 1,594,099	5,118,757	2.25
1878-79	Real Estate Improvements Personal	2,700,835 1,173,170 1,608,551	5,481,546	2.25
1879-80	Real Estate Improvements Personal	2,696,931 1,196,630 1,514,171	5,407,732	2.25
1880-81	Real Estate Improvements Personal	3,497,564 1,226,499 1,880,098	5,804,161	2.00
1881-82	Real Estate Improvements Personal	3,264,779 1,233,081 1,721,622	6,239,482	2.00

ASSESSMENT ROLL OF 1853-4.

The following interesting article on the assessment of 1853-4 is taken from the *Times*. It was the first assessment made in the county.

A little blank book not much more than six inches square and half an inch thick, on file in the office of the County Clerk, contains the duplicate assessment roll of Humboldt County for the fiscal year 1853-54. The County Assessor at that time was D. D. Williams. He received $10 per day and was employed but little over two months in making the assessment. The assessment was under the direction of the Court of Sessions, at that time performing functions similar to those now vested in the Board of Supervisors.

The late Judge J. E. Wyman was presiding Judge of the Court at that time. Lewis K. Wood was Clerk of the Court and ex-officio Auditor.

The total assessment roll was $582,560, about one-tenth of present assessment. The largest tax-payer was the Eureka Mill Company, whose property was valued at $110,000. Bowles, Bowles & Codington were heavy merchants of Uniontown, and built the store now occupied by A. Brizard. Their assessment was $8,150. Mr. Bowles became a large property owner, and a plateau near Arcata is called Bowles' Prairie to the present time. C. S. Ricks & Co. were estimated by Assessor Williams to be worth $6,700, and were assessed accordingly. Roskill & Co. were a heavy firm at that time, being assessed for $15,000.

William Roberts was considered one of the rich men, his property being valued at $7,400. John A. Kneeland, from whom Kneeland's Prairie was named, owned property valued at $5,050.

Wiley, Mills & Co. were proprietors of the American Hotel, Uniontown, which was assessed for $1,600. Mr. Wiley has continued a citizen of the same town ever since, and in 1881 conducted the weekly newspaper at Arcata.

Among those who are at present blessed with large shares of this world's goods a few were here twenty years ago and were not in as affluent circumstances as at the present time.

Joseph Russ kept a butcher shop in partnership with Mr. Adams. The firm was assessed at $1,000.

The firm of John Vance & Co. was assessed at $1,600.

Jonathan Clark's belongings were valued at $3,100.

It is amusing to compare this little note-book with the three large-sized volumes necessary for the enrollments of the assessments of 1880-81, and interesting to note by a glance at the pages of each how some have been favored, and from small beginnings have become proprietors of great landed tracts or owners of saw-mills, sawing logs into money for them. A great many whose names are on the little book have crossed the last river to the land where in the great book the good and evil actions of each one in this world is assessed at the proper valuation.

POPULATION AND INCREASE.

In 1852 the population of Trinity County, before Humboldt was taken off, was 1,764.

Klamath, before Del Norte was formed from it, 530.

In 1860 Klamath was 1,803, Del Norte 2,022, Humboldt 2,694.

In 1870 Klamath was 1,686, Del Norte 2,022, Humboldt 6,140.

In 1880 Del Norte 2,499. Increase in ten years, 628. Humboldt 15,515, an increase of 9,375. But it must be borne in mind that part of this large increase came from the territory of Klamath, annexed during the time.

The county has steadily advanced in wealth and prosperity, and will compare favorably with any of the rural counties in the State.

FINANCIAL CONDITION OF THE COUNTY.

It will be seen from the following statement, prepared for us by the County Treasurer, L. T. Kinsey, that the funds of the county are in sound condition and the Treasurer's office ably managed.

The receipts for the year ending December 1,
1881, were $246,183.13
Balance on hand Dec. 1, 1880 .... 28,946.45

Total receipts....................... $275,129.58
Total disbursements for year 1881..... $249,599.87

Balance on hand Dec. 1, 1881 .... $25,529.71

COUNTY DEBTS.

The bonded debt of Humboldt County is given at $125,000, bearing nine per cent. interest, which amounts to $11,250, payable annually. The bonds are known as wagon road bonds, and were issued under Acts of February 28, 1874, and February 12, and March 28, 1876, in the following amounts:—

Wagon road bonds 1875... .... $60,000
"   "   " 1876................. 45,000
"   "   " 1877................. 10,000
"   "   " 1878................. 10,000

These bonds run for twenty years, but ten years from date the Supervisors begin to provide for their redemption by levying a tax of five per cent. of the whole amount of the bonds, increasing the levy for this purpose with each year until the bonds shall be canceled. When such tax shall be collected the bonds may be called and interest stopped. The bonds of 1875 were taken at $97.50 on the $100; and those issued under the act of 1876 brought all the way from par to $105.74, being issued in parcels. Besides these bonds there is a floating debt of $7,245.16, making the total debt of Humboldt County $132,245.16, less $2,996.30 available for payment of the debt. This leaves a debt of $29,248.86 to be provided for in the next sixteen years.

Mining in Humboldt County.

Early Mining Scenes—Klamath and Trinity Mines—Gold Placers of Humboldt—The Gold Bluffs—Beach Mining, Etc.

Few of the early residents of the county can have forgotten the "gold bluff" excitement of 1852, when, by all accounts, old ocean himself turned miner and washed up cart-loads of gold on the beach above Trinidad. It was represented and generally believed that any enterprising man could take his hat and a wheelbarrow and in half an hour gather up gold enough to last him for life! But as shown in previous articles, this excitement led to the early settlement of the county.

Placer mining is followed with some degree of success on the Klamath and Trinity Rivers, but gold digging is of nominal importance in comparison with agriculture.

The Klamath River country north of the redwoods is the least accessible part of the county. It is more mountainous and contains the only parts of the county which are rocky. The only mining in the county is here, and has been carried on since the early days of the gold excitement.

Quartz mining is now chiefly occupying attention, and valuable mines have recently been discovered. Hydraulic mining has been carried on to some extent; there are twenty-three miles of running ditches, and, during 1880, 3,790 inches of water were used daily. This hydraulic mining meets with no such embarrassments as meet the industry in the Sierra Nevada. There are no bottom-land farms upon the Klamath to be destroyed, so it has free scope for its operations.

A "bench" claim at Big Bar, eight miles below Orleans, has been worked successfully by the the hydraulic process for some five years. This latter process, Judge J. P. Haynes says is revolutionizing the old Klamath mining region. Prospecting has been directed more recently towards the high bars and beaches on the Klamath, which the Judge says he believes to be one of the best mining regions in the State, and one, moreover, which has hardly been scratched for mining purposes. The mining properties are mostly owned by private parties who are content to pocket their own dividend. Their shares in the bank or the bar is not gazetted in the market.

A SPLENDID MINING DISTRICT.

Orleans Bar, upon the Klamath, is known to many old miners. The gold belt, which runs transversely through the Western United States from Colorado, seems to terminate here at the coast. Placer mining has taken a new start, and a large amount of capital is being invested in new mining enterprises. There is little or no speculation in engaging in that industry, for, with capital and good judgment and a strict adherence to business principles, the returns are as sure as any other legitimate enterprise.

Mr. T. M. Brown, Sheriff of Humboldt County, has at Orleans Bar a claim consisting of 405 acres, the bank of which is not more than from forty to eighty feet deep, with a bed of pay dirt, from ten to thirty feet deep. This is considered one of the richest claims in the State; at present there is a small ditch of some five miles in length, and only about eighty feet pressure. The water is conducted through an eight-inch pipe. In this primitive way the claim pays from $8 to $10 per day to the man.

The beauty of this property is that the "slickens," which is such a serious question in some other portions of California, cannot injure any one, as there are no farming lands to destroy between here and the ocean. With an outlay of say $25,000 Camp Creek, which is quite a stream, can be turned onto this property, which has a pressure of from 150 to 200 feet. Judging from a report we saw recently, made by a mining expert this must be an excellent property.

Gold has been found in all parts of the county. Lately on Dobyn's Creek fine specimens of gold quartz were found indicating that somewhere on the streams or in those mountains there is gold to be found. This creek and some other small streams have in their beds small bits of quartz and gold-bearing sand, and we learned that the colors had been found in many places and some gold but not in paying quantities. The best paying mines of the Trinity Section now being worked are at Scott's Bar. The largest piece of gold found on Scott River weighed 197 ounces, and was worth $18.74 per ounce, or $3,504.38. It was in the shape of a fish, seven inches long, and was found by James Lindsay and T. L. Wade, January 27, 1855, while running a cut into Whiting Hill.

THE STARVATION TIMES.

The starvation times on Salmon River forms quite an interesting chapter in the history of this region. So great was the fear of wintering in this comparatively unknown region, that probably not half a hundred men were to be found on the stream in December of 1850.

These had all provided themselves with an ample supply of provisions, and passed the winter very comfortably. As soon as it was suspected that the worst part of the winter had passed, miners began to flock in from Trinity River, Trinidad and Humboldt, and some came up Sacramento River and over through Scott Valley. This was in the latter part of January and during the month of February, 1851. Many of these, especially those from Trinidad and Humboldt, came unprovided with supplies, expecting to find them on the river, and knowing that there were pack-trains at those points preparing to bring in provisions. The result was that, although a few small trains arrived with supplies, the provisions were soon eaten up and there was a crowd of several thousand men without anything to eat.

At this juncture, early in the month of March, a terrific

THE GOLD BLUFFS AND BEACH MINING.

snow-storm set in and so completely blockaded the mountain trails that it was impossible for pack-trains to pass through to their relief. Men lived on mule meat, on sugar, and sometimes on nothing at all. Those who took their rifles and went hunting met with poor success. One man killed two grouse and was offered eight dollars each for them and he declined the trade. The extremity to which some of them were reduced was very great, and for nearly a month not a pound of food came to their relief. Finally packers got as far as Orleans Bar, and men who had made a trail through the snow took small packs on their shoulders and carried them over the mountains to their starving friends. It was nearly the last of April before a train of mules made its way clear through to Salmon, and found a most hearty welcome. Hundreds of the miners who had been snowed in had made their way over the mountains, some to Orleans Bar, some to Trinity, and others to Scott Bar and the newly discovered mines at Yreka Flats, suffering terribly on the way, and at last reaching these places in a starving condition.

GOLD PLACERS OF HUMBOLDT.

There are thousands of millions of dollars in gold-dust lying waste along the ocean beach of Humboldt County. From Table Bluff to the Klamath River, a distance of sixty miles, is an almost unbroken gold-bearing sand beach, exclusive of Gold Bluff beach mining claims. This deposit has accumulated from the crumbling debris of the gravel banks that cave upon the beach and from the discharge of the Klamath River. The process is going on continually, and there is not a panful of sand along this whole distance but what will show the color, and in many places, where the action of the water has been just right it is yellow with gold in streaks. There are more than a thousand acres of this gold-bearing sand between Table Bluff and Klamath River, unclaimed by any one, in fact is outside of the U. S. Survey. It contains from fifty cents upwards to as high as $100 to the ton.

THE GOLD BLUFFS.

John Chapman, Esq., is one of the fortunate owners and successful operators in the region of the Gold Bluff mines. A good idea of these mines may be formed from the illustration he has had made and inserted in this work.

Gold Bluffs are situated on the beach twenty-three miles north of Trinidad and nine miles south of the mouth of Klamath River. In the early days of the wild gold excitement of California, Gold Bluffs was one of the notoriously rich placers. To-day it holds a quiet reputation as a steady paying property that nothing seems to affect. The amount of treasure that has been taken from the two claims runs into the millions, and still the deposit is no more exhausted than on the day it was discovered by the pioneer, E. Du Bertrand, of Trinidad.

The gold-bearing gravel bluffs extend about eight miles on the beach, and in many places they are a perpendicular wall of unbroken gravel three and four hundred feet high. Every winter, after the parching heat of summer has cracked the earth, the soaking rains of winter cause huge slabs of earth and gravel to cave and split off the perpendicular face of the bluff, millions of tons, falling upon the beach. At high tide the surf washes to the base of the cliff, which is subjected to incalculable washing and swashing during the heavy storms. The cakes of gravel become dissolved and are ground to pieces and carried about by the action of the water.

BEACH MINING UNSUCCESSFUL.

From time to time efforts have been made and considerable money invested in the attempt to save and secure the fine gold that is to be found in large quantities along the beach from Little River to Crescent City. The gold is very fine, a mere scale, and to separate it from the sand is just what has baffled the skill of all inventors. Many machines have been invented, which, it was claimed, would accomplish the desired result, but on a trial on the beach, each in their turn have proved failures. The last to try the experiment were W. W. Stow, Jr., Captain Harford, and others, and the machine used was Professor Plant's Gold Separator. After a good deal of prospecting and experimenting the field was abandoned. The beach for many miles is covered with layers of black sand in which the fine gold is found, and although the greater portion is taken up, it could be obtained doubtless for a very small figure, and one which would pay a company largely if the machine could perform the required work.

The parties who have been working the beach mine below Crescent City, known as the Lockhart Mine, have suspended operations, for the reason that they could not make it pay. In years past there has been a great amount of gold taken out in the vicinity of this claim, but there was always a difficulty in getting machinery that would save it, and in some instances almost as good prospects could be obtained from the tailings as from the sand that had been worked.

The effect has usually been that southerly storms cast up great banks of sand, the gravel, mostly, finding some other place of deposit; while the heavy northerly winds which usually prevail at intervals during the summer, act upon this sand-beach like an immense gold pan in the hands of a skillful miner, washing off the gray sand, leaving the black sand containing the gold upon the beach. The weather and wind are carefully watched by the owners of these beaches, and when the gray sand begins to go out, that is the signal for active operations. The pack mules are driven up from the range, the men are re-engaged, and the sand is scraped together upon the beach as fast as it appears and packed up to the washing box and dumped in piles, to be washed out at leisure. The eight miles of gravel bluffs is at present owned by John Chapman and one other company, and it may be truthfully said that either one is a princely fortune.

THEORY OF THE FORMATION.

This deposit has given rise to many theories, but nearly every one holds the idea that at some remote period the Klamath River discharged its waters into the ocean at this point, and with much apparent plausibility. Another theory is that it is the former bed of the Trinity, and that the Klamath and Trinity at one time had separate and distinct channels, at least as far as the present coast-line. A few miles north of the present mouth of the Klamath is a distinctly marked line of gravel which bears as strong evidence of having been a former river bed as does the Gold Bluff section, and which extends inland and northward toward the Klamath Lakes, the source of the Klamath River. This is said to be the former bed of the Klamath, separate and distinct from the Trinity, and that the latter river found its way into the ocean at Gold Bluff. This old gravel bed has been a matter of speculation among practical miners for many years. It is distinctly marked and well defined for thirty-five or forty miles inland from the coast, to where it intersects the present channel of the Trinity River a few miles above its junction with the Klamath. A preliminary survey was once made which proves that the waters of the Trinity River can be brought on to the whole line of this gravel field. The millions of dollars that have been gathered from the sand beach at Gold Bluffs, which was first washed by the surf from the crumbling debris of the cliffs without any perceptible diminution of the Bluffs, gives but a faint idea of the immensity and value of this vast gold deposit—from two to eight miles wide, and thirty-five to forty in length. The country produces everything immediately at hand needful wherewith to develop this field.

THE OSSAGON.

This is the name of the placer that was opened on the upper or northern edge of the Klamath gravel bed on the coast, and adjoining the Upper Gold Bluff claim. It is nine miles south of the Klamath River. The name is a corruption of the Indian designation, which is articulated by the Klamath Indians, "Osh-she-gan." The mine is owned by a stock company known as the "Eureka Gold Mining Company," and all the stock is owned in Eureka. A dam was built and water brought on from a small creek bearing the name of the mine. The dam and other works were thrown up hastily as is too frequently the case in such enterprises, and the company was calculating upon a rich return from a trifling outlay. But the winter rains came, washed out their dam, it having been made of soil with nothing to stay it, and otherwise destroyed the improvements such as they were.

The works were reconstructed and a strong dam built, 250 feet in length, thirteen feet high, and had a holding capacity of 80,000,000 cubic feet. The ditch was half a mile in length, and at the pressure box had 150 feet elevation. The sluice was composed of sixty boxes, twelve feet long, three feet wide, and six blocks or ripples to the box. There were sixty boxes, each twelve feet long, composing the sluice, and six blocks in each box; multiplying sixty by six gives 360 of these huge blocks.

This Ossagon Creek is but one of many that are available on and near the Klamath gravel bed, and timber is to be had on every hand. The many attempts that have been made to work over the gray sand lying along the beach have proved as many failures. The action of the surf grinds the gold so fine that no machine has yet been invented which succeeds in saving it. But in no case have efforts to work the gravel from the inland field, failed to meet with good success. It is river gravel, and the gold coarser, and this difference is more noticeable as the distance from the coast increases.

This mining region offers an encouraging field for the practical and scientific prospector, for the men of small means who wish to take a prospector's chances, or for the representative of heavy capital.

The rich placers that have been found on the Trinity, the Klamath and their tributaries, are conclusive evidence that the "Black Bear" is not the only rich gold bearing quartz lode in this section. These mountains are veined with rich quartz, and a careful, patient and intelligent prospecting will bring many of them to light.

Coal was found on Mad River as early as 1854, but no paying veins were discovered. At a later date, it was found on Eel River. At Point St. George, several years ago, a shaft was sunk, and a good quality of coal obtained; for want of capital the work was abandoned. It is similar to all the coal on this coast—lignite or brown; and as it does not occur in the carboniferous formation of the earth, it can hardly be called true coal.

Petroleum, which is very nearly allied to coal, has been found quite extensively in several places in the county. The first vein located was at Petrolia, which was in 1864. This vein was so rich with petroleum, that several gallons flowed from it daily. Some of the wells yielded several hundred barrels of the crude article, but none of the wells turned out to be flowing ones. The production was slow and limited, and the business not being considered very profitable was at last abandoned.

Copper in well-defined lodges has been discovered in the south part of the county. When these mines were discovered there was a great excitement and rush for claims, everybody ignoring the rule that it requires money to successfully operate in copper mining. Del Norte has several successful copper mines; one is now worked.

Iron ore was discovered as early as 1854, by United States Surveyor Murray, on Eel River. At later dates other bodies have been found all along the coast. No serious attempts have ever been made to develop them, except in Del Norte County.

INDIANS AND THEIR RESERVATIONS.

Klamath Indians—Names of Various Tribes—Indian Wars and Treaties—Their Disappearance—Indian Reservations—War Claims, Etc.

THE Indians of the section, originally called Trinity County, were estimated in 1854 at 10,000, and divided into several bands which were subdivided into numerous ranches of families. Their languages were divided into six general divisions: The *We-ott* and *Pot-ta-wott Co-nill* occupied lower portions of Eel and Mad Rivers and the bay country.

The *Tu-lick Si-ti-quo* ranged along the coast and the Klamath from Port Trinidad to Bluff Creek, a small stream eight miles above the confluence of the Klamath and Trinity and some sixty miles from the ocean.

The *Oar-rook Ar-rah* occupied a territory extending along up the Klamath some ninety miles, being bounded on the north by the Shasta.

The *No-ten-ta-yuh No-oo-stoh*, or Trinity Indians, occupied the Trinity from its junction with the Klamath to its South Fork, and were also scattered over the Bald Hills and on Redwood and Mad Rivers.

The *Patch-wies* were a small band located on New River and upon the main Trinity above the South Fork and extending through all the country embracing the head-waters of Panther Redwood, Mad, and Eel Rivers. This also included a wing of a powerful tribe known as the *Win-toon*, or "Mountain Diggers."

KLAMATH INDIANS.

The Indians known by the general term of Klamath River Indians included all those mentioned and that occupied the river between the Shastas and the sea. The Klamath River Indians were the finest specimens of physical manhood to be found among the natives of California, powerful and fierce, and gave the whites trouble from the time they first placed foot on their hunting grounds.

Indian difficulties will be treated of in the order of their occurrence, and facts and causes related with as close an adherence to the truth as is possible when information is drawn solely from the testimony of the whites. It will be seen, however, that even then the record is by no means creditable to our boasted civilization. We shall not attempt to give a full history of all the Indian difficulties. Our space would not allow recital of even of a small part of the difficulties and encounters with the Indians. We will give a few leading items which show something of the state of affairs in this part of California and the trials of the pioneers. These Indians had no chiefs in the common acceptation of the term. But Indians who were wealthy in their own peculiar goods and had many relatives were very influential in their districts. Among these may be mentioned *Ken-no-wah-i*, or "Trinity Jim," *Zeh-frip-pah*, who lived on the Upper Klamath, *No-roo-kus* and *Kaw-tap-ish*, on the Lower Klamath. These last mentioned were the firm friends of the whites in early times. Many difficulties were adjusted by their intervention and assistance.

The settlement of the white man soon brought about seemingly inevitable conflicts. The Indians were interrupted in their fisheries; lands were plowed up where they had obtained their grass, seeds and roots; their game was killed; trees and shrubs were burned, which furnished nuts and berries, and last but not least, says the *Times* of that date:

"They are ill-treated and abused, had white men ravish the squaws and whip and beat the men."

INDIAN MURDERS AT MARTIN'S FERRY.

In 1851, Blackburn, his wife and three men were in charge of the above ferry. Blackburn and wife occupied a small shake shanty on the river-bank. One day Mrs. Blackburn, a noble woman of the brave pioneer class that have been led by love to follow the footsteps of their idol into the very heart of the wilderness, noticed that the stock of bullets had become exhausted. She immediately moulded a large quantity, and by this prudent act and her afterward heroic conduct saved the lives of herself and husband that self-same night. No trouble had been experienced from the Indians for some time by the occupants of the ferry-house, and they retired to rest that night with little thought of the bloody deed the savages purposed to commit. As the shadows of night blended into a universal gloom, the Indians gathered in the forest about the abode of their intended victims, and waited until their eyes were closed in peaceful slumber and the place was wrapped in a mantle of silence.

When the night had sufficiently advanced to assure them that their victims were asleep and that they would not be interrupted in their hellish deed by the appearance of belated travelers, they crept stealthily to the tent where the three men lay sleeping, and commenced the work of death. Two of the men were instantly killed, while the third sprang to his feet and rushed from the tent with a cry for help. He had taken but a few steps when the cry was hushed upon his lips, and he fell to the ground dead beneath the knives of his pursuers. The agonising cry of the wounded man awoke from their slumbers the occupants of the house, who knew too well its dreadful import. Hastily barricading themselves, they prepared for defense. Their arms consisted of two rifles and a revolver, and with these Blackburn kept the savages at bay throughout that long and terrible night, his noble wife reloading the weapons as fast as he discharged them.

With the coming of the morning there appeared on the opposite bank of the river A. E. Raynes, William Young, and

LAUREL GROVE DAIRY RANCH, BEAR RIVER, 17 MILES FROM FERNDALE, HUMBOLDT CO. CAL. RICHARD JOHNSTON, PROP.

William Little, who had stayed that night at a cabin a few miles distant, and had come at the request of its occupants to see if Blackburn had any extra arms, as they feared an attack by the Indians. Blackburn made his appearance from the house and greeted them with a sad voice, saying, "I'm glad to see you boys; they are all killed but myself and wife." When he had ferried them across the stream they went to examine the scene of conflict.

SAD MEETING OF FATHER AND SON.

They saw a body lying about 100 yards from the house and hastened to the spot. When the body of the dead man was turned so that they could see his face, Blackburn sprang back with the cry, "Great God! it is my father," and so it was, killed by heartless savages in sight of the cabin of his son, whom he had not seen for ten years. The old gentleman had accompanied a pack-train from Trinidad, and when they encamped that night some ten miles from the ferry, he had pushed on alone, and had fallen before the knives of the Indians that lay concealed in the forest, awaiting the time for the attack upon the cabin.

The three men volunteered to push through to Trinidad for assistance, to administer to the Indians a chastisement they would not soon forget, while Blackburn and his dauntless wife remained on guard at the cabin. They lost the trail in the darkness and lay all night in the redwood forest, until daylight enabled them to again find the trail and push on for help Arriving at Trinidad the next day, they were joined by only ten men, and the little party of thirteen started back to the ferry to attack at least three hundred savages.

A number of miles above Trinidad lies a body of water on the low land between the mountains and the sea, known as the Big Lagoon. When the party arrived at this point they came upon a number of Redwood Creek Indians in canoes, whom they decided to attack. They therefore fired upon the canoes, when the savages jumped into the water and swam ashore. A brisk battle was maintained for some time, the men using their animals for protection. The superiority of guns over bows was soon demonstrated, and the Indians withdrew with the loss of two or three braves. The party continued the contest, and going on up the river, located Happy Camp, as heretofore related.

McKEE'S INDIAN TREATIES.

In 1851 the Government appointed three Commissioners of Indian affairs in California, with instructions to make treaties with all the tribes in the State. They were Col. G. W. Barber, of Kentucky, Dr. O. M. Wozencraft, of California, and Colonel Reddic McKee, of Virginia. They divided the State into three districts, Southern, Sacramento, and Klamath. Barber taking the first, Wozencraft the second, and McKee coming into this section. They made treaties right and left, promising enough in the way of blankets, cattle, etc., to have swamped the whole Government. McKee came up the Klamath in 1852, and many amusing stories are told of him and his method of treaty-making. He was a self-important man, and to impress the Indians with a sense of his official dignity, and to convince them that he was a great *tyee*, wore a flaming red vest. This sanguinary garment was the envy of every Indian heart and the focus of every Indian eye whenever its wearer appeared among them. The treaty was concluded in due time, the consideration to the Indians for the relinquishment of their claim to the lands outside of the strip set apart for a reservation being 200 head of cattle.

It is a custom among the aborigines to exchange presents upon the conclusion of a treaty, and old Tolo, one of the chiefs, set his heart upon the envied vest. He could scarcely restrain his impatience to sign the document, and when he had affixed his cross he turned eagerly to the agent, threw off his upper vestment, and exclaimed, "Me take um vest." "What for!" asked the astonished official.

"Me sign um treaty, you make um me present. Me take um vest."

McKee did not relish the idea of exchanging his badge of authority for the dirty and he feared otherwise objectionable garment of the chief, and so he said, "I give you my name and you give me yours. You be McKee and I be Tolo."

The chief consented to take the name, though he preferred the vest, and was thereafter known as McKee. The bad faith which has characterized the dealings of the Government with "the nation's wards" was not wanting in this instance. The promised cattle did not appear. The whites invaded and occupied the reservation as well as the ceded territory, while young McKee went into the ranching business in Scott Valley. No wonder the Indians became dissatisfied, and no wonder they should have little faith in any promises made to them in the future.

THE INDIAN WAR.

The Indian war, if it can be properly so termed, was brought on by the whites, under the most aggravated circumstances. The facts are, as we are informed, says the *Times* of 1855, that about the 10th of December, 1854, a ruffian attempted to commit an outrage upon the person of an Indian woman, who was accompanied by an Indian boy. The woman clung to the boy and the white man drew his revolver and shot the boy down, who afterwards died from the wound. The man after bullying around for sometime, left for parts unknown. The Indians thinking to get revenge, killed an ox that had formerly belonged to this man, but learning that he had sold it, they offered to pay the present owner the value of the steer, which was refused.

The Indians became frightened and by their conduct filled the minds of the miners with suspicion, they attempted to disarm them without paying the value of the arms; and upon the Indians refusing to surrender them the miners proceeded to burn the Indian ranches with their winter's supply of provisions, which they defended by killing the whites engaged in so doing.

INDIAN WAR CLAIMS.

At a session of the Legislature in 1856 an act was passed requiring the Governor of the State to appoint two Commissioners to examine all claims held by citizens of Klamath, Siskiyou and Humboldt Counties for services rendered and for supplies furnished in the suppression of Indian hostilities in the years of 1852, 1853, 1854 and 1855.

In pursuance of this act, Governor Johnson appointed E. J. Curtis, of Siskiyou County, and Walter McDonald, of Klamath, as such Commissioners. Mr. Curtis subsequently resigned and A. M. Jones, of Siskiyou, was appointed to fill the vacancy thus caused. Each Commissioner was to receive $3,000 as compensation for discharging their duties.

INDIAN TREATY.

In August, 1857, Major Heintzelman succeeded in getting into Council the head men of the Klamaths with the Copas, Honags, Yougatneks and Talawas, which he had recently removed on to the reservation, at which time a treaty was made in which they agreed to bury all animosities that have heretofore existed between them—to live together in peace and submit any difficulties that may arise between them to the officer in charge of the reserve for settlement.

WHY INDIANS DISAPPEAR BEFORE THE WHITES.

The rancheria on Indian Island was attacked on Saturday night, February 20, 1860, by an unknown party of men, and, with the exception of three or four that escaped, *the whole tribe*, with many Mad River Indians stopping there, were killed. It may be well imagined that this unexpected attack on the Diggers so near town, says the *Times*, accompanied with such a terrible and indiscriminate slaughter, produced considerable excitement. In the midst of it, news reached town that the ranches on South Beach had also been attacked the same night, and the whole number of Diggers there exterminated. It was afterward reported that a considerable number of Indians on Eel River were killed at the same time. The ranches at Bucksport and on Elk River were not disturbed. As there were only squaws and children at these places, except two old bucks, it would seem that the design at first was only to kill the bucks. The killing appears to have been principally with knives and hatchets or axes. The whole number killed at the different places on that night did not fall far below *one hundred and fifty*, including bucks, squaws and children.

Three days before, a large ranch of Indians above Eagle Prairie, on Eel River, was attacked, and twenty-six Diggers killed, mostly bucks, and among them some that were known to be desperate villains. The next day another ranch opposite "The Slide" was attacked, but we did not learn how many were killed or taken.

GRAND JURY REPORT.

Some effort was made by the authorities to punish the perpetrators of these murders. The following report of the Grand Jury, in April, 1860, shows no one was punished: "We cannot close our report without commenting upon the massacre of Indian women and children lately committed in this county. We have endeavored, by summoning before us a number of citizens of this county whom we supposed could give us some information, to enable us to bring to trial the persons engaged in this revolting crime; and after a strict examination of all the witnesses, nothing was elicited to enlighten us as to the perpetrators. We would express our condemnation of the outrage, and regret our investigations of this matter have met with so deplorable a result." D. MASTEN, Foreman.

J. Ross Browne, in speaking of these Indian troubles, says: "I am satisfied, from an acquaintance of eleven years with the Indians, that had the least care been taken of them, these disgraceful massacres would never have occurred. A more inoffensive and harmless race of beings does not exist on the face of the earth, but wherever they attempted to procure a subsistence they were hunted down; driven from the reservations from the instinct of self-preservation; shot down by the settlers upon the most frivolous pretexts, and abandoned to their fate by the only power that could afford them protection."

The massacre of Indians still continued, and in February, 1861, thirty-nine Diggers were killed by the settlers on main Eel River, above the crossing of the old Sonoma trail. It seems that the few settlers at Kentinshaw, at the beginning of winter, in order to avoid danger to their stock from snow, moved down on main Eel River at the point mentioned. Not long after some of them returned to look after their houses, etc., and found that the Indians had destroyed all of them. Thereupon a company started in pursuit of the offenders, taking along some friendly Indians to assist them. They found the band that committed the damages and killed the above number of males.

Of course the Indians retaliated as best they could, and the settlers were driven from the interior. It was estimated that 9,000 head of cattle were killed by Indians. Another war was inaugurated, in which the local volunteers participated.

For many years the Indians in this State were abused and defrauded of their natural rights, and sometimes cheated out of Government bounties. Their domestic happiness was disturbed by lawless adventurers, and they were driven from their favorite fishing-grounds and hunting-places, under a pretense of Indian hostilities, when the primary object was to get possession of choice locations, and incidentally make money out of the Government pending disturbances.

These encroachments upon the natural rights of the Indians aroused their dormant passions and savage nature, until they became dangerous foes to the white race, and caused much suffering, and for a time retarded the growth and prosperity of the country. Latterly they have been more peaceable and contented; many have been collected upon the reservation, and under promise of protection become happy and industrious.

INDIAN RESERVATIONS.

Under the Act of Congress passed in 1864, it was provided that not more than four reservations should be set apart for Indians of this State and two Superintendents. These were accordingly established as follows: Round Valley (Mendocino County), Hoopa Valley (Humboldt County), Smith River (Del Norte County), and the Tule in the southeastern part of the State. The last two were leased from settlers.

Congress in July, 1868, authorized the abandonment of the Smith River Indian farm and the removal of the Indians to the Hoopa Valley Reservation in Humboldt County. The route from the former to the latter place is by a devious mountain trail, probably the most difficult on the Pacific Coast to travel or drive stock over. There were many rivers and mountain streams to cross, and a portion of the way led along the sea beach, utterly impassable except at low tide and in moderate weather. The first twenty miles only, from Smith River to the foot of the first range of mountains, had ever been traveled with wagons. The entire distance from there to Hoopa was but a serpentine trail through mountain fastnesses, deep gorges, and over rocky cliffs.

JOHN CHAPMAN, THE MOUNTAINEER.

John Chapman, of Humboldt County, was employed, an experienced mountaineer, well acquainted with the route, with the crossings, and with the various tribes of Indians, through whose country they were obliged to pass. He acted as special Indian Agent or conductor in the matter of removal of Indians and stock. He was a good interpreter, an experienced guide, and packer. He furnished a train of pack mules and several practical packers.

It was found no easy task to move Indians, cattle, horses, colts, and a pack-mule train, all at the same time, over a narrow mountain trail; consequently, Mr. Chapman, Henry Orman, Jr., the Agent at Smith River, and B. C. Whiting, Superintendent were frequently separated, each having about as much responsibility as a division commander.

The sick and blind Indians, (thirty-eight in number,) besides a portion of the baggage, were hauled from Smith River to the foot of the mountains, in wagons. This was about twenty miles, and as far as wagons could go; from thence to the Klamath River (a distance of twenty-four miles) the sick were carried in boxes, packed on each side of a mule, as Californians carry smoked bacon or salmon.

From the mouth of the Klamath the sick were taken in Indian canoes up that river to its junction with the Trinity, and then up the Trinity River to Hoopa Reservation, where they were landed.

The balance of the Indians, together with the train of pack mules, the Government horses, colts, and cattle, were driven over the mountains, a distance of about ninety miles further, making a total of 134 miles.

KLAMATH RESERVATION.

In 1856 the President by proclamation reserved as a military reservation for the Indians, a strip of land on the Klamath River, one mile on each side and extending from its mouth about twenty miles up the stream, and containing 25,000 acres. It belongs to Del Norte County, but is about a mile north of the Humboldt line.

The number of Indians officially reported on this reservation is upwards of 1,000. But the settlers claim that there is not over one-tenth of that number on the reserve. The settlers complain against the maintenance of the Klamath River Reservation, covering and locking up the mouth of a navigable river, from which they have been forcibly expelled by the United States, and the presence of a military post that, from all appearances, has been devoting itself to the work of instigating the Indians to acts of aggression against the whites that are upon the free public domain.

HOOPA VALLEY RESERVATION.

This reserve has an area of about 38,000 acres, and the valley is estimated to contain about 2,500 acres of arable land. With the assistance of the Smith River Reservation Indians, who are industrious and experienced in farm operations, a large crop of grain and vegetables has been raised in the valley. The reservation is under a fine state of cultivation and highly prosperous, and the Indians are orderly and contented—a decided improvement over the state of affairs with them, when dissensions and bloodshed prevailed to a great extent. There is a U. S. Military Post here, called Camp Garton. This reserve is also coveted by the whites.

INDIAN TRADITIONS.

The Bay Indians have a tradition that the Humboldt Bay was produced by an earthquake, which swallowed up the land, and destroyed a large and powerful tribe of Indians, only a few escaping—which statement is almost corroborated by the evidences presented to us, viz.: Trees buried to the depth of 200 feet and more; palpable proofs in the immense fissures found in the hills to the southeast of Arcata, which appear to have been made within a century. When Humboldt was first settled, the Indians held meetings, at which they offered sacrifices to the Great Spirit, that he would hold the world together.

THE TOWNS AND VILLAGES.

Description of Each Village—When and by Whom Settled—Rapid Growth—Present Condition, Etc.

During the year 1851 the population of the county did not increase much, if any, the speculative population leaving about as fast as the industrial came in. Business languished in all places except Arcata, which carried on the trade with the mines with undiminished vigor. In the year 1852 the population increased rapidly, business flourished, and everything wore an air of prosperity. The trade with the mining increased, agriculture was prosecuted with vigor and success in all parts of the county, and the lumbering business increased rapidly. Although speculation was the order of the day, yet the different towns immediately commenced such industrial pursuits as seemed most natural for it. Union and Humboldt both opened trade to the mines, and Eureka commenced shipping piles and square timber, and before the close of the year quite a number of cargoes of these materials had been sent to San Francisco from the sloughs in her vicinity.

The other two towns made strenuous efforts to build up a trade with the mines, but in the case of Humboldt Point, was unsuccessful, trains invariably leaving and going to Arcata whenever there was no inducement held out to them to go to the former place, and in July, 1851, the last train left Humboldt Point for the mines, and since that time Arcata has enjoyed that monopoly almost alone.

BUCKSPORT.

Bucksport was laid out in 1851, by the lamented David A. Buck. It immediately took a position in the ranks of the then rival towns of the Bay. In 1854 the Masons erected a handsome hall, two-story, with school room on the first floor. Dr. J. Clark erected a handsome residence fronting directly on the Bay. At this time the four towns of the Bay were Bucksport, Humboldt, Eureka, and Union. The first three had one store each and Union seven large stores.

Bucksport was made the port of entry, and in 1856 contained a church, two hotels, saw-mill, store and private residences.

Fort Humboldt was erected on a bluff in the rear of the town site, commanding a view of the entrance to the Harbor.

HUMBOLDT POINT.

Early in the year 1850 it was the general impression that Trinity River emptied into the ocean and formed a bay at its mouth, and as the mines on that river were reported to be amazingly rich, it was but reasonable to suppose that if any man could find this bay and lay out a town on it he could make his fortune by selling lots; and as it was the time when the speculative mania was at the meridian of life in California, there was no lack of men who were ready to embark their lives and property on a perilous voyage of discovery for the chance of becoming city proprietors, and consequently rich.

In January, 1850, several vessels were fitted out in San Francisco for the purpose of exploring the coast and searching for the mouth of Trinity River, as mentioned by Buhne, Howard and others. Humboldt Bay and the mouth of Eel River were both discovered soon afterwards, and the party which discovered the latter thought it was the mouth of Trinity, got their vessels into the bay at its mouth and prospected some distance up for gold. These adventurers soon explored the country contiguous to the bay, occupied Humboldt Point and laid it out in 1850 for a town site.

Union was settled soon after, and Eureka sprang into existence soon after her; each place claimed a large tract of land for its site, and thus before autumn the whole margin of the bay was claimed as city property and a great portion of it actually surveyed and laid off into streets, blocks, etc.

TRINIDAD VILLAGE AND HARBOR.

It is claimed by the residents of this place that this is the best outside port on this part of the Pacific Coast, and it appears they have good grounds for such claims. Its position on the coast certainly would be a most favorable one for a port of refuge. It is easy of access from the open sea at all times. Those who have carefully watched the direction and break of the sea in heavy storms, assert that a break-water, extended from a certain point on Trinidad Head to what is known as Pilot Rock, would completely and effectually shelter the mooring of the harbor.

Pilot Rock is over 300 feet across the base, and is 112 feet above high water. The whole length of break-water would be 2,000 feet, with an average depth from shore to rock of about seven to eight fathoms. This it is claimed, by those who have watched the action of the heavy sea for years, would be all that is necessary to make this a perfectly safe harbor in any and all storms.

There are many reasons and arguments favorable to Trinidad being an available open seaport. She has depths of water at her moorings to accommodate the largest vessel that floats, and thirty feet of water at her wharf at low tide. The cost of making a break-water would not be great, and the relative benefits which would accrue appear to be such as should justly bring about an early and serious consideration of this work.

The tonnage of this port may be estimated at 7,000 tons for last year. The number of cargoes about forty.

TRINIDAD EXPORTS IN LUMBER FOR 1881:

Lumber, feet	18,000,000
Posts	38,000
Shingles	8,000,000
Shakes	800,000
Wool, pounds	15,000

HOME OF THE LATE ALEXANDER ROBERTSON, SEVEN MILES SOUTH OF BRIDGEVILLE, HUMBOLDT CO. CAL.

DESCRIPTION OF THE TOWNS AND VILLAGES.

Trinidad is about twenty miles above Eureka. It is the site of the extensive operations of the Trinidad Mill Company, composed of Messrs. Hooper Bros., of Stewart Street, San Francisco. They have an extensive saw and shingle mill; they also have a railroad, and do all their logging by steam, which is well worth the while to see; the logs are hauled to the railroad track by a donkey stationary engine, then by locomotive to the mills. The railroad is four miles long.

The town has 200 inhabitants, who are nearly all engaged in the lumber business. The steamer *Mary D. Hume* makes Trinidad her first call from San Francisco up on her way to Crescent City.

Gen. B. F. Butler's brother's buildings, which were built in 1851, when the gold excitement was at the highest, are still here in a good state of preservation. Trinidad then had some 3,000 people; twenty or thirty pack-trains went out daily to the mines at Sawyer Bar, Klamath, and Gold Bluff, and the Upper Trinity Country.

The town now has several stores and other business houses. Our artist has given a good view of this town situated on an elevation and backed up by the beautiful redwoods which extend for some twelve or fifteen miles into the interior. The lumber business is the chief support at present, although there is still considerable mining, and the pack-trains can still be seen with their loads bound for the mines.

A Lodge of Good Templars is located here. They own their hall and lot upon which it is built, besides the two adjoining lots, and both as a Lodge and as individuals have done much noble charity work in the community.

The Occidental Hotel is kept by W. Watkins and affords a pleasant stopping place.

ORLEANS BAR.

The village bearing this name was selected as the county seat of Klamath County in 1856. Between the junction of Trinity River with the Klamath and the mouth of the Salmon, the mountains recede from the river somewhat, forming a basin consisting in places of large bars at the river's edge, then successively bottoms, higher benches, table-lands, and red hills rearing up into mountains. On one of these bottoms, on the right side of the Klamath, about sixteen miles above the mouth of the Trinity, and right below that of the Salmon, stands the town of Orleans Bar.

The bar from which the place takes its name was christened by Captain Tompkins and Bob Williams, in 1850.

A party in the spring of the same year went up from the mouth of the Klamath, which had just previously been discovered, by sea in canoes, and two or three towns were laid off. The river being swollen, it was supposed to be a navigable stream and the party concluded that "New Orleans Bar," as it was first called, would be about the head of navigation. As the season advanced the river dried up to a small stream and the town dried up also.

During the spring and summer of 1851, after the Gold Bluff bubble had bursted, the crowd of disappointed adventurers who had arrived at Trinidad in search of golden sands, started for the Klamath and Salmon Rivers. Orleans during this summer was quite a prominent point but toward fall the whole region of country was abandoned, the adventurers just mentioned having gone to the mines without any intention of hard labor, and not finding gold scattered about on the surface left for other sections.

After 1852, the mining population in that section had, as a general thing, been steadily on the increase, and confidence as to the richness and durability of the mines had also been increased in proportion to the experience in working them.

Orleans was a central point for the section of country mentioned, and will yet become quite a flourishing inland town. It is pleasantly situated and the climate, although warm in the summer, is not sultry; there always being a cool ocean breeze sometime during the day. The dissolution of old Klamath County, which demolished Orleans Bar as a county seat has not affected the place as much as many suspected it would. The mining, stock-raising, and farming industries make it about as flourishing as ever, if not so high-toned with official dignitaries.

There is an abundance of good, rich paying mining ground in that section, which only needs capital and water-ditches to develop. The place met with a serious disaster by the great flood of 1861, in the loss of many valuable mining improvements, from which it is now gradually recovering, the slowness of such recovery being due to the disadvantages of having no wagon road, or other mode of communication, with the balance of the world, except on the hurricane deck of a mule.

HYDESVILLE.

Hydesville sprang up in 1858, on a place called by the euphonious name of Goose Prairie, on Van Duzen Fork of Eel River. It derived its name from Mr. Hyde who formerly owned the land upon which the town stands. Pine's Hotel was the first erected there. The first general merchandise store in the place was built by Dr. M. Spencer, who kept it for many years.

In 1859, there was a wagon and carriage shop, a blacksmith, saddler, carpenter, shoemaker, a livery stable, and one store kept by I. Manheim & Co. The school was taught by W. H. Mills, and had thirty-four pupils. Cooper's Mills were turning out twenty-five barrels of flour per day. They were located about three miles distant on Yager Creek and propelled by water-power.

Hydesville is now considered the fifth town in the county, having a population of 300 people. It is situated on high table-land nearly 300 feet above the general level of Eel River Valley. It has a fine farming country to back it. Mr. J. W. Sweasey keeps the Pioneer Hotel. There are two general stores. S. F. Bullard, the General Superintendent of the Humboldt and

Mendocino Stage Line, resides here. Stages pass here daily.

Samuel Strong's pleasure resort is located about nine miles from Hydesville, and is fitted up for the comfort and enjoyment of guests, and fully described elsewhere.

J. A. Coyle is the dealer in stoves, tinware, glassware, crockery, hardware, and a large general stock of agricultural implements. His business place is located on the main street.

D. Gibson & Co. are the principal dealers in dry-goods, clothing, boots and shoes, hats, caps, etc. They also keep a general line of ladies' and gents' furnishing goods and a large general merchandise stock, wholesale and retail. The members of the firm are David Gibson and Louis Hessing.

ROHNERVILLE.

The town obtained its name from Henry Rohner who still resides there and is a successful business man. In 1859, there was but one store here, kept by Rohner & Feigenbaum, and a hotel erected by Brower & Woodruff. Now it has a population of 510 people. This town is situated twenty-two miles southeast from Eureka, and is pleasantly located in the rich valley of Eel River, one mile north of the stream. The principal wagon road of the county passes through the place. It has an excellent farming and grazing country on one side, and redwood timber on the other, to back it.

A. M. Gill is the principal merchant having a large stock of general merchandise. It can be truthfully claimed that Rohnerville has acquired as large, if not a larger trade with Trinity, than any other point in Humboldt County. Train loads of merchandise leave here weekly for trading points on the Trinity River, and to that portion of Trinity County lying between Hay Fork Valley and the South Fork Mountain, to the south. A great portion of the furs and skins coming from Western Trinity find a market at Rohnerville.

The *Rohnerville Herald* is issued every week by Charles E. Gordon, who publishes more local news for an inland town than any other paper. It is a live paper in a live town. There are two hotels, one extensive saw and grist-mill, churches, schools, and all needed business houses. Land in the vicinity is held at high prices. In the valley and improved, it is valued at from $30 to $75 per acre. Rolling hill-lands in the vicinity have a rich, dark, loamy soil, and are excellent grain lands, and are valued at nearly the same price as the valley. St. Joseph's College, an institution of learning belonging to the "Society of the Precious Blood of Christ," is in the suburbs.

There are four church societies, United Brethren, Congregational, Methodist and Catholic. The Odd Fellows and Masons have large societies and halls. There is also a large public hall for meetings and exhibitions. An abundant supply of pure spring water is furnished by the water-works.

FERNDALE.

Ferndale has a population of some 350. Francis Creek, a swift little stream runs through the town, affording splendid facilities for drainage. It is connected by daily stage with Eureka, and is located some eighteen miles south. It is beautifully situated on the south side of Eel River Valley, about one mile beyond Salt River, at the foot of the range of hills bounding Eel River on the south. This flourishing town is delightfully situated, well built, public spirited, and is improving.

Ferndale is well situated for a business place, having the farmers on the south and west side of the valley, and on the other the settlers of the Bear River and Mattole sections. This valley is about twelve miles in length, and on an average from four to eight miles wide. This may properly be called the cream of Humboldt County as an agricultural district.

A post office was established in 1860, S. L. Shaw postmaster.

The *Ferndale Enterprise* is ably managed by Dr. T. A. Alford.

A. Putnam is one of the substantial merchants of the place. His residence forms one of the illustrations for this work.

Messrs. Russ, Searls & Putnam have a fine brick building, and the largest store in the county. Mr. Joseph Russ, the senior partner, has about 50,000 acres of land in this vicinity, and is the owner of over 2,000 dairy cows, which are rented to dairymen with land enough to support a certain number of cows. This firm are also in the forwarding and commission business and are one of the large dealers in butter on the coast.

Roberts Hall is fitted up for general use, and is owned by D. K. Roberts.

A. Bearding has a large store of merchandise and general agricultural implements and does a large trade.

Ferndale Hotel is kept by W. J. McCollum. It is a first-class stopping place and can easily accommodate fifty guests. Everything is conducted by an experienced proprietor who knows how to keep a good hotel.

There are now three fine churches in Ferndale, Methodist, Congregational, and Catholic. There is a free reading-room and library of 200 volumes, and an excellent school under charge of Prof. L. B. Lawson, who has introduced a method of teaching penmanship by a new and shorter process than any now in use. He is about publishing a book on this subject.

The village has several stores and business houses. The business of the town is rapidly increasing.

It has the usual quota of professional men. Among them may be mentioned A. A. Glasscock, M. D., a skilled physician and surgeon, who has an office and residence on Church Street.

PORT KENYON AND SALT RIVER.

Salt River is a small stream but is navigable for a short distance for deep water craft. Ferndale is situated on this stream, and Port Kenyon is the shipping point. Centerville is at the mouth of Salt River. Port Kenyon is four miles from the mouth of the river. J. G. Kenyon, the original owner of the land upon which the shipping point known as Port Kenyon is situated, struggled long and bravely to establish the fact of the navigability of the bar. He finally enlisted T. P. H·

DESCRIPTION OF THE TOWNS AND VILLAGES.

Whitelaw of San Francisco in the matter, and the result was a staunch and well-constructed steamer of excellent sea-going qualities, the *Thos. A. Whitelaw*, which cost about $45,000. The *Whitelaw* made weekly trips for some two months, but was soon afterward withdrawn. Mr. Kenyon has lately started a store at a point called Washington Corners.

TABLE BLUFF, HOOKTON AND SPRINGVILLE.

Table Bluff is on high rolling land overlooking the south end of Humboldt Bay and the Pacific in the distance. It has one good hotel, two general stores, and a Granger's hall. A mile north is the stage station of Salmon Creek, and the grain warehouses of Hookton, and lumber yards are near by.

Hookton is the shipping point for Ferndale, Rohnerville, Hydesville, Petrolia and Springville, where the farmers haul their grain, butter, etc., and lumber from the mills in the vicinity; the steamers *Los Angeles* and *Humboldt* coming down from Eureka for this freight.

The village of Fairhaven lies on the south end of Humboldt Bay, and has some extensive ship yards and lumber mills.

Springville is another small place between Rohnerville and Table Bluff, where the Springville saw and grist-mills are located. There is a hotel, kept by L. Gilligan, a livery stable and a general store, etc.

GARBERVILLE.

This small village is situated in the south end of the county, on the east side of Eel River, on a healthy plateau about two hundred and fifty feet above the bed of the river and a quarter of a mile distant from the same, shaded with sociable, mossy old madrones and oaks. The business consists of one livery stable, two hotels, two blacksmith shops, one general store, two saloons, a shoemaker's shop, and last, but not least, just out of town a few steps, a newly-fledged tannery. The town has one principal street, and standing at the southern end of the town proper, the course of Main Street lies in direct line with the north star, so strangers visiting the town may have the pleasure of knowing in advance that the sun rises in the east and sets in the west.

A grist-mill has lately been constructed and also a bark-mill and a saw-mill. The town is named for J. C. Garber, Esq., one of the early settlers and principal merchant of this vicinity. He is an enterprising and influential citizen.

CENTERVILLE.

This place was located on the sand but a few steps from the ocean at a point formerly called False Cape. It was thus located on account of its proximity to the slough which passes along nearly parallel with the coast to the mouth of Eel River. As early as 1859 a store and hotel comprised the business.

A. Bearding, who was on the "*Cameo*," whose career is given in poetry in another place, kept the hotel. Bearding was at one time worth several hundred thousand dollars in town lots at the mouth of the Klamath River. (See Biography.)

BRIDGEVILLE.

This town, situated on the Van Duzen, is some twenty-five miles east of Hydesville. It has two hotels, blacksmith shop, store and a few dwelling houses, and has an air of thrift. Nature has done her part toward making this place most favorable for spanning the stream. The river is narrow, the banks high, and large rocks put on either side, forming perfect buttresses, from which the bridge rises in a graceful arch far removed from the dangers of high water.

This is the second bridge that has spanned the Van Duzen at this point, the former one was swept away by a freshet. There was a sad accident connected with its destruction. Several men and a lad were standing upon the bridge at the time watching the water as it rushed down the cañon, when the bridge was struck by a large log, gave way and went crashing into the foaming torrent, the men made their escape but the poor lad went down with the bridge and was drowned.

BLOCKSBURG.

The town was named after the enterprising business man B. Blockburger. He has had our artist sketch the town so as to show the business of both sides of the street. The town shows a business thrift, and several new buildings have been erected during the last year. In the center of the view of the town may be seen the "pack-trains," which give a very good idea of the manner merchandise is transported into the interior, where roads are poor. The town has a public hall and several stores and shops. A race track is laid out on a flat among the willows.

The business of general merchandise is conducted by B. Blockburger, who has an extensive trade in that locality, and is a popular and influential citizen.

A first class hotel is kept here by H. H. Ticknor, a prominent citizen. Guests receive the best of attention.

SHELTER COVE.

This is at the extreme south corner of the county. It is the natural shipping point for southern Humboldt and northern Mendocino. It has a natural open port, easy of access and vessels often lay here in time of heavy northers. The improvements consist of an ample warehouse and two staunch lighters. It is a strange, wierd place, and is well calculated for a seaside resort.

There are about 300 acres of good plowing land, consisting of table-land immediately on the beach and side hill, rising gently above it. Back of this rising higher and more abrupt, higher and higher the grassy hills ascend in a semi-circular form, having the little table flat on the beach for its center, till they reach the timber and chaparral-lined summits of the high ridges.

The sea breaks with awful force upon the rocks north of the harbor and has played some singular freaks. In many places it has cut underground chambers, and when the surf comes rushing in, the angry, boiling and foaming waters may be heard roaring and bellowing through these salty caverns with sullen sound, while the ground quakes with the untold force of the suddenly checked breakers.

Numerous and extensive shell mounds indicate many hundreds of years of feasting upon the shell-fish which abound on the rocks, by the aborigines. Shelter Cove was at one time thickly settled by the Indians.

The fortieth degree of latitude passes five miles below the harbor, and the same forms the southern county boundary line of Humboldt County.

The harbor is a perfect shelter from the heavy north winds, but storms from the south have full play, though the expense would not be great to make a break-water that would shelter an ample anchor ground.

The exports from Shelter Cove for 1881 were: 220,000 pounds of wool, 8 bundles deer skins, 2 bundles pelts, 13 cases merchandise, 2 boxes eggs, 1 bundle furs, 16 bundles leather, 1 box seeds, 11 kegs butter, 13 sacks dried fruit.

PETROLIA.

This little village is situated five miles from the beach. Its location is a quiet place with mild climate, while the pepperwood, alder, cottonwood, madrone and buckeye form a pleasing background. Viewing the valley from Petrolia, there is no apparent outlet, the point of observation being entirely surrounded by an amphitheatre of hills. The hills are open on every side except looking south. It commands the trade of both Upper and Lower Mattole Valleys, whose fertility is as rich as any in the county. Within a few miles of the ocean beach, it is fanned by the cool sea-breezes, but escapes the southerly gales so prevalent in winter, and the barrier formed by the hills completely breaks the force of the "northers." The town is steadily growing, new business is springing up, and many and varied improvements are continually being made; there are two general stores, one hotel, two saw-mills, and a grist-mill, and other shops and business places. It has but one saloon, and it seems as if that was starving to death; a thing worthy of note in a California town. It has a fine large school house, attended by 108 scholars. There is a church here, but we were unable to obtain any statistics.

On the river about a mile above town, is a saw-mill, run by water-power, having a sawing capacity of about 5,000 feet. The timber is pine and spruce, no redwood. On a branch of the Mattole, also about a mile above town, is a small flouring mill, known as Langdon's mill, which furnished flour for this section of the valley. About the only produce which can be disposed of from this section is butter and cheese, wool, beef, mutton and pork. The best fruit in the county grows on Bear River and the Mattole, but it is too great a distance from market for profit.

ARCATA VILLAGE.

The name of "Arcata" was given to this place, formerly called Union, in March, 1860. The *Times* of that date said:—

"No name could be more appropriate for a village containing such a sociable and fun loving people than that of Union. Some romantic people about there, ran away with the idea that 'Arcata' is a legitimate digger word, and means 'Union.' This is not correct. It means a certain place in town where the diggers were once in the habit of congregating, which in our language would be about the same as 'down there' or 'over yonder.' To some, 'Union' may sound as sweet by any other name, but not so with us. Therefore, other people may call it what they like, but we shall call it 'Union.'" Notwithstanding the opposition to the new name, it easily stuck fast and became popular.

In 1854, had twelve or fourteen stores carrying large stocks of goods, besides saddle and harnessmakers, jewelers, gunsmith, tin shop, and several blacksmith and wagon shops all doing an active and lucrative business.

The first officers of Arcata village were elected in April, 1856, under the order of the County Judge, incorporating the village. The following were elected trustees: W. C. Martin, A. H. Murdock, T. J. Titlon, and Byron Deming; Assessor, J. P. Whaley; Treasurer, K. Stern; Marshal, William Wall. But in May the act of incorporation was declared void.

There were four towns on the bay in 1855, viz., Humboldt, Bucksport, Eureka, and Union. The first three boasted of one store each, while the latter had seven large wholesale establishments, with harnessmakers, saddlers, jewelers, tinsmith, and blacksmith, with a brisk trade with the mines and plenty of money.

Mad River Canal was cut through in 1854, but no logs were taken through the canal until a raft was pushed through belonging to L. Larkin.

In 1856, Arcata was connected with the ship channel by a plank road and rail track two miles in length, passing over the intervening marsh or flat. At the end of the rail track was built a fine wharf and warehouses.

In 1856, Arcata had nine wholesale and retail stores, besides hotels, drug stores, tin, harness and gun shops, church, etc. The town was laid off after Spanish style with a plaza, around which are the principal business houses. Titlon & Serights erected a grist-mill in 1857.

There were two private schools in 1856, one of girls, kept by Miss Hart, and the other for "young lads and girls," kept by Miss Webb. Now there are large public schools in flourishing condition.

SUNDAY LAW IN 1856 IN ARCATA.

"After the first day of June, 1856, we, the undersigned merchants, pledge our word and honor to keep our stores closed on

FARM RESIDENCE OF G.A. DUNGAN, ON THE ISLAND, 3½ MILES FROM FERNDALE, HUMBOLDT CO. CAL.

DAIRY RANCH OF JESSE WALKER 6 MILES FROM PETROLIA, NEAR THE STAGEROAD HUMBOLDT CO. CAL.

DESCRIPTION OF THE TOWNS AND VILLAGES. 161

Sundays and transact no kind of business whatsoever, on that day.

ROSKILL & Co.,
A. JACOBY,
JOHN A. WHALEY,
MANHEIM & STERN,
I. J. NEWKIRK,
H. I. DART,
H. FLEISCHMAN,
S. LEWEY,
ROSS & McLEAN,
BYRON DEMING,
H. W. McNAY,
WILLIAM C. MARTIN,
BOWLES & CODDINGTON.

Union, May, 1856.

Arcata is now an incorporated town situated at the head of Humboldt Bay, about seven miles distant from Eureka in a straight line, and about twelve miles by land. The town site was located in 1850, as related in the general history.

It is built upon a plateau sufficiently elevated to command a view of Eureka and all of the bay north of the entrance, and of the beautiful prairie lying to the west and north. There are two large saw-mills, one flouring mill, and two shingle-mills, and quite an extensive tannery, owned by Thomas Devlin.

There are three churches—Presbyterian, Methodist and Catholic.

The mines on the Klamath as far up that river as the mouth of the Salmon, portions of those on the last-named stream and the Trinity River, also New River, draw their supplies from Arcata. It also enjoys a large and flourishing trade with the country round about.

The fine agricultural and fruit lands that surround it are of wonderful fertility, possessing a soil that is literally inexhaustible. The vast redwood forests in the background, generations will not exhaust.

It has numerous pleasant residences and quiet homes, as will be seen by our illustrations. Its business houses are numerous and flourishing.

A. Brizard has a large substantial stone store. It is one of the largest mercantile houses in the county.

Robert Burns is an extensive hardware merchant of Arcata. He is the principal dealer in hardware, stoves and tinware, and his trade extends over a large extent of country.

The Burns Block, situated on the corner of the street, is an extensive building. The upper part is occupied by societies. His residence is one of the most elegant houses of Arcata, located on elevated land, and on a corner lot, its situation is prominent, and commands an extensive view. All three of these are represented in our history.

The Marsh House of Arcata, is a quiet, neat and homelike place in which to stop permanently or transiently. It is a temperance house. While the table is set with all the good things of the season and market, yet they are prepared with a careful hand and strict reference to the laws of health. Besides this the proprietor, Dr. W. H. Marsh, has attached to the house a system of electro-magnetic, Turkish, Russian and steam baths, which, with his application of them, will do almost a miracle in restoring to a healthy condition those who by neglect, have allowed their systems to get out of order.

CITY OF EUREKA.

Eureka was settled in mining times and received at that time a large, floating population. In 1854 it experienced a set back in lumbering and other lines of business, which made hard times and diminished her population. Early in 1856, the county seat was moved to Eureka and the following spring business revived. Since that date its course has been steadily onward until it is now a city of 3,000 people, estimated.

Eureka was incorporated April 18, 1856, and the first election of officers was as follows: Trustees, James T. Ryan, C. S. Ricks, A. S. Rollins, J. M. Eddy, and George Graham. C. S. Ricks was President of the Board, and J. M. Eddy, Secretary.

It contained in 1848, six steam saw-mills, one steam flour-mill, six stores, four hotels, several private boarding houses, five drinking saloons, two drug stores, two fruit stores, two shoemaker shops, three blacksmith shops, two livery stables, one wagon and carriage manufactory, two butcher shops, one saddle shop, one tailor shop, one paint shop, one tannery, one barber shop, about a dozen carpenters, Daguerrean rooms, one surveyor and civil engineer, four lawyers, two physicians, four Federal officers, two preachers, and the Humboldt *Times* office. Of societies there were, the Humboldt Library Association, one lodge of Masons, one of Odd Fellows, one division of Sons, and the Ancient and Honorable Order of E. Clampsis Vitus.

The first church was a rude structure, surrounded by logs, stumps and brush and had the title of "The Church." It was used as the place of public worship for all denominations, a hall for Sons of Temperance, singing school, school house, public speaking and various gatherings. To-day it has five churches and numerous schools.

It is situated on the eastern shore of Humboldt Bay about five and a half miles above the entrance from the ocean. It is the principal shipping point of the county. It is built upon an eligible site, on nearly level ground, gradually sloping to the northwest, affording fine drainage. Its water front is very good and has a continuous line of docks for a distance of eight blocks, where vessels of all kinds find ample room for loading and discharging cargo.

Eureka is the commercial depot for all the towns in the county, except Trinidad. At her warehouses are received the supplies for the mining camps on the Klamath, Salmon and Lower Trinity Rivers. In point of ship building Eureka is not excelled by any port on the coast of California. The U. S. Land Office is located here, and C. F. Roberts is Register.

The Humboldt County Bank has been established since 1875 and has a paid up capital of $200,000; J. W. Henderson, President, and W. M. Huntoon, Cashier. It has an excellent reputation as an eminently safe and well-managed institution.

There are five church edifices, Methodist, Congregational, Episcopal, United Brethren and Catholic. Nearly all of the benevolent organizations that have an existence in the State, have societies in Eureka.

The public school buildings are large and substantial, one fifty by seventy feet in size, two stories, containing four rooms, and the others, three in number, one-story buildings, hard-finished, and all supplied with patent desks.

The Young Ladies' Seminary is a large, handsome three-story building, well furnished throughout, supplied with all the modern conveniences of a comfortable home, and the school-room is furnished with patent desks.

The Catholic Institute is a handsome two-story edifice, and is alike supplied with every convenience for the comfort of those in attendance. The sites of both these institutions are exceptionally beautiful, commanding fine views of the bay, the ocean and a great diversity of hill, valley, plain and mountain.

The main resource of the city is in manufacturing lumber, shingles, etc., there being seven steam saw-mills and several shingle-mills within the city limits.

The town is regularly laid off; the streets and business houses are lighted with gas.

The city is watered by artesian wells, the water being pumped into tanks and distributed through the city in pipes. The works were constructed by John Vance, Esq., in 1873.

The buildings are principally wood, although there are several brick business blocks in the town.

The *Times* and *Telephone* are published daily and weekly, and the *Democratic Standard* weekly.

There is a free library and reading-room. There are now nine hundred and forty-one books in the library. During the year 1881, 7,515 books were taken from the library.

VANCE'S HOTEL.

This hotel forms one of our illustrations and is an ornament to the city. It is conducted by John Vance, the owner. It fronts 110 feet on G Street and 120 feet on Second. It has an elevation of seventy feet to the cupola, from which a fine view of the surrounding country, bay and town can be had. The building has three stories—lower story is fifteen feet to the ceiling, second fourteen and the third eleven feet. There are ninety-six rooms and a parlor. The rooms are all supplied with gas and water, good beds, stationary marble wash-stands and call-bells. Part of the number of rooms are heated by hot-air pipes. The building terminates in a Mansard roof, with cottage windows in the upper story. The windows of the lower story are double sash, with panes of plate glass.

The table is supplied with the best the market affords. There is a barber and bath rooms connected with the building, where persons may be neatly barbered, or get hot, cold or steam baths, at usual rates.

There is also a saloon in the same building, but not conducted by the hotel proprietor. It is a first-class hotel in every respect. A free 'bus runs to the steamer landing, which is only a few blocks distant. The W. U. Telegraph Office is in the office room of the hotel.

CHAMBER OF COMMERCE.

A meeting of business men was held in February, 1882, for the purpose of forming an association to be known as the "Chamber of Commerce of the City of Eureka," for the purpose of rendering such aid and encouragement as in their judgment may be just and proper toward the development of the natural resources of Humboldt County and to encourage all legitimate commercial undertakings.

John Vance, Esq. presided at the meeting, and suitable rules and regulations were adopted. The following gentlemen were then nominated and unanimously elected Directors for the present year: John Vance, William Carson, W. J. Sweasey, P. H. Ryan, Fred. W. Bell, Jonathan Clark, J. E. Jansen, W. L. Mercer, and W. H. Pratt. The Chamber then adjourned and a meeting of the Board of Directors was called to order, and organized by electing John Vance President, J. E. Jansen Vice-President, Fred. W. Bell Secretary, and W. H. Pratt Treasurer. A committee consisting of the President, Secretary and Treasurer was appointed with instructions to prepare a memorial to Congress, urging the necessity of Government aid for our harbor as also the pressing need of declaring Eureka a Port of Entry.

The city contains many pretty residences and homes which we have illustrated, as well as substantial business blocks which space will not permit mentioning.

HOW TO REACH EUREKA.

Eureka is accessible to the outside world, in addition to the overland stage route, of which we have given a description, by two steamship lines. Goodall, Perkins & Co., are agents of the Pacific Coast Steamship Company, and are represented by the steamship *Los Angeles*.

The steamer *Humboldt* is owned by a home company, and is a new, commodious, and elegantly fitted steamship, George Paton commander, who is one of the most careful captains on the coast. The officers and assistants are very gentlemanly and courteous to passengers. Captain Paton is always willing to answer as regards the coast, and give general information.

W. J. Sweasey, a prominent citizen of Eureka, is part owner and manager of the vessel. She was built at Eureka, in October, 1875. The vessel is all wood, but is considered the safest steamer on the route.

Eureka has mail communication southward along the coast over a stage road; northward, along the coast to Oregon; northeasterly, up the Klamath River to Siskiyou and Oregon, and eastward to the Upper Sacramento Valley.

The census of 1880 showed a population of 15,511 in the county. The several towns have a population as follows: Eureka, the chief port on Humboldt Bay, 2,639; Arcata, at the head of the Bay, 702; Trinidad, 104; Ferndale, 178; Rohnerville 500; Springville, 103; Garberville, 50; Hydesville, 143; Petrolia, 78; Blocksburg, 121.

SKETCHES OF FORT HUMBOLDT.

BY A FORMER RESIDENT OF THE FORT.

In giving a history of the early days of Humboldt County, the establishment of Fort Humboldt and its occupation by two companies of the Fourth U. S. Infantry, should not be forgotten. Indian disturbances had been frequent, the early settlers became alarmed, and urgent requests were made for troops to the officer commanding the Pacific Department. The Fourth Regiment U. S. Infantry had been sent to California in July, 1852. The regiment reached Benicia Barracks in August of that year, its ranks depleted by at least 100 dying of cholera.

Two companies, B and F, were selected to go to Humboldt Bay to establish a post for the protection of the then sparsely settled region. The troops sailed from Benicia the latter part of January, 1853, in the little steamer *Goliah*, commanded by her owner, Captain Wright. Brev. Lieut. Col. R. C. Buchanan commanded the troops. The officers under him were Lieutenants Scott, Underwood, Bonnicastle, Crook, and Dr. Deyerle. Lieut. L. C, Hunt joined the command some weeks later.

Lieutenant Underwood was accompanied by his wife, and a few camp women followed their husbands to this almost unknown region. Some anxiety and nervousness were felt by the weaker sex at least, in regard to "crossing the bar," and entering Humboldt Bay. Wrecks had been frequent, the channel was a shifting one, and not well understood at that time. It did not allay the fears of the timid, to see the ghostly remains of vessels wrecked at the entrance of the bay, their spars still visible, as a warning to mariners that they too might share their fate. But the little *Goliah* steamed right in without signaling for a pilot, giving her passengers a slight shaking up, as she "crossed the bar."

All eyes eagerly turned to the shores of the new home, to see what kind of a country this was. The impression was decidedly a pleasant one, the beautiful trees, and shrubs, and verdure, in contrast to the barren hills about Benicia.

Colonel Buchanan was authorized to select the most desirable location for a fort, and to proceed at once to put up buildings suitable for his command. At this time Eureka was little more than a swamp. The writer of this article, remembers well the hospitable reception given the troops upon their arrival there. The families of the late Hon. James Ryan and F. S. Duff were then living in primitive style, in quarters similar to those of "Mr. Peggotty," in "David Copperfield." The ladies of these families welcomed the new-comers and extended to them the hospitalities of their home.

Bucksport at that time, was a rival of Eureka, and at this point Colonel Buchanan decided to locate his post. The high bluff, about a quarter of a mile back from the bay, seemed as though intended for a fortification. The forests on two sides of this bluff, furnished an abundance of timber, the California redwood being most desirable. Tents were pitched upon the smooth plane of the bluff, leaving the center for a parade ground. Building began at once, the men of the command furnishing the labor. The plan was to put up a frame, fill in with hewn logs, then weather-board and plaster inside. The first house was built in this manner but it was found to be expensive and unnecessary in this climate. A good weather-boarded house, plastered inside, was sufficient protection for the coldest weather of the bay.

FIRST BIRTH AT HUMBOLDT.

The first house completed was assigned by courtesy to Lieutenant Underwood, whose wife and young son were made as comfortable as possible.

This son, now an honorable officer in the naval service, was the first child born to an officer at Fort Humboldt. He was born in a tent pitched in the yard adjoining the little house in which lived Dr J. Clarke, one of the early settlers at Bucksport, the Dr. sharing his house as far as possible, with the family of Lieutenant Underwood.

The Huestis family then lived at Bucksport, also the Molony's, who had a hotel there. Captain and Mrs. Tickuor lived near Table Bluff, and Mr, Dupern was a citizen of the Bay. The Martins and Wymans were then living at Uniontown, now called Arcata.

Game of all kinds was abundant, and beef could not be obtained, only at long intervals. A contract was made with the celebrated hunter, Seth Kinsman, to furnish elk meat so many times a month to the command. This was found to be a substitute for beef, the men not tiring of it as of venison.

KINSMAN, THE OLD TRAPPER.

The old trapper, Kinsman, is still living, and is identified with the first settlement of Humboldt. His stories of adventures with Indians and grizzlies, would fill a volume with thrilling tales. The writer remembers well the old trapper and his violin. He used to enliven their parties by playing for dancing. His "Arkansas Traveler" was inimitable.

Lieutenant Crook now a full Brigadier General, and the finest officer for Indian service in the army, was then a young man just from West Point. He was fond of hunting, and very desirous of trapping a bear. Tracks of bears were frequently seen in the woods adjoining the fort, and the young Lieutenant was at length rewarded by finding Mr. Bruin in the trap, so skillfully laid for his capture. The news created no small excitement at the fort. The bear was shot, and his carcass furnished food for those who enjoyed the coarse meat.

Elk and deer were seldom seen in the vicinity of the fort, but upon one occasion a herd of elk was seen upon the bluff south of the fort, and had a good sportsman been in readiness with his rifle, he could easily have brought them down. But they only took a survey of the landscape and bounded away with their horns in the air.

The water was found to be excellent, to the delight of all. The water at Benicia was rather distasteful, being from cisterns, and collected for the year from rains that fell in the winter months. The climate of Humboldt Bay was similar to that of San Francisco, a little fire being agreeable nearly every day in the year.

BEAUTIFUL WILD FLOWERS.

The wild flowers were most beautiful about Bucksport. They began to bloom in February, and it was a delight to the newcomers to find them increasing in variety and beauty, as the months went by. Early in March was found in the woods back of the fort, a species of cyclamen, or arrow plant, now seen in Eastern conservatories. A shrub or bush grew near the post with clusters of beautiful pink flowers, and bore a fruit not unlike the currant, which made a fine meat jelly. The same shrub may sometimes be seen in gardens or yards at the East, and is there called the Oregon Currant. Near the post was a pond, with marshy ground about it, where grew a sort of May-flower, a species of azalea with delicate salmon-colored and pink blossoms, quite fragrant too. The California poppies were abundant, but the most beautiful specimens of these were brought from the Eel River neighborhood by the officers who occasionally visited that locality.

WILD BERRIES PLENTY.

The salmon berries were a great novelty, a very tempting looking fruit when seen upon its vine, but very perishable and only good when taken from its vine or bush with great care and eaten immediately. It resembled a large Antwerp raspberry in form and size, but of the most beautiful salmon color. A few were to be found of a deep, ruby color, and these interspersed among the salmon-colored ones, made a very tempting-looking dish. The salmon berries grew on vines that were ten or fifteen feet high. The Indians used to gather them by pulling down the bushes with a forked stick, picking the fruit into baskets woven from rushes that they wore upon their heads. They would then bring them to the fort to sell, or exchange for flour or hard tack. If they found a purchaser in some one not squeamish in their ideas of neatness, the fruit was emptied, and the flour received in exchange, returned in the basket to their wigwams, in turn to serve again as head covering.

The Indians were very friendly with the troops, visiting the garrison almost daily. The presence of the troops gave security to the settlers, and emigration was materially increased from this time.

Colonel Buchanan did not neglect the settlers in more remote regions, as detachments were frequently sent out, the moral effect being very beneficial. Desertions were frequent soon after the arrival of the command upon the bay; the soldiers being tempted by the mines not far distant, and for some time they eluded capture. But finally a stop was put to their desertions, by several being taken, tried by Court Martial, and severely punished. A garden was soon prepared and planted, which yielded a bountiful supply of vegetables of all kinds, so that the men were made very comfortable in a few months.

A DISTINGUISHED POST.

Fort Humboldt became a very popular post, and it is to be regretted that the Government saw fit to abandon it. Many officers distinguished in the service, have at times, been stationed here. Of those who accompanied Colonel Buchanan to establish the fort, only Lieutenants Bonnicastle and Crook are living; the former resigned from the service some years ago and is now living in Louisville, Kentucky. Colonel Buchanan died two or three years since in Washington. Dr. Deyerle died at Benicia the same year that the post was established.

Lieutenant Underwood, who afterward located and built Fort Gaston, California, died in Utica, New York, in 1863. Lieutenant Hunt is now full Colonel of one of the Infantry Regiments of the army.

General Grant was at one time stationed at Fort Humboldt. A number of officers who were at Fort Humboldt at the breaking out of the war, joined the Southern Confederacy. Among those who left were Major Rains, Dr. Guild, Lieutenants Hardcastle and Rundell. General Rains died recently in Georgia. Dr. Guild, who was Medical Director on General Lee's staff, died a few years since in California.

Captain Lovell, afterward General Lovell, was left in command of the post in 1861. He remained loyal to his Government, and was transferred to the East, where he did honorable service, and after the war was over died in Louisville, Kentucky. His oldest son is an officer in the army at this time.

Soon after the fort was established, Eureka began to look up, and in a few, short years a thriving town had been built upon the marshy ground that had seemed so uninviting in 1853. In later years the garrison depended very largely upon the supplies obtained at Eureka.

PRIMITIVE SHOPPING.

No doubt many of the inhabitants remember the little cart drawn by a mule, driven by a soldier with the Garrison ladies, taking a straw ride to Eureka to buy a roast of beef, perchance and other supplies for their comfort. Many pleasant families were then living at Eureka. The Eddy family were there, and the army ladies enjoyed much hospitality from their hands. The writer has never visited Humboldt Bay since 1861, but has heard of the prosperity of the country with great pleasure.

Certainly no more healthful locality can be found. The climate is equable, never having the extreme heat of the Sacramento Valley, and no malarial troubles exist here as in the interior. Eureka is now the largest town in Northern California. When she shall enjoy rail facilities what may we not predict for her growth and prosperity? May her oldest inhabitant live to see and enjoy that time.

Chas. W. Long

H. H. Buhne

HUMBOLDT PIONEERS

Jonathan Clark

Frank S. Duff

C. Wasgatt

THE HUMBOLDT COUNTY PIONEER SOCIETY.

Organized January 22, 1876; Reorganized and Incorporated May 12, 1881.

BY W. F. HUESTIS.

NEARLY a generation has passed since the original white members of this society set foot upon the then savage and forest shores of Humboldt Bay and vicinity, and before another generation shall lapse, all of our pioneer citizens above referred to, will in all probability have gone to that "waveless shore," whence they

"Who once reach it shall wander no more."

Prompted no doubt by the laudable desire to preserve some memorial of the early settlement of this portion of our fair domain, as well as for the accommodation of the annalist of future years, the initiatory step for the organization of a Pioneer Society for Humboldt County was taken on the 8th day of January, 1876, in the city of Eureka. At the meeting of pioneer citizens held on that day at the office of Maj. E. H. Howard, in pursuance to given notice, signed by Judges J. E. Wyman, and A. J. Huestis, Maj. E. H. Howard, Capt. H. H. Buhne, and F. S. Duff; Judge Huestis was chosen Chairman, and Maj. Howard Secretary.

Following an earnest expression of interest very generally participated in by those present, in the object and establishment of the society, and a hearty exchange of personal recollections and bits of Pioneer history, a committee was selected to draft a Constitution and By-laws, to be submitted at an adjourned meeting to be held on the 22d day of the same month. On that day the second meeting of pioneer citizens was held in the City Hall on Third Street, when the committee selected at previous meeting, submitted their draft of a Constitution and By-laws which were duly considered and adopted as a whole.

The election for permanent officers of the society for the first year, provided for in the Constitution, was then held, and resulted in the selection of A. J. Huestis as President; James Hanna, Byron Deming, and J. E. Wyman, Vice-Presidents, E. H. Howard, Secretary; R. W. Brett, Treasurer; C. W. Long, Marshal; and I. Cullburg, C. S. Ricks, George Graham, Joseph Russ, F. S. Duff, and A. Brizard, as a Board of Directors.

The society being duly organized, the first business transacted by it was the acceptance of an invitation tendering a complimentary reception by the young ladies of the "Humboldt Young Ladies' Seminary," which was held at that institution on the evening of January 28, 1876. The reception was largely attended by pioneers and their families, and reported by the city press as a most enjoyable affair.

The first appearance of the society in public was on the 4th day of July, 1876, when, with its beautiful new banner for the first time unfurled to the breeze, on one side of which is a very clever representation of pioneer life, and on the other side is the motto *Per tot discrimine rerum*, it constituted a prominent feature of the procession had on that day in the city of Eureka, in honor of the Centennial Anniversary of American Independence.

On the 10th of September, 1877, the society celebrated its second anniversary in a becoming manner, consisting in a procession in the morning, literary exercises at Buhne's Hall in the afternoon, and a ball in the evening. This gathering of the pioneers, embracing many whose names and acts are intimately associated with the earliest history of Humboldt County, was a highly interesting one, and was successful in attaining one of its principal objects—that of drawing together so large a number of the first settlers of the county. The poem from the pen of Mr. Charles Comstock, a confirmed invalid of this city, was an interesting feature in the exercises at the hall, and shows unmistakable evidence of the cultivated mind of its author. Some estimate of its merits and character may be formed from a perusal of its opening and closing stanzas, which are herewith presented; did allotted space permit, it would be reproduced in full:—

THE HUMBOLDT COUNTY PIONEERS

"From our place on Life's rugged hill to-day
 Downward we cast our glances o'er the way,
 Winding back through the misty vale of years,
 And dim, we see the *forms* of Pioneers."

"Some we see by the baby fingers led
 Of children's children, and many a thread
 Of silver hair among the dark we trace,
 But oh! we miss many a well known face;
 Have they forgot the vanished days of yore?
 We call and wait in vain, for they come no more;
 For besides each village, town and city,
 There grows a rival without rivalry—
 Thither with tears, one by one we bear
 The forms we love; the patient Mother there
 Is resting after the toils of life;
 And men who once were foremost in the strife
 Now slumber with those never waking bands,
 In the silent city of the folded hands;
 Oh, Pioneers, the way how oft ye tread
 Between the cities of the living and the dead!
 But whilst those roofs of sod ye rear so fast
 Let, among you in memory of the past,
 Friendship's bond be closed 'till the hour shall come,
 When the heart grows chill and the lips are dumb,
 And the reaper Time with his garnered years,
 Gathers these, the *last* of the Pioneers."

But little, if anything, worthy of note is embraced in the history of the society from this period of its existence down to the 14th day of April of the present year. On that day there was a meeting of the society, at which a move was made with the view of rendering the organization more potent for the attainment of the objects for which it was formed. Several changes in the organic law of the society were suggested, among which, was one to exempt the wives and daughters of Pioneers from the payment of the admission fee then imposed.

It was also ordered that the society celebrate its next and fifth annual meeting on the 13th of the following month. A committee was appointed to report at such meeting, a plan of reorganization with a view of incorporating under the laws of the State, if deemed necessary for the best interests of the society.

Fifteen or twenty applications for membership were received, and a committee appointed to report a membership list. This meeting was regarded as a very important one for the society, because of the action had, looking to the enlargement of its field of labors, as well as an increase in its membership. At the annual meeting above referred to, there was a large attendance, and much interest manifested.

A new Constitution and Articles of Incorporation were deliberated upon, and adopted; and the election of officers for the ensuing year also held, which resulted in the selection of Jno. Vance, as President; C. W. Long, A. Wiley, and J. H. Dungan, Vice-Presidents; W. F. Thurstin, Secretary; J. S. Murray, Jr., Treasurer; Geo. H. Tilley, Marshal; and James Hanna, E. K. Howard, Geo. Graham, Joseph Russ, Jno. H. Kimball, Isaac Minor and J. A. Whaley, as a Board of Directors.

The celebration of this annual meeting, was concluded with the evening's festivities, consisting of a grand ball, the partaking of the good things so abundantly spread upon the tables at the Vance House, and the responding to toasts. The ball which was largely attended, and enjoyed in the good old-fashioned way, was also a financial success; the supper amply met the demands of the assembled throng, and the responses made to the toasts proposed were prolific in reviving the memory of departed days, which were fraught with dangers and hardships incident to pioneer life.

In short, it can be truthfully said, that this demonstration of the Society of Humboldt County Pioneers, was successful in all respects. That its triumph on this occasion may be an indication of its future career is the wish of all, who would have no unmerited blot cast upon pioneer effort; for it should not be forgotten, that it was that grand and conquering army of adventurers, who, braving all opposition, has laid the foundations of our society, our schools, our homes, and our churches. As the founders of new communities, they hold a just claim upon the gratitude of those who, following in their footsteps, have been able to reap so bountifully of the blessings vouchsafed by the honorable toil of the hardy pioneer. Embracing as this society does, many of the actors themselves in our earlier history, it should be able to command the most reliable sources of information, and personal memoirs of eventful interest, which are now almost wholly unknown outside of its ranks. With these and other desirable objects at its command, it is to be hoped that the Society of Humboldt County Pioneers, will be a united and prosperous body, in its efforts to advance the interest and perpetuate the memory of those "whose sagacity, energy, and enterprise, induced them to form a settlement in the wilderness."

CLASSIFICATION OF MEMBERSHIP.

Under Article II of the Constitution, (1) "Any person who was a resident of the territory now known as the county of Humboldt prior to the 1st day of January, 1855, (2) or was a resident of Trinity County at the time Humboldt County was a part thereof and has since become a resident of Humboldt County as now established, (3) and his or her descendant of full age, (4) and the husband or wife of such person or descendant, (5) and members of the First Battalion of Mountaineers California Volunteers, honorably discharged, are eligible to become members; (6) honorary members may be admitted without these qualifications, and life members on such terms as may be fixed by the By-Laws."

The following is a list of the contributing members of the society up to date, with their nativity, and dates of arrival in the State and county, as far as ascertained. The number preceding the name of each member indicates his status of eligibility.

		Native of	Date of arrival in the State.	Date of arrival in the County.
1	Averell D. D...	Maine...	December, 1849	June, 1850.....
1	Allard Richard..	New Hampshire	February, 1853	December, 1853.....
1	Brizard Alex..	France...	Sept., 1848...	August, 1853.....
1	Brown J H...	Illinois...	August, 1850..	January, 1851.....
1	Bull J. C., Sr..	Massachusetts..	Nov., 1850....	May, 1851.....
1	Ball J. C., Jr...	"	"	"
3	Baine H. H.....	Denmark...	June, 1849...	April, 1850.....
3	Bahne H. H., Jr.	California...		Born in County, 1855
3	Bahne A. M....	"		" 1860
4	Bullock N......	New York...	July, 1854...	July, 1860.....
1	Brett R. W.....	England.....	1849	April, 1850.....
1	Beckwith L. C..	Connecticut...	December, 1849	July, 1851.....
1	Barnum G. N...	New York...	April, 1854...	April, 1854.....
2	Brown T. M....	Tennessee...	October, 1849.	March, 1850.....
1	Callburg L......	Sweden...	Nov., 1853...	Nov., 1853.....
1	Clark Jonathan..	Indiana...	Nov., 1849...	June, 1850.....
1	Comstock H. S..	Pennsylvania...	April, 1853...	Nov., 1854.....
4	Comick Harris..	New Brunswick	July, 1857...	July, 1857.....
1	Daniels H. S....	New Hampshire	February, 1853	January, 1853.....
1	Denning Byron..	Vermont.....	July, 1850...	March, 1851.....
1	Dart H. J......	Connecticut...	May, 1850...	October, 1852.....
1	DeHaven J J....	Missouri...	August, 1849.	June, 1853.....
1	Duff F. S......	New Brunswick	July, 1849...	" 1850.....
1	Dungan J. H....	Kentucky...	February, 1852	February, 1853.....
1	Eagle W. C.....	Ireland.....	October, 1849.	Nov., 1852.....
1	Fay Geo. M.....	Connecticut...	August, 1852..	October, 1852.....
1	Fay Nahum.....	"	Nov., 1852...	April, 1853.....
1	Foss T H.......	California...	April, 1850...	August, 1852.....
3	Foss T H., Jr...	California...		Born in county, 1855
1	Fater M. P......	Ohio.....	Sept., 1851...	Sept., 1851.....
1	Gartman Henry..	Germany...		" 1854
1	Gardner C. J....	Massachusetts..	April, 1850...	January, 1853.....
1	Graham Geo.....	Virginia...	July, 1852...	March 1853.....
1	Graham Thos. R.	Mississippi...	December, 1853	December, 1853.....
1	Gunson James...	Ireland.....	August, 1854..	October, 1854.....
1	Hale Edward....	New York...	December, 1849	March, 1852.....
1	Hanson John....	Hanover.....	July, 1849...	Sept., 1853.....
1	Hanna James....	Pennsylvania...	May, 1850...	February, 1854.....
3	Hanna Wm. P...	"	Sept., 1850...	October, 1857.....
1	Hasty Cyrus L..	Maine.....	June, 1852...	July, 1852.....
1	Hitchings B. B..	New Brunswick	Nov., 1859...	Nov., 1860.....
1	Howard E E.....	New York...	Sept., 1849...	April, 1850.....
1	Huestis A. J....	New Hampshire	October, 1849.	June 1850.....
1	Huestis W. P....	Virginia.....		"
1	Jackson Chas....	"	May, 1854...	June, 1854.....
1	James Otto E...	Denmark.....	August, 1850..	January, 1851.....
1	Jones D. R......	Wales.....	April, 1850...	June, 1850.....
1	Kelsey B. B.....	Maine.....	Sept., 1849...	March, 1853.....
1	Kelcher John....	New Brunswick	March, 1852..	January, 1853.....
3	Kelcher Jas. T...	"	July, 1868...	July, 1866.....
1	Kimball J. H....	Massachusetts..	March, 1850..	March, 1855.....
1	Kimball Geo H...	California...		Born in County, 1854
1	Kimball J. B....	"		" 1856
1	Kingston Henry..	Pennsylvania...	July, 1853...	August, 1853.....
1	LeMian J J B...	New Brunswick	May, 1850...	March, 1853.....
1	Lowell David B..	Maine.....	Nov., 1851...	January, 1852.....
1	Light James.....	"	October, 1846.	August, 1850.....
3	Light W. A.....	California...		Born in County, 1856
3	Long Chas. W...	New Brunswick	August, 1850..	Sept., 1850.....
3	Long C. E......	California...		Born in County, 1857
1	Long W. S......	Pennsylvania...	October, 1854..	October, 1854.....
1	Lucie Moses.....	Massachusetts..	July, 1849...	July, 1850.....
1	Molony M. F....	California...		Born in County, 1853
1	McKone W. J...	Australia...	August, 1849..	January, 1852.....
1	McKenna James.	California...		.....

* Indicates deceased members.

BIOGRAPHIES OF THE COUNTY PIONEERS.

	Native of	Date of arrival in the State.	Date of arrival in the County.
Munson Daniel	Maine	May, 1852	May, 1853
Murray J. S.	Scotland	August, 1843	December, 1850
Murray J. S., Jr.	Great Britain	"	May, 1851
Murray Hon. D.	California	....	Born in County, 1854
Monroe Aloazo	Connecticut	February, 1850	June, 1852
Markle A. P.	New York	Nov., 1852	February, 1853
Minor Isaac	Pennsylvania	March, 1852	December, "
Minor T. H.	California	....	Born in County, 1856
Morrison Donald	New Brunswick	1849	June, 1850
Osgood B. P.	Massachusetts	January, 1850	October, 1852
Pardee A. L.	New York	"	August, "
Peuter P. P.	Ireland	April, 1854	" 1855
Pollard B H. C.	Kentucky	1850	1853
Patrick Marshall	Illinois	1852	1853
Ricks C. S.	Indiana	August, 1849	July, 1850
Ricks Thos. P.	California	....	Born in County, 1853
Ricks C. N., Jr.	"	....	" " 1857
Ricks H. L.	"	....	" " 1859
Richardson Chas.	Maine	Nov., 1853	Nov., 1853
Russ Joseph	....	March, 1850	" 1852
Russ Ira A.	California	....	Born in County, 1861
Robinson W. S.	Virginia	1850	" 1852
Rohner Henry	Switzerland	1849	1851
Roylor A. B.	Indiana	Sept., 1850	March, 1851
Routhmeyded L.	New Hampshire	March, 1853	July, 1853
Schmidt J. C.	Wirtemburg	Nov., 1850	1850
Smiley J. C.	Maine	February, 1850	January, 1853
Stokes B M.	Virginia	Sept., 1854	1854
Stokes J. P.	Missouri	1854	1854
Sweasey Michael	Indiana	August, 1853	August, 1855
Spear A. C.	New York	July, 1851	July, 1852
Skera H. P.	California	"	Born in County, 1856
Showers J. O.	New York	1850	February, 1851
Scott H. P.	Germany	July, 1849	January, "
Tilley Hon. H.	Rhode Island	Sept., "	May, 1850
Tydd Peter	Ireland	1852	February, 1853
Visgee John	Nova Scotia	July, 1850	" 1852
Walsh Thomas	Ireland	February, 1851	March, 1853
Whaley J. A.	New York	December, 1849	June, 1850
Whaley W. A.	California	....	Born in County, 1860
West W. A.	Connecticut	1849	1851
Waite B. L.	New York	Sept., 1850	March, 1851
Warren Jno. P.	Ohio	Sept., 1852	Sept., 1854
Wigenga Chase.	Maine	....	1852
Wyman J. E.	Massachusetts	May, 1850	May, 1851
Wyman W. H.	California	....	Born in County, 1854
Wiley Hoasoa	Illinois	October, 1849	December, 1852
Wiley Austin	"	" 1852	October, 1853
Wiley A. J.	California	....	Born in County, 1857
Winsler Louis	Germany	1851	1852
Ward Gabriel	Prussia	Sept., "	March, 1853
Watson Jno. A.	New Hampshire	October, 1851	February, 1852
Young Jno. T.	Connecticut	" 1849	May, 1860

HON. A. J. HUESTIS.

Among the public men of Humboldt County, there are few better known, and none more universally respected, and esteemed, than A. J. Huestis. Born in New Hampshire on the 23d day of February, 1806. At the age of twenty-two, and for three years thereafter, he was a student of the Wilburham Academy, Massachusetts, of which Dr. Wilbur Fisk, was Principal. From thence he attended the Wesleyan University, at Middletown, Connecticut, on leaving which, in 1834, he married Miss Annie Minerva Chaffee, who still survives, to render him wifely aid and comfort in his declining years. The first year of his married life was spent in New Jersey, where, during that time, he conducted a private school. From thence he moved to Virginia where he at once engaged in the educational enterprise of building the Buckingham Female Collegiate Institute, of which he was for several years President, his wife being governess and teacher, for the same period. Resigning his control of this institution and placing it in charge of the M. E. Church, he moved west in the year 1848, to the State of Iowa, where he energetically engaged in the most important educational enterprise of his life, resulting in bringing into existence the Iowa Wesleyan University.

In 1849, he resigned the Presidency of the last-mentioned institution, and moved to this State, (by the overland route), arriving at Sonoma in October, of the same year. In June, 1850, he located in the territory now included in this county, where he has ever since resided.

With the exception of two years in the traveling ministry, fifty years of his life has been spent in the local ministry of the M. E. Church.

Although always constant in the field of denominational duty, he has repeatedly been called to an active participation in secular affairs, and the administration of various official positions in civil life. He was the first Superintendent of Public Instruction for this county, and the first President of the Society of Humboldt County Pioneers. He was twice elected County Judge, and subsequently, in 1866-67, represented this county in the State Legislature.

During his residence in Virginia he experienced a first slight attack of paralysis from which he soon recovered without any permanently serious results. After an interval of several years he suffered the second attack of the same malady, but without its impairing the natural vigor of intellect or body which has ever marked his individual character; and now, under the weight of nearly fourscore years, he survives the third and most violent attack of all, which (occurring some fifteen years ago), though adding somewhat to those infirmities incident to age, has not diminished his wonted relish and interest in those questions of moral, mental, and material progress, which are so largely identified with the age.

With a reputation for wisdom in council, and honesty of purpose; an impressive speaker, and able writer, the "simple story of his life," with its honors and experience, commands the uncircumscribed respect of all.

HON. JONATHAN CLARK.

The subject of this sketch was born in Crawfordsville, Indiana, in the year 1826 ; and is therefore fifty-six years of age. He comes of good Revolutionary stock, being a lineal descendant of Abram Clark, one of the signers of the Declaration of Independence. At the age of fifteen years he went to Iowa where he attained his majority, studied medicine as a profession, and entered upon active practice immediately after receiving his diploma. In 1849 he came to this State, overland, where he arrived in November of that year. For four months he followed mining, in which occupation he was successful. At the end of this time he made his way to Humboldt Bay. He arrived on the brig *Reindeer*, on the 16th of June, 1850, and immediately commenced the practice of his profession. On the first day of November, 1853, he was appointed acting Assistant Surgeon U. S. A. and assigned to duty at Fort Humboldt, California, under the command of Col. R. C. Buchanan, of the Fourth U. S. Infantry. On the 6th day of June, 1863, he was commissioned Surgeon of the First Batallion of Mountaineers, California Volunteers, Lieut.-Col. S. G. Whipple, commanding and served in that capacity during the Indian wars of 1863-4-5. At the close of the war he resumed the practice of medicine in this city, and continued in active practice until 1870, when he retired from practice on account of the pressure of his private business. He was the first Postmaster on Humboldt Bay, having been appointed in 1851, and was also the first Notary Public ever appointed for this place. In 1855 he was elected a member of the Board of Supervisors, and at the next general election was re-elected to the same office. In 1857 he was appointed County Treasurer. In 1874 he was elected a member of the Common Council for the city of Eureka, and in 1876 was re-elected to the same office. The same year he was elected a member of the California Assembly from Humboldt County. While a member of that body he was very active introducing a number of bills and being a member of several committees.

He introduced a bill for the completion of the Kneeland Prairie and Round Valley Wagon Road, also the Coast Wagon Road, leading from Ferndale to the county line, via Petrolia. Also, Authorizing the Construction of the Grizzly Bluff and Camp Grant Wagon Road.

He is the author of the Humboldt County Road Law, and amended the Klamath County Dismemberment Bill so as to secure an adjustment of the affairs of the county. He is also the author of the Humboldt County Hospital Law, and he procured an amendment to the act incorporating the city of Eureka. He introduced a joint resolution asking for a mail route from Eureka by way of Ferndale to Mendocino County. He served on the State Hospital Committee, the Committee of Public Morals, of Commerce and Navigation, and was also a member of the Centennial Committee. As a Representative he was active, cautious, and untiring in his exertions to guard the interests of his constituents. His term of service was successful and in the main satisfactory to the people of his county.

In 1878 he was elected Mayor of the city of Eureka and served his term of two years, declining a re-election.

In person Doctor Clark is large, his height being five feet eleven inches, and his weight 190 pounds. He has accumulated a good share of property, and is the proprietor of "Clark's Addition to the city of Eureka."

He is a Protestant in religion and in politics a staunch Republican.

HON. JOSEPH RUSS.

From difficulty to triumph, from poverty to wealth, from obscurity to prominence by the sole aid of his own energy! Such is the history of Joseph Russ. He was born in Washington, Lincoln County, Maine, on the 19th day of December, 1825. He resided there until he was ten years of age, when his parents moved to Belmont, Waldo County, where Mr. Russ attained his majority. He then made a start in the world on his own account and resided for a time at Dartmouth, Massachusetts. Two years after he moved to Fall River, where he engaged first in teaming, and afterward in merchandising. He does not seem to have been satisfied with the result of his venture for we afterwards find him at Appleton, Maine, where he purchased an interest in a saw and stave mill, connecting with them a grocery store. He remained in Appleton three years when the great event which changed the current and determined course of so many men occurred.

The news of the discovery of gold in California, reached the East, and Mr. Russ was one of the many thousands who determined to try their fortune in the great West. Mr. Russ purchased the materials for a large business house ready framed, and prepared to put up immediately upon landing, and having put this on the bark *Midas*, he embarked on the same vessel for a voyage around Cape Horn. At Tuckawana he purchased a large quantity of flour and took this also. The voyage around the Horn was made in five months without difficulty or accident, and on the 15th day of March, 1850, Mr. Russ was in San Francisco.

He at once sold his house and flour without realizing much profit, and with a small sail boat containing six passengers, set sail for Sacramento. Here he sold his boat to some government officers and started for Georgetown, El Dorado County, but could get no further than White Oak Springs. At this place he was employed to take charge of a steam saw-mill, for which he received the modest salary of two hundred dollars per month. He remained here two months and then left for the purpose of building a bridge across the American River. Having finished this he took a contract to build a bridge across the Cosumnes River and Daly's Slough.

His next venture was to buy goods, take in a partner, and open a store at Volcano, Amador County. In speaking of this enterprise Mr. Russ says in his peculiarly quiet, humorous way, "we did an excellent credit business, and left the profits on the books where they still remain uncollected." Of course this business did not continue long. Mr. Russ and his partner closed up business, and Mr. Russ purchased a number of beef cattle and drove them to a place on the Yuba River, then known as Onion Valley, where he sold his cattle at a fair profit and went to mining. He continued mining about four months with good success. From there he went to Sacramento Valley, put up a large amount of hay which he took to Colusa, and opened a hay-yard. This venture proved profitable, and Mr. Russ purchased a number of teams and commenced freighting goods from Colusa to Shasta City. While engaged in this business he was attacked with chills and fever. He closed out his business and departed for Placerville.

Here he purchased a drove of cattle and started for Humboldt in the fall of 1852. He first remained at Rohnerville, then visited Table Bluffs, but thinking there was some valuable territory on Eel River, near where Ferndale now is, he determined to explore it. Accordingly he purchased a skiff hauled it to Eel River and set out for Centerville. The party

RES. OF JAS. E. MATHEWS, 5TH ST. BET. D & E STS. EUREKA, CAL.

RES. OF J.L. SOUTHMAYD, COR. OF BROADWAY & CEDAR ST. EUREKA, CAL.

arriving at the mouth of Eel River, made their boat fast and went into camp. After three or four days spent in the most toilsome labor, they reached the present site of Ferndale, where they went into winter quarters, subsisting chiefly on elk meat and potatoes, the little flour obtainable being scarce at fifty cents per pound.

On the site of the old camp ground, Mr. Russ now has a fine brick store which is well stocked with all kinds of goods, and the constant ticking of the telegraph apparatus may be heard at almost any time of the day. A wonderful change for twenty-four years! In the spring of 1853, Mr. Russ went to Sacramento with Mr. Berry Adams (now of Arcata), and returned with a large drove of beef cattle. Soon after their return to Humboldt County Messrs. Russ and Adams opened a meat market in Eureka. After two or three years this business was discontinued, and Mr. Russ followed the rush to the Salmon River mines, where he remained three years. At the end of this time he went to Oregon and purchased a large drove of cattle which he brought to Bear River in this county. He started a meat market in Eureka in 1859.

In 1870 he erected the saw-mill of Russ & Co., in which he still owns a large interest. While at Salmon River he was elected Justice of the Peace. His native good sense and clear judgment stood him in stead while holding this office, and in a great measure compensated for the lack of special reading, so necessary to properly filling a judicial position.

In 1873 he was elected to represent Humboldt County in the California Legislature. His well-known character for thoroughness and sincerity, as well as his high social position at home, made him respected among his fellow members, and gave him at once an acknowledged position and much influence in the House. He was active and zealous in the work of the session, and the Canada Thistle Bill, as well as the Humboldt County Road Law of that session were due mainly to his efforts.

In 1875 he was the Republican nominee for the Senate by acclamation. He received a flattering vote, running far ahead of his ticket in Humboldt County, but, owing to the weakness of his party in Mendocino County, as well as the great popularity of his opponent, Judge McGarvey, in his own county, Mr. Russ was defeated by a small majority.

Mr. Russ still resides near Ferndale on his farm. His possessions are very large. He owns some 50,000 acres of land, over which roam some 3,500 head of cattle, 2,000 of which are dairy cows; 13,000 sheep, 400 hogs, fifty horses, and twenty-five mules. The land is divided into twenty-one dairy ranches.

His meat market in Eureka is a very large establishment, and his store at Ferndale, with his mill at Eureka, represent a very large capital, and do an extensive business, giving employment to about 300 men, thus being a great benefit to the common people. He has never failed in business, although not always as successful in his ventures as he would have wished.

He is now one of the largest land-owners and wealthy men of California.

He is a great friend of education, has contributed liberally to every educational institution that has ever been erected in Eureka and the county, and is now the principal stockholder in the Humboldt Seminary of Eureka. In person, Mr. Russ is five feet eight inches in height, and stoutly built. His complexion is dark and his whole appearance indicative of great strength and vigor. He is yet in the prime of life, and his general health excellent.

He was married in 1854 to Miss Zipporah Patrick, a native of Illinois, but a resident of Humboldt County, an excellent lady, and has been blessed with thirteen children, ten of whom are still living.

In 1876, accompanied by his family, he visited the Centennial, and made an extensive trip to the scenes of his childhood in Maine. Socially, Mr. Russ is affable, cheerful, and hospitable. There is a quiet humor about him which is very agreeable without being at all showy, and which makes him a very desirable half-hour companion.

The long continuance of his business associations shows that he wears well, and the regard his employes have for him shows that he does not abuse the power his wealth gives him.

He is a Protestant in religion, and in politics a strong Republican. Mr. Russ is, in every sense, a self-made man. He is pleasantly situated in his house, surrounded by his family.

In 1880 Mr. Russ was one of the delegates from California for the Republican party to the Chicago Convention; he was instructed to vote for Blaine, and continued to do so until Garfield's nomination was assured, thus showing his *true* Republican spirit. He has figured prominently in politics for some time, and is honest in his purpose.

ELIAS H. HOWARD.

E. H. Howard was born July 10, 1818, near Poughkeepsie, County of Duchess, New York. After some years spent at school at Burlington, New Jersey, he was matriculated in the University of the City of New York, from which he was graduated in the Class of 1837, receiving one of its commencement honors. In the same year entered on the study of law at Richmond, Virginia, in the office of Sidney S. Baxter, Attorney-General of the Commonwealth. Soon after he became editor and proprietor of the *Richmond Herald*, a paper devoted to news and literature and published in the interest of an association of young men mostly engaged in professional studies, and which was afterwards continued as the *Richmond Lyceum Journal*. In May, 1840, Mr. Howard was admitted to the bar of the Supreme Court of the Commonwealth of Virginia, and located in practice in the circuit of L. Summers, Superior Court Judge. Was in the same year married to Miss Elvira A. daughter of Col. R. Willburn, of Parisburg. Was appointed District Attorney for the county of Logan and elected member of the State Convention in 1841.

Mr. Howard removed to the West, and in 1844 settled in Sheboygan, Wisconsin. During his first year's residence there he was occupied on special duty as assistant to Lieut. Joseph D. Webster, U. S. corps of Topographical Engineers, (since Brigadier General U. S. A.). Mr. Howard then resumed practice of his profession in partnership with Elisha Fox Cook and at the beginning of President Polk's administration was commissioned Postmaster for the city of Sheboygan, which office he held until near its close, February, 1849, at which time he resigned and in the following spring started for California with his family (wife and child), by the Santa Fé and Gila route. On reaching the Gila River at the Pima Villages he determined to test the practicability of navigating the stream, and accordingly he launched the body of his wagon, which had been purposely modeled for amphibious service, and now was to be tried on a new element, as a family barge on the Nile of Arizona. The after-part was a cosy apartment handsomely fitted and upholstered and specially appointed for family use. Having embarked, with Dr. J. M. Ball, of Louisville, Kentucky, and the Rev. Mr. Stephens, a Baptist clergyman of Hannibal, Missouri, as *compagnons tes voyage*, Mr. Howard successfully made the passage, arriving at Fort Yuma in three and one-half days from place of embarkation: a distance, by the river's course, of 225 miles.

FIRST WHITE CHILD BORN IN ARIZONA.

On this part of the journey, September 20, 1849, a little rumpus happened by reason of a *stowaway* being found aboard. A lady was at the bottom of it. But as Mrs. Howard declared the stranger to be her best beloved, and that she would be responsible for *his* fare as well as good behavior as her own darling *babe*, he was at once admitted to the honors of the ship, and voted to be the first child born of American parents in Arizona.

Arriving at San Diego Mr. Howard was compelled to a delay of one month, for passage to San Francisco. The Panama line sailed monthly and the last steamer had then just left port up the coast. By permission of Major Heintzleman,* Mr. Howard occupied quarters in the Mission Church at the head of San Diego Valley. In this venerable sanctuary was his first house-keeping in the State. He has told the writer, that 'he always feels a twinge that necessity compelled him to profane with the fumes of the trencher and the kitchen, that altar which had been dedicated in clouds of incense to the Virgin and St. James; but after all, poetic sensitiveness had no business to intrude itself at such a time.

On the month following (December), having reached San Francisco, he at once entered into law practice associated with Stephen J. Field, Esq.;† their office being on the corner of Clay and Montgomery Streets, in what was then known as the "Belden Block."

* Commanding a detachment of soldiers on escort duty to Mexican Boundary Survey.
† Now Justice of the United States Supreme Court.

March 19, 1850, he formed a co-partnership with Lieut. Douglass Ottinger * in an expedition up the coast. Under the auspices of the "Laura Virginia Association," the schooner *Laura Virginia* was dispatched with Ottinger as master, and it is due to this expedition that the first re-discovery of, and entrance from the ocean was made to, the harbor now known as Humboldt Bay.

From its contingent fund the L. V. A. as an acknowledgment of the special services of Ottinger & Howard in this enterprise awarded to each the amount of $1,500, or its equivalent.

NAMING OF HUMBOLDT BAY.

At a meeting held April 17th on (now) Humboldt Point, of which Captain Ottinger was Chairman, and E. H. Howard, Secretary, it was thought to be time to fix on some name for the bay. Various names were proposed. Among others, "Ottinger," "Folsom," "Laura Virginia;" but all were voted down. The Secretary then presented the name of "Humboldt," in honor to the great philosopher and traveler, whose visit to the Central and South American States on the Pacific had enlarged and enriched the field of enthnological and physical science, but as yet had not been recognized by any local appellation bearing his name.

It was adopted without opposition.

THE FIRST ALCALDE.

At the same meeting E. H. Howard was elected Alcalde; in 1852, was elected Public Administrator for the County of Trinity, then including the present territory of Humboldt; in 1856 and 1857, was District Attorney, and in 1858 and 1859, County Superintendent of public schools.

In 1864, he was appointed to county office which the records do not clearly state.

In 1854, was a candidate for District Attorney, Walter Van Dyke, Esq., his competitor, and was defeated by a majority of forty-three. He was candidate for the Assembly in 1863, A. Wiley, Esq., his opponent, being elected by a handsome majority.

For several years Mr. Howard was Chairman of Republican County Committee, and previous to the Grangers' Organization in the county, was President of the "Farmer's Union."

Until 1873, Mr. Howard had always lived upon his farm on Humboldt Bluff, at which time having leased his place, he removed to Eureka, where in the enjoyment of that competence which makes him independent of wealth, he, with his family of wife and daughter now reside on a pleasantly situated homestead at the corner of G and 6th Streets.

He held the office of Police Judge for the city, to which he was elected in 1876, for a term of two years.

At the commencement of the Rebellion, he was a "Douglass Democrat," since which time he has prominently contributed to

* On leave of absence—of Revenue Cutter *Frolic*.

the organization and support of the Republican Party, and the defense of its principles. The writer of this (who has enjoyed the acquaintance of its subject for over thirty-five years), has failed to get Mr. Howard's consent to what he had further prepared touching his personal characteristics.

But at the risk of his displeasure we will add that Mr. Howard is a gentleman of varied and cultivated attainments, deliberative and sound judgment, a graceful writer, of warm attachments, and never disposed to surrender his own convictions for the sake of popular success. In the several public positions he has occupied, ability and faithfulness have marked the discharge of his duties.

Mr. Howard has six children living—daughters, Laidee (Mrs. Fred Axe), Bertha (Mrs. Thomas Tomlinson), and Helen Howard, and Gila, Thomas, and Norman Howard.

JOHN VANCE.

John Vance, Esq., is in the prime of life, having been born in the province of Nova Scotia, October 1, 1821. His father was a ship-builder of the vicinity of St. Johns, New Brunswick. He had the advantages of a common-school education, and at sixteen years of age he began to learn the trade of ship and house carpentering. In the meantime he attended the night sessions of the St. Johns' Mechanics' Institute. At the age of twenty he had finished his trade and struck out for himself, as a builder and contractor, and located in Roxbury, Massachusetts.

He remained in Massachusetts until 1849, when he joined the tide of adventurers for California. He took passage in the steamer *Ohio*. The vessel put into Havana and was detained and condemned. The passengers were transferred to the *Georgia*, Capt. Rogers was in command, who has since been lost at sea. After crossing the Isthmus on foot they re-embarked in the *Panama*, Capt. Baily. He reached San Francisco July 6, 1849, and engaged in house and mill-building. He afterwards mined on Yuba, at Foster's Bar, in the spring of 1851, with very good success.

He came to Humboldt Bay, July 24, 1852, and has ever since been actively engaged in mill-building, lumbering and railroad construction, and other general business. He has built houses, mills, steamboats, ships, hotels and railroads, and says he finds in the latter the most intellectual field for mental labor of any other undertaking in his experience.

Mr. Vance has a fine tract of some 5,000 acres of timber on Mad River, and on it is a saw-mill that will cut 40,000 feet per day. He has a railroad seven miles long to transport the lumber to lighters on Mad River Slough, whence his steamer *Ada* hauls them to Eureka for shipment. He also has a saw-mill in Eureka with a capacity of 30,000 feet per day, and gets the logs for it by hauling them seven miles on his railroad from Mad River Slough where they are put in the water and made in a raft and towed with his steamer *Ada* to Eureka, where they are manufactured into lumber of all kinds.

His mills are fully described elsewhere, but we will add an item here in reference to the shingle capacity of the Mad River Mill where, on February 17, 1882, W. G. Randall and the sawyer, E. B. Rittenhouse, cut a larger number of shingles than had ever been cut before in Humboldt County in a day's run, running the figures up to 65,000. We think this has never been beaten, though they say that if the machine had been in first-class order they could easily have made it 70,000. They challenge the sawyers of the county to equal it.

Mr. Vance erected a bridge for his railroad across Mad River, in 1875, at a cost of $10,000, but in the winter of 1877-8 it was swept away. He was still determined to have a superior bridge, and in the summer of 1878 he re-constructed it at a cost of $15,000. It is a fine structure, and the only Howe truss bridge in the county. It is inclosed with redwood and is fireproof. It forms one of our finest illustrations.

Mr. Vance is a public-spirited citizen and has done much to develop the resources of Humboldt County. He was the first to construct a railroad. His lumber and shingles are found in the markets of Australia, New York, Mexico, Central and South America. He has been sending lumber to Tahiti for the past twenty-five years. In Arizona and all along the Pacific slope south can be found lumber bearing his brand.

To conduct all of Mr. Vance's business matters requires a clear head and great executive ability. He keeps employed about 150 men, forty work-oxen, and twenty horses, in his various business enterprises. He requires and uses a telephone line of twenty-two miles. His hotel is described elsewhere.

Mr. Vance is in politics a decided Republican, and in religion he believes in being useful to himself and his fellow-men.

ISAAC MINOR.

It is really pleasant and instructive to young men to read the biographies of successful and prominent men. Their examples should be imitated by all who complain of being roughly handled by fortune and nature.

Isaac Minor is one of the many examples, proving that even if unsuccessful at first, by energy a person may attain a competency, and become a useful and influential citizen.

Mr. Minor was born on a farm in Fayette County, Pennsylvania, in 1830, and followed farming until of age. He left Uniontown, Pennsylvania, by way of New York and the Isthmus, for California, the passage consuming two months and ten days, owing to detention on the Isthmus. He reached San Francisco, March 4, 1852, and like nearly everyone else at that time, proceeded to the mines. He went to Tuolumne County and was tolerably successful, and in December, 1853, he came to Humboldt County, where he has since resided and been actively engaged in business. For the first six years he engaged in packing and trading with the mines and interior towns. He then settled on a ranch and engaged in stock-raising until the Indian war broke out, in 1862-3, when by Indian raids and the war he lost all he possessed.

His loss did not dishearten him and with commendable energy he next located on his farm one mile from Arcata, which is represented in the sketch we have made of his property which forms one of our largest views. The farm is composed of 140 acres of rich bottom-land, producing wheat, oats, barley, and potatoes, which will average per acre, of wheat, 60 bushels, oats 100, and barley 80 bushels; of potatoes 100 sacks per acre. In the view of his farm, at the side of his residence, will be noticed the orchard of 100 apple trees, 25 cherry, 12 plum, 12 pear, etc. At the right of the view will be seen the railroad as it passes through his farm, and the distant timber-belt forming a fine background. He keeps some stock on the place, generally 100 head of cattle, 30 hogs, 30 thoroughbred rams, and 15 horses.

He was married in 1855 to Miss H. C. Nixon, a native of Pennsylvania. They have six children living, Theodore H., Isaac N., David W., Mary E., Bertie A., and Jessie I. Minor. That fearful disease, scarlet fever, claimed six children, Alice L., Florence, May, Lottie F., Maggie L., and Sarah L. Minor.

He engaged in the lumber business in 1875, in company with N. H. Falk, and built two steam mills near Arcata. First the Dolly Varden and next the Jolly Giant. Both of which he sold to Chandler, Erington & Co., of Santa Cruz. In 1881, in company with Isaac Cullberg and James Kirk, built the Warren Creek Mill, which has a cutting capacity of 35,000 feet per day. It is six miles from the shipping point to which the lumber is carried by the railroad owned and operated by Yocum & Fernald.

HON. CASPER S. RICKS.

C. S. Ricks was born at Rome, Perry County, Indiana, in 1821. After the age of fifteen years he engaged in the business of flat-boating on the Ohio and Mississippi Rivers until about 1842. He then removed to New Orleans, where he was engaged in the lumbering and commission business until the year 1847. After a short interval spent at Natchez in the superintendence of a saw-mill, resumed his former occupation at New Orleans. In 1849 he came to California by the Isthmus route, arriving in San Francisco after a passage of thirty-five days, on the 13th day of August. Immediately thereafter went to the mines on the Yuba, remaining there about four months and meeting with moderate success. After leaving Yuba he was variously occupied in different parts of the State until he came to Humboldt Bay, where he settled (at Eureka) about the 1st day of July, 1850.

His first venture at the latter place was with a general assortment of merchandise, in which he opened business under the firm of Crozier & Ricks. This firm at once acquired an undivided one-half interest in the original town site of Eureka. Soon after, having purchased the interest of his partner therein, Mr. Ricks devoted his energies and special attention to develop and secure to Eureka those natural advantages of location, which he foresaw would soon enable it to distance and defy all competition from rival business points on the Bay. By liberal advancements in land and money, Mr. Ricks had stimulated the establishment and growth of manufacturing enterprises, of which lumbering has been chief, and largely contributed to invite early investments which have proved a source of permanent success to the owners therein, and prosperity to the town. In 1854 he attended at the session of the Legislature in the interest of the town site location of Eureka, and successfully exerted his influence towards the passage of the Act "to provide for the disposal of lots in the towns and villages on the public lands in the county of Humboldt."

In 1855 he represented the county in the Assembly of the State Legislature, to which position he was chosen his own successor for the second term. At the first term was passed the act locating the county seat at Eureka.

He was also, in 1861, appointed to fill a vacancy as District Attorney for Humboldt County, which office he held for one term. Subsequent to the more active participation in public affairs, his time and supervision have been given chiefly to his private interests, and particularly to the improvement of his real estate in the city.

EUREKA WATER-WORKS.

Deserving of prominent mention is the construction of water-works, with elevated reservoirs, supplied from an artesian well, by steam power, and distributing by three miles of mains the best of water to the principal business part of the city. While it is remunerative as an individual enterprise it greatly adds to the private convenience of citizens and to the general security in case of fires. His son "Lem" is superintendent of them. The "Palace Stables" built, stocked and equipped by Mr. Ricks, is one of the largest and most complete in its appointments of any on the coast, and is conducted under the personal care of his son Thomas F. Ricks.

To the numerous dwellings which he had built before, Mr Ricks, within the last ten years, has added two fire-proof brick blocks, one of two stories, having three capacious rooms on the first floor for business purposes, with suits of office apartments on the second floor; the other block containing six large business subdivisions, with open, ornamental and attractive fronts, and all situated in the very heart of trade.

Mr. Ricks is probably the largest owner of improved real estate situated in the city. He has always been among the foremost in affairs of public enterprise and in his own private concerns, devoting the acquirements of a varied business experience in early life so as to pluck success from opportunities which others might altogether fail to see. His extensive and almost sole interest being within the limits of the city, Mr. Ricks' natural ambition is to contribute, as far as may be, towards its growth and prosperity. To this end he has not hesitated to risk pecuniary investments, although they might not prove of immediate profit to himself. Mr. Ricks, however, never shelters himself behind a pretense to unselfishness in his

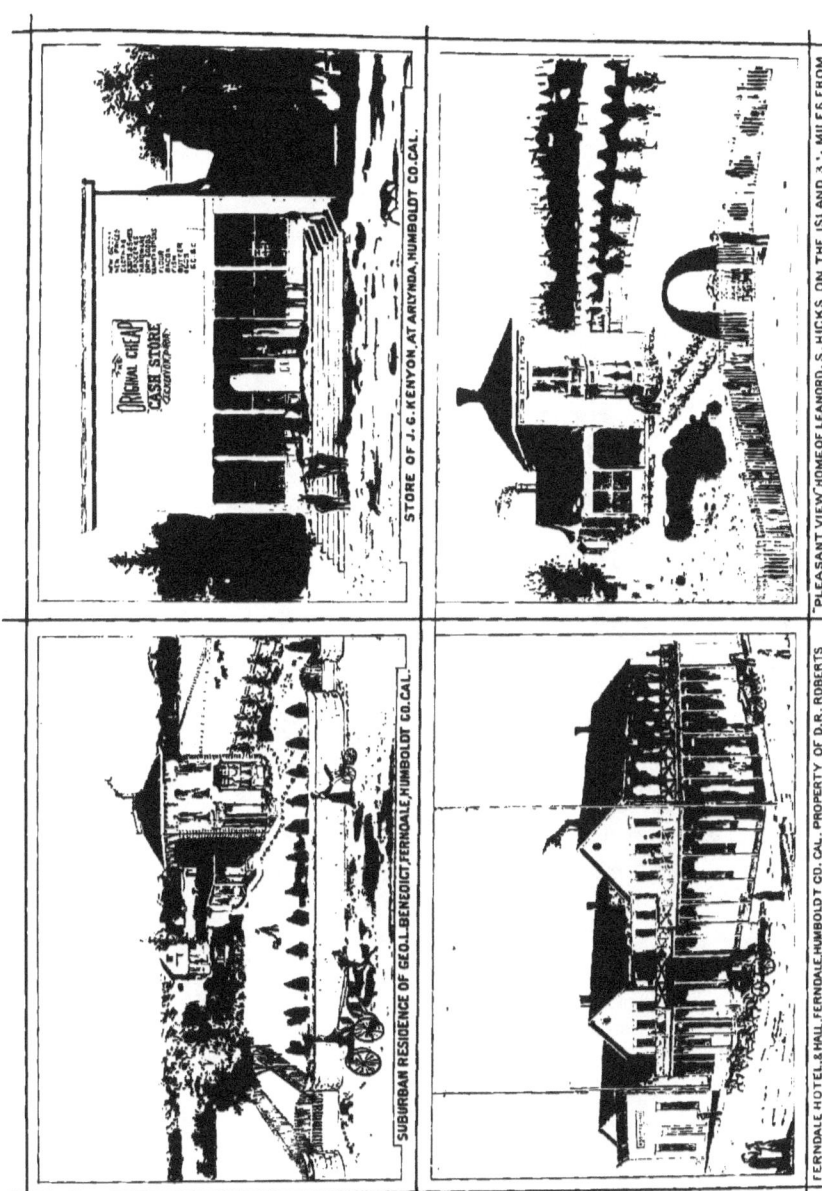

aims for personal success. For *this* he strives within the limits of legitimate business methods, and as a useful and active citizen, has practically shown that those methods cannot well be independent of the public welfare.

In politics Mr. Ricks is a Democrat. In 1854 he visited the East, where he was married to Miss Adaline A. Fouts, of Clark County, Indiana. He has a family of three children.

JAMES HANNA.

James Hanna was born on the 2d of February, 1806, in that part of the county of Philadelphia then called the District of Southwark and now included within the limits of the city. Both of his parents were from the County of Down, Ireland. He received such education as the private schools afforded and in 1820 was placed as a clerk in a large merchandise house, where he remained until 1826, having during the intervening time made two voyages to the West Indies as supercargo. In the latter part of the same year he made his first political speech. It was hostile to General Jackson, then a candidate for the Presidency. As far as it was delivered the speech was most uproariously received and the speaker pitched out of the hall. This treatment, of course, intensified his admiration of Jackson and the kind of democracy he established!

In 1829 he commenced the study of law and was married to Clarissa Sidney, grand-daughter of Betsey Ross, who assisted in designing and made the first American flag as established by Congress. In 1832 he was admitted to the Philadelphia bar and elected as a Whig to represent the county in the Legislature of the State. The next year he was the Whig candidate for the State Senate and was defeated. In 1835 he was again nominated by the Whig party for the Senate, and received a certificate of election. He was admitted to a seat but was afterwards ousted, his election having been contested.

In February, 1850, he left Philadelphia and by the way of the Isthmus and sailing vessel from Panama, arrived in San Francisco in May of the same year. His eldest son had preceded him, but his wife and eight children remained in Philadelphia. The family, excepting his wife, who died, were afterwards all united in San Francisco.

In January, 1854, he left San Francisco for Humboldt County and arrived in Eureka on the 2d of February, where, with his children and several of his grand-children, he still resides. He has been District Attorney of the county for one term, and one year he volunteered as a candidate for District Judgeship against the Know-nothing nominee. Mr. Hanna received a majority in this county, but Trinity County, at that time a much more populous county, gave a larger majority for the opposing candidate who was a resident of that county.

As long as there was a Whig party he was a member of it, then voted for Bell and Everett and afterwards became a Black Republican. He was always and perhaps is yet a Stalwart, always voting as he was ordered from *regular* headquarters without reading his ticket. He, however, once voted under protest. He was required by the Whig party to vote in the Congressional District in which he lived for the less objectionable of two Democratic candidates for Congress. He kicked but submitted to the harness. He voted a ticket endorsed Democratic, but before touching it he put on his gloves. Notwithstanding this precaution he fancied for a month afterwards that his fingers smelt.

H. H. BUHNE.

H. H. Buhne was born in Flensburg, Denmark, June 27, 1822. His father was a seafaring man, owning at one time thirteen vessels and their cargoes. Young Buhne attended school until he was sixteen years of age, when he embarked in a seafaring life as cabin boy. One year after was promoted, and the following year shipped in a whaler for the South Pacific. After a cruise he returned to his native home in Denmark, in 1845, with a full shipload of oil and bone.

On the 7th of June, 1845, he began a course at a navigation school, and October 20th received his diploma and went to sea on the same whaler ship he previously made a cruise in, and was promoted to first mate and officer of the first boat. They set sail for the South Sea, October 28, 1845. On their passage out, calling for fresh water and provisions, they were shipwrecked on Cape Verde Islands. In the afternoon they anchored under Fort St. Luz, but in the night a heavy sea caused the vessel to drag her anchors, and she went ashore. The vessel was a total wreck, and two days thereafter nothing was to be seen of her. From there they went on board a small schooner for the Island Salt, another of the Cape Verde Islands. After their arrival they embarked in the Bremen bark *Active* for Rio Janeiro. He there shipped before the mast on a bark commanded by Captain Fallesen, for Hamburg, Germany. When they arrived at Hamburg he returned home, about the first of May, 1846.

After remaining at home a couple of months he left for Bremen and shipped as third officer in the whaling ship *Clementine*, Captain Hashogen commanding, for the Arctic Ocean. After a cruise in the *Arctic* they left there about October 8th.

SAN FRANCISCO IN 1847.

They arrived in San Francisco in November, 1847. When they entered the Golden Gate they looked for San Francisco where their chart located it, and saw only a few houses, and one ship lay at anchor. They looked then over towards South Saucelito, where they saw two large buildings, and three vessels were lying at anchor. They then concluded to anchor there instead of San Francisco, as they inferred it was the largest business place. After they got to anchor Captain Richardson came on board and told them that the largest business place was at "Yerba Buena," now called San Francisco. The next day they hove anchor and sailed to Yerba Buena and cast anchor close to a Boston barque that was loading with hides and tallow. While there he became acquainted with a family named Ellis, and with the old pioneer "Bob Parker." Also got acquainted with Captain Sutter, on board of the first steamer that was ever built in or run on the San Francisco Bay. It was built by the Russian Government, and presented to General Sutter. While in San Francisco the ship's doctor, Heyermann, deserted and went on the little steamer to Sonoma, and Mr. Buhne and a boat's crew, accompanied by a constable, pursued him. They came near him several times, but the Dr. was always provided with a fresh horse by the ranchers, and as Mr. B. says, the Dr. would laugh at them on their jaded steeds, and flee faster than before. After a chase of two days they returned to Sonoma without the fugitive. When Mr. B arrived at Sonoma he found that his boat's crew had deserted and he and the constable were left alone to get to San Francisco as best they could, and finally, after camping on Mare Island one night, they arrived the night following on board of their ship in San Francisco. After three weeks spent in San Francisco they sailed for Magdalena Bay on a whaling voyage, and had fair success. A voyage was taken to the Sandwich Islands whence they arrived the middle of March of 1848. There Mr. B. left the ship *Clementine* and re-shipped as second officer on the Dutch ship *Zudipole*, Captain Meier commanding. On the first of April they set sail for Okhotsk Sea and the Bay of Kamtchatka for a whaling season. After the season was ended they sailed for the Navigators' Islands, and arrived there in the latter part of December, 1848. While there they were informed of the discovery of gold in California, and after a couple of weeks they sailed for Talcowana, on the coast of Chili. They shipped a part of their oil and whalebone for Amsterdam, where they opened negotiations for carrying passengers and freight for San Francisco. Here Mr. B. was promoted as first officer of the ship *Zudipole*, and sailed with passengers and freight for Valparaiso where forty more passengers came aboard, and in the first part of April they sailed for San Francisco with about thirty cabin passengers and one hundred and twenty in the steerage, and a full load of freight.

In the first part of June, 1849, they were safely anchored in San Francisco Bay. Mr. B. remained a short time on the vessel and then concluded to change his life from a sailor to that of a miner. He says that was the greatest mistake of his life. He and his party left San Francisco for the dry diggings at Auburn. The day after he arrived in Sacramento he purchased a couple of mules to pack the mining outfit, and succeeded quite well in loading the first mule, but when they came to load the second mule they found they had more goods than he could carry, but they continued to load goods on until they had, as Mr. B. says, "more goods on the upper deck than on the lower one," and the consequence was that the mule commenced bucking and was not contented until all the load was strewn over the plains of Sacramento. The mule ran away. After a hard chase they succeeded in overtaking him, and commenced re-packing. By this time they had learned to humor the mule's whims and not overload him. After several days they arrived in the mining vicinity of Auburn, where they commenced to dig gold, and had very fair success as long as it lasted. After mining about a month he was taken down with the fever and dysentery. After a fourteen days' sickness he finally got into Auburn and found two persons in a tent, one who had been third officer with Mr. B. on the *Zudipole*. He took up his quarters with them until a friend from his native town who was teaming from Sacramento to the mines, placed them in his wagon and hauled them to Sacramento and assisted them on board a little steamer which took them down to Benicia, and on arriving there they got aboard a schooner and went to San Francisco, where they arrived about the middle of October, 1849. They went to a boarding house kept by Edward Young and Clavieter, who had been a shipmate of Mr. Buhne. The house was managed by Young & Clavieter, both of whom had been shipmates of Mr. Buhne.

FIRST VIEW OF HUMBOLDT BAY.

After his suffering six months, and his money all spent he left his sick bed and went on board the *Laura Virginia*, Captain Ottinger commanding. He shipped as second officer, and the second day out they passed Eel River and saw from the masthead the Bay of Humboldt. They went to anchor about four miles southwest of Table Bluff, and to the best of Mr. Buhne's recollections, the next day two schooners hove in sight, and anchored at the mouth of Eel River, near the *Laura Virginia*. One of them proved to be the *General Morgan*, of San Francisco, which put out a boat and started for Eel River Bar. The *Laura Virginia* at the same time put out two boats, one with Captain Ottinger in command, and the other with Captain Swain in command (who lives at present on a farm on Elk River, Humboldt County). The intention was to follow the *General Morgan's* boat into the mouth of Eel River. Captain Swain's boat capsized in the breakers on the bar. Captain Ottinger turned back to the vessel in his boat and asked Mr. Buhne to go in command of his boat to the rescue of those who were in the breakers. He succeeded in saving the crew with the exception of a gentleman who was drowned before he arrived.

They started north, and arrived at Trinidad Bay the day following. They left some of the passengers there to explore the coast south and north of Trinidad Bay, and the vessels continued north in search for the mouth of Trinity River. They were rewarded by finding the Klamath River, which they supposed was the mouth of the Trinity River. As the sea was rough they continued on their course, and the day following cast anchor in Crescent City Bay, where they found the brig *Kamehameana* loading with piles, and the schooner *Patigonian* high and dry on the beach. After remaining a couple of days, started on their course south again, and sounded the bar of the Klamath, but had orders from the captain not to enter the river. They then sailed for Trinidad, and arrived there on the 8th of April, 1850. Here learned that the party who had been left to explore the country south of Trinidad, had seen a good entrance into Humboldt Bay, and the next day they set sail for the entrance.

FIRST BOAT ENTERS THE BAY.

When off Humboldt Bar the *Laura Virginia* came to anchor on the afternoon of the 9th. The morning following, Captain Ottinger asked Mr. Buhne if he thought it safe to cross the bar in the ship's boats. He said he thought it was. He then asked him if he would take one of the boats and enter the bay? He answered him by stating that if he would stay by him with his boat he would try. About 9 o'clock, A. M., they set out in their boats for the bar. After Mr. Buhne got inside the breakers with the poorest boat, Captain Ottinger turned about and struck out for the vessel. Mr. Buhne was compelled to continue his course into the bay. The boat was filled twice before they got inside the bay. When in the bay they went onto Humboldt Bluff (now called Buhne's Point), and saw a fine entrance to the bay.

When on the Bluff, about 400 Indians came running along the beach flashing their *pololtos*. One of the company called out to Mr. B. to hurry down as that was a sure war sign, but upon his getting down the Indians had them surrounded; they were very friendly.

They then started for the north Peninsula in their boat, the Indians following in their canoes, and upon their arrival, kindled a fire to cook their dinner, which consisted of roasted salt pork and hardtack. The Indians were very anxious to trade with them, but they possessed nothing except a sailor's knife which they traded for a couple of smoked eels. By that time ebb tide was making, and they started to take soundings of the channel. After that they went on board the vessel and reported to the captain what they had done. In the afternoon (same day), they took all the passengers who could get into the boats with their baggage and provisions without overloading the boats, and started again for the bay.

Mr. Buhne was in command of the first boat, and Captain Swain was in command of the other.

When off the bar, the passengers were frightened, and did not wish to proceed further. Mr. B. told them that if they did not go on that evening, he would not bring them the next day. The other boat came along side and they held a meeting and appointed a chairman, and balloted to determine whether to enter or not. The majority were in favor of entering, and they proceeded, the other boat following. Mr. Buhne landed safely after entering the bay near where the light house now stands, at about 7:30 P. M.

NAMING OF HUMBOLDT BAY.

After supper, the subject came up of naming the bay. Quite a number of names were suggested by different parties; some proposed to call it Buhne's Bay, but Mr. Shaw, now of San Francisco, proposed the name of Humboldt, in honor of Von Humboldt. The next morning they took soundings of the bay and located towns. Among the rest was one called Humboldt City, now Buhne's Point, which he now owns as part of his fine farm.

Five days afterwards Mr. B. went out with a boat's crew and piloted the schooner *Laura Virginia* into the bay. It was the first American vessel ever entering the Bay of Humboldt.

FIRST HOTEL ON THE BAY.

After remaining a week in the bay he left for San Francisco, and purchased cooking utensils and a tent and returned on the 1st of May as a passenger on the *Laura Virginia*, where they arrived on the 5th of May, 1850. Landed at Humboldt City and pitched their tent and made ready to keep hotel. Everything went off nicely except they were obliged to keep watch on account of the Indians, because they would steal all they could lay hands on.

One evening Mr. Buhne received an arrow wound between the second and third rib from an Indian's bow. He thought he would die, but recovered. His venture as a "canvas hotel" did not remunerate him as he expected. He concluded to go piloting on the Humboldt Bar, and, making a few hundred dollars, went to San Francisco and purchased a stock of groceries, loaded them on the schooner *Caroline*, Captain Sterling, for Humboldt Bay. He was shipwrecked and lost all of his goods and clothing. He started for Sonoma on foot and took passage on a steamer for San Francisco. He was sick and without a cent or a friend. He met the captain of the brig *Newcastle*, who had been in Humboldt Bay, and told him of his distress. He took Mr. Buhne on board his ship to remain there until he recovered. When he recovered, he shipped on a little schooner as mate, bound for Humboldt Bay.

After arriving he started packing to the Trinity River. On their first trip the Indians killed fourteen mules, surrounded them in the woods on Grouse Creek and kept up the battle for four hours. When the Indians ceased fighting, they continued on their journey to the mines on Trinity River, and after a fatiguing trip returned to Humboldt Point. He says that he was satisfied with his packing experience and did not desire to repeat it.

In July, 1851, Mr. Buhne went to the mines on Trinity River and worked on the Big Bar and also Cox's Bar. While there he was not financially successful, became disgusted, and one fine morning he packed his blankets up and put them on his back and struck out on foot for "Union Town," now called Arcata, and from there he took a little sail boat for Humboldt Point. Mr. Buhne says he was so disgusted with his past expeditions that he concluded to try his hand at hunting elk and deer; was pretty successful. Mr. Buhne took charge of the brig *Colorado*. He shipped as commander.

SHIPWRECK AND NARROW ESCAPE.

While he was in command of her, Captain Brunerhoff, of the barge *Holmes* asked Mr. Buhne to assist him to get his ship to sea. He reluctantly consented as the ship was drawing too much water to cross the bar in safety. But Captain Brunerhoff was determined for Mr. Buhne to accompany him, so on the morning of the 2d of July, 1851, they attempted to cross the bar and were cast in breakers on the South Spit. They cut away the masts and spars and threw the deck-load overboard to ease the vessel, and still she pounded and soon the hold was full of water. In the night it became very rough and the breakers were washing her decks all night. The next day they attempted to launch a boat, and by doing so stove the bows of the boat. Mr. Buhne and one of the sailors of the vessel jumped into the boat to bail it out. When the mate who had hold of the painter was going to drop the boat under the stern of the vessel, a breaker struck it and jerked the painter out of his hand. The boat then capsized and the sailor and Mr. Buhne scrambled upon the bottom of the boat and were drifting out to sea when the breakers washed them off into the water. The sailor caught hold of Mr. Buhne and he put him upon the upturned boat once more. That was repeated three times in succession when Mr. Buhne found his strength was leaving him, and the last time he put the sailor on the forward part of the boat where the painter was and took the other end of the boat. The next breaker washed them off and he never saw the sailor again. Mr. Buhne got on the bottom of the boat again and as he says "made the boat as comfortable as he could and went drifting out to sea."

The next morning the boat drifted ashore about four miles south of the wreck, and when he came to his senses he found himself lying in the boat "high and dry" on the beach. He says he got out of the boat and attempted to walk but found he had not strength to carry him. He then crawled up behind the sand-hills on the sunny side and fell asleep.

After awhile some Indians awakened him and he asked them to assist him to get across to Humboldt Point. At first they could not be persuaded to assist him, but after a brief powwow among themselves they motioned for him to get up and follow them; but when they found his total inability to arise, two of them came to his assistance and by putting his arms on the shoulders of two Indians they finally succeeded in dragging him half-way across the sand-spit, when his strength left him and he dropped upon the ground. While lying there three of the Indians who had a single-barrel shot-gun went off behind a sand-hill and he became convinced that they intended to shoot him where he lay.

After they had the gun loaded they went to the beach as he supposed to see whether there were any white men around and as luck happened two of the sailors, who had gotten ashore from the wreck, were in search of Mr. Buhne's body. One of the sailors took him upon his back and after carrying him some two miles came to where there chanced to be a boat, and brought him across to Humboldt Point.

After about a week's careful nursing under Dr. Clark's care, he recovered. While he was lying on the beach all parties supposed him to be drowned and all the vessels in the bay put their flags half-mast in honor. When they learned of his safe return the flags were hoisted to the mast-head and it is safe to say that never were flags hoisted with more pleasure than on that occasion.

When he recovered he left the brig *Colorado* and engaged himself to the numerous mill-owners of Humboldt Bay to pilot the ships in and out of the bay, in which he was very successful, considering they had nothing but a ship's boat to cross the bar in.

The 10th of November, 1852, Messrs. Ryan and Duff brought the tug-boat *Mary Ann*, of which Mr. B. took command soon after her arrival. While piloting he had many narrow escapes, but fortunately none terminated disastrously to him or his boat. At the present time Mr. Buhne is part owner of the tugs in the bay, the *Mary Ann* and the *H. H. Buhne*.

At one time Mr. Buhne owned the bark *Watcher* that plied between San Francisco, Japan, China and Australia. It is from this venture that he dates his successful financial career.

He owns some 1,000 acres of farming and grazing land and 4,000 acres of good redwood timber land, also is part owner in four different vessels, and one-third owner with D. R. Jones & Co. in two saw-mills, and one-sixth interest in the Fresh-Water logging railroad, and a two-thirds interest and senior partner in the hardware business of H. H. Buhne & Co., and other valuable property in the city of Eureka.

He has a fine residence of which we have made an illustration. Mr. Buhne is a public-spirited citizen and a self-made man in all meaning of the name.

In height he is six feet, one and a half inches, and weighs 208 pounds, and he is well proportioned and enjoys good health. He is of light complexion, but years have changed his beard and hair to a gray tinge. He bids fair to enjoy his many possessions for years to come.

In 1853, April 10th, he was happily married to Mary Margaret Ohlson, who was a native of Flensburg, Denmark, by whom he has had five children, all of whom are at home at the present time. Their names are Mary, Henry, Alexander Humboldt, Sophia and Georgia Buhne.

HON. J. E. WYMAN.

Judge Wyman was well known. Perhaps there is not a man, woman, or child in the county that has not heard his name repeatedly.

He was a pioneer. We who are enjoying the blessings of our civilization can scarcely understand what is meant by "pioneer." It means labor, privations, vexations, embarrassments, failures, with which this generation is unacquainted. It means indomitable courage, Herculean labor, broadness of ideas,

and a spirit of prophecy and heroism. Judge Wyman did not subdue the forest, nor break up the wild lands, nor drain the swamps, nor build ships or railroads, nor open up mines; but he was a builder, and in a sphere that was essential to the welfare of the county.

Justus Edwin Wyman was born in Woburn, Mass., October 21, 1823; afterwards removed to Maine and was educated in the college at Gorham in that State. At the age of nineteen years he went to sea, and during his maritime life made several voyages across the Atlantic. He subsequently resided in New York; studied law with Judge Lott Clark, and was admitted to practice before the Supreme Court of that State.

In the spring of 1850 he came to California by way of the Isthmus, landing in San Francisco the day after the big fire, in May. Mined on the Feather, Yuba and American Rivers during the summer and winter of 1850; and in the spring of 1851 moved to Arcata (then Uniontown), Humboldt County, where he engaged in mercantile pursuits and the practice of his profession.

In 1864 he removed to Eureka, having purchased the Humboldt *Times*, and was engaged in this business up to the time of his death.

During his residence in Humboldt County he served as County Judge for fourteen years. Having joined the order of Odd Fellows at the age of twenty-one years, he remained an active member of that order until the time of his death, a period of thirty-six years.

Was one of the founders of Anniversary Lodge, I. O. O. F., of Arcata, and Fortuna Lodge of Eureka. Was a member of Mt. Zion Encampment; of the Veteran Odd Fellows of San Francisco, and a member of Humboldt Chapter Royal Arch Masons. He was also a member of the Society of Humboldt County Pioneers.

He died November 5, 1880, after a long and painful illness. All that remained of a kind and doting father and affectionate and loving husband, a true friend and a noble man, passed from the gaze of mortal eye.

JOHN J. DE HAVEN.

The subject of this sketch was born March 12, 1845, in St. Joseph, Buchanan County, Mo., which place his parents left in the spring of 1849, for California, and reached Sacramento in August of that year, crossing the plains. He resided there from August, 1849, to May, 1853, when he came to this county which he has since made his home.

In 1862 he commenced work as a printer, and worked at his trade for four years. While working as a printer in the office of the *Humboldt Times*, he for part of the time acted as editor and displayed ability in preparing articles and managing the paper.

He read law with the late Judge J. E. Wyman and was admitted to the Bar in March, 1866, and now occupies a leading place among the attorneys of the county.

He was married in 1872 to Miss Z. J. Ball, a native of Ohio. They have two children, Jotham J. De Haven and Sarah Louisa De Haven.

In 1867 he was elected District Attorney, which office he resigned in 1869, to take his seat in the Legislature, having been elected to the Assembly that year.

He was elected to the State Senate in 1871 and served two sessions. He has since been engaged in the practice of his profession in Eureka. In 1878 he was by a few votes defeated as a candidate to the Constitutional Convention from his county. In politics Mr. De Haven is Republican.

ALEXANDER BRIZARD.

A. Brizard was born in Bordeaux, France, March 17, 1839. At the age of four years his father, being a sea captain, moved his family to Lima, Peru, where he located and embarked in a stage line from Callao to Lima, until 1848, when he reached San Francisco and was soon afterward followed by his family, who arrived September 25, 1849. Thence he left for Humboldt Bay, arriving August 25, 1850, and located at Arcata. Soon after Alexander accompanied his father to the Trinity mines.

STARVATION TIMES IN THE MINES.

In the winter of 1852 and 1853, while Mr. Brizard was at the mines on the Trinity River, the snow was so deep that all communication between Uniontown (now Arcata) and the mines was shut off, and consequently all provisions at the mines were soon exhausted. One dollar a pound was charged for flour, and only five pounds could be obtained by one person. It soon gave out, and all other provisions, excepting barley, which the merchants sold at sixty-five cents per pound. This was ground in a coffee-mill and made into a paste, and was all they had to eat excepting the mules and jacks, with now and then a fox or deer or wild cat.

Early in the winter they killed all the Jacks and mules, and salted them down for future use. They endured these hardships from November, 1852, until March, 1853, when a pack-train came in loaded with provisions. Flour was seventy-five cents per pound, and all else in proportion. No one died from starvation, however. In 1857, Mr. Brizard concluded to embarked in a more lucrative pursuit, and engaged in packing at a good salary, and in 1858, secured a position with Roskill & Co., who were then the leading merchants of Arcata. Then when they disposed of their business in 1859, he engaged with Spencer, Manhism & Stern. They carried on the business until the death of Mr. Stern, when the firm dissolved, selling out to Mr. Brizard and James C. Van Rossum in 1862. In 1865, they purchased the business of William Codington & Co., and followed the business until 1871, when Mr. Brizard bought out his partner and carried on the business until 1875, when he was burned out at a loss of $40,000 with only $10,000 insurance. He soon opened a store by the material assistance from parties in San Francisco, who had confidence in his business abilities.

In 1879, he purchased his present store, of which we have made an illustration. He also has three other stores in Humboldt County in the interior, and one in Trinity County, and one in Siskiyou County. He owns, or is interested in the above stores, five in number. He also has an interest in a pack-train of 100 mules, used for transporting merchandise to the interior to the branch stores.

He has a farm of 400 acres of first-class timber land easy of access.

He married Miss Maggie Henry in 1871, who was a native of Iowa. They have three boys, named Paul Alexander, Marcial Browne and Henry Francis Brizard.

Mr. Brizard is a very energetic and wide-awake business man, and deserves great credit for his successful career. He is a generous citizen, and all public charities find in him a generous support.

T. M. BROWN.

The subject of this sketch has the honor of having held the office of Sheriff for a longer period than any other man in the State. He came to Trinity River in March, 1850, and to this section long before any county organizations, and has resided in parts of the territory which formed Shasta, Trinity, Klamath, and Humboldt. He has witnessed all the changes that have taken place in this part of the State and participated in them. He has assisted in developing the resources of this section both in agriculture and mining. He has now a valuable mining claim near the old county seat of Klamath which we have described elsewhere.

Mr. Brown was Sheriff of Klamath County for thirteen years and of Humboldt four years, making a term of seventeen years. This fact speaks volumes for his ability and integrity, and nothing we can say will add any luster to his career.

He was born in Overton County, Tennessee, January 26, 1820, and followed a pioneer life on the frontier of Illinois and Missouri.

He left Harrison County, Missouri, by the overland route, in 1849, consuming over five months on the journey, reaching Sacramento October 5, 1849. He re-crossed and returned with his family in 1860.

He was married in 1847 to Miss S. J. Poynter who was born in Kentucky. They have one child, Martha J. Brown.

CHARLES WILLIAM LONG.

C. W. Long was born on a farm in Kingsclear, York County, New Brunswick, February 26, 1826, and followed the business of farming until 1845, when he engaged in the lumber business. He then worked two years at carpentering previous to starting for California, which he did from St. Johns, December 13, 1849, on board the bark James via Cape Horn, and arrived in San Francisco, August 24, 1850, after a passage of 254 days.

He came to Humboldt on the first steamer, the Sea Gull, that entered the harbor on September 25, 1850. She was afterwards wrecked on Humboldt Bar. He has resided in Eureka since coming here, except about eighteen months of 1855-56, when he engaged in farming in Hoopa Valley, at that time in Klamath County. In 1850 he engaged first in lumbering and afterwards in 1852-53, in general merchandising and again tried lumbering in 1855.

He was married to Miss Francis Ann Snider in 1854, a native of New Brunswick. She died November 10, 1874, and he married Mrs. Matilda Angeline La Grange, October 28, 1878.

The children's names are Charles Edwin, Katie, Harriet, Mary E., and Milton Long.

HENRY ROHNER.

Henry Rohner, whose history we give in brief, was born in Switzerland, in the year 1820. He was raised on a farm, and at suitable age learned the printer's trade, and in 1847, at the age of eighteen, emigrated to the United States, landing at New Orleans, where he followed his trade for two years.

In 1849 he went to Louisville, Kentucky, from whence he went to Sacramento, and in 1851 to Humboldt County, where he has since resided, making himself an honorable name and fortune, and rising from obscurity to a position of prominence and trust.

At St. Joseph, Missouri, with four others, they purchased a yoke of oxen, wagon and outfit for the journey overland, their route being across the plains, by Fort Hall and Truckee River to Sacramento, arriving on the 18th of September, 1849, just four months from the time of starting. He walked the whole distance except a half-day when he was sick, traveling mostly from 2 A. M. until noon. Five men composed the party and owned jointly the team and outfit. At the end of the trip they had left of their store, two pounds of bacon, five pounds of flour and a little coffee.

Mr. Rohner mined on the Yuba, Feather, and Trinity Rivers with moderate success. In the fall of 1852, he located a place on Eel River, and operated in the Trinity River mining region. He has resided in Humboldt County since, at or near Rohnerville, excepting a few months at Arcata in 1854, and nine months at Eureka in 1855; also resided at the latter place from October, 1865, to October, 1867.

In 1862 he commenced merchandising at Rohnerville, under the firm name of Rohner & Fagenbaum, continuing till 1865. Since then he has followed farming, and general merchandising in Eureka, under the firm name of Rohner & Ellery.

He owns an interest in the saw and flouring mills at Springville, manufacturing 20,000 feet of lumber and forty barrels of flour daily.

Mr. Rohner has 200 acres of valuable land situated near Rohnerville, twenty miles from the county seat and eight miles from water communication. He raises on an average sixty-five bushels of oats, thirty-five of wheat, sixty-five of barley, fifty of peas, and four tons of potatoes per acre. He has an orchard of 120 trees, mostly apple. He generally keeps about four cows, thirty sheep and seven horses.

He married Miss Mary A. Bulkely, a native of Pennsylvania, in 1861. They have four children, two boys and two girls named: Annie, Henry, Lizzie, and Frank Rohner.

The village of Rohnerville derives its name from him. He was Postmaster there when engaged in business. He built the first house there used for merchandising.

W. S. ROBINSON.

On the left bank of the Van Duzen River, at Bridgeville, we found the fine farm of W. S. Robinson, which he bought in 1870, from Mr. Silas Hogland, and which comprises 1,520 acres of good grazing land, of hilly formation. The residence is pleasantly situated and the surroundings improved. It has an orchard of 120 trees attached, which brings a variety and an abundance of fruit to the owner. Mr. Robinson is engaged in stock raising. He keeps all kinds of stock, but his greatest pride is taken in his flock of 1,600 sheep, which are of a high grade and amongst which can be found some fine merino sheep.

Mr. Robinson married, November 18, 1862, Miss E. L. Albee, and they have three boys and six girls.

He is one of those men who started life with nothing, and made a capital with hands and energy. We will give a short sketch of his life.

Born on a farm in Virginia, February 4, 1828, he was brought up thereon until 1836, when his parents moved to Tennessee and afterwards, in 1843, to Missouri. He stayed with them until 1850, when he concluded to emigrate to California. He came by ox-team via Fort Laramie and Bridges and Salt Lake City, and Truckee River, and arrived in Nevada City, California, September 26, 1850.

Mr. Robinson mined awhile at different places, but not finding it very profitable, he left the mines and went to Colusa in 1851, where he teamed between that and Shasta City. Hearing that Humboldt County was a fine place to settle down, he, in 1852, disposed of his property and in company with Mr. Joseph Russ and others, came to this county. At first Mr. Robinson resided in Ferndale for two years, then moved to Union (Arcata) where he stayed nine years; then to Eel River where he remained five years; then to what is called the "Redwood House," where he remained two years, and then to his present home, of which we have made an illustration.

C. A. DUNGAN.

It is a well-known fact, that most of the prosperous men in this country, are men who were brought up to hard labor. Here we introduce another of those men who toiled until they conquered. Mr. C. A. Dungan, lives on a farm owned by him, consisting of 222 acres of land located within nineteen miles of the county seat, two miles from water communication, and within three miles of Ferndale. He was born in Harrison County, Kentucky, July 18, 1829. Before coming to this coast, Mr. Dungan worked in several States as a farm hand until 1850, when he left Lee County, Iowa, his last stopping-place, and came across the plains to California, and arrived at Hangtown (Placerville), August 29, 1850. It took him over four months to accomplish the trip.

The first job he got was to make shakes at $2.00 per day and dinner. The other meals he had to cook himself. Afterwards he mined in several places, but what money he made in one he lost in the next; so after stopping in several places as Nevada City, Forest City and Downieville, he at last took his course to this county, where he arrived in May, 1853. At first Mr Dungan engaged in salmon fishing, and in 1858, bought his present farm, which is of a deep, rich soil, a clay loam, and averages—oats from sixty to 125 bushels, wheat from thirty to eighty, and potatoes from three to fifteen tons per acre. He also owns sixty acres of land two miles away from his residence, and an orchard close by containing 150 apple, twenty pear, twenty-five plum, and fifteen cherry trees. He keeps ten head of cattle, 253 sheep, and nine horses on hand at present. Mr. Dungan's home is presided over by his amiable wife, whom he married in 1863. She was a native of Illinois, where she was known as Miss Mary L. Jenkins. They have two boys and two girls named Eleanor, Garland Albert, Joanna, and George Cuy Dungan.

NATHANIEL BULLOCK.

The careful readers of our history will find a description of the large saw-mill of J. Russ & Co. One of the partners and the head book-keeper of this large business is Nathaniel Bullock, a native of Yates Center, Orleans County, New York, where he was born September 26, 1834.

Mr. Bullock is a Notary Public for Humboldt County and agent for the Union Insurance Company.

His residence is an ornament to the village of Eureka, where he resides. His wife, Sarah M. Hinestis, is a daughter of one of the pioneers of Humboldt. She was born in the State of Virginia, and their children are: Minnie A., Nellie C., Blanche, Curtis, Bertram N., and Russ R. Bullock. They were married in 1864.

Mr. Bullock's motive in coming to California was to improve his health, which he has accomplished in the fine climate of Humboldt. He left his native State in June, 1860, coming by way of Nicaragua, which formed a very pleasant and agreeable trip.

He arrived in San Francisco in July, 1860, from whence he went directly to Arcata, where he stayed until November 1861, after which he came to Eureka, where he lives now. He was engaged in diverse occupations; at one time he mined, at another he farmed, and at another he was engaged in a mechanical business, and is now book-keeper and manager for J. Russ & Co's. market. He has been a member of the firm of J. Russ & Co. in the lumber business since 1875.

ISAAC CULLBERG.

In bringing the different citizens of this county before the public we must not omit to mention Mr. Isaac Cullberg, a prosperous merchant who resides in Arcata. He is a native of Ootenburg, Sweden. He went to Antwerp, Belgium, at the age of twenty-one, and remained there nine years as a clerk; during four years was engaged in merchandising. In March, 1853, he arrived in Philadelphia; from thence he went to Platte City, Missouri, and with ox-train across the mountains to Sacramento, and by way of Shasta to Hayfork and this county. He located in Arcata in November 10, 1853, and engaged in farming for three years, and in April, 1857, engaged in mercantile pursuits, in which he has become successful, and is classed among the prominent business men of the county.

He was married in 1860 to Mrs. H. M. Fales, who was born in Woburn, Mass.

HON. AUSTIN WILEY.

A. Wiley came to California from Cincinnati, in 1852. In October, 1853, he came to Humboldt Bay, and entered the Humboldt *Times* office as a printer in 1854; and, in company with Walter Van Dyke, bought the paper in 1855. He bought out Van Dyke in 1857, and moved the paper from Arcata to Eureka in 1858.

He was elected to the Legislature from this county in 1863; was Chairman of Committee of Indian Affairs in the House.

In April, 1864, he was appointed by President Lincoln Superintendent of Indian Affairs for California. He located the Hoopa Indian Reservation in August, 1864, which virtually terminated the Indian war that had been going on in the counties of Trinity, Klamath and Humboldt, for a few years.

In 1865 he bought a one-fourth interest in the San Francisco *Morning Call*, and occupied a position on the editorial staff for a little more than one year, during which period he served for four months, by appointment, as School Director for the Eleventh Ward. He sold his interest in the *Call* in 1866, and removed back to Humboldt, where he engaged in lumbering, merchandising, and farming with varied success until December, 1880, when he assumed control of the *Arcata Leader*, which he published for one year. On the 21st of December, 1881, he, in company with Will L. Heney, commenced the publication of the daily and weekly *Telephone*, in which business he is engaged at the present time, and which is described elsewhere.

JOEL SCOTT WHITMORE.

Joel Scott Whitmore was born in Oceanville, Hancock County, Maine, where he had a good opportunity to learn the details of lumbering, continuing there till 1852, when he came to California, stopping in Trinity County, where he resumed his former occupation of lumbering. The first business he engaged in was a job of logging for Messrs. Sturdivant & Whitmore. We next hear of him in Humboldt County, in 1861, locating on Bear River Ridge, engaged in raising cattle and dairying. He rented a farm for two years of Joel Burnell, one mile from Hydesville. Afterwards rented for two years, the Langdon Mill, near Hydesville. He then started a team for freight, which he followed for two years. He then rented a place of Sturdivant & Whitmore for two years, a ranch and mill property.

He soon after took up a ranch just outside of the redwood country in the Bald Hills, where he rented 2,000 sheep of Salmon Brown for two years; in the meantime he bought 2,000 acres of land contiguous to the Brown Ranch; cultivates fifty acres for hay; keeps a feed stable and public house.

This place is forty-three miles from Eureka, thirty from Hookton, the nearest shipping point, eighteen from Hydesville, and four from Bridgeville Post-office. A daily mail passes each way on the overland route.

Mr. Whitmore says the county was kept back from settlement up to 1870. Previous to that date stock was killed and run off, houses robbed and many lives lost, making improvements or permanent settlements very hazardous; since that date that section has progressed rapidly.

Mr. Whitmore has now one of the most valuable farms in that part of the county. His residence is in a beautiful locality, at the foot of a mountain covered with a dense growth of forest, the whole forming one of our best views, to which attention is called. He keeps 2,000 sheep, and usually a dozen horses and twelve cows, besides hogs and poultry. He cultivates about fifty acres, the balance being used for his stock. His orchard consists of 125 trees, all young and of all varieties, such as apple, peach, plum, cherries, apricots and prunes.

They have had children as follows: Frank Leland, Lowena Frances, Carrie Agnes, Anna Louisa, Myrtle, Willie Edwin, and Joel Cushman Whitmore.

ABNER DOBLE.

Abner Doble did the first blacksmith work on Humboldt Bay, where he landed August 1, 1850. He had a small shop somewhere about where Eurk a now stands, but no streets were laid out. He made an ox-yoke ring and staple for J. Ryan, and received fifty dollars for it. Since that time rings and staples have come down in price! Abner Doble was born in Shelby County, Indiana, and reached San Francisco June 25, 1850. He went to Humboldt Bay and returned with a load of lumber, which he sold on thirty days' credit, and at the end of that time the purchaser failed. Being without means he was unable to return to Humboldt as he intended, and went to work in San Francisco. He was prospered and now conducts a large iron establishment at 13 and 15 Fremont Street. He is the owner of a large ranch of 15,000 acres in Fresno County, where he has spent a great deal of money in introducing water and preparing the land for market.

W. F. HUESTIS.

The subject of this sketch, an early pioneer, and the present Secretary of the Society of Humboldt Pioneers, was born in Buckingham County, Virginia, July 24, 1836. Like most old Californians, Mr. Huestis has experienced the ups and downs of pioneer life in its varied forms. With him exposure, trials, struggles, fortunes and misfortunes have not been strangers. In 1843 his father, the Hon. A. J. Huestis, moved with his family to Mt. Pleasant, Iowa. An institution of higher learning, of which he was the founder, and now known as the Iowa Wesleyan University, admitted the son to the advantages of early intellectual training, and supplied those educational equipments with which, as a mere lad, he was to enter on the new sphere about to be opened to him on these distant shores.

By the overland route, in the great exodus of '49 to California, he made the toilsome journey, and arrived at Sonoma late in the fall of the same year. Early in the spring of the following year, he was again on the move, and in June, 1850, with his father, located in Humboldt County, where, with a slight exception, of time, he has resided ever since. The dangers and hardships of travel, and the trials of pioneer life, were not lost in their influence on his character. Though but a mere boy, not unfrequently had devolved on him the duties of a man. He had been taught to share the risks and responsibilities of 2,000 miles of a wilderness journey, and the early development of his mental manhood, and robust self-reliance, was but the natural offspring of rugged experience during this formative period of his active life. At the age of twenty-one Mr. Huestis visited Santa Clara County, where he was engaged to teach in one of the district schools of that county. Fulfilling this engagement and returning to Humboldt, he again engaged as teacher in one of the public schools.

About this time he was selected by a nominating convention as a candidate for the office of Superintendent of Common Schools for Humboldt County, and, although the ballot did not record a popular victory, yet he won a compliment for himself under defeat, by the display of an energy and tact in the canvass that would have been creditable to maturer years.

With an ambition that was not content to be idle in the ranks of private life, Mr. Huestis soon became identified with local politics, in which he always took an active part. As a field more favorable to his desire for political observations, and for more enlarged experience in public affairs, Mr. Huestis, at the commencement of the session of the Legislature of 1859-60, paid a visit to the State Capitol. Without the usual help of an extended acquaintance with its members, or the prestige which personal influence or political affiliations as a pronounced partisan might give, but by a tact and affability all his own, he secured a situation in the organization of the Senate, that introduced him to a succession of appointments in the State Legislature, from year to year, only ending in 1877.

In 1865-66, Mr. Huestis was Deputy Clerk of the United States Circuit Court and U. S. Commissioner at San Francisco.

In 1867, his name was submitted for nomination as State Senator from the Twenty-seventh Senatorial District, comprising the counties of Humboldt, Klamath and Del Norte, Hon. L. H. March being the rival candidate. An obstinate ballot for two or three successive days resulted as it had begun, with a tie vote; Mr. Huestis, in the interest of what might be considered as a concession due to an older candidate, authorized the withdrawal of his name, and thus broke the dead-lock that threatened the harmony of the party. Mr. March was then unanimously nominated, and no one entered the campaign more vigorously for his election than Mr. Huestis.

About this time he received from Governor Haight the appointment of Assistant Adjutant-General of the National Guard of California, with the rank of Major, which position he held for two years.

In 1877, Mr. Huestis became the nominee of the Republican party for the Assembly; but the extended prevalence of the "Dolly Varden" defection in the Republican ranks, and the sharp antagonisms engendered in the contest for nomination were unfavorable to his success, and the result was the election of his rival. To one of less perseverance these adverse experiences might have persuaded to retirement; but no such alternative occupied his thoughts. The active arena of politics had now developed a surer balance and command of his own powers, and the several occasions wherein he had experienced defeat in the past, were but preparatory steps rendering his success more certain in the future. An intercourse and contact with public men for nearly twenty years had given him a pretty good chance to form correct opinions concerning them, and probably convinced him that certain opportunities being offered, he might, with equal, if not greater claim to fitness, fill a position of higher trust and dignity than he had yet sought. That opportunity soon came. In 1878 a Convention for the revision of the State Constitution had been authorized by a law passed by the preceding Legislature. Mr. Huestis matured his plans and admitted but few to his counsels. The result was that he received the nomination from the Non-partisan Convention for the Third Congressional District, as one of the delegates at large, to the Constitutional Convention, and was elected. To the tempest of abuse and envious detraction which fairly blistered its own tongue in the intensity of its personal venom, showered upon him by his enemies during the canvass, Mr. Huestis paid but little attention. He had no weapons to soil in an engagement of that character, but chose to wait the coming occasion, when by addressing himself to the grave demands for intelligent action on propositions involved in framing the organic law of the State, he might silence the flippancy of petty political opponents, and compel from envy a just recognition to merit.

In the organization of the Convention Mr. Huestis was

assigned to a membership on two of its committees: "*Education*" and "*On Pardoning Power*." He introduced the first proposition before that body on Revenue and Taxation, and some of the best features of Article XIII. of the New Constitution relating to that subject, were adopted as presented by him. On frequent occasions during the protracted session, he brought to his service on the floor of discussion, the fruits of conscientious study and close application, which always commanded the attention of his hearers.

Imbued with right principles, and showing himself a clever manager and practical parliamentarian, he was justly regarded by his associates, and the representatives of the press, having seats assigned them in the Convention, as well able to sustain the dignity of his place. As will be seen by this brief sketch of his life, Mr. Huestis has known what it is to meet and overcome difficulties, and to win success. From the close of the Convention to the present time he has abstained from active political affairs, devoting his attention to those private interests, which, long neglected, now demanded his closest business care.

In 1861, Mr. Huestis was married to Miss Amanda, daughter of Captain J. C. Bull, of Arcata. He now resides in the city of Eureka.

JOHN ANDREW WATSON.

John A. Watson, a pioneer and prominent citizen of Humboldt County, reached California in October, 1851, having left Brunswick, Maine, for the then distant shores of the Pacific, taking the Nicaragua route and reaching San Francisco in thirty days.

He was born in Dover, New Hampshire, December, 1829, and experienced the usual trials of boyhood days and early manhood, in his New England home.

Following the usual plan pursued by new-comers at that day, he proceeded to the mines of El Dorado County, in search of a fortune, and after spending some time about Mud Springs he went to Trinity County, where he resided from February, 1852 until July, 1863.

He entered the United States service in July, 1863, and continued until the close of the war, and was mustered out at Old Fort Humboldt in 1865. A view of this noted fort is given in our frontispiece.

He was elected County Clerk of Humboldt in 1868 and served for six years, until 1874.

At the close of his term as Clerk he was appointed Deputy Collector of Customs for that district, which position he now occupies. During his official life, by his strict fidelity and faithfulness he secured the highest esteem and confidence of all in whose society his duties have brought him. He is also engaged in the real estate and insurance business in Eureka.

In 1868 he married Annie E. Seaman, a native of New York, and sister of Harry Seaman, Esq. They have one child, Nellie Watson.

WALTER VAN DYKE.

Walter Van Dyke, who was connected with the Humboldt *Times* in 1856-78, is a lawyer by profession. Coming to Humboldt County during its earliest history, he practiced in the courts until he purchased an interest in the *Times*. The publication of the paper interfered with the practice of his profession, and he was compelled to give up the former. He served as District Attorney of the county in 1855. In 1861 he represented Humboldt, Mendocino and Del Norte Counties in the State Senate. In 1863 he removed from Humboldt County to San Francisco, where he would have a wider field in the practice of his profession. He now resides in East Oakland, and has a law office in San Francisco.

L. M. BURSON.

L. M. Burson was one of the first settlers of Humboldt County, having arrived on the first vessel that ever crossed Humboldt Bar, the schooner *Laura Virginia*, in April, 1850. He was elected District Attorney in 1856 and again in 1858, and represented the county in the Legislature in 1859.

PIONEERS OF TABLE BLUFF.

Amongst those who came to Table Bluff during the years 1852-53, were N. Dupero, who located the claim furthest west on the bluff, and after improving and occupying it seven years, moved to San Francisco.

The next place located on the bay side of the bluff was that of J. D. Mires, and was known as Mires' Landing, a shipping place to and from Eureka. Mires sold and went to San Diego. Captain Wright, an old man, preëmpted the shipping point on the south side of the bluff for freight to and from Eel River. Wright's mind became deranged and he wandered off and died. His body was found some five or six months after. Richard Wolfenden occupied the claim adjoining on the east. He went to Mexico. Elisha Clark joined Mires on the east. Captain Johnston kept the lighthouse a few years and died. The adjoining claims were those of G. H. Brown, William Espie and Allen Hawks.

FIRST HOTEL AT TABLE BLUFF.

The first hotel was kept by John Van Arenam, which at that time was the only hotel south of Eureka, and was largely patronized, as many as fifty being at dinner at one time. Van Arenam and wife were buried a few rods from the house. The oldest daughter married at the age of thirteen and the other at fourteen, and both now reside in the county.

Jackson Sawyer owns the claim next north of the last mentioned, which is described elsewhere. J. P. Alboe located south of Jones' Landing. He with two others graded a track for a railroad for lumbering purposes in the timber north of Salmon Creek. He was killed by the Indians.

Two miles southeast of the bluffs were the claims of C. Garrett, who afterwards went to the mines, and E. Bulkeley, who was Sheriff of Humboldt County in 1872-75.

Sketches of Prominent Citizens.

HON. JOHN P. HAYNES.

JOHN P. HAYNES, the present Superior Judge of Humboldt County, was born in Breckinridge County, Kentucky, on the 3d day of December, 1826. In his childhood, his mother, then a widow, removed to Elizabethtown, Hardin County, Kentucky, where he was raised and educated. In his seventeenth year he entered a store as a clerk and salesman, in which business he continued for almost three years. About this time the Mexican war broke out, and the young men of the county at once proceeded to organize a company of volunteers for the service. The subject of this notice took an active part in organizing the company, and was elected Lieutenant. The quota of the State was filled so quickly after the call of the Governor, that this company with scores of others was rejected. Young Haynes with ten or twelve others of his company then joined Company C, Capt. Rowan Hardin, which was attached to the 4th Kentucky Volunteers, under command of Col. John S. Williams, more popularly known as "Cerro Gordo Williams," from his gallantry in the battle fought at that place. He remained in the service until the close of the war. On his return home he commenced the study of law, and in due time entered the law department of the University of Louisville, and graduated in 1851.

A few months afterwards he started for California, via the Isthmus, and arrived in this State early in 1852. He remained in San Francisco a short time, and then started for the northern part of the State, arriving in Klamath County in the spring of that year. During the summer and fall he was engaged in mining on the Klamath.

At the election in November of that year, he was elected District Attorney of the County.

In 1853, he removed to Crescent City, which about that time became the county seat. Here he commenced the practice of his profession, and was re-elected District Attorney. Upon the removal of the county seat to Orleans Bar, he resigned the office.

Upon the organization of Del Norte County soon afterwards, was elected District Attorney of the new county. He continued in the practice of his profession in Del Norte and Klamath until 1858, when he became a candidate for District Judge, and was defeated by Hon. William R. Turner, by a majority of two votes. The following year he was elected Senator by a large majority, from the 12th Senatorial District, composed of the counties of Del Norte, Klamath and Siskiyou. At the expiration of his term, he resumed the practice of his profession in Del Norte, meantime making some ventures in mining without much success.

On the 1st day of February, 1868, he was appointed, by Governor Haight, District Judge of the 8th Judicial District, composed of the counties of Klamath, Humboldt and Del Norte, to fill a vacancy occasioned by the resignation of Judge Turner.

He was elected by the people to the same office at the Judicial election, in 1869, and re-elected in 1875. He held the office of District Judge until it was abolished by the New Constitution, and at the first election under the new instrument was elected Superior Judge of Humboldt County, which office he now holds. In politics the Judge is a Democrat, not ultra in his views, and has abstained from taking an active part in politics since he has been on the bench. To this fact, in some measure, may be attributed his repeated election to office, in a district with a large political majority against him.

In June, 1869, he removed with his family, consisting of his wife and daughter, to Eureka, the county seat of Humboldt County, where he now resides.

LOUIS T. KINSEY.

L. T. Kinsey is the present faithful Treasurer of Humboldt County, to which responsible office he was elected in September, 1877. Proving to be the right man in the right place, he was re-elected in 1879, and his term of office will expire January 1, 1883.

Mr. Kinsey is a native Californian, having been born in Yreka, Siskiyou County, December 17, 1852, where he resided until 1857, when his parents moved to Humboldt County and located a stock ranch near Centerville, where they remained about two years when they removed to the town of Eureka where he has since resided.

Mr. Kinsey engaged in the drug business in Eureka and continued in that line two years. He then associated with W. J. McNamara in the clothing business under the firm name of McNamara & Kinsey.

He married Miss Jenny Hart in 1872, who was a native of Santa Cruz County, in this State. They have one child Charles H. Kinsey.

J. B. CASTERLIN.

The subject of this sketch has charge of the public schools of Humboldt County, under whose able administration they are in a flourishing condition.

He was born February 22, 1845, in Seneca County, New York. His early life was spent on a farm, but he eventually drifted west, and resided for a short time in Michigan, Iowa, and Nebraska. He left Fremont, Nebraska, in January, 1872, and came to California by railroad. He made his home in Hydesville and engaged in teaching there until 1881. He then moved to Arcata, where he has since resided.

He married Miss M. A. Reed in 1871. She was also a native of New York.

JOHN SMITH THOMSON.

J. S. Thomson is the efficient County Clerk of Humboldt. He was appointed to fill the office of County Assessor of Klamath County in 1862. He was elected to the same position and served in 1863–64. He was the only Republican ever elected.

While discharging his duties he was obliged to have an escort on account of the dangers from Indian attacks, who were at that time very hostile. He filled his office creditably and removed to Arcata in 1865, accepting a position in a store as clerk, where he continued to reside until 1879. That year he was elected by the Workingmen's party to the office of County Clerk, which he now holds.

J. S. Thomson was born in Lawrence County, Pennsylvania, June 9, 1833. At the age of fifteen he began to learn the carpenter's trade. He went to Iowa in 1852, and in 1859 he set out for California with ox-train, consuming six months' time on the road and arrived at Orleans Bar, October 4, 1859. He engaged in mining and ferrying at that place on the Klamath River. The ferry was washed out in the flood of 1861.

He was prominently identified with Klamath County and its interests until he came to this county in 1865. He proves an honest and efficient officer and stands high in the estimation of the citizens of Humboldt.

C. WAMGATT.

Capt. C. Wasgatt, a well-known resident of Hydesville, first became acquainted with this county in March, 1851, when he was wrecked on Humboldt Bar, in the schooner *Susan Warkwell*, which was the same vessel in which he came from Massachusetts. Two passengers and the cook were lost, but Mr. Wasgatt escaped unharmed, after remaining in the water fourteen hours on the wreck. Soon after he located in Eel River Valley.

Captain Wasgatt was born in Mt. Desert, Hancock County, Maine, August 28, 1801. He was born on a farm and followed various occupations until he was twenty-three years of age when he shipped as a sailor before the mast, and followed sea-life. He was promoted to Captain of the schooner *Bangor* in 1828, which was wrecked the following year. He afterwards shipped as mate, and soon after as Captain undertook successfully several hazardous voyages.

He left Salem, Massachusetts, as Captain of the *Susan Warkwell*, for San Francisco, and came around Cape Horn, making the trip in one hundred and fifty-three days, reaching San Francisco in the spring of 1850. He followed coasting until wrecked as stated.

After settling in Humboldt he followed farming until about 1866, when he sold his farm and went to reside with his daughters in Hydesville, where he now makes his home.

He was married April 12, 1832, to Miss Betsy M. Bowditch, of Salem, Massachusetts. They have lost one child, named Ellen, and the following are living: Sarah Ann, Louise, Cornelius, and Abbie Wasgatt.

A. BERDING.

In Ferndale we can also find the fine residence of one of the pioneers of California; a "forty-niner," as the people call him. Mr. A. Berding owns several houses and lots in the town, and 765 acres of land (partly timber and partly farming land of good quality), outside the city limits. No one passing through Ferndale can fail to notice the nice store belonging to Mr. Berding; he is one of the most prosperous merchants in the county.

Mr. Berding's family consists of his wife, formerly Mrs. M. M. Blum, of Germany, and five children, three of them, viz.: Josephine Gertrude, Clement Robert, and Christina Sophia, being his own, and two, viz, Henry C. and Lena Blum, those of his wife of a former husband.

Mr. Berding was born in Oldenburg, Germany, December 8, 1827. His father was a farmer, but he attended school until thirteen years of age, when he went into a store as a clerk, where he remained until nineteen years of age. He left then and went to Rio Janeiro (South America), where he clerked for two years, after which, April 14, 1849, he and two of his friends chartered the Bremen brig *Adelgunde*, Captain Beling commander, and loaded her with merchandise, which they intended to sell in San Francisco, thus showing an enterprising and wide awake business spirit. They had also goods belonging to several other merchants of Rio Janeiro on board. The trip was pleasant, they rounded the Horn in safety, with the exception that the vessel leaked some, so that the sailors were obliged to pump "for dear life," as Mr. Berding says, and arrived in San Francisco, September 15, 1849. There Mr. Berding sold his merchandise and went to mining in Tuolumne County. In 1852 he made a short trip to Mexico, returning the same year, and afterwards kept on mining until 1856, when he retired with fair success.

In 1857 Mr. Berding came to this county, where he kept a store in Centreville; in 1864 he went to Oregon, where he stayed one year, and in 1866 he settled at his present abode where he is still engaged in general merchandising.

HENRY HYDE TICKNOR.

Traveling through Humboldt County by the "overland route" and stopping at Blocksburg, the traveler will receive a cordial welcome and the best of accommodations for man and beast, at the Blocksburg Hotel, which is owned by the subject of this sketch, Henry H. Ticknor.

In the genial proprietor of that mansion, the strangers and the people of California can greet one of the oldest pioneers of this State, whose history may prove interesting to many readers of our book.

Mr. Ticknor was born in Washington County, New York in 1814, where in his early youth, he occupied his time partly in school, partly in working on his father's farm, and in boating on Lake Champlain. The last of these occupations struck his particular fancy; for when fifteen years of age he went out to follow the life of a sailor. He remained such for twenty years, until August 4, 1849, when he arrived in San Francisco, as mate of the bark *Strafford* (which belonged to the New

J. P. Haynes
SUPERIOR JUDGE

T. M. Brown
SHERIFF

T. F. Thomson
CLERK

OFFICERS OF HUMBOLDT COUNTY 1882.

J. B. Casterlin
SUPT. OF SCHOOLS

L. F. Kinsey
TREASURER

G. H. Shaw
ASSESSOR

York Mining Company, and was afterwards used as a prison ship at Sacramento). Capt. Wm. L. Cullin was the commander.

The trip from New York was very pleasant and interesting, for the bark stopped at St. Catherine's and San Juan Fernandez Islands, where all on board paid a visit to Alexander Selkirk's Cave, all of which proved a good subject for "Robinson Crusoe."

At San Francisco, Mr. Ticknor lost his fancy for the sea for a while, the gold fever taking a hold on him. He accordingly went to mining on Dry Creek, Sonorian Camp, where he had very good success, averaging an ounce a day. When the rainy season commenced, he again went to sea, in the ship *Pacific*, staying this time two years on board.

In 1852, Mr. Ticknor came to this county, where he determined to settle for good. He occupied himself with agriculture, for twenty years in Bucksport Township, then went to Hydesville, and finally, after four years' sojourn there, came to his present home where he has ever since resided.

While in Hydesville he owned a farm of 170 acres which he traded off for a sheep ranch of 960 acres, called "Neapes' Peak Ranch," twelve miles from Blocksburg. After four years he kept a hotel in Akler Point, where he stayed two years.

Although there were many troubles with the Indians from 1860 until 1870, he never had any difficulty with them. The Chief, "Coon Skin," was friendly and protected him from all depredations, not even losing a single head of cattle through all the troubles.

Mr. Ticknor owns a farm of 160 acres, besides his hotel, which he bought in July, 1881. His property is so well known for its excellency, that we need not make any further remarks.

Mr. Ticknor was married in 1850, to Miss Martha Creen, of London, England, whose good judgment and industry does much in adding to their prosperity.

BENJAMIN BLOCKBURGER.

Our readers cannot fail to notice the view of the village of Blocksburg, named from its founder, Mr. B. Blockburger, an enterprising merchant and business man.

Mr. Blockburger is a native of Hillsborough, Illinois, where he was born May 1, 1828, and brought up until eighteen years of age, when he enlisted in the Third Regiment of Illinois Volunteers, with which he went down to the Rio Grande. Afterwards he lived in several of the Southern States until 1853, when he stopped at St. Joseph, Missouri.

Mr. Blockburger was married in 1850 to Mrs. Margaret Harkey, of North Carolina. She died in 1852.

In the spring of 1853, he joined a train going to California; they set out April 10, 1853, and stopped at Sink of Humboldt, where he remained with the worn-out cattle for six weeks, while his train went on. He then started on foot towards Placerville, where he arrived six hours ahead of the teams August 26, 1853.

Mr. Blockburger mined in several places with fair success until 1866, at which time he came to this county, where he first engaged in ranching and dairying. In July, 1872, he started the business in Blocksburg, where he built the first house the year before. He has been engaged in general merchandising and wool-buying ever since, and is the prominent citizen of that section.

DOMINGO ZANONE.

Another worthy citizen, of whom this county can justly be proud, is Mr. Domingo Zanone, who lives near Petrolia. His farm consists of 4,550 acres. School and church within about four miles.

It is within thirty miles of water communication and forty miles of the county seat. The land is splendid pasture ground, mostly rolling hills, and part of it which is cultivated produces good hay and vegetables. There is also a small orchard attached to it.

Mr. Zanone's home affords a splendid view of the ocean and is presided over by his wife, who is a native of Italy, and to whom he was married in 1874. Her maiden name was Miss M. Madalena Ghio. She is the mother of three girls, all of them are living.

Mr. Zanone has seen a great deal of this world; he was born in Genoa, Italy, March 9, 1828. He followed farming until he was grown up and about to be drafted into the army; not wishing to fight the battles of crowned heads, he said adieu to his native country and went to the United States, where his father had gone before, and returned to Italy in order to send all his sons to the United States. While in the East he worked in a foundry at Pittsburg, Pennsylvania.

He left New York October 18, 1849, in a sailing vessel, for California. It took him eight months to accomplish the trip on account of sundry misfortunes which we will briefly relate: The vessel made a stop at Rio de Janeiro, Valparaiso, and Chili. At Rio de Janeiro the vessel sprung a leak and yellow fever was so bad that the captain returned two-thirds of the passage money to the passengers, who took passage in a packet-line to Buenos Ayres and from there crossed the Pampas Plains and Andes Mountains to Valparaiso, making the trip in forty days. There they took passage for San Francisco where they arrived ninety-three days after, June 1, 1850.

The first job in California was to pack bricks at $1 per hour. He worked two days in that capacity, then started for the gold mines, at Oroville; afterwards he bought some stock in the White Rock Flume Company, but was swindled out of all of his money. After residing in Sierra County for awhile he again went to Oroville, where he mined for seven years with very good success; but losing again most of his money, he stopped mining in 1857 with $10,000 and purchased a farm on Dry Creek, Butte County, where he raised stock.

In 1865 he came to this county. He was the first person

who drove stock down the coast. He is still engaged in stock-raising, owning at present 1,000 cattle, twelve horses, and five mules.

He is also a stockholder in the Humboldt County Bank, and part owner of the steamer *Ferndale*. He is very generous in promoting all public enterprises, and an honorable citizen.

ALEXANDER GILMORE.

The residence of Mr. Alexander Gilmore, situated in the city of Eureka, is an ornament to the city and forms one of our illustrations. The owner, the subject of this sketch, was born in St. George, New Brunswick. At the age of thirteen he was thrown on his own resources, but with only his hands as sole capital, he has succeeded, through thrift, energy, and hard toil, to secure a competency.

He left New Brunswick in 1850, on a bark which made the trip to San Francisco in about six months. The voyage was rough, but pleasant, and the bark arrived safely at her destination in June, 1850.

Mr. Gilmore went straightway to the mines, but had poor success, so in 1852 he directed his steps to this county where he took up fine timber lands. He owns now 960 acres of good redwood timber land on Mad River and 240 acres on Jacoby Creek.

Mr. Gilmore is one of the well-known men in this county, and is log surveyor for the county, appointed by the Supervisors, who put unlimited trust in him. He is married and has six children, four boys and two girls. His wife is also a native of New Brunswick. His children are named Daniel, Jennie, Carrie, Frederick, William and James Gilmore.

FRANKLIN Z. BOYNTON.

The subject of this sketch was born December 28, 1828, in the town of Weathersfield, Winsor County, Vermont, and lived upon a large farm near Black River; remained upon the old homestead until 1846, then went to Boston, Massachusetts, and remained there until 1849.

February 3, 1849, sailed from Boston harbor in the bark *Drummond* for California, via Cape Horn; in fifty days from time she left Boston, made the harbor of Rio Janeiro, where he remained three weeks, and had the privilege of seeing the Emperor, Dom Pedro, his palace, Floral Gardens, and other public buildings. At Callao saw the ruins of the old city of Callao which was destroyed by an earthquake. Also, visited the City of Lima, and the famous cathedral built by Pazarro Emanuel.

In August, 1849, he arrived in San Francisco, and then to Sacramento, which was then a city of tents and framed buildings covered with cloth; from Sacramento went to a place then called Mormon Island, on the American River, where he engaged in mining for two or three months.

He was taken sick with lung fever and returned to San Francisco, where he remained until the spring of 1850, and then went to the old Mission of San Jose and rented land and farmed upon a small scale, raising mostly vegetables, which were sold in San Francisco in the fall, at the rate of twelve and a half cents per pound for potatoes, fifty cents per head for cabbages, and other things proportionately high.

He tried farming in San Joaquin County, but the season proved too dry. He was there when the famous bandit and horse thief Joaquin was making his raids; had all his stock stolen by him; sold out in the fall and went to Crystal Spring Valley, in San Mateo County, where he was engaged in farming for five years. Being unable to secure a valid title to the land at that time, it being held under a Spanish grant, he abandoned the place in 1857, and moved to Humboldt County and located on Eel River Island, where he has followed the occupation of farming to the present time.

His farm consists of 300 acres of rich bottom-land, situated between Eel River and Salt River, bordering on Salt River. It is four miles from Ferndale, and nineteen from the county seat; the land is all level, the soil clay loam; average crop of wheat, forty-five bushels per acre, highest yield, eighty bushels; average crop of oats per acre, seventy-five bushels; highest yield, 130. He has 225 acres under cultivation, balance in pasture and timber. There are 500 fruit trees upon the place, consisting of apple, plum, pear, cherry, etc. He usually keeps twenty head of cattle, fifteen horses, fifty sheep, and seventy-five hogs.

He was married to Miss Emily Ann Kinneston February 7, 1850, have four children living, three boys and one girl, by this marriage, Rollin Dewan, Franklin Hirani, Cyrus Harvey, and Annie Harriet Boynton. His wife died February 9, 1876, and he again married May 10, 1877, Mrs. Malvina M. Morgan.

CHARLES F. ROBERTS.

C. F. Roberts is another of the prominent citizens of Eureka, and is Register of the United States Land Office at the present time. He was appointed such in January, 1872, re-appointed February 15, 1876, and again February 15, 1880.

He is a man who has worked his way up in the world by his own energy and unaided efforts. At present he owns a farm of 3,500 acres, forty miles from Eureka, and another of 1,360 acres within twenty miles. He raises stock on those farms, usually keeping forty head of cattle, 2,500 sheep, five horses and two mules. The land which is partly cultivated produces an average crop of oats, barley, potatoes and corn, and the orchard of 100 trees, a variety of fruit. His residence (of which we have made an illustration) is in Eureka.

Mr. Roberts was born in Hartland, Somerset County, Maine, April 7, 1843. In his youth he attended school in the winter time and worked on the farm during the summer. In 1861 he enlisted in the Second Maine Regiment to serve his country in the late civil war. In 1863, being honorably discharged from the army, he left Bangor, Maine, for New York, which city he left the day of the great riot, June 13, 1863, for California. He came via Panama, and arrived in San Francisco, August 12, 1863. In September of that year he went to Carson City, where he was employed in a lumber yard.

In 1866 Mr. Roberts came to this county and went to work as a common laborer, in the woods. Since that time he has risen to his present standing and is a valuable acquisition to the county.

In 1863 he was married to Miss Alesia J. Bragg, a native of Maine. They have three children named: Ida A., Guy L., and George Fred. Roberts.

THOMAS BAIR.

In the beautiful village of Arcata, stands the pleasant home of Mr. and Mrs. Thomas Bair, and their children, Thomas and Fred. Bair. The residence is finely situated and constructed of modern style with neat yard and surroundings. It commands many fine views of the surrounding country and Humboldt Bay; Eureka can be seen in the distance.

Mrs. Bair was born January 1, 1854, her maiden name was Allie Boyne, she was married to Mr. Bair in 1876.

Mr. Bair was born September 26, 1844, he is a Missourian by birth, and was brought up on a farm. When nine years old he lost both his parents, and soon after came, via Truckee route, out to California, in company with his uncle, where he arrived at Red Bluff in the fall of 1853.

Mr. Bair was first engaged in packing from Red Bluff to the mines, he afterwards resided in Idaho and Montana, and in the fall of 1867 located in Arcata where he now resides.

Mr. Bair is proprietor of a store at Fort Gaston, situated on the Klamath River, he also has a place of business in Arcata. As he is still engaged in packing to the interior, he owns a fine lot of pack-mules, 170 in number. It may be amusing and interesting to our readers, to read a little description of such a train, we will therefore give a short sketch of one. There are generally from twenty to fifty mules in a train, it takes about one man to ten mules, and when everything is ready for a start it is highly amusing to see them loaded with goods of every description. One mule is always used for carrying the cooking utensils and is called the "kitchen mule."

SAMUEL STRONG.

Mr. S. Strong is a native of Ohio. When four years old, in 1827, his parents moved to Illinois, where his father took an interest in the lead mines and erected a mill. Mr. Strong, Jr., stayed with his parents until 1850, and assisted his father in business, he then came across the continent, per mule and horse train to Placerville, where he arrived, after a three months' journey, July 29, 1850. He mined at different places with poor success until 1853, when he came to this county, where he engaged in farming at different places until 1877, when he moved to his present home.

His wife, formerly Miss Maria G. Johnson, he married October 6, 1858; she is a native of New Hampshire; they have one daughter, married.

A BEAUTIFUL PLEASURE RESORT.

The readers of our book must not omit to look at the illustration representing a Humboldt County pleasure resort, of which Mr. Samuel Strong is the enterprising proprietor.

The place comprises an area of 426 acres, it is situated ten miles from Hydesville and thirty-five miles from Eureka. The Overland Stage delivers and takes mail for Eureka and San Francisco daily. As a summer residence for invalids and pleasure seekers it has no equal in the county. It is delightfully situated on the east side of Van Duzen River, up in the redwoods, above the fog belt, where fishing and hunting can be had in abundance. The house has a large parlor with organ, etc., and seventeen sleeping rooms.

The accommodations are first-class, a very good table is set by the landlady, who supervises the cooking, and the traveler will always be welcomed by the landlord, Mr. Strong, who is ever willing and anxious to make it comfortable for his guests and their teams. A fine orchard is attached to the grounds, where fruit of several kinds can be had, it contains 100 trees, and shrubs for smaller fruits. The grounds which are beautifully laid out, are fixed for croquet games, etc., and swings can be found for the amusement of children.

EDWIN P. VANCE.

E. P. Vance, born in New Brunswick, August 21, 1836, was raised on a farm. When twenty-one years of age he concluded to go to California, and accordingly took passage and came via New York and Panama direct, making the trip in thirty-one days. He arrived in San Francisco November 1, 1858, and intended to go to the mines, as there was a great gold excitement at the time on Fraser River, a second thought though induced him to come to Eureka instead, and to start a saw-mill there. He did so with good success.

In 1861 Mr. Vance returned to New Brunswick and stayed four years, during which time he married, in 1863, Miss Mary Welch, of New Brunswick. Their children are named Esther E., Louis J., George P., Charles E., Mary, and Kate Vance.

Having once tried the climate of California, he could not resist his desire again to settle therein, and in 1865 he came again to Humboldt County, this time bringing his family with him. He settled where he lives now, within one quarter of a mile of Table Bluff Post-office, where he is engaged in farming.

His farm comprises 290 acres, located within eleven miles of the county seat, and is composed of loamy soil extending over valley and hills. The land will produce 75 bushels of barley and oats, 180 bushels of potatoes, 30 bushels of wheat, or 40 bushels of peas per acre.

He also owns an orchard of 300 trees, 14 head of cattle, 30 hogs, 12 horses and mules.

LEONARD S. HICKS.

Within two miles of Ferndale is the home, farm and residence of Mr. Leonard S. Hicks, who is a native of Vermont. Mr. Hicks came to this county April 8, 1854; he was first engaged as a mechanic, then went to the mines in October, 1855, where he worked for three years with good success; afterwards returned to Humboldt County and engaged in farming and stock raising for the last fifteen years, which he still follows.

His residence is pleasantly situated within one mile of Eel River, and four miles of the sea coast; He owns an orchard which yields all kinds of fruit and berries; and land which will yield as much as 100 bushels of oats per acre, and fifty bushels of wheat. The climate is one of the best in the State, the soil unsurpassed. The country is fine, forests of redwood abound, the hills offer splendid grazing grounds for the stock.

Mr. Hicks is married; his wife is a native of New York; they have one child named Leonard Hicks.

CLEMENT CHARTIN.

Not far from the Blue Lakes can be found the hotel and farm of Mr. Clement Chartin, a native of France. He is an energetic man, and has brought to himself a comfortable living by a close attention to business, hard work, and good judgment.

Mr. Chartin was born January 2, 1827. His parents were poor, and were obliged to make him work hard from the time he was twelve years old. He worked on the farm until he was twenty-three years old, living mostly on black bread of that country. He desired to see the world, and went to work as porter in a wholesale house for three years, then to Paris, where he worked as coachman for four years, then worked ten years for an English family; then traveled through most parts of Europe.

He next went to Egypt on the Suez Canal, where he kept a restaurant for two years, then went to Jerusalem, where he stayed for six weeks, then returned to Paris. There Mr. Chartin received some recommendations for New York. He left France on the steamer *William*, and on reaching New York took a position for three months at Delmonico's, the celebrated *restaurateur*. Afterwards he took a position with Mr. Frank Page, Congressman, at Washington, where he filled many times the glasses of many of our prominent men and foreign representatives with whom he could converse in French. He left Central City, Colorado, for San Francisco, where he arrived August 1, 1869.

In 1871 Mr. Chartin came to this county, where he is now engaged in farming and hotel business. He owns 300 acres of land of average good quality; also, a good orchard of a variety of fruits. His pleasure resort at Blue Lakes is described elsewhere.

In 1858 he married Miss Antoinelle Deschatre, a native of France.

DAVID R. ROBERTS.

David R. Roberts, the owner of "Robert's Hotel" in Ferndale, was born December 8, 1838, in Wales, England. When twelve years of age, his parents, who were respectable farmers, moved to Wisconsin, where they settled near Racine. Ten years after, in 1860, young Roberts joined an ox train going across the continent and arrived after a five months' journey, at Chico, Butte County, California.

Being brought up a farmer, he engaged in that worthy occupation first. He stayed in Chico four years, then moved to this county, where he at first tried boring for oil, near Petrolia, which proved a failure; so he moved to Ferndale in 1865, where he now resides. There he farmed at first, then started a livery and feed stable; in 1870 he opened the Ferndale Hotel, and after a successful run of two years, he leased it and attended to his stable only. In 1879 he built the "Robert's Hall, "and purchased a half-interest in the "Enterprise Sawmill," situated on Salt River, below Port Kenyon.

The hotel is well known, and is one of the best in the county. The host, J. W. McCollum, is always accommodating to his guests. He keeps two horses and a carriage at their disposal.

Mr. Roberts married Miss Mary Blanche Francis, of Nevada City, California, on March 17, 1868, but the following year she was taken away from her grief-stricken husband. After being a widower for two years, he married Miss Mary Pugh, a native of Wales, England. They have a son named Ellis Roberts and a daughter named Annie Roberts.

SALMON BROWN.

Near Bridgeville, we find the pleasantly situated house and large sheep ranch of Mr. Salmon Brown. The ranch consists of 3,340 acres, which is of a very good quality, and would produce large crops if Mr. Brown would use it for that purpose. As it is, it returns a large average of oats, and affords splendid grazing for Mr. Brown's 2,000 sheep and ten horses, and other stock. The county seat is within fifty miles, and water communication within forty miles.

Mr. Brown is a native of Hudson, Summit County, Ohio, where he was born October 2, 1830. He lived on a farm until eighteen years of age, when he started life on his own hook; going to Kansas, and from there to New York State, where he arrived in 1855, and married in 1857, his wife being a native of Essex County. Her maiden name was Miss Abbie C. Hinkley. Mr. Brown and wife stayed in her native county until 1863, when he had a longing to go West again, and consequently went to Iowa, from which State he, in 1864, emigrated to California. The trip overland per ox-team, was rather rough. They were six months coming, and twice in peril of losing their lives; first through outlaws, who gave them a hard chase, and the second time through a band of 250 Sioux, who fortunately did not attack them.

Mr. Brown and family arrived in Red Bluff, October 1, 1864, where he went to sheep raising with good success, but not being

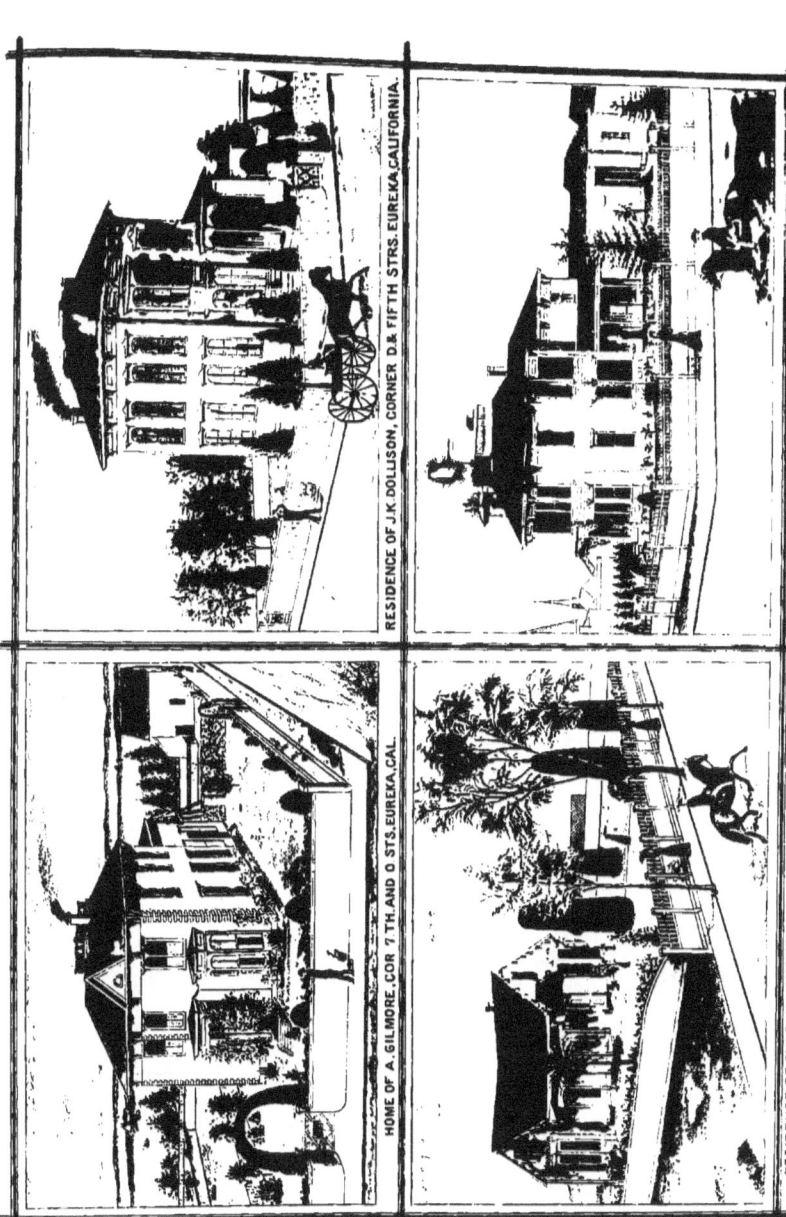

satisfied with the location there, he again moved to Tehama County, and in 1870, moved to his present home and farm. Mr. Brown's family consists of seven children, two boys and five girls, whose names are respectively: Minnie E., Inez, John, Edward, Ethel, Agnes S., and Nellie Brown.

THOMAS STEWART.

On the north bank of the Bear River, a short distance from Capetown Post-office in this county, we find a pleasant home and property which belongs to Thomas Stewart, who has taken great pains in beautifying the same.

As Mr. Stewart is kind and entertaining towards strangers, we took advantage of his hospitality, and, after viewing his farm, which is divided by the river, and contains 619 acres of splendid grazing land, sat down in order to listen to the story of his life, etc., which we will give here for the benefit of the citizens of his county.

Mr. Stewart is a native of Edinburgh, Scotland, where he was born December 9, 1827. At the early age of six years he went to sea as a cabin boy with his uncle, and at the age of eighteen he ran away from the ship while in Quebec, and went as a sailor before the mast for three years on the great lakes. Afterwards he worked for seven years in the coal mines of Illinois, then went to Cape Girardeau County, Missouri, where he stayed two years, and where he was financially ruined in 1862 by the soldiers of Jeff. Thomson.

Being compelled to start life anew, he set out from Illinois with an ox and horse train across the plains, via South Pass, for California, but spent the winter of 1863-64 in Ogden. In the spring of 1864 he continued on toward California, where he arrived at Hydesville in November, 1864.

Mr. Stewart has followed the business of dairying since he arrived in California, and now owns 100 fine dairy cows and twenty-five young cattle and nine horses. On his farm he has an orchard of 125 trees, bearing apples, pears, peaches, cherries and plums. He is a self-made man and has seen a great many hardships, such as only a sailor and frontiersman can see.

He has had many narrow escapes. At one time he undertook to rid the county of grizzly bears, being engaged for that job by Mr. Russ nearly two years; he slew a great many, and found them to be tough customers; into one of them he had to fire thirty-two bullets before he brought him down; it proved to be a very fat specimen.

Mr. Stewart married Miss Eliza Moorhead, a native of Ohio in 1852, and has one child, a girl named Emma E. Stewart.

ERNEST W. DENT.

In no other county of California have we met with as many men who have traveled over the greater part of the world, as in Humboldt County. Among them we may mention Ernest Wm. Dent, who can justly be proud of his experiences in life.

He was born in Calcutta, East India, in 1857. After receiving a liberal education, he served in a tea broker's office, in London, England, for nearly one year and a half. At the age of eighteen he left England for China, where he procured a position with the firm of Hohl & Co., of Amoy, Formosa. He left after three and a half years' service and went to Shanghai, where he worked during tea season. In 1878 he left Shanghai for Ceylon, where he was Assistant Superintendent of the celebrated Blackwater tea and coffee estate; which position he had to leave in 1879 on account of ill-health, the climate not agreeing with him.

He left Ceylon and came directly to Eureka, via Halifax and New York, making the whole trip in four months, and arriving in Eureka, April 26, 1880. He then went to his present home, which is situated within one and a half miles of Ferndale, and within twenty miles of the county seat. He owns 180 acres of land, and occupies himself at present with dairying, owning twenty-five head of cattle, two hogs and eight horses.

Mr. Dent thinks of experimenting as soon as he can get the seeds, to see if he cannot grow tea in this county. He understands the business thoroughly, and we wish he may succeed and give this county the honor of being the first in the United States which produces this valuable article.

Mr. Dent was married to Miss Laura Ferrill, of this county, in 1881.

CHARLES A. DOE.

A short distance from Petrolia is situated the residence and farm of Mr. Chas. A. Doe. It is on the west side of the north fork of the Mattole River (see illustration). The location is very healthy, free from extreme heat or cold.

The farm consists of 1,070 acres of land, forty of which are cultivated and the rest used as pasture land for Mr. Doe's stock, consisting of some 100 head of cattle, fifteen horses and two mules. There is also an orchard of 100 fruit-bearing trees on the land, part apples the rest in pears.

Mr. Doe, who has had a good many ups and downs in life at various occupations which we will describe further on, is now peacefully settled and surrounded by an interesting family of five children named: Charles P., Annie L., Susan N., Blandie M., and Nelson H. Doe.

His history is as follows: Born on a farm near Windsor, Kennebec County, Maine, January 29, 1839; he left it when fourteen years of age; worked for two and a half years at the tanner's trade, and after finishing his apprenticeship went to Mobile, where he assisted in getting out a raft of cypress for that town.

In 1858 he went as a sailor, but after arriving in Portland, Maine, got tired of a sailor's life and made arrangements to go to California. He made the trip to San Francisco via Panama in twenty-four days. It was an unpleasant trip; three passengers died on the way.

At first Mr. Doe went into the lumber business, and soon after went to Dogtown, Butte County, then to Chico Ridge, where he built and run a saw-mill for one and a half years, when it was destroyed by fire. He then left for his old home in Maine, December, 1861, where he married a year later, Miss Hannah S. Noyes, with whom he moved to Pennsylvania, where he located on Oil Creek, near Titusville.

In 1864 Mr. Doe set out for California again, and arriving in San Francisco, he made his home in Oakland for one year and then came to Humboldt County, where he now resides. He tried to bore for oil near Petrolia at first, but when he did not even get water after boring 1,400 feet deep, he gave up the attempt and went into stock-raising and farming, which proved to be a profitable undertaking.

HORACE S. CASE.

Mr. Horace S. Case, whose home is also illustrated in this book, is another of the so-called self-made men of the coast. He says: Since thirteen years of age I was obliged to "hew my own timber;" but now have succeeded in possessing myself of a fine home and considerable of this world's goods.

Mr. Case's house and farm is located within a short distance of Hydesville. The house is sheltered from the winds of winter and is built on a spot one mile northeast of the town, which for its rural beauty may be called "romantic." The farm consists of 660 acres of land of the best soil in the county. It will produce most any crop a man may desire. It averages sixty bushels of oats per acre and fifty tons of beets; the ground is mostly black loam, partially level and partially hilly.

As Mr. Case is engaged in dairying he owns a considerable number of cattle and stock, amongst which we find 55 fine dairy cows, 600 sheep, 7 horses, and 2 hogs. He also owns an orchard of 400 fruit trees, apples, pears, plums, cherries, prunes, and all kinds of small fruit for table use. He has such confidence in the quality of his land that he tried raising alfalfa. He may be said to have introduced alfalfa into the county, of which he has now five acres growing nicely.

Mr. Case was born in Pennsylvania, November 5, 1832. Being brought up on a farm he followed farming until 1852, when he came per pack-train via St. Joe, Missouri, and South Pass to California, making the trip in eighty-two days, and arriving at Yreka, Siskiyou County.

He commenced his career in this country with mining, which he followed until 1854, but not having much success, he the same year ran a pack-train from Crescent City back into the mountains and diverse other places, going as far as British Columbia sometimes. In 1863 he engaged in mining and merchandising at Canyon City, Oregon, where he married Mrs. Eleanor C. Cooper, in 1864. She is a native of Canterbury, England. They have one son named George W. Cooper also a daughter named Eleanor Case.

Mr. Case came to this county in 1866.

AMASA M. GILL.

Turning our attention to Rohnerville, Humboldt County, we there notice Mr. Amasa M. Gill, who is one of the prosperous merchants of that place. He is a wide-awake gentleman and business man. As it may be of interest for many of our readers, we will give his history.

Mr. Gill was born May 16, 1848, at Mallorytown, Leeds County, Ontario, where his father's family resided until 1857. His father was in California from 1852 to 1857, when he returned home and took them to Wisconsin where they lived for three years. In 1860, Mr. Gill, Sr., who got a liking for California at his previous stay there, resolved to try his fortune once more in the golden State; so he, with his family, left Evansville, Rock County, Wisconsin, on the 4th of April, 1860, and journeyed across the plains, per ox-team, until they reached Eureka, which happened November 6, 1860, just seven months and two days from the day of starting. As Mr. Amasa Gill was then too young to stand guard or drive ox-team, he had all his time to himself and therefore enjoyed the trip immensely, not being able to appreciate the dangers or hardships of it.

Mr. Gill worked on his father's farm until 1865, when he was seventeen years of age, then made himself useful by teaching schools at different places in the County. He then went to San Francisco and San Jose to attend the State Normal School; after which he taught school in Placer County, and finally, in the summer of 1873, came to this town where he engaged in the drug business which he sold out in 1876, when he bought his present business.

The same year Mr. Gill was married to Miss Ida J. Look, of San Francisco, born in Westfield, Wisconsin. They have two children named James Selah, after his grandfather, and Jennie Florence Gill.

THOMAS DEVLIN.

In the village of Arcata, corner of Ninth and K Streets is located the large residence of Mr. Thomas Devlin. The railroad passes directly in front of it.

Mr. Devlin is an enterprising business man and tanner of Arcata, whose tannery is to be found on Eighth Street near J Street, and is described elsewhere. He has 480 acres of land containing an abundance of oak trees which furnish him the bark, necessary to manufacturing first-class leather. Near his residence is an orchard of 150 fruit trees bearing apples, plums and pears; and a number of varieties of berries.

Mr. Devlin is a native of Perth, West Canada, where he was born June 13, 1834. He lived on a farm until he became an apprentice to a tanner which happened when he was eighteen years old. He learned for four years, and became a skillful and efficient tanner. He followed this calling in diverse States East, until he reached New York, when he concluded to go to California. He left Watertown, New York, in April and arrived in San Francisco, May 18, 1861, after a journey of thirty days, by way of Isthmus of Panama. The journey across the Isthmus was pleasant, but from there to San Francisco it was almost unbearable, the boat was too crowded. The whole trip lasted thirty days.

Mr. Devlin did not care to go to the mines, as he had an unpleasant experience in that line, by buying stock which proved worthless. He went first on a dairy ranch near Marysville, then went to Healdsburg where he stayed until 1866 and afterwards came to Arcata where he located for good.

Mr. Devlin is a self-made man, he had only his hands as capital, when he started life in California, and now has quite an amount of property and an interesting family. In 1861 he married Miss Hannah Daven, of Ogdensburgh, N. Y. The union proved a happy one, and was blessed with seven children named: Catherine L., William Grant, Lizzie, Nina Jane, Thomas D. Wallace and Bruce Devlin; the last two being twins.

ROBERT W. ROBARTS.

One of the finest houses in Ferndale which we have illustrated is owned by Robert W. Robarts, a young man of business habits and energy. From the verandas of the residence, one can enjoy many fine views, as the house faces the hills which are covered with timber and ferns; his orchard near by furnishes him with an abundance of fruit.

Mr. Robarts owns also the livery stable in Ferndale, where he keeps twenty-five fine horses and numerous buggies of style and comfort. The little farm of ten acres, Mr. Robarts devotes to the production of vegetables, etc., for his private use. As Ferndale is only eighteen miles from the county seat and has its church and school, one can easily perceive that Mr. Robarts' judgment in locating himself was a good one.

Mr. Robarts, although only twenty-two years of age, having been born in County Kent, England, May 30, 1860, is already a man of family, having in 1879 married Miss Amelia Francis, a native of Ferndale. They have two children, named Grace M. and Robert F. Robarts.

Mr. Robarts came to California in 1876, he landed at San Francisco but soon came into this county where he started business as a butcher, but after eighteen months disposed of it and went out of active business until 1881, when he bought his present business and commenced to build his residence. He is the brother of Mr. Percival Robarts, whose biography will be found elsewhere.

S. LEWIS SHAW.

"Ferndale" is the name given to the beautiful residence of Mrs. Isabella Armitage Shaw, the wife of S. Lewis Shaw, deceased. The residence is an ornament to the county, and one of the handsomest of our illustrations. Mrs. Shaw devotes a large share of her time in beautifying the place. She has only one living child, named Joseph Armitage Shaw, who graduated at the State University in Berkeley, with high honors, and holds at present an important position on the railroad.

The founder of the home, whose death the county mourns, was a native of Vermont, where he was born March 22, 1818. He was brought up on a farm until fourteen years of age, then learned the cabinet trade; but after finishing his apprenticeship, he thought that he had more love for art than anything else, and therefore took lessons and became quite an adept at portrait painting and photographing.

Before coming to California, he located in Nashville, Tennessee, where he became acquainted with the lady he afterwards married.

He made the trip across the continent in a wagon train, and arrived in Sacramento in 1850, three months after he started. He mined for a while; but being unsuccessful, he went to San Francisco where he opened an extensive photograph gallery, which proved very successful. In 1853 Mr. Shaw was persuaded by his brother, who was one of the discoverers of Humboldt Bay and returned with glowing accounts about it, to dispose of his gallery and to settle in this county. He at first farmed near Table Bluff, but afterwards came to Ferndale where he acted as first postmaster. The village takes its name from his farm, which he named "Ferndale."

Mr. Shaw died November 22, 1872. He was a kind husband and indulgent father. He had three children, two of whom are resting with him. Being an artist, he was not as successful as he would otherwise have been at farming, yet he left a good farm of 160 acres, and succeeded in laying the foundation for a good home and competency for his family. The products of his farm are wheat, barley, oats, and potatoes. The orchard has fifty apple trees, all kinds of pears, peaches, plums, cherries, etc.

GEORGE L. BENEDICT.

That Ferndale is one of the nicest spots in Humboldt County is proven by the fact that there are so many good residences in and around it. Within the outskirts of the town, we find Mr. George L. Benedict's residence, which is one of the handsomest homes that surround Ferndale. It is on the Rohnerville and Ferndale road, is delightfully situated near the foot-hills and is sheltered from the coast winds.

Mr. Benedict was born in Otsego County, New York, May 22, 1842, on a farm; was taken to Broome County when seven years of age, and remained there on a farm until 1861. As soon as the civil war broke out, he left his home in order to participate; and he showed his love for his country by serving her until the war was over, in 1865. He was in the battle of Bull Run and several other minor engagements.

After the war Mr. Benedict returned to Broome County, but having acquired a desire for traveling, he visited several of the Southern States, and finally made up his mind to come to California.

He left Broome County and arrived in San Francisco November 1, 1872, after a pleasant trip of thirty days' duration by the way of the Isthmus.

Mr. Benedict was first engaged on a dairy ranch at Lake

Tahoe. And finally, in 1874, lived at "Little Nigger-head Prairie," after having previously visited this county, and finding it what he desired, came to his present home where he is engaged in dairying. He owns 1,000 acres of land, grazing and farming, quite a number of cattle and other stock.

In 1881, Mr. Benedict married Miss Katie Dorsey, who is a native of Trinity County, California.

PERCIVAL W. ROBARTS.

Within three-fourths of a mile from Ferndale is the home and residence of Mr. Percival W. Robarts. His family consists of himself, his wife, formerly Miss Florence N. Smith of Quebec, Canada, and their son, named Henry St. Albans Robarts.

Mr. Robarts' business is that of raising fine Merino sheep. His flock is small, only fifty in number, but of exceedingly fine stock of the Spanish Merino breed. They were purchased in Haywards, Alameda County, and thrive well in our county. At the late 9th District Fair, Mr. Robarts was awarded the first premium on all his sheep, his buck "Restless," being undoubtedly one of the best in the State. Sheepmen prefer home raised bucks to those raised in warmer climates. Mr. Robarts has quite a number of home-raised bucks on his farm, which are very fine animals. The farm consists of 262 acres of fine, rich soil, which produced at one time eighty bushels of oats per acre. There is a small orchard containing various kinds of fruit trees.

Mr. Robarts came to this county in 1880. He is a native of Kent, England, where he left in 1874; he resided in Canada before coming by the way of Panama, to California. The trip was unusually pleasant.

A. PUTNAM.

Mr. A. Putnam deserves to be mentioned amongst the enterprising residents of this county. He owns one of the attractive homes in the pleasant village of Ferndale, where he is engaged in merchandising. Mr. Putnam is a native of Nova Scotia, where he was born November 19, 1847. He was raised on a farm, but when fourteen years of age, went into the business house of his brother-in-law, where he remained until sixteen years of age. In March, 1867, Mr. Putnam thought he might make his fortune in California, and accordingly left Halifax, and journeyed across the Isthmus toward the Golden State, where he arrived in April, 1867, being just thirty days on the trip. So far as we can judge he has succeeded to his satisfaction in establishing himself in business, and has become a worthy citizen of his town and county. After landing in San Francisco Mr. Putnam went to the mines for a short time during the White Pine excitement, but made most of his fortune since in raising cattle and merchandising in this county, to which he came in 1870. He married Miss Mary Johnston in 1877, who was a native of Humboldt. They have two children named William Mason, and Edwin Putnam.

JOHN ANDERSON.

Mr. John Anderson was formerly of Alsen, Schleswig, Germany, where he was born February 5, 1846, and is now, a citizen of this county worthy to be mentioned amongst the enterprising men. He went to sea when fourteen years of age, and was ten years before the mast, then was made an officer, which position he held five years. He visited all parts of the world, but while stoping at Japan, resolved to settle down in California. Accordingly he took passage on the *City of Tokio* which made the trip in twenty-one days, arriving in San Francisco, June 29, 1874. He located at first on Mad River where he was engaged in sheep raising. In 1878, he made a visit to his old home in Germany staying ten months, and then came back and bought Mr. John Duncan's farm for $7,000, on Eel River. It is four miles from Table Bluff near the ferry on the Rohnerville Road, and easy of access to all parts of the county. There is a small orchard of thirty trees, forty acres of fine farming land cultivated, and 236 acres or grazing land in Mr. Anderson's possession. On his land he usually keeps twenty cows, twenty hogs, 400 sheep, and three horses. Mr. Anderson married Miss Mary C. Lind of Schleswig, Germany, in 1882.

GEORGE H. SHAW.

Undoubtedly all the people of Humboldt County will be acquainted with their genial County Assessor, George H. Shaw, who was elected by the New Constitution Party in 1879, and is holding that position still, to the satisfaction of his fellow-citizens.

Mr. Shaw is a Kentuckian, born November 22, 1831, but had lived in several States before he came to California. He lived in Kentucky until 1836, in Illinois until 1846, and Iowa till 1852. From there he came to California by the way of Council Bluffs, thence to the north side of Platte River, Salt Lake, Humboldt and Downeyville, making the trip in six months, not without coming in contact with the Indians and the other general hardships attending such a journey.

He mined in Downeyville and several other places with medium success. In 1860 he went to Virginia City, Nevada, where he was one of the first Councilmen of that city, in 1860. He held that honorable position for four consecutive terms, until he left the State, in order to come to this county.

He established himself six miles from the county-seat in 1865, where he owns now a fine farm of sixty acres, and an orchard. He also owns 530 acres of land not cultivated. His home farm is of an excellent character, of free black soil, producing large crops averaging eighty bushels of oats, three tons of hay, and five tons of potatoes. He has at present twenty head of cattle, fifty hogs and six head of horses. In the orchard are 200 apple, ten cherry, and thirty plum trees.

Mr. Shaw was married in 1872, to Miss Margaret A. Farrill, a native of Sonoma County, California. They have three boys: George Henry, Frank Clinton, and James Clifford Shaw.

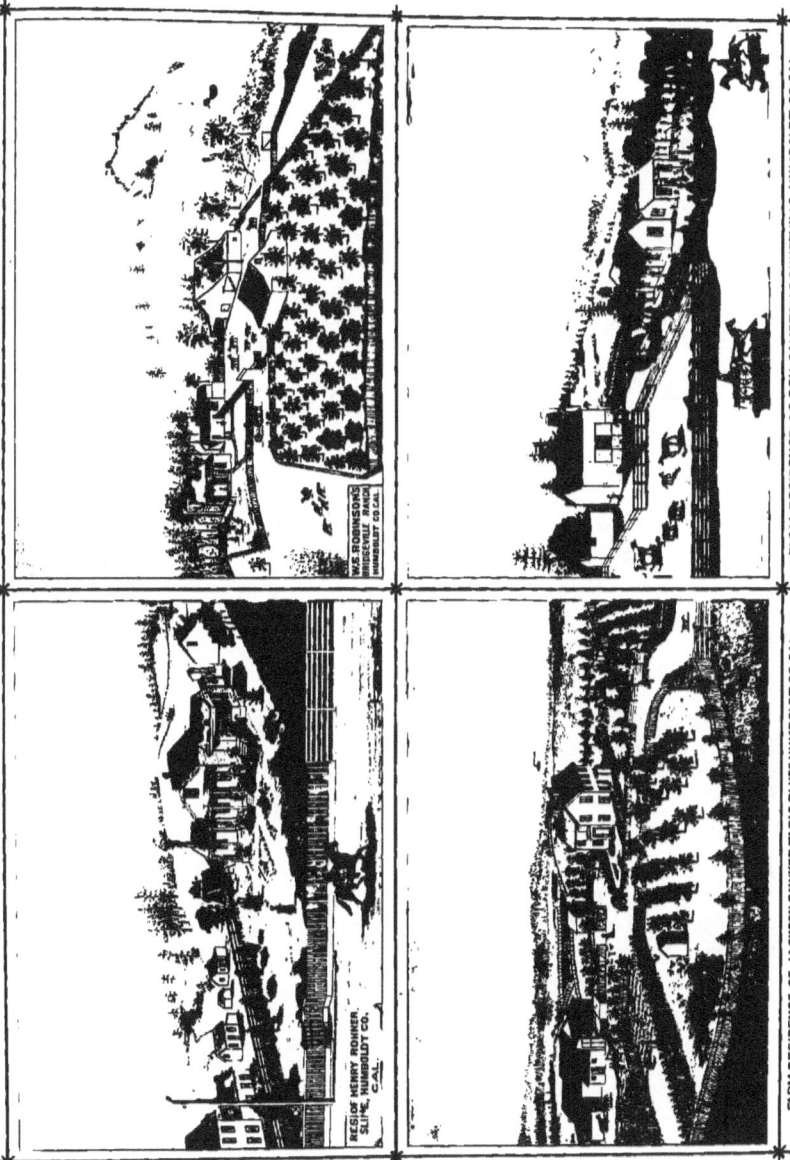

GEORGE H. GRAY.

Another thrifty citizen, Mr. George H. Gray, was born in Rush County, Indiana, November 30, 1832. When five years old, his parents took him to Illinois where they settled on a farm in Adams County, sixteen miles from Quincy.

In 1854, Mr. Gray came by way of north side of Platte River, and Salt Lake, to California; he had a pleasant journey, and arrived at Diamond Springs, October 4th, in the same year. He mined for three years at the Springs; realized $2,000 the first year and losing that amount in the next two years. Afterwards he went to Volcano where he had better luck, and left in order to take up a farm at Santa Rosa; he stayed there until 1859, when he moved towards this county where he has been a citizen ever since.

In 1869 Mr. Gray married Miss Martha C. Creighton; she is a native Californian, their two children are named George H. and Mary C. Gray.

Mr. Gray now owns a farm of 275 acres, the land is black loam, with clay sub-soil; it averages fifty bushels of oats, and twenty of wheat; of potatoes, five tons per acre. His residence, which is pleasantly situated, is surrounded by an orchard of 300 fruit trees and bearing apples, peaches, plums, and pears, as represented in our sketch. It is within one and one-half miles of Hydesville, and twenty-five miles distant from the county seat.

Mr. Gray is chiefly engaged in stock-raising, he owns at present 15 head of cattle, 18 hogs, 1,500 sheep, and 12 horses, also one mule.

RICHARD JOHNSTON.

The subject of this sketch was born April 16, 1822, in Eneskellen, Ireland. In 1841, with an older brother, the family emigrated to Sidney, New South Wales. In the year 1849 he came to California. San Francisco was a few scattered houses and tents. Gold was the one absorbing topic. Every day brought shiploads of people rushing for the mines. Vessels were deserted, and all hands went to the mines. Mr. Johnston made his way to Marysville from Sacramento in a whale boat and footed it up to Park's Bar and Foster's Bar. He was tolerably successful this year and returned to San Francisco. Here he decided to return to Sidney, and was eighty-four days on the way, calling at the Sandwich Islands.

After remaining a short time he determined to return to California and took passage in March, 1850. On board the vessel he became acquainted with the lady who afterwards became his wife. On his arrival he was married to Miss Mary Lancaster, of Lancashire, England, who was accompanying a married sister to her husband then in California. They were sisters to John Lancaster, now owner of Bolton Grange, owned at one time by the Tichborn family. Mr. Lancaster and his brothers are owners of large coal and iron mines, and manufacturers of steel. One of her brothers is considered an expert in the manufacture of Bessimer steel. Mr. John Lancaster was the owner of the yatch *Deerhound*, and rescued a part of the crew of the Rebel cruiser *Alabama*.

He was married by the noted street preacher, Rev. William Taylor, on the 3d of July, 1850. Mr. Johnston went again to the mines with little success, and returned to the city but found it very difficult to obtain employment. But after a while opened a store of dry goods, &c., at the corner of Stockton and Clay streets. But Mr. Johnston says he came to California to mine, and as the Salmon River mines were then coming into notice, he concluded to go. He started for Trinidad, leaving his wife to dispose of the goods and follow on. At the mines everything in the shape of provision was from one dollar to a dollar and a half a pound, and the most that any miner or company of miners were making was not more than eight dollars per day to the pound, and some not half that amount; the greatest portion not making anything, and were the very picture of wretchedness, with not much to eat and very little money. He then went on to Trinity River and worked a week. The gold was scale gold and weighed very light; they only had an ounce apiece for their week's work. They then moved from there up to Weaverville, which was quite a contrast from Salmon River, everybody looked well and cheerful. Mrs. Johnston was the first married woman that lived in Weaverville. He opened a boarding-house and trading post, and as it was customary in those days, kept a bar. He afterwards built one of the largest log buildings in the State, called "Sidney Hall." After several mining operations he returned to Humboldt in the summer of 1856, and rented a dairy farm on Eel River.

In 1857 he moved onto the place where he now has a valuable property of 1,392 acres of good grazing land, on Bear River, capable of supporting between two and three hundred cows. It is divided into two dairies, and is fully described elsewhere. He keeps 200 head of horned stock. He has five children, three sons and two daughters.

ALEXANDER ROBERTSON.

Alexander Robertson was born in Perthshire, Scotland, in the year 1823. At the age of twenty he emigrated to America, and settled near the town of Simcoe, Canada West, where he married Miss Jennette Forbes, and engaged in lumbering and farming.

Not being very successful, and California promising a more extensive field of operations, in the spring of 1850, he started with a party to cross the plains, arriving at Salt Lake without meeting any serious drawbacks, remaining there three weeks being hospitably treated by the Mormons. The balance of their journey was attended with all the horrors of overland travel; being at one time near the verge of distraction for want of water, the thoughts of suicide were seriously entertained by some of the party. On another occasion it was left to vote whether they should go on or not, and being carried in the affirmative, they proceeded, and the result was they had cause to regret it. Their water gave out, and with swollen tongues they toiled on and would undoubtedly have perished if a slight shower had not providentially fallen. Every expedient was resorted to, for the purpose of saving a few drops of that precious fluid. At night they lay down in their tracks, and the rising sun only revealed to them another day of desperation. Out of water, out of provisions, they subsisted altogether on what food fortune threw in their way. Mr. Robertson, with a Delaware Indian as guide, was some distance in advance of the main party, following the trail defined by an occasional bean, which must have dropped from a dilapidated sack carried by the party preceding them The Delaware killed a small bird, of the duck species, which they almost instantly devoured without removing the feathers or subjecting it to the action of fire. Eventually as a last resort "they gave their horses their head" and they found a spring and thus ended their sufferings.

He was engaged in mining for several years, with fair success. Then went to Elk Valley, in Del Norte County, where Crescent City now stands, and took up 160 acres of farming land, and a vessel arriving from the East about that time, loaded with freight and passengers, made things lively and soon the town of Crescent City sprang up. Mrs. Robertson and child joined him December 24, 1855, arriving by way of the Isthmus of Panama.

After thirteen years of prosperity he concluded to remove to Humboldt County, where he arrived on the 19th of May, camping on the present location of his ranch, having brought with him a large number of cattle, and making it a permanent home, selling off his cattle and stocking his ranch with sheep. The ranch now contains between 6,000 and 7,000 acres of deeded land, nearly all under fence.

On the 28th day of April, 1880, he was one of the party surveying a road around what is known as Whitmore's Bluff, on the Van Duzen River. The party wishing to cross a deep ravine, could save a long trip around by jumping across on the logs which lay partly over it. Several had got over and Mr. Robertson, who, though over fifty, always felt as young and active as anybody, made the jump forwards and about five feet down. He felt something give way within him. Those near noticed a change in his face as of pain and weakness; he became sick and vomited some. He was taken to Mr. Whitmore's house, where after lying down he never moved again. His loss was deeply felt not only by his family but by a wide circle of neighbors and friends.

Mr. Robertson took an active interest in all public improvements and always had an open hand in forwarding the same. Liberal to a fault, he was kind and sympathetic in his neighborly intercourse. He died in the fifty-eighth year of his age. Since then the ranch has been carried on by Mrs. Jennette Robertson successfully, and now affords pasture for 5,000 sheep of fine quality. Mrs. Robertson has four children. The older son, Mr. Alexander Robertson, Jr., is now engaged in sheep-raising near Garberville, this county, has four children, and is doing well.

The Robertson ranch is located on the Overland Stage Road, seven miles from Bridgeville, which town is the post-office of the surrounding country.

LORENZO PAINTER.

Of the many go-ahead and enterprising men of Humboldt County, Mr. Painter stands conspicuous. He was born in Columbiana County, Ohio, December 27, 1817, on a farm, where he lived till seventeen years of age, when he left for Kalamazoo, Michigan, traveling the distance, 350 miles, on foot, where he lived eighteen months. He then went to Cass County, Michigan, where he learned the carpenter's trade. He afterward went to Van Buren County and engaged in mercantile and lumber business.

In 1864 he started for California with a drove of horses, being fifteen months on the way, wintering on the Humboldt River, and arriving at Napa County, July, 1865. He bought a farm in Santa Clara County, raised one crop and sold out and returned East by way of Panama. After doing mercantile business at South Haven, Michigan, a short time, running two vessels from there to Chicago, he starts a second time for California, coming by railroad to San Francisco, thence by steamer to Humboldt Bay, arriving in July, 1870.

RIO DEL HOUSE.

After looking the country over, he located near Eel River, a place now called Rio Del Ranch, where he has a mineral spring and public house, prepared to accommodate parties seeking a pleasure resort. The natural inducements to draw visitors are, being almost surrounded by mountains which shut out the cold fogs, mineral spring, hunting, fishing, bathing, and sailing on the river. See view of this fine resort.

Mr. Painter has a half section of land equal to any in the county, mostly level, and an orchard of 700 trees, of most kinds of fruits as well as berries. He has forty head of cattle, 140 hogs, eight sheep and eight horses.

He was married to Miss Elizabeth Bourman in 1838, a native of Ohio. They have one girl, named Louisa Painter.

JACKSON SAWYER.

Jackson Sawyer was born near Mooresburg, Montour County, Pennsylvania, December 25, 1824, of Scotch-Irish parentage. When eighteen months old, both parents died and he was adopted into a very worthy family named Kerr, where he remained until twenty-one years of age, during which time he learned the practical part of farming. He was always fond of books and had access to a much better library than was common in farm houses. Like most boys raised on a farm, he thought the life of a farmer too slow and plodding and resolved that he would become a machinist.

He went to Pottsville, a mining town in the anthracite coal regions of Pennsylvania, and worked about one week when one of his eyes was cut by a piece of steel from a chisel which destroyed the sight. In the spring of 1852 he worked in the rolling mill in Danville. The iron business at this time was not very good and he set out for California, taking the Panama route. The passage to the Isthmus was pleasant, which he crossed partly by railroad, and by boat, and on foot.

He arrived in San Francisco May 2, 1853; after remaining in the city three or four days he went to the Weaverville mines, by boat to Sacramento, thence by stage to Shasta, and on to Clear Creek. He worked with rocker with very moderate success, and health failing he left for San Francisco.

MR. SAWYER ARRIVES IN HUMBOLDT.

About August 1st, he started for Humboldt Bay to work for James T. Ryan, where he worked but a short time. At Eureka he engaged to work for a man, called "Long Jones," in 1852. After some three hours' sailing they arrived at his cabin, a sort of connecting link between a cabin and a wood pile. Jones' place was a boating point at that time. He kept a boat and carried freight and passengers to and from Eureka, as the trail around the bay in winter was almost impassable. Settlers from Eel River Valley would turn their animals into Jones' pasture and go by water. Freight at that time was $7 per ton. Jones kept a few staple articles for sale, such as salt pork, sugar, and flour. The supplies were not very abundant in the grocery line, as much of Jones' coin was spent on cards and whiskey. Flour was sold that winter as high as $40 per barrel.

In the winter of 1853-54 he gave $200 for a claim to the place now known as Hookton. He thought as he was not able to do hard work, that in the course of time, it would grow into a place of business that would afford a living. He didn't think the place of much value for farming but put in a crop of six acres. He improved the shipping facilities as fast as required. During the summer of 1855 the Government had the land surveyed.

The Land-office was at Marysville. He inquired of the Surveyor what he would be required to do to secure the prospective business point of Hookton. He directed him to enter the high land, the marsh being fractional it would be thrown on the high land. But failing to secure the shipping point, he lost all interest in the place and traded it for a heifer, and the heifer for a hive of honey-bees, valued at $60. He then secured a pre-emption on the 160 acres where he now lives, making various improvements as fast as his means would permit him.

There were several favorite camping places for the Indians on the bay side of Table Bluff. They never remained long at any one place, moving around sometimes for fish, at other times for clams or whatever might suit their fancy. When moving by water they used canoes to carry their goods, but if by land the squaws were made to serve as beasts of burden. All the trouble the whites had from the Indians in this section was their stealing and constant begging. They were always cold, always hungry, and could never get enough for what they had to sell. If the Indians judge the moral standing of the white race by the conduct of some white men of early days, their estimate must be low.

One of the annoyances of pioneer farming was the large flocks of crows and blackbirds. They picked up the grain when sowed and often the ground required to be resown. One of the greatest troubles of those days was the bears. They had no respect for a fence but would tear it down whenever they came to it. They were very destructive animals to have on a farm, eating and tramping through the grain, rolling down large patches as flat as a floor. Bears were very fond of pork and they could dispose of quite a large hog at one meal. Whatever remained after their hunger was satisfied they always covered up with fern or grass or whatever else came handy. It was no pleasant amusement to get out nights and help the dogs scare the bears from the hogs. He says he "recollects one night he had to get up three times for that purpose. He always found them willing to run and he was always willing to let them go."

CHARLES S. COOK.

One of the energetic business men of Humboldt County is Mr. C. S. Cook, who was born March 12, 1846, in Tompkins County, New York, who like most of the early emigrants to this country by the overland route suffered almost incredible hardships while on their way seeking to obtain a competency and a home in this land of gold. His boyhood life from the age of sixteen until twenty-one was spent on the Michigan Central Railroad, running from Detroit to New Buffalo. Afterward we hear of him in Morrow County, Ohio, from whence he starts for the Pacific Coast, in February, 1852. On May 1st we find him at St. Joseph, Missouri, on the way with an ox-team which he drove across the plains, which at that time was a great undertaking, consuming almost four months' time, arriving at Foster's near Oregon City, August 22, 1852. He was attacked with the cholera on Green River and came very near dying. His first business was mining at Althouse, in Southern Oregon, where he met with good success. He came to Petrolia, Humboldt County, in 1859, and engaged in dairying and raising stock. He has a very productive farm of 1,600 acres, turning off yearly five tons of butter and from 800 to 1,200 bushels of oats, and about forty tons of hay. It is located fifty miles from the county seat, 150 miles from railroad and two from church and schools. He has an orchard of 150 trees of apples, pears and plums. He has 150 head of cattle, thirty hogs, eight horses and two mules.

He married Miss Ann E. Walker, who was a native of Illinois, in 1857. They have two boys whose names are Levant and George W. Cook.

J. O. KENYON.

J. O. Kenyon was born in Upper Canada, of American parents, on the 23d of March, 1833. He then removed with his parents to York State when about two years old. When about fourteen years old he commenced giving ventriloquial entertainments, and traveled extensively through the northern States and Canada.

In the year 1855 he came to California and traveled through all the mining camps and towns of California, Oregon and Washington Territory. In the year 1857 he purchased 800 acres of land in Eel River Valley, Humboldt County, and settled there.

In November, 1869, he invented the fluid pencil, or what is substantially the same, and now known as the "McKinnon Fountain Pen." Mr. Kenyon holds letters patent for the pencil.

In May, 1858, he started for the Frazer River mines, during the first gold excitement. When he arrived at Victoria, B. C., he abandoned the idea of going to the mines on account of unfavorable reports, and then went to Puget Sound, Seattle, W. T., and invested in town lots, which are now in the city of Seattle.

In the year 1856 Mr. Kenyon went to San Francisco and entered into an agreement with Messrs. Whitelaw & Hawley by which they were to run their steamers regularly between San Francisco and Eel River for the term of two years, which was the first establishment of Eel River navigation. In this he met with many discouragements, and in order to induce the parties to undertake the venture it became necessary for him to advance considerable money for the construction of a warehouse and wharf at "Port Kenyon," which derives its name from Mr. Kenyon. He also sold lots to about thirty families on which they have built homes.

In March, 1879, he started the first cash store in Humboldt County, south of Eureka, and has continued in the general merchandise business ever since. The steamers having ceased to run to Port Kenyon, he removed his store one and a half miles east of Port Kenyon, on the Eureka and Ferndale road. This place is called "Arlynda." Arlynda is an Indian word, signifying merchandise or property.

ROBERT BURNS.

This biography presents to the good people of Humboldt County a prominent and successful business man—one who by correct habits of living, industry and frugality made himself a name, and set an example that others may safely follow, especially young men. We find that in early youth he learned a trade and adopted such habits of living, which was the secret of success in after life. He early made the Bible his study, and its precepts his guide. Having musical talent, he improved and used it in God's praise.

Mr. Burns was born in Manchester, England, January 16, 1832. At the age of fourteen he went to learn the tinner's trade, working three and a half years, when he with his father's family left Old England and sailed for the New, May, 1849, and after a voyage of forty-five days landed in Boston, Massachusetts, July 10th. From there he went to Fall River, Massachusetts, where he worked a few months at his trade. From there he went to Providence, Rhode Island, where he worked one year, then back to Fall River where he worked three and one-half years. He then did business for himself in Somerset and Pawtucket, where he exercised his musical talent as a member of a quartette choir in the Congregational Church.

In 1857 he caught the gold fever, and the 19th of July prepared to go to California. In 1858 he left Pawtucket and took passage on a steamer on the Sound for New York, where he secured a passage on board the steamship *Moses Taylor*, sailing the 1st of August, 1858, arriving at Aspinwall in nine days. After crossing the Isthmus of Panama he took a steamer for San Francisco, arriving August 28, 1858, and after one day he went to work for Morris & Doberzinsky, making gas-meters, where he stayed seven months.

From there he went to Humboldt County and worked for Major Murdock, of Arcata. After seven months he went back to San Francisco and worked for Messrs. Locke & Montague, till February, 1861. On February 5, 1861, he went by steamer to Eureka, from there he went to Arcata, where he purchased the stock and trade of the only tin shop in Humboldt County, of I. J. Newkirk, for about $800, conducting the business successfully ever since.

In the year 1862 he helped to raise a company of militia to protect the people from the Indians of Humboldt County. In July, 1865, he was elected Captain, and held the office for two years, receiving his commission from Governor Low. In May, 1870, he visited New England on an excursion train of the Central Pacific Railroad.

September 15, 1873, he married Miss Jennie Pouleur, a native of Lille, France. They have two boys named Robert and Paul Burns. On July 9, 1875, his store and four of his other buildings were burned.

In May, 1878, he took part in a musical festival in San Francisco, representing Humboldt County, and was appointed one of the "Bouquet of Artists."

In 1869 he became a member of the Anniversary Lodge, No. 85, I. O. O. F., in Arcata, which has a fund of $10,000. It has a membership of 131. He has had the honor of representing the lodge three times in the Right Worthy Grand Lodge of the State.

He has conducted the Presbyterian Church choir four years, in a very successful manner.

He has 340 acres of timber and marsh land which is eight miles from the county seat; churches and schools within two minutes' walk from his house. He also has several building

DAIRY & FARM OF SAMUEL T. YOUMAN, 500 ACRES, DEL NORTE CO. CAL.

JOSEPH G. ANTHONY'S HOME & MILL, SMITH RIVER VALLEY, DEL NORTE CO. CAL.

BENJAMIN CAMPTON.

Benjamin Campton was born June 8, 1849, in Wisconsin, and came to California when but three years old, so that it may be said that he is almost a native of California. He, as most others who came by the overland route, had a tedious time, being six months on the way, and with others, came by the Fremont route, arriving at Shasta City September 25, 1852. His first business was general farming, which he continues till the present time. In 1857 he went to Rohnerville, Humboldt County. He farms 100 acres of land, consisting of black loam, with clay bottom and is very productive, averaging sixty bushels of oats, sixty bushels of barley, and forty bushels of wheat per acre. It is located twenty-two miles from the county seat and one-fourth mile from church and school. He has an orchard of 100 trees, consisting of apples, pears, plums, cherries and peaches. He usually has on the place about ten head of cattle, ten hogs, and eight horses.

In 1873 he was married to Miss Sarah Melissa Kay, a native of Michigan. They have four girls named Mussadora, Gertrude, Lucy and Pearl Campton.

WILLIAM CAMPTON.

William Campton, a pioneer resident, was born near Mineral Point, Lafayette County, Wisconsin, November 13, 1846, where he was engaged in farming and stock-raising. He came to the Pacific Coast by way of the Fremont route, meeting with the usual hardships of a journey across the uninhabited country, much of it a desert, to this land of plenty, arriving at Shasta City September 25, 1852. In 1857 he came to Rohnerville, in this county, and has followed farming ever since he arrived in the State. He has 160 acres of rich, black loam land, giving an average yield of forty-five bushels of oats or barley, and thirty-five of wheat per acre. He has an orchard of 150 trees of apples, pears, peaches, plums and cherries. He generally keeps ten hogs, ten head of cattle and about a dozen horses.

He married Miss Ellen Lindley in 1874, who was a native of Oregon. They have two children, one boy and one girl, named Benjamin Forrest Campton and Ada Louisa Campton.

The farm is located twenty-two miles from the county seat and only one-fourth mile from church and school, thus possessing many advantages for residence.

SETH KINMAN.

One of our most striking illustrations is that of the noted Seth Kinman and his "buck-horn chair" which was presented by him in person to President Buchanan. This celebrated hunter and presidential chair maker was a native of Union County, Pennsylvania, where he was born September 20, 1815. In April, 1849, he left his home with rifle, Colt's six-shooter, knife and fiddle. On the journey he acquired the title of "Arkansaw" from the fact that he could play the "Arkansas Traveler" better than any one else. He reached Sacramento and visited the mines, but concluded that the country was full of gold, and at the rate it was then being taken out, would not be worth much after a while, so he turned his attention to hunting. In the spring of 1850 he joined Major Reading's company on its way prospecting the Trinity River. In the fall of 1850 he returned East, and in 1852 he again came to California and pushed immediately for Humboldt Bay. He made a contract with Col. R. C. Buchanan to furnish meat of bear and elk for the Fort, which contract he faithfully executed.

He made a second visit East, and returned in October, 1854, to this county and built a small house, where Hon. J. Ross now lives, and afterward took up a small place near Table Bluff, for his mother's home. In the spring of 1855 he took up a ranch on Bear River, which was near a pond still called Kinman's Pond. Here he resided and acquired his skill at chair making, which gave him national renown.

We learn that Mr. Kinman is preparing a history of his life for publication, and we deem it best to only give the above brief outline of his career.

KINMAN'S CHAIR ON EXHIBITION.

The chair received many flattering notices from the San Francisco press, where it was on exhibition at a fair. Some leading gentlemen of that city, among whom was Peter Donahue, took charge of the matter and procured a free passage both for the chair and Kinman to Washington. The San Francisco *Herald*, in speaking of the buck-horn chair, concludes as follows:—

"Seth Kinman is about as extraordinary as the chair. He is the beau ideal of one of the advance guard of civilization, or Rocky Mountain hunters, being in the prime of life, over six feet high, a large pair of whiskers, buckskin pants, ditto coat, and a heavy bowie-knife attached to a belt around his waist. Here," says the *Herald*, "is part of his conversation while showing the chair: 'Anybody can make a chair, but I take credit for the design of this. I kill deer and elk meat up in Humboldt County. My range is from Bear River Valley into Oregon. This winter I killed considerable meat, so I thought I would take it easy and set about making this cheer with the view of sending it to Washington for "old Buck." After I got it finished though, the boys up there in our parts thought it would do to travel on, so I thought I would try and go on with it to Washington myself, and left my mother and four children behind and started with nothing but my rifle and powder-horn. Nobody has ever set in this cheer and never shall till after the President does. I was told that they would help me get through with it, and here I am to see. If they don't why I will have to put back to Humboldt County. I would like to see the President though, and I have several friends in Washington. Jim Denver is an old friend of mine; it was him who recommended me to go in Humboldt County for game. Here s the chicer, gentlemen; the more you see it the better you'll like it.'"

THE BUCK-HORN CHAIR PRESENTED.

The *Washington Union*, May 23, 1857, says: "The handsome buck-horn chair which was brought from California by Seth Kinman, of Humboldt County (a real Rocky Mountain hunter), was presented this afternoon to the President of the United States, in the presence of a large number of delighted spectators, not a few of whom were ladies. Mr. Kinman was the observed of all observers, and many were the complimentary remarks that were made of him.

Immediately after the entrance of the President Mr. Kinman was introduced to him by General Denver. Mr. Kinman thereupon addressed the President briefly, and feelingly, alluding to the reverence in which he held him as a statesman, and expressing the pleasure with which he hailed him as Chief Magistrate of the Union.

"He himself was a Pennsylvanian, and was born in Uniontown. When quite a youth he had gone to the Great West, since which time he had been a pioneer. He had twice crossed the Rocky Mountains and had come to the city of Washington with that chair, pointing to the curiously-fashioned massive antlers at his side, which was securely fastened with iron of their own State, Pennsylvania, to present it to the President, and he hoped that he would accept it."

"The President responded in the courteous manner for which he is so distinguished, and said that he had no doubt that Mr. Kinman was honest and sincere and brave like the people of the frontier, to which he belonged, who could be led by kindness but never could be driven by force. He would accept the chair with a great deal of pleasure, and would keep it as a momento of the occasion. He would now sit down in it. It is needless to add that in the act of sitting he was loudly applauded. General Denver then introduced to the President Dr. O. M. Wozencraft, of California, who spoke on behalf of the Californians."

The chair occupied a central position in the celebrated east room, and was the greatest attraction of the President's mansion. The Washington letter-writers to the papers throughout the country spoke of it in the highest terms. In Frank Leslie's newspaper for June 3, 1857, the front page is devoted to a picture of Kinman and his buck-horn chair. He is represented in full buckskin rig, rifle, powder-horn, etc. He stands in an easy and natural position, reclining on his old rifle. The chair occupies a separate cut. Our portrait is from an original photograph.

Seth Kinman, in return for his buck-horn chair, presented to the President, received a Government appointment to assist in removing the Indians in California and Oregon to their reservations.

Kinman made a chair out of elk-horns which he took to Washington and presented to Abraham Lincoln, in 1864. He made one out of grizzly bears' remains and presented it to Andrew Johnson in the White House, September, 1865. The next was made of elk-horns and presented to President Hayes in 1876.

HON. JAMES E. MURPHY.

The Hon. James E. Murphy is acting Judge of the Superior Court of Del Norte County, having been elected to that arduous and responsible position in 1879, for a period of five years. Although he has but fairly entered upon the duties of the office, it is the unanimous opinion that a wise selection has been made by the voters, and doubtless the position which he occupies will prove a creditable one to himself and satisfactory to the people who elected him. He is a lawyer of acknowledged ability, and has proven himself the possessor of those noble traits which enables him to easily discriminate between right and wrong.

He was born in Calais, Maine, January 12, 1846. He is of Irish descent, his ancestors having emigrated there in 1816. He moved with his parents to Del Norte County in 1860. Here he attended the public school at Crescent City for one year, when having become proficient in all the studies taught in the public schools in that place, he was sent by his parents to St. Thomas Seminary, an ecclesiastical college situated then at the old Mission Dolores, San Francisco. Here he remained about four years, receiving a thorough classical education. He afterwards taught the public schools at Crescent City, Smith River, and Happy Camp. Happy Camp being a mining town, he taught school during summer and mined during the winter.

In 1866-67 he read law and was admitted to the Bar before Judge Turner. He is not only learned in his profession, but is a gentleman of superior literary tastes and acquirements.

In 1867 he received the nomination for District Attorney by the Democratic party and was elected. In 1869-70 he represented Del Norte and Klamath Counties in the Assembly. In 1871 he was again elected District Attorney for Del Norte. From 1873 to 1878 he represented Del Norte County in the Legislature, occupying the position of Speaker *pro tem* during the last two sessions.

He was the author of the Bank Commission Bill, which has worked incalculable benefit to the people of California.

At the election of delegates to the Convention to revise the Constitution of this State in 1878, he was chosen delegate to that body, which assembled at Sacramento and framed a "New Constitution," which was adopted by popular vote of the people.

There is probably no man in the State of the age of Judge Murphy that has been elected to so many responsible positions as he has. He is now thirty-six years of age, and has been a member of the Legislature at four sessions, thrice District Attorney, once a Constitution maker and now a Superior Judge.

EDGAR MASON.

Edgar Mason was born in Cape Girardeau, Missouri, May 17, 1849. While yet an infant, in 1852, his father's family emigrated to the Golden State, crossing the plains and arriving at Marysville in the fall of that year. The next year they came to Crescent City, then a thriving little village just budding out and bidding fair to be a rival to the largest city in the State. At that time Crescent City was in Klamath County, out of which Del Norte was carved in 1857. What education Mr. Mason received was in the public schools of Del Norte County which in those days were under the management, at different times, of several able professors, some being graduates of Yale College and Edinburgh University.

He has made Crescent City his home ever since the time of his first arrival in 1853, with the exception of an absence of two years when he was in the lower part of the State pursuing the study and practice of dentistry for which profession he was educated. In the year 1870 he returned to Crescent City where he first commenced the practice of dentistry for himself.

He was married in 1871 and settled down for a quiet, steady, uneventful life. Although he has met with success as a dentist, yet the small income which was derived from the practice of that profession was not sufficient to keep up his expenses, and ill-health having overtaken him, he was in a measure forced to abandon that business as a means of livelihood.

Having devoted some time to reading law, he was elected District Attorney of his county in the year 1875, which office has occupied his time until now. During the six years he has held the position, he has contributed largely to the advancement of local interests. He has met with unprecedented success in the prosecution and conviction of criminals in Del Norte. Before his election it was often said, "if you want to commit a crime go into Del Norte, no one is ever convicted there." He was instrumental in sending six men to the State Prison in the year 1880. It is a notable fact that not a single criminal prosecution for a crime amounting to a felony has been necessary for about eighteen months last past.

Mr. Mason is one of the prominent and permanent citizens of his county. He has always been a Democrat. He is a member of the Masonic fraternity, and has filled the highest positions in his lodge.

FRANK BURTSCHELL.

Frank Burtschell was born in Germany in 1825, residing on a farm till twenty-two years of age, when he came to New York City in 1846, where he lived for two years. In 1848 he went to New Orleans, and from there to Philadelphia, and New York in 1851; from there he went back to Germany, staying six months; then returned to the State of New York in 1852, remaining for one year; then started for California by way of Nicaragua route, coming to San Francisco in the fall of 1853, where he stayed two years.

In 1855 he went to Weaverville and kept a restaurant with good success; after a year and a half came to Del Norte County in 1856, and was in the Cushing House for four months. He then bought the house and has been engaged in keeping a hotel since.

He has a farm of 644 acres in Smith River Valley, eighteen miles from county seat, one mile from the mouth of Smith River, three-fourths of a mile from school, and five from church. His farm is for dairying; keeps ninety head of cattle, sixty hogs and four horses. He has an orchard of 150 trees of various kinds.

He was married to Miss Eliza Brougham in 1860, who was a native of Ireland. In 1865 he married Miss Carolina Mosher. They have six girls.

Among our illustrations will be found a view of the hotel of Mr. Burtschell, situated on Front Street, Crescent City. This hotel is now first-class in every particular. A few of its advantages are that it possesses extensive facilities for accommodating a large number of guests, and is provided with large and well-ventilated rooms and excellent beds. The proprietor's long experience in attending to the comforts of the traveling public will not fail of appreciation. We advise any one visiting Crescent City to make their home at this hotel.

HENRY WESTBROOK.

Mr. H. Westbrook is one of the active and prominent farmers of Del Norte County, having derived his knowledge of farming in early life in Germany, and many years of practical farming in Del Norte County. He was born in Westfog, Prussia, in 1829; he left his native home at the age of twenty, and landed in New York City in April, 1849. He came direct from New York to Naperville, Du Page County, Illinois, where he engaged in farming for three years.

In April, 1852, Mr. Westbrook started overland for Oregon. The mode of travel was by ox teams exclusively; this slow mode of travel required much patience for that long distance of five or six months. When on the Platte River, that dreadful disease, cholera, made its appearance among the company, and the road was frequently marked with the grave of one of its victims. He continued with the company until they reached Salmon Falls; here he started in company with four others ahead of the ox train; making good time, he reached Oregon City in October, 1852. He remained here only about two months, when like many others who had cast their lot in Oregon, he started for the gold mines of California; he arrived at Sailor Diggings, Oregon, in the latter part of December, 1852. Sailor Diggings was then one of the lively mining camps of the Pacific Coast, but provision was very scarce, and Mr. Westbrook and many others lived on nothing but acorns and wild meat for two months. He remained at Sailor Diggings for one year; the Rogue River Indians being very troublesome, he returned to the Willamette Valley, where he remained for two years, and again returned to Sailor

Diggings. The day before Mr. Westbrook arrived at Sailor Diggings the Rogue River Indians had broke out and indiscriminately slaughtered most of the inhabitants. Here the miner was found killed with his own pick; here the defenceless women were tomahawked in their houses, and their children's brains dashed out against the walls. Such atrocious crimes were too horrible for the subject of our sketch to pass by without resenting, and he enlisted the next day as a soldier to fight the Indians. The war lasted for six months, and Mr. Westbrook being unsuccessful in mining he resolved to quit the mines.

He came to Smith River Valley and took up a part of the ranch that he now owns. The original tract of land was 160 acres, but he has added to his farm until he has 1,600 acres, fifteen miles from Crescent City, 150 miles from any railroad; but has water communication with the entire world, the Pacific Ocean being the western boundary of his land.

He has the best arranged dairy ranch in northern California, his churning being done with water-power from an overshot wheel, the water being brought a distance of three-quarters of a mile. He also raises wheat with an average yield of forty bushels to the acre. On his dairy ranch he milks 225 cows which produce 32,000 lbs of butter annually.

It is not to be supposed that Mr. Westbrook has lived alone all this time; he was married to Mrs. O'Laughlin in 1856. Mr. Westbrook has two sons, William and Henry; William, the oldest, like his father, is engaged in farming and dairying, while his second son has chosen the legal profession. He is a young man of bright intellect and promising future, and will no doubt win laurels of which his father and mother may feel justly proud.

J. G. ANTHONY.

J. G. Anthony arrived in San Francisco March 3, 1850. He engaged in mining at Grass Valley, Nevada County, with but little success. On his first arrival, he worked in Meigg's planing mill in San Francisco for some time. He was born in Carolina County, Maryland, in 1830, where he lived with his father, who was a miller, during his boyhood. He resided, before starting for California, at Wilmington, Delaware. He sailed from New York in 1853, and came by Nicaragua. He resided at Grass Valley two years, came to this county in 1850 and engaged in milling at Smith River. His farm consists of 320 acres, fourteen miles from Crescent City. It is very desirably located, being only three miles from water communication with markets, and half a mile from school and church. On the place is a valuable orchard of fruit trees consisting of the most choice kinds of apple, besides plums, pears and other fruits; about 140 acres is suitable for cultivation, the balance forming excellent grazing land. He keeps forty head of cattle and forty sheep, and usually about forty hogs, six horses, and other stock.

He married Miss Emma C. Bailey in 1860, who was a native of Knox County, Illinois. They have three boys and two girls, whose names are Ella, Mark, Joseph, Kate and Fred Anthony.

SAMUEL WINTON.

Mr. S Winton was born in Sangamon County, Illinois, November 26, 1835, and moved with his parents to Kane County, Illinois, where he remained until seventeen years old, then moved to La Fayette County, Wisconsin.

He started from Lafayette County, Wisconsin, April 4, 1860, and was five and a half months on the road, and arrived at Ashland, Rogue River Valley, Oregon, September, 1860. He was engaged in farming for one year, then he mined four years with but little success. In 1865 he engaged in farming which he followed for ten years. He has been engaged in dairying ever since. He has 120 acres of land, fourteen miles from Crescent City and two miles from water communication, and half a mile from school, and one mile from church. He has eighty acres of farming land, and forty acres of timber, situated in the redwood forest ten miles from Crescent City. In his orchard are 150 choice fruit trees, apples, cherries and plums. He keeps about thirty head of cattle.

He married Miss Cordelia Beam in 1855, who was a native of La Fayette, Wisconsin. They have three boys and four girls, whose names are Howard, Thomas, Sara E, George, Charley, May and Mina Winton, who are all living with their parents at the present time.

H. F. SIMON.

H. F. Simon, a pioneer of California, was born in Tilseit Prussia, in 1827. He sailed from Antwerp in 1850, and came by New York and Panama to San Francisco, in 1850; was a saddler by trade, which he followed for ten years. In 1861 he went to Montana and from there to Brice, Idaho, where he remained for five years, working in the mines with good success. In 1862 he was in the saddlery business in Crescent City. From 1876 to 1879 he was engaged in merchandising at Smith's River, in Del Norte County.

S. T. YOUMANS.

Among the substantial enterprising men of Del Norte County we find Mr. Youmans; well qualified by his early training to stand in the front ranks of the agriculturists of the county, born of Quaker parentage in Schoharie County, New York, instructed in the details of farming, he is just the man to develop the resources of the county where he makes his home. Instead of going to the mines as many before have done, he engages in farming where his experience and skill tell with good results. He resided in Schoharie, New York, till March 5, 1852. He then went to Otsego County and followed farming from 1852 to April 17, 1858, when he sailed on the steamer *Philadelphia* from New York to Havana. There he changed to the steamer *Grenada*, and when about twenty miles from Aspinwall the vessel collided with a schooner, but no lives

DEL NORTE COUNTY OFFICERS

were lost, and arrived in San Francisco May 15, 1858. He came to this county in 1858, residing in Crescent City one year, driving team in a logging camp. He then located on a farm three miles from the mouth of Smith's River, where he has 200 acres of prairie land, very rich, producing, on an average, eighty-five bushels of barley and eighty bushels of oats per acre. It is located eleven miles from the county seat, three miles from water communication, 200 from railroad, one from school house and three from church.

He has a productive orchard of 120 trees of different varieties. He has rented his ranch, but reserves his residence. He has 100 head of cattle and five horses.

He married Miss Ruth Sweat, in 1842, who was a native of Albany County, New York. They have one boy and three girls. Their names are Alvonia, Harriet, Amanda, and May E., who are married. Samuel Youmans remains at home with his parents.

FRANCIS FRANCIS.

Francis Francis, of Ferndale, a pioneer settler, was born in Wales, in the year 1818, and came to the United States in 1841, and went to work in the coal mines of Pennsylvania. He became tired of the Eastern States, and determined to find a home on the frontier of the far West, and in 1843 he arrived in the town of Galena, Illinois, and went to work in the lead mines near that town, where he worked for about three years, when he married an excellent young lady of English birth and good parents, the daughter of his partner in business, and for two years lived very happily in Galena and then moved to Kentucky, where he remained until 1850 when he returned to Galena with his family, and when he saw them comfortably settled and provided for he started to the new gold-fields of California.

Traveling across the plains in a wagon takes all the romance out of that part of one's life. Once on the way provisions were short and they were obliged to go on half rations for five weeks, until they could get a fresh supply. It required about six months for the trip, and he arrived at Nevada City in the fall of 1850, with rags around his feet, his boots having worn out, destitute of clothes and dead broke. He then said if California would only afford him enough to eat and wear he would be satisfied. He began to look around and first went to work on Gold Run, but soon tired of that, thinking more could be made elsewhere. About this time his wife and little girl came to California by the way of Panama. This journey was full of adventures from the first, but the roughest experience was at Panama. One steamer had arrived the day before with 1,200 passengers, and their steamer had 1,000 passengers aboard; and of course every available conveyance was quickly engaged, and it was her lot to ascend the Chagres River in an open canoe, which took a whole week, and at the end of this long, tiresome journey she was obliged to sit all night in a terrific rain-storm with her little girl in her lap, and no protection but an umbrella. The next day she crossed the mountains on a mule and went aboard the steamer *Tennessee* which brought her safely to San Francisco. Those were the days of slow mail communication, and although she had written some time before starting, he had not received the letter, and she was much disappointed at not meeting her husband. But being a brave little woman, she made her way to Nevada City where her husband was much surprised and overjoyed to meet her. Here they lived very happily for six years. Mr. Francis for some time prospected on the Yuba, but without success. He then went to Shelby Hill where he took a claim which turned out tolerably well. He was one of the firm which brought the Snow Mountain Ditch to Nevada City, and was partner with the Lillard boys in the Nebraska Mine, and also owned an interest in the Cayuga Mine.

Hearing of the wonderful resources of Humboldt County he sold all his possessions in Nevada County and started for Humboldt, and with his family landed in Arcata, then called Uniontown, in 1856. In a short time concluded to settle where the town of Ferndale now stands; but it then was very sparsely settled. He bought a claim of S. W. Shaw, of San Francisco, and also took claims adjoining. Ferndale is built on the northwest corner of the claim.

FERNDALE WATER-WORKS INTRODUCED.

He did some farming and kept from eight to ten cows for dairy purposes, and when the town began to grow he supplied customers with milk. Water being scarce in town, and there being plenty of water on his place, he built tanks and began to supply the town with water in 1875. The next year he built a reservoir and laid pipe down to town, which is about a quarter of a mile. In the spring of 1877 Mr. Francis died, and the business, which has been increasing every year, has been managed by his wife, and now almost the whole town and some in the suburbs are supplied from this reservoir.

FIRST CHILD BORN IN FERNDALE.

They had a family of ten children, six of whom are living. Eugene Francis, Mrs. Clara Brice, which was the first white child born in Ferndale, Mrs. Amelia Robarts, Henry Francis, Frederic Francis, Decima Francis. The youngest is about sixteen years old.

The farm contains 220 acres, and is designated as "Brook Farm," and forms one of our illustrations. Forty acres of the place are farmed, 100 acres are pasture-land and the rest timber land. A tenant has twenty cows on the place, conducting a dairy. Mr. Francis was County Assessor in 1868-69.

J. HETHERINGTON.

Among the residences of Eureka will be found the home of J. Hetherington, who is a comparatively new-comer of Humboldt County, where he arrived April 7, 1877. He was born in Carlisle, England, and came to America at an early age, settling in the town of Webster, Worcester County, Massachusetts. He served his adopted country during the late war, in the Twenty-first Regiment of Massachusetts Volunteers. Since coming to Humboldt he occupied the store on the corner of F and Second Streets, in Eureka, doing an extensive tailoring business. He was very prominently identified with all musical matters of the county.

E. C. CUMMINGS.

E. C. Cummings was born in Oneida County, New York, August 18, 1837, and lived on his father's farm till seventeen years old. He then engaged in teaching school, which he followed for five years. He then went to Coldwater, Michigan, and farmed for one year. He started from Peoria, Illinois, for California, via New York and the Isthmus of Panama, being twenty-eight days from New York to San Francisco, where he arrived May 19, 1861.

He kept books two years for a fruit and produce house in San Francisco, and spent the year 1863 in Inyo County, prospecting and fighting Indians. In April, 1864, he went to Idaho and spent four years in mining with fair success. He resided in San Francisco in 1861-2; in Inyo County in 1863; Idaho, 1864-5-6-7; in Oregon in 1868.

He came to Humboldt County February, 1869, where he has resided ever since, teaching school at first for several years.

In 1873 he was elected Superintendent of Schools, holding the office for two terms, and until 1878. He gave up the profession of school teaching and engaged in the furniture and undertaking business in Ferndale.

In 1868 he married Miss A. A. Hill, who was a native of California. They have three boys and one girl, whose names are, Mary May, George Elliott, Charles Edwin, and Willis Everette Cummings.

H. D. SMITH.

The subject of this sketch resides in Capetown, thirty-five miles from Eureka. He was born in Truro, Province of Nova Scotia. He came to California by way of Boston, New York and Panama, arriving in San Francisco April 29, 1863. Upon his arrival he went to French Camp, San Joaquin County, and worked there on the first combined header and thresher in the State, for Mr. Baxter, now an extensive farmer, in Merced County, and inventor of other improved machinery.

He left there in August, 1865, and arrived at Eureka and began farming with Mr. Dixon, on Eel River, and continued there for two years. At present he has a farm on Bear River of 160 acres. During 1867-8 he followed the business of logging. In the winter of 1869 he resided in Sierra Valley, Plumas County. While there he took charge of Meiggs Brothers' stock ranch. He returned to Humboldt County in June, 1869. In January, 1870, he was in partnership with Mr. Putnam, and rented a dairy ranch from Mr. Joseph Russ for a term of three years. In the spring of 1874, in company with Adam Putnam and J. Smith, he drove 1,000 head of cattle from Humboldt County to Oregon, and remained there three years. He then sold out at a fair advantage. From Oregon he went east, and from there took a trip home, during the winter of 1877-8. He returned to Humboldt County in the spring of 1878. During that summer he drove a band of beef cattle from Humboldt County to Napa City.

He was married in 1878 to Miss Carrie Flint, and they have two children named, Robert H. Smith, born September 28, 1879, and Agnes E. Smith, born October 8, 1881.

He was employed on one of Mr. Russ' ranches during the fall of 1878, and in the fall of 1879 bought the property of Mr. Russ on which he now resides.

JONATHAN FREESE.

Jonathan Freese came to Humboldt County in June, 1853. He was born in Orono, State of Maine, and reached California by way of Panama. In Humboldt he was engaged for a good many years in the lumber business. On the 14th of October 1875, he met with a serious accident, which, unfortunately terminated fatally. He was at his logging claim watching the men as they were rolling a log upon the trucks, when by some means the dog on the chain became loosened, tearing out a piece of wood and throwing it with great force. The piece struck Mr. Freese in the stomach, knocking him senseless, and injuring him to the extent that he died in ten minutes. A courier was dispatched for Dr. Schenck, but it was too late to be of avail.

Mr. Freese was one of the pioneers of Humboldt; one who came to this county in its infancy, and shared the trials and triumphs of his time. He came with a band of California's bravest, sturdiest men, having in their bosoms hearts of oak when called upon in time of need; the kindest of the kind when called upon to aid suffering humanity; men who have undergone the heat and burden of the day. But he is no more. The great Father, in his infinite mercy has taken one of the most enterprising citizens, a kind and affectionate husband and father. What a feast death has had within the past few years, dining off the lives of our old pioneers! How many of those faces, so familiar for the past quarter of a century will meet us with a smile and word of good cheer no more. Through a period equaling almost an average lifetime these active, energetic men have played their part—a very active and important part, too—and have built up fortunes for themselves as well as for others. Many of them made names that deserve to live honored for what they did and what they tried to do. But one by one, as the leaves fall from the tree in autumn, they have faded from our view.

Although the band of true-hearted pioneers was small at first, yet their numbers have been thinned so that but few remain to repeat the story that should be most dear to the hearts of all—the founding and settlement of our county.

Mr. Freese leaves a wife and three children to mourn his loss. The sympathies of the public are extended to his sorrowing family in their bereavement.

Mr. Freese's name frequently occurs in the early history of the county, and his record, either private or public, is of spotless purity. He was a member of the Common Council of the city of Eureka at the time of his death. He was elected County Treasurer in 1861, and was a member of the Board of Supervisors in 1859.

His wife and three children, Benjamin F., Adele A., and Charles W., are living in their own residence in Eureka.

FREDERICK AXE.

Frederick Axe was born in Philadelphia, January 17, 1840. From the age of nine to that of fourteen years, the principal opportunities of education of his life he obtained from the public schools of the time. At the latter age he engaged as an apprentice to the business of silver plating, in which he was employed until at the age of twenty-two, when he enlisted as private in Company "C," Second Regiment of Infantry of Pennsylvania Res., belonging to what was known during the war as Governor Curtin's pet division. Under this command his first ten months in the "tented field," proved no holiday service, having shared the heat of conflict in the battle of second Bull Run, and the fierce encounters with the enemy during the seven successive days and nights in the execution of Gen. McClellan's order for change of base from Chickamauga to Harrison's Landing, at the camp near Fredericksburg, Virginia. He got a discharge from his company on the condition of joining another arm of the service, which he did, by enlisting in Battery "M," Second Regiment, U. S. Artillery, on the 10th day of December, 1862, for the period of three years. On the expiration of his full term he received his discharge from the regiment, Lieut. Col. William H. French, commanding, indorsed with the highest testimonial as to character that could be awarded to a soldier in the ranks.

An official list of twenty-two battles and skirmishes in which Mr. Axe was engaged while in this command accompanies his discharge.

With an aggregate of four years "to the front" in the bloody field of the Rebellion, though luckily he survived without a memorial scar of the strife upon his person, it may be said with equal truth, that during the long period of that severe experience, not a single act of dishonor or reproach is recorded against his reputation as a soldier and a man.

The close of the war found Mr. Axe in California, where for the first two years he served in the position of horse guard at San Quentin Prison, after which he settled at Eureka, Humboldt Bay, where he has acquired a moderate property, and permanently established his home.

In the private relations of life Mr. Axe is noted for his retiring modesty of manner, and in his home circle as an affectionate husband and father. He was married at Eureka, October 29, 1873, to Laidee, daughter of E. H. Howard, Esq., and has a family of three children.

EUREKA POST-OFFICE.

Recommended by the leading influence of the community without respect of political distinctions Mr. Axe was commissioned as Postmaster of Eureka, Feburary 10, 1873, J. A. Creswell being Postmaster-General. During Grant's administration, the office became one of the third class, to be filled by Presidential appointment, and his subsequent commissions, under President R. B. Hayes and C. A. Arthur of dates November 8, 1877, and January 7, 1882, respectively, is a sufficient recognition of the thorough competency, as well as fidelity, with which Mr. Axe has discharged his trust.

The following editorials from the press of the city may fitly conclude this sketch. "To say that he has been an efficient officer will scarcely express it. * * We have never known him to lose his temper on a single occasion. He is always affable and courteous—has a pleasant word always upon his lips, and is ever attentive and obliging. His manner of conducting the business not only meets with the approbation of the people, but he has received many flattering testimonials from the department for his attention, promptness and correctness. We do not know of a single man in our community as well calculated to fill the position. He has caused to be constructed in Eureka City a fine building, especially designed for a post-office. He has done this wholly at his own expense, and it is an ornament to the city, and a monument to the enterprise of the builder. * * Great credit is due him and we know our people will award him all praise."—*Times Weekly*. "For the erection of this fine building we owe much to the worthy zeal and spirit of our efficient postmaster, Mr. Fred. Axe."—*Dem. Standard*.

This fine structure is represented on another page in connection with the residence of Mr. Axe.

JOSEPH PORTER ALBEE.

J. P. Albee, a pioneer of Humboldt, was born in Huron, Ohio, May 20, 1815, and was raised on a farm. In 1838 he settled in Michigan, and in the fall of 1847 moved to Illinois, and in 1850 came overland to California with three men and two four-horse teams, and engaged in mining in Hangtown with good success.

He came to Humboldt in 1852 with a band of cattle. He went to Weaverville and came back with his family, in November, 1853, and settled on Table Bluff, where he kept a hotel, as mentioned on page 182. In 1855 he had a pack train running from Arcata to Klamath, and in 1855 removed with his family to Redwood Creek where he planted a large orchard, built a large hotel, and accumulated a handsome fortune. His early life in the western wilderness made him familiar with toil and privation. His indomitable spirit qualified him for a successful pioneer of Humboldt.

He married Miss Caltha Putnam in August, 1839, who was

a native of Huron County, Ohio. The family consisted of four boys and four girls: Anna M., Electa L., Mary C., Sophia, Daniel D., Joseph C., Lincoln H., and George B. Albee. He was a man of the purest private character among his friends and neighbors. He was kind and humane to the Indians and had no fear of being killed. He always rode a gray horse, and said the Indians knew him and the horse and would not shoot him.

MURDER OF J. P. ALBEE BY INDIANS.

"Not contrary to the expectation of many people on this Bay, news reached Arcata of the probable murder of J. P. Albee, by Indians, at his farm on Redwood. He left his family in Arcata on Saturday, November 1, 1862, going alone to his place, with the intention of looking after his stock and taking care of his farm. This was the last seen of him alive. On Thursday following, about noon, Mr. Faulkner and a man in his employ named Ramsey, went from Minor's place down to Albee's in search of mules. When they came near the house they saw a squaw on the lookout. She gave the alarm immediately when she discovered the two men. Five bucks were then seen to break from the garden, running towards the road above where the two men were, with the intention of cutting them off. Faulkner and his companion succeeded in getting ahead of them, however, and were getting well out of reach when they were fired upon by another Indian who had headed them off. They were passing under a bank, and within a few feet of the Indian when he fired, but fortunately missed his aim, the ball whizzing in frightful proximity to Ramsey's head. This much for them. After they had gained the hill they looked back and discovered the house on fire. Not knowing that Albee was at his place, Faulkner went on to Hoopa Valley. From there news reached Arcata on Saturday when a party started out immediately in search of Mr. Albee. They found all his fine improvements, the labor of years, in ashes, and a few hundred yards from the house, close to his plow, where he had been at work, pierced with two bullets and an arrow, they found the body of J. P. Albee. He had evidently been dead for several days. He was buried where he was found, not being in a condition to move. The subject of this melancholy sketch was no stranger to the people of this and adjoining counties. He came here with his family in 1853, lived a while in Eureka, from whence he moved to Table Bluff. Not finding sufficient range for his stock there, he moved to Redwood in 1856, since which time he had resided there with his family. He had ever been a warm friend to the Indians, and so confident was he that they regarded his friendship, it was with difficulty he could be induced to allow his family to be moved into town, after so many frightful massacres had taken place in localities less exposed than his own. He leaves a wife, one married and three single daughters and four boys to mourn.

In many respects Mr. Albee was a remarkable man. Unaided by education, he was a man of force of character and great strength of will. No obstacles in his path deterred him from the one idea of executing what he undertook; no argument could change a once established opinion. His judgment was eminently sound, his integrity unquestioned. Peace to his ashes.

JAMES C. SMILEY.

J. C. Smiley one of the earliest settlers and member of the Society of Pioneers of Humboldt County, was born in the city of Brunswick, Maine. Leaving his native State, he took passage to California on the bark *Sarah Moore*, and after a passage of six and a half months, arrived in San Francisco about the first of February, 1850. Like most young men who came to the State at that early date, Mr. Smiley had marked out his plan of operations for the immediate future, and to leave out of it the usual venture of mining enterprise would fall short of filling the "bill." He accordingly went to Wood Creek, in Tuolumne County, where one season's trial with sluice and rocker proved quite sufficient, to the end of rewarding him with lots of experience, but with little of the "dust." Returning to San Francisco, he remained there eighteen months.

He came to Humboldt Bay on the bark *General Wool*. Here he at once entered upon the erection of a saw-mill which, after its completion, in 1854, was known as the Smiley & Bean Mill. While Mr. Smiley's interest was connected with this mill it was twice partially burnt, and while engaged in putting on the roof the second time he marvelously escaped damage from the explosion of the boiler beneath, which otherwise left its wreckage about the premises of shattered machinery and timbers. Mr. Smiley immediately went to San Francisco, where he purchased a new boiler, which was shipped on the brig *Judson*, Ross, master, and at last (such were the aspects in those days of coast navigation) after a passage of seventy-eight days, was landed at Eureka. After the mill was again put in running condition, Mr. Smiley sold out his interest.

In 1863, in company with Frank S. Duff and the late Alonzo Monroe, he went to Reese River, Nevada, the company taking with them the machinery for the lumber manufacturing business in that place. This enterprise did not prove a success, nor did that of quartz-mining, in which he afterwards engaged, sufficiently satisfactory to keep him away from Humboldt, to which place he returned in 1865, where he has since permanently resided.

By profession Mr. Smiley is a house and sign painter. The designs and executions of the numerous works in the last-named branch of his art, to be seen in the city, are the highest testimonials to his skill, which, of the former, the principal hotels and private residences of the place, done under his contracts and supervision, are abounding proofs of the taste and thoroughness of a master in his profession.

No one of our citizens is more highly respected for the generous and exemplary traits that belong to his private life, nor any one less ambitions of the tempting emoluments and honors that may attach to official position.

Mr. Smiley is a bachelor, and with the exception of what is excluded by that term, is living in the enjoyment of all that an ample fortune can command.

JAMES E. MATHEWS.

J. E. Mathews is one of the stirring business men of Eureka, who came in 1871, and opened a variety store and news depot, and has conducted a profitable and constantly increasing business.

J. E. Mathews was born in the city of New York, February 22, 1845. His early life was that of newsboy, in New York and Brooklyn, and with his early energy he was the first to arrive in Brooklyn with extra *Heralds* containing the news of the firing on Fort Sumpter in 1861. The first money he earned was in selling the Brooklyn *Eagle*. In 1858, the Rev. Henry Ward Beecher had him arrested for striking him with a "shinney block" or ball. It was the custom of the boys while waiting for the *Eagle* to be issued at three o'clock to go on Columbia Street Hill and play "shinney." Rev. Beecher generally came along about that time, and one day young Mathews accidentally struck the reverend gentleman, who grabbed him by the coat collar and took him up to the top of the hill and turned him over to a policeman, but no charge was preferred for the boyish sport and accident. During the war he was employed on steamers running from New York to Havana, Mexico, New Orleans and Charleston. In April, 1865, on the coast of Florida they met a gunboat painted lead-color, but on returning from Havana the same boat was painted black, with flag at half-mast. From this tug they first learned of the assassination of President Lincoln. On arrival in New York City the body was lying in state and an immense number of people in line, extending from City Hall to Battery, to view the remains.

In 1864, while in Havana, he was offered by a lady, the situation of overseer on a plantation in Matauras, Cuba. But on account of age, being only nineteen, and a dislike to leave his native country, he declined the position, although every inducement was held out to him. He afterwards worked in a glass factory as glass blower.

On an hour's notice he set out for California from New York, December 10, 1867, and arrived in San Francisco January 23, 1868, on the steamer *Constitution*. He engaged in business on steamers running from San Francisco to other ports on the Pacific Coast. He was engaged in selling charts of Grant and Colfax and Seymour and Blair, in San Francisco, in the fall of 1868, and came to Eureka in March, 1871. His early life and later experience has peculiarly adapted him for the business in which he is now engaged.

He married Miss Linegar, in San Francisco, in 1873, who was born in Australia, but arrived in California at the age of six months. They have three children, named Ella Rose, Charles James, and Mary Gertrude Mathews.

ALONZO MONROE.

Alonzo Monroe, a pioneer, was born October 21, 1821, in Fair Haven, Connecticut. He was left an orphan at an early age, and went to New York City to live with his grandmother. He learned the engineers' and machinists' trade in the Novelty Iron Works. He went to New Orleans in 1843, and followed his profession until 1849. He started from there in 1849 in a schooner for California and arrived in San Francisco in February, 1850. He proceeded to the mines of Feather and Yuba Rivers. He was oftentimes very successful and as often lost all.

He came to Humboldt County in the fall of 1851, as a volunteer to fight the Indians. He returned to Trinity County, where he followed mining until 1853. He then engaged in butchering in Weaverville and Ridgeville until 1855, when he came to this county permanently. He was one of the Supervisors of Trinity County in 1855.

He married Miss Anna M. Alboe October 7, 1856, who was a native of Hillsdale, Michigan. There are six children, named Joseph Porter, Alonzo Judson, John W., Charles A., Horace P., Nettie S., Henry W. T., and Caltha J. E. Monroe.

Mr. Monroe drove a band of cattle from Oregon in 1859, and settled at Table Bluffs, and the next year drove them to Bear River. He sold a part of them and engaged in merchandising in Hydesville, under the firm name of Manheim & Co. Mr. Hyde gave them an acre of land if they would build a store on what was then called "Goose Prairie." He removed with his family to Eureka in March, 1861, and there remained until August, 1863, when he went overland to Reese River, Nevada, driving two span of horses. He discovered and named a good many mines, among them "Eureka." He endured in these trips incredible hardships incident to a new country. One night camping in the sagebrush without fire or food he lay down in his blankets and suffered from the intense cold.

He sold his mines in Nevada for a good price and returned to San Francisco in 1870.

He built a hotel on the corner of Second and E Streets which was burned January 1, 1876, and rebuilt of brick in April of the same year. He was a very resolute and courageous man, and no ordinary discouragements would keep him down. He was honored as a man of public spirit and integrity. He was stricken with paralysis in 1875, which affected his mind of late years, and gradually failing, he died March 20, 1882.

The funeral obsequies were attended by an unusually large number of citizens, both at the church and at the grave. The remains were attended from the residence to the church, and thence to the grave (The Eureka Cornet Band acting as escort) by Humboldt Lodge, F. & A. M., and the Humboldt County Pioneers. The funeral services at the church were of a most appropriate nature, and at the grave the beautiful burial service of the Masonic Order was observed.

S. G. WHIPPLE.

Captain S. G. Whipple, one of the early settlers, commenced the publication of the *Northern Californian* at Union in 1858, and merged with the *Times* in 1860. In 1863, during the Indian troubles, he was commissioned as Major of the Battalion of Mountaineers, and was afterward promoted to a Colonelcy. At the close of the service he was mustered out, and placed in charge of the Indian Reservation at Hoopa as agent, serving a term in that position; he then enlisted in the regular army, as Captain, and is now stationed at Fort Klamath.

JOHN BURMAN.

John Burman, one of the old pioneers, was drowned in Mad River, at the crossing of the upper old trail, on the 1st of March, 1857. The deceased came to this bay early in 1850, with the party that came up the coast in the *Cameo*. The party landed at Point St. George, present site of Crescent City, and he with Nelson Jenkins, Van Thulen and Peterson coasted down in whaleboat in search of the mouth of the Trinity, the object of all the numerous adventures cruising about this coast at that date. They ran into Eel River, supposing it to be the Trinity, and then returned to their party, and afterwards the deceased piloted the schooner *J. M. Ryerson* into Eel River, the only vessel that had ever been in there. He was one of the original parties who located and laid off Union, and resided there. He was a native of Sweden and about thirty-three years of age at the time of his death.

WILLIAM HARRISON WOODBURY.

William H. Woodbury was born at Salem, Essex County, Mass., Feb. 2, 1830. At the age of fourteen years, shipped before the mast, on the barque *Guy Head*, of Boston, bound for Australia, the Society Islands and California. He arrived in San Francisco in the spring of 1854, where he left the vessel and worked at painting, paper-hanging, and such other work as he could obtain. After working about a year he became restless ashore, and shipped for sea again, and continued until the latter part of June, 1855, on the steamer *America*, at which time the steamer was burned in the harbor at Crescent City.

He then lived at Crescent City, where he engaged in boating and whale-fishing until 1857, when he engaged as clerk in the grocery store of F. Nauke; here he continued until 1861, when he engaged with Dr. H. Smith and Wm. Coburn in salmon-fishing, near the mouth of Smith River. The flood of 1861 and 1862 came and washed fishery buildings, boats, and everything to sea, leaving nothing to show where the fishery had been.

He next started a small cigar and stationery store, and after carrying this on for a few months he entered into a co-partnership with T. S. Pomeroy in the grocery business, which was continued until the death of Mr. Pomeroy in 1865, since which time he has been carrying on business by himself. During his residence at Crescent City he has held several offices, having been elected Constable at twenty-one years of age, and afterward Justice of the Peace.

He was appointed postmaster at Crescent City June 12, 1865. He was assessor of Del Norte County for seven years, and became thoroughly acquainted with its resources. He is active in all the secret and benevolent societies, and is a leading member of the Masons and Odd Fellows, as well as the United Workmen.

He was married to Elmira Fleming June 12, 1865, and has three children—girls, aged fourteen, twelve and ten years.

WILLIAM SAVILLE, ESQ.

William Saville first saw the light of day in Old England, being the eldest son of an eminent British barrister. In early life he pored over the pages of Blackstone, but being of a roving, rollicking disposition, he abandoned the law office for "a life on the ocean wave and a home on the rolling deep," which latter occupation he followed for several years, graduating from an ordinary seaman to sailing master. He, however, getting tired of a seafaring life, landed in Crescent City in the year 1855, being then about twenty-eight years of age. Since that time he has been engaged in various occupations, and has filled many positions of public trust. He was one of the first Supervisors of Del Norte County, and has served one term as District Attorney of said county, and while practicing at the bar is said to be a very effective and exhaustive talker. His hearing having become somewhat impaired, owing to the effects produced from the bursting of a cannon in close proximity to him in some naval engagement while in the British navy, he forsook his lucrative practice at the bar and now occupies the position of Treasurer of Del Norte County, which he has filled for several successive terms. He is a whole-souled fellow, and his hand is always open to the needy. He resides in Crescent City, although he is largely interested in business in other parts of Del Norte County.

J. K. DOLLISON,
NOTARY PUBLIC,
Court Commissioner, Real Estate and Loan Agent, and Conveyancer.

CITY LOTS, FARMING AND TIMBER LANDS FOR SALE.

OFFICE:—No. 130 Second Street, Vance Block, Eureka, Humboldt Bay, California.

ATTORNEYS OF HUMBOLDT COUNTY.

The following is a complete list of the attorneys of this county as they appear on the roll of the Superior Court:—
James Hanna, C. G. Stafford, W. H. Brumfield, S. M. Buck, J. J. DeHaven, J. D. H. Chamberlin, G. W. Tompkins, R. B. Dickson, J. H. G. Weaver, G. W. Hunter, Ernest Sevier, E. W. Wilson, J. M. Melendy, T. H. Foss, Jr., J. K. Miller, P. F. Hart, G. W. Hopkins, E. G. Anderson, A. J. Monroe, R. W. Miller, James N. Shibles.

HUMBOLDT COUNTY COMMON SCHOOLS.

First School, Present Condition, Private Schools, Financial Prospects, etc.

THE early educational interests of Humboldt County have no obtainable statistics. Suffice it to say, the first organized free school was at Arcata (then Union). This district was organized in 1852, with fifty pupils, while Humboldt County was a part of Trinity County. In the school year ending October 31, 1854, there had been three common schools, or public schools, kept in the county, as per report of school officers. There were 180 children of age entitled to school money.

In the district of Union (Arcata) there had been a school taught nine months by Mrs. A. E. Roberts.

In the district of Eureka there had been a school kept three months during 1853, by George W. Gilkey.

In the district of Bucksport there had been a common school kept three months by Miss Louisa Wasgatt. In addition to the public school at Union there had been a private school kept for a portion of the year. Hon. A. J. Huestis was elected Superintendent of schools in 1855. In November, 1855, Bucksport school district was organized, including Bucksport, Table Bluff, Pacific, and Eel River Townships.

Maj. E. H. Howard succeeded Huestis, and during his administration the formation of new school districts was the principal matter of interest, and procuring suitable teachers. It was a matter of great interest in early times when mails were uncertain, to get the Superintendent's reports to the State Department in time to secure the county's share of the State money.

FIRST SCHOOL DISTRICT.

In 1856 there were only three schools organized under the common law: one at Bucksport, one at Eureka and one at Arcata. At Bucksport the citizens erected a fine school house, which answered the purpose of a village church. The second story had been finished off by the Masonic fraternity for their meetings. At Eureka, also, there was a school building.

Arcata had not shown an equally public spirit in this respect, although a school had been kept once and the number of pupils was greater than at the other places. But the next year Messrs. Jowby and Martin of the Trustees purchased Mr. Henry White's house for the sum of $800, one-half in hand, one-half in sixty days and had caused the same to be temporarily fitted up for the reception of the school, and it was occupied by Mr. Dusty as a school house in 1857.

Henry H. Severns was the next Superintendent. He reported in 1860 the total number of districts as nine; the number of children in the county 502; moneys received from the State, $803.04; and the expenditures for all school purposes $7,036.

Rev. W. L. Jones was the next Superintendent. He was an energetic, earnest Superintendent, and did much for the schools. At present he is at Hilo, Sandwich Islands, in charge of a private institution. J. B. Brown was appointed Superintendent when the Rev. W. L. Jones resigned, after which he was elected continuously until he refused to accept the office. Too much cannot be said of J. B. Brown as a teacher and Superintendent, for fourteen years he had charge of the schools in Eureka. These schools have flourished and prospered under his supervision. These schools compare favorably with schools of the larger cities of the State.

E. C. Cummings, the next Superintendent, had been engaged for several years as teacher in various parts of the country. Previous to his term of office he had been a member of the Board of Education, he was re-elected to the office. E. C. Cummings had no opposition to the office at the first election. At the close of his official term he withdrew from the profession. Perhaps no county in the State has developed more than Humboldt during the last decade. Twenty-four school districts included all Humboldt County could boast ten years ago; now she has fifty-six, and employs eighty teachers. The school affairs of the county are now ably managed by J. B. Casterlin.

For 1882, the Superintendent apportioned from the State School Fund, of Humboldt County, the sum of $158.50 to each teacher assigned to the several districts, and an additional sum from the same fund, of $7.95 per capita on the average daily attendance as shown by the last annual report. Ten per cent. of the State Fund of each district was set apart for library purposes. There was also apportioned from the County School Fund, $13.50 per teacher.

The following is the total apportionment:—

No. of Districts	State.	Library.	County.
56.	$25,403.08	$2,320.77	$1,066.50

DUTIES OF COUNTY SUPERINTENDENTS.

The powers of the County School Superintendents are greater than they were in the beginning. In 1855 they were required to aid the School Trustees in the examination of teachers—a duty which would have been rather hard to perform in case two or more Boards of Trustees had held examination at ten o'clock of the same day. County Superintendents are now required: To apportion all school moneys; to report to the State Superintendent on blanks furnished; to fill all vacancies in the Boards of Trustees by appointment; to draw requisitions for all warrants on the school fund; to visit schools; to preside over Teachers' Institutes, and to secure the attendance thereat of competent lecturers; to issue temporary certificates in certain cases; to preserve all school reports, and to grade the schools. The County Superintendent is *ex officio* Secretary and member of the Boards of Education.

CLIMATE AS AFFECTED BY WIND CURRENTS AND FOGS.

Healthfulness, Fogs, Rain-fall, Temperature, Meteorological Table, etc.

The climate of Humboldt County differs considerably from most any other county in the State. It presents many phases, and even within a few miles there can be found wonderful diversities, not to say extremes, of climate. Along the coast the atmosphere is always more or less laden with moisture, and the winds are almost constantly blowing, hence it is necessarily cold in that section at all seasons of the year.

Just inside the first range of mountains the air is shorn in a measure of its moisture, but is still damp enough to keep the temperature reduced greatly and to make it really the most pleasant place in the county to live, it being that happy mean where the wind is shorn of its chilling fog, and the heat of the midsummer's sun is tempered by passing through a stratum of moist air.

Farther in the interior the air is shorn of all its moisture and becomes arid and parches the vegetation as it passes over it. The summer's sun pours its unimpeded rays into those valleys in a merciless manner, as if fully determined to prove to mankind that it can shine more fervidly to-day than it did yesterday. And yet it is not so very disagreeable, and those accustomed to it really enjoy its pelting rays.

On the coast the usual fogs of the summer season set in about the first of May. This phenomenon is of almost daily occurrence till the middle of August, and is an important factor in the growth of grass and crops along the sea-coast. About the first of May the trade-winds set in from the north-west and prove a great agent in the modification of the climate on the coast, serving to reduce the temperature wherever it penetrates among the valleys of the interior. These are the breezes which bear on their wings the burdens of mist and fog which are so refreshing to the growing vegetation along the coast, making the season much longer in that section than farther back, and adapting it for grazing and especially for dairying purposes.

These great fog-banks form every day off the land, caused perhaps by the meeting of cold and warm strata of air. In the afternoons this fog comes inland with the breeze which commences about noon daily. This moisture-laden air is not deleterious in any way to the health of the inhabitants along the coast, except, perhaps, those affected with lung or bronchial troubles. It is a fact, on the contrary, that the most healthful portion of the year is that in which the fogs prevail. These fog-banks spread over the country in the afternoons and continue all night, but the early morning sun is apt to dispel them. Sometimes, however, there come several days in succession when the sun is shut out from the view of man altogether along the coast. It is then generally dreary and cold, and the wind whistles and sighs through the branches of the giant redwoods in a mournful, disconsolate sort of way, and the dash of the breakers against the rocky strand gets to be a very melancholy swash, monotonous and irksome, and the heart of man longs for a gleam of sunshine almost as the prisoner pines for liberty. But it is not always thus gloomy, for there are many days, during the season, of unexcelled beauty and loveliness—days when the sun shines in unalloyed brightness from out the blue empyrean of heaven's own vault, mantling the world in a sheen of silver.

The following table showing the range of the barometer and thermometer at Humboldt Bay was prepared for this work by W. P. Daykin, Esq.:

Month.	1878		1879		1880	
	Barometer	Thermometer	Barometer	Thermometer	Barometer	Thermometer
January..	29.30	49	31.00	47	31.30	49
February.	29.30	50	28.00	47	29.30	45
March ...	31.00	53	31.00	51	31.00	49
April	30.00	54	30.00	55	31.20	48
May	31.20	58	31.00	58	31.30	53
June.....	30.00	59	30.00	57	30.00	55
July	31.24	62	31.00	61	31.30	61
August ..	31.00	61	30.30	61	31.00	61
Septem'r	30.00	59	30.30	56	30.00	57
October..	30.00	61	31.00	57	31.00	56
November	31.00	54	30.00	50	30.00	50
December.	31.00	50	31.00	49	29.30	52
Average		56		54		53

The average rain-fall is much more in Humboldt than in San Francisco or Sacramento. It is a fact, there never has been a year yet when the crops and grass were an entire failure for want of rain. The season of rain in this section may be said to commence in October and end in May. It is rare that it rains more than a day or two at a time, and the intervals range from a few days to several weeks. This is truly the beautiful season.

According to the rain record of R. E. Foster, at Bucksport, the rain-fall for ten years has been as follows:—

1873................28.45 1874................36.66
1875................22.95 1876................43.03
1877................28.18 1878................50.94
1879................21.02 1880................48.02
1881................38.61 1882................38.19

The average rain-fall for the past ten years was 35.11 inches.

The average fall, in inches, for the seasons and the year at different localities is:

Places.	Spring	Summer	Autumn	Winter	Year
San Francisco....	6.64	.13	3.31	11.33	21.41
Sacramento......	7.01	.00	2.01	12.11	21.73
Humboldt Bay...	13.51	1.13	4.87	16.28	35.79
Fort Yuma......	0.27	1.30	.86	.72	3.15
San Diego.......	2.74	.55	1.24	5.60	10.43

Snow is very rare on the coast and in the valleys, and never remains for many days except in the Klamath Valley, where there is sometimes a month's sleighing during the winter.

DAIRY, MILL & FARM OF HENRY WESTBROOK, SMITH RIVER VALLEY, DEL NORTE CO. CAL.

Business in Early Days.

First Express Lines, Post-Offices, Ferries, Bridges, and Modes of Travel.

One of the indispensable institutions of the early days was the mounted express. Without it business could scarcely be carried on, so slow was communication by means of pack-trains. The express consisted chiefly of letters, papers, gold-dust, and small packages, all goods of any bulk or weight being carried by the packers. There was no post-office until 1853, and all mail was brought and carried by the express companies. At first the price for each letter carried to Trinity was three dollars, and half that sum for a newspaper.

FIRST EXPRESS LINE.

The first express ever introduced into the mines of this county was when A. E. Raynes began to run between Trinidad and Bestville in the spring of 1851. Before that the people had been completely isolated from the outside world. Occasionally a few letters were brought in by a pack-train and others carried out.

FIRST POST-OFFICES.

In June, 1853, the following offices were appointed: Union, H. H. Murdock; Eureka, H. W. Bean; Bucksport, J. Clark; Trinidad, L. B. Gilkey. But no provision was made for transporting the mails other than the small receipts of offices. Mails were very irregular, often were received only once in four weeks. Leland & McComb were the pioneer express men of Humboldt Bay. They ran an express from the bay to Crescent City, Gold Bluff, etc., and John N. Utter was Superintendent.

In 1854, Adams & Co. established an Express and Banking House in Arcata, and fitted up a portion of the County Clerk's office for that purpose. It was under the superintendence of B. H. Wayman. It ran daily from Bucksport via Eureka to Union. John Vance, Esq., was agent at Eureka.

Messrs. Filley & Co. commenced in November, 1854, to run an omnibus from the steamboat-landing to Arcata.

Strawbridge & Co. established an express in 1854, having a route from the towns of the bay to Klamath, Trinity, and Salmon River mines.

Messrs. Chism & Co. brought into the county, in 1857, the first Concord Coach to run between Eureka and Eel River.

FIRST FERRIES AND BRIDGES.

In the spring of 1851, to accommodate the travel between Trinidad and the Salmon River mines, a ferry across the Klamath some five miles below the mouth of the Trinity was established on the regular road to Bestville. The proprietors were Gwin R. Tompkins and Charles McDermit. This ferry was placed in charge of a man named Blackburn, and was usually known as Blackburn's Ferry. H. W. Lake, in 1861, constructed a wooden bridge across the Trinity, near the hotel in Hoopa Valley. It was fourteen feet wide and considered a substantial structure. John F. Martin put up a wire suspension bridge across the Klamath in 1861, three miles below Weitchpeck, at a cost of about $4,000. Length of span in clear, 298 feet, width, eight feet, height above water, ninety-one feet. It is a fine and substantial structure.

PACKING TO THE MINES.

Packing to the Salmon and Trinity mines from Trinidad began in 1850, and among others engaged in it were E. P. Rowe, Abisha Swain, Charles McDermit, Charles D. Moore, F. F. Marx, and E. W. Conner.

Over 400 mules left Arcata in the week ending April 11, 1857, loaded for Klamath, Salmon, Trinity and Hoopa Valleys. Six hundred mules, heavily freighted, left Arcata during the week ending August 1, 1857, for Weaverville, Trinity, Klamath and Salmon, at an average of 275 pounds to the animal. The amount of goods taken out by these 600 mules would be 165,000 pounds. This gives a good idea of the extent of the early packing trade of Humboldt, which is still conducted quite extensively from Arcata.

OVERLAND ROUTE.

During the season of 1873-4 the Legislature authorized Humboldt County to issue bonds for the construction of a road from a point about eight miles east of Eureka to Round Valley in Mendocino County. This road was known as the Kneeland's Prairie and Round Valley Road, and was completed under this act as far as Blocksburg, a distance of seventy-four miles. It was afterwards extended to a point 100 miles southeast from Eureka. The amount of bonds issued for the construction of the road was $125,000. The road is ten feet wide, with turnouts fifteen feet wide, and fifty feet long within sight of each other. By the terms of the contract all curves were required to have a radius of thirty feet. The completion of this highway has been very serviceable to the county in the way of inducing and affording facilities for immigration. It is traversed daily (except Sunday) during the season, from April to December, by the stages of the Humboldt and Mendocino Stage Company, which bring the United States Mail through from San Francisco, the schedule time being three days in summer and four days in winter.

The Humboldt and Mendocino Stage Company has laid out a large sum of money in fitting up and equipping the route, and have succeeded in making it popular. S. F. Bullard, of Hydesville, is Superintendent of the line. Bullard & Sweasey are the proprietors.

SECRET AND BENEVOLENT AND LITERARY SOCIETIES.

Masons, Odd Fellows, Good Templars, Knights of Honor, Sons of Temperance, Workmen, etc.

THIS county has a good class of inhabitants, and in habits of thrift and industry are far ahead of many other counties in the State. Society is, however, somewhat divided into groups, caused by the great mixture of nations and habits of life. In early times people were more united and harmonious in their associations. The early settlers well remember the long trip taken to visit a friend. Since the organization of the county, the population has slowly but steadily increased.

SOCIETY, PAST AND PRESENT.

In early times society was disorganized, and disagreements among settlers were common, but of late years peace and quiet have been the rule.

In early times the settlers were without the thousand attractions and comforts of a home, cut off from the pleasures of society and association of ladies, living in hotels, boarding-houses, cabins, back-rooms of stores, offices, and, in fact, in all kinds of unattractive places. It is no wonder that the early miners and business men turned eagerly to the amusements of the day for the needed relaxation. Saloons, with their clinking glasses, convivial songs and inviting music, were among the first adjuncts of a new town.

The miner, when his day's work was done, the merchant, when released from the busy cares of trade, the happy delver who had "struck it rich" and came to town to spend his "pile," as well as the penniless "bummer" all sought the cheerful rooms where music and liquor were plenty, and where the games of chance formed an attraction, even to him who simply watched the fitful changes of fortune. Music was in demand, and he who had any instrument from which he could invoke harmonious strains was certain to find an opportunity to do so for an ample remuneration. Violins, guitars, and other light-stringed instruments that were easily transported, were the first to find their way into the mining camps. The place that was able to secure anything approaching to the magnificent proportions of an orchestra was certain of an overflowing patronage.

Gambling saloons were the first to don fine raiment; even when in shake buildings with canvas walls, an attempt was made at ornamentation, to render them attractive to the eye, and inviting by contrast with the general crudeness of their surroundings. Church organizations were slow in forming. They came next after the secret societies. Among the first organized were those about Arcata and Eureka.

FREE AND ACCEPTED MASONS.

The Free and Accepted Masons erected a neat and eligible hall at Bucksport in 1854. The lower part was occupied as a school-room.

In 1856 a lodge was organized in Arcata. The Masonic Lodge at Arcata celebrated the 24th of June, 1856, by a procession in regalia from their hall to the church, where an address was delivered by A. J. Huestis, of Bucksport. There was a ball in the evening at Murlock's Hall, and a supper by Capt. Ball, of the American.

The Masonic Lodges of the county united in celebrating the 24th of June, 1857, at Eureka, the Arcata Lodge joining them on the steamer *Glide*. At the school house an appropriate address was delivered by E. H. Howard, Esq.

Eel River Lodge was instituted September 11, 1860, at Hydesville under dispensation of N. Green Curtis. The financial condition of this lodge is good, and has expended large sums for charity. All the lodges are in a flourishing condition.

The following is a list of Masonic Societies of the county, with the time and place of meeting and officers for the first of the year 1882:—

Myrtle Lodge of Perfection, No. 10—14th Degree—A. and A. Scottish Rite of Freemasonry. Stated meetings on the first Monday of each month at Masonic Hall, Eureka. S. M. Buck, T. P. G. M., J. S. Murray, Jr., Secretary. Regular Convocation of Humboldt, R. A. Chapter, No. 52, meets at the Masonic Hall on the second Monday of each month. John A. Watson, M. E. H. P, W. P. Hanna, Secretary. Humboldt Lodge, No. 79, F. and A. M., will hold their stated meetings at their hall, corner of Second and G Streets, Eureka, on the first Thursday evening of each month. J. D. H. Chamberlin, W. M., John S. Murray, Secretary. Eel River Lodge, No. 147, F. and A. M., will hold their stated meetings at their hall in Rohnerville, on the first Saturday evening of or next preceding the full moon. S. H. Crabtree, W. M., F. B. Simonds, Secretary. Ferndale Lodge, No. 193, F. and A. M., will hold their stated meetings on Saturday evening on or next succeeding the full of the moon in each month at 7:30 o'clock. K. Geer, W. M., James Howard, Secretary.

ODD FELLOWS' LODGES.

The Odd Fellows annually celebrate the organization of the first lodge of the order in the United States, Washington Lodge, of Baltimore, No. 1. This was chartered by the Manchester Unity, February 2, 1820. Since that time over 1,000,000 persons have been initiated into the order in America. The introduction of Odd Fellowship into California in 1849, by the formation in Sacramento of an Odd Fellows Association for the relief of the destitute, is one of the brightest pages in the history of the State. Since then the order has grown to giant proportions here, with more than 20,000 members.

April 25, 1859, was held the first celebration of the Odd Fel-

SECRET AND BENEVOLENT ORGANIZATIONS.

lows of this county, consisting of the two lodges of Eureka and Arcata. At eight o'clock in the morning the procession formed in front of the Hall, in Eureka, and preceded by the Eureka Brass Band, they marched through the principal streets of the town, when they embarked on the steamer *Glide* for Arcata. Arriving in Union at eleven o'clock, they were joined by the members of the order there and all paraded through the streets, making a fine appearance. The procession then moved to Masonic Hall, where Anniversary Lodge, No. 85, I. O. O. F., was organized. At two o'clock they went to the Methodist Church, where an oration was delivered by Mr. Benedict.

Humboldt Lodge, No. 77, is located at Eureka, and was organized September 6, 1858, being the first of the order in the county. Its stated meetings are held at its hall every Monday night. For the first few years its growth was slow, and its members had many adverse circumstances to contend with. Eventually they were overcome, and subsequently its career has been one wherein its usefulness has only been equaled by its prosperity. Its membership numbers 218 persons, and the value of its property, consisting of a fine hall, real estate, cash, etc., is about $15,000. The aggregate sum disbursed by this society for relief and charity is $18,479,00. Mount Zion Encampment was organized on the 24th of May, 1867, at Arcata. It was removed in 1872 to Eureka. The total membership at the present time is eighty-seven. The property of the lodge is its lodge-room, furniture, securities and coin, in the total value of $3,110, and the disbursements of the lodge in the dispensing weekly benefits and other fraternal contributions since it was organized are $9,201. Its stated meetings are at Odd Fellows Hall, corner 2d and F Streets.

Fortuna Lodge, No. 221, was organized August 30, 1873, and holds its regular meetings in the hall of the I. O. O. F. With a record of 135 members, $9,000 in coin, bonds and mortgages; $19,562 disbursed in charities, the society may well be called benevolent and prosperous.

Eel River Lodge, No. 210, was instituted October 15, 1872, at Rohnerville, by authority of a dispensation granted by A. C. Bradford, then Grand Master, D. D. G. Master J. E. Wyman officiating. A goodly number of brothers from Humboldt and other visitors were present. The greatest number of members at any one time was eighty. Present membership, thirty-five. In 1876 about fifteen members living in the vicinity of Hydesville withdrew from this lodge for the purpose of forming a lodge in that town. This they did, and it is known as Hydesville Lodge, No. 250. The lodge owns a good hall, 28x60 feet in size, and a well located and laid out cemetery. It is free from debt and its property is valued at $2,632.00. It has distributed in benefits, charities, etc., about $3,000.

The Odd Fellows in Eureka are making preparations to build a Hall, which will serve as a permanent meeting place for lodges and the Encampment. Contract let to J. Simpson for $18,950.

The American Legion of Honor meets at their hall in Eureka. The objects of this order are to unite fraternally all persons of sound bodily health and good moral character who are socially acceptable and between eighteen and sixty-five years of age. To give all moral and material aid in its power to its members and those dependent upon them. To educate its members socially, morally and intellectually. To establish a fund for the relief of sick and distressed members. To establish a benefit fund from which, on the satisfactory evidence of the death of a member who has complied with all its lawful requirements, a sum not exceeding $5,000 shall be paid to the family, orphans, or dependents, as the member may direct. There was a lodge of the Legion of Honor instituted at Ferndale in July, 1881.

Bay City Lodge of United Workmen was organized, June 21, 1879, and it has now eighty-three members. Its objects and aims are the promotion of a fraternal feeling among its members, and to provide for the families of deceased members by paying $2,000 at the death of each to the widow or other relative. Several lodges are now organized in the county.

Humboldt Bay Mutual Relief Association is in a flourishing condition. The following prominent citizens are Directors to serve for the ensuing year: William Carson, C. F. Roberts, John A. Watson, George Graham, C. W. Long, J. H. G. Weaver, H. Dorman, Thomas Vance, H. Kingston, H. Connick, I. R. Brown, J. D. H. Chamberlin.

Lincoln Lodge K. of P. was organized and dedicated under auspices flattering to the cardinal aims of the order: "Friendship, Charity and Benevolence." Its stated meetings are held at the Pythian Castle, on the southeast corner of 3d and E Streets, Eureka. There are fifty-seven members in this lodge. Its property consists of lodge-room, furniture, money and mortgages, equal to $3,725, and its financial condition is prosperous. It has expended for beneficiary and charitable purposes $4,250.25. The Knights of Pythias of Eureka and Arcata united in a grand hurrah time. The occasion of the celebration being the installation of the officers of North Star Lodge, No. 30, of Arcata. After the conclusion of the proceedings the Knights partook of supper at Richert's Hotel, over 100 persons being at the table. It is said that this was one of the largest gatherings in the history of fraternal societies of the county.

Aurora Lodge K. of P. meets at Ferndale, and we believe there are other lodges in the county in flourishing condition among them Lincoln Lodge, No. 34.

Humboldt Bay Council A. S. of H., was instituted at Eureka July 23, 1881.

Eureka Branch of Land League was organized March 15, 1881. It has seventy members, and its meetings are held monthly at the hall of the Catholic Church.

The Grand Army of the Republic formed an organization in June, 1881, of the old soldiers about Ferndale. J. N. Adams, Commander, G. L. Benedict, Adjutant.

A Band of Hope was organized in Eureka by C. S. Haswell, in 1878. It was designed for children, and was very successful in point of numbers. It has recently been resuscitated and its field of labor enlarged so as to include adults as well as children. It is called Garfield Lodge, and at present has 103 members.

No Surrender Loyal Orange Lodge, No. 143, grants sick, funeral and other benefits. It meets first and third Saturdays of each month. It was organized February 21, 1877, and has 120 members; and lodge furniture, coin and securities, valued at about $3,000.

There are numerous other secret and benevolent organizations in the county, but from the list already given a stranger will learn that the inhabitants are of a social nature.

TEMPERANCE ORGANIZATIONS.

Probably the first temperance organization was an order started in Arcata in 1857, called the "Reformed Drunkards." Soon after the Sons of Temperance held numerous meetings, and flourished for a time. The first organization was at Eureka in January, 1858, called "Morning Star" Division. It met in Murdock's Hall. The Rev. P. H. Shafer officiated as Deputy W. P.

On the ruins of the Sons was built up the Good Templars. The last meeting of the order elected for the northern district the following officers for the year 1882: D. C. T. and D. D., W. F. Brown, Eureka; D. V. T., Sister Campton, Rohnerville; D. S.; A. M. Gill, Rohnerville; D. F. S.; G. W. Hopkins, Arcata; D. T., Sister Julia Stearns, Arcata; D. M.; A. J. Coyle, Hydesville; D. I. G.; F. Cabarus, Trinidad; D. O. G.; W. B. McClane, Arcata.

At the session of 1882 the Ferndale Lodge reported a membership of forty-two; the Port Kenyon Lodge, twenty-four; North Star Lodge, twenty-nine; Mountain Lodge, twenty-seven; Hydesville Lodge, forty-nine; Humboldt Lodge, eighty-four; Rohnerville Lodge, forty.

The Good Templars in Humboldt County are banded together for the purpose of combatting the fell-destroyer—intoxicating liquors—together with all its concomitant baleful evils and influences. Lodges are flourishing in all parts of the county, but we were not able to obtain reports from the organizations.

AGRICULTURAL SOCIETY.

A preliminary meeting of citizens to organize a County Agricultural Society was held September 28, 1860, at Hydesville, of those "interested in the progress of Agriculture, the Mechanical Arts and the general Development of the Material Resources of Humboldt County." This meeting adjourned to October 13th, and the following officers were elected: Dr. Jonathan Clark, President; Samuel Strong, Vice-President; William Olmstead, Treasurer, and William J. Sweasey, Secretary.

June 1, 1861, the Society held their first annual meeting at Brett's Hall, Eureka. The first fair was held at Hydesville on October 8, 9, and 10, 1861, and turned out to be a success.

The Society held its last fair at Rohnerville, October 4, 5, 6, and 7, 1881. It is now called the Ninth District Agricultural Association, and is composed of the Counties of Del Norte, Humboldt and Mendocino. The premiums were divided into five departments, viz: live-stock, mechanical products, agricultural products, fruits and miscellaneous, the latter including household fabrics, fancy work, painting and drawing, etc. The highest prize, $25, is offered for the best display of agricultural implements. The following are the members of the Board for 1882: G. C. Barber and F. Z. Boynton, Ferndale; H. S. Case and Robert Porter, Hydesville; T. D. Felt, Rohnerville; Henry Rohner, Springville; E. C. Newton, Smith River, Del Norte County. Officers are, G. C. Barber, Ferndale, President; S. H. Crabtree, Rohnerville, Secretary; Morris Levinger, Rohnerville, Treasurer.

THE EUREKA GUARD.

The Eureka Guard was organized and became a part of the National Guard of the State of California in March, 1879, with about forty names on the roll of membership. The officers elected for the term were Alexander Campbell, Captain; J. B. Brown, First Lieutenant, and W. P. Hanna, Second Lieutenant. In the rank and file were many who had served in various positions in the army during the "late unpleasantness." The work of drilling was at once commenced, and it was not long before the company could execute many evolutions in a creditable manner. Lieutenant Brown was commissioned Captain; William P. Hanna was promoted to First Lieutenant, and James T. Kelcher, Second Lieutenant. Under this set of officers the company has moved for nearly two years. Captain Brown, during that period, has given all the attention possible to this command, has spent valuable time and money, and, with the assistance of his officers, has made great improvement in the company. Much interest has been taken by all, privates as well as officers, and the Eureka Guard to-day stands second to no company of militia in the State. Their arms, accoutrements and property are in splendid order, their armory supplied with everything necessary, and their execution of the manual and knowledge of tactics would rank among the first.

The annual election for commissioned officers of the Eureka Guard was held in December, 1881, at the armory. Forty-nine members of the company were present and voted. Major Pierce H. Ryan presided by order of Brigadier General J. C. Wall. J. W. Freese was elected Captain, W. P. Hanna as First Lieutenant, and Jas. T. Kelcher as Second Lieutenant—the officers elect for the ensuing term.

Churches of Humboldt County.

Date of Organization, First Members, Officers, Present Membership, Location, Present Condition.

FIRST SERMON PREACHED.

It is beyond doubt, that the church history of this county begins with a meeting appointed for divine worship at Bucksport, early in the summer of 1850, on which occasion the Rev. A. J. Huestis preached the sermon. These services were continued every Sabbath, with few exceptions, until 1853, when as a field for missionary work the M. E. Conference supplied Humboldt by the appointment of regular pastors of which, at Eureka, the Rev. James Corwin was first. The first class in Eureka was formed by the Rev. Chas. Hinckley, November 27, 1859. The school house now standing and still used as such, on the corner of G and 3d Streets, did duty on the occasion of religious exercises and lectures, for all denominations.

The first Methodist church building in Eureka was built and dedicated in 1859. The bell for this church was obtained through the efforts of the pastor in charge, Rev. Chas. W. Hinckley, and was first hung from the top of a large stump near where the building now stands. Mr. H. was accustomed to do his own bell-ringing, and, what is not always the case, also to preach his own sermons; and it may be added, no one found fault with the tone of the bell or of the preacher.

Afterwards this building was sold and removed from the lot, and in 1866 the present one was erected in its place, incurring a heavy debt, which was not discharged until August, 1872. The Rev. Ed. J. Jones was then pastor and mainly instrumental to this result. During the pastorate of the Rev. Dr. Haswell the church building was much improved. There are sittings for about 600, gallery and floor. The parsonage, situate on the adjoining lot, is a modest, unpretentious cottage, well furnished, and affords the usual comforts and conveniences of modern dwellings. The aggregate value of the church property is $6,500.

The first Trustees were G. D. Wilson, A. J. Huestis and B. L. Waite. The present number of members is seventy-nine, but its highest number has reached one hundred. A good library belongs to the Sunday-school of about 300 volumes and the school is in a most prosperous condition, having now 210 scholars. Within the twelve years last preceding about $14,000 have been distributed for salaries of pastors, and benevolent contributions. S. H. Rhoades is now the pastor.

Rohnerville M. E. Church was organized in 1852, by Wesley Harrow. He preached near Eel River on a place owned by Robert Roberts. In 1853 the services were conducted by two local preachers, J. Burnell and Mr. Stringfield. In 1854 the church was connected with the Eel River circuit, and James Corwin was appointed the first regular pastor. This charge has been quite prosperous, having as high as fifty-five members in past years, and at present forty-six. The present pastor is H. H. Stevens. The property is valued at $2,000. The society owns a church parsonage, and a barn and the ground on which they stand. They are free from debt and in tolerable good condition. The church will seat about 150 persons. The parsonage is neat and attractive in design, and most pleasantly situated.

FIRST CHURCH BUILDING ERECTED.

The M. E. Church at Arcata was organized in 1850. Rev. Asa P. White, the pioneer preacher of California, pitched his tent of blue cloth in San Francisco in 1849. He commenced his labors in Arcata in the same tent where afterwards stood Kirby's stable, and there organized this society.

The present minister is John B. Chisholm, and the membership is forty-four. The society has a church and parsonage valued at $2,200, and the society is in a flourishing condition.

Christ Church, Eureka, was organized June 1, 1870. Its stated services are held on every Sunday, and other services as the rector may appoint. On the evening of June 8, 1870, the members of the parish met and elected a vestry, which organized by the election of Thomas Walsh, Senior Warden, and Robert Searles, Junior Warden. The vestry then called the Rev. J. Gierlow to the rectorship of the parish.

The church was consecrated on the 5th day of February 1871, by the Rt. Rev. W. I. Kip, D. D. The Rev. J. S. Thomson was elected rector January 1, 1872, and was followed by Rev. J. H. Babcock and Rev. W. L. Githens. The Rev. H. D. Lathrop, D. D., of the Church of the Advent, San Francisco, accepted a call and entered upon the duties July 14, 1878, and still continues as rector. This church with rectory occupies one-quarter block, handsomely inclosed and improved with attractive shrubbery. The architect of both was I. W. Fairfield, and the designs represent those styles common to the rural churches of England.

A chime of five bells, the gift of the present Mayor of Eureka, T. Walsh, rings out from its pinnacled tower their weekly invocations to worship and in the surprise of the moment, takes the stranger back beyond the tall redwoods and the mountains, to his distant home. The interior appointments are in harmony with the surroundings. The east window to the rear of the desk is a splendid mosaic of stained glass of diamond pattern. The value of church and parsonage is not less than $7,500, and financial condition good.

The United Brethren in Christ Church is situated at Rohnerville. The first minister sent here was Israel Sloan, who organized the first class on Eel River in 1862. His memory is dear to the people of Rohnerville, where he was buried in the old cemetery. In 1865 the second class was organized. The first minister was Rev. J. B. Hamilton. The society have a comfortable church, a good parsonage, and two camp-grounds, one on Eel River, the other about one mile north of Springville, and is entirely free from debt. The membership is eighty-seven. The present minister is C. F. Lane.

The M. E. Church at Ferndale was established during Indian troubles and planted amidst many difficulties. The country was a forest and the circuit was large, embracing Petrolia and Rohnerville; the minister in charge frequently exposing his life to the dangers of savages and the crossing of swollen streams in the course of his itinerant duties. Dr. Morrow organized the church in 1860. Rev. F. H. Woodward is now in charge. There are now seventy-five members and twenty-seven probationists. The church property consists of two lots, church, parsonage, etc., also camp-meeting ground; altogether of the value of $4,400, and this without any debts or liabilities.

First Congregational Church in Eureka was organized October 30, 1860. No record shows the names of the first Trustees, of which Dr. Jonathan Clark was President. It was in the charge of Rev. W. L. Jones, as first pastor. Its present minister is the Rev. C. A. Huntington. The greatest number of members appearing on the official minutes of this church is sixty-three, and the present membership consists of twenty-four persons. The church building and parsonage attached are neat and attractive in general appearance, and for their respective uses well furnished, and handsomely situated on the corner of 4th and G Streets. The church property is valued at $6,000, and is out of debt.

Ferndale Congregational Church was organized March 17, 1876. Its first meeting of the society was held in a small hall; at the present time it is the owner of a large church building. On July 24, 1881, it was free from debt and dedicated. Dr. Warren preached the dedicatory sermon. Mr. Strong gave a brief resume of the work done by the society for the past five years.

Hon. Joseph Russ has aided this society very much in donations. It received from this source the lumber for the entire building, a fine bell, and about one-sixth of the whole debt. Its first pastor was Rev. E. O. Tade, and its present one is Rev. Phillip Combe. Mr. A. Berding, Mrs. J. M. Lewis, and Dr. F. A. Alford were the original members. Its present and greatest number in membership is forty-one. The property, consisting chiefly of church building and lot is valued at $5,000.

The Presbyterian Church at Arcata was organized January 1, 1861. Rev. Alexander Scott was first pastor. He preached in the Methodist Episcopal Church for about sixteen months previous to the erection of the church. The membership consisted at that time of three persons only. B. Wyman, George Danskin, and Sarah Nixon, the last named still remaining as an active member. Fifty-five is the present number of members. The church was dedicated March 31, 1861. It and the parsonage are pleasantly situated, occupying one-quarter of a block under neat inclosure and with attractive surroundings. It has two organs and a library of 200 volumes, valued at $2,500. The disbursements for salary of pastor and benevolent purposes, are about $1,100 annually, and for the twenty-two years since the organization of the church, has reached a total of $24,000. Its financial condition is perfect. The Rev. James S. Todd, the present pastor, occupied this charge in 1868. He left the place in 1877, but returned to it again in 1880.

United Brethren in Christ Society meets in its own house of worship regularly on every Sabbath. It was organized in the year 1877, with G. W. Burtner, pastor. Its present membership numbers twenty-seven. Its property consists of a neat little church and parsonage comfortably furnished, and the lot on which they are situated, and is of a total value of $1,500, unembarrassed financially, and in good condition.

ROMAN CATHOLIC CHURCHES AND SCHOOLS.

The Roman Catholic Church at Eureka was organized in 1858, the Rev. Father Thomas Crinion being the first in charge. The present pastor is the Rev. C. M. Lynch. The church polity of this denomination secures for it a unity in its secular as well as spiritual relations that is unknown to Protestant churches taken collectively. The membership in Eureka and attending the ministrations of the Catholic Church, numbers about 1,200. The church building and parsonage are neat in appearance and pleasantly located, the former affording seats for about 400 persons. The total value, $5,000. The church was erected in 1861.

Besides the above, the Catholic Churches in the county are as follows: Ferndale Church, built in 1878, with seating capacity of about 200; assessed valuation of property, $650; number of Catholics in the vicinity, 200. Table Bluff Church built in 1860, and numbers in attendance about 150 from the vicinity. Property valued at $800. Rohnerville Church was built in 1871 with sittings for about 150. There are also churches organized at Arcata and Trinidad.

St. Joseph Convent of Mercy, situated in Eureka; occupies one block, and unexceptionally commands one of the most diversified and beautiful views of the city and bay, as well as the further landscape, that can be found in the place. Its inclosures are adorned with whatever of foliage and shrubbery and flowers that can render it a charming retreat to the occupants, and the building itself is a prominent feature among the improvements of the town. The Institute, in charge of the Sisters of Mercy, enjoys deservedly a high reputation for their care and thoroughness of training; number of Sisters nine; pupils, sixty. The value of this fine property is about $10,000.

Newspaper Enterprises.

First Newspapers, Failures and Triumphs, List of Papers of Humboldt County from 1854 to 1882.

EARLY in the year 1853, among the few who endeavored to form a settlement and build up Humboldt County, came Dr. E. D. Coleman. He was a man of nerve and ability, possessed of a good education and a literary turn of mind. Union, now Arcata, and Eureka grew rapidly, the former taking the lead and holding it for some years. When the prospects for Union were the brightest, when the tide of immigration had set northward and was fast flowing into Humboldt Bay, Dr. Coleman conceived the idea of starting a newspaper and furnish reading matter for the inhabitants of northern California. With every fresh influx of people the more favorably did he look upon the matter, until he determined to put his plan into execution, and on the second day of September, 1854, he presented to the people of Humboldt County the initial number of

THE HUMBOLDT TIMES.

As Eureka was the most central point the paper was published at that place. The commercial, agricultural and mining interests of this section were then in their infancy, in fact barely opened. The harbor was second only to that of San Francisco, from Panama on the south to the Straits of Fuca on the north. Steamers entered the port on an average of once a month, and mail facilities were little better than none at all. With all conceivable obstacles before him, the Dr. began his task. The *Times* was independent in politics, and was devoted purely to the interests of the people. It was ably edited, its columns well filled with choice reading matter, and its typographical make-up excellent. Toward the close of the year, Union had made such rapid advancement and attained such proportions, the county seat being located there, the *Times* was moved across the bay and published at Union, December 23, 1854.

On the 22d of December, 1855, E. D. Coleman sold out the *Times* to Walter Van Dyke and Austin Wiley, the former taking editorial charge, the Doctor taking his departure from the county and locating at Washington, D. C. These gentlemen carried on the paper until January 23, 1858, when W. Van Dyke transferred his interest to A. Wiley, the junior partner, and again took up his profession, that of attorney-at-law.

As time rolled on the business interests experienced a change of base. The great timber resources were being opened on a large scale. Mills for manufacturing lumber were established at Eureka; the county seat was removed from Union to Eureka; it was made the principal shipping point, and immigration and the increase of business caused the village to make rapid strides in the march of progress and take upon itself the habiliments of a town. The business finger indicated Eureka as the objective point, and at the close of the fourth volume Mr. Wiley moved the *Times* office back to Eureka August 28, 1858, where it has been published without an omission up to the writing of this. June 9, 1860, Mr. Wiley transferred the paper to Walter Van Dyke and L. M. Burson.

In 1858, when the *Times* was moved from Union the citizens of that place were in no manner of means pleased with the change, and at once made arrangements for the publishing of another paper. Accordingly, on the 15th of December, 1858, the *Northern Californian* made its appearance with S. G. Whipple as editor and proprietor. After running about eighteen months, the owners were satisfied that there was neither business nor patronage in the county sufficient to warrant the publication of two papers, and the *Californian* was merged into the *Times*, July 14, 1860, L. M. Burson withdrawing from the last-named paper and S. G. Whipple associating himself with Walter Van Dyke as publishers of the *Times*. The paper was carried on by the two gentlemen above named until March 30, 1861, when W. Van Dyke withdrew, having transferred his interest to S. G. Whipple. August 16, 1862, Mr. Whipple sold out to A. Wiley and Walter Bohall, Mr. Wiley again taking charge as editor. In April, 1864, Mr. Wiley having been elected to represent Humboldt County in the Legislature, J. E. Wyman was placed in charge of the editorial columns, the ownership remaining the same, and on the 27th of May Mr. Wiley transferred his interest to J. E. Wyman, the firm being Wyman & Bohall. August 19, 1865, J. E. Wyman purchased Mr. Bohall's interest.

Business, which at that time was at a standstill, soon began to pick up and improve. A large number of people settled in the county, new industries were opened up, and the march of progress was onward and upward. The mail facilities were greatly improved, lines of steamers were placed on the route between the bay and San Francisco, and an era of prosperity was inaugurated. Under the management of J. E. Wyman, the *Times* was Republican in politics, and pursuing a consistent course, steadily worked into the good graces of the people. In 1873 a telegraph line was built from Eureka, connecting with the Western Union at Petaluma, and arrangements were made by J. E. Wyman to publish a daily paper at Eureka. The line was completed and in working order the latter part of the year.

DAILY HUMBOLDT TIMES.

First number was issued January 1, 1874. For protection, as well as to be placed in a position to receive the latest and most reliable news from all parts of the world, the *Times* joined the Associated press, and received all dispatches from that source. On the 1st of January, 1875, W. H. Wyman, a son of the proprietor, was taken into the business, and the firm was from that time known as J. E. Wyman & Son. The *Daily Times* rapidly grew in favor, and from time to time was enlarged to suit the increasing business. November 5, 1880, J. E. Wyman, the senior partner, who had been connected with the paper since 1864, died, and in September, 1881, W. H. Wyman assumed entire control, and is at the present time publisher and proprietor.

The *Humboldt Times* is one of the oldest papers published on the coast, and has a complete file of the publication from the first issue, which is in itself a valuable record and a correct history of the current events that have transpired for over a quarter of a century. It has sailed the sea that all journals have to cross; it has met adverse winds, and encountered heavy swells; it has suffered strong opposition, but pursuing a straightforward, honorable course, it is now the exponent of the people of Humboldt County, and ranks among the leading interior papers of the State. A large amount of capital has been invested in the business; it is supplied with steam power, power presses, etc., and is complete in every respect.

OTHER JOURNALS.

Since the county was organized a host of papers have been started, but most of them failed to make the business pay, and one by one they, like the rose, withered and died.

One of the early papers was the *Sluice Box*, published at Orleans Bar in 1856, by Frank Ball. The first numbers were filled with local hits and humorous illustrations.

VIEW OF KLAMATH COUNTY JAIL.

One of the illustrations in the *Sluice Box* was entitled "A View of Klamath County Jail, erected in 1852, built of oak wood." The picture was a sketch of a large oak tree, with a staple and chain attached. It represented two verdant sons of Erin who were indicted for jumping Chinamen's claims and were handcuffed and fastened to said jail by means of the chain. It seems they were victims of "misplaced confidence," having surrendered themselves on the supposition that the county had no jail, and expected that the sheriff would board them at the hotel. They were ready to plead guilty and make amends after being out all night.

December 1, 1856, the publisher of the *Sluice Box* determined to discontinue his little sheet which had become a great favorite with its readers. In his valedictory he says: "Our work is done, our mission is ended, and now with a clear conscience and dust in our pockets, we vacate the editorial chair and retire to the shades of private life." He asked no odds of the public and had no thanks to render for past favors. Hear him: "Perhaps, dear public, you think we ought to thank you for your liberal support and for paying us so promptly. Not a bit of it. The boot is on the other foot, and you know it. You know very well that we did not start it to make money or gain a livelihood, but for our own pleasure, nevertheless you bought it, and for a wonder paid for it, and got your money's worth, and we hope will profit by the advice we have given you from time to time." He takes his final leave after this fashion: "And now, dear public, we must close. If we have hurt any one's feelings, we forgive 'em; if we have done any person injustice, we will accept their apologies, and hoping the Lord will take a liking to you, we bid you a last farewell."

VARIOUS JOURNALS STARTED.

The *Northern California* was published at Union, in December, 1858, by S. G. Whipple, and merged into the *Times* July 14, 1860.

The *Casket* was started in Arcata in 1860, but was issued for only a short period.

The *Humboldt Bay Journal*, Democratic in politics, was first published September 1, 1865, Rev. J. W. Hines, editor. In December of the same year the editorship passed into the hands of J. E. Baccus, Jr., who conducted the paper until the time of its demise, April 20, 1867.

The *Humboldt Bay Democrat* began its career October 24, 1868, with L. M. Music & Co. at the head, and lasted three weeks.

The *National Index*, Democratic, appeared June 27, 1867, and suspended March 14, 1868.

The *Northern Independent* was laid before the public July 22, 1869, A. M. Parry, publisher. The tone of the paper was Independent, with Democratic tendencies. Later on the paper passed into the hands of Eugene Russ, who carried it on until August 15, 1872, when the obituary was pronounced.

The *West Coast Signal*, D. E. Gordon, editor and publisher, appeared February 15, 1871. It was Independent in politics, with Republican leanings. October 7, 1876, the *Daily Evening Signal* made its appearance. The *Signal*, as a daily and weekly, was published by Mr. Gordon until March 17, 1880, when it suspended.

The *Age*, a small daily paper, was started in 1876, by W. H. Clipperton, as a free advertising sheet, but failing to make it pay, it was suspended. The material was purchased by J. A. Betteridge, and after refitting the office Betteridge & Sinnerton, December 23, 1876, commenced the publication of the *Evening Star* as an advertising sheet. Afterwards a regular price was charged for subscription, and April 20, 1878, publication was suspended.

The *Evening Herald* commenced publication March 22, 1879, W. B. Thorpe, proprietor. The paper was issued only a few months, when the office was removed to Arcata.

The *Leader* was commenced at Arcata, August 2, 1879, by W. B. Thorpe. Shortly after the close of the first volume the paper suspended, the editor moving away from the county. December 11, 1880, it was revived, Austin Wiley taking charge. It was published one year and again suspended.

The *Eel River Echo* was commenced by W. H. Runnels at Robnerville, in 1878, and after nearly two years' struggle, was compelled to suspend. The material was moved to Eureka, where A. J. Bledsoe commenced the publication of the semi-weekly *News* in 1881. The *News* suspended after being in existence three months.

FERNDALE ENTERPRISE.

This paper, a seven-column folio, 24x36, was established May 11, 1878, by W. G. Jones & Co. The *Enterprise* was an outgrowth of the indomitable spirit of energy that has ever characterized the citizens of Ferndale and Eel River Valley in their determination to be surpassed by no other portion of the county. The paper, though founded by inexperienced and youthful men, soon became a power in the county and did much toward demonstrating the possibility of navigating Eel River entrance by ocean steamers. It has labored unremittingly to advance the material interests of southern Humboldt and always has been found with the people in all vital questions of civil or religious polity, numbering among its supporters men of all parties and of all sects. November 19, 1880, the firm of Jones & Co. was succeeded by the present proprietor, F. A. Alford. He, also a novice, being by profession a physician, a graduate from the noted school of Bellevue Hospital Medical College, New York City, in 1869, brought new life and vigor to the *Enterprise*. Almost immediately a Gordon job press and full outfit of job type were added, and other important changes made in the office and in the paper. The business was reduced to a system under the new regimé, the most important feature being the collection of all bills the first of each month, by a regular collector. No dead advertising matter has been allowed to remain in its columns under any circumstances. It is well supported by home and foreign advertisements, being recognized as occupying a field unfilled by any other publication, supplying a section some fifty miles square. Independent in politics, the editorials are always outspoken on all questions of interest, and aim to be radical in their conservatism. The *locals* have made the paper a recognized standard for local and county news, doubling the circulation in a year, which now averages about 800. January 1, 1882, the office was removed to a building of its own, and fitted up with every convenience. It is now situated south of the Pioneer Livery Stables, on Main Street, and presents a handsome front, twenty-eight feet in width. It occupies rooms 16x32 feet, and 12x20 for composing and press rooms and offices. The first papers from the new quarters was issued January 6, 1882, and is a fair specimen and representative paper of southern Humboldt.

THE DEMOCRATIC STANDARD.

The *Weekly Standard* was established in June, 1875, by R. V. Cladd & Co. In June, 1877, it was purchased by the present publisher, William Ayers, Esq., who shortly afterwards changed its title to "*The Democratic Standard.*"

In the spring of 1878, it commenced the discussion of the greenback financial doctrine, to which it has adhered ever since, being the first greenback paper published in California. The main feature and effort of the paper has been the description of the various sections of the county, together with the discussion and agitation of bay and harbor improvements. In this self-allotted task it has been untiring, letting no opportunity pass that would serve to give the subject a fresh stirring up.

It is a representative northern California paper, gleaning all important items from the northern tier of counties into its columns. Its publisher makes it a point to travel over some portion of the territory it serves, every year, to study the country, its needs and capabilities, and get acquainted with its inhabitants.

The ultimate aim of the *Standard* is to leave no stone unturned in the effort to make Eureka the port of supply, export and import, for the whole section of country in semi-circle from 100 to 150 miles surrounding Humboldt Bay. From its columns we have gathered much valuable information, used in compiling this History.

DAILY AND WEEKLY TELEPHONE.

The *Telephone* was first issued December 21, 1881, by Messrs. Wiley & Henoy, proprietors. It is 21x28 inches in size, with six columns on a page. It is the most complete daily paper ever published in the county. Its initial number contained seventy-two local paragraphs, all of them readable and newsy. The firm has made an independent telegraph arrangement, and has secured the services of a competent telegraphic correspondent in San Francisco.

It has daily and weekly editions. A. Wiley was associated with Walter Van Dyke twenty-six years ago on the *Times*. The publishers are practical newspaper men and very well know how to manage and make a successful journal. It is bright, and keeps up with the demand for local items and late news.

ROHNERVILLE HERALD.

The publication of the *Herald* was commenced at Rohnerville, Humboldt County, on the 2d day of November, 1881, by Charles W. Gordon, at the age of 19 years, who had been a resident of the county since 1873. The people of Rohnerville demanded a newspaper, and the present publisher took advantage of the opportunity, and has found the venture a successful one. The subscription list had reached nearly 450 on the 1st day of March, and the paper shows a very liberal advertising patronage. It is the official organ for publication of land notices in eastern and southern Humboldt and is published at $1.50 a year. The publisher declares his paper to be Independent-Republican. It is a creditable paper, and does honor to the people of Rohnerville and vicinity, who are determined to have a paper of their own in which to set forth the advantages of that prosperous village.

Journalism of Del Norte County.

Just after Crescent City sprang into existence, on June 10, 1854, was issued the first number of the *Herald*, which for seven years was a weekly visitor to its friends, and a vigilant and earnest factor of the growth and welfare of this section of California.

The press and material were shipped from San Francisco by the editors and proprietors, Messrs B. Y. Feehtig and U. B. Freanor. It was a twenty-column paper, published weekly, at a subscription price of ten dollars per annum. The very first issue contained an article upon the subject of a wagon road to connect this place with southern Oregon—a question which still gives rise to discussion. It professed to be "independent" in politics, but really had a very decided Democratic inclination. In September, 1854, Mr. Feehtig withdrew, and S. H. Grubler assumed his place. Under the new management the tone of the *Herald* was unaltered. The last issue by Grubler & Freanor was June 4, 1856, when T. S. Pomeroy entered the partnership and took editorial charge. This co-partnership continued until August 19, 1859, when Freanor withdrew, and the paper remained in the exclusive control of the latter. He continued at its head until the completion of its seventh volume, June 8, 1861, when he removed to Jacksonville, Oregon, with the entire office.

T. S. Pomeroy came to Crescent City in 1853 as Clerk of Klamath County, when the seat of Government was removed to this place. In 1856 he was appointed County Judge to fill a vacancy. In 1861 he established in Jacksonville the *Southern Oregon Gazette*, in connection with O'Meara, now of the San Francisco *Examiner*. This was in the dark days when the Union toppled upon its foundation. The *Gazette* was too pronouncedly "Secesh," and was refused admission to the mails. This action of the Postmaster General ended its life. After a lingering and painful illness he died here. He was an active positive man of many virtues and few faults.

The Crescent City *Courier* issued its first number September 12, 1872, with Walter B. Thorpe as editor and proprietor. Under his management the *Courier* flew the Republican colors, and was the only paper that has ever in Del Norte assumed openly the partisanship of any political party.

In his issue of March 7, 1874, he announced the sale of the paper and bid an affectionate adieu to the scenes of his early life. From here he went to Eureka, and subsequently to Arcata, where he established the *Arcata Leader*, but sold his property there and went to Sacramento, and thence to Washington, D. C. At last accounts he was still at the National Capitol. On the 14th of March, 1874, without interruption, the *Courier* appeared with Mason & Tack as proprietors, the former, Wm. B. Mason, making the editorial salutatory and introduction. This firm was beyond question the strongest that has solicited support for a paper in Del Norte. Both were typographers and neither was unfamiliar with pencil and scissors. Both had and still have, a large circle of warm, sincere friends.

Wm. B. Mason, the senior partner, spent nearly all his life in Crescent City, and has led a life such as is seen only in the shifting scenes of a "far West." A school boy here of long ago, he has grown to man's estate with many of its virtues and none of its vices. Frequently, in various capacities, has he been called upon as a servant of the people, the last time being as Assemblyman from this county to the Legislature of 1879 and 1880, to which he was elected as a straight Republican.

On the 12th of November, 1879, Silas White resumed the publication of the *Courier* which he continued until the 9th of February, 1881.

The *Del Norte Record* was first started as a free monthly, April 19, 1879, by J. E. Eldridge, and was published weekly, beginning May 13th, and in September of that year it was slightly enlarged. With the second volume, May 8, 1880, the paper was enlarged to its present size, twenty-eight columns. On the 5th of February, encouraged by success thus far and the business prospects of the future, the *Courier* was bought and consolidated with the *Record* after its last issue on the 9th. The editor does not feel that the field of his labors warrants the advocacy of any set of party tenets and still abstains from the expression of party views, and has taken up the cudgels neither for nor against opposing factions nor men.

The paper is a valuable sheet. The editor came here many years ago, and has grown grey as the town matured in years.

SCHOOLS OF DEL NORTE.

The following is a list of school districts of Del Norte, and the amount of money to which each is entitled in 1882, as apportioned by John Miller, Superintendent of Schools.

Districts.	State.	Library.	Total.
Crescent	$1,009.11	$26.16	$1,035.27
Bradford	370.94	41.22	412.16
Happy Camp	311.16	34.57	345.73
Rowdy Cr	251.37	27.93	279.30
Lincoln	249.07	27.68	276.75
Redwood	242.17	26.91	269.08
Elk Valley	267.47	29.72	297.19
Fort Dick	244.48	27.16	271.64
Total	$2,945.77	$241.35	$3,187.12

DEL NORTE COUNTY OFFICERS, 1882.

Superior Judge..J. E. Murphy
Assemblyman...W. B. Mason
Sheriff.........C. E. Hughes
Clerk and Auditor.P.H. Powler
Treasurer.........Wm. Saville
District Attorney.Edgar Mason
Assessor....W. H. Woodbury
Cor. & Pub. Adm...J. F. Frantz
Co. Surveyor..A. H. Cleveland
Supt. Pub. Schools.John Miller
Deputy Sheriff....Jos. Eudert
Deputy Sheriff..J. E. Eldredge
Deputy Sheriff.Jeremiah Lane
Co. Phys'n. Dr. J.W. Robertson

FIRST BATTALION MOUNTAINEERS, CALIFORNIA VOLUNTEERS, SERVICE OF THE UNITED STATES.

Prepared by Hon. J. Clark.

Rank.	Name.	Date of Commission.	Date of Rank.	Remarks.
FIELD.				
Lieut.-Col., and Commanding Humboldt Military District	Stephen G. Whipple.	April 27, 1863	April 27, 1863	Headquarters Humboldt Military Dist., Ft. Humboldt, 1863; Ft. Gaston, 1863-4; Ft. Humboldt, 1864-5.
Major	William S. R. Taylor	June 2, 1863	June 1, 1863	Resigned in 1864.
Major	Charles W. Long	Oct. 3, 1864		Promoted Major Oct. 3, 1864, vice Wm. S. R. Taylor, resigned. Command of Ft. Gaston 1864-5.
STAFF.				
First Lieut. and Regimental Adj., and A. A. A. Gen., Humboldt Military District	Acquila W. Hanna	June 19, 1863	June 19, 1863	January 1, 1865—Out of service by general order from War Department, mustering out extra Lieutenants on Staff-Appointments.
First Lieut., Co. F, and Regimental Adj., and A. A. A. Gen., Humboldt Military District	Alpheus W. Randall		January, 1865	January, 1865—Appointed, vice Acquila W. Hanna, mustered out of service.
First Lieut. and Regimental Quartermaster	William H. Pratt	June 5, 1863	June 5, 1863	January 1, 1865—Out of service by general order from War Department, mustering out extra Lieutenants on Staff-Appointments.
SURGEON.				
Surgeon	Jonathan Clark	June 5, 1863	June 4, 1863	In charge of Hospital at Ft. Baker, 1863, Ft. Iaqua, 1863-4, Ft. Gaston, 1864, Ft. Humboldt, 1864-5.
Assistant Surgeon	Theodore D. Felt	June 19, 1863	June 19, 1863	Declined.
NON-COMMISSIONED STAFF.				
Sergeant Major	William P. Hanna			
Commissary Sergeant	John T. Bost			
Band Master	Roswel Tupper			
LINE.				
Captain Company A	Charles W. Long	Feb. 9, 1863	Feb. 9, 1863	In command of Ft. Baker in 1863, Ft. Iaqua, 1863-4. Promoted Major Oct. 3, 1864, vice Wm. S. R. Taylor, resigned.
Captain Company B	George W. Ousley	Feb. 9, 1863	Feb. 9, 1863	In command of Camp Curtis in 1866, Camp Anderson, 1864, Ft. Gaston, 1863.
Captain Company C	Abraham Miller	April 4, 1863	April 4, 1863	In command of Burnt Ranch, Cal., in 1864.
Captain Company D	William C. Martin	August 19, 1863	August 19, 1863	Detailed as Mustering Officer in 1864.
Captain Company E	John P. Simpson	Feb. 28, 1863	March 2, 1863	In Command of Camp Grant, Cal., in 1863-4-5.
Captain Company F	Robert Baird	July 1, 1863	June 30, 1863	In command of Camp Forks, of Solomon, and Camp Lincoln.
First Lieutenant Company A	Knyphausen W. Geer	April 27, 1863	April 27, 1863	Promoted Capt., Co. A, Oct., 1864, vice Chas. W. Long, promoted. Command Ft. Iaqua, 1865.
First Lieutenant Company B	Isaac W. Hempfield	April 27, 1863	April 27, 1863	In Command of Camp Fawn Prairie in 1863. Resigned, 1864.
First Lieutenant Company C	John A. Watson	June 5, 1863	June 4, 1863	Adjutant and A. Q. M. and A. C. S. at Ft. Gaston.
First Lieutenant Company D	R. F. Herrick	Dec. 4, 1863	Dec. 3, 1863	
First Lieutenant Company E	W. W. Skinner	June 18, 1863	June 18, 1863	
First Lieutenant Company F	Alpheus W. Randall	August 20, 1863	August 20, 1863	In Command of Ft. Jones, 1863, Camp Lincoln, 1864. Jan., 1865, detached from Co.; appointed Regimental Adj, and A. A. A. Gen., Humboldt Military Dist.
Second Lieutenant Company A	Leonard C. Beckwith	April 27, 1863	April 27, 1863	Resigned in 1864 to accept appointment of Indian Agent, Hoopa Valley Reservation.
Second Lieutenant Company B	Edward Hale	April 27, 1863	April 17, 1863	Resigned in 1864.
Second Lieutenant Company C	Thomas Middleton	June 5, 1863	June 4, 1863	Promoted First Lieut., Co. A, vice Knyphausen W. Geer, promoted.
Second Lieutenant Company D	William N. Tuttle	Dec. 5, 1863	Dec. 5, 1863	
Second Lieutenant Company E	W. W. Frasier	June 18, 1863	June 18, 1863	
Second Lieutenant Company F	Henry B. Mathewson			
Second Lieutenant Company B	John S. Hughes		1864	Vice Edward Hale, resigned.

The First Battalion Mountaineers, California Volunteers, were mustered into the service of the United States for the suppression of Indian hostilities in Northern California, serving during the years 1863, '64, and '65. The following counties are entitled to the credit of raising the companies comprising the Battalion: Humboldt County, Companies A and B; Trinity County, Company C; Mendocino County, Company E; Siskiyou County, Company F; Northern Counties, at large, Company D.

OFFICERS OF HUMBOLDT COUNTY, FROM 1853 TO 1882.

PREPARED FOR THE COUNTY HISTORY BY D. CUTTEN, ESQ.

Date	Assemblymen.	County Judge.	Sheriff.	County Clerk.	Treasurer.	District Attorney.	Assessor.	Date.
1853		J. E. Wyman...	Peter Lothian	L. K. Wood...	M. Spencer...	Joel Burnell...		1853
1854	A. H. Murdock..	J. E. Wyman...	Peter Lothian	L. K. Wood...	M. Spencer...	W. VanDyke...	D. D. Williams...	1854
1855	C. S. Ricks...	J. E. Wyman...	Peter Lothian	L. K. Wood...	A. H. Murdock.	W. VanDyke...	D. D. Williams...	1855
1856	C. S. Ricks...	J. E. Wyman...	Wm. I. Reed...	L. K. Wood...	H. W. McNay...	L. M. Burson...	Jacob DeHaven	1856
1857	H. W. Havens	J. E. Wyman...	Wm. I. Reed...	L. K. Wood...	H. W. McNay...	E. H. Howard...	Jacob DeHaven	1857
1858	E. L. Davis...	A. J. Huestis...	A. D. Sevier...	Elisha Clark...	Jesse Wells...	L. M. Burson...	Jacob DeHaven	1858
1859	L. M. Burson...	A. J. Huestis...	A. D. Sevier...	Elisha Clark...	Jesse Wells...	L. M. Burson...	Jacob DeHaven	1859
1860	Wm. B. Hagans	A. J. Huestis...	B. VanNest...	A. W. Hanna...	Jon. Freese...	J. E. Wyman...	Hock Hills...	1860
1861	Geo. H. Work..	A. J. Huestis...	B. VanNest...	A. W. Hanna...	Jon. Freese...	J. E. Wyman...	Hock Hills...	1861
1862	Geo. H. Work..	A. J. Huestis...	B. VanNest...	A. W. Hanna...	J. H. Davis...	G. W. Tompkins	Reese Wiley...	1862
1863	A. Wiley...	A. J. Huestis...	B. VanNest...	A. W. Hanna...	J. H. Davis...	G. W. Tompkins	Reese Wiley...	1863
1864	A. Wiley...	J. E. Wyman...	Joseph Tracy	Jas. M. Short...	David W. Nixon	S. M. Buck...	Stephen Goff...	1864
1865	A. J. Huestis...	J. E. Wyman...	Joseph Tracy	Jas. M. Short...	David W. Nixon	C. S. Ricks...	Stephen Goff...	1865
1866	A. J. Huestis...	J. E. Wyman...	Joseph Tracy	Jas. M. Short...	David W. Nixon	G. W. Tompkins	Stephen Goff...	1866
1867	C Westmoreland	J. E. Wyman...	Joseph Tracy	Jas. M. Short...	David W. Nixon	G. W. Tompkins	Stephen Goff...	1867
1868	C Westmoreland	J. E. Wyman...	W. S. Barnam	John A. Watson	David W. Nixon	J. J. DeHaven.	Francis Francis	1868
1869	J. J. DeHaven..	J. E. Wyman...	W. S. Barnam	John A. Watson	John Kelcher.	J. J. DeHaven.	Francis Francis	1869
1870	J. J. DeHaven..	J. E. Wyman...	A. D. Sevier...	John A. Watson	John Kelcher.	James Hanna..	A. N. Guptill...	1870
1871	Joseph Russ...	J. E. Wyman...	A. D. Sevier...	John A. Watson	John Kelcher.	James Hanna..	A. N. Guptill...	1871
1872	Joseph Russ...	J. E. Wyman...	E. Bulkeley...	John A. Watson	John Kelcher.	Wm. H. Mason.	A. N. Guptill...	1872
1873	B. C. Hurlbutt..	J. E. Wyman...	E. Bulkeley...	John A. Watson	John Kelcher.	Wm. H. Mason.	A. N. Guptill...	1873
1874	B. C. Hurlbutt..	J. E. Wyman...	E. Bulkeley...	W. J. McKenna	John Kelcher.	Geo. A. Knight.	A. W. Randall	1874
1875	Jonathan Clark	J. E. Wyman...	E. Bulkeley...	W. J. McKenna	John Kelcher.	Geo. A. Knight.	Wm. Wallace†	1875
1876	Jonathan Clark	C. G. Stafford.	J. C. Bull...	W. J. McKenna	D. C. Scott...	Geo. A. Knight.	Wm. Wallace	1876
1877	Joseph Russ...	C. G. Stafford.	J. C. Bull...	W. J. McKenna	D. C. Scott...	Geo. A. Knight.	Wm. Wallace	1877
1878	Joseph Russ...	C. G. Stafford.	T. M. Brown...	W. J. McKenna	L. T. Kinsey..	Geo. A. Knight.	Wm. Wallace	1878
1879	W. B. Stoddard	C. G. Stafford.	T. M. Brown...	W. J. McKenna	L. T. Kinsey..	Geo. A. Knight.	Wm. Wallace	1879
1880	W. B. Stoddard	J. P. Haynes*	T. M. Brown...	J. S. Thomson.	L. T. Kinsey..	E. W. Wilson...	Geo. H. Shaw	1880
1881	G. C. Mudgett.	J. P. Haynes	T. M. Brown...	J. S. Thomson.	L. T. Kinsey..	E. W. Wilson...	Geo. H. Shaw	1881
1882	G. C. Mudgett.	J. P. Haynes	T. M. Brown...	J. S. Thomson.	L. T. Kinsey..	E. W. Wilson...	Geo. H. Shaw	1882

Date	Surveyor.	Supt of Schools	Administrator.	Coroner.	Supervisors.
1853	J. S. Murray...				First meeting of Board held May 7, 1855...
1854	J. S. Murray...		H. J. Wyman		
1855	J. S. Murray...		Wm. Roberts		John Quick, Joseph S. Bowles, Jonathan Clark...
1856	Joseph Seeley..	A. J. Huestis...	James Light..	Byron Deming.	Jonathan Clark, H. S. Daniels, J. P. Langdon...
1857	Joseph Seeley..	A. J. Huestis...	James Light..	Byron Deming.	John M. Eddy, David Masten, Abner D. Sevier...
1858	J. S. Murray...	E. H. Howard.	R. M. Williams.	J. N. Hume...	Jesse Duugan, Wm. C. Morten, Jonathan Freese...
1859	J. S. Murray...	E. H. Howard.	R. M. Williams.	Amos Crane...	Jonathan Freese, Wm. C. Martin, Seth Chism...
1860	J. S. Murray...	H. H. Severens.	R. M. Williams.	Amos Crane...	Wm. C. Martin, Seth Chism, A. P. Guthrie...
1861	J. S. Murray...	H. H. Severens.	R. M. Williams.	Amos Crane...	Seth Chism, A. P. Guthrie, H. S. Daniels...
1862	J. D. Kinsley...	W. L. Jones...	R. M. Williams.	B. Deming...	A. P. Guthrie, H. S. Daniels, Seth Chism...
1863	J. B. Kinsley...	W. L. Jones...	R. M. Williams.	B. Deming...	Seth Chism, A. N. Guptill, John Dolbeer...
1864	J. S. Murray...	W. L. Jones...	R. M. Williams.	H. D. Ley...	Seth Chism, A. N. Guptill, John Kelcher...
1865	J. S. Murray...	W. L. Jones...	R. M. Williams.	H. D. Ley...	A. N. Guptill, Wm. Carson, Thos. Hart...
1866	W. W. Skinner	W. L. Jones...	J. O. Kneeland.	Byron Deming.	Wm. Carson, Thos. Hart, S. W. Morrison...
1867	W. W. Skinner	W. L. Jones...	J. O. Kneeland.	Byron Deming.	S. W. Morrison, Thos. Hart, Geo. H. Tilley...
1868	J. S. Murray...	W. L. Jones...	A. J. Tyrrell...	L. Lewis Shaw	S. W. Morrison, Geo. H. Tilley, Seth Chism...
1869	J. S. Murray...	W. L. Jones...	A. J. Tyrrell...	L. Lewis Shaw	Geo. H. Tilley, Seth Chism, S. W. Morrison...
1870	J. S. Murray...	J. B. Brown...	C. B. Whitman	Wm. Todd...	Seth Chism, S. W. Morrison, W. J. Sweasey...
1871	J. S. Murray...	J. B. Brown...	C. B. Whitman	Wm. Todd...	S. W. Morrison, W. J. Sweasey, John W. Cooper...
1872	R. F. Herrick..	J. B. Brown...	John A. Whaley	A. W. Randall.	W. J. Sweasey, John W. Cooper, G. C. Barber...
1873	R. F. Herrick..	J. B. Brown...	John A. Whaley	A. W. Randall.	John W. Cooper, G. C. Barber, H. S. Daniels...
1874	R. F. Herrick..	E. C. Cummings	J. A. Thomson	John L. Eby...	G. C. Barber, H. S. Daniels, Geo. S. Williams...
1875	R. F. Herrick..	E. C. Cummings	J. A. Thomson	John L. Eby...	H. S. Daniels, Geo. S. Williams, G. C. Barber...
1876	R. F. Herrick..	E. C. Cummings	J. H. Kimball.	J. H. Kimball.	Geo. S. Williams, G. C. Barber, Stephen Hill...
1877	R. F. Herrick..	E. C. Cummings	J. H. Kimball.	J. H. Kimball.	G. C. Barber, S. Hill, A. Wiley, J. O. Dinsmore, D. A. Demerritt...
1878	R. F. Herrick..	J. B. Casterlin.	J. H. Kimball.	J. H. Kimball.	S. Hill, A. Wiley, J. O. Dinsmore, D. A. Demerritt, Seth Chism...
1879	R. F. Herrick..	J. B. Casterlin.	J. H. Kimball.	J. H. Kimball.	J. O. Dinsmore, Geo. H. Tilley, S. Hill, D. A. Demerritt, S. Chism...
1880	R. F. Herrick..	J. B. Casterlin.	O. H. Spring..	O. H. Spring..	S. Hill, J. Hannah, E. M. Dowell, J. O. Dinsmore, Seth Chism...
1881	R. F. Herrick..	J. B. Casterlin.	O. H. Spring..	O. H. Spring..	S. Hill, J. Hannah, E. M. Dowell, J. O. Dinsmore, R. W. Stevens...
1882	R. F. Herrick..	J. B. Casterlin.	O. H. Spring..	O. H. Spring..	S. Hill, J. Hannah, E. M. Dowell, J. O. Dinsmore, R. W. Stevens...

Court of Sessions from 1853 to 1861.

1853—J. E. Wyman, J. N. Borden, S. L. Shaw. 1854—J. E. Wyman, A. D. Sevier, D. F. Gilbert. 1855—J. E. Wyman, H. P. Janes. D. F. Gilbert. 1856—J. E. Wyman, H. P. Janes, D. F. Gilbert. 1857—J. E. Wyman, A. J. Huestis, F. S. Duff. 1858—A. J. Huestis, A. Hanna†, J. H. Kimball. 1859—A. J. Huestis, John F. Moore, Benj. T. Jameson. 1860—A. J. Huestis, J. H. Kimball, James S. Florent. 1861—A. J. Huestis, J. H. Kimball, J. M. Cox.

* Superior Judge. † Appointed. ‡ Resigned. § The first named was Chairman.

www.ingramcontent.com/pod-product-compliance
Lightning Source LLC
Chambersburg PA
CBHW030009240426
43672CB00007B/885